379.73
P875d

DISCARD

The Dilemma
of Education
in a Democracy

The Dilemma
of Education
in a Democracy

Richard H. Powers

Regnery Gateway
Chicago

Copyright © 1984 by Richard H. Powers
All rights reserved. Manufactured in the United States of America.

No part of this book may be reproduced in any form or by any electronic or mechanical means, including information storage and retrieval systems, without permission in writing from the publisher, except by a reviewer, who may quote brief passages in a review.

Published by Regnery Gateway, Inc.
360 West Superior Street, Chicago, Illinois 60601-0890

Library of Congress Catalog Card Number: 81-85568

ISBN: 0-89526-662-8

This book is dedicated
to Ksenija.

379.73
P875d

CONTENTS

Introduction 1

PART ONE   *Our Students and Our Colleges*

1 Slogans of Deceit: "Access" and "alternatives" 23
2 Diversity: Students and Institutions 33
3 Diversity Within a Single Institution 51

PART TWO   *Decline and Indifference*

1 Teachers and Administrators 59
2 Innovative Definitions of "Success" 65
3 "No one writes anymore" 71
4 Parental Attitudes 77
5 "Different styles of learning" 89

PART THREE   *Equality*

1 "Compensatory opportunity
   and full cognitive equality" 101
2 The Dictates of Justice 107
3 The Very Nature of Man 113
4 Not All of Us Are Enslaved 117
5 The Prevailing Delusion 123

PART FOUR *The Denial of Freedom*

1 Education is a Form of Compulsion 131
2 "We shall have to prohibit
  such poems" 139
3 Through Just Prejudice 147
4 The Perennial Question 153
5 No Simple, No Superficial Thing 163
6 Standards of Decency 171
7 The Logic of Intolerance 177

PART FIVE *Curriculum*

1 Licensed Foolishness 189
2 The Foreign-Language Crisis 199
3 Science and Mathematics 205
4 Reading and Writing in
  Elementary and Secondary School 209
5 History in Elementary and
  Secondary School 219
6 The College "Core" Curriculum 227
7 Reading: The College Years 235
8 The Summary of All Advices 243

Conclusion *The Role of Parents* 247

Introduction

In the spring of 1983 President Reagan was told by the National Commission on Excellence in Education that "if an unfriendly power had attempted to impose on America the mediocre educational performance that exists today, we might have viewed it as an act of war." The commission, appointed eighteen months earlier by Education Secretary T. H. Bell, also noted that "for the first time in the history of our country, the educational skills of one generation will not surpass, will not equal, will not even approach those of their parents."

This assessment of our educational plight was not new. The facts have been before us for a long time. Not that there was nothing new about the report. It bore witness to the fact that for the first time in this century we have a national administration which is hostile to our educational establishment rather than a dedicated ally. For the first time ever our federal government has placed academic excellence at the top of its agenda for educational policy.

The National Commission recommended a number of reforms. It suggested compulsory instruction in secondary schools: four years of English, three years of mathematics, science and social studies and a half year in computer sciences for all students, plus two years of foreign languages for the college bound. It called for schools to establish standardized achievement tests and for colleges to raise admission standards. It urged that the school day and the school year be lengthened. It pointed out the need for higher academic standards and recommended higher pay for teachers, and that pay be based on merit.

The academic recommendations made by the commission were similar to those made, unavailingly, in *1893* by a group of leading authorities, and those made in vain a half century later by James Bryant Conant in his famous report on the nation's schools. During this entire century the enemy within, which has done so much to impose mediocrity on American children, the educational establishment, has vehemently and explicitly condemned and ridiculed such recommendations, and has gleefully and successfully subverted them. Under the system they, aided and abetted by their allies in the federal bureaucracy, have created, fewer than 3 percent of 1983 high school graduates met the academic requirements suggested by the commission.

For some time now the evidence of our national failure to educate the young has been overwhelming. The accumulation of facts which demonstrates this failure is staggering. The educationists, who advanced the theories and administered the policies which have accompanied the decline of our schools, have insisted for years that the practical meaning of all this evidence is a mystery beyond understanding because the possible reasons for the decline "are so many and so uncertain." They have cried up the danger that an excited and ignorant public might jump to conclusions which in its innocence seemed obvious to it, and then engage in wanton destruction, or even turn to "reactionary policies," or, worst of all, adopt "simple solutions." Until very recently their fright seemed to be unfounded. Seldom has a catastrophe so great had such small consequence for those with so large a share in the responsibility for it. The most despicable villains in the piece have been our professional educators, for among the guilty only they may be said to be profiteers. Not that they have been the source of our ills; quacks do not invent dread disorders. They offer easy remedies for ills which seem to be incurable by rational means, or curable only at a price which cannot or will not be paid. In hard times they flourish, and in education they have flourished for a very long time. Recently it seemed that this time might be ending, although this did not justify the expectation that education would improve.

By 1982 public education in this country was losing both financial support and the confidence of taxpayers. Big-city and small-town schools were facing unheard of spending controls. There was a growing willingness to shift public resources to non-public schools, and a concomitant unwillingness at both the state and federal level to continue with wasteful, non-productive, and counter-productive expenditures. These were perfectly reasonable responses to the shabby performance of public education. Wasting less on incompetent institutions makes simple sense. But citizen understanding is limited. The fundamental causes of our plight are hardly perceived.

The habitual self-righteous assertiveness of the educational establishment when confronted with the consequences of its misfeasance was unshaken. Its spokesmen continued to recite their tricky nostrums with undiminished sanctimoniousness, to repeat again and again that schools "have not changed fast enough," that the system "is out of synch with our youngsters," and that teachers "must go with the flow." In the uproar which followed the commission's report, however, these spokesmen were silent. The ideology of the educational establishment is unchanging, but its leaders are adept in adopting new disguises and different strategies. This adroitness is now being tested by an unusual circumstance. An incumbent president seems bent on making the condition of our public schools a political issue in a national campaign.

Washington politicians and the media do not merely embrace the issues they exploit, they crush them. A few days after the report of the National Commission on Excellence in Education was made public the "education issue" was on its way to becoming a summer spectacular. Presidential aspirant Walter Mondale unveiled an $11 billion program "to improve the public schools." His rivals for the Democratic nomination, vying with him for the support of the National Education Association (NEA), the largest teachers' union, and a bountiful source of Democratic campaign workers and national convention delegates, promptly entered the bidding. Senator Ernest E. Hollings promised every teacher a $5000 a year federal pay raise, at a cost of $14 billion. Senator John Glenn, the "moderate" Democratic hopeful, made the most modest proposal. He promised only $4 billion. The leaders of the NEA (since their rise to influence among the most effective warriors against the compulsory academic curriculum, standardized achievement tests, merit pay, or any other policy which might contribute to excellence) were not placated. Their analysts computed that federal spending on elementary and secondary education would have to rise to $23.1 billion to carry out the commission's recommendations.

Overnight there was an "educational quality" bandwagon. Derek Bok, president of Harvard, secure enough in his eminence to be both consistent and candid, was almost alone in repeating the educationists' longstanding mystifications. He declared that the public perception of schools besieged by an erosion of discipline and plummeting student academic performance was largely erroneous. "The schools have not failed," he said. "They have taken our national goals seriously and have opened their doors to a diverse population. . . ." By and large, however, the educational establishment appeared to have forgotten the dogmas which have united them for generations. Brazenly it proclaimed that how we got into this mess was less important than how we get out of it. Educationists were mute about the academic suggestions made by the commission, but in a chorus exhulted that bilions of additional federal dollars would be needed if they were to be carried out.

Dennis Gray of the Council for Basic Education warns against this orgy of overindulgence. He predicts that "tomorrow we're going to have a terrible headache because the problems aren't going to be solved," and he is surely right. Without understanding how we arrived in our present condition we will not have grounds even for believing that improvement is possible. All of our experience and all of the facts of contemporary American life and politics inform us with near absolute certainty that our federal government neither can nor will do anything to support academic excellence in our public schools, but does have the capabiiity, and the propensity, to do great harm.

The reasons for the parlous condition of our educational system are no mystery at all. The facts are clear enough, but our political system ensures that the facts, being what they are, do not matter at the federal level, nor, in many instances, at the state level. The facts are irrelevant because they are unacceptable to the various elements in our society who, working together, have the political power to insist that they be disregarded. Education is a subject of general concern about which there is no informed or coherent discussion. There can be no informed or coherent discussion because Americans do not share a general culture which would give them a common basis for comprehending the true nature of the problem.

There is hardly anything new to be said about education. There is a body of knowledge which can fairly be described as "the accumulated wisdom of our civilization." Familiarity with it is so absent that this wisdom is of no service to us, and for this we pay an awful price. Now, the public has not rejected this wisdom. Rather the self-serving philosophy of the educational establishment, whose leading spokesmen dominate our most grandiose "philanthropic" foundations and who have sat on the highest thrones at HEW, has a virtual monopoly in all public discussion of the problem. Critics of this pilosophy have been stereotyped as elitists, reactionaries, Christian fundamentalists, and racists. In the press and on television (particularly on public television) they are treated with the same patronizing contempt which characterizes comment about pro-life, anti-busing or anti ERA groups. To propound the relevance of the educational views of the greatest thinkers of our civilization is to invite the kind of dismissal from the ranks of moral and intellectual respectability otherwise reserved for culprits who do not hate Jerry Falwell.

In the pages that follow close attention will be paid to the thoughts of men from the past. Quotations in themselves, no matter what the source, of course, should not take on the authority of Revelation. What authorities have written can only be judged by the reader in the light of his or her experience and understanding of things. I will quote because I would not pretend to originality in matters where our common heritage provides ample wisdom, whether or not we are capable of comprehending or using it for our purposes.

My endeavor is based upon the presumption that those who compare the thoughts and conclusions found here with those with which they have become familiar through press reports and television will understand "educational questions" better. It is my intent to make clear that lay persons should not feel uncertain or be overcome by self-doubt when their instincts and their common sense are outraged by what they hear from public school principals and superintendents. It is my purpose to explain why suspicion and doubt are appropriate responses to what they hear about education from spokesmen of the Ford or Carnegie foundations, or the deans of any school of education. The chapters which are descriptive and those which relate how we have arrived at our present condition explain our failure. If they succeed in their purpose the reader will be able to judge with some confidence the sense and practicality of the reforms which are touted and the panaceas promised by educationists and by politicians. Above all it is hoped that this work may have an influence in determining the attitudes and practices which readers adopt regarding the education of their own children.

Sound education could not be cheap, or even cheaper than the education we have, but the cost of what we have is enormous—and indefensible. The glib smugness of our humorless "post-Watergate morality" pervades discussion of all public things. The oil companies, the auto industry, the telephone companies, the electrical power companies, real-estate developers, and politicians, all engaged in essential work and providing necessary services, are fair game. When former President Carter's popularity in the polls dropped, he attempted to gain ground by attacking any available minority more affluent than the average. But whatever one pays for an automobile, for oil, for a home, one gets something for one's money which serves a strict purpose. In none of these instances is one cheated so blatantly and so completely as in educational purchases; in none is one so completely without recourse; and in none will the damage be so permanent and so irrevocable.

And in none of the other cases is one characterized as a bigot or a fuddy-duddy if one criticizes and complains. The richest, the most powerful, the most oppressive, and beyond all comparison the most incompetent institution in the country is the educational establishment. No other matches it in public-relations skills; no other profits so greatly from the ignorance which it fosters and enforces. No other controls and decides the destiny of so many, and no other levies contributions so large on family incomes.

During the last 20 years a shambles has been made of public-school and higher education in the United States. Our system was never very good, but it had real virtues and accomplished real things. These virtues and accomplishments have been lost. Every change has brought a decline in equal opportunity for the children of the poor, of minorities, the lower-middle-class, and much of the middle-class. Changes have been wrought in the name of greater justice; but despite uncounted millions spent on federal, state, and local programs, the gap in achievement between children from poor families and those from more affluent backgrounds continues to widen. Escalating costs ensure that very soon the best college or university education will be beyond the reach of all but the affluent, and the tiny minority, which grows proportionally smaller each year, of poor children with exceptionally high scores on standardized tests.

In history many a disaster was inevitable; our educational disaster may be one which was. The United States was the first nation to follow the Prussian example of establishing a free common-school system. By 1870, practically every native white American could read and write. Out of 28 million Americans over the age of 10, the nation's nearly six million illiterates were almost all either black people (3.6 million) or white immigrants from the countries of southern Europe (2 million). For the most part, rich and poor white children attended the same public schools (although a trend toward private schools for the rich was already apparent in the larger cities). Foreign observers were impressed to note that free schools permitted all to reach the threshold of the liberal professions, and that the sums spent on public education were much greater than the war budgets of the largest European states.

But peculiarities in the system were questioned or criticized. The complete lack of centralization at state and federal levels was found striking by all European observers, though not universally condemned. Many were astonished that the law itself prevented public schools from teaching or instilling religious beliefs and morals, and derided "this absolutely false principle." One thoughtful observer concluded that American education, so democratic and seductive at first glance, was in reality singularly arbitrary and despotic, and led to a decline of family feeling, and, among parents, to a general indifference about the instruction itself. The most striking and most appalling feature was the general encouragement given children to express opinions on subjects far beyond their competence. One visitor reported that he had actually had an eyewitness account of a class in which 10-year-olds were asked to explain their views on whether blacks should be permitted to vote in the South, and that the class listened with respectful attention to one of the children as he babbled on for some 30 minutes. Another related that in a class he had observed 13-year-olds had been asked to judge the political conduct of Milton with respect to the death of Charles I, and that in the ensuing discussion the principle of capital punishment had been debated at length. Other visitors mentioned letters from 12- and 14-year-olds expressing their views on questions of discipline and education "which were printed seriously" in newspapers. The germs of a later-day disaster were thus present from the beginning.

By 1876 there were some 545 colleges, universities, and other educational establishments, including theological seminaries, in the United States. Ninety of the colleges and universities had been founded by the state governments. The large number of such institutions occasioned the comment from abroad that "the means of instruction is far greater than the number of those capable of profiting from it." Foreign critics of our elementary system did note that secondary and higher education had, until then, escaped the false theories which harmed elementary institutions. An American author explained the reason: "The people as such are not interested in education from which they do not profit." In 1876 only 3 percent or 4 percent of the population went beyond grammar school. Free public secondary education was generally available to the talented and ambitious poor who were fortunate enough to come from circumstances in which they were encouraged to continue their education. But secondary schools, even the large number which were publicly supported, were free from democratic and popular pressures.

The older secondary education in the United States was conservative in that it accepted the existing order of society and called upon the child to assert himself within its framework. But it was democratic in that it assumed that large numbers from every class of society were capable, by native endowment, to enter with some degree of hope into the world of academic competition—the mastery of subject matter, and discipline of mind and character. Poor but ambitious parents were delighted to have a child, or children, who excelled in this competition. Children were judged by educational standards, and these standards were not subject to redefinition to suit the capabilities of the average child. Then the United States began to develop free public secondary education on a large scale, and was one of the nations to take the lead in making secondary school attendance compulsory.

By 1890 27 states required compulsory attendance, and by 1918 all states did. By the 1920s the legal age for leaving school was close to today's mean of 16 years and 3 months.

The period between 1890 and 1900 was an era of mass immigration of non-English speaking, illiterate people. By 1911, more than 50 percent of the public-school population of our 37 largest cities was first-generation Americans. During the First World War the mass influx of subliterate blacks from the South to the industrial North began. In 1890 about 10 percent of all adolescents entered high school; by 1914 40 percent entered, and about 25 percent finished. Today about 80 percent finish high school.

By the end of World War I our secondary schools were dominated by an increasing number of pupils who were not only unselected but who were also unwilling—in high school not because they wished to learn but because the law forced them to go. The free school, once a splendid opportunity for those who chose it, now held a captive audience. As the 20th century progressed, high schools filled with a growing proportion of doubtful, reluctant, untalented, unsuited, unfit, and actually hostile pupils. Average ability and interest declined greatly. Between 1870 and 1955, a period during which our population increased 4 times, the public school population increased 80 times.

In 1893, a group of leading educators undertook a study of high school curricula in the United States and made recommendations based upon its review. The group found that there were then some 40 subjects taught somewhere nationwide, but that 13 of these were offered at very few schools. The basic curriculum was based on 27 subjects. The group recommended a set of four alternative courses for secondary schools—a classical course, a Latin-scientific course, a modern language course, and an English course. The curricula varied in accordance with their relative emphasis on the classics, modern languages, and English. All required four years of English, four years of foreign language, three years of history, three years of mathematics, and three years of science. There is a close similarity between these recommendations and those made a half century later by James Bryant Conant, in his survey of high schools, as a minimum program for "academically talented boys and girls." Three decades have passed since Conant's recommendations fell on deaf ears, during which time we have moved in enormous steps further along the route from which he hoped to turn us.

In the older education the teacher was measured by what he or she could do with a bright girl or boy. At the end of the 19th century one of the traditional educators, Charles William Eliot, wrote in this vein: "The policy of an institution of education, of whatever grade, ought never to be determined by the needs of the least capable students." Obviously, this philosophy would have been difficult to maintain in the conditions which developed in the United States. The difficulty was not faced at all. Instead of regarding the mediocre, the reluctant, or incapable students as obstacles, or as special problems in a school system devoted to educating the interested, the capable, and the gifted, American educators entered upon a crusade to exalt the academically uninterested and ungifted child.

A new ideology justified this course, one which proclaimed that the old ideal of education was archaic and futile, and that a "truly democratic" system was one which would meet the child's immediate interests by offering a series of "practical" and "useful" things. For the first time in the history of education teaching came to be measured, not by what could be done with the best, but by what could be done with the worst.

Public money was spent accordingly. In the words of the late Richard Hofstadter, ours is the only educational system in the world which is dominated by professionals "who joyfully and militantly proclaim their hostility to intellect, and their eagerness to identify with children who show the least educational promise." For a long time now our professional educators have assumed and rejoiced in the idea that, for practical purposes, representatives of our most numerous and most deprived classes are incapable of academic excellence. Because most are incapable, the opportunity to achieve academic excellence has been denied to almost all of those who are capable.

The crucial question was the academic curriculum. Educational theorists justified the view that *academic* subjects were irrelevant for the mass of secondary school students. In 1911 there were one million high school students, in 1941 more than six million. Latin, taken by 49 percent of all high school students in 1911, was taken by 7.8 percent in 1949. Modern language enrollment fell from 84 percent to 22 percent. In both instances the total number of enrolled students dropped while the student population increased six-fold. Algebra enrollment fell from 57 percent to 27 percent; geometry from 31 percent to 13 percent. Total mathematics enrollment fell from 90 percent to 55 percent, total science enrollment from 82 percent to 33 percent. In 1911 more pupils were studying foreign languages, or mathematics, or science, or history, or English—any of these—than all non-academic subjects combined. By 1941 some 274 subjects were offered in high schools, only 59 of which, using the most inclusive definition imaginable, could be classified as academic subjects. And the most violent stages of the revolution were still to come, for in 1941 almost all children with the aspiration to pursue higher education still enrolled in academic subjects. The changes in secondary education had done relatively little harm to the children of the more affluent, more sophisticated, or more ambitious parents.

During the 1940s and 1950s the leaders of our educational bureaucracy, with the aid and support of the United States Office of Education, largely succeeded in making completely dominant the values of the crusade against intellectualism which had already won so many victories. A very large percentage of those in our high schools were, and today a still higher percentage are, unsuited or incompetent to deal with the academic curriculum. A significant minority of young people always have and always will lack the mental endowment to succeed or to benefit very fully from that curriculum. Our educationist's first response to the influx of masses of incompetent and disinterested students was to provide "alternative" education in the form of a wide choice of "practical" courses and non-college preparatory high school programs. These programs were then "enriched." In the next stage, the academic curriculum was denigrated as archaic and elitist, to be imposed on or required of no one. The consequence of these policies has effectively denied the advantages of the academic curriculum to the *majority* of our young, who could benefit from it, and in practice has been highly discriminatory: It has denied opportunity to the talented children among the socially and economically underprivileged.

Shortly after the end of World War II the United States Commissioner of Education announced that only seven out of ten youths were entering senior high school, and that only four of these graduated. In spite of 40 years of trying to increase the "holding power" of schools, large numbers of young people were still not completing their secondary education. "Enriching" the curriculum ten-fold had failed to accomplish its purpose—a purpose which itself was passing strange for so-called "educators." The Commissioner concluded that the curriculum had not been enriched enough. The Office of Education then issued its first manual on "Life Adjustment," which revealed an important discovery: the needs of the great majority of American youth were not being adequately served by secondary schools. Proof of this was that 20 percent were being prepared for college and 20 percent for skilled occupations. The remaining 60 percent came almost entirely from unskilled and semi-skilled families with low incomes, who provided a poor cultural environment. These young people made low grades, scored lower on intelligence and achievement tests, lacked interest in school work, and were "less emotionally mature—nervous, and feel less secure."

The public servants who wrote the manual did not mean to be unkind. They declared that "these characteristics are not intended to brand this group as in any sense inferior." Inferior or not, a majority of the nation's children were written off as unfit, not only for academic studies that prepare for college, but even for vocational education leading to "desirable skilled occupations," whether mechanical or clerical. The authors did not bother to note that almost every child from an affluent or even an educated background was in a college preparatory program, that it was an oddity for one of them to be found even in the privileged 20 percent preparing for the "skilled professions," intending to become, for example, a bricklayer or a secretary. National educational policy was, then, to be based upon the premise that 60 percent of our youth are unfit for any professional or skilled work, and that all of this 60 percent happened to be born into deprived circumstances.

Before long these same educators declared that their ideals should be applied not only to the unfit 60 percent. What was good for them would be good for all American youth, however competent or gifted. The only learning which has practical meaning in the real world thus came more and more to be a privilege of those young people from educated and affluent homes where speaking and writing correctly were learned from everyday example, and in which the reading of books began by the age of ten and continued through life.

The following statement, given wide currency and notoriety by both Arthur Bestor and Richard Hofstader, expresses a point of view which for years now has dominated departments of education, and which today is more widely held by public school principals and superintendents than any other. Soon after the publication of the paper which contained these remarks the author, a junior-high-school principal, was appointed to a like post in the affluent township of Great Neck, Long Island, where *far fewer* than 60 percent of the children came from low-income, unskilled or semi-skilled families.

> Through the years we've built a sort of halo around reading, writing, and arithmetic. We've said that they were for everybody . . . rich and poor,

brilliant and not so mentally endowed. . . . Teacher has said that these were something "everyone should learn." The principal has remarked, "All educated people know how to write, spell, and read. . . ."

We've made some progress in getting rid of that slogan. But every now and then some mother with a Phi Beta Kappa award or some employer who has hired a girl who can't spell stirs up a fuss about the schools . . . and ground is lost. . . .

When we come to the realization that not every child has to read, figure, write and spell . . . then we shall be on the road to improving the junior high school curriculum. . . .

Between this day and that a lot of selling must take place. But it's coming. . . .

We cannot all do the same things. We do not all like the same things. And won't. When adults finally realize the fact, everyone will be happier . . . and schools will be nicer places in which to live.

If and when we are able to convince a few folks that mastery of reading, writing, and arithmetic is not the one road leading to happy, successful living, the new step is to cut down the amount of time and attention devoted to these areas in general junior high school courses. . . .

These comments were made in the midst of a revolution which even then had largely succeeded in emasculating the curriculum which the writer proposed to bury.

No sensible person ever believed that everyone could benefit fully from the academic curriculum. *Everyone* cannot benefit fully from any form or kind of education. Those who believe in the academic curriculum, which indeed may be defined as the only kind of public school education which serves the best and highest interests of a majority of all children, are dedicated to the notion that the opportunity to have its advantages should be denied to no one capable of benefiting from it. That learning to read and write "was the road to happiness" was a thought with no more standing among traditionalists than the view that illiteracy is bliss can be presumed to have among educational "enrichers." The inability to read and write is a handicap, the grave consequences of which are in direct proportion to the social or economic background of those with the deficiency. Those who believe in the academic curriculum are unhappy that so many of those who are unsuited or unfit for it are unsuited or unfit not because they are untalented but because of their background and environment. A large majority of the children of the affluent once were capable of benefiting from it, and *did* benefit from it. A large majority of their underprivileged contemporaries were unfit and unsuited. *Yet the pool of natural talent in both groups has always been roughly equal.* This has been a tragedy and a disgrace.

A significant percentage, probably one-third, of all young people do lack the mental endowment to succeed in or benefit very fully from an academic curriculum—although a very large percentage of these, through the first ten grades, would benefit more from it than from any other "schooling." College, and the academic curriculum which ought to be the preparation for it, is for an elite, but not for a narrow elite. In 1940 80 percent of the young people from affluent families attended some kind of college or university. They were certainly not an "intellectual elite." Yet almost all of them could and did meet more rigorous academic standards than exist today.

In the 1950s, only half the best-qualified students attended college, and half of those who did attend college were less qualified than an equal number who did not attend. Differences in economic and social background, not of ability or performance, were the most decisive factors in determining who did and who did not attend college. Today economic barriers to higher education are still high. Among the young of middle-range ability, two-thirds of the affluent go to college, while less than one-third of the poor attend. But, as we will discover, ability and achievement have even lost much of the relevance they once had, and today our essential problems are quite different. In the late 1950s observers devoted to the principle of equal opportunity were concerned about the injustice of having a college population one-half of which was less competent than a group of young people, equally numerous, who were not in college at all. Such critics did not espouse anything so meaningless as "college for all," but rather a system in which opportunity was equal and in which factors relevant to academic performance would be decisive in determining who would receive its advantages.

Many questions have been raised about tests of all sorts. Because so many do so poorly on all standardized examinations there is a large audience which is glad and willing to believe that such tests are invalid. And because achievement tests also measure the performance of our educational system, the educational establishment has been loudest in discounting them. Confusion about such matters in the mind of the general public is therefore widespread and inescapable. Without, at this point, taking up this whole matter in detail, a truncated discussion of it may clarify certain issues, and answer the question raised in some minds by reference made to the "incompetent," to discuss tests which do not measure achievement but, instead, talent.

Intelligence tests have been used less and less by our educational establishment. These tests are subject to misinterpretation, misunderstanding and abuse. Like all objective standards, their results reveal things which some find disagreeable and unacceptable. Their proper use requires sound judgment and some subtlety of mind, but they were and are a means by which natural intellectual ability or the lack of it can be measured and discovered. For practical purposes there is no better single means of identifying intellectual promise among the economically and culturally unprivileged whose presence, manner, bearing, style, and speech give evidence of mediocrity or less. The virtual suppression of such tests by educational institutions, for a variety of reasons including surrender to the criticism of affluent activist parents of untalented children and the complaints of misguided or demogogic spokesmen of minority groups, has had the effect of denying an opportunity for recognition of the talented young who need it most, and is one step of many to remove objectivity from influence over practical educational policy and thus to increase injustice.

In recent history, our government itself used such tests. During World War II certain levels of intelligence, as measured by a standard IQ test, were required in order to qualify for certain kinds of specialized training. Only those enlisted men with a specific score, or higher, could qualify for Officer Candidate School in the Army of the United States. The effect of this regulation was democratic. It denied the opportunity for a commission to many who, because of background or education or influence, would have won appointment to the School, and it qualified many who had no such influence. The same level of IQ required by the Army for appointment to Officer Candidate School was the same as that long generally regarded as the dividing line between those capable and incapable of succeeding in the traditional high school curriculum. Before 1965 few prestigious colleges or universities accepted students with a lower score, and when they did it was not often the children of the poor. About 40 percent of the population achieve this score. Thus, by this measure, 40 percent of all youth have the talent which qualifies them to succeed in the academic curriculum in high school—leaving aside how many others might benefit from it. This is double the number deemed fit by life-adjustment educators. IQ distribution in the general population is very much less class-related than is achievement. The percentage of high-IQ children from semi-skilled and unskilled parents is within the same range as among the children of more favored elements within the population. Distribution is race-related, partly because a higher percentage of blacks and members of other minority groups (including some which are white) suffers from particularly deprived circumstances, and succeed less well than others in fulfilling their genetic potential.

On the other hand, superior intellectual ability exists and can be identified by these tests in every ethnic minority group. Achievement is, generally speaking, both class- and race-related. These bare facts have led to the illogical charge that achievement and IQ tests are themselves a form of social and racial oppression. The reason some social and racial groups score lower than the native white population is certainly, to one degree or another, a consequence of their relatively deprived circumstances. If there were no measurable differences between achievement levels within these groups and those who enjoy more favorable circumstances, the evidence for social and racial injustice would be much reduced or nonexistent.

Present academic policy is, in one sense, quite democratic. It is comforting to a majority of all parents of every class and background. A majority of young people of every class and background lack the ability to succeed in the traditional high school curricula. By effectively denying it to all our youth, we have determined that its advantages be available only to the fortunate few who receive them from their home environment, or who attend exclusive and expensive private schools. But some 40 percent of all parents, of every class—quite a substantial minority—should realize that present educational policy cheats them and cheats their children. And we are all cheated, whatever the innate intellectual abilities of our own children, by a system which wastes the talent of the nation's youth.

PART ONE

Our Students and Our Colleges

1 Slogans of Deceit: "Access" and "Alternatives"

In the 1920s 40 percent of the population finished high
school. Today high schools have largely abandoned the idea
that the pupil should know anything in particular in order to
win a diploma, and 80 percent finish. The student who has
spent 12 years in school is felt to have "earned" some kind of
diploma, and it is thought "unfair" to send him away empty-
handed. In 1920 8 percent of the 18- to 21-year age group was
enrolled in colleges or universities. Today 40 percent of those
who graduate from high school attend some kind of college or
university. Some 2,500 colleges and universities, with budgets
totalling more than $24 billion, enroll 7,600,000 students. In
1950 half of college and university students attended public
institutions. Today about 80 percent do. In the 1950s half the

students who entered four-year institutions of higher learning finished. By 1970 two-thirds of those who entered did not finish. Meanwhile, the most common reason for not finishing changed, from the failure to meet required standards to simple disinterest. By 1970 (and the trend has continued) colleges failed fewer and fewer students, and today any person with a high-school diploma, and often without one, has an enormously wide range of institutions of higher learning which will accept him.

We have had a huge increase in the number and proportion of students enrolled in colleges and universities, students whose preparation, natural abilities, and attitudes parallel those of students who flooded into the high schools in the 1920s. That two-thirds of this new type of college student dropped out before finishing a four-year program has been used to justify the destruction of the higher education curriculum.

Not that students have dropped out because traditional standards were maintained, however. Declining student achievement has been accompanied by grade inflation so great that achievement, had there been no other measure, might have seemed to be increasing. Colleges have reduced the number and jazzed up the content of basic courses, weakened graduation requirements, and added a host of academically less demanding electives. Grades have lost much of their former meaning and students are able to get through college more easily and with less preparation but with higher grades than ever before. Absenteeism from classes has reached incredible levels. At our large urban public institutions students hold demanding part-time, even full-time, jobs while enrolled in a full-time schedule of classes, and find that their grades, if they pick and choose their courses, suffer little, if at all. The total number of hours required to obtain the baccalaureate degree has been cut back, semesters have been shortened, and vacations lengthened. All of this began in the mid-1960s, just at the time when students who were beginning to be less well prepared than any who had preceded them flooded into our institutions. Collectively, these trends have undermined the rational and intellectual foundations of higher education.

In colleges and universities across the country general education requirements have dropped by 22 percent during the last decade. This movement parallels a steady drop in the competence of entering college students. Less qualified students when they enter, less is done than ever before to correct their deficiencies. Requirements in English, history, literature, foreign languages, and mathematics have all declined appreciably. And the decline in percentages reveals only a small part of the trend. The requirements which have been kept have been watered down beyond recognition. A huge variety of new courses have been invented and defined so as to fit traditional categories. "Foreign language" requirements are met by reading works in translation. Science departments have designed freshman courses, for which their own majors can receive no credit, fitted to the ability and interest levels of students unprepared for introductory college-level courses of the type which prepare the student to go on to the next step in the discipline. A majority of entering college freshmen are unqualified to take introductory college science courses which in the 1950s were required of every freshman.

There is no end in sight. In 1978, at the University of South Florida, where the average competence of entering freshmen is well below that required at better private institutions (not to speak of prestigious ones), 200 members of the freshman class became "instant sophomores" before setting foot in a college classroom or taking a college course. They did so by taking part in the "credit-by-examination process," called the College Level Examination Program. Organized during the 1967–68 academic year, CLEP had only 1,400 takers at first. Since then the number has soared. Today some 100,000 students are taking 250,000 CLEP examinations annually. The pass rate is 74 percent, and the results are accepted by more than 1,800 colleges as substitutes for course credit. CLEP promoters say that they have "only begun to scratch the surface," but even now most public colleges and universities participate, as do many large private institutions with low entrance requirements.

That 1,800 American colleges and universities have given

hundreds of thousands of credit hours for these examinations is a major academic scandal. In the overwhelming majority of cases these hours of credit have been granted to students already highly disadvantaged when compared to their contemporaries who attend prestigious private colleges and universities. Almost all students at such institutions have greater academic skill, more general knowledge, and more "practical" abilities when they enter college than does the average graduate of the institutions which are likely to give away college credit for the purpose of "cutting down the expense and the time it takes to earn a degree."

In the name of opening up "access" to higher education to all young people, especially to the poor and to minority groups, we have transformed our institutions. We have duped those sections of our population who are the least sophisticated and the most credulous in educational matters. We do now give degrees to those who want them badly enough, but "access" has not been given to higher education; something has been substituted for that education. The sleight of hand has befuddled almost everyone, and the most befuddled remain those who have been most exploited. They cry out plaintively that "a degree does not guarantee a good job." Employers, however, are not befuddled. They require competence, and they have been quick to recognize how meaningless a guarantee a B.A. degree is that the holder knows or can do anything at all.

The leaders of the federal educational bureaucracy, who had played a decisive role in the destruction of the high-school curriculum, have done all in their power to destroy the college and university curriculum. In the first instance they based their policies on the premise that 60 percent of the young were unfit for academic studies. This premise was veiled in terms which deceived or misled much of the public. They continued to be absolutely indifferent to the interests and concerns of those capable of being educated, whatever their percentage might be, and addressed themselves solely to the problem of the two-thirds of our masses of college students who do not finish.

The Newman Report, prepared for the Secretary of Health,

Education and Welfare by a committee headed by a Stanford University administrator, Frank Newman, appeared in 1971. A response to critics who demanded "reform" because of the dropout rate in colleges, the report was widely acclaimed in the press as the best of the large number of recent studies on education. Certainly no other report was to be so useful to the anti-intellectuals at the top of our educational bureaucracy. Our whole system of higher education was criticized on grounds that denigrated education itself. The report declared:

> [I]t is not enough to improve and expand the present system. . . . The system . . . resists fundamental change, rarely eliminates outmoded programs . . . ignores the differing needs of students, seldom questions its goals, and almost never creates different types of institutions.

When this statement was issued colleges and universities had already turned themselves inside out, making fundamental changes, eliminating unpopular programs, all in the name of meeting the "needs" of students. Most remarkable of all was the charge that there was an absence of "different types of institutions." The plethora of "different kinds of institutions" which call themselves colleges and universities in the United States are so varied and dissimilar that the terms themselves have little meaning except when used in reference to specific institutions.

When the Newman Report was issued Sidney P. Marland was United States Education Commissioner. His views were directly related to those of that Report. Marland believed that it was his job to effect a completely new system of education. He announced that the changes he had in mind would "take time" and cost "billions of dollars in public funds." He called for two goals for high schools: to give every student a saleable skill or to prepare him for college.

If one did not know his definitions of "saleable skill" and "college" this might have seemed somewhat reasonable. The ability to push a broom for eight hours a day is a saleable skill, but few dreamed that Mr. Marland had such "skills" in mind. He did. He proposed that states be allowed to use money allocated for vocational education for more "relevant" programs, on training for saleable skills which are not usually honored by the name of "vocation," but which would be suited to those unfit either for vocational training or for college, who, according to the philosophy of the federal educational bureaucracy, make up 60 percent of our young, including almost all of our young who are poor or non-white. As far as can be discovered, no child of a top bureaucrat has ever been thought to fit into the "in no way inferior" 60 percent. In his first major speech after his appointment Mr. Marland described general education, which imparts an introduction to that body of information which middle- and upper-middle-class children possess, but which their inferiors do not have, as "irrelevant pap." But the definition of "college" carried in such minds needs to be understood by the public.

The authors of the Newman Report noted the enormous expansion which had taken place in higher education in the United States—that more than one-third of the young between 18 and 21 were in college, that the percentage was growing, and that there was also a marked shift from private to public institutions of higher learning—and declared, although it was demonstrably untrue at the time, that there was a growing lack of "diversity" among colleges. This was so because most colleges were trying harder and harder to become as much as possible like the 100 or so most prestigious institutions. They concluded that America had built its system of higher education on the assumption that if more and more young people could be persuaded to go to institutions that looked more and more like Harvard, society would get better and better.

This was a misleading simplification in part, of somewhat more validity if applied to what had been going on in the 1950s, and in part was a simple untruth. The diversity in American institutions has always been exceedingly great, which has led, for one thing, to vast confusion in the minds of the public as to what higher education is; and the expansion in recent years has meant even greater diversity, not less. And nothing is less certain than that diversity is good. Society might certainly not have gotten better and better if more and more young people could have been persuaded to attend institutions as much like Harvard as possible. No one really knows what kind of "education" will make people "better and better." But certainly such a Harvardian development would have meant that more Americans were better educated than they would have been otherwise. One might believe that every young person with talent and ambition to benefit from it should have the opportunity for the very best possible education. Many in this country have associated the best with Harvard, or with a few schools of similar reputation. These models are certainly not perfect ones, but popular opinion is correct in preferring them to any others known to it.

The Newman Report made much humorless fun of practices and assumptions which were invented and presented as having real existence. It declared that there were two points of view worth noting. One view was that our nation had made a serious mistake in attempting to fit half of its young people into an institution which was designed for an intellectual elite. The other point of view which the authors found worthy of notice held that we should do a better job of opening access to higher education to all young people, especially to the poor and minority groups, and that we should change institutions, or create new ones, to meet the needs of the new clientele. In political terms it may be said that these two points of view expressed the interests of those who wished to cut wasteful spending and those who wished to see levels of spending maintained or increased. The conclusions reached in the Newman Report suggest that the interests of both groups were influential, but that the spokesmen for poor and minority groups were more influential.

The authors of the report did not recognize the existence of another point of view, one that presumed "higher education" had a specific content, which, whatever its other virtues or defects, had greater "practical" usefulness for the children of the poor and of minority groups than any other, and that no "alternative" systems had any practical usefulness at all in the educational sense. That "alternative" systems ensure that a larger share of public educational expenses will go to the political interest groups which dominate urban communities, the densely populated states, and the federal government is true. The principle of Bread and Circuses is not an educational principle, however, even when "higher education" becomes one of the circuses. Higher education should be the birthright of all our young people who have not been born or made unfit for it. That is an educational principle, even if, as the Newman Report would suggest, it is not a principle which has political viability.

Critics who declared that we had made a mistake in attempting to fit half our young people into "an institution designed for an intellectual elite" should have been partially content with the recommendations of the Newman Report. It accepted the view that the children of the poor and of minority groups were unsuited for such an institution. But this did not lead to a recommendation to cut spending. The authors were moved to their greatest concern by a fact which, on the face of it, might have been a sign of health. They were disquieted to discover that two-thirds of those who enter college did not complete a four-year program, and that at large state colleges the dropout rate was even higher. Their solution was astonishing.

The authors of the Newman Report proposed that more alternative institutions be created, where students would not be expected to learn the same way as at Harvard or at its imitators, and they pleaded for institutions which would allow students to learn "in other ways than sitting in classrooms and reading books," and from which, by implication, they would not drop out until they had finished. This, the authors explained, would provide "access" for the poor and for minorities, and allow the Harvards to serve the intellectual elite.

Mr. Newman, after 1974 the president of Rhode Island University, declared in a 1976 interview that "the university is the way to assure yourself that you are in the upper class" in

England, and that in the United States, more egalitarian, in the past "if you could somehow get into that marked group, then you were separated out from the rest of society." Today, he noted, young people going to college do not have that kind of guarantee:

> Even if you go to college you have to make your own way. The combination of that fact with that of the cost means you simply have to raise some serious questions about the value of going to college.

This conclusion, presumably, he addressed to the less affluent and the poor. The article reporting the interview included the information that Mr. Newman was spending $25,000 on the education of his son, who attended the Massachusetts Institute of Technology, where, at last report, students both sat in classrooms and read books.

The recommendation for "alternative" institutions was a solution which shrewdly exploited the claim of minority spokesmen that traditional educational standards were a disguised form of racism and oppression. The recommendation had the merit of quieting fears that total funds expended on higher education might be reduced so as to have some rational relationship to the cost of educating those among the young capable of benefiting from higher learning. If followed, there would still be greater expenditures, and more jobs—new institutions suited to those incapable of pursuing traditional higher learning would be established, and "elitists" institutions would be left to their own devices.

Our institutions of higher learning have always been enormously diversified. At the time recommendations were made for more "alternative" institutions a large majority of our colleges and universities were already alternatives to anything which could possibly be described as elitist or archaic in curriculum and standards. For a long time, much too long it might be thought, there had been institutions geared to students of the lowest levels of academic competence, and these institutions had been increasing in number and size at a rate to fully meet the demand of such students for a college education.

2 Diversity: Students and Institutions

A generation ago an important descriptive work, *The American College*, edited by Nevitt Sanford, was published. In ideological outlook the authors typified the liberal academic viewpoint of that day. They felt that our institutions of higher learning were not doing a good job of liberal education. The proof of this was the conservative and reactionary ideas, or political indifference, and shallow material interests, and a lack of interest in the "finer things" of college-educated Americans. The evidence for this was that they voted for Eisenhower instead of Stevenson, that they did not go to concerts or the theatre enough, and that they preferred their sons to be bankers rather than poets. The authors said that "if one supposed that the main business of a college was to nurture students who had intellectual and scholarly interests," he might well wonder how such students fared at even our best institutions in which they were so sadly out-numbered. On the other hand, the authors were surprised that this evidence of "failure" did not seem to lessen the general public's willingness to support institutions of higher learning. They observed that even though our culture placed relatively little value upon learning or the intellectual life, and had little understanding of, or sympathy for, "what professors are trying to do," the general public did seem to regard college as one of the greatest goods, and that for the great mass of the middle-class students going to college was second in importance only to getting a job and getting married. The belief was that "you have to go to college to get anywhere these days." For the great middle-class college was a social necessity, and for the lower classes a means of social advancement.

The discovery that the general public had little interest in improving colleges should not have been surprising. The au-thors discovered that the main effect of four years of college was to make students more like one another. This was, after all, what the general public wanted and expected. Colleges and universities, even Harvard and Yale, long ago would have with-ered and died if they had depended upon support from parents who wished to see their children transformed into intellectuals with scholarly interests. What professors were trying to do did not matter for so long as their subversive efforts were ineffec-tive, or nearly so.

Colleges and universities traditionally have been institutions into which students of great diversity enter to be developed in such a way that they will possess qualities which are desired by those who support higher learning. In spite of the radical di-versity of our institutions, the quality of students, faculty, and standards, their goals, although varied, all include some intro-duction to our civilization and the material environment, and to some degree are specialized so as to focus on preparing the student for a particular social role. Some idealists have thought it appalling that, realistically, colleges could be looked upon primarily as personnel offices, feeding properly certified em-ployees into business and the professions.

But certainly a significant function of college has always been to train young people to respond with a disciplined attitude to work not of their own devising, providing employers and professional schools with a good yardstick for determining who would perform well for them. And although today very many professors actually ask whether or not colleges should be willing to do this, and, indeed, think that their highest function is to inculcate an unwillingness to participate in or collaborate with the "system," colleges and universities would not exist if our society did not expect them to make their students more competent and more useful.

Colleges and universities, to one degree or another, some very little and some a great deal, increase the usefulness and competence of those who attend them. Some very little, and some a great deal, inculcate social and personal skills which are useful in life, and necessary in most "good" jobs. Until 1960 all studies of taste and opinion suggested that one of the greatest chasms in our society was between those who had been to college and those who had not. What poor and lower-middle-class students mainly learned, and which was most useful in life of what they did learn in college, they learned from their more affluent fellow students. Disadvantaged students learned most and were changed most at institutions of higher learning in which they were most outnumbered by their social and economic superiors. The kind of institution which they attended, not the college degree itself, determined the extent to which the opportunity for social mobility presented itself.

The democratization of education has meant the creation of colleges so uniformly lower-middle-class in style that the very notion that college marks a decisive social change—as it must if it is to have future meaning for those from such backgrounds—never enters the students' minds. Students at such institutions assume that all they need to become upper-middle-class is the right job, and that this job will be available once they have accumulated enough course credits to graduate. They presume that, outside of scientific fields, courses will not teach them the things they will need on the job. They simply want to accumulate enough credits to get the job. What they fail to realize is that the courses which seem most irrelevant to them, and which are the most difficult for them, are, in fact, the most useful. They have little sense at all of the fact that promotion into the occupational-cultural elite depends most upon social and intellectual skills, to which the course of studies they are most likely to pursue contributes little or nothing.

Once upon a time it was possible for a lower-middle-class college to have intellectual eminence, such as the City College of New York did in the 1930s, and to compensate to an important degree for the virtual absence of more sophisticated upper-middle and upper-class students. But CCNY had a clientele which was highly sophisticated about the potential benefits of high-level performance in scholarly and scientific pursuits, which prized intellectual attainment, and, most necessary of all, had the political influence to ensure public support for this kind of institution. High academic standards were expected and respected. No such institution has been able to survive the democratization which has taken place since 1960. Politics has made them extinct. Such institutions would have been appropriate models for the new public institutions of the 1950s and 1960s. Instead they failed even to survive as honorable institutions.

Mark Twain once pointed out that if Shakespeare had been born on a barren unvisited rock in the ocean he would have produced nothing, that in Turkey he would have produced something, and that in France, he would have produced something better. College environments differ in the same way that a barren unvisited rock in the ocean differs from Paris, and almost as much. One important characteristic which makes prestigious private colleges and universities, and some of the older state universities, different from the newer public institutions is that in the latter, upper-middle-class students who could enlarge the career as well as the cultural horizons of their fellow students are not present. Faculties are nearly as different as are students in these two kinds of institutions. Although, tragically, the differences are becoming less and less.

There has always been a "backward" country in American higher education. Once this was mainly in the countryside, teacher's colleges in which not only were there no broadly educated professors, but also no member of the faculty who in his own schooling had encountered such a person. This is now a common phenomenon throughout our recently created public institutions of higher learning, particularly in urban areas. David Riesman noted, more than 20 years ago:

> Today there are so many institutions in which almost the whole faculty consists of first generation collegians. . . . In such settings tastelessness and laxity may not only feed on themselves but also renew themselves in the oncoming generation of teachers. . . . Thus many colleges can do little to alter the parochialism of the culturally impoverished whom they equip with a diploma and other symbols of respectability.

Professors in general also live lives quite isolated from highly competent people in the upper reaches of the worlds of business, medicine, law, or politics. In the "backward" country of higher education the typical professor, who by profession, either certified by a degree in sociology, psychology, political science, or history, or self-appointed because of an "advanced" degree in anything at all, is an "expert" in contemporary American society and politics, but has never met on intimate friendly terms a successful independent businessman or lawyer, a congressman or a surgeon, an army or a police officer, or an executive in a large company. His isolation from the world of achievement and work is practically complete. He is of less help than other lower-middle-class students in suggesting career goals to students.

Institutions of higher learning differ greatly in the kinds of background common to their typical students. As a consequence they also differ in the kinds of academic skills their students have. Here the differences are nearly unimaginable. The diversity of entering college students is striking among institutions and among students entering the same institution. Many of our colleges are now designed for students of low ability, and most of their students fit. But such institutions do not turn away students of high ability, and colleges with low standards will almost always have students of a very wide range of ability. The lower-middle-class or poor student of high ability is unlikely ever to overcome the consequence of having, almost always in complete innocence, chosen such an institution rather than another, which in many cases would have been available to him had he understood the difference. Understanding standardized tests and test scores and their use by colleges and universities is necessary if one is to sort out some of these differences.

In 1947, President Truman's Commission on Higher Education recommended the score of 100 on the ACE Psychological Examination as the threshold for entering a college or university. In part this recommendation grew out of a concern, long since outdated, that too few of our brightest and too many of the dull were attending college. The recommended threshold was significantly lower than that demanded by better private institutions, many of which took very few students under 110 and then as exceptions to their general policy. Some schools required a score of 120. On the other hand, in 1954 the mean score for entering freshmen at institutions of all kinds was 94. The average college freshman in the country had a significantly lower score than that recommended as the threshold by the President's Commission (although its recommendation was to admit students which most of our better institutions would not accept). At the same time college students who successfully pursued disciplines leading to the professions came almost exclusively from those who had scored above 110. All in all, one of the most impressive and important facts was the diversity among colleges in respect to the students they attracted or selected, and this is true to this day.

In 1938 a study was made in the variations in scholastic aptitude and achievement among 49 Pennsylvania colleges. The results revealed a condition which, if it has changed at all in more than 40 years, has changed in the direction of even greater diversity. Great diversity was found not only among student bodies, but also among students majoring in various subjects. On a general culture test, in 3 of the 49 colleges not a single student equalled the mean score of students in the college with the best-prepared students. One-fourth of all college seniors, clustered mainly in a few colleges, made lower scores than the sophomore average, and nearly 10 percent of all college seniors, clustered mainly in the same few colleges, did less well than the *average* high school senior. School status, defined as time spent and courses passed in school or college, thus had no necessary relation to any body of ideas understood and available as a result of education.

This remains to this day the fundamental truth about our system of higher education. A college degree, in itself, tells us nothing about what the holder knows or can do. Most seniors at some high schools are better educated, in the formal sense of having a broader knowledge of our culture as well as superior language and mathematical skills, than are most graduates of many of our colleges.

In recent years the Scholastic Aptitude Tests (SATs) have largely replaced the ACE examination as a means of determining academic eligibility or competence. Essentially, they are achievement tests, standardized measurements of verbal and mathematical reasoning ability. The scores are used by colleges and universities as a basis for comparing students, whose high school grades cannot usefully be compared because of the diversity of standards and programs in the high schools. The tests are conducted by the Educational Testing Service of Princeton, New Jersey. College Board Scores, or SATs, are weighed by almost all colleges and universities in determining who is admitted among those who apply. In every state in our nation there is a number, in some states a large number, of public and private colleges and universities to which students can obtain admission with very low scores, and almost no students are denied admission to college itself because of poor performance on these tests. However, many students are denied admission to the college of their choice because of deficiencies which the tests reveal.

Many students from poor or modest circumstances are admitted to and granted scholarships to our best colleges and universities because these tests enable them to demonstrate their superiority and promise in comparison to their peers. The tests demonstrate a student's ability, or lack of it, to function in a college or university which maintains meaningful academic standards.

Indeed, what these scores mean, and what they reflect, are subject to a variety of conflicting interpretations. The scores do predict the possibility, or the impossibility, that the student perform well, they reveal the competence, or the lack of it, to meet reasonable academic standards in a college or university. They test something as real, as relevant, and as measurable, as the time it takes a baseball player to run from home to first, or the accuracy and velocity with which he throws from right field to third base.

In recent years, SAT results have been a measure of the decline in public-school education in the United States. Here they concern us only insofar as they reveal further evidence of the diversity of our college population. Today about 1.5 million students take the tests each year: one-third of all high school graduates, and two-thirds of the freshman class in colleges and universities. The test-taking group is made up of our best students; students with no intention of attending college do not ordinarily take them. The decline in performance which they reveal, extreme as it has been, is much less than the decline which they do *not* measure—that in the performance of students who have been tracked into vocational or "non-college" programs.

The highest national average achieved by students taking the College Boards was in 1963, when the average score was 478. The decline has been steady since. In 1966–67 the average score was 466, in 1971–72 it was 453, in 1975–76 it was 431, in 1979–80 it was 424. In 1980–81 it rose one point, to 425, and fell back to 424 in 1981–82. Further decline in the future, if the tests are not tampered with, is predictable on the basis of a study completed in early 1983 which revealed declining scores for high achievers during the 70's among 8th and 11th graders. High school students in the nation's largest cities rank far below the national average, with cities comprising 50 percent minority population more than 60 points lower. Only 15 percent of blacks score above 400, and only 2 percent above 500. Again, all of these figures refer to the *best* students in high school, not to the total population, or even to half of it. And during the year 1963, when the average score was the highest, that score, 478, was not high enough to gain entrance to better private colleges or universities in any part of the country. It was well below the score which was generally thought necessary to perform adequately, much less successfully, in respectable institutions of higher learning. In the early 1960s scores of 600 or better were required to gain admittance at our more prestigious colleges and universities, and scores of 500 or better were required generally by institutions with little or no serious claim to academic excellence.

No college or university can rise very far above the average level of the preparation, ability, and motivation of its students. What students can be required to learn is limited by what they are capable of learning—and this is determined by what they know and can do when they enter. Academic goals are no more than abstractions. What actually happens in the classrooms of any college or university is decided, in the first place, by the kind of student who attends. Today there are many institutions of higher learning at which the average SAT score of entering freshman is below 450; there are others where it is above 600. In Atlanta, Newark, and Washington D.C. the average score for high school graduates taking the College Board test is under 350. There are colleges with significant percentages of students with even these kinds of scores.

3 Diversity: Within A Single Institution

The diversity among students majoring in different subjects is so great that B.A. degrees granted by the same institution differ as radically from one another as do typical degrees from institutions with entirely different levels of average graduates. A college whose average freshman has greater knowledge and competence than the average senior at another institution may have departments in which the average senior is less knowledgeable and competent than the average freshman at the inferior institution. The time spent in college and the number of courses taken tells us nothing specific about what a person knows or can do. Unless we know the student's major, the time the student has spent and the number of courses he has taken tells us very little about what he knows or can do even if we know the college or university he attended. Even grade averages of graduating seniors have little use as a basis of comparison between students attending the same institution, because standards vary so between departments, and because departments at the same institutions attract students of very different levels of competence. There are very few public colleges or universities at which "alternative" education is not available for those who fail to qualify for anything resembling "higher" education.

The following description is of the student body of one of our recently founded public universities. Located in one of the major Eastern cities, the students of this university compare favorably with those of similar institutions, and are superior to those of some. In a typical year during the 1970s the average SAT score of an entering class of 1500 was 480. At this university the four point grading system is used: $4 = A$, $3 = B$, $2 = C$, $1 = D$. At the end of four semesters 52 of the 1,500 students had a cumulative grade point average of 3.5 or above. Although nearly half of the 1,500 were graduates of urban high schools in the city in which the university is located, only two of these 52 good students came from such a school. The average SAT score of these 52 was 566.

The performance of these 52 students in two departments is instructive. Majors in history in this group had an average SAT score of 660. Majors in sociology in this group had an average SAT score of 492. This pattern of grades existed at every level of performance. Students in history with grades falling between 2.75 and 2.5 had an average SAT score of 540; those in sociology an average of 425.

The history majors, who had an average SAT score of 502, received an average grade of C+. The sociology majors, who had an average SAT score of 456, received an average grade of B. Sociology majors had lower SAT scores than average entering freshmen, and on the average received higher grades than students majoring in any other discipline with a large number of students. History majors had higher SAT scores than the average entering freshman, and received lower grades than the students majoring in any other discipline with a large number of students. The key to understanding what the graduates of this institution know and can do is not how long they attended college or how many courses they took, or grades they received, but the subject in which they majored. Nor is this a matter of special knowledge or skills. What some students can do better than the others, as revealed by this information, is to read with greater understanding and to write more understandably. The difference in their knowledge is about quite general things which are useful for any person to know.

There was a time when, exceptional cases aside, only the untalented and bored daughters of the wealthy were so privileged that they could devote college years to the study of the fine arts. To some observers this seemed perfectly reasonable, since by and large such young people possessed high-level verbal and social skills, as well as considerable sophistication and general culture. They did not need the academic experience which their social and economic inferiors could not do without. But today the subliterate poor pursue such programs at public expense. At the university which we have been using as an example, twice as many students major in the fine arts as in chemistry, physics, and mathematics combined. Students majoring in the fine arts, with SAT scores under the 480 average of entering students, receive an average grade of B. Students in chemistry, physics, and mathematics, whose average SAT score is well above 480, receive an average grade of C+.

All departments at this institution had considerably inflated their grades in the ten-year period previous to the entrance of the students under discussion. Departmental grade averages had commonly risen from the 1.6–2.1 range to the 2.6–3.3 range. During the same period the competence of entering students, as measured by SAT scores, had declined. These students, who, on the average, have never qualified for admittance to one of the nation's better institutions of higher learning, but who once, nonetheless, did work defined as "average," now do work described as "good."

In some disciplines semi-literate students can and do successfully complete degree requirements, although they could not possibly do so in other disciplines at the same college or university. This cannot be explained by differences in talent or natural aptitude which fit some students for some intellectual pursuits and not for others, but rather by the availability of departments which make no demands and have no requirements which ordinary opinion would presume to be prerequisite for any activity which received college or university credit. Colleges and universities accept students at different levels of academic competence, and at any institution the least competent of those accepted will find departments whose standards they can satisfy.

Now, most of these students do not begin college with the intention to choose the easiest possible route to a degree. Some come intending to follow a pre-law or pre-medical program. Some intend to become biologists or chemists, or to major in mathematics. When many discover, as they quickly do, that their intentions are unrealistic, they find that there are "alternatives," which they can pursue with success, with little effort, and with the B.A. degree still the prize. Having done so, they are included in the percentage of Americans described as "college educated." Today they are a majority of this nebulous category.

Because differences between institutions are so little understood, statements in the press by educators about SAT scores are frequently misleading, and often dishonest in the impression they mean to convey. For example, recently it was widely reported that, among others, one of the better small colleges in the country had dropped the requirement that applicants for admission submit SAT scores. A spokesman for the college explained that it had been discovered that less than one-third of the school's honor students had entered with above average scores, and that one-fourth of its top students had lower than average scores. Faculty members had also included on a private list of students they "could do without" a significant percentage of high SAT achievers.

To the uninitiated, this certainly must have seemed important evidence against the reliability of the tests. The real reason for dropping the requirement that SAT scores at this college may have been one of any number. Quite possibly, in a time of declining applications for admission and much-increased operating costs, the institution may have discovered that it could no longer turn away applicants from affluent families who could afford to pay full tuition, but who had lower SAT scores than had been required in the past. Today this is a commonplace problem, although few, if any, colleges advertise that they have been forced to lower their entrance requirements, that they have become less exclusive. As for the facts given by this college about scores and classroom performance, they should have been known and expected. They were meant to mislead.

This college had in the past admitted students with SAT scores which averaged somewhat above 600. Many students at such an institution with "below average" scores, say 580 or 590, have always performed very well, and many with better than average scores, say 650 or 660, or even 750, have done less well. This had no necessary effect at all in deciding whether or not applicants for admission ought to be required to submit SAT scores or that students below a minimum score ought not to be admitted. *SAT scores measure achievement.* A significant percentage of students with scores over 625—most of them in fact—come from backgrounds which give no incentive to excel academically in college, and many do not. They do as well as they care to, often with very little effort. The typical professor often does resent them, and if permitted "privacy" would welcome the opportunity to name them on a list of those he "could do without." At such an institution it is also to be expected that a number of students who had been indifferent to academic performance in high school will make greater use of their intellectual abilities in college courses and do very well in them. Such students often do fall in the 550 to 600 range when they take their SATs in high school, a category "below average" at this college, but in the top 5 percent of high school graduates nationally. One could teach a lifetime at such an institution and never see or hear of a student who entered with a verbal SAT score of 603 who performed at a level equal to that of a student who entered with a score of 750 when both exerted themselves to the limits of their respective abilities. SAT scores tell who can and who is not able to do respectable college-level work, and how well they will be able to do it. If we mean by a college education the command of a body of information and a level of competence and sophistication which employers, to take an unpopular example, once took for granted in a graduate from an institution of the kind in question, we know that a high school graduate with a verbal SAT score of 485 is not likely to achieve either.

At the end of the 1960s it was widely believed that "open admissions were on the way." This too was a promised "alternative." For public institutions, at least, the prophecy came true, although in most cases in a manner not predicted. In a handful of tragic cases reputable urban institutions were destroyed by adoption of the practice. In most cases admission policies were modified in ways which enabled institutions to avoid so radical a step. Open admissions, in the widest sense, espoused by militant blacks who were among the first to demand it, meant that with a high school diploma, and sometimes without one, any student could enter any college.

The state of California was credited with coming closest to open admissions—with its three-tiered system, which accepted any high school graduate into its community colleges, those in the top one-third of their class into the state colleges, and the top one-eighth into the university complex, with a chance for those who did well on one level to move up.

Although recognized as closest to open admissions, the system was not accepted by egalitarians. The very principle of "merit" condemned it. Militants charged that the system worked against blacks and Mexican-Americans, and from a "population percentage standpoint," the charge was proved. Indeed, any merit system of accepting students into college was, and is, bound to give preference to the offspring of the white middle-class. It is equally true that a majority of white youngsters have always been and still are eliminated disproportionately from a chance at higher education. In both cases, however, those who do not strive for higher education, who do not seek to enter it, have to be counted as "eliminated" to make the charge of discrimination "true."

That open admissions might not increase candidates for admission was not considered. Discussion about the matter included much comment about the difficulties and the enormous obstacles, and the need for a huge change in national priorities without which there would never be "enough money, teachers, equipment, or classroom space." These difficulties were only imagined, for there were no large numbers of blacks, Mexican-Americans, or, if anyone cared, whites, seeking admission to colleges and universities which were closed to them. There were, to be sure, millions of blacks, and many more millions of whites, who reached college age incapable of meeting admission standards of any kind which were based on merit. Somehow this came to be viewed by some as a problem which could be solved by open admissions. Legalizing infanticide might just as logically have been offered as a solution to overpopulation. The presumption that millions were waiting for the legal right to murder their infants, and would do so at once if legislation were passed which permitted it, would have been no more foolish than the expectation that open admissions would increase the number of those already swarming into higher education.

4 Diversity and Public Policy

In 1981 federal loans, grants, and other aid paid one-third of all college tuition, and room and board bills. Between five and six million students, one half of all those in college, received help amounting to $14.8 billion. This aid is granted without distinction. It is granted to high school graduates who are academically incompetent. It is granted without regard to the quality of institution attended. Any high school graduate can gain admission to some college, and a large percentage of our colleges do not qualify as places of higher learning. Institutions are recognized as colleges and universities on the basis that they have so defined themselves, and our government defines anyone who attends such a place as a student. The only qualification the student must meet for aid is "need."

A majority of the students receiving federal support are not qualified to be in college, and in any case are not pursuing programs of any real value to themselves or to society. There are, indeed, thousands upon thousands of students to whom, under different conditions, it would be reasonable to give more assistance than they are getting, but most of these students are attending institutions and pursuing programs which do little, and can do little for them.

Early in 1982 the Reagan administration proposed to cut overall federal aid to college students in half by 1983. The administration did not address the problem of "diversity" among our students and our institutions. The proposals did not appear to be related to educational policy but to be determined solely by fiscal concerns. Not that any relevant educational detail mattered. Howls of protest rose from hundreds of American campuses. Senator Kennedy, addressing a cheering convention of the National Education Association, described the Reagan government as the "most anti-education, anti-teacher, anti-student administration in our national history." He told his audience that everyone must work together to defeat the President's effort "to keep teachers from teaching, and students from learning." And Congress came to the rescue. Federal student aid in loan subsidies, for example, which had grown from $600 million in 1972 to $6.8 billion in 1981, was actually cut to $6.4 billion for 1983.

Educationists responded to the President's proposals with frenetic hyperbole and populist demogogery. Jean Mayer, president of Tufts University declared:

> It appears the Administration's programs present a policy of getting upper-middle class students into private colleges, middle-class students into state college, black students into black colleges, and I suppose, poor young people nowhere.

Kenneth Ryder, president of Northeastern University, warned against the federal government's turning its back on thirty years of "responsibility to help promising young men and women help themselves go to college." He added:

If we don't invest now, Japan's cars and computers will still be outperforming and outselling ours in the 21st century, and the Soviet missiles and space technology will be outmaneuvering ours in the decade of the 90's.

The sad fact is that we could reduce federal support to college students by eighty percent and not cut off aid to a single student who will ever contribute to the performance of our cars, computers, or of missiles, or to space technology. Half of all college students, and all colleges, are subsidized by the federal taxpayer. Theoretically there is nothing unreasonable about this. What is unreasonable is that this subsidy is not connected in any way to the competence or performance of these students, nor to the programs they are pursuing, nor to the quality of the institution they are attending.

The president of Dean Junior College in Massachusetts was among those who protested against the immorality of the proposed budget cuts. There are hundreds of colleges like this institution, which is eighty-eighth percent "tuition drive." Twenty-five percent of the admitted students have verbal SAT scores below 380. The school has no policy of requiring minimum grade point average for staying in school and continuing to receive aid. And its students receive the same kinds of aid, in the same proportion, and in the same percentage, as those with verbal SAT scores of 650 attending our most demanding academic institutions.

In the 1960's, when large sums first began to be available to colleges and universities, existing institutions transformed their policies in order to share in the largess. Until then most of the leading educational institutions carried some twenty-percent of their students on scholarship, and could do so again. At present at many, thanks to federal money, it is about forty percent. If the federal government limited its support to students with as much academic promise as is required to gain admittance to such institutions the cost of sustaining students on scholarship which deserving schools could not support unaided would be a small fraction of what the Reagan administration's minimum proposals would have provided.

The example of Princeton is instructive. Princeton had about 12,000 applicants for the freshman class of 1982–83, and admitted about 2,000. In recent years Princeton, like others among our top institutions, has been able to admit "blind," that is without having to consider the ability of an applicant to pay, or not to pay, the cost of college. Having admitted the number of students to fill the available vacancies the next step has been to determine the amount, if any, the student needed to support his education, and then to grant this in full. The federal government has provided the lion's share of these funds. The pressure on admissions at Princeton, where only students with considerable academic ability even apply, has guaranteed that this aid does go to highly selected and unusually competent young people. Also, Princeton students who do not progress toward a degree in a satisfactory and timely fashion are dismissed, and aid to them ceases. There are some two or three dozen colleges and universities in the country which are, very roughly, similar to Princeton in these respects. There are possibly two or three hundred other institutions with a sizeable proportion of students competent to do college work, and with programs of study which are at least minimally respectable, although a sizeable minority of those who attend these schools are quite unworthy of subsidy as "students." There are nearly two thousand or so other institutions of "higher learning" in our land, at some of which the average student reads at the seventh grade level.

Students with verbal SAT scores under 450 do not apply to Princeton. They understand that they will not be accepted. They do not apply to Duke, to Purdue, to Bates, to Wake Forest, to Texas Christian. But in every state there are a number of schools which will accept them, some quite as expensive as those which will not, and where, therefore, if their parents are not affluent, they may qualify for six, seven, or eight thousand dollars a year, and where, performing at a level which would result in academic dismissal at any of two or three hundred other colleges or universities in the country, they may remain year after year.

The same lack of discrimination has prevailed with respect to graduate study, and the Administration's proposal to bar graduate students from the Guaranteed Student Loan program was universally condemned by the educational establishment. In 1981–82 about 700,000 graduate students took advantage of this program. At Harvard, for example, 70% of the graduate students had done so, and President Derek Bok was terribly upset by the suggestion that these funds be halted. But he was not so uncivil as to compare Harvard graduate students with those at East Tennessee State or at Southeastern Massachusetts University. Instead he pronounced that a program which kept poor students out of the fields of college teaching, the ministry, and advanced science would be "really catastrophic," and would enact a "price that the nation could ill afford to pay." In the first place graduate students regarded as potentially fit to teach at the college or university level have never lacked for institutional support to pursue their studies, not to speak of those identified as likely to make significant contributions in the "advanced sciences." President Bok's reference to the federal duty to train the ministry may, out of politeness, be termed eccentric. The administration's proposal was indeed inept, but in the ensuing furor the real issue was not mentioned by anyone.

At Tuft's University, for example, the administration's proposals would have reduced by $13 million in 1982–83 the $31.1 million which had been available in 1981–82, and $8 million of the estimated loss would have been in loans to graduate students. At Tufts much of the graduate work is worthy of support, some of it not. Many of the students receiving aid are worthy of it, many not. Some of the programs they are pursuing will provide graduates in fields where they will be needed, some will not. There are many other schools at which little or none of the graduate work is worthy of support, and almost none of the graduate students. There are many fields which no student has a "right" to pursue if he can neither pay the cost nor demonstrate the kind of promise which will win him institutional support. In no European country (and in all of them higher education is almost exclusively public), is admission so open, and in none of them are students permitted to enter fields at public expense without any regard for the need for graduates with that training.

If we limited federal subsidy to needy students with a total Verbal and Mathematical SAT score of 1100, with a bonus of 200 points to those from particularly disadvantaged backgrounds, to such students who attended colleges and universities who admitted no students with lower scores, and required them to maintain a C+ average in academic subjects while receiving the subsidy, and made similar and relevant stipulations for graduate students, teachers would do more teaching, and students more studying, than we have seen in a long time. In the short run federal support would decline much more than the Reagan administration proposed. In the long run we could hope that it might become greater than it has ever been. But, given our politics, these are senseless dreams.

Part Two

Decline and Indifference

1 Teachers and Administrators

The decreasing ability of our young people to qualify for the opportunities which meaningful "higher" education might offer is not the fault of colleges and universities. Colleges and universities have, some more, some less, degraded themselves to match the qualities of the students who are available to them. Elementary and secondary schools have failed us, insofar as we believe that it is their function to develop academic skills. What the public does not fully comprehend is that public-school administrators and teachers, by and large, do not see this as their function.

Average public opinion about what an educated person is and knows is quite naïve. Generally speaking, the public does think of such persons as ones who can write and speak correctly, who can understand the written word with better than average facility, and who have a general knowledge of the past and present above the ordinary. The public does think that teachers are educated in this sense. It may think of teachers as more "unrealistic," less "practical," more "theoretical," and more "liberal" than the average, but not as unlettered, ungrammatical, and semi-literate. It does not think of them as belonging to a group which did poorly in school. The public is not aware that elementary and secondary educators, teachers and administrators both, have long been academically less fit than college graduates who enter any other profession. A 1980 study revealed that the average SAT scores of senior education majors was 48 points *below the national average* in mathematics and 35 points *below the average* in verbal skills. Only students intending to go into ethnic studies and home economics scored lower.

Educators, as a group, do not believe in the educational values which the general public, even if vaguely and uncertainly, takes for granted. As a group they reject these values because they did not and could not meet the standards which are a part of those values. Most teachers and administrators in our public schools were dropouts from the academic major degree programs during their first two years in college. As undergraduates they shifted to the pursuit of degrees in elementary or secondary education upon finding academic disciplines too difficult or too demanding. Doing poorly, or failing, in the effort to carry out an original plan to major in English, history, mathematics, physics, or chemistry, having difficulty with degree requirements which included the study of foreign languages, sciences, and mathematics, they shifted to education as a major because it was easy, because degree requirements did not include foreign languages or standard science and mathematics courses, and because they could be "certified" to teach almost any subject by taking four courses in it while not required to fulfill even half the requirements for majoring in it. They learned that indeed there were "opportunities for success within the system," and "different styles of learning." In education courses they were taught that their previous difficulties had not been a consequence of their own deficiencies, but had been due to unreasonable demands and false judgments made by elitist defenders of outmoded theories of education. They received indoctrination in a philosophy which soothed them, built up their self-confidence, and enabled them to take an aggressive and militant stance against theories and practices which had branded them as incompetent.

As teachers they empathize with their own kind, the slow, the inept, the indifferent. They conduct classes as they wish classes had been conducted for them. They are utterly incapable of applying the effort and discipline required to achieve concrete results in the classroom, much less of having respect or understanding for what can be achieved. They cannot be expected to make the judgments which are required, to associate themselves with values which long ago had been applied to them and which they failed to meet. To give into their hands the power of deciding what a child ought to be able to do, or not be able to do, is to condemn children in their charge to a terrible form of exploitation—to make children objects to be used in repaying the world for inner resentments and jealousy which result from the typical teacher's longstanding, and completely justified, feeling of insufficiency. It is as if we were to choose for coaches of athletic teams those who in their youth had been most clumsy and inept, and who in compensation had developed life theories which ridiculed athletic endeavors; and further, as if we then let such coaches decide whether winning or losing was important or irrelevant, and whether or not there should be sanctions applied to the coach whose teams were defeated and defeated year after year after year.

There are, of course, other kinds of teachers. A small minority were excellent students in college. A larger group did rather poorly in academic subjects because they did not apply themselves but developed no resentment against students who performed better or against departments which asked more of them than they were willing to do. They took the easiest route, were honest with themselves about why they had done so, and were not drawn to or seduced by the ideology preached in Education courses.

But there is nothing unfair about applying the harsh evaluation here made to the teachers and administrators who practically everywhere dominate our public schools. Principals and superintendents are almost exclusively of the type described. Their ideology is prevalent, it rules, and seems to be in no danger of being overturned. Almost all of those who pass through graduate schools of education, and who go from them to responsible positions in our public-school system, were in college unqualified for or found incapable of pursuing academic subjects. Resentment against academic standards and against all measurements which identify or reward talent is common among them. Nothing is more natural than that they adopt a philosophy which denies the validity of measurements which judged them inferior. Education, the very purpose of which is the development of talent, has fallen into the hands of a body of individuals who would deny its existence insofar as educational policy is concerned by insisting that it can neither be measured or identified. While far from perfect, conditions were very different before World War II. It would have been exaggerated to describe conditions in the 1950s in the above manner. But for nearly a generation of public schooling, this is an accurate picture.

The majority of our elementary and secondary public-school teachers, and principals and superintendents almost entirely, are the products of schools of education. Through the lobbying efforts of the administrative bureaucracy, working with schools of education, almost every state has established certain requirements for teachers and administrators—the completion of courses which only departments or schools of education offer, or which they offer more cheaply and "conveniently" than other colleges or universities can or will.

In many states the graduates of one or two schools of education play a dominant role in making education policy and in supplying administrative and teaching personnel. In Massachusetts, for example, the Boston University School of Education is a major influence. Not long ago the dean of that school, Robert Dentler, attacked President Silber of Boston University for having stated that a natural aristocracy of talent and virtue should hold a position of leadership. Dean Dentler is typical, a representative example of those who lead our schools of education. In keeping with our times, he was one of the experts appointed by a federal court to oversee the implementation of desegregation decrees, and has also served as a member of a court-appointed secondary school commission, in which capacity he worked to eliminate or destroy two of the oldest and most prestigious public classical high schools in the United States.

In his attack upon talent and virtue as tests for leadership, Dean Dentler declared: "We know today that there is no such thing as a natural aristocracy." He spoke to the only kind of audience which shares this privileged knowledge—professional educators. He urged a group of representatives from schools and departments of education to stop imitating academic departments which prided themselves on the elitism of selecting only the brightest students. He explained: "Elitism is flawed, not because people are equal in abilities, but because these abilities are too numerous, changeable, and immeasurable . . . to provide the basis for group membership or status attribution."

His audience applauded this restatement of its common faith. They would not need to stop doing what they had never done. For nearly half a century schools and departments of education have had less talented and less capable students, according to any measure ever devised or applied, than any other category of undergraduate or graduate college or university students.

2 Innovative Definitions of "Success"

In a 1976 Gallup Poll, conducted following widespread publicity of new evidence of declining SAT scores in the nation's
schools, most respondents declared that more intensive teaching of the basic skills would be the most effective step to halt
the decline. Sixty-five percent of the total sample were in favor
of a system which would require all high-school students to pass
a standard, nationwide examination to get a diploma. The educational establishment was quick to respond to this frightful
suggestion. Eight years before only 50 percent of the public
had favored such a requirement. The danger was growing.
John Ryer, President of the National Educational Association,
issued a general attack upon standardized tests of any kind. He
declared that SATs were wasteful, inadequate, and destructive,
and that "They don't measure what is being taught and what

is happening to our students. They ought to be dispensed with once and for all." He believed that it was important to measure "what students know," but that standardized tests were not the answer. Mr. Ryer's bald statement that students were not being taught to develop their verbal or mathematical reasoning ability was certainly accurate. His conclusion that the solution was to suppress tests which revealed that schools were not doing what they were created to do was logical given his constituency. He headed the most powerful of the teachers's unions, and represented those whose incompetence is made apparent by the test results. He and other leaders of his organization have annually dismissed declining achievement scores as insignificant.

Consistent with the tradition among those who have held the office, Harold Hodkinson, Director of the National Institute of Education, the educational and research arm of the U.S. Department of Health, Education and Welfare, responded to the press furor with the following comment:

> Reports of the decline have been presented as if the schools are going to hell in a hand basket. . . . I think it's just not a fair criticism. . . . That's not to say . . . that there are not areas for improvement. . . . But certainly, if you compare them to almost any other educational system in the Western world and consider the magnitude of the job they're asked to do . . . the schools have done, I think, an incredibly good job.

As for the decline in scores, Mr. Hodkinson said: "I think people are looking for a simple-minded answer to a very complex problem."

Every country in the "Western world" likely to occur to the layman, and some not likely to, educates its young of average and above-average ability much more successfully than we, and in all such countries problems which parallel our own do exist. Mr. Hodkinson's veiled reference to the blacks and minorities in his statement that we are incomparably more successful "when you consider the magnitude of the job," was misleading even to those who understood the implication. The decline in achievement has been among our academically superior students. During the period of decline the size of the student population, the male-female ratio, or students' academic standing has not changed significantly among those who take the tests. Throughout the period of decline it has been the top one-third of our high school seniors—from families in the top one-third of the economic pyramid—who have taken the tests.

In the face of the constant decline of scores for 13 consecutive years, at the end of 1976 the Educational Testing Service appointed a task force to investigate the problem. A former United States Commissioner of Education, later a vice-president of the Ford Foundation, Harold Howe II, was made vice-chairman of the group. In the course of the general public discussion of the problem, some commentators had brought up the drop in foreign-language enrollment, teacher militancy, a lower drop-out rate, and the elective curriculum all as possible causes for the decline. Mr. Howe contributed to this discussion by declaring that the national interest demanded his philosophy of education remain in ascendency. He responded testily to the comments he was hearing. "I am sure about one thing about this phenomenon: as of today nobody knows the cause." He warned that

> hasty measures for reversing the decline run more risk of disservice to American youth and American society than of doing anything useful. What worries me is that we may overreact and introduce in schools a regimentation of learning that denies what we know about individual differences among children and the importance of motivation in producing learning and also denies the significant values of schooling unmeasured by tests.

After 1976 test scores continued to decline. An obvious solution was to change the tests, to establish new norms, to end the possibility of comparison with the past by suppressing the evidence which permitted it. This we may now expect. Early in 1981 it was announced that Gregory R. Anrig, then serving as Commission of Education for the Commonwealth of Massachusetts, would take office as President of the Educational Testing Service in September. Mr. Anrig believes that our public schools are "remarkably successful" in the things that matter most, or, in Mr. Howe's words, in "the significant values of schooling unmeasured by tests." These include feeding children, monitoring their health, providing counselling, and giving training to youngsters with academic, emotional, mental, and physical handicaps. Thus, a "life-adjustment" educationist *par excellence* has been chosen to head a body whose function has been to devise and administer tests which are meant to identify our academically talented youth. The SATs have been delivering bad news for many a year; the messenger may not survive.

By the time Mr. Howe made his comments many facts had accumulated. A few months before, the General Accounting Office had discovered that $1.8 billion spent annually in an effort to close the gap in the educational levels between children living in low-income areas and other children had not worked. In 15 school districts in 14 states the gap between the achievement level of the educationally deprived children and that of average children of the same age generally *increased* while students were in the program. Sixty percent of the children in the program fell behind children of the same kind who were not in the program. The gap increased between them and "average" children.

Despite these results, "school officials in the investigated programs generally thought Title I reading activities were successful." Given the teachers and administrators involved in this special reading program, and without regard to their dependence upon the funding, it was and is quite certain that students in their care will fall further behind students in regular classes, even though the performance of students in the regular classes has declined and still declines each year. The decline in all reading levels is a consequence of the fact that teachers who themselves read poorly do the teaching, and that the methods they employ are unsound. Teachers trained as "specialists" in reading are generally less competent even than the average elementary school teacher, some of whom know through experience better than to adopt the "methods" of the specialists.

It may be a mystery why the taxpayers' money should continue to be spent on a counterproductive program. It is no mystery, however, that the expenditure of nearly $2 billion for the unrealized purpose of closing the gap between the educational achievement levels of children living in low-income areas and other children could be judged "successful" by teachers, school officials, and federal bureaucrats. The cash nexus is not to be forgotten, but that is not our subject: It could be judged successful because those involved in the program have a different agenda. They have their own definition of "achievement levels." Nearly half of the seven million children who were damaged by the program were non-white. Our educators are not dedicated to improving the academic achievement of the non-white population, but rather in aiding that population to improve its "self-image." This they truly seem to expect can be accomplished by encouraging the notion that membership in a minority group is in itself a cause for self-congratulation, and that customs, habits and tastes common to the group should be cherished. This is the other side of the page on which it is written that any vestigial feelings associated with white, Anglo-Saxon, Protestant culture should be a source of shame and embarrassment to the descendents of that truly privileged element.

The tragic conditions which prevail in our largest cities, and particularly in those with large minority populations, is reflected in the intolerable statistics in Atlanta, Newark, and Washington, D.C. The per capita expenditure in our major cities where the scores are lowest is roughly double that spent in some 30 states, and the per capita expenditure for minority students in these cities is higher than for white students in the same cities. Everywhere scores have declined as expenditures have risen sharply.

A study out of the Stanford Center for Research and Development in Teaching, on the subject of "institutional racism in urban schools," tells a familiar story. The authors found that in urban schools, students who were the lowest achievers reported getting the most praise from their teachers, and that most of the misled students were black or Mexican-American. Minority students were said to have completely unrealistic images of their own achievement. The study found that black students in general were receiving assignments that were not sufficiently challenging, that minority students were receiving completely unrealistic grades: "they simply show up for class and get a C."

Surely our schools do pamper the incompetent. It is less certain that they mislead them. Very rarely, if ever, is the minority student fooled by praise or grades into thinking that he or she is performing at the same level as competent white students. They know that they do not, and that they cannot. Encouraged to think in this way, they adopt a self-serving ideology which justifies their incompetence, places the blame for it on "society," and denigrates "performance" as a servile surrender to oppression. In 1975 the Conference on College Composition of the National Council of Teachers of English adopted a policy statement which embodied this ideology: Standard English was simply a "prestige" dialect, and the insistence that the minority young learn to speak and read standard English was an act of repression by the white middle class. Students were declared to have a "Right to Their Own Language." One of the college teachers who helped to draft the declaration explained: "We tend to exaggerate the need for standard English. You don't need much standard English skill for most jobs in this country."

Students denied the opportunity to master standard English because their teachers refuse to teach them do lose the possibility of reaching higher-ranking jobs where standard English prevails. The author's response to this was that she and her colleagues were "idealistic," and that "the important thing is that people find themselves through their own language."

3 "No one writes anymore"

It has been said that the answer to the question "Why can't Johnny write?" is that his teacher can't write either. Certainly it may be suspected that so many secondary teachers have gone on record to the effect that "standard" English should not be imposed upon the inarticulate because of their own incompetence. Public school teachers are inadequately educated and are dramatically deficient in writing skills. About half of the teachers who apply for English teaching jobs, and a high percentage of those who hold such jobs, are unable to pass basic tests in grammar, punctuation and spelling. More than 50 percent of the nation's secondary school English teachers did not major in English during their college years, and those who have majored in English during recent years have found it possible to go through college without taking a single course in English composition, or even a course in which they read the language's major writers.

As reading scores drop an angry public may insist on more "remedial reading" taught by trained "reading experts." Almost everywhere this is already being done. Millions are also spent on "bilingual" education, a procedure which slows and postpones command over English, particularly as the teachers in these programs are rarely competent in any language. These programs do, however, provide a source of patronage to politicians with minority constituencies. Cynical members of a minority community may at least take pleasure in the thought that some tax money reaches their pockets. Meanwhile, parents concerned about the reading skills of their children have no source of satisfaction. The "expertise" of these teachers derives from the "knowledge" that standard English, and the demand that students learn to speak and write it, is a form of class and race oppression. Experts of this type are particularly dominant in communities which we describe as "deprived": in urban public-school bureaucracies, and within English departments of public institutions in states with large minority populations. The philosophy is thus most dominant among administrators and teachers in public schools where the students are most in need of the learning which such administrators and teachers are ideologically dedicated to refusing them. Experts of this type are so prevalent among those with the academic credentials for dealing with reading problems that they overflow into almost all communities, even those with almost entirely native-white student bodies. For not only minority students are given assignments which are not sufficiently challenging; this is true for almost all of our school children. Everywhere they are likely to get a C if they simply show up for class. At best, teachers of remedial reading strive to lessen the discomfort of those who have reading "problems" by subverting the very goal which leads communities to engage them and to undertake the burden of paying their salaries.

The policy in vogue for blacks and minorities is part and parcel of the manner in which reading is generally regarded.

A common response of educators in the face of the declining ability to read is to question the value of reading itself. The superintendent of schools in one of our major Eastern states has declared that students who cannot read should be granted high school diplomas, stating that "some students will never learn to read in spite of everything that had been done for them and they should not be punished for their failures." In his view "a diploma should be based on attendance and not on academic achievement."

It must be said that his suggestion that diplomas be granted for attendance reflects a realistic acceptance of what has long been common practice. (Usually, however, the practice is disguised by the system known as "tracking," a subject to be treated later in this book.) His theory of punishment is quite innovative. If "education" has any concrete meaning, any relationship to particular and definable goals, and has any similarity to any other human activity, his theory implies that employees who simply cannot make themselves come to work on time, or baseball players who cannot hit, or typists who cannot type, should not be "punished" as employees, as baseball players, or as typists.

Other education experts reached more practical conclusions. A group at Berkeley, after spending considerable time, effort, and taxpayers' money, decided that reading should not be taught in the schools until children reached the age of 12. The "fact" which led to this conclusion was that only a minority of children learn to read earlier without serious difficulty. Unfortunately they had no control group of illiterate 12-year-olds upon which to test the hypothesis that such children would learn with any less difficulty. In any case, other facts might have led to even more practical suggestions had they been considered: for example, only a minority of high school students have learned to read well even by the age of 18. But central in this kind of thinking is the indifferent, seemingly unconscious, sacrifice of the vast number of children who *can* learn to read at five and six. We have yet to drop physical fitness programs because some children run faster than others. We have yet to hear suggestions that we put blindfolds on those who can see, for the theoretical benefit of the sightless. Singing lessons have not been banned for the better mental health of the tone deaf. And swiftness of foot, at least, can be increased in almost all by effort and practice. Yet we would deny children the right to read in order to mollify those who cannot learn to read well.

In a similar vein, but applying the suggestion to young adults in "higher education," a leading professor of linguistics at a well-known college in the Northeast recommends that thought be given by colleges and universities to the suggestion that students not be required to read or to write. Noting that many high school graduates could do neither, he said:

> An interesting problem has arisen in education during the past couple of years. Kids are asking for example: "Why should we learn to write? There is no need to write. No one writes anymore." And, in a way, they have a point. Very few people write . . . or need to write.

Here we have the professor revealed naked in his typical ignorance, either no more familiar with the world about him than the most unsophisticated "kid," or completely cynical about the possible usefulness of "higher education" to those whom he teaches. The inability to write parallels, and is usually a direct consequence of, the inability to read. Among contemporary youth the inability to write often has an even more fundamental cause: the inability to organize thought well enough to speak correctly and coherently.

Very few in our world, it may be said, need to read or write, and very few do. Those in the bottom third of our social and economic pyramid, for the most part, cannot and need not for the jobs they hold. Very few people write or need to write, depending upon how one defines "need." Very few people hold interesting and responsible positions in industry, business, government, or the professions. That is also true, but these very few can very often read and write, and most of them "need" to. Among those who are not *made* to learn in school, and so do not, a high percentage could have learned and would have learned if schools had required it of them, and some among them might have risen as high in the world as a college professor, who, perhaps, is capable of reading and writing, and who, assuredly, would permit no authority on earth to decide that his own children were incapable of learning to do the same, or that it was an indifferent matter, the mastery of which would be left to the free decision of pre-adolescents. What should strike the layman, however, is that implied is a theory of education ready to absolve elementary schools, high schools, colleges and universities from requiring or expecting that its students learn to read and write. Incomprehensible as it may be to the lay public, this is the theory which dominates the educational establishment up to and including our secondary schools.

Learning to read is difficult for a significant percentage of human beings. There is no reason to believe that this percentage will ever change much. What has changed is the attitude towards those who do not find it easy. The methods practiced in teaching reading up until 20 years ago were sound and remarkably successful. No one then thought of condemning teaching of a subject because some pupils could not or would not learn it. Lack of success in teaching the lowest quartile to read may be no greater today than it ever was: the difficulties encountered with this group result from a combination of genetic and environmental deficiencies. This is not new. At all times, but for exceptional cases, genetic deficiencies can be presumed in this group whatever the socio-economic background.

4 Parental Attitudes

Horace Mann, of glorious memory, argued for the school as a common social institution because the population of our country was diverse and dispersed, badly needing education in the rudiments as well as in a sense of national culture. Common sense might inform us that today our population is more diverse and more dispersed than Horace Mann could have imagined, and that the need for education in the rudiments and a sense of national culture is absolutely enormous. The program of our educationists, however, is based upon entirely different premises. Theodore M. Sizer, the former dean of the Harvard School of Education, and then headmaster of Phillips Academy (Andover) writing in 1978, informed the public that "conditions today are just the reverse," and that what "America needs today is not more homogenizing institutions but fewer." How many

77

among the public could recognize in this statement a disguised plea to pamper the underprivileged and to encourage their ineptitude, and to sanction the privilege of academic education as a birthright of the well-to-do? In the politics of educational policy it is just that.

Once upon a time the first 12 years of school were highly structured and generally uniform throughout the United States. By and large in mathematics, English, history, foreign languages, and in the sciences the same materials were used from grade to grade. Expectations were common, and the performance required for success was roughly the same everywhere. In more affluent communities, and in the more "advanced" sections of the country, demands, requirements, and performance were indeed higher than in less-favored communities or sections. But in my own youth, before World War II, I attended public schools in New Jersey, Louisiana, Florida, and Pennsylvania, and the material presented and the performance level demanded varied but little in these schools—all of which were in large towns or small cities. Fourth-grade mathematics was the same in Louisiana as it had been in New Jersey. In the junior year of high school the same Shakespeare plays and the same novels were assigned in Pennsylvania as had been in Florida. In all of these schools it was presumed that every child was capable of learning, to the point at least of doing passing work. Grading was in all cases rigorous, in the sense that most students received C's, a minority B's, and a very small minority A's. About one-fourth of the students received mostly D's and F's. The student of average ability who studied hard and regularly did B work. A brilliant student who did very little work might receive A's and B's in English or history but did poorly or failed in foreign language and science courses. The dull but industrious student made C's. Students of limited ability who made little or no effort failed.

In all of these schools a small group, some 10 percent or 15 percent of each class, was identified as superior in its ability and willingness to do the tasks required. Identification was made on the basis of performance in classes. A majority of the students in this group came from the most affluent and best educated families in each of the towns. But nearly half of this group came from different and quite varied backgrounds. They demonstrated that they belonged to the academic elect and this was fully accepted. To be sure they did not often gain entrance into the social life of their affluent colleagues, and no glorification of the class structure which gave these results is intended. Insofar as its legitimate function was concerned, the schools were democratic. They were engaged in imparting knowledge—information and skills which one had to have if one were to have a reasonable chance for "success" in life, and for any chance at all to enter any of the learned professions. Every student, without regard to background, was expected, and insofar as possible, required, to meet the same standards. The able and motivated students, without regard to background, were given an opportunity, which many of them seized. To be sure, at each of these schools, a majority of the children of the poor were neither particularly able, or much motivated. To these the whole school experience was often boring. A majority of the children of the comfortable or rich were no more able, but were more skilled, and satisfactory performance was within the capacity of most. By and large these schools did the one useful thing they could do. They taught useful and necessary things, and they enlarged the opportunities of those who needed most to learn what was taught. Teachers, to be sure, did not have the freedom to decide to follow a different agenda.

Massachusetts was the first state to try and discover why SAT scores kept dropping. The conclusions of the report made for the Massachusetts Department of Education in 1976 revealed more ability to present statistics honestly than is usual in a report sponsored by such an agency. The authors of the study noted that during the period of decline there had been a marked increase in enrollment in elective courses, plus a shift from basic skills to courses fostering creativity and emphasizing decision-making and "inter-personal" relations. They concluded that "substantial curriculum changes initiated in the past decade" appeared to have contributed to the drop in scores. The magnitude of these changes was only surmised. It was greater than almost anyone suspected. In the Spring of 1983 a report prepared by the National Institute of Education revealed that the percentage of students enrolled in general as opposed to academic subjects jumped from 12 percent in the late 1960's to over 42 percent by 1980. But the cautious and qualified statement in 1976 by the Massachusetts Department of Education of the obvious was immediately attacked as reactionary and therefore dangerous by leading spokesmen at the highest reaches of the educational establishment. These attacks ensured that the report would have no practical effect, and it did not. The facts proved irrelevant; they were facts nonetheless.

Declining student achievement and grade inflation are largely the result of a widespread and pervasive shift in social and educational values in the 1960s. This shift did not result from a widespread reversal of opinion or ideology among educators. The victorious ideology had long been ascendent in leading schools of education, had long been dominant within major foundations, and had always ruled supreme within the federal educational bureaucracy. Within many, if not most, colleges and universities, however, the faculty representing this philosophy, centered mainly in departments of education, sociology and psychology, and had been a minority, although its viewpoint was well represented among college administrators in advising and admissions. These long-time critics of academic standards and the traditional curriculum in the late '60s gained ascendency in public institutions of higher learning and in many private ones. Already ascendent in elementary and secondary schools, their philosophy now gained nearly absolute influence at these levels.

The critics of excellence sided with a student revolt against standards, and joined by many parents, won victory at all levels and almost everywhere. An enormous and successful push was made to make education in the nation's high schools, more than ever before, a practical preparation for low-level occupations, and to move in the same direction in public higher education. Collectively these trends undermined the rational and intellectual foundations of education. The resulting shift from basic and common academic requirements to a vast array of electives has been the most direct contributor to the decline in both schools and colleges. Student achievement progressively declined in subject areas where the number of electives increased. At the college level in the natural sciences, where requirements were not reduced for majors, achievement scores actually rose between 1965 and 1974.

All the great critics, Edmund Burke once wrote, "have taught us one essential rule." If ever we should find ourselves unable to understand or disposed not to respect philosophers whom all of the learned have admired,

> not to follow our own fancies, but to study them, until we know how and what we ought to admire, and if we cannot arrive at this combination of admiration with knowledge, rather to believe that we are dull than that the rest of the world has been imposed upon.

Given everyman's pride and prejudice regarding his own judgment, Burke's suggestion is quite unappealing, even insulting. The first lesson in the demagogue's primer prescribes slogans which comfort and appease this pride and prejudice. In education the critics of excellence exploit it shamelessly by declaring that distinctions cannot and should not be made, that learning should be painless and "fun," and suited to the "individual." This does seem convincing to most parents, most of whom resented the standards they had been asked to meet during their own public schooling, which certainly had not been fun, or much suited to their individuality.

Traditionally in this country ambitious and industrious parents of modest or poor economic condition had faith that "education" was the road to higher status for their children. This faith was long founded on solid evidence. The public school and public university provided access to both affluence and status to thousands of able and industrious young people from poor but stable and ambitious families. Until at least 1960, parental aspirations were more decisive than talent or performance in determining whether or not high school graduates from poor families attended college. Until World War II our public schools generally, whatever their weaknesses and faults, demanded and rewarded performance, and distinguished clearly between those who would not or could not learn to read and write, master or not master the common body of information requisite for intelligible discussion of commonplace topics and issues. The children of the poor who excelled in these schools often "succeeded" in life. The last generation of Americans who attended schools predominantly of this type were parents of school and college students during the period when these institutions were revolutionized. During their tenure as parents our educational system was transformed, and policies adopted which led to the progressive decline in the achievement level of our young. Their role in all of this is understandable.

The old system was never "popular." By the late 1930s the majority of high school students were untalented, unmotivated, and uninterested. When they became parents the boredom and resentment of their school days was not forgotten. In the late 1930s the graduating seniors in a high-school class who excelled in the academic curriculum were rarely much more than 15 percent of the total. In a graduating class of 200 in a small city only 20 or 25, usually no more than 10 or 12 of these from low-status families, had excelled. The system benefited the majority of students, certainly much more than the system which has taken its place. The 10 or 12 from low status families who excelled were the glory of the system, and one of the most tragic consequences of the changes which have taken place since is that today there are virtually no such examples. Once the motivated and talented poor had a much greater opportunity to identify and prove themselves. Now, by and large, we have an educational system which sacrifices the talented, of every background, in an effort to appease and placate those uninterested in, or incapable of, being educated.

Most of those who attended our public secondary schools

after attendance became mandatory almost everywhere were bored and uninterested. Nothing has changed this, and nothing ever will. Most saw no sense in the requirements made of them. Most, when they became parents, looked back and saw little benefit in the schooling they had received. For the vast majority of high-school graduates, who did not excel, who did not, as a result, attend top colleges or universities, who did not go on to higher education at all, or who attended second- or third-rate institutions, where academic subjects requirements seemed as boring and as irrelevant as in high school, "education," in the academic sense, seemed unrelated to life and work. Those who did not excel, and who came from poor and lower-middle-class backgrounds, the bulk of this group, achieved very different levels of economic success in later life, although almost never high status. Those who succeeded most, as small businessmen, in real estate, as building contractors, or in the high-paying trades, achieved higher levels of self-confidence with their success, and as parents denigrate an educational system which they had resented and whose judgments and values seem proven false by their own economic advancement.

Such parents rarely aspire to have their children attend prestigious institutions of higher learning, even when the cost is within their means. In many middle-class suburbs and in many small cities and towns such parents are the most influential in deciding public-school policy. They want schools which do not hassle their children as they were hassled at the same age. They want their children to be as carefree as the children of the affluent seemed to be to them during their own school years. Wives and mothers in families of this kind, whose school experiences paralleled those of their husbands, are particularly prone to resent academic demands or standards which might brand their offspring as inferior to any other child. The more affluent the family has become the more insistent and active the mother is likely to be. The self-assurance which is the product of success, combined with the certainty, justified by that success, that academic studies are "stupid," makes them vigorous combatants.

The vast majority of graduates did not excel under the old system. Those who did not excel, but who succeeded in life, were a small minority of that vast majority. For most of those who did not excel, eventual income was low to modest, their kinds of employment enormously varied. In general they come to see little or no relationship between elementary and secondary education and opportunity. In their experience school was a place where things were expected of them which were difficult or impossible to do in a respectable or praiseworthy manner, things which to them bore no conceivable relationship to a predictable or imaginable future. Most of these demands seemed to require little effort from their more fortunate contemporaries, those from affluent and educated backgrounds. Poor and uneducated parents with such memories do not commonly understand why their own children, however much these children disappoint them in other respects, ought to be tortured by the same kind of demands which made their own school experience so humiliating. In retrospect their own boredom and resentment was justified, and they see no reason for their own children to repeat the suffering. They, when encouraged to do so, come to believe that their days in school would have been happier had they been left to go at their own pace, to follow their own interests, and been able to escape comparison with those who excelled them in learning.

The life-adjustment educators are their natural allies. These educators share and give respectability to the anti-intellectual attitudes of such parents. They assign responsibility for the discontent or poor performance of any and all children to the school. They preach that every child should be content, and that every child should succeed and will succeed if the schools are properly run. This view conforms closely to the feeling which the average parent has about his or her experience in school, and, possibly more important, it frees them and their children from any responsibility for boredom or poor performance and places blame on the school itself.

Parents who form the majority of the public have limited education, and generally unsatisfactory school experiences.

Although they vary greatly in income most have low to middle incomes, and few of the minority who have enjoyed significant economic success achieve comparable status. Much less numerous, but of very real influence in the successful fight to defeat traditional schooling, have been parents who are both college-educated and affluent, and who hold prestigious positions in the professions, government, education, and business. Significant numbers in this group do, in part, owe their station in life to excellent performance during their school and college years. This is particularly true of those in the professions—among them, lawyers, doctors and scientists. But for the most part this class sees little or no connection between its academic performance in school and college and its station in life, and, in fact, there is little connection. Most owe their station to birth, to the good fortune to have been born into families where correct English was spoken, and insisted upon, in which a high level of literacy was general, in a milieu characterized by self-assurance and security. For those from this class who attended public schools, and in much of the country most of them did, the academic side of secondary schooling was undemanding. Generally speaking, above-average performance cost them little effort, for most classes were more or less boring but not particularly onerous. Their academic concerns were largely limited to achieving grades and scores high enough to assure them entrance into the colleges which had high financial rather than high academic requirements. "Education" itself was hardly given a thought. Their niche in life required that they attend a certain kind of college or university, where the friends they made and the associations they formed were the most critical matter. Pronounced intellectual interests or a serious concern to achieve academic distinction were inappropriate, and were not given parental or peer approval.

A generation ago parents of this privileged background were not much concerned about curricula details in the public schools attended by their children. They had little need for such concern. The college preparatory program was quite rigid, determined by admission requirements which were much the same at any college or university which their children wished to attend. Programs which existed for "non-college bound" or for "vocational" students neither threatened nor concerned them. Neither they nor their children asked many questions so long as the school prepared its academic graduates to meet the entrance requirements for the higher education they sought. In the 1960s considerable changes took place in the attitudes of such parents, and many of them allied themselves with their children in the general revolt against academic excellence. A detailed analysis of the reasons for this is a huge and separate subject; a summary which is simple, brief, and accurate is nevertheless possible.

These parents did not make the demands on their children which their parents had made on them, and they were much more lax in enforcing the demands they did make. The skills and self-discipline of affluent children sank to lower levels because of changes in their upbringing at home. At the same time, educationists brought about important changes in the schools, the consequences of which such parents did not foresee. Schools required less and less of their charges, and did less and less to correct the deficiencies of the pupils who attended them. Affluent parents, with little or no experience to make themselves believe that the academic side of schooling had much meaning and with little or no realization of the academic deficiencies of their own children, did not observe that these deficiencies were of a kind closely related to their future economic well-being, even their future social status. Certainly their own position in life had not seemed to have much relationship to SAT scores, or to have been determined by whether or not they had had distinguished academic records in college. Downward mobility was not something much feared in our society among the affluent. In the immediate post-World War II period there was almost no experience with it among the comfortably born. In the early 1960s it was unforeseen that the affluent classes would produce significant numbers of young suited only to driving cabs, serving as carpenter's helpers, making leather bags, jewelry, or candles, or working at various levels of the welfare-state bureaucracy. It was predictable enough in the behavior and attitudes of those of high school age in the 1960s. A rebellion against discipline and irrelevance among the spoiled young of the affluent met with little resistance in the suburbs of the major cities in the East. Parents proved allies. Their own attitudes toward "meaningless" learning found justification in the attitudes of their children.

One theory holds that the movement of privileged youth in the 1960s was a kind of Oedipal revolt. Spokesmen for the "youth movement", however, have been able to point out that very many of its leaders were close to their parents, and had learned many of their basic attitudes at home. In fact the essential characteristic of that youth, an assertive self-assurance about the infallibility of its moral and intellectual judgments, was a direct product of its privileged status and upbringing. In the 17th century, Moliere commented that the nobility knew everything without having had to learn anything. Until recently this was a privilege of members of our affluent classes, particularly of the newly affluent. Never, I imagine, were middle- and upper-middle-class parents so determined, as they were in the United States in the '40s and '50s, that the appetites of their children be satisfied.

5 "Different styles of learning"

The degradation of democratic dogma is either the cause or the consequence of much that we see about us today. Democratization of our society has led to the degradation of everything. Dogma, when it prevails, serves prevailing interests, and in a democratic society the prevailing ideology serves mass appetites. This has had little to do with the equalization of material advantages. Quite possibly the reverse will prove true. The masses, as well as the barbarian rich, can be placated by the gratification of everyman's primary prejudice—that he is as good as any other man, that he is born, and remains during his whole life, worthy of all the respect and consideration due any other man, without regard to any other fact than that he lives and breathes. There is enormous profit in surrendering to this, and exploiting it is a major industry in our society.

Our relentless pursuit of "happiness," and the popular view that this benighted state is won by avoiding discomfort also helps to explain. Parents want the "best" for their children, and the general view is that the best thing is to be free to be oneself, free from restraints, from standards, from judgment, from failure, from criticism, free to be "equal" without the necessity to be compared in any respect whatsoever to any one else; that is "best," because that is "happiness." Universally our deepest worry is that we or one of ours reveal any signs of inferiority. The success of the educationists is in part because they promise that no one will be exposed.

Recently a new assistant principal in a wealthy suburb of a large American city, possessor of a brand new Ph.D. from a major Eastern university, attracted notice in the press when he declared that concern about school achievement was a country-wide "nightmare." It was so bad, he said, that some students were studying three and four hours a night. Apparently he took for granted that the public understood that such suffering and toil was wrong, although many parents must have wondered, given the example of the study habits of their own children, whether the picture he painted was accurate. In any case, his purpose was to reduce the amount of studying. All this studying was bad "because only a few can get the highest grades and many who work hard can see no sense in it." No reporter asked whether there might be a profit to students which came from working hard and thus learning more, even if not as much as those who were more talented. The expert was asked if the fact that only a few students got the highest grades did not simply reflect that some students have more ability than others. He gave the stock institutional answer. Intelligence, he replied, was a "very slippery concept."

Having constructed an imaginary "problem"—students working too hard, and most finding the effort of no value—the principal reached his agenda, the cure was proposed. The solution was to ask less of students, to do things in such a way that students "gain a good opinion of themselves, have them learn that they are valuable and worthwhile persons—then they will perform better." Anxious to apply the lessons he had learned in winning his doctorate, he explained:

> The first thing is to expand the curriculum offerings so that there are more opportunities for success within the school system. Different rates of learning should be considered. Also the school should develop evaluation procedures which are helpful to the individual rather than procedures which are group comparisons, and which tell a student little or nothing about his learning.

This describes what many, if not most, high schools have been doing during the last decade. The policies proposed are those which for a long time have been a major cause for the dropping achievement levels of high school students.

Recently a study, conducted at taxpayers' expense by the American Institute for Research for the U.S. Office of Education, "revealed" one of the most poorly kept secrets of our time. Expensive educational innovations of the previous 20 years, including team teaching, open classrooms, the use of paraprofessional aides, and ways to "individualize" instruction had, separately and in combination, contributed to the decline in student achievement. Compared to students enrolled in programs which were less innovative and with less emphasis on individualization, those who had been subjected to more up-to-date procedures did not perform as well. A federal research psychologist who oversaw the study exclaimed: "I just hope it doesn't put a damper on future innovations." The press relayed the information that some "federal and public education officials" were troubled. They feared that the publication of the results would further fuel the "back-to-basics movement," hurt funding of new education projects, and add to the general dissatisfaction with the public schools.

Funding, indeed, has become a problem. But no facts seem likely to defeat the reluctance to understand them or to act in accordance with them. The educational system which prevailed

20 years ago was unable to survive increased community participation and control. A trend toward participatory democracy was bound to weaken a system which discriminated in favor of ability and excellence. By the end of the 1970s, better-off and better-educated parents were everywhere transferring their children to expensive independent private schools, in the hope that their children might be taught to read and write. Very soon the federal government, through the agency of the Internal Revenue Office, began to plan steps to slow or halt this movement by questioning the tax-exempt status of these institutions on the grounds that they were not racially balanced. At the same time, parent involvement in public schools was greater than ever before, and those involved spoke as one, in the same voice as the educational establishment. In the late 1970s the head of the Massachusetts Parent Teacher Association, holder of the office for the third time during a 17-year span, declared: "Schools have improved tremendously in the last 10 to 15 years, particularly in the skills of teachers and their attention to individual student differences, and that attention pays off in student growth and development." She explained that there was "confusion" about basics—reading, writing and arithmetic. She found that the "farther away people are from schools, the more they talk about the three R's." She noted that the PTA was developing a new organization which would support close involvement of parents "with her views" with their schools, and pointed out that the federal government had made generous grants to study school-community relations across the country. Both developments, she promised, would be helpful in the fight to prevent a return to the three R's.

Different styles of learning, different rates of learning, attention to the individual student—these are the magic phrases which mask the anti-intellectualism of our present-day educationists. These phrases are, consciously or unconsciously (it matters little which), self-serving for those within and without the educational system who bandy them about. They are enormously confusing even to those parents who are most suspicious about what seems to them to be going on in the schools.

Ambitious and industrious parents with the old-fashioned faith in "education" as the road to higher status for their children have not disappeared. Such parents have a full sense of the wide separation which exists between them and the well-educated. However, although they wish their children to "learn," they do not know exactly what or precisely why. They have no coherent or fixed convictions, either received or acquired, to guide them in educational matters, or, indeed, in most matters. Naturally inclined to trust authority, they have been incapable of responding critically to educational policies which seem both suspect and mysterious to them; that these policies have the support of leading educators, and of experts generally, fills them with self-doubt. Natural allies of the three R's, they are rendered mute when prominent educators pronounce that reading and writing should be deemphasized.

To the question "What makes schools work?" educationists answer: "individual attention." To be sure, once upon a time this was at the heart of school policy, at least until high school. For many years the different economic and social classes were given "attention" by providing "vocational," "general," and "college preparatory" programs in our secondary schools. But before high school, in theory and largely in practice, students were treated individually. For no greater attention can be given to student differences than to give students different grades. In contemporary educational jargon the opposite is meant. "Individual" attention means conducting schools in such a manner that no student or parent can easily determine on the basis of any record how one student compares with any other student. The goal striven for by the life-adjustment educator is this: that every student be content, and every parent be convinced that whatever his or her child is achieving is an exact fit with the child's abilities and interests. In this system children go at their "own pace." This "pace" is determined by the child's motivation, interest, and ability. These qualities are judged by the teacher, who is encouraged to decide that whatever the child does, without pressure or guidance, is satisfactory. No child is compared to another child. Each child is treated as though he were perfect or incorrigible. Parents receive evaluations which, usually without the parents either knowing it or understanding it, do not describe the student in relation to any normative standard, nor in comparison to any other student, but in relation to the teacher's private and subjective judgment of the child. "Satisfactory," "Good," and "Excellent," in this system of grading are given as freely to the poorest as to the best students. By this device the school hides the judgment which it passes on the majority of students: they are not learning but we have decided that they are incapable of doing any better.

In the language of our educationists this process provides more "opportunities for success." It permits different styles of learning as well as different rates, and it includes evaluation procedures "which are helpful to the individual rather than ones which are group comparisons, and which tell a student little or nothing about his own learning." The practical result of treating children on the basis of this kind of distinction is to shield teachers and school administrators from the parental concerns which arise when each child's rank in class is more or less known, and when comparisons between what students achieve in one school and in others can be learned.

In theory, these procedures enable individual children to learn more and with greater efficiency than would be possible if all children were treated alike. In fact, by refusing to establish any normative standards as to what it is desirable for every child to learn, "learning" becomes a word without meaning, simply an adjective to describe whatever a child is doing, or not doing. Permitting principals, counselors, or teachers to determine, in a limbo in which the only concrete objective is to give the student "a good opinion of himself," that "education" is different in every individual case is at best mindless.

At the elementary level these procedures have a disastrous and usually permanent effect on the performance of children. Only those with privileged backgrounds which cause them to value academic performance and who are highly motivated to excel in such matters are at all likely to learn or to work at the level of their ability. The average child, even if fairly well-motivated, is soon bored when no standards are set and when there are neither rewards nor punishments for what he or she does or does not do. The motivated but slightly below-average child is quickly confused and soon indifferent. The unmotivated superior child is simply lost.

At the high-school level, assigning students according to individual competence and providing courses varied enough to serve diverse interests, usually mean two things: first, different programs, which usually match students to their parents' social and economic standing—"vocational" programs, "general" programs, and "college preparatory" programs; second, more up-to-date procedure, usually called "tracking." Courses in subjects like mathematics, English, and history, which all students take, are given in classes in which students are divided according to ability, and the courses given on three different "levels." These procedures, either separately or in combination, segregate students with skills, ability, and aspirations from those less favored either by nature or circumstance. The authority to discriminate is in the hands of guidance counselors and that part of the faculty which teaches the academic curriculum. Guidance counselors are notorious for being both sensitive and realistic: sensitive to pressure from affluent and articulate parents, whose children are rarely placed in "vocational" programs or assigned to "Level III" English; and quite realistic about what is best suited for the crude, rowdy and unskilled children of the poor. Affluent and articulate parents thus have no reason to complain. Where there are such parents, numerous courses in contemporary music, cultural anthropology, experimental theatre, and the sociology of sex and race discrimination are provided for those among their offspring who are "bored" by traditional academic subjects, but who certainly do not belong in the machine shop or in mechanical drawing. Poorer and less sophisticated parents with ambitions for their children, who insist that they take academic subjects, often never discover, or discover too late, that in Level II or III English and algebra much less is done or asked than in Level I. They receive evaluations which inform them that their offspring are performing in a "satisfactory," "good," or "excellent" manner. Students in all three levels receive the same grades in the same proportions. Students in the remedial Level III thus often appear on class Honor Rolls when students in the advanced Level I do not, although the levels of competence and performance of these students is the opposite of what this implies.

The old-fashioned theory of public interest was based on the axiom that the general interest should take precedence over selfish or individual interests. Here too a return to "basics" might be salutory. The public should, and must if we are to educate our young, judge public schools in the light of what they do for the average and above-average child. Other children must be required to adjust to the kind of school which can do most for the most. The majority has its rights, and in educational institutions, designed, according to any rational theory, to give it the opportunity to develop its talents, its rights come first.

The proper way to deal with different levels of learning ability in public schools is to conduct classes so that average students must perform at the level of their ability to do work which is graded "average," requiring below-average students to work harder than others in order to be judged satisfactory, and pushing above-average students to achieve excellence. Such a system teaches every student, by daily experience, how his ability compares with that of others. No system ever devised fools children about this in any case; efforts to obscure or to deny these differences are hypocritical, and demoralizing for less talented children. The charade serves only to make their sense of inferiority more acute. It is made to appear that their condition is so bad that it must be hidden from them. Children do not learn at the same rate, and do vary widely in ability to master subjects which are difficult. However, there is a group of skills, and a body of information and knowledge, without which effective living is not possible in our world. Acquiring these skills and mastering this information and knowledge are important to every American. These are not things some people need and some people can do without. Every person benefits from as much as she or he can get out of them, no matter how little this may be in comparison to others.

Children should be taught to do their best and to accept their limitations. Failure to excel in the classroom can be compared to the failure to make the varsity football team in spite of every effort. Parents of a mediocre athlete may often charge the coach with favoritism, or prejudice against their child, but they rarely demand that football be abolished. The ability to play football is not one of life's requirements, however. Playing it with remarkable skill may have rewards; playing it poorly, or not at all, is irrelevant in most lives. Speaking and writing coherently and correctly; the ability to read and understand serious writing; having a large fund of general knowledge and information; all are relevant to all human existence, and the highest level one can achieve in these areas is important, no matter how low it may be. It is an advantage to be in the 80th percentile rather than the 60th, and in the 20th rather than the 10th.

The exceptionally bright child does deserve special attention. The less content and rigor in the academic program, the more members of this group will be bored. The traditional academic program did not bore brilliant young people. Often, to be sure, they were bored in class itself when it was conducted at a pace which permitted the average student to keep up, and bored by the teacher whose powers of understanding and analysis were limited. But the content of courses, the subject matter itself, was worthy of the best among them.

The disciplined student of exceptional ability could and did earn top grades without strain or worry. If his brilliance was ever likely to be of worth to him he realized, and was given some adult assistance in reaching this understanding by a parent or an exceptional teacher, that public schools could not be conducted solely for his kind. He learned tolerance for those, including most of his teachers, who were not so favored by fate as he. He learned that he must act in such a way as to make his superiority respected rather than obnoxious. He learned that superior intelligence was not the only important quality, and that without other human qualities it was a worthless gift. There was a time when such attitudes were taught in the homes of the elite, or of the wise.

If schools are what they should be, in terms of curriculum and standards, and if the student body has the range and proportion of abilities roughly the same as those found in the general population, the mentally competent but below-average, the average, the above-average, and the brilliant belong together in the same classes. All benefit from being together, at least until high school, and for the large majority in high school as well.

PART THREE

Equality

1 "Compensatory opportunity and full cognitive equality"

The 18th-century discovery that every human being, by the mere fact of birth, and without any special qualification whatsoever, possessed fundamental rights—the so-called rights of man and the citizen—and further that, strictly speaking, these common rights are the only ones that exist, has borne mature fruit in our time. Ortega y Gasset commented that it took the people many generations to believe that they were sovereign. Today the ideal has become reality, not only in legislation, but in the heart of almost every American as well. The sovereignty of the unqualified individual has passed from a theory and become the psychological state inherent in the average man. The characteristic of our age is the power of the commonplace to proclaim its rights and impose itself wherever it will. The masses have taken nearly total social power, and we are in the process of achieving a cultureless society. No traditions or institutions offer adequate or viable protection against the tide. Our educational institutions simply mirror the general will.

The prideful presumption of the 18th century was embodied in the Religion of Humanity. This religion provided the ideological base for the moral absolutes which democracy imposes. These absolutes were first enshrined in the slogan of the French Revolution: Liberty, Equality, and Fraternity. "Fraternity" had a short life. "Liberty" and "Equality" both appeal to basic human conceits and their life has been vigorous and long. Democratic dogma decrees that there can be no proscription against these "rights," no compromise. Anything withheld from their full demand is so much fraud and injustice. If we have a folk wisdom this is it.

In this chapter we will examine "equality." To begin with, let us recognize that by far the greater part of conscious thinking, including philosophical thinking, is an instinctive activity. The moral, or immoral, intentions of every philosophy constitute the real germ of life from which the whole plant develops. A philosophy prospers insofar as it dignifies widespread interests and appetites. "Equality" is universally and dogmatically established in democratic rhetoric as always and absolutely desirable. The responsiveness this has elicited is all the proof we need that the fruits of equality gratify popular tastes, but tells us nothing about the morality, or immorality, of the philosophic intent. The good or evil embodied in a wish is not defined by the intensity of the desire to gratify it.

These observations may seem to range far afield from the matters which have been discussed in previous chapters. They do not. Public discussion of education is so permeated with the ideology of individualism that few feel comfortable in approving anything which is said to limit freedom or to deny equality. Nevertheless, true education requires that freedom be limited, and that inequality be measured and granted privilege. We are confronted by an educational establishment which is not interested in true education.

We have a surfeit of treatises by members of the educational establishment, but one book in recent years earns our special attention. When it appeared, this work was hailed as likely to have as much effect on American education as anything written in the last 50 years, one which would influence educational policies for years to come. A collaborative effort which consumed the talents of numerous educational experts for several years, the project was funded by the Carnegie Corporation, the Office of the Secretary of Health, Education and Welfare, the U.S. Office of Economic Opportunity, the U.S. Office of Education, the Guggenheim Foundation, and, particularly, Harvard University. The title was *Inequality*; its principal author was Christopher Jencks.

The practical result of the ideology of the educational establishment has been to make students more equal by retarding the development of all, and retarding the development of the most able most severely. This might be thought to be merely the by-product of policies which, although clearly destructive in their results, have honorable purposes. One might suppose that our educational leaders are sincere, although, given the results of their policies, stupid and incompetent. The authors of *Inequality* made clear to us that such thoughts or suppositions are mistaken. The mean level of ignorance which we are approaching has been intended, and Jencks and his fellows hope to achieve it much more fully. Equality is the goal, the ultimate good. The only way in which this can be achieved is to reduce everyone to the level of the lowest. The results are not accidents at all.

From one point of view, equal opportunity is a matter of justice. Accordingly, education ought to be universally available so that those with talent have the occasion to prove their worth, and ultimately achieve status and assume responsibilities in society which accord with their abilities. The stewards of our young decry such a purpose. They are not concerned with our burgeoning failure to accomplish this, but with the fact that we have succeeded even as little as we do. Ordinarily this admission is not made so explicitly. Apparently emboldened by the patronage of the most elite and prestigious of our foundations and institutions, as well as by the federal agencies which embody public virtue and enlightenment, the authors of *Inequality* were blunt. Contemptuous both of history and facts by habit, secure in their professional eminence, they could be smug in the assurance that, even if their most extreme proposals were paid little heed, things were going their way.

The authors begin with the assumption that the purpose of education is to make people "end up alike." What they end up like is irrelevant, except that they be the same. They are primarily concerned with inequality between individuals, not inequality between groups, because when we compare the degree of inequality between groups to the degree of inequality between individuals, inequality between groups often seems relatively unimportant. They write:

> It seems quite shocking, for example, that white workers earn 50 percent more than black workers. But we are even more disturbed by the fact that the best paid fifth of all white workers earn 600 percent more than the worst paid fifth. From this viewpoint, racial inequality looks almost insignificant.

The use of such words as "shocking" and "disturbed" reveals a state of agitation, but about what? To be sure, group inequality may be, mainly or altogether, a product of man-made environment, and subject to reform or modification. But individuals are unequal, and "reform" will not change that. And education, if it educates, will increase and make more evident inequality between individuals. The only way to make inequality less evident would be to deny opportunity to the more able while giving special attention to the less able. This indeed describes much current practice, and occurs with deliberate intent. The authors explain: "For a thoroughgoing egalitarian, however, inequality that derives from biology ought to be as repulsive as inequality which derives from socialization." Not only is socialization—and this means nothing less than history and experience—"repulsive," but so is human biology. In the name of an abstraction, "equality," we will overcome both.

The authors make specific suggestions. No summary could do them justice. They write:

> Another possible strategy for reducing cognitive inequality is to accept both genetic and environmental inequality as inevitable but to alter the relationship between them. This means trying to allocate the most favorable environments to those individuals who start life with the fewest genetic advantages. By implication, of course, it also means allocating the least favorable environments to those who start with genetic advantages. If, for example, some students have more trouble than others learning to read, this strategy implies that the teacher should ignore the fast readers and give the slow learners extra help. If this does not help, a remedial teacher should be called in to provide intensive help of a kind not available in the regular classroom. Taken to its logical conclusion, this strategy would imply that anyone who was reading above the norm for his age should be sent home. . . .
>
> For analytic purposes, it is . . . useful to distinguish between "equal opportunity" (i.e., treating everyone alike) and "compensatory opportunity" (i.e., helping the neediest). Unfortunately, conceptual clarity is precisely what the advocates of compensatory opportunity (including ourselves) feel they cannot afford. "Compensatory opportunity" is a slogan devoid of political appeal, which "equal opportunity" is still capable of rallying widespread support. Advocates of compensatory opportunity have therefore felt obliged to pretend that "equal opportunity" really implies compensatory opportunity. We see no reason for abandoning this sleight of hand. . . .

A society committed to achieving full cognitive equality would, for example, probably have to exclude genetically advantaged children from school. It might have to deny them other advantages, like denying them access to books and television. Virtually no one thinks cognitive equality is worth such a price. Certainly we do not. But if our goal were simply to reduce cognitive inequality to, say, half its present level, the price might be much lower.

In Hitler's Germany mental defectives were gassed. Here we have a proposal much less extreme for an even more heinous purpose. The state is to drive the most able students, or half of them, from the schools. Given the admission that the authors feel that they cannot afford "conceptual clarity," we can suspect that they might brand such children so that they could not sneak into libraries undetected. Busing obviously qualifies as "a sleight of hand" which does indeed help us achieve "full cognitive equality." They feel that it is not good for us to know the secrets in their hearts. If, however, we judge prophets by their works we will not be misled. The evidence is all about us.

A book which suggested that we limit the intellectual development of the above-average young person, that we should transform our educational system to deliberately pursue this purpose in the name of equality, was hailed universally in national magazines and in our most prestigious newspapers. The suppression of excellence was offered as a national policy and applauded by educational leaders. Organized and legal repression of humanity's singular gift was proposed as reform, and praised as humane. To be sure, there was little or no conceptual clarity in the public discussion of the book. Very few laymen read the book, and even those who read reviews of it remained in the dark about its essential purpose. That remained a conceptual secret of the sectarians who belong to the establishment elite. If this group were without power and influence the ideas it holds would be unworthy of notice. But general confusion about some of the most fundamental facts of life gives its members decisive authority over educational policy in this country.

2 The Dictates of Justice

Nothing new needs to be said about education, but the accumulated wisdom of the ages does not pass as currency in our public transactions. That the concept "equality" could be put to the uses we have described, and that this could then pass without comment, reveals how great our difficulty is, how completely we are released from all past authorities, even from common sense. At no stage do our educational institutions provide the basis for informed discourse of fundamental problems. Today many admission officers of both public and private colleges and universities, hard pressed to find qualified students, argue that less weight should be given to SAT scores than in the past. They explain that because of changes in high school curricula students no longer take traditional courses. They ask: How can students answer questions on subjects they have not taken, and what does it matter if they cannot? The college curriculum itself no longer requires the background secondary schooling once provided. Even among university faculty members under 40 the vast majority have no comprehensive knowledge of our intellectual heritage. Yet, except for small pockets among the clergy of a few denominations, university faculty members far outdistance any other group in their familiarity with the past. A large majority of our best educated Americans regard either Jerry Brown or John Anderson as "intellectuals." Very few among them have been equipped to compare shallow and self-serving contemporary shibboleths to the thoughts of men respected by the ages.

It is said that all philosophy—the investigation of wherein consists the happiness and perfection of man considered not only as an individual but as a member of a family, of a state, and of the great society of mankind—is a footnote to Plato. St. Augustine profoundly influenced the major intellectual tradition of our civilization. Thomas Hobbes is one of the truly great figures in the history of political thought. Edmund Burke is one of the most original and influential of modern political theorists. Sigmund Freud presumably needs no introduction. T. S. Eliot will assuredly be remembered centuries after the name of every contemporary educationist has passed into oblivion. No exercise is so futile as to discuss fundamental questions such as "equality" without knowing or caring what any other personage, however eminent and wise, has had to say about them. There may have been a time when it would have been gratuitous to review ancient orthodoxy and time-honored canons for an educated audience. Today nothing can be taken for granted, and so we will call them to mind.

Only 30 years ago there was some public concern because half of our brightest young people of college age did not attend college, and because half of those in college were less able than this group which did not attend. To be sure this anxiety was not widespread and was politically inconsequential. The concern did demonstrate that there were many who still believed that in the upbringing of the young the first duty of society was to identify the talented and educate them accordingly. This belief is based upon a particular view of man, the view of man which characterized our civilization until recently, and to which we owe its most remarkable achievements. It is the view which originally justified the very notion of universal and compulsory education. It comes down to us from Plato.

Plato addressed the question of how society could be reshaped so that man might realize the best that is in him. He depicted a soul in man composed of reason and appetite, and taught that it was the business of reason to rule in behalf of the entire soul. Man alone of all creatures possesses reason, a quality which enables him to live well, or fittingly. This judgment has long been reflected in the phrase "Western man's determination to live according to his intellect." Human excellence, in Plato's view, was the excellence of an essentially social creature, a citizen. Thus the goal of the commonwealth was to bring reason and appetite into accord by training, to produce men and women of the best possible type. His ideal was a society in which every individual achieved, through training and education, the fullest comprehension of truth possible for each.

Human inequality is perfectly obvious. The result of any moral, social, or political theory which denies the fact or the relevance of this inequality can only be injustice, because this denial must work to limit the development of the more talented, and so, in impoverishing humanity, be unjust. On the other hand, in the real world the individual's position in the social hierarchy is determined only roughly, if at all, by individual merit. This is equally unjust. True human inequality is the fact determined by fate, social inequality is largely a product of human institutions. Plato did not quarrel with fate, but in his ideal state he eliminated social injustice. The best would rule.

The eternal dilemma of politics has been how to ensure that it is the best who lead and govern the rest. To clear minds, that the worst should rule has always seemed the greatest injustice. It seemed self-evident to Plato that the wisdom which any society possesses as a whole is due to the knowledge residing in the smallest part, and that if a state is constituted on natural principles this is the part which takes the lead and governs the rest. If the excellence of the state depends upon the universal observance of the principle that each should do his own proper work, everyone then ought to perform the function for which his nature best suits him. Justice dictates that each citizen should possess and concern himself with what properly belongs to him, and that no one assume a role for which he or she is unsuited or unfit.

In the real world every individual, more or less, inherits his or her station in life, is usually fixed in this place, and generally transmits it to the next generation. Plato recognized the practical difficulty. Parents transmit their privileges and disadvantages to their children. He did not propose to deform the privileged.

Plato divided men into three categories: ordinary men of iron and brass, extraordinary men of silver, and exceptionally superior men of gold. It followed that

> the first and chief injunction laid by heaven upon the Rulers is that, of all the things of which they must show themselves good guardians, there is none that needs to be so carefully watched as the mixture of metals in the souls of the children. If a child of their own is born with an alloy of iron or brass, they must, without the smallest pity, assign him to the station proper to his nature and thrust him out among the craftsmen or farmers. If, on the contrary, those classes produce a child with gold or silver in his composition, they will promote him, according to his value. . . .

Translated into educational policy in the 19th century, this became "equal opportunity." Public education made available to all was to make careers open to talent. The child of humble origins, in whose composition gold or silver was mixed, was to be given access to education, and reach whatever level his natural talents qualified him.

Plato recognized that one of the most difficult of all responsibilities imposed upon those who ruled was that of moving inferior children born to them down into other classes, and promoting from other classes any child who was good enough to hold superior rank. In ideal circumstances education would train reasonable and virtuous rulers, who would be governed by the principle that every citizen be set to the task for which nature fitted him, and justice dictated. This was the very purpose for which the state existed. For as long as modern education was under the control of men and women who regarded it in something like this light the system did provide an important means of upward mobility in some European countries and in the United States. Public education was meant to and did serve justice. During the last 20 years the decrees of our courts and federal policy, both responsive to our huge urban and ethnic constituencies, have surrendered to egalitarianism. Increasingly, public education serves injustice.

3 The Very Nature of Man

In a democracy in which the dispossessed and deprived hold the balance of political power, it is inevitable that egalitarianism saturate public life and affairs. The plight of education is not rooted in peculiar causes but suffers from a common malady.

Every person's attitudes and ideas regarding social and political issues stem, coherently and logically or not, from a particular understanding of basic human nature. This understanding reflects an image of self. Public discussion of education in our society is trivial and foolish because educationists subscribe to a view of human nature which is shallow and absurd. Catering to the popular will, they necessarily conform to everyman's passionate feeling that he is the equal of every other man. This universal prejudice explains public policy. On this subject Thomas Hobbes, one of the greatest figures in the history of political thought, is a source of wisdom.

Hobbes' aim as a thinker was to bring all he could discover about the nature of the world and man to bear upon the solution of the practical question of how life can be best regulated. He was dominated by a determination to ground a theory of morality in the facts of human nature, and to build a thoroughly rational system of human conduct which would provide for the public welfare. To prescribe for man one must first decide what man is, and what men think of themselves. In his great work, *Leviathan*, Hobbes devoted one-third of the chapters to this subject.

Hobbes studied man, and his first conclusion was that men were equal in the faculties of body and mind. Now that human beings are unequal to one another is painfully obvious, or, to some, joyfully apparent. They are radically unequal in every quality of any practical concern or importance, innately so, and natural inequalities are determined irrevocably at the moment of conception. Environment may, in time, partly compensate for deficiencies or destroy potentiality, may moderate or increase natural inequality, but extreme inequalities are natural and universal, and could only be overcome by artificial measures which reduce all to equality with the poorest human specimen. Inequality which is not innate is just as real and just as much a matter of practical importance, and no amount of wishing or wringing of hands will change the reality or lessen its importance. Equality does not exist between the good and the bad. The well brought up child of good, prudent, and prosperous parents who transmit to their offspring a healthy mind and body and a sound education and the deprived and neglected child of parents who have nothing to transmit which would not better have been uninherited are not equal. Hobbes was not blind to these facts. He understood that men are truly unequal, but recognized that the key to good governance, to prosperity and peace, is to be found, not in the understanding of what men are, but in acknowledging what men think of themselves. He observed that no man is so unequal that he will easily accept, or admit the justice of, unequal right to advantage and privilege. Men are equal in this one sense. Hobbes pointed out the practical result of this egotism:

> From this equality of ability, ariseth equality of hope of obtaining our ends. And therefore if any two men desire the same thing, which nevertheless they cannot both enjoy, they become enemies; and in the way to their end (which is principally their own conservation . . .), endeavor to destroy, or subdue one another. . . .

Men are not equal but believe themselves so, and no man who is less fortunate than another, in possessions, in affections, or in rank, can ever feel that these differences are just. Thus Hobbes believed that without the suppression of individual wills a state of war existed, of every man against every other man, and the life of men "nasty, brutish, and short." To give free reign to average human envy insured chaos, and the end of civilization. Democracy legalizes this envy and makes it supreme.

There is no possibility of civilization without rank and hierarchy. There has never been a civilized society in which there have not been differences in rank, power, and education, and no chance at all that there ever will be. The pride of every man does put men at war with one another. There can be no peace without subjection, of one kind or another, to beliefs and traditions, or to armed police. Heirarchy need not mean extremes of exploitation and cruelty. Subject to the sovereignty of the democratic fury to end all discrimination we move towards rather than away from such conditions.

The very nature of man determines that an untaught, or uncultured, majority can only be envious of distinctions, be they based on merit or not. That the state guarantee to all the security which the prudent, industrious, and able plan and save for, and remove, not only the suffering, but even the inconveniences of imprudence, shiftlessness, and ineptitude is democratic justice. That every American, regardless of income, should have identical medical attention and care, that beauty contests should be banned if the winners cannot be drawn by lot, that in the schools no one should be graded, or that everyone should go to college, are all notions with vast democratic appeal. They cannot be resisted if we have no body of citizens, an elite, which understands the source of such feelings, and is thus able to take a stand against them, and with moral conviction. More than a century ago the distinguished, and popular, English novelist, Anthony Trollope wrote:

> There is no duty more manifestly incumbent on the superior than that of bearing, if not with patience, at any rate with dignity, the evils which come with the inferiority of lesser men. That they should sacrifice excellence in order to placate the inferior should be unthinkable.

We cannot survive without the best, and we must educate them. In America today there is no segment of private or public life which is not in crying need of more competence, more ability, and more wisdom. Nothing can be done to remedy this unless the political forces which determine policy in our society are better understood, at least by some.

4 Not All of Us Are Enslaved

Our government was founded on the principles of justice which Plato thought self-evident. Like Hobbes, our Founding Fathers understood that government exists to protect inequality. James Madison, the "master builder" of our Constitution, believed that he had constructed a document which protected talent from the jealousy and resentment of the majority. Madison, indeed, shared the time-honored view that out of the inequality of men arose the very need for government itself. He noted that the diversity in the faculties of men, "from which the rights of property originate," was an insuperable obstacle to a uniformity of interests. In his words, "the protection of these faculties is the first object of government." Egalitarian democracy, he recognized, was thus incompatible with government. The majority would ever deny that such faculties have rights at all, or that they even exist.

Jefferson was committed to democratic rule because he believed that American circumstances created an opportunity unique in human history. In previous human experience men had "been steeped in the vices" which their situation had generated. He looked upon America as a kind of Garden of Eden. In this virgin land everyone, "by his property, or by his satisfactory situation," would be interested "in the support of law and order." He concluded:

> And such men may safely and advantageously reserve to themselves a wholesome control over their public affairs, and a degree of freedom, which in the hands of the *canaille* of the cities of Europe, would be instantly perverted to the demolition and destruction of everything public and private.

John Marshall, the first Chief of Justice of our Supreme Court, remarked that Jeffersonian democrats were either speculative theorists or absolute terrorists. Jefferson was foolishly optimistic. Democracy, as it has evolved in the United States, according to his theory could only result in the demolition and destruction of everything public and private. Those who forget Jefferson's condition of a vast majority with a vested stake "in the support of law and order" are indeed "terrorists."

The presumption that democracy was incompatible with civilization was also commonly taken for granted by 19th-century liberals. They took for granted that private property was the basis of civilization, and did not believe that private property rights or natural inequality could survive the unrestrained will of the majority. The Supreme Court was established as a check upon that will, and throughout much of our history provided it. More recently it has become an instrument for imposing that will. As a practical matter the issue is now uninteresting because irrelevant. Madison's presumption that property is a product of virtue and talent is held in public contempt. Only a masochist would openly strive to revive it. An effort to restore respect for talent and virtue may not be so hopeless.

Lest we forget, "Fraternity" was the third magic word in the slogan of the French Revolution, and had equal place with "Freedom" and "Equality." Fraternity meant compromise and understanding between unequals; it was the key to harmony between classes. Faith in reason equaled belief in the ability of men to sacrifice their interests to their opinions, that is, to overcome individual or class selfishness and to act for the general good. "Fraternity" was an early casualty of experience, but the concept was at the heart of Enlightenment thought. Modern egalitarianism has its roots in that ideology, but that ideology was not egalitarian.

The Rights of Man and the Citizen, passed by the French National Assembly in August of 1789, is one of the most important documents in the history of the Religion of Humanity. It begins: "Men are born and remain free and equal in rights. . . ." Nevertheless the authors did not aim at destroying the security of property. They intended to make it more secure, making it more legitimate by strengthening the connection between it, virtue, and talent. Article Six defined the law as the expression of the general will, and stated: "All citizens being equal in its eyes, are equally eligible to all public dignities, and employments, according to their capacities, and without other distinction than that of their virtue and their talents."

The authors did not espouse egalitarianism. Like Plato, or Madison, they equated justice with distinctions based upon virtue and talent. They took for granted that when the security of property and equality were in conflict equality must yield, that otherwise security would vanish and society lapse into savagery. Democracy, they understood, would enthrone equality, but they did not foresee its victory. They established propertied suffrage. Fraternity, they speculated, would unite the classes in the harmonious pursuit of the general good, some as active citizens, some not.

The best should rule. Anything else is unjust. Careers should be open to talent, and one's role or station in life should be determined by one's capacities, with regard only to talent and virtue. Anything else is unjust. Closely related, these two notions are universally disruptive and subversive. Judged by these standards there has never been a just society, and if men are taught these dogmas every man's natural conceit will cause the vast majority of any society to be discontented with its place. Upward mobility, which equal opportunity is meant to provide, has been, relatively, a characteristic of U.S. society. Relatively, however, this opportunity has had less and less to do with what individual Americans become. In general, the sons and daughters of our educated and wealthy elites do some things in life, and the sons and daughters of our ignorant and degraded slum dwellers do other things. Environment decides and limits possibilities and aspirations. Civilization makes it inevitable that this be true at laast to some degree, and could not survive were it not true at least to some degree. But if justice is said to require that every individual be placed in the function and station which capacity, with regard only to talent and virtue, entitles him, in our society, as in any other, almost all men and women are given legitimate grounds for loud complaint.

Liberal ideology justified the aspirations of a middle class which had proved its worth but which had not yet won political power. In power, the middle-class limited the vote to property owners. Leaders of this class did not believe that limited suffrage gave property a special privilege; rather, it recognized ability. Their revolution merely brought government into conformity with natural law and ancient theory. One of the leading liberal statesmen of the 19th century informed the poor: "If you want the vote get rich." For "equal opportunity" did not satisfy democratic aspiration for very long. The hierarchy of every society is like a pyramid, broad at the base and narrow at the top. Even if utopia could be achieved, and the connection between talent and virtue and role and station be absolute, democratic feeling would not be assuaged. Mass resentment and discontent reject the legitimacy of making distinctions, and a democracy makes an end of distinction.

It ought to go without saying that in our dealings with one another we should recognize equality where it exists, but it needs to be remembered that we ought to recognize real inequalities where they exist. Men's vanity does indeed make them prone to exaggerate real inequality. On the other hand, envy leads them to deny its existence. Democracy translates this envy into power. A mean and cowardly trait, this envy is the common deformity of the unfortunate, of those we entitle the "culturally deprived." In our democracy the weight of government enforces their demands. Public policy reflects their wishes in those matters which affect them directly, in education as a prime example. This may be inevitable. It is not inevitable that every last one of us be drowned by popular culture, or that judgments based on ignorance and envy be unanimous. Not all of us are enslaved by the necessity that our thoughts and acts be approved by mass prejudice and passions. Few of us are required to view and to present the events and issues of the day in terms which will assure us the greatest possible share of the national television audience. The thralldom of our monolithic culture does make escape difficult, and we need to recognize that our public educational system is one of the keepers of the prison. The diversity of the faculties of men may be an insuperable obstacle to a uniformity of interests, but this diversity is submerged when the faculties of all are stunted by a climate, and by institutions, which deny them nourishment. Our public educational institutions do this deliberately.

5 The Prevailing Delusion

Sigmund Freud, in his own way, repeats much of what other great men have written. His name may not add, may even, for some, detract, from the weight of the words we quote here. The reader may, however, heed the counsel of Francis Bacon: "Read not to contradict and refute; nor to believe and take for granted; but to weigh and consider." Freud put the matters we have been discussing in different terms. Some men will always share Plato's concern that society be reshaped so that man might realize the best that is in him, enable him to live well, or fittingly, according to his intellect. Self-knowledge, the recognition and acceptance of reality, is among the virtues most revered by Western civilization. But this has never been, and can never be, a popular goal. Freud described the ways men guard against pain, and emphasized the method which operated most energetically and thoroughly:

It regards reality as the source of all suffering, as the one and only enemy, with whom life is intolerable and with whom therefore all relations must be broken off if one is to be happy in any way at all. . . . Each one of us behaves in some respects like the paranoic, substituting a wish fulfilment for some aspect of the world which is unbearable to him, and carrying this delusion into reality. When a large number of people make this attempt together and try to obtain assurance of happiness and protection from suffering by a delusional transformation of reality it acquires special significance. The religions of humanity, too, must be classified as mass-delusions of this kind. Needless to say, no one who shares a delusion recognizes it as such.

The concept "equality" is the keystone of the prevailing delusion.

Man's body is doomed to dissolution and decay, and the external world is cruel and indifferent. To moan and groan endlessly about what is permanent and necessary is cowardly and repulsive. Freud noted, however, that the suffering which comes to us from our relations to other men is perhaps more painful than any other. We tend, he wrote, to regard it as a kind of gratuitous addition, although it cannot be any less fatefully inevitable than the suffering which comes from elsewhere. In man's political relations with others, differences in ability, in material success, in status and power, are the sources of unhappiness. Fate makes us unequal and civilization embellishes these inequalities.

Equality is a delusion by means of which those mistreated by fate deny reality. The doctrine meets the need of those who do not wish to be answerable for anything, and enables them to lay the blame for themselves somewhere else. More than a century ago Friedrich Nietzsche pointed out that intellectuals who cater to these tastes are in the habit of taking the side of criminals. He identified these professional caterers to democratic resentment, in Europe and America, who belonged

> among the levelers . . . being eloquent and prolif-
> ically scribbling slaves of the democratic
> taste . . . only they are ridiculously superficial, above
> all in their basic inclination to find in the forms of
> the old society as it has existed so far just about the
> cause of *all* human misery and failure—which is a
> way of standing truth happily upon her head. . . !
> The two songs and doctrines which they repeat
> most often are "equality of rights" and "sympathy
> for all that suffers," and suffering itself they take
> for something that must be *abolished*.

Levelers have abolished, insofar as they have succeeded, suf-fering, as they understand it, in the classroom. National heroes, of our or any other nation, are degraded in textbooks, because such men represented or served the special interests of "re-pressive" societies. Great literature, "so-called," they say, is de-nigrated because all literature in the past has taught class values and served class interests. The text of all human history is dis-appearing under their interpretation, which condemns all greatness as petty and vile. They are, Nietzsche noted, "at one in their tough resistance to every special claim, every special right and privilege (which means in the last analysis *every* right: for once all are equal nobody needs 'rights' any more)."

Nietzsche noted a kind of pity, prominent in his day, and dominant in ours, which if listened to closely was a hoarse, groaning, genuine sound of self-contempt. His own pity was of a different kind:

> It is not pity with social "distress," and with "society"
> and its sick and unfortunate members, with those
> addicted with vice and maimed from the start, al-
> though the ground around us is littered with them;
> it is even less pity with grumbling, sorely pressed,

> rebellious slave strata who long for dominion, call-
> ing it "freedom." Our pity is a higher more far-
> sighted pity: we see how man makes himself
> smaller. . . . And *our* pity—do you not comprehend
> for whom our *converse* pity is when it resists your
> pampering and weakness?

The longed-for dominion has been largely won, and its public name is "equality." It would be callous and vulgar to defend all the social and intellectual inequalities and all that leads to them. But to attempt to base the struggle against any or all of these inequalities upon the abstract demand for equality in the name of justice faces an obvious objection. Nature began the unjustice by the highly unequal way in which she endows individuals physically, for which there is no recourse. Culture and civilization have their source in these differences and can only survive if they are respected. The resentment which the favored must bear with dignity is not that which is theoretically justified by unrewarded talent and virtue, but the instinctive resentment of the unfavored against the fact of natural inequality.

The power of truth evaporates when popular delusions capture authority, when subjection to these delusions becomes the only license to be heard. In a society with democratic institutions, leaders, in order not to lose authority, yield to the masses more than the masses yield to them, and in time the laws themselves reflect the rebellious and destructive passions of the masses. No one better than Freud has summed up how inevitable it is that the unfavored members of civilized societies develop hostility to culture, instinctively strive to destroy it, and in an unfettered democracy will ultimately succeed.

The sacrifices that civilization demands of men in order to make communal existence possible are heavy and onerous for most. Therefore, Freud wrote:

> Culture must be defended against the individual
> and its organization, its institutions and its laws, are
> all directed to this end; they aim not only at estab-

lishing a certain distribution of property, but also at maintaining it; in fact they must protect against hostile impulses of mankind everything that contributes to the conquest of nature and the production of wealth. . . .

So one gets the impression that culture is something which is imposed on a resisting majority by a minority that understands how to possess itself of the means of power and coercion. Of course it stands to reason that these difficulties . . . are conditioned by the imperfections of the cultural forms that have so far been developed. . . . One might suppose a reorganization of human relations should be possible, which . . . would remove the sources of dissatisfaction with culture. . . . It seems more probable that every culture must be built up on coercion and instinctual renunciation; it does not even appear that without coercion the majority of human individuals would ever be ready to submit to the labor necessary for acquiring new means of supporting life. One has, I think, to reckon with the fact that there are present in all men destructive, and therefore anti-social and anti-cultural, tendencies, and that with a great number of these people these are strong enough to determine their behavior in human society. . . . It is just as impossible to do without government of the masses by a minority as it is to dispense with coercion in the work of civilization, for the masses are lazy and unintelligent, they have no love of instinctual renunciation, they are not to be convinced of its inevitability by argument, and the individuals support each other in giving full play to their unruliness.

The minority defenders of culture grow fewer and weaker. In all broad questions which directly affect all individuals and classes this minority is increasingly impotent. Even local influence is denied it, as no authority with the power to resist the national consensus is permitted to stand. Anything but compliance is hopeless against the power of the central state. That minority cannot rule. One may still hope that it might become imbued with the higher and more farsighted pity of which Nietzsche spoke, and that pampering and weakness might be resisted.

PART FOUR

The Denial of Freedom

1 Education Is a Form of Compulsion

Indoctrination and the pressure of popular opinion may result in almost universal outward conformity to a belief in equality. Nevertheless, widespread inner resistance to this foolish doctrine will always be present. The evidence, and human conceit, ensure that an attack on this article of faith will strike a responsive chord in many hearts. The dogma of liberty, or freedom, is more formidable, and to attack it is to invite opprobrium without limit. The evidence is rusted over with neglect and superstition, and human instincts combine to rebel against the thought of compulsion. In this matter, as in so many others, having left the great past unremembered, we wander confused and troubled in the howling present, and on no issue have we forgotten so much as in the question of individual freedom.

When we do not learn from the past we remain forever beginners. Those whose knowledge is gained solely from contemporary teachers remain prey to arguments worn out in the service of delusion and sedition, and in English statesman Edmund Burke's words, "being unacquainted with the conflict which has always been maintained between the sense and nonsense of mankind, know nothing of the former existence and the ancient refutation of the same follies."

Education and freedom are contradictory terms. That confusion about this truth could arise is one of the most striking phenomenons of our time, marked though it be by bizarre bewilderment and amnesia with respect to so many truths demonstrated by all previous human experience. Perplexity in this particular instance can only be explained by the almost universal fancy that freedom itself is an unalloyed good (a presumption which will require separate attention). But to educate is to train, to discipline, to form, to develop and cultivate mentally and morally. Education by definition presumes an authority which decides the purpose, the content, and the methods of teaching. A system which does not deny individual freedom to the student and the teacher is not an educational system at all.

Plato declared that the truly formative kind of education with which society must be most concerned is that which leads "you always to hate what you ought to hate and love when you ought to love from the beginning of life to the end." He believed that this education must begin with the young and tender, for it is then that human beings can best be molded and take the impression we wish to stamp on them. The more self-confident a society is, the broader the agreement about its purpose among the dominant groups within it, the more categorical are the prevailing doctrines about children and their upbringing. Public education in our civilization was everywhere established with the purpose of molding youth into moral, useful, and competent adults. Compulsory education was based upon the elitist presumption that left to their own devices individuals would fall into error and society into chaos.

Leaders of the Reformation in 16th-century Germany made

the first systematic effort to develop a system of compulsory public education in the hope of developing new and better impulses in the young. They established schools to train children in the liberal arts and in Christian discipline, where they would be raised "to become responsible men and women who can govern churches, countries, households, children and servants." These Protestant leaders understood and foresaw every practical problem. They realized that their purpose could only be accomplished by a carefully trained cadre of teachers operating under the aegis of strong-willed governments. These teachers were compelled to swear to articles which prescribed teaching methods, curriculum, and texts. All schools had a uniform teaching program and list of books. Uniformity was mandated so that no able scholar would escape detection, and so that none would arrive at the university unprepared. Identical books and teaching methods were prescribed in order to permit common examinations throughout the state, so that the talent of teachers and students could be evaluated "by comparing them." The brightest students were moved up from lower to higher schools, and stipends were provided for the talented poor.

Conforming the young to the approved type was the chief aim of this education, but the selection of an intellectual elite was a goal no less energetically pursued. On the one hand these leaders quoted Plutarch: "Moral virtue is a habit long continued"; on the other Quintillian: "Nature brought us into the world that we might attain to all excellence of mind." One goal encompassed self-restraint induced by disciplined habits: modest speech and demeanor, punctuality, conscientious performance of assigned duties, and avoidance of idleness and loose chatter. The other involved ensuring that the best minds be developed and their potential contribution not be lost to society. Compulsory attendance protected the most able young from short-sighted or ignorant parents. The passage from lower to higher schools was determined by sensible discrimination. The Spanish humanist Vives provided the principle:

> Because individuals are variously endowed with
> mental gifts and aptitudes teachers must make care-
> ful discriminations so that no sluggish mind is ov-
> ertaxed, which would only lead to frustration and
> rebellion, and no able intellect remains unchal-
> lenged, a sad waste of human resources.

The fondest hopes and most energetic efforts of these reformers ended in disappointment. The first venture of its kind,
it failed. The experiment has been repeated and repeated. Degrees of success and of failure have varied widely, but everywhere that democracy has become ascendant accomplishment
has declined. Remission, not compulsion, tolerance, not discrimination, are characteristic of the egalitarian ethos. Insofar
as today's practical politics are concerned, the educational program of Protestant leaders of the 16th century is of only theoretical interest.

Nevertheless, modern national systems of universal and compulsory education were founded on the same principles, and
the principles are as relevant today as they ever were for the
parent who wishes his children to be educated. Philip Rieff
writes:

> Meaningful interdicts must be taught; we humans
> are not born with them. On the contrary, the hu-
> man is born criminal. To praise the infantile is to
> praise criminality. You and I, fellow teachers, are
> the real police, whether we like it or not.

No culture, Rieff notes, can survive without police of this sort,
priests, teachers—whoever explains and interprets the limits
and rules of human behavior, defines the circle, within which
is the essential safety, from the danger of living outside it. Rieff
concludes:

> The real alternative to such authorities is in the
> hands of armed opponents of all authority. . . .

> Where authority is no longer mindful, and no
> longer deeply felt, first by the authority-figures
> themselves, then all power to armed nihilists is
> more than likely.

In our democracy nihilists are armed somewhat differently. Some form battalions as "public-interest" groups, some are armed with magazines and newspapers, others with public agencies or judicial office, others merely with tenured teaching posts. The most powerful are those who control and manage television and the movie and entertainment industry. All combine to enhance and pamper infantilism and nihilism. The authority-figure who is mindful and confident is not a viable candidate for superstardom in our mass society. You and I, fellow parents, are the only police, whether we like it or not.

Education is a form of compulsion, the systematic denial of freedom. This is a truism so taken for granted that for centuries it was the common premise of thinkers of widely divergent ideologies, times and places. John Stuart Mill and Thomas Jefferson were as convinced of it as were St. Augustine and Martin Luther; Jean-Jacques Rousseau as much as Thomas Hobbes; T. S. Eliot as much as Lenin. First let us return to Plato.

In Plato's ideal republic those with the wisdom to understand the good govern. They exercise all authority because only they are fit to rule, only they are capable of enthroning wisdom in human life. All others must be schooled by them in civic virtue, based not on immediate knowledge, but on correct belief. Left to itself the broad public will ever arrive at corruption. Philosophy and political power meet together, because otherwise there would be no rest from trouble. Only by training can society achieve the goal of producing men and women of the best possible type. Plato demonstrated the need for this compulsion. He asked what the innocent young, uninstructed in true wisdom, would learn from observing the world about them. He pictured the scene, the timeless tumult:

> Whenever the populace crowds together at any

public gathering, in the Assembly, law-courts, the theatre, or the camp, and sits clamouring its approval or disapproval, both alike excessive, of what is being said or done; booing or clapping till the rocks ring and the whole place redoubles the noise of their applause and outcries. In such a scene what do you suppose will be the young man's state of mind? What sort of private instruction will have given him the strength to hold out against the force of such a torrent, or will save him from being swept away down the stream, until he accepts all their notions of right and wrong, does as they do, and comes to be just such a man as they are.

Today the only possible source of strength to hold out against the force of this torrent is private instruction, which begins in the home. The enormity of the task explains the passive surrender of many parents, and the self-doubt causing the capitulation of many more.

That our public institutions will cater to democratic whim and prejudice is now inevitable. The opinions of majority combinations are defined as wisdom. It is, Plato wrote,

> as if the keeper of some huge and powerful creature should make a study of its moods and desires, how it may be best approached and handled, when it is most savage or gentle and what makes it so, the meaning of its various cries and the tones of voice that will soothe or provoke its anger; and having mastered all this by long familiarity, should call it wisdom, reduce it to a system, and set up a school. Not in the least knowing which of these humors is bad or good, right or wrong, he will fit all these terms to the fancies of the great beast and call what it enjoys good and what vexes it bad.

Our educationists have made this study. They have learned

what soothes and what provokes. Their definitions follow. Difficult is translated "irrelevant," backward or delinquent are transposed into "special" or "exceptional." Respect for excellence becomes "elitism." Resistance to demagogic rhetoric is slandered as "racism." Inequality merely reflects "environment." Insistence upon standard English is "repressive." Intelligence is "a slippery concept." The results of standardized tests are "misleading." Encouragement of whims and fads is "providing for individual interests." Objective grading of accomplishment is "unjust." The average representative of every politically significant racial, ethnic, or religious minority is to be unmolested in the prideful expression of every inherited habit, cultural or linguistic, in order to enhance "self-esteem."

True education is a strenuous and systematic effort to give the whole character of the pupil a shape and quality wished for by the educator. A parent who does not, insofar as possible, undertake to decide for his children the question of whether they should be truthful, industrious, sober, respectful, and educated, and to do so without allowing them to hear the other side, is a pedagogic cretin, and a society which does not, through its public institutions, do the same, has abdicated its highest function. Not one man in a million is capable of making a significant addition to what is already known in these matters. Yet in education we have come to operate on the premise that compulsion is evil, and that discussion should take its place. We take for granted that people, nay children, when they know what is good for them generally do it. This breaks with every tradition, even our own.

2 "We shall have to prohibit such poems"

Thomas Jefferson, the most democratic of our Founding Fathers, was a democrat in a theoretical sense, and in a special context which has long since has ceased to bear practical relevance. He imagined a democracy in which everyone, by his property or by his satisfactory situation, would be interested in the preservation of law and order. The main thrust of his educational schemes was no different from that of Plato. He planned educational institutions so that "worth and genius" could be "sought out from every condition of life" by selection based on scholarly attainment in the earliest years. The minority which proved itself would attend the university. He believed that "that form of government is best which provides most effectually for a pure selection" of society's guardians.

139

Benjamin Rush, signer of the Declaration of Independence, proposed the mode of education proper in a republic, and outlined a plan for public schools in Pennsylvania. The citizens of Pennsylvania came from many different kingdoms in Europe. By producing one general and uniform system of education, schools would render the people more homogeneous, "and thereby fit them more easily for uniform and peaceable government." Rush noted that the principle of patriotism "stands in need of the reinforcement of prejudice." This the schools would provide. As for religion, he was adamant:

> Do we leave our youth to acquire systems of geography, philosophy, or politics, till they have arrived at an age in which they are capable of judging for themselves? We do not. I claim no more for religion. . . .
>
> I must beg leave upon this subject to go one step further. In order more effectually to secure our youth the advantages of a religious education, it is necessary to impose upon them the doctrines and discipline of a particular church.

Adam Smith, proponent of freedom from governmental restraint, believer in the invisible hand which guided so many natural forces in the service of man's best interest, thought education too serious a matter to leave to chance. A man without the proper use of his intellectual faculties was, "if possible, more contemptible than even a coward, and seems mutilated and deformed in a still more essential part of the character of human nature." Therefore, he believed, the state should impose "upon almost the whole body of the people the necessity of acquiring the most essential parts of education, by obliging every man to undergo examination before being licensed for adult employment." Of aspirants to middling, or more than middling, rank anf fortune, he would have required evidence of successful study of philosophy and the higher and more difficult sciences before permitting them to fill any honorable office of trust or profit. Mme. de Stael, one of the most unrestrained enthusiasts of the Religion of Humanity, observed that political equality could not subsist unless differences of education were classified "with even more care than feudalism put into its arbitrary distinctions."

Compulsory public education originated in the desire to instill moral principles, and to identify talent which could be trained for leadership. That the life of no nation could ever be carried on satisfactorily without constant and direct reference to moral and religious considerations was simply taken for granted. Philip Rieff asks, regarding the contemporary college student, "Who is to teach our students that reverence and justice they should have sucked with their mother's milk, and heard at their father's feet, long before they reach us?" He recalls the law ordered by Zeus, "that he who has no part of reverence and justice shall be put to death, for he is a plague of the state." Today only some of the least educated seem to understand this, as we see from their suspicion and resentment of much of the public wisdom, but we will search in vain for our Zeus. Modern educational institutions were established to instill that reverence and justice which Zeus commanded, by elites who did not doubt their premises. They took for granted that men cannot be governed, or govern themselves, without reference to the most important part of human nature. They recognized that every significant aspect of human existence, public or private, is intimately connected with the intellectual, moral, and religious life of man, that the legislator, or the teacher, or the lawyer, or the doctor, who is not a mere hack, needs a creed as much as a priest does.

Writing at the end of the 18th century, Edmund Burke noted that far from thinking a national religious establishment unlawful, the majority of the people of England hardly thought it lawful to be without one. Education conformed to the conviction, and was placed in the hands of ecclesiatics, in all stages from infancy to manhood. His French contemporary, De Maistre, predicted that education which did not rest upon religion would do no more than pour poisons into the state.

Purpose, not indifference to the result, and, therefore, authority, not freedom, is simply presumed by the very concept education. Children will be taught as those who control educational institutions wish them to be taught. The connection between indoctrination and education is inescapable. Early in the 20th century Charles Peguy described one of the major accomplishments of secular and republican education in France. Before 1789 and the Revolution all education had been in the hands of the Church. By Peguy's time, for more than a generation education had been public and secular, stamped with the ideological impress of "Liberty, Equality, and Fraternity." He wrote:

> Children are taught that until the 31st of December, 1788, the children of France were born utter idiots, but that since the 1st of January, 1789, they were born intelligent and free. To make them believe this piece of nonsense, they get hold of them young, and it is a serious matter, because they do believe it.

All of those who have proposed state education have presumed society to be a wise master. All presumed leadership by an elite. Mass democracy meets none of their conditions. The multitude can never be philosophical. It is bound to disapprove of the pursuit of wisdom as a source of distinction. Our educational institutions represent the multitude, and are dominated by individuals skilled in pleasing that "huge and powerful creature." Institutions or customs which are desirable and right require guardians who know in what way they are good. When levelers hostile to culture gain control over education, "freedom" becomes a means of protection against the interference of minority defenders of culture; it becomes a means of mutilating talent in order to achieve greater equality. Freedom in education today is simply a phrase which describes the power of the multitude to impose its prejudices and its definitions. In John Updike's phrase: "Freedom is just another word for nothing else to do." This power is firmly established. We need not make a virtue of every fact. Our children are not beyond our influence. Nor is our society yet such a wilderness that every dissenting voice is lost. The national majority, through the agency of the federal bureaucracy and the courts, has transformed the purpose of education and ended the compulsion and restraints which served its original purpose. The logic of that compulsion and restraint is no longer applicable to public policy. It is worth reviewing because insofar as it is found convincing it may moderate public policy, and determine some private opinion and policy.

If not blinded by the illusion of perpetual progress, one might conclude that once the best possible education had been established any change would be for the worse. What was believed about the laws of physics in the days of Aristotle is no longer important. What was true about morals in Aristotle's day is still true, and always will be true. The Ten Commandments may not be timeless, but tens of centuries have not proved that they are not. What Kant wrote about the immorality of lying, indulgence in drugs, or even masturbation may be as relevant today and tomorrow as when he published it two centuries ago. Sanity, Orwell reminded us, is not statistical. Truth is not invalidated by being denigrated by sociologists and psychologists who sanction whatever is done widely enough to make praising it profitable. If Plato makes sense to us we need not fear making him our guide. He gave explicit advice regarding what the young should know, and not know.

The ignorant have no single mark before their eyes at which they must aim in all the conduct of their lives. This must be supplied to them, in the first place as children. In discussing primary education Plato began with the mind. The ideas a child takes in at an early age are likely to be indelibly fixed. Under this heading Plato considered the legends, myths, narratives, and tales upon which children are likely to be raised. Story telling, he noted (in our terms elementary schooling, or, often more important, television watching), begins at an early age, at a time when character is being molded and easily takes the impress one stamps upon it. We, may, of course, allow our children to listen to any stories that anyone happens to make up, or anyone wishes to choose for them. We may be indifferent to the possibility of their receiving into their minds ideas often the opposite of those we had thought they ought to grow up with. This may be true because we have no fixed notions about what our children should think or become. If we are not indifferent, nor uncertain, we will not permit this freedom. We will, in Plato's words, make it our "first business to supervise the making of fables and legends, rejecting all that are unsatisfactory." In education few things are so important as seeing to it that the first stories a child hears shall be designed for the best possible effect on character. Logically, therefore, Plato proposed that poets, on pain of expulsion, should be compelled to make their poetry express the image of noble character. Rules had to be made, because otherwise we will find

> both poets and prose-writers guilty of the most serious misstatements about human life, making out that wrongdoers are often happy and just men miserable; that injustice pays, if not detected; and that my being just is to another man's advantage, but a loss to myself. We shall have to prohibit such poems and tell them to compose others in the contrary sense.

Plato did not wish to have the future rulers of society grow up among representatives of moral deformity, and understood that proper training in early youth is what makes a man quick to detect any defect or ugliness in art or nature. With that kind of training, "all that is ugly and disgraceful he will rightly condemn and abhor while he is too young to understand the reason; and when reason comes, he will greet her as a friend with whom his education has made him long familiar."

Disreputable as it may sound, the suggestion to prohibit and condemn was once generally followed in our culture, the sense of all this once understood. Well into the 20th century in most parts of the United States public conformity to community standards was rigidly enforced upon all who taught the young. "Moral deformity" disqualified candidates for teaching posts. Teachers, by definition, are models, and it was understood that the fact of their employment gave a stamp of approval to their ideas, their actions, and their character. Maligned and ridiculed as it was by intellectuals, the Hayes Office insured that at least in the movies, then a cultural force nearly as powerful as television today, wrongdoers were never happy, virtue was rewarded, and justice triumphed. School committees did oversee the content of school libraries, and did prohibit works which made "serious misstatements about human life." Judgments, indeed, were sometimes unwise, as they must be in these or any other matters. To shirk the responsibility to pass such judgments is to betray the young to their worst impulses.

Lack of conviction about the meaning of such things as "moral deformity" explains much of the parental passivity about what is presented or permitted in the schools. Fear of being characterized as ignorant, primitive, or reactionary if one proposes limits on freedom explains as much or more. It is the timidity of those with convictions which needs to be overcome. Parental authority ought to be taken for granted.

The legitimacy of parental authority is a natural target of our educationists. That authority directly challenges their own freedom. Plato declared that there are certain beliefs about right and honorable conduct which all ought to be brought up from childhood "to regard with the same kind of reverence that is shown to parents." This put matters in their proper context. Whoever uttered the axiom, "Honor thy father and mother, that thy days be long in the land," had a far better conception of the essential conditions of national health and prosperity than did the author of the motto, "Liberty, Equality, and Fraternity." Thomas Hobbes asked a question all parents should ask themselves. Declaring that in a well-ordered society it was necessary that children be obedient to their parents, and that children be so taught, and noting that this was, after all, in accordance with the Fifth Commandment, he asked: "Why should men desire to have children, or to take care to nourish and instruct them, if he were afterwards to have no other benefit from them than from other men?" Put in terms which suit our times, who would choose to have children if they are to be putty in the hands of others, who wish to form them into creatures loathsome to our sight, and our own voice to be without authority or privilege? And why does any parent stand for it?

3 Through Just Prejudice

Everyman's conceit that he is as good as any other man is the source of almost universal discontent and resentment with civilization. The social and economic pyramid, broad at the base and narrow at the apex, places the few above the many. The doctrine of equality condemns this distribution, and justifies rebellion against it. The doctrine of freedom provides the means of destruction. Hobbes, who presumed that the function of government was to maintain necessary distinctions, to provide peace and stability so that civilization could thrive, insisted upon the obvious. The actions of men proceed from their opinions. Therefore the well-governing of men's actions consists in the well-governing of opinions. Thus it was the office of the sovereign, and his duty, to examine what doctrines are conformable, or contrary, to the defense, peace, and good of

147

the people. The poison of seditious doctrines threatened always to return men to the state of war, and life which was "nasty, brutish, and short," and no law but the will of the strongest.

Hobbes named two such doctrines in particular, that every private man is judge of good and evil actions, and that whatever a man does against his conscience is sin. The first false doctrine encourages the natural disposition of men to debate and dispute all commands and restraints, and to obey or disobey them as seems appropriate in light of their individual interests. The second false doctrine, equally repugnant to civil society, depends upon the presumption of making each individual judge of good and evil. If no one need obey the edicts of civilization further than it shall seem good to his own judgment and passions we are back in the state of war, a war of every man against every other man. He concluded that:

> It is annexed to sovereignty to be judge of what opinions are averse and what conducive to peace, and consequently, on what occasions, how far, and what men are to be trusted withal, in speaking to multitudes of people, and shall examine the doctrines of all books before they be published.

Education, in the first place, is the transmission of standards of culture. It does not begin with free discussion of those standards, but strives to impose them. It does not encourage questions, but provides answers. Whatever moral standards we have are imposed by authority and tradition. They are a form of "prejudice," in that, as far as most individuals are concerned, they have not been arrived at by means of reasoning and personal judgment. Were each man put to live and trade on his own stock of reason we should not expect much common morality. In the best of times the individuals who compose a nation avail themselves of the general bank and capital of the ages. As Edmund Burke wrote, "prejudice," in this sense, previously engages the mind in a steady course of wisdom and virtue, and does not leave man hesitating in the moment of decision, skeptical and hesitating. "Prejudice renders a man's virtue his habit: and not a series of unconnected acts. Through just prejudice, his duty becomes a part of his nature."

No theory of morality yet devised has, indeed, prevented an enormous mass of people from deliberately doing all sorts of things they ought not to do, and leaving undone all sorts of things they ought to do. A large proportion of men and women would not be improved in the least by the freest of free discussions. The vast majority of mankind forms its opinions in a quite different way than by discussion, and is attached to them because they suit its temper and meet its wishes. The certain result of unlimited freedom of thought is to produce unlimited skepticism on many subjects in the vast majority of minds. Where there is unlimited skepticism there can be neither honor nor justice, no standards and no truth—might makes right, and the will of the strongest is law.

Plato spoke of Guardians who would rule in the ideal republic, and who would be responsible for and would direct all education. In the real world, as Freud tells us, it is only by the influence of individuals who can set an example, whom the masses recognize or accept as leaders, that they can be induced to submit to the labors and the renunciations on which the existence of culture depends. Educational establishments were established with the presumption that they would be directed by or be responsive to such leaders. Modern democratic leaders represent and are submissive to the masses, and we cannot expect public institutions to impose standards or to demand renunciations.

Our schools, from the earliest years, conduct education in accordance with the two doctrines which Hobbes declared to be false—seditious doctrines which threaten always to return men to the state of war. The discussion which he would not have permitted is a method for deliberately encouraging the remissions he feared, with the results he predicted. Plato too described the natural consequences of plunging into philosophical discussion. He sees the young confronted by the question: "What does honorable mean?" The student gives the answer he has been taught, and his teacher argues him out of his position. He is refuted again and again on many such points, and is reduced at last to thinking that what he called honorable might just as well be called disgraceful. He loses his old respect and obedience:

> And when he has disowned these discredited prin-
> ciples and failed to find true ones, naturally he can
> only turn to the life which flatters his desires: and
> we shall see him renounce all morality and become
> a lawless rebel.

The result is the inversion from civilization to barbarism—from a refusal to do what is not done to the routine performance of precisely that.

The morality of the vast majority of all men and women is to do what they please up to the point at which custom puts a constraint upon them, arising from fear of disapproval and its consequences. With a very short memory we Americans can remember numerous forms of behavior which were once severely condemned and are now commonly accepted in respectable society, and, in many instances, now encouraged by the bureaucratic state with monetary rewards and subsidy. Attitudes and practices regarding every conceivable aspect of family life have been revolutionized in hardly more than a generation, and every change has reduced constraints and enlarged freedom to do as one pleases. Having illegitimate children is now one of our largest female professions, and in some of our great cities more than half of all children born each year are born out of wedlock. Yet it would be an unusual American who would even mention this phenomenon if asked to list our most serious "social problems." The custom of looking upon certain kinds of behavior or practices with aversion, learned through education, is the essence of morality. Such disapprobation does not become customary unless it is imposed upon mankind at large by an elite who have the means to make other people adopt their principles and even their taste and feelings. Once custom-

ary attitudes toward abortion, divorce, chastity, sloth, ignorance, excellence, and crime and punishment are of this sort.

For most things there is an explanation to suit every fancy.
Nevertheless some explanations are much better than others,
and often the best has very little appeal. Experience, even so
many centuries ago, warned Plato that democracy was always
in danger of turning into despotism. It took no prophet to see
that democracy was subject to falling into the hands of politicians ready to minister to its thirst for liberty, and that once
certain extremes had been reached the demand for more would
become insatiable. Then, Plato predicted, a period would come
at which law-abiding citizens

> will be insulted as nonentities who hug their chains;
> and all praise and honor will be bestowed, both
> publicly and in private, on rulers who behave like
> subjects and subjects who behave like rulers. In
> such a state the spirit of liberty is bound to go to
> all lengths. . . .
>
> It will make its way into the home. . . . The par-
> ent falls into the habit of behaving like the child,
> and the child like the parent: the father is afraid
> of his sons, and they show no fear or respect for
> parents, in order to assert their freedom. . . . To
> descend to smaller matters, the schoolmaster timidly
> flatters his pupils, and the pupils make light of their
> masters. . . . Generally speaking the young copy
> their elders, argue with them, and will not do as
> they are told; while the old, anxious not to be
> thought disagreeable tyrants, imitate the young and
> condescend to enter into their jokes and amuse-
> ments . . . and I had almost forgotten the mention
> of the spirit of equality in the mutual relations of
> men and women. . . .
>
> Putting all these items together, you can see the
> result: the citizens become so sensitive that they
> resent the slightest application of control as intol-

erable tyranny, and in their resolve to have no master they end by disregarding even the law, written or unwritten.

4 The Perennial Question

Education, in the first place the transmission of the standards of culture, in our civilization was for centuries a function of the Christian church. In the intellectual climate of the 18th century men became accustomed to ask of Christianity whether or not it was true. After the upheaval of the French Revolution the question changed, and in the early 19th century there were many who inquired whether or how Christianity could contribute to the reconstruction of society. Men asked how strong it was, not how true; they asked how much social weight it had; not whether it could save souls, but how it might bring about social and political order. Conservative thinkers declared that a return of social peace depended upon the revival of Christian faith. Chastened disciples of the Enlightenment saw the need for a "pure" religion, uncontaminated by supersitition. For the descendents of the *philosophes* this represented a new emphasis, growing out of changed circumstances. They did not break with their mentors, none of whom had been democrats.

We associate with the 18th century the diffusion of confidence in a new Heavenly City. Because he possessed reason and free will, man was perfectable. The presumption upon which this optimism was based was that natural man was good. Once the necessary institutions and environment had been created, enabling man's reasonableness and native goodness to find expression and to give it authority, all would soon be well, or much better. Under the impetus of great scientific advancement, faith in man's capacity for almost unlimited progress reached dizzy heights by the end of the 19th century. As political institutions became increasingly democratic this disastrous illusion became the bedrock of popular ideology. It was a logical, if not inevitable, development, but nonetheless an aberration of Enlightenment ideology.

Voltaire, who truly hated organized Christianity, wished his valet to attend Mass. The man who is so famous for his defense of free speech never thought in terms of democratic institutions, or of a society ruled by the popular will. He believed rather that the greatest service which could be rendered to the human race would be to separate stupid men from intelligent men forever. No one, he wrote, should be forced to suffer the absurd insolence of being asked to "think as your tailor and your washwoman do." He went much further. He did not believe the masses worthy of receiving education. By this he meant

> the mass which has only its arms with which to live. I doubt that this order of people will ever have the time or the capacity to learn—they would die of hunger before becoming philosophers. . . . It is not the worker who needs must be taught, it is the good middle class. . . . That enterprise is difficult enough and big enough.

For the masses established religion could provide all the education needed.

Jean-Jacques Rousseau wrote that public instruction "under rules prescribed by the Government and under magistrates established by the sovereign" is one of the most fundamental maxims of legitimate government. Having worked out for himself something which seemed to him to be the natural religion, Rousseau "saw no harm in making its simple articles of faith part of the contract whereby society is founded." In any case, he wrote, "the truly tolerant person does not tolerate crime in the least; he tolerates no dogma that renders men wicked."

Mme. De Staël, who was widely admired among 19th-century liberal idealists, a devotee of liberty whose own religion was a faith in the capacity of enlightened men for disinterested behavior, noted that for philosophers the day of miracles was past. Yet she saw the need for connecting morality with the idea of God. Her own morality, based on reason, and the "philosophic spirit," could never, she believed, become the religion of the masses of any nation. She was convinced that only traditional political and religious institutions could provide the necessary sanctions for public-spirited and moral behavior in the masses. She too advocated a state religion.

In the sequel the only state religion that can be said to have emerged was the religion of nationalism, but for some time basic assumptions did not change. One of the first major legislative acts in the history of modern education was the Elementary Education Bill, passed in France in 1833. Sponsored by the Minister of Education, Francois Guizot, a Protestant and a liberal, the measure required every French commune in which there was no Church or other primary school to establish a public elementary school. The law required that primary education include moral and religious instruction, and made the parish priest an ex officio member of the committee established in each commune to oversee and control the new schools. Guizot defined the purpose of the measure: "to calm and quench the people's thirst for action, as dangerous for itself as for society, to restore in their minds the inner sense of moral peace, without which social peace will never return."

The Prussian system of elementary education was widely admired in the United States during the 19th century, and the Prussian schoolmaster was widely credited with the victory of Prussia over France in 1870. That victory itself was celebrated among progressive elements in the United States. This too is revealing.

Following the defeat of the Prussian revolution of 1848, the ruler, Frederick William IV, turned his attention to education as means to establish mental health among his people. He announced that first of all every one of the teachers' colleges must be removed from large cities to small villages, "in order to keep them from the unholy influence which is poisoning our times." In 1854 he issued a series of controls regulating the whole course of training for prospective elementary teachers, as well as prescribing the curriculum for the elementary schools themselves. The purpose of the normal school was declared not to be the teaching of facts, but rather to shape the mind of the future teacher for his function, which would be "to train the youth into Christian and patriotic modes of thought and into domestic virtue." The assigned reading of the normal school student was to be restricted to works which by reason of their content and attitude were likely to lead to "orthodox Church life, Christian morals, patriotism, and reflective consideration of Nature."

In bringing such matters to the fore there is no hidden agenda. This book contains no religion whatever. It expresses no opinions of my own upon religious questions. Neither Guizot nor Frederick William IV are models for our time. Neither passed muster in his own. The perennial question remains: Traditional religious beliefs do not survive in contemporary culture, and without such beliefs what happens to values? In the 19th century, and in part of the 20th, in the United States local communities imposed these beliefs. Today the central state imposes the will of the freedom-loving majority, in the name of civil liberties, to suppress them in the schools.

The term "traditional religious beliefs" should mislead no one. Orthodoxy is of no concern here. Ultimate values, and in large measure prescribed standards of ideal behavior, have never been in much dispute in our past culture. Major thinkers, Christians and non-believers, have been quite unified in their view of what human behavior ought to be: Plato, St. Augustine, Hobbes, Locke, Voltaire, Mill, Marx, Lenin and Freud differ mainly in what they thought it possible to achieve, and how. The source of the difficulties to be overcome Freud and Hobbes assigned to natural human instincts, which they believed severely limited human possibilities. St. Augustine and Calvin attributed the condition of the world to original sin, which condemned most of humanity to degradation.

Mill and Lenin blamed the degradation of the vast majority on history, and proposed to change man by changing his environment. This disrespect for experience and life, or history, is the source of our own utopian public doctrines about what is possible and how it is to be achieved, an ideology more utopian even that that of Lenin, fanatical utopian though he was. It is the presumption that freedom is the road to a better world which distinguishes our public faith. For both Mill and Lenin compulsion would come to an end, sometime in the future. In the meantimes very severe dosage would be required. Lenin wrote:

> Freed from capitalist slavery, from the untold horrors, savagery, absurdities and infamies of capitalist exploitation, people will gradually *become accustomed* to observing the elementary rules of social intercourse that have been known for centuries and repeated thousands of years in all copy-book maxims; they will become accustomed to observing them without force, without compulsion, *without the special apparatus* for compulsion which is called the state.

Mill wrote in *On Liberty* that the "complete spirit" of his liberal ethics was found in "the golden rule of Jesus of Nazareth." This rule would reign in Lenin's golden future, after a period of dictatorship during which the wicked would be exterminated.

Mill, more effete and less bloodthirsty, was equally clear-eyed: Coercion by means of education was necessary in order to instill correct values.

In the latter half of the 19th century, Mill became the most influential spokesman in the English-speaking world for the notion that the wise minority are never justified in coercing the foolish majority for their own good, and for the presumption that the removal of restraints usually improves character, that out of free and untrammeled discussion truth emerges victorious. His essay "On Liberty" is to this day probably the most frequently assigned piece of writing in college and university courses. Our courts are servants of his doctrines, the public media glories self-righteously in the freedom which his theories declare unquestionable. And yet Mill, sometimes foolish and often shallow, was neither a simpleton nor inane. He presumed certain conditions before liberty could be made policy. His requirements are forgotten. That his theory of individual liberty should ever be made the basis for educating the young was contrary to his own very explicit statements on the subject.

Mill did presume that, potentially, most human beings might reach a plateau at which their conduct in all matters might be regulated by the results of free expression. He even seemed to believe that this plateau had been reached by a majority of the adult Englishmen of his day. It was, and is, fair to ask where Mill found any class of persons whose views or whose conduct on subjects of concern to them were regulated in the main by the results of free expression, to ask what proportion of human conduct was and is due to ignorance and what to weakness or appetite. In our own time what single governmental policy of major importance has been brought into being by mere discussion? Democratic government is simply a form of compulsion. The minority gives way not because it is convinced that it is wrong, but because it is convinced that it is a minority. But whatever the weaknesses in Mill's logic, he did declare: "Liberty, as a principle, has no application to any state of things anterior to the time when mankind have become capable of being improved by free and equal discussion." He went further. Plato wrote that philosophical discussion at an early age would lead pupils to renounce all morality and become lawless rebels. Mill gave the same warning, but broadened it to include more than the young:

> If you once persuade an ignorant or half-instructed person, that he ought to assert his liberty of thought, discard all authority, and—I do not say *use* his own judgment, for that he can never do too much—but *trust* solely to his own judgment, and receive or reject opinions according to his own views of the evidence;—if in short, you teach him all the lessons of *indifferency* . . . the merest trifle will suffice to unsettle and perplex their minds. There is no truth in the whole range of human affairs, however obvious and simple, the evidence of which an ingenious and artful sophist may not succeed in rendering doubtful to minds not highly cultivated, if those minds insist upon judging all things exclusively by their own lights.

The context in which Mill constructed his absolute condemnation of the suppression of any opinion is also neglected. In the "progress of human affairs," as Mill would have it, governments became representative and were becoming democratic. The time when the ruling power would emanate from the periodical choice of the ruled was at hand. He did not believe that arguments used in the past to limit the power of kings and aristocrats provided an adequate basis for limiting the power of governments which were democratic. Mill was perturbed to note that many democrats seemed to see no need to limit governments which expressed the will of the majority. He feared the future tyranny of majorities, and the real subject of his essay on liberty was the need for protection against the tyranny of prevailing opinion and feeling. He feared that the stupid majority would coerce the wise minority. His tactic, the construction of an argument meant to convince the majority to resist

its natural inclination to intolerance, was a child's sand castle
built to stem the incoming tide. His arguments in favor of individual liberty have proved most influential in fostering the
indifference he so detested. The educational system he believed
necessary never came into being. For Mill proposed coercive
means for improving the quality of majority opinions. The only
possible agents of this coercion resemble Plato's guardians.

For all his theoretical devotion to freedom Mill was convinced
that no great improvement in the lot of mankind was possible
until man began to think differently. He concluded that the
vast power of education and opinion have over human character should be used to bring about better thinking, and that
what was needed was "an effective national education." In this
he was at one with the authoritarian Christian reformers of
Reformation Germany. He wrote:

> Is it not almost a self-evident axiom, that the State
> should require and compel education, up to a cer-
> tain standard, of every human being who is born
> its citizen?

Presuming compulsory education, and Mill meant not practical
but moral education, his ethics, taught as a religion, could become universal. Mill did recognize a serious difficulty:

> Granting that in ten years the children of the com-
> munity might by teaching be made perfect it seems
> to me that to do so there must be perfect people
> to teach them.

He complained that "if given absolute power tomorrow," he
would fail from the impossibility of finding "fit instruments."
The fatuousness of presuming that every "teacher" have the
freedom to decide what ethics should be taught, and by what
means, did not occur to Mill, much less that pupils make choices.
Neither teachers nor pupils were a part of his decision-making
process.

Mill utterly rejected traditional religion and all sanctions based upon ceremony, authority, and faith. He did believe that if all men thought correctly, they would think the same, and he proposed indoctrination by the state in correct thinking. The notion that the untaught passions of individuals express themselves in truth was as ridiculous to him as to his contemporary Frederick William IV of Prussia.

There is no way in our world to make men believe in God and in a future state of existence. Nevertheless the character of our morality depends upon conceptions we may form about the world in which we live. If we presume the existence of God and a future state, one course of conduct will be prudent, and if we presume otherwise, a different course of conduct will be prudent. This was once generally understood. John Locke would have outlawed atheists from the commonwealth. Mill represented the viewpoint, commonly and energetically preached in the 19th century, that morality is, or can be, independent of such beliefs. Today this is the conventional wisdom, all the evidence against it notwithstanding.

Government alone cannot govern. Separation of church and state may have been, as some thought it was, "an act of unexampled madness." The most thoughtful of those who brought it about, and those who later celebrated it as a progressive step, believed that education by the state would inculcate a higher form of morality. Implicit, or explicit, in the thinking of Mill and others like him was the presumption of an elite which would direct and guide the educational establishment. The modern democratic industrial society created conditions quite different from anything envisioned by the prophets of progress, and made a mockery of their expectations of state education. On the other hand, only in our own time have the extreme predictions of those who foresaw disaster been fulfilled. But no one believed that education could be entrusted to the kind of state that we have, one in which the foolish majority rule the wise minority, and in the exercise of their power define virtue, and "education."

5 No Simple, No Superficial Thing

The centuries-long and deep influence of Christianity in Western culture would be incomprehensible if it had no persuasive message, if it did not offer something profoundly meaningful and relevant—a view of human existence which, in the light of human experience, is coherent and convincing. Christianity is, as Burke said of another ancient institution, "the result of the thoughts of many minds in many ages. It is no simple, no superficial thing, nor to be estimated by superficial understandings."

Many young Americans today know little about Christianity that they have not learned from watching Mike Wallace hector Oral Roberts, Johnny Carson wisecrack with Billy Graham, or Bill Moyers simper with Reverend Coffin. The more advantaged may have sat through a college course on the "sociology of religion" and mastered the term "opiate of the people." Others may have been led by clergymen in protest against energy rates or in favor of rent control. The most advantaged of all, the young who have attended Yale, Princeton, or Harvard, have observed the salaried Christians at their institutions gain celebrity status as apologists for criminals and terrorists, domestic and foreign. The lesson is that there are two categories of Christianity. One appeals to ignorance and superstition, and is made up of dupes; the other encourages contempt for every establishment, and is made up of a privileged and arrogant self-righteous elite.

The more educated they are, the more likely older Americans are to resemble characters in a John Updike novel, who have "the same milky kindness, the same preposterous view of the church as an adjunct of religious studies and social service, the same infuriating politics, a warmed-over McGovernism of smug lamenting. . . ." But, whatever the plight of its organized churches, however irrelevant, superficial, or vainglorious the most familiar of its ordained spokesmen, Christianity is a source of wisdom and guidance. The most literate elements in our population, those with the most formal education, understand this least, and are in most need of knowing it. Their "education" explains their deficiency. The central teachings of Christianity are not to be discovered in the attitudes and activities of those professionals who create the most sensation, and therefore attract the most media attention. Christianity too addresses the question of freedom and liberty, constraint and censorship, and reaches conclusions which are not, and never can be "popular."

Freud wrote of the injustice of natural inequality, for which there is no help. Plato wrote of men of iron and brass, and men of silver and gold. The terminology is different, but both thinkers address the fact that some men are capable of culture and others not, that some are capable of understanding virtue and others not. The terminology of Christianity is different still. St. Augustine wrote that we should look for three things in assessing a man's value: natural ability, training, and the use to which he puts them. But St. Augustine knew that fate decided these things. The logic of the story of the Fall is compelling. It explains the world. The gravity of the wickedness of the first act of disobedience condemned the whole of mankind. In St. Augustine's words:

> The result is that there is no escape from this justly deserved punishment, except by merciful and undeserved grace; and mankind is divided between those in whom the power of merciful grace is demonstrated, and those in whom is shown the might of just retribution. . . . Now there are many more condemned by vengeance than are released by mercy. . . .

Natural inequality, men of iron and brass, on one hand, men of silver and gold, on the other; on the one hand, the damned, on the other, the saved; and in each case many more of one than the other. The practical wordly consequences are the same: a social order based on these distinctions. Martin Luther wrote:

> The kingdom of the world, which is nothing else than the servant of God's wrath upon the wicked . . . should not be merciful, but strict . . . in fulfilling its work and duty. Its tool is not a wreath of roses or a flower of love, but a naked sword. . . . It is turned only against the wicked, to hold them in check and keep them at peace, and to protect and save the righteous. Therefore God decrees . . . "You shall take the murderer from my altar, and have no mercy on him."

In Madison's words it is the first object of government to "protect the diversity in the faculties of men, from which the rights of property originate." This can fairly be said to be a Christian point of view. Writing in 1525, Luther clarified matters which in democratic times are inevitably confused:

Although the severity and wrath of the world's kingdom seems unmerciful, nevertheless, when one sees it rightly, it is not the least of God's mercies. Let everyone consider and decide the following case. Suppose I had a wife and children, a house, servants, and property, and a thief or murderer fell upon me, killed me in my own house, ravished my wife and children, and took all that I had, and went unpunished, so that he could do the same thing again, when he wished. Tell me, who would be more in need of mercy in such a case, I or the thief and murderer? Without a doubt it would be I who would need the most that people should have mercy on me. But how can this mercy be shown to me and my poor miserable wife and children, except by restraining such a scoundrel, and protecting me and maintaining my rights, or, if he will not be restrained and keeps it up, by giving him what he deserves and punishing him, so that he must stop it? What a fine mercy it would be, to have mercy on a thief and murderer, and let him kill, abuse, and rob me!

Luther recognized that secular authority is by no means to be found in Christianity alone, and that the intrinsic legitimacy of this authority does not derive from the fact that those who exercise it are Christians. Pagans, he noted, can and do speak well on the subject. Secular rule is established to restrain the wicked, who outnumber the virtuous "a thousand to one" even in a nominally Christian state, and who must be forced to keep the peace, "and be silent against their will." *Governments exist to deny freedom to the majority, in act and word.* The logic is the same for both cases.

St. Augustine noted that corrupt thought, corrupt lives, and corrupt conduct are so dangerous that the most learned men assert that countries come to ruin through them, even when cities still stand. The severity and wrath of the world's kingdom, therefore, could not be limited merely to denying the freedom to steal and murder. He described the corruption which ensues when the state is interested not in the morality but in the docility of its subjects, when the state is regarded not as the director of conduct but as controller of material things and provider of material satisfactions. In such a state, laws punish offenses against a man's property, but not offenses against a man's personal character. No one is brought to trial except for an offense against another's property or person, but everyone is left free to do as he likes about his own, or with his own, or with others, if they consent. Then, he observed, there will be theatres full of fevered shouts of degenerate pleasure, and every kind of cruel and degraded indulgence. And the popular view will be that "anyone who disapproves of this kind of happiness should rank as a public enemy: anyone who attempts to change it or get rid of it should be hustled out of hearing by the freedom-loving majority, and removed from the land of the living."

The first duty of a Christian government was to declare war on the wicked and give peace to the virtuous. Society was seen as a war waged between the good and the bad, and not only against the evil in the sense of legal criminals, those who attacked life and property by theft and homicide, and the honor of private individuals by libel and injustice, but against the wicked, a thousand times more dangerous, who by their speech and writings undermined morality. No doctrine which tended to contradict the established laws of morality, to shake belief in them, pervert their sense, if only by implication, could be a matter of public discussion. The code of the moral world was regarded as outside the competence of private men.

St. Augustine lived long before the Christian state, we long after it. He had interesting things to say regarding the difficulties and responsibilities of believers living in the midst of a ruling, freedom-loving majority, those whose fearful arrogance and greed, whose detestable wickedness and impiety brought destruction on the earth. It was not, he wrote, easy to find anyone who regarded such men as they should be regarded, who, when he met them, treated them as they should be treated.

Men evaded their responsibility to instruct and admonish them, because the task was irksome, because they were afraid of giving offense, or that they themselves might be done harm in worldly matters, either in respect to what they sought to gain or dreaded to lose. Men had not the heart to offend those whose lives of shame and crime they detested; rather they delighted in flattery and popularity, and dreaded the judgment of the mob. He wrote:

> In this matter a uniquely heavy responsibility rests on those to whom this message is given by the prophet: "He indeed will die in his sin, but I will require his blood at the hand of the watchman." For "watchmen," that is leaders of the people, have been appointed in churches for this purpose.

Discontent with contemporary civilization has periodically resulted in the idealization of past times and places. In the conservative and clerical reaction which followed the French Revolution, the Middle Ages, much abused as the Dark Ages during the Enlightenment, became the Age of Faith, a time when princes and peasants lived in loving harmony under the benign jurisdiction of the universal church. Every class was seen as performing its divinely ordained function. Every little nobody had not thought himself the equal of his inherited betters, or presumed to rights and privileges reserved by God for his masters. Moral soundness and social stability was conferred upon the period by historians who detested the anarchy of their own time, which they attributed to modern individualism. Such men dreaded the future, and in time events proved them prophets. But Christian ideology is not recalled here out of yearning for any past time or place, much less for a Church which would appoint "watchmen." But every citizen, much more, every parent, is a watchman. St. Augustine reminds us that indifference is cowardice. Luther explains that it is a crime.

American historians, purveyors of democratic ideology in one form or another, write of the democratic origins of Calvinist religious authority, and explain the development of American institutions, in part, by Calvinist influences in our culture. At best this is misleading. John Calvin, the most profoundly influential of the Protestant reformers, whose *Institutes of the Christian Religion* is one of the major works of Christian theology, was said by the 19th-century skeptic, Ernest Renan, to have been the most influential man of his generation because he was the most Christian man of his time. Calvin noted that the forms of government are considered to be of three kinds: monarchy, the dominion of one man; aristocracy, the dominion of a few; and democracy, in which power resides in the people at large. He commented that the transition from monarchy to despotism is easy, from aristocracy to oligarchy not much more difficult, "but it is most easy of all from democracy to sedition." His doctrines demanded rigorous public control over individual social behavior and speech.

Civil government, according to Calvin, was as necessary to mankind as bread and water, light and air, and to entertain a thought of its extermination was inhuman barbarism. It was needed so that every person might enjoy his property without molestation, and so that men might transact their business together without fraud and injustice. Again, this was not all: "Its objects also are, that idolatry, sacrileges against the name of God, blasphemies against His truth, and other offenses against religion, may not openly appear and be disseminated among the people. . . ." Calvin explained that if Scriptures did not teach this it might be learned from heathen writers, for not one of them had treated the office of magistrate, of legislation, and civil government, without beginning with religion. All had understood that no government was well constituted unless its first object be the promotion of piety, and that all laws are preposterous which merely provide for the material interests of men. Calvin, echoing St. Augustine, emphasized that this objective must be pursued with particular energy, because "the rage of universal innovation, and the desire to escape with impunity, instigates men of turbulent spirit to wish that all the avengers of violated piety be removed out of the world."

All states are supported by reward and punishment, and Calvin insisted that when these two things are removed all the discipline of human societies is broken and destroyed. Rulers exist to execute judgment and righteousness. He explained: "*Righteousness* means the care, patronage, defense, vindication, and liberation of the innocent: *judgment* imports the repression of audacity, the coercion of violence, and the punishment of the impious." Education might also be defined as the care, patronage, defense, vindication, and liberation of the young; and certainly education requires judgment, which surely does import the repression of audacity, the coercion of violence, and, to adjust Calvin's terminology to our secular age, the suppression of falsehood.

The denial of the freedom to blaspheme, that is to revile, to abuse, to profane, anything or everything regarded as sacred or necessary, common to Plato, Roman law, and Catholic and Protestant Christianity, is based upon the same understanding, recognition of the fact that the desire to escape with impunity from the demands and requirements of civilized existence is so general that men will welcome and embrace seditious doctrines, doctrines which flatter and justify their appetites and resentments. In Geneva it may be said that Calvin allowed nothing. The wearing of rouge and the eating of sweets were both crimes. Such facts are not arguments which support indifferency. Quite different judgments may be made about particulars without turning from or rejecting the basic assumptions which Calvin shared with so many other thoughtful and wise men.

6 Standards of Decency

Of all contemporary phenomena the most incomprehensible to an American who awakened after a 30-year sleep would be popular entertainment. A Sex Pistols "concert" might well seem a vision of Hell. Such a person could hardly guess that this group was but one of a number who were part of a "cultural revolution against oppression," who were expressing anger "at those who aspired to power over the people." Then he would discover that films of a sort once associated with the smokers of the most plebian fraternal organizations were appearing at neighborhood theatres, and being brought into family living rooms by cable television. If he watched one of the annual television award shows he could observe the self-congratulation with which its "artistic" leaders bestow honors upon themselves, for the courage of such innovators as Norman Lear, who have managed to subvert so many canons of outmoded decency, now named "hypocrisy," for such profit.

Wide awake, indeed, he would discover that other changes were consistent with those he found in the world of entertainment, but his wonderment might increase to learn that since 1973, when the Supreme Court gave its approval, there had been an average of one million legal abortions per year in the United States. Surprised to learn that colleges and universities no longer dismissed students for overt homosexuality and exhibitionism of perverse sexual behavior, but rather sanctioned and promoted "gay" student organizations and public functions, he would be prepared to discover that the Surgeon General of the United States had testified that our laws forbidding the entry of homosexuals into the United States were based upon outmoded prejudices that such persons were abnormal, and that according to "the latest opinion such persons are healthy." Many of the changes he found, he would learn, had received their sanction from the Supreme Court, and that in the opinion of a late Chief Justice, Earl Warren, "the evolving standards of decency that mark the progress of a maturing society" had required a continual reassessment of the meaning of our civil liberties.

No politically powerful segment of our society has a belief in any moral standard which it agrees ought to be enforced by any public sanctions whatsoever. Our god is the public appetite, and we foster obscene practices in propitiation of our master. Liberation is the new morality. Our liberators are gods, and no gods have ever been so lavishly or so willingly rewarded by the public.

Today we are obliged to consider the question of censorship. What is not mentioned in the press or on television might as well never happen or not exist. What is mentioned is, for all practical purposes, the truth. Discussion of many of the most crucial issues of our time is suppressed by silence, others are hidden behind misinformation. This is not censorship. What does not interest, titillate, or indulge the appetite of a large consumer group or politically powerful minority will be very little seen or heard. The audience selects and chooses by itself and is polled regularly and frequently to ensure that its desires are met. Censorship means the denial of the right to publish or to say certain things, or to do certain things, because of the judgment that they are harmful and dangerous. The question needs to be considered, not because the democratic state is a fit censor, or a desirable one, but because individuals need more understanding than very many have that civilization itself requires censorship and censors. What then did it mean when the founding father laid down that Congress "shall make no law . . . abridging the freedom of speech, or of the press"?

John Locke to whom, in very large part, we owe the theory of our Constitution, was an apologist for the English revolution of 1688, which overthrew a monarchy based upon divine right and replaced it with a monarchy based upon a contract between the ruler and the nation. According to Locke's theory of government, the corruption and viciousness of some men is one of the reasons which make it necessary to leave the state of nature, and so men quit that state "for the mutual preservation of their lives, liberties, and estates, which I call by the general name—property." Men give up the freedom of the state of nature, and consent "to be regulated by the laws of society." In doing so they do not subject themselves to arbitrary power, but retain the right to judge whether government properly serves the purposes for which they created it. Should it cease to protect private property, or should it, indeed, invade private property, government becomes illegitimate and may, with justice, be overthrown. Upon these premises Locke established certain civil rights, the first of which was the freedom to criticize the government. Thus we have the First Amendment to our Constitution.

Locke recognized that it could be said that his hypothesis laid the basis for frequent rebellion. To which he answered:

> Nor let anyone say that mischief can rise from hence as often as it shall please a busy head or turbulent spirit to desire the alteration of govern-

ment. It is true that such men may stir whenever they please, but it will only be to their own just perdition. For till the mischief be grown general . . . the people, who are more disposed to suffer than right themselves by resistance, are not apt to stir. . . . I grant that the pride, ambition and turbulency of private men have sometimes caused great disorders in commonwealths, and that factions have been fatal to states and kingdoms. But whether the mischief has oftener begun in the people's wantoness, and a desire to cast off the lawful authority of their rulers, or the ruler's insolence and endeavors to get and exercise an arbitrary power over their people, whether oppression or disobedience gave the first rise to the disorder, I leave it to impartial history to determine.

We have examined the conclusions of a number of thoughtful men who believed that the evidence of history gave the opposite answer from that deduced by Locke. But only by gross misrepresentation, if not only by insolence and wantoness, can Locke be made the source or authority for contemporary libertarianism. What Locke established was the denial to government of the power to suppress speech and writing critical of its actions. Busy heads and turbulent spirits he left to their own just perdition. He did not give them protection against the judgment of private employers. The preposterous notion that they should be guaranteed the unmolested privilege to spread sedition as tenured and salaried public employees is not suggested. Locke would not have allowed atheists to live within the commonwealth, because, recognizing no law, such men were beyond the law. The product of a Puritan home, he often spoke with great approbation of the severity with which his father had raised him. The culture of which he was a part was severely inhibited, and the meaning it gave freedom severely limited. Freedom, in any case, presumes limits which cannot be abridged. When the founding fathers laid down that Congress "shall make no law ... abridging the freedom of speech, or the press," the power was denied to Congress. The power was not denied to the states or to any other political jurisdiction, a limitation not removed until the 20th century. In their day all public entertainment, all printed matter, and all individual behavior, judged contrary to public morality, was censored and subject to severe sanctions. Not until 1933 did our federal courts exonerate James Joyce's *Ulysses* from the charge of obscenity, and then when a judge "after long reflection" reached the considered opinion that nowhere did the work "tend to be an aphrodisiac." D. H. Lawrence's *Lady Chatterly's Lover* waited almost a generation longer for its exoneration, and Henry Miller's works until 1963.

All of this is not to declare, for example, that *Ulysses* and *Lady Chatterly's Lover* ought still to be under ban, although the harm our deprivation might have done us in these instances might be thought to have little weight in the balance of good and evil consequences of the cultural changes which the sanction of the courts reflected. What might be considered is rather the transcendental authority which today is given to the market place. How and why has it happened that our "constitutional rights" have come to include the privilege of exploiting mass appetites and indulging perversity, both for profit? If we eulogize this right, let us at least recognize that what we worship is mammon, the cupidity of the moment, the rage of the hour; and explain to ourselves why it took a century and a half and more before this right was read into our Constitution. As the majority will has gained in authority our "civil liberties" have inevitably been redefined and redefined again. It is perfectly logical to presume that the taboo against incest will be the next important remission, and that we will fall below the apes.

Hugo Black, in his time one of the Supreme Court judges most revered by the liberal establishment, refused to view pornographic movies that came before the court. Individual judgment was unnecessary for him. Every book, every newspaper article, every movie was protected by the First Amendment. This absolutist view, in its ultimate consequences, denies to our society the power to transmit standards of culture, to educate the young. It is one symptom of a vast change.

Within memory of Americans not yet old, in many areas of the United States, in most places outside of large cities, female school teachers could not smoke, drink, or use vulgar and obscene language in public, could not have children out of wedlock, could not live in open adultery, and were denied the freedom to be slovenly and filthy in appearance. In many communities church attendance was required, and denominational choice limited. Except for the right to smoke, male school teachers were in much the same fix. In the classroom the teacher had no freedom to attack or question religion or established institutions, no privilege to undermine prevailing ethical or moral standards, no right to encourage revolt against parental authority. Teachers did not enjoy the freedom to choose materials slanted to accord with whatever subversive doctrines they found comforting as individuals. Repression and censorship were the rule. Judgements made in these matters were sometimes reasonable, sometimes not, but in general the right to make them was taken for granted. By now this confidence has so eroded that, although the avengers of violated piety have not yet been removed "out of the world," they are reduced to impotence. The process was long.

For many years educated Americans have not had to know the facts to know who was wrong and who was right in a conflict between the American Legion and the American Civil Liberties Union. Any pleas for censorship, or repression, or control, have long been associated in the minds of our most literate Americans with the ideology of simple primitives or vulgar barbarians. In a real sense true education long ago ceased to be a topic seriously discussed. The logic of intolerance faded from our collective memory. Today circumstances require that some, at least, relearn it. The authors of our Constitution and the Bill of Rights took it for granted.

7 The Logic of Intolerance

Justice Oliver Wendell Holmes, known as the "great dissenter," who sat on the Supreme Court from 1910 to 1932, is venerated by liberal hagiolaters. In one of his most saluted minority opinions, before disputing it, he spelled out the logic of intolerance:

> Persecution for the expression of an opinion seems to be perfectly logical. If you have no doubt of your premises or your power and want a certain result with all your heart you naturally express your wishes in law and sweep away all opposition. To allow opposition by speech seems to indicate that you think the speech impotent, as when a man says he has squared the circle, or that you do not care

whole-heartedly for the result, or that you doubt
either your power or your premises.

If an individual finds himself in fundamental disagreement
with the conventional wisdom of the day, and finds much that
is permitted and condoned in every-day life disordered and
degrading, and yet has no doubt of his premises and cares
wholeheartedly for the result, what is his responsibility? He has
not the power to persecute error, not to express his wishes in
law and sweep away all opposition. He need not surrender to
indifferency. He may find the courage to be intolerant of opinions he loathes and knows fraught with danger. He can speak
and act in accordance with his own convictions.

If a man knows that the earth is a spinning globe revolving
about the sun, and if he loves his neighbors, he will act to
prevent all the members of his community from embarking in
a rocket navigated by a man who presumes that the earth is a
flat stationary object. As a last resort he might assassinate the
navigator to save the others.

The extremes of tolerance now guaranteed by our courts, in
response, it must be understood, to the will of the freedom-
loving majority, have limits still. Certain knowledge and absolute conviction, as always, set those limits. Certainty dictates
intolerance. The way of life of a public-school teacher may flout
community standards viciously and contemptuously, he or she
may indoctrinate the children in their charge outrageously.
Depravity and exploitation are protected, in part by the courts,
more by the parental confusion and indifference which saps
resistance. But if a teacher, who came to believe that the bite
of a rabid dog was God's greatest gift, an immediate passport
into heaven, succeeded to convert children to this faith, and
then sought to expose willing disciples to mad dogs, not many
communities would honor that teacher's religious freedom or
academic privilege. Toleration is the product of uncertainty
and doubt. There is much about which man will eternally be
without certain knowledge. There is much else about which
certainty must be presumed. The evidence requires it. In such

matters toleration is craven, and less than human. Holmes did not assume that speech is impotent, nor did he suggest that the man who says that he has squared the circle should have the freedom to teach mathematics in the public schools. Parents who do not doubt their own premises, and want a certain result with all their hearts, *can* express their wishes in laws for their children.

Holmes's dissent was in a case in which the Supreme Court upheld the conviction of an obscure man who had written and surreptitiously published a silly leaflet of no demonstrated influence whatsoever. Holmes, having stated the logic of intolerance, sought to confute it in this renowned passage:

> But when men have realized that time has upset many fighting faiths, they may come to believe even more than they believe in the very foundations of their conduct that the ultimate good desired is better reached by free trade in ideas—that the best test of truth is the power of thought to get itself accepted in the competition of the market. . . . That at any rate is the theory of our Constitution. It is an experiment. . . . While that experiment is part of our system I think that we should be eternally vigilant against attempts to check the expression of opinions that we loathe and believe fraught with death, unless they so imminently threaten immediate interference with the lawful and pressing purposes of the law that an immediate check is required to save the country.

This hyperbole may have had some justification in Holmes's understandable irritation with his brethren over their stand in the case at issue. In the sequel his fanciful interpretation of our Constitution prevailed. It has also gained enormously in latitude, a consequence not to be laid at his door.

The sequel cannot be blamed on Holmes because the character generated by his culture was in many respects as severely inhibited as was that of our Founding Fathers. He lived in a time when the notion of enforcing public morality by law was still firmly embedded. In 1903, the Supreme Court upheld the Mann Act, which provided punishment for any person who in any way brought about the transportation of a woman across state lines for "immoral" purposes. Now we live in a world in which the only generally accepted definition for "immoral" seems to be "what Nixon did." In 1903, in this law, it meant sexual intercourse between a man and a woman who had no marriage license. The Eighteenth Amendment, the purpose of which was to deny to Americans the freedom to imbibe alcoholic beverages, became a part of the Constitution in the same year that Holmes wrote his famous opinion. Freedom, as we have come to know it, was not a problem he had to confront. It is pertinent to recall that only recently had the Constitution been amended in order to remove one of the checks against democracy which had been established by our Founding Fathers. United States Senators had been elected by direct democratic suffrage for less than a decade when Holmes wrote his dissent.

The theory of our Constitution, in view of the most radical of our Founding Fathers, was a democracy in which everyone, by his property or satisfactory station, would be interested in the preservation of law and order. To the most conservative, democracy was a "beast." Our founders set up an experiment in representative government which was quite undemocratic. Judged in accordance with the views of every one of them that experiment has failed. Not one of them saw truth emerging from democratic tumult. Together they fashioned a Constitution based upon the presumption of leadership by an elite, with permanent institutional checks upon the will of the jealous majority. Democracy, long since, has imminently threatened the immediate interference with the pressing purposes of law, as they understood them.

The last time that Establishment intellectuals publicly considered the merits of suppressing thought by means of the police was in the period just before World War II. Some concern was expressed at that time that the free dissemination of Nazi ideology was a menace to liberal democracy. The only memorable contribution to that discussion was made by the historian Carl Becker.

There was a manifestation of free speech which Becker thought a far greater menace to liberal democracy than was the free dissemination of any foreign ideology. The speech which he regarded as socially vicious, to the point of endangering all liberties, functioned chiefly as an instrument of the competitive business economy. He meant advertising. Writing years before the advent of television, he remarked that modern methods of communicating thought were more subtle and more effective than any ever known before, while the verification of the truth or relevance of the thought communicated was far more difficult. There issued daily from the press and radio a deluge of statements that were false in fact or misleading in implication, which were made with no other purpose than to fool most of the people for the economic advantage of the few. In keeping with this ideological premises, Becker concluded that the evil could not be cured by creating a board of censors pledged to exclude lies from oral discourse and printed matter. He did recognize that neither could the danger "be cured by waiting while truth crushed to earth pulls itself up and assembles its battered armor."

Becker blamed the problem on the "competitive business economy." Those who largely controlled the avenues of expression were not seeking truth, but profits. Thus freedom of speech would not cease to be used for purposes that are socially vicious until it ceased to be profitable. He concluded that "the essential thing is either to abolish the profit motive or divert it into socially useful channels. This artless suggestion, Becker's obsession with the evils of advertising, his characteristic academic anti-business resentment, do not make his analysis memorable. He did, however, identify the nature of our predicament: We will wait forever for truth to pull itself up and assemble its battered armor. He wrote: "The liberal democratic political mechanism functions by enacting into law the common will that emerges from free discussion. Thus the circle seems completed:

for curing the evil effects of free speech we must rely on a public formed in large part by the speech that is evil."

There is no ready solution to this. To propose that we put an end to democracy is as impractical as Becker's suggestion that we transform human nature, although certainly not as impossible or as unlikely as an ultimate development. What those in our world who know what it is that they should not do, and what all ought not to do, should understand from this is that it is not in the laws which emerge from free democratic discussion that they should expect guidance regarding either justice or morality, and that the popular consensus is the last thing which should make them doubt their own premises.

Carl Becker invented a dilemma: for curing the evil effects of free speech we must rely on a public formed in large part by the speech that is evil. But "free" speech can only be evil; the public is not formed by the speech that is evil. Television and the movies certainly contribute to the lowering of our cultural standards, as an ever-larger audience is captured by what appeals to the lowest tastes, and as more and more of the young know less and less that they have not learned from it. But in the absence of censorship there could be no other result. Culture is something which is imposed on a resisting majority by a minority which understands how to possess itself of the means of power and coercion.

Constant exposure to advertising does dull sensitivity to the immorality of lying for advantage or profit. Becker was not wrong about that, but he wildly exaggerated its moral influence. The impact of advertising on our democracy is indirect. Television programs, certainly the most powerful cultural force in our society, do seek profits, not truth. Profits depend on designing programs, including the "news," which the public will watch, and in the process be captured for advertisers. As far as watchers and listeners are concerned, the advertising is incidental, and for the most part irksome. The only speech that can attract mass audiences is the speech which conforms to mass appetites and prejudices. The only profit is in what does appeal to a mass audience, and the level of profit is determined by the size of the audience. Nothing is more democratic. If democratic liberal assumptions about human nature, and the power of truth to get itself accepted in the competition of the marketplace were sound, all popular entertainment would be quite different. The television industry is not the culprit. It has no power not conferred upon it by the pleasure-loving majority.

The purchasing power of any group determines the degree to which its appetites and resentmens will be encouraged by the public media. Television shows designed for the teen-age market are structured to meet the most primitive impulses toward defiance. These programs confirm the view that children need not honor and obey their parents; they celebrate the sexual superiority of youth to age; they feature the meanness and ineptitude of adult authority; the mockery of the old (often characters in their early 50s), and the depravity of the Establishment. Theft is laughed away in the euphemism "rip-off." Successful people are depicted as pompous and grasping, the well-educated as vacuous snobs, and powerful people as connivers. Crass appeal to prurient interest is ordinary. The essence of their sermon is the ease with which traditional values may be flouted, and the pleasures to be enjoyed in doing so.

In ancient Rome the government provided public spectacles, which included lions against Christians, women against dwarfs, and men against one another, in mortal combat. Private theatres emptied, until they offered live sexual performances, mutilation, and murder. Then, in the competition of the marketplace, they survived.

Those who already know what is not to be done are weaker among us today than ever before. They can scarcely make themselves heard. Incapable of originating authority, they can only work to confirm it. Self-respect depends upon and is derived from a respect that is not for self, but for models from which everything is copied. To be able to recognize your superior, to know when you ought to honor and obey, to recognize at what point submission in good faith and without mental reservation becomes a part of wisdom and courage, is supremely difficult, and must be taught by example. Our culture engenders in the young an attitude of mind which renders them incapable of recognizing the fact that to obey a real superior, and to submit to real necessity and to make the best of it, is one of the most important of all virtues—a virtue absolutely necessary to attainment of anything great and lasting.

Only parents can transmit the interdicts, and only those parents who know what ought not to be done. The beleaguered family, in shambles as it is, is the last institution in which they survive. Among the less sophisticated classes, those most impregnated with traditional values have fought a losing battle. The ferocity of fundamentalist Christian parents in their opposition to the teaching of evolution a half-century ago, to sex education in the schools a generation ago, and to busing more recently, is largely because they have seen these controversies as defense of their homes and families. They have struggled to save the religion of their children, indeed to save the family itself, from the ravages of emancipated intellectuals and atheistic cosmopolitans, and they have suffered defeat after defeat. At the same time they have been subject to an unrelenting storm of insult and derision from the liberal establishment, with the educationists generally the most impudent and offensive. They have lost every battle because they have not had the resources required for so unequal a struggle. They have had too much respect for authority not to be confused when authority itself betrayed them, not to be disheartened when every elite scorned them. In the last analysis, resisting license, they were outnumbered.

Any society, any group of human beings united in some purpose, will strive to enforce ideological unity. Through the agency of the state the most powerful constituency will endeavor to enforce the kind of unity which best serves its interests. What matters is the kind of ideology: what does it permit men to do, and what does it require that they not do? What men are taught and may come to believe determines much of their behavior. Democratic ideology's appeal to freedom is universally seductive, but masks its own kind of despotism. There is the despotism of ignorance and subjection to instinct, there is the despotism of learning and reason. The greater an ideal, the more tyrannical it will be. But the moral measure of any despotism is the measure of its achievement. What manner of men and women does it produce? What manner of behavior does it tolerate, and not tolerate?

The parent who does not think speech or example impotent, and who cares for the result, will exert what power and influence he has. What is not censored or forbidden is approved. Children can assume nothing else. True culture does not ask ordinary mortals to make extraordinary renunciations; it does, however, impose limits. Societies perish not so much from the absence of truth as from the presence of error. Even the unjust suppression of a perfectly harmless activity is of little loss, compared to the harm that thoughtless leniency may cause.

The most important and the most inalienable of duties is that of instructing the young, educating them to hate what they ought to hate and to love what they ought to love from the beginning of life to the end. Parents, in the realm of their jurisdiction and influence, must assume this responsibility and perform this duty. This means parental control over what the child reads, sees, and hears, and what the child does not read, see, or hear. It means objecting to what the parents find wrong in the schools which they support and which their children attend. It means not sending their children to colleges and universities whose programs and activities, and what is permitted and not permitted, makes no sense to them, and seems foolish or intolerable.

The ideology of license and remission is the ultimate and inevitable consequence of democracy. We can only restrain the tyranny of the majority by whatever individual personal influence we have as private men and women. The question of governmental forms is not a practical issue. Democracy is a given, and anything for which it may be exchanged in the future will surely not improve our lot. The pressing question is whether or not the decrees of the mob will determine the cultural level of everyone, whether or not there will remain among us any at all to whom the evidence of the human potential for greatness has not been lost.

PART FIVE

Curriculum

1 Licensed Foolishness

What is the proper course of study for the young, what should be the method and the content of formal education? What should be the curriculum during the elementary and secondary grades, and in the colleges and universities? What standards of performance should be demanded, and how uniformly should they be applied? These are questions of vast generality. The answers depend upon ideology. In the real world every interested faction will propose answers which serve its interests, putative or real. The questions are political in the profoundest sense, and politics determines the answers. In our system the majority will decides. We suffer the inevitable consequences.

A quarter of a century ago Walter Whyte, in *The Organization Man*, made a gloomy forecast. He noted that the anti-intellectual sector of the education establishment has usurped the word "democratic" to justify the denaturing of the high school and college curriculum. Once the uneducated had had the humility of ignorance. Now they were being given degrees and put in charge. The delusion of learning on their part, he believed, would produce disastrous consequences. By 1985, he predicted, not only would those who controlled the educational establishment be themselves the product of stringently anti-intellectual training, but laymen, equally the products of the social adjustment type of schooling, would have no other standards by which to evaluate the education of their own children. Events moved much more rapidly than Whyte expected.

Lay ignorance—and the consequent failure to discuss, much less think about, what should be studied, and why—is the mortal failing of American education from the primary grades through college. Paul Gagnon writes: "It is the airy avoidance of thought about such things that allows American educationists to proclaim that 'the liberal arts have failed,' that content and order in a traditional curriculum no longer matter to the training of 'competent Americans.'" Gagnon repeats the familiar litany. Many college freshmen, after 12 years in the public schools, are unable to speak or write correctly or coherently; few are able to read more than the simplest prose; the large majority have never heard of the Enlightenment, of the Reformation, or the French Revolution. They know nothing of the deterioration of Athens and Rome, of Czarist Russia and Weimar Germany, and next to nothing of the history of technology, industry, labor, of fascism and Stalinism, of how we found ourselves in two world wars, or even in Vietnam. Almost none can as much as identify Jane Austen, Dickens, Walter Scott, Milton, Blake, or Shelley. They have been asked to read very little, to reflect and to write hardly at all. Almost nothing relevant to them as citizens or as intelligent human creatures has been prescribed.

Four years later hundreds of thousands of such young people receive college and university degrees, having improved their reading and writing proficiency very little, still with hardly a suspicion of what education might have meant to them. They are likely still to have no notion of music before the Beatles, of theater before *Hair*, of more than a half dozen contemporary works before *Fire on Ice*. They know no foreign language. They know no foreign culture, unless we so dignify what can be absorbed in tendentious courses about semi-literate or illiterate ethnic sub-cultures, whose members we once cruelly wished to assimilate, and whom we now placate with attention in higher education to their eating and courting habits. Of poetry and philosophy, of anything in Christianity, Judaism, or Islam deeper than the pieties or excesses, they are innocent. Their requirement in the humanities may well have been met by three credit hours in ballads of the 1950s, a workshop in urban graffiti, and a course in the philosophy of prostitution (tape recorder supplied for required interviews with real, live, philosophizing prostitutes). At 21 or 22, they are sent forth as cultural paupers, cheated for life by an educational establishment which abandons its students and calls that abandonment liberation. Having been required to confront nothing, they are unaware of the everyday choices offered them by the modes of thought evolved over centuries. Philosophy, history, literature, political and economic theory set men free to choose for themselves. Our schools pretend to educate while encouraging students to evade those subjects.

The mass and complexity of contemporary society makes it harder than ever before to be wise. Yet it is more necessary than ever before that some, at least, keep hold of the perspectives of history, and to know the source and course of ideas and institutions. Paul Gagnon writes that for private life the technological society, with its threat of alienation, or boredom, at work, has now "made indispensable to everyone a personal culture, a furnished mind, practiced sense, skilled hands." It would be foolish to hope for "everyone." But it is indispensable that *some* have these qualities, and that these some be more than a tiny and isolated irrelevant minority. In a special way technological society requires men who find honor in what they are and know. Without personal cultivation and the power to avoid being duped and brutalized by the mass media and amusements on the part of any segment of our society degradation will be universal.

In this chapter, curriculum proposals will be made and explained. They are not offered in the expectation, or even the hope, of reform. They are offered to parents who may be anxious, willing, and able to guide their children, and to bring whatever influence they have to see their offspring educated as they think they ought to be. They are proposals which may serve as a model to which practice can be compared, and to which conformity can be sought. But before these suggestions can be made and explained a more detailed review of the curriculum revolution which put us in our present state is in order. The more parents know of these details, the better armed they will be.

The destruction of the traditional curriculum, on the grounds that "the liberal arts have failed," begun in the middle 1950s and completed by the early 1970s, was justified by arguments long in vogue among educationists. Writing near the end of this period of "curricular ferment and reform," Daniel Tanner, a leading authority on the secondary curriculum, exulted. Long before Walter Whyte had predicted, the "licensed foolishness" he had described was ascendent. Tanner gloated to see so much recognition of the need of the curriculum to take account of the problems of contemporary society, the problems and needs of the learner, and growing emphasis on "open-ended learning." Educationists had made, and were making, great contributions in developing textbooks which rejected "the arbitrary and dogmatic representations of knowledge that have placed a premium on rote learning and regurgitation. They have rejected the traditional approaches of treating subject matter as a corpus of inert and unchallengeable factual matter to be passively absorbed for the examination."

Pleased, Tanner noted a variety of new approaches, though admittedly of unequal merit, and though the claims of none were "empirically substantiated," all shared the virtue of rejecting the traditional approaches that conceived of knowledge as bodies of information to be arbitrarily and dogmatically handed down to students from higher authority. This conception of learning, in giving undue emphasis to rote learning, had "provided students with false impressions of what knowledge and schooling are all about." The methods coming into vogue promised to produce better citizens, who would be capable of reaching decisions which would "improve the quality of our democratic society." Tanner used as evidence of the error of traditional approaches the student protest movement, which, he explained, reflected the low priority which had been given the "felt needs of the learner." He wrote of the need for curriculum "relevance and coherence," in an epoch of "exploding knowledge and growing academic specialization."

By the early 1970s, these theories had been implemented across the nation in every discipline. Millions upon millions of federal and state dollars had been spent to subsidize the overthrow of conventional courses and methods. In every instance the result was the same—a decline in student interest and performance. In no case was a single promised result achieved. Yet every experiment was declared to be a "success," and almost everywhere the traditional curriculum was overthrown, permanently.

Important aspects of the debate which arose in face of the growing evidence that Johnny could not read or write have been covered earlier, but more now needs to be said about the English curriculum itself. The victory of educationist ideology was overwhelming in the most important discipline of all. These theorists were able to exploit the public concern and to shift the blame. The changes in methods and curriculum of a decade or more were not the explanation for declining performance. What was needed, they insisted, was a revolution. And they got one.

The crisis in the late 1950s gave final victory to those who had long claimed that the traditional approaches for developing effective writing ability had been mistaken. By the end of the decade educationists succeeded in imposing the view that "traditional approaches had failed." By their "investigations" they demonstrated that "prescriptive grammar as a separate discipline has little effect upon written and oral language skills." Researcher Henry C. Meckel, for one, complained that, nevertheless,

> many English teachers continued to assume that
> drill in traditional grammar will automatically be-
> come transformed into written and oral skills, and
> that grammar skills are best attained by making
> language conform to various atomistic rules and
> constructs.

Models emphasizing "personal and social growth" were proposed, designed to overcome "the inertia of tradition," which,
appallingly, remained in those schools "which continued to adhere to curriculum stressing formal drill in grammar and the
study of literary works that were largely irrelevant to life and
outside the main currents of changing society."

By the mid 1960s demands increased. Not less emphasis, but
total exclusion of traditional grammar, became part of the
agenda. Teachers of high school English, or, at least, their official spokesmen, criticized the still-surviving tendency of some
teachers to impose a fixed and "correct" standard of English
on their students. In 1966, educators participating in the highly
publicized Dartmouth Seminar, a conference sponsored by the
Modern Language Association and the National Council of
Teachers, among others, announced that "prescriptive grammar had been discredited." It was now "agreed that emphasis
on traditional grammar not only had a negligible effect on
improvement of writing, but served to squander time that might
better be spent on writing." In keeping with these discoveries
reforms followed, more "pragmatic" approaches, which were
accompanied with ever lower performance in writing, by ever-
larger percentages of students.

Educationists had long insisted upon the need to develop the
secondary curriculum in English "according to student needs,
experiences, and interests," and that subjects be chosen in the
fields of "citizenship and family living." This battle against the
study of traditional literary works, "largely irrelevant to life,"
took longer to win than the campaign against "prescriptive"
grammar." In its early history the College Entrance Examina-

tion Board relied on lists of prescribed classics as the basis for the English examinations. In 1965, fighting a losing battle against the proliferation of courses and subject under the rubric "English," a Commission established by the Board recommended that the scope of secondary English programs be defined as the study of language, literature, and composition, written and oral, and that "matters not clearly related to such study be excluded from it." Educationists complained that this was reactionary, that it went counter to progressive trends, that it seemed to omit drama as a performing art, journalism, and the "newer mass media." In fact the door had been opened for such things, and for much more, by surrender to educationist ideology in the most essential matter. In its same 1965 report the Commission bowed to the inevitable, and confessed that the "folly" of prescribing a definitive list of literary works for all secondary schools had become clear. The Board had long assumed such authority, and performed possibly its greatest educational service in doing so. Now its own Commission on English asked: "Who can claim the authority to draw up such a master list? Or to require it, once drawn? . . . What conceivable principles can govern inclusion or exclusion?" The mind of man might have been struck dumb at such questions!

Educationists had long decried the "folly" of making choices. In their view, Daniel Tanner explained, prescribed lists failed "to take into account the tremendously diverse population of students attending public schools, not to mention the specific needs of the disadvantaged." They declared that "essentialists" who would prescribe lists were guilty of not recognizing that "to isolate literature from social studies is to isolate literature from life." The Commission, in deciding that literature itself was a word "inconceivable" to define, effectively licensed giving comic books, detective stories, hobby magazines, union pamphlets, business letters, advertising copy, indeed anything written, parity with the works of Shakespeare, Tolstoy, Homer, and Dante. In the absence of principles to govern inclusion or exclusion, such choices followed naturally and logically.

Writing in 1971 Daniel Tanner noted with displeasure that

"the notion that there should be a universally prescribed canon of literary works to be read by all secondary school students persists in some quarters to this day." By then, however, his concern was groundless. Those holding to such a notion were no more than a defeated and despised remnant.

Traditionally, formal education before college was limited to a few subjects. Of these, English was given first priority, and history second. History was the prime target and first victim of the anti-intellectual onslaught against the traditional curriculum.

Until World War I the secondary public-school curriculum included ancient history, medieval and modern European history, English history, and American history and government as a four-year sequence. A report emanating from the professional education establishment, published in 1916 by the Committee of Social Studies on Reorganization of Secondary Education, advocated "modernizing" the curriculum in order to develop "the learner's potential for more effective membership in society." The proposals of this report, which were widely adopted, downgraded history but did not radically undermine its position, leaving it intact for college-bound students. But between the two World Wars, to quote a prominent educationist, "increasing enrollments gave sufficient cause for a reassessment of the secondary curriculum."

In 1944 the National Education Association's Educational Policies Commission issued its "Education for *All* American Youth," which gave special attention to the "social studies" in general education, and proposed a program of "common learnings," designed to help youth "grow in six areas." These were: (1) civic responsibility and competence; (2) understanding the operation of the economic system and of the human relations involved therein; (3) family relationships; (4) intelligent action as consumers; (5) appreciation of beauty; (6) proficiency in the use of language. All of these things were to be accomplished by suppressing the study of history and substituting the "social sciences," in the form of courses in "everyday" economics, "consumer skills," and "the family." The proponents agreed in admitting that the social sciences should not be expected to imitate the "rigorous exactitude" of traditional disciplines, but declared this to be their virtue, because "social and political life is shaped by emotions and manifold variables and unknowns, which allow for societal change and improvement." What little history that remained in the curriculum was expected to reform itself. American history was not eliminated, but the traditional method of teaching it, uniform coverage, chronological completeness, and rote learning, were all deplored. One authority declaimed:

> There is a need for new and promising changes in the fields notorious for their didactic-memoriter methods, which are known to be deadening to the student. . . . The current movement rejects the factual-descriptive-chronological treatment of subject matter characteristic of the traditional curriculum. . . .

He was, however, confident that, because the traditional curriculum failed to meet the "relevancy criterion demanded by so many students," it was doomed. This was an accurate prediction. By the middle 1970s the typical college freshman knew virtually nothing about anything that had happened on earth before his 14th birthday which was not a part of his own immediate experience. And by then he would be able to go through four years of higher education without suffering embarassment for his ignorance or being required to repair it.

2 The Foreign-Language Crisis

For some months following the Soviet invasion of Afghani-
stan in 1979, the staff of the United States Embassy in Kabul
did not include a single person capable of speaking or writing
even simple Russian. In Teheran before the overthrow of the
Shah no American in our Embassy could read the daily press,
or even the posters plastered about the city. In Cairo the same
is true today. This is a matter which might be thought relevant
by any educational "pragmatist." Except for Russian, under no
conditions would these languages be appropriate subjects of
study in secondary American schools, or even in undergraduate
higher education. Russian certainly would be, and the mournful
fact of our national incompetence in foreign languages stems
from deficiencies in our secondary curriculum. These deficiencies, of course, have their source in a more general malaise.

Shortly after World War I, a university scholar, writing on Voltaire, commented that almost all educated Americans had read *Candide* in French. Today, even if we restricted the appellation "educated" to the graduates of our most select colleges and universities, those granted degrees during the past 12 or 15 years are for the most part incapable of reading anything at all in any foreign language (nor have many read *Candide*, even in English). This result was hurried along by the expenditure of millions of dollars in support of curriculum reform which promised to increase bilingualism.

Prior to World War II, the objective of secondary school foreign-language instruction was to develop the ability of students to read and write the language. Foreign-language study, required for all in the college preparatory program, was thought as well to increase the student's mental discipline, and to strengthen his command over English. The development of real proficiency in reading and writing the foreign language was not often achieved, although students who took four years of French often acquired a real proficiency in reading. The best students did. It would have been unreasonable to have expected anything more, and in no other discipline was average success noticeably better. The method did improve the mental discipline of the students who made a serious effort in the language. Indubitably it improved the competence of these students in their own language.

After World War II, high-school enrollment in foreign languages continued its long decline, and in 1950 the proportion of students in foreign languages, which had been 40 percent in 1916, fell to 14 percent. Early in the 1950s concern that our high schools were not producing "bilingual" students, and the rapid trend away from foreign-language study, assisted educationists in their campaign against traditional language instruction itself. Oral proficiency, they promised, could be acquired effortlessly and painlessly by new methods. Emphasis on speaking the language would attract students, because the subject matter—"daily living"—would be relevant. That secondary schools should try to produce bilingual students, or could accomplish this if they did try, was an ignorant notion. Nevertheless "revolutionary reform" followed.

The result was not an increase in bilingualism, but a sharp decline in the ability of students enrolled in foreign-language courses to read the language, and no improvement in their ability to speak it. Effortless by design, the new methods denigrated "mental discipline." Avoiding translation and ignoring formal grammar, it contributed nothing to the better understanding of English. The study of Latin, a "dead" language, was an unlamented victim of the revolution, enrollment dropping to 4 percent of high-school students in 1970. This could happen because by 1950 educationists declared that the doctrine of mental discipline was "generally discredited," and no one worthy of notice responded. Evidence that the study of Latin had made an important contribution to the ease and correctness with which generations of educated Americans expressed themselves in writing English was blithely dismissed "in the light of recent research."

Until the early 1950s, the Modern Language Association took the position that secondary schools should concentrate on reading skills, but then reversed itself and endorsed an audiolingual or aural-oral approach. The danger to foreign-language programs was severe. Declining enrollments had already resulted in many fewer secondary teaching positions in foreign languages, and future prospects were alarming. By joining with educationists in the crusade for reform, and by making specious promises which responded to a public concern, the tide might be turned. For a time it was.

In response to the outcry over Sputnik, the National Education Act was passed in 1958. Along with the sciences and mathematics, foreign languages were recognized to be essential to our national interest. Tens of millions of dollars were made available for "improving" foreign-language instruction. The money was passed out to those willing to adopt "reforms." There were few refusals. Following passage of the act high school enrollment in foreign languages nearly doubled, reaching 25 percent by the mid-1960s. By the early 1970s, decline had set in again. Today a large proportion of colleges and universities have ceased to require high school foreign-language credits for admission, and have dropped undergraduate foreign language requirements for the B.A. degree. High school enrollment has dropped below the 1950 percentage.

The "national need for functional fluency" provided the rationale for radical change, "the old approaches having failed." Functional fluency was an incompassable goal for our high schools. This did not matter to theorists and ideologues. No method will ever be found adequate to teach high school students of average ability, self-discipline, and motivation "functional fluency" in a foreign language in classes that meet four or five times a week, nine or ten months a year, for four years. The methods introduced, the Direct Method and the Aural-Oral Method prominent among them, came into being "as a reaction to the inadequacies of the traditional grammar-translation method." These new methods, characterized by their "painlessness," guarantee that virtually nothing is learned. Despite all of the financial support, despite the purchase of wastefully expensive equipment, all comparative studies have demonstrated that the traditionally trained student performed significantly better in reading and writing, was less likely to become bored and more likely to persist in the language, and that neither group acquired significant speaking ability. Nevertheless the "revolutionary" methods are firmly established and permanently entrenched, and the foreign-language skills of our educated population are lower than ever, and still declining. Foreign-language majors in our colleges and universities with median grades graduate without working proficiency in the language they have "studied," and the top 20 percent of these majors have only "a limited working proficiency."

An Italian child, brought up with a German governess and a French tutor, and later sent to a private school in England, may never have been drilled in irregular verbs or in tense endings, and may never have spent hours memorizing vocabulary and genders, but may achieve functional fluency in four languages without having labored as those who have mastered several languages primarily by the traditional and "disreputable" grammar-translation method. But for the child without governesses, tutors, and the privilege of attending private schools in two or more countries, the only likely option is the one which American high school and college students are now largely denied.

3 Science and Mathematics

The subject here is what *every* educated man and woman should know, and what skills they should have mastered. Traditionally, formal education during the first eight years included English, history, geography, and mathematics. During the secondary phase foreign languages and sciences were added.

Over the last generation the sciences have maintained higher levels of competence and standards in colleges and universities than have other disciplines. But during these years a smaller and smaller percentage of students have reached the college and university with the capability to major in these fields. This too has been the end product of curriculum "reform," in physics, in biology, in chemistry, and in mathematics.

In response to the clamor following Sputnik that too few of

our able young people were entering scientific fields, in 1960 a new high school physics course was designed by the Physical Science Study Committee. Federal and foundation support made it possible for "progressive" communities throughout the United States to adopt the course designed by this group. In the sequel it was discovered that students taking conventional courses in physics scored significantly higher on SAT tests than those who had been privileged to take the PSSC course. The designers of the course, who had predicted better scores on this very test, reversed themselves and demanded changes in the test to favor PSSC students. These changes were made. Test scores then showed no significant difference between conventional and PSSC products, and comparisons of college grades revealed no differences. Some defenders of PSSC complained that many teachers had been skeptical of the course, and had failed to discard all of the conventional content. Others were convinced that had there not been a body of such teachers, PSSC results would have been disastrous.

The main purpose of this reform had been to make physics "more relevant and interesting," and to attract more "good minds" to the discipline. After five years' experience the percentage of high school seniors enrolled in physics courses declined from 25 percent to 20 percent. After seven years, in spite of sharply rising enrollments, the actual number of college juniors majoring in physics declined by more than 15 percent. Among the top 1 percent of high school seniors, the percentage of young men choosing physics for a college major dropped from 18.8 percent to 11.1 percent; and among young women from this group from 4.1 percent to 1.6 percent.

Millions of dollars were spent to achieve this result. Subsequently the National Science Foundation fostered the design of similar courses in biology and in chemistry. The money spent equaled that squandered on the physics course, and the results were as bad. Those who designed the biology course, prepared for the possibility that its students might fare worse than conventional students on the biology test prepared by the College Entrance Examination Board (as indeed they did), prepared a test of their own designed to measure "understanding of scientific principles and scientific reasoning capability." Their students were outscored by conventional students on this test as well. But in all instances results were judged to be irrelevant. Conventional courses continued to be swept aside, to be replaced by courses founded on a failed premise. Advocates of the new chemistry responded to the evidence with the declaration that there "was no external criteria . . . with which the new course can usefully be compared." Mysticism had infected the most prosaic of our scientists, chemists.

No other discipline has been rocked by so much controversy, no other discipline has been subject to greater revision and reform, than mathematics. There is no evidence that any revision or any reform has effected any improvement in the cognitive process, college performance, or career motivation of U.S. students, but there is overwhelming evidence that there has been a steady impairment of traditional mathematics skills and mastery of concepts. Comparisons between the performance of our high-school seniors and those of England, Belgium, Japan, or Israel, for example, suggest that our schools are gravely deficient. Upon the most recent revelation that the high-school seniors of some seven or eight other nations surpassed our own in mathematical skills, it was shown as well that in all of these countries more homework was assigned there than here, and that in the nations whose students surpassed us by the greatest margins the amount of homework assigned was greatest of all. A national spokesman for the educational establishment was prompt to announce, and the press prompt to quote without question, that those fully familiar with the data, and expert in the interpretation of it, had concluded that the problems of students in the United States were probably the result of too much homework.

The sciences and mathematics are a special sphere, and few parents are competent, or capable of achieving competence, to pass authoritative judgment on this part of the curriculum. But they can observe the standard of performance and effort demanded in these disciplines, they can insist on knowing how a school's graduates compare with those of other schools on national standardized achievement tests. They can inquire of the mathematics and science departments of the colleges their children hope to attend what preparation and what mastery are practical prerequisites for majoring in these fields.

4 Reading and Writing in Elementary and Secondary School

The family is the primary, the school the secondary, channel of culture. For the moment, however, the elementary and secondary curriculum will be discussed in isolation, the curriculum appropriate for young people destined to attend colleges and universities. For many centuries following their founding the purpose of universities was to educate a minority. This minority was selected on the basis of promise demonstrated in earlier schooling. The purpose of the university was to prepare an elite whose personal temperament and ability qualified it for being educated to practice certain professions. In spite of contemporary circumstances, this model is not out of date. In the following analysis of the elementary and secondary curriculum we have in mind *all* students, but the goal of this education is to identify and prepare an elite suited for higher education.

No effort is made here to construct a complete curriculum. The study of mathematics, from grade 1 through 12, four years of science and four years of a foreign language in high school, are taken for granted. In the discussion of literature and ideas much will be said of "great books," but no list of such books is to be offered. They are the books judged to be great by the general consensus of the informed and competent over generations or centuries. In this connection F. Scott Fitzgerald, in 1940, complained to see the hard-earned money which had paid his daughter's tuition at Vassar spent on a course like "English Prose since 1800." A person, he wrote, who "can't read modern English prose by themselves [is] subnormal." Times have changed, but an amendment will do: courses in "contemporary" literature, in English or in translation, do not belong in a secondary or undergraduate college curriculum.

Education is, in part, a process by which certain skills are imparted, but moral and intellectual development through self-understanding is its ultimate purpose. In our times this places a peculiar burden on education. Contemporary youth is, in historical terms, remarkably free of restraints upon its appetites, and at the same time radically ungrateful and wholly ignorant with respect to all that has made possible the ease of its existence. When the child has little experience that there are limits, he does not learn that external restraints exist. He acquires the habit of not considering others, especially not considering them to be superior to himself. This feeling of another's superiority can only be instilled in him by someone who forces him to give up some desire, to restrict himself, to restrain himself. He then learns this fundamental discipline: "Here I end and here begins another more powerful than I." Ortega y Gasset noted that the ordinary man in past times was taught this elementary wisdom by the world about him. The form, the content, and the method of formal education, from beginning to end, must be designed to impart this wisdom.

Educationists have succeeded in giving a pejorative meaning

to methods which displease them: "regurgitation," memoriter-regime," "factual-descriptive-chronological treatment," "adult imposed standards and tastes." Nevertheless, through the years of elementary education, most of secondary education, and no small .part of college and university education, learning is a patient process of the mastery of details, minute by minute, hour by hour, day by day, week by week. The 18-year-old who has achieved a decent realization of his or her potential, and has become competent to benefit from higher learning, will have worked long and hard. There is no royal road to learning through an airy path of brilliant generalization. Without going through the patient process of the mastery of details there can be no real intellectual development, or even a desire for it. As Alfred North Whitehead wrote years ago, the apprehension of general ideas, intellectual habits of mind, and pleasurable interest in mental achievement can be evoked by no form of words, however accurately adjusted. The patient process is the only road, and the motivation to enter upon it is inherent in no one. Only those guided to it, and conducted along it, have any chance of acquiring its rewards.

The essence of elementary education is language, and nowhere is the patient process more required. The novelist Edith Wharton, born to considerable affluence and high social position, had parents with few intellectual interests. She declared, however, that her own development as a writer owed much to them. Her greatest debt to them was their use of English. She learned reverence for the English language as spoken according to the best usage. Her parents spoke their mother tongue with scrupulous perfection, and insisted that she do the same. They also stressed two other elements in her education: modern languages and good manners. With the virtual disappearance of such parents—and in our past they were not peculiar to the upper classes—it would be utopian to expect public institutions of learning to operate on similar principles. The fact remains that nothing so useful or so practical could be learned in the early years of schooling as what could be learned if students were drilled in traditional grammar, and taught to conform their speech to the maligned "various atomistic rules and constructs."

English teachers never assumed that drill automatically did anything. Many did discover how little can be accomplished at all significantly to alter gross language difficulties among unmotivated students. In many schools the teaching of conventional grammar was "chiefly a waste of time." By discontinuing it the "teaching" of English became a still greater waste of time. The most efficient means of bringing about improvement, no matter how little that improvement might be, was discontinued. For the vast majority of our school population lack of self-discipline, the inability to speak, read, or write, and general and appalling ignorance of many things which could have been learned by rote, are the deficiencies which make up the most serious "life-relevant problems."

A Teddy Kennedy may go far without the ability to speak coherently or correctly save the aid of a memorized, ghost-written script. Most Americans are condemned to live and work within limitations fixed by their mastery, or lack of it, of a "fixed and correct form of standard English." This is not a consequence of mere snobbery, but a practical necessity, and should it become less true than it now is our society will be the worse for it. Modern educationists have made much of "mute and inglorious Miltons," mute and inglorious because denied educational opportunities. How mute and inglorious Abraham Lincoln, for one, might have remained had he fallen into their hands!

The French elementary school, as it existed before democratic pressures forced the government to recognize "the special needs of different communities," provides a model of what ought to be done in these years. During the first two years, when the children were six and seven, in an average six-hour school day, two hours were devoted to reading, a half-hour to writing, and a half-hour to grammar. In grades three and four the same total time was spent on language, with the emphasis slightly shifted. Less time was devoted to reading and more time to the formal study of grammar. In the fifth and sixth grades half the school day continued to be devoted to reading and writing, but the study of formal grammar replaced reading as the primary concern of the class. During the seventh and eighth grades primary emphasis on the French language continued, although the time devoted to it in class was much reduced. Throughout all eight years, French was recognized as the most important subject taught in school. The hours assigned to it were inviolable. Any other subject might be slighted or sacrificed in order to increase the time for drill in reading (silent or aloud), and writing (penmanship, spelling, grammar, and composition). At the age of 13 or 14 every able student had learned to speak and to write his native language correctly.

The antithesis between liberal and technical training is fallacious, at least through the first ten grades. If our "disadvantaged" were sentenced to the kind of language program envisaged above, their career or job "opportunities" would be enhanced to a degree which will never be reached by the route of "job training," or by "vocational" schools. But command over language is equally relevant to our subject—intellectual development and self-realization. Alfred North Whitehead, in *The Aims of Education,* gave particular attention to what the student should be learning between the ages of 12 and 15, in preparation for the time between 16 and 21 when more intellectual development would be taking place.

Whitehead too recognized that of the things which children can learn in the early years of schooling, and what is most useful for them to learn, command over language is the most essential of all. Only those who can read well at 16 are prepared for the intellectual development which should begin to take place. Therefore he proposed that from the age of 11 onwards there should be a gradually increasing concentration on precise knowledge of language, and that the 3 years between 12 and 15 should be dominated by a mass attack. Within this period, he believed, we could ask that children achieve a thorough command of English, the ability to read fairly simple French fluently, and complete the elementary stages of Latin. Such a measure of attainment was well within the reach of the ordinary ·

child, "provided he had not been distracted by the effort at precision in a multiplicity of other subjects." More gifted children could go further. The study of French and Latin were to be undertaken, in large part, as a means to achieve better command and understanding of English. The potential of ordinary children has not changed since Whitehead made his proposals.

James Conant made similar, if less ambitious, recommendations. In his *The American High School Today*, published in 1959, during the "post-Sputnik" age when the public and the government grew briefly interested in "the development of academic talent," Conant suggested that all students, even the "untalented," be forced to take four years of English in high school. He proposed that some, if not all, pupils begin a foreign language in junior high school, and a four-year sequence in one foreign language in high school for all academically talented students. The educational establishment charged that Conant "virtually ignored the ordinary student and the disadvantaged." It did not matter. His recommendations were completely ignored.

So much for the formal study of language. Education ought to be planned so a definite result, itself worth having, is achieved. Education should turn out a pupil with something he knows well and can do well. The educational method of the literary curriculum is the soundest we can possibly adopt for the elementary and secondary years of schooling, that is, the study of our most habitual method of conveying to others what we feel, what we know, and what we think. The technique which is acquired is verbal expression.

Reading and writing are not merely mechanical skills, nor is speaking. The mechanics are learned by drill and exercise, rote and practice. They are learned by a long process, over years. On the other hand, intellectual development does not wait until the age of 16. Command of language opens up the world of literature, and the literature appropriate to the elementary and secondary years of schooling must be considered. Because confusion is also rampant here, the first thing that needs to be emphasized is that the study of literature is functional. Lest we forget, the ultimate task of education is to make the pupil like and dislike what he ought, in C. S. Lewis's words, "to train in the pupil those responses which are in themselves appropriate, whether anyone is making them or not, and in making which the very nature of man consists."

Education assumes the doctrine of objective value, the belief that certain values are really true, and others really false. It assumes, as Lewis explains, that

> to call children delightful and old men venerable is not simply to record a psychological fact about our parental or filial emotions, but to recognize a quality which *demands* a certain response from us whether we make it or not. . . . And because our approvals and disapprovals are thus the recognitions of objective value or response to objective order, therefore our emotional states can be in harmony with reason (when we feel a liking for what ought to be approved) or out of harmony (when we perceive that liking is due but cannot feel it). No emotion is, in itself, a judgment. . . . they can be reasonable or unreasonable as they conform to Reason or fail to conform. . . .

The educational function of literature is to teach virtue, to bring about harmony of the emotions and reason. If derangement were not so widespread there would be no perplexity about this. Plato, we recall, declared that a rational society will make it its "first business to supervise the making of fables and legends, rejecting all that are unsatisfactory." In Roman times Horace wrote that it was the function of the poet

> to set the bounds of public and private property, and the limits of the sacred and secular, to prohibit promiscuous concubinage, and found the rite of marriage; to establish the civic order and record the laws; it was in these performances that the

honor and renown of the divine bards and poems
came into being.

For centuries this was the unquestioned presumption of our
literary tradition. In the 17th century, John Dryden, in his
Introduction to Virgil's *Aeneid,* wrote that the design of epic
poetry was "to form the mind to heroic virtue by example."
The function of tragedy was "to purge the soul from pride . . . to
expel arrogance, and to introduce compassion." In the 18th
century, all art was defined as didactic. For Voltaire its function
was to civilize men; for Diderot the greatness of a work of art
was measured by the clarity with which it taught a moral lesson.

In his *Autobiography* Anthony Trollope summed up the
method and the purpose of his life's work. He put the matter
simply. No 20th-century reader should be embarrassed to approve his sentiments. If they seem "dated" one should ponder
by what logic have they been overturned. Trollope wrote:

> I have always desired to "hew out some lump of the
> earth," and to make men and women walk upon
> it just as they do walk here among us,—with no
> more of excellence, nor with exaggerated base-
> ness,—so that my readers might recognize human
> beings like themselves. . . . If I could do this, then
> I might succeed in impregnating the mind of the
> novel-reader with a feeling that honesty is the best
> policy; that truth prevails while falsehood fails; that
> a girl will be loved if she is pure, and sweet, and
> unselfish; that a man will be honored as he is true,
> and honest, and brave of heart; that things meanly
> done are ugly and odious, and things nobly done
> beautiful and gracious. I do not say that lessons
> such as these may not be more grandly taught by,
> higher flights than mine. Such lessons come to us
> from our greatest poets. . . .
>
> I have ever thought of myself as a preacher of
> sermons. Any writer does, and must, teach whether
> he wish or no.

Dryden compared "trifling" literature to great: "One raises the soul and hardens it to virtue; the other softens it again, and unbends it into vice." Great literature teaches virtue, but all books are not worthy. Human education is a thing of habits established, of tendencies confirmed and tendencies repressed. Thomas Carlyle wrote:

> Book-writing is of two kinds: one wise, and may be among the wisest of earthly things; the other foolish, sometimes far beyond what can be reached by human nature elsewhere. Blockheadism, Unwisdom, while silent is reckoned bad; but Blockheadism getting vocal, able to speak persuasively, —have you considered that at all?

Thus there are, indeed, "principles of inclusion and exclusion" for choosing works to be assigned as literature to the young we wish to educate. Discrimination and judgment are required, but the parent who has followed this discussion with sympathy and consent should be consequent. Such parents should not hide their light under a bushel. They should act for the sake of their children, and become censors.

There are secondary considerations. Planning the difficulty of what we require be read needs careful attention. All reading should be challenging, and the degree of difficulty should be progressive. Serious books are not understood until the reader has had a certain experience of life, and has seen and lived at least a part of their contents. The student may learn little at 14 from a book which will broaden his understanding at 18. The communication of ideas requires a similitude of thought and language. In Gibbon's phrase, "the discourse of the philosopher would vibrate without effect on the ear of the peasant."

5 History in Elementary and Secondary School

Educationists long charged that the study of history, with its demand of mastery over detailed information, when required year after year in the elementary and secondary curriculum, had the effect of denying youth "the opportunity to investigate life-relevant problems," and further, that this denied them their "rights as citizens." In good time they succeeded in all but eliminating the study of history in elementary and secondary schooling. This process was aided by the presumption of "an explosion of knowledge" and the resultant creation of new disciplines and sub-disciplines which made "inter-disciplinary approaches necessary." Now, education would not be education if it were not relevant to the learner and to life problems. Personal and social growth is not an invention of educationists; "essentialists" have always striven for it. Traditionalists believe that, given what students snould and can learn, a reasonable assessment of the economy of time dictates a curriculum restricted to essentials, and that history is such a discipline.

Observing the common man of the 20th century, Ortega observed: "These spoiled masses are unintelligent enough to believe that the material and social organization, placed at their disposition like the air, is of the same origin, since apparently it never fails them." They do not see that behind the benefits of civilization are marvels of invention and construction which can only be maintained by great effort. They simply insist upon the benefits as if they were natural rights. In past centuries when there were famines the mob went in search of bread, and frequently smashed the bakeries. In the early days of the Industrial Revolution the "Luddites," gangs of the unemployed, roamed about, smashing machines and factories. On a greater and more complicated scale, the masses today adopt the same attitude toward the civilization by which they are supported. The study of no other subject can do more to innoculate the individual against this primitivism than the study of history. More frequently than not teachers trained in the "new" disciplines of sociology and psychology are carriers of the disease.

In the post-Sputnik period traditionalists were able to make their voices heard, if only briefly, and to no avail. Conant's 1959 book recommended that our high schools restore history to something of its former place in the curriculum, and to do so at the expense of the "newer disciplines." Others proposed that the social-science requirements in grades 7 through 12 be limited to history and geography. One panel of scholars suggested that current affairs be eliminated, because the purpose of such studies would be best achieved "by the study of history, whose subjects, more remote in space and time, render easier objective analysis of conflicting opinions and interests." Arthur Bestor, who became the best known of the "essentialists," recommended that the high schools teach ancient history, medieval history, early modern history, and world history of the 19th and 20th centuries in a four-year sequence, and American history and

American constitutional history in a two-year sequence. He excluded all of the other "social sciences" and the whole litany of "life adjustment" courses.

History, Carlyle noted, lies at the root of all science, and is man's earliest expression of what can be called thought: "It is a looking before and after; as indeed the coming time already waits, unseen, yet definitely shaped, predetermined and inevitable, in the Time come: and only by the combination of both is the meaning of either completed." The present appears as chaos to the man without knowledge of the past; he is at sea without rudder or compass. This is but one side of the coin. Moral education is impossible apart from the habitual vision of greatness. The sense of greatness is the groundwork of morals. And, in Whitehead's words: "The sense of greatness is an immediate intuition and not the conclusion of an argument."

A leading 20th-century historian of Renaissance art, Bernard Berenson, wrote that the history of art should be the history of the humanization of the completely bipedized anthropoid. A visit to the zoo would be a fitting beginning for the study of history. Our anthropoid cousins should be an encouragement to us. If after the zoo the Paris Opera or the Louvre were visited, the Congressional Library, or the Smithsonian Institute, the human creature might feel some elation. After the entertainment of the zoo some might find the other institutions "irrelevant" and "boring." A nation made up exclusively of such men and women will have reverted to barbarism. Civilizations rise and fall. Their health and survival depend upon their ability to transmit the values and beliefs which sustain them widely and profoundly to succeeding generations.

We are all creatures of time and place, limited in understanding, suffering from parochial prejudice, motivated by self-interest which is more or less unenlightened. To live at the human level, to have ideas, is to both overcome, insofar as that is possible, and to recognize these limitations at least to some degree. Knowledge of the past is an essential requirement if we are to succeed at all. And there is more. To have ideas, to form opinions, is identical to appealing to the authority of reason, submitting oneself to it, accepting its decisions. No questions are more disputed today than social and political issues. Those who wish to have the right to opinions on these matters must accept the conditions and presuppositions which underlie all opinion—to study and learn the facts, and to respect them. Otherwise ideas are in effect nothing more than appetites in words. The study of history is the beginning of there being something more than that, and it can produce an enrichment of intellectual character more quickly than any alternative discipline directed at the same object.

History, through the elementary and secondary grades, is a patient mastery of detail, minute by minute, hour by hour, day by day, and during these years a great deal can be learned. The French example, in this instance still in place, is an excellent model. In the elementary grades a simplified and pictorial history gradually instills in the pupils' minds the idea of time, indispensable to genuine history instruction. In grades 7 through 10, through the ages of 11 to 15, there is a program for history, geography and civics which is required of all school children regardless of the school attended.

The courses in history are designed to present the sweep of history over long periods, placing the most important facts in their setting, punctuated by the essential dates; making clear what larger significance these facts and dates have, what makes them stand out, why they have a life of their own. They are structured to present and bring back to life the most significant persons and make real the characteristic ways and conditions of life in each era. The teaching is to be concrete, in order to result in knowledge of the most important facts and essential dates, dates and facts well related to their time, and solidly rooted in the memory. The courses are as follows:

Grade 7
Antiquity

I.   Introduction to History
     The life of prehistoric man
     History: generations, centuries, millenia, dates

II. The East
Three types of civilization
Egypt
The Jews
A maritime people: Cretans or Phoenicians

III. Greece
Geography
Homeric Greece
Greek religion
Greek colonization
The Persian Wars and the maritime empire of Athens
Life in Sparta and Athens in 5th and 6th centuries
B.C.
Alexander's empire and Hellenistic civilization

IV. Rome
Italy and its early inhabitants. The site of Rome
The origins of Rome
Conquest of Italy
The Roman Republic: basic ideas on government and
on economic, social and religious life in 3rd cen-
tury B.C.

Grade 8
The Middle Ages

I. From the 5th to 11th centuries: the East dominant;
the West fragmented
Byzantine civilization
Islam and Arab civilization
The great invasions. The fragmentation of the West
Charlemagne's Empire
Decay of Carolingian Empire and further invasions
Birth of France and of the German Holy Roman Em-
pire

II. The Rise of Western Europe (11th through 13th centuries)

Feudal society
The Church
France and England from 11th to 14th centuries
Evolution of civilization, economic development and
the expansion of cities. Life in the countries and
towns; the universities; Romanesque and Gothic
art

III.   The 14th and 15th centuries
The West in Crisis
Epidemics, wars; economic, social and religious up-
heavals
The Hundred Years' War and its effects on France
and England
Europe at the end of the 15th century
The nation-states
The Italian city-states and the origins of the Renais-
sance
New Economic conditions
What happened elsewhere (Islam and the Far East)

Grade 9
The Renaissance and Early Modern Times

I.   The new perspectives of the 16th century
The voyages of discovery; the colonial empires
Economic and social transformations
Humanism and the Renaissance
France in the first half of the 16th century and the
struggles against the Hapsburgs
The Protestant Reformation and the Catholic Ref-
ormation
Spain, England and France in the second half of the
16th century and the beginnings of the 17th cen-
tury

II.   The 17th century
The Dutch Republic; its merchants and painters

England to 1713

The rise of the absolute monarchy in France: Louis XIV and Richelieu, Mazarin and the Fronde

Character and results of major European wars

The reign of Louis XIV: absolutism; foreign policy; the end of the reign and its difficulties

Rural and urban life in France during the 17th century; the "Century of Louis XIV"; Versailles

III. The 18th century

New discoveries, science and inventions; economic changes; the rise of colonial empires; the slave trade

The new faces of Europe; the major powers

Character and results of major international conflicts

Arts and letters in France and Europe

One or two examples of Enlightened Despots

The crisis of the monarchy in France. Attempts at reform

The birth of the United States of America

Grade 10
The Contemporary Era

I. The Revolution and Empire

The major phases and leading figures of the Revolution

The development of the Consulate and Empire; Napoleon

The results and legacy of the Revolution and Empire

II. The 19th century to 1914

Liberalism and Nationalism; the revolutions of 1848

The unification of Italy and Germany

The industrial revolution. The working class; Socialism

Political and social evolution of the major European states

European Imperialism

The United States and the Far East
Conditions of life at the beginning and end of the 19th century

III. From 1914 to the present
The war of 1914–19: causes, course and consequences
Between two wars: the Revolution of 1917; the U.S.S.R., Lenin and Stalin: the depression and weakening of the democracies; totalitarian Italy and Germany
The Second World War: causes and consequences; the Cold War, decolonization, the traits of the new civilization.

This four-year cycle of courses parallels a four-year sequence in geography, and another in civics covering the political, economic and social life, and the administrative structure, of France. The study of geography is systematic, and includes examination of relief, climate and vegetation, rivers, population, agriculture, and industry, as follows: grade 7, Africa; grade 8, The Poles—America—Asia—Oceania; grade 9, Europe (except for France) and Soviet Asia; grade 10, France—Her place in Europe and in the World.

All of this is required of every French school child, many of whom leave school at the end of the 10th grade. Grades 11 and 12, designed for the academically talented, build upon these foundations. Making the adjustments which are appropriate, simply by exchanging the United States for France in the geography and in the civics curriculum, provides us with a model. It is not offered as a practical suggestion for any school system to follow. It is a model which reveals to us what an able student ought to learn and can learn during these years, one to be compared and contrasted with a standard curriculum in our public schools, and what our able young can and do learn from that.

6 The College "Core" Curriculum

For many centuries following their founding in the Middle Ages, universities were conservative institutions. Their traditional purpose was to educate a minority for practicing one of the "liberal" professions. This minority was selected on the basis of the promise demonstrated in their earlier schooling. The sum total of liberal studies included but three professions, the church, medicine, and law—law taken in the broad sense to include administration. The purpose was not to provide a general higher education for the population as a whole, or even for many. The purpose was to prepare an elite, whose personal temperament and ability qualified its members for being educated to practice certain particular professions.

Traditional society and culture were static. There prevailed a religion and philosophy which was taken to be the expression of ultimate and immutable truth, wisdom, and morality. Therefore intellectual and moral education could be imparted complete, once and for all, in the early years of life, to the minority which had been selected to receive higher education. Education was authoritarian. It was founded upon sacrosanct doctrine and was handed on to students by certified masters, who in turn certified the competence of those students to whom they awarded degrees.

In the course of the long period during which higher education remained traditional there were additions to the body of knowledge. For the most part these additions were not new ideas, but acquisitions of already existing bodies of knowledge derived from other civilizations, living or dead. These enlargments left knowledge itself still limited and static. No institutions were so little affected by the dynamic intellectual, technological, and scientific developments of the 16th, 17th, and 18th centuries as were universities. In the 19th century, however, the vast expansion of knowledge and the spread of liberal ideology and representative institutions brought real change.

Dante, it is said, knew practically everything there was to be known in Western Christendom in the year 1350. Goethe knew the greater part of what there was to be known in the year 1800. Not much more than a generation later it became impossible for the most powerful intellect to master more than a fraction of what there was to be known. The accelerating pace of change in science and technology and institutions created circumstances in which the university student was required to specialize in order to acquire knowledge with sufficient thoroughness to enable him to use it in professional life. This specialization had a high price. As the 20th century progressed, the most educated, in the formal sense, came to suffer as much as did the uneducated from parochialism and ignorance. Once the central purpose of higher education, intellectual and moral education declined until it became vestigial, and finally, insignificant. We have arrived at a time when it is painful to hear, or read, "educated" people discuss the most elementary problems of the day. In Ortega's phrase, "they often seem like farm hands trying with thick clumsy fingers to pick up a needle lying on the table."

We will never return to the authoritarian education of the Middle Ages. The very idea of doing so is obstinate and perverse. And the "explosion of knowledge" forced proper modification in higher learning. That is indisputable. But knowledge, not wisdom, "exploded." What Dante or Goethe could tell us about science, technology, or economics would now be useless. Either, most certainly, could speak to us with more wisdom than we are in the habit of hearing about the most difficult and complex problems of our everyday lives. Every man and woman, in our time or in any time, ought to know as much as their powers of comprehension permit of what Dante and Goethe knew. Ultimate and immutable truth, as they relate to wisdom and morality, *are* limited and static, at least in the sense that no "education" can ever hope to raise many to the levels of understanding which the greatest minds have achieved in the past. Education, in this fundamental aspect, remains essentially static.

Modern higher education consists of preparing students for the learned, and not so learned, professions, and of scientific research and the preparation of future scientific investigators. Although only a small minority of those who attend colleges or universities today prepare for the learned professions, or for scientific careers, the overwhelming majority pursue programs which are designed to qualify them for some profession. Nevertheless the student is nearly always required to take some courses of a general character, such as literature, philosophy, or history. This relic is the paltry remnant of what constituted higher education proper and entire. It was once understood that the study of the liberal arts was not an ornament of the mind, but the repository of convictions which became the effective guide of his existence. In his *Mission of the University*, Ortega y Gasset wrote:

> Life is a chaos, a tangled and confused jungle in which man is lost. But his mind reacts against the

> sensation of bewilderment; he labors to find "ways,"
> "roads," through the woods, in the form of clear,
> firm ideas concerning the universe, positive con-
> victions about the nature of things. The ensemble,
> or system, of these ideas, is culture in the true sense
> of the term; it is precisely the opposite of external
> ornament. Culture is what saves human life from
> being a mere disaster; it is what enables man to live
> a life which is something above meaningless tragedy
> or inward disgrace.

Today our educational system has abandoned almost entirely
the teaching or the transmission of culture, and the vast majority
of our students pass through institutions of higher learning
without being touched by it.

Society needs good professionals—lawyers, doctors, engineers. Cardinal Newman's mid-19th century ideal of the university as "a place of teaching universal knowledge" no longer
accommodates our needs. Professional training can no longer
be excluded from the undergraduate curriculum. Good professionals are needed, but society needs before this, and more than
this, men and women of culture, men and women who have a
decently coherent picture of the great movements of history
which have brought humanity to its present pass, some understanding of how speculative philosophy and religion speak to
eternal human problems, an understanding of self and others
enhanced by a familiarity with great literature.

Years ago, T. S. Eliot noted that in the United States the
education of college students was impeded by the fact that one
could never assume that any two of them had studied the same
subjects or read the same books. It was, he thought, obvious
that when you have no agreement that there is any body of
knowledge which any educated person should have acquired
at any particular stage, the idea of wisdom disappears. Only a
proper system of education can unify the active and intellectual
life of a society. You cannot expect continuity in politics, or
reliable behavior on fixed principles persisting through changed

situations, unless there is an underlying political philosophy. You cannot expect continuity and coherence in literature and in the arts unless you have a certain uniformity of culture expressed in a settled agreement as to what everyone should know to some degree, as well as a positive distinction between the educated and uneducated.

Until World War II the undergraduate programs in the arts and sciences at many private colleges and universities emphasized the great cultural disciplines, and in 1939 roughly half of all college and university graduates majored in fundamental subjects. By 1954 the number had dropped to 26 percent. The main business of colleges and universities had become vocational training. Nevertheless traditional degree requirements in the cultural disciplines were, by and large, maintained for all students.

As late as the mid-1950s the student enrolled in a pre-professional major at many, if not most, of our more reputable undergraduate liberal arts colleges had to meet quite considerable and specific degree requirements. Nearly half, but less than half, of the 36 to 40 courses ordinarily required for graduation were taken in the major and in related subjects. Often, 18 of the remaining courses were specified. A typical pattern was: foreign languages—four semesters in one language; history—two semesters of Western civilization, two semesters of American history, and one or two semesters of advanced electives; English—two semesters of composition, a two-semester survey of literature, one or two semesters of advanced electives in literature; social sciences—two semesters chosen from among political science, economics, sociology, or psychology; philosophy and religion—two or three semesters. Non-science majors were required to take in addition two semesters each in two sciences, or two semesters of one science and two semesters of mathematics.

The student revolt of the late 1960s destroyed this remnant. Within five or six years these 18 or so courses had been reduced by half at most colleges and universities. Almost everywhere the foreign-language requirement had been abolished. In history, philosophy, religion, and literature the requirements were slashed, and, at least as important, no particular courses were specified for meeting the requirements which survived. What core requirements remained had often been made meaningless by the expansion in offerings in the cultural disciplines, which to survive at all became diluted and bloated. The number of hours required to fulfill the major, pre-professional or not, changed little, if at all, but the remaining half, or more than half, of the student's formal education was now served cafeteria style, and every dish was served for which there was a demand, or for which a demand could be created. And in the great cultural disciplines themselves the major lost meaning. By the late 1970s there was hardly a medium- or large-sized college or university in the country, save a few exceptions, primarily in the South, at which offerings in these disciplines had not become swollen in the hope of enticing every taste.

All of this was not new. More than a century ago Harvard inaugurated an elective system from which students could select at pleasure their own program of studies. Henry Cabot Lodge remarked that under the previous compulsory plan

> a certain amount of knowledge, no more useless than any other, and a still larger discipline of learning, were forced on all alike. Under the new system it is possible to escape without learning anything at all, by a judicious selection of unrelated subjects taken up only because they were easy or because the burden imposed by those who taught them was light.

In Lodge's day, however, entering Harvard students had a better command of English and more familiarity with the great cultural disciplines than the average college or university graduate today, and the total number of courses open to a Harvard College undergraduate were fewer in number than those offered in sociology and psychology courses alone at many present-day institutions.

Today, mostly elective courses in literature, history, languages, philosophy, and religion attract only a handful of students. The Dean of Humanities at the City College of New York describes a particularly baneful example of what followed the great liberation from requirements:

> In desperate measures redolent of Madison Avenue, the faculty created sexy courses to attract students: gay literature, Jewish fertility. Then they tried to sell the courses with gaudy posters or notices. In the sweaty gym during registration too many of the faculty were no better than barkers at a circus side show touting the attractions awaiting behind the tent flap.

At least one private institution has adopted a policy of postponing registration in courses until the second week of classes. During the first week professors are on display to the customers, who have the opportunity to sample 20 or more courses, and then choose their favorite 5 for the semester. Today, throughout the country the non-science and non-professional courses actually taken by most undergraduate students do nothing for their intellectual development and add nothing to their fund of useful knowledge.

At most institutions of higher learning students still have decent choices. Although relatively few students choose them, fundamental courses are still offered. But the examination of the degree or major requirements put forth in the college or university catalogue reveal little about their true meaning until the available options are studied carefully. There is no consumer protection for the student unless he assumes the responsibility for himself, or his parent assumes it for him. A specific example of what courses two different students might take at the same institution and receive the same degree follows. Three of our "better" medium-sized private institutions have provided the data, and the results are quite typical. The student example making the choices which students most often make has not chosen any of the "individual study" courses widely available and which often do have significant enrollment. Urban graffiti and the philosophy of prostitution, which have been mentioned, are from this large and varied category. The expense of sending a student to any of the three institutions for four years is over $40,000, and rising.

Each student is presumed to be majoring in either one of the sciences or mathematics, in some pre-professional field, like business administration, or some subject, like sociology, other than one of the traditional cultural disciplines. The courses they choose are the only ones in these disciplines which they will take during their four years of higher education. The first student chooses, in history: ancient Greece, Renaissance and Reformation, Europe, 1815 to the present, 20th-century United States; in English: Shakespeare, Milton, the continental novel, the Victorian novel; in social sciences, foundations of political thought: Plato to Locke, history of economic thought, American Constitutional law; in philosophy, formal logic, foundations of modern philosophy; in art, history of art, Renaissance to the present. The second student chooses, in history: childhood in America, working-class women, the Harlem Renaissance, the American cowboy; in English: children's literature, detective fiction, lesbian literature, studies in cinema; in social sciences: battered women, prison rights, popular culture; in philosophy: media aesthetics, the philosophy of sexuality; in art: introduction to ceramics.

The student who makes choices like or similar to our second example is a typical member of the vast majority of our present-day graduates. Not one college graduate in 25 resembles our first example. Both students receive the same degree. Taxpayers totally support public institutions of higher learning and substantially subsidize private ones. By and large they ask no questions. But parents have a special responsibility, and rights.

7 Reading: The College Years

In order to live with assurance, freedom, and efficiency it is necessary to know an enormous number of things. But we all have a limited capacity for learning. The young cannot learn all that we should like them to know. The student's dimensions are, first, what he is—a being of limited learning capacity; and, second, what he needs to know in order to live his life. The nucleus of the college curriculum should thus be the subject matter which can be required with absolute stringency—what the good student can really learn. The parent and the student must pick and choose from the tropical underbrush of subject matter offered at our institutions of higher learning that which is strictly necessary for the life of the person who is now a student.

Only some are capable of benefiting from higher education,

and only a few from benefiting fully. In George Gissing's words: "Teach as you will, only a small percentage will profit from your most zealous energy." But zealous energy is required if those few are to benefit and is today most required at the point at which the decision is made to include or to exclude what is read or not read (which in higher education means what courses will be given or taken). Higher education is not shepherding. It must meet the needs of the few. Above all it must help them to discover themselves. Great literature is the royal road.

Long ago John Dryden distinguished readers into three classes according to their capacity for judging literature. We may distinguish our students in the same way. In the lowest form he placed those who were as

> our upper-gallery audience in a playhouse, who like nothing but the husk and rind of wit . . . these are mob readers . . . they are but a sort of French Huguenots, or Dutch boors, brought over in hordes, but not naturaliz'd; who have not two pounds per annum in Parnassus, and therefore not privileg'd to poll. Their authors are of the same level, fit to be . . . masters of ceremonies in a bear garden. Yet these are those who have the most admirers. But it often happens . . . that, as their readers improve their stock of sense (as they may be reading better books, and by conversation with men of judgment), they soon foresake them.

This is the class which our institutions have placated, on the basis of the principles which insist that it is inconceivable to establish principles that could govern inclusion or exclusion in establishing a master list of worthwhile books or courses, and that schools and colleges must take into account the diverse population of students and their varied interests. These are demogogic, not educational, principles. It gives the deciding vote to those who, as John Stuart Mill put it, "are not entitled to an opinion." The practical effect of their nearly universal application is that very few in schools and colleges read better books, and to guarantee that almost all of them remain "mob readers."

Were they required, or were they given the opportunity, to read better books, mob readers might improve their stock of sense. Dryden wrote:

> There are a middle sort of readers such as have a farther insight than the former, yet have not the capacity of judging right . . . a company of warm young men, who are not yet arrived so far as to discern the difference betwixt fustian, or ostentatious sentences, and the true sublime. . . . Even these too desert their authors, as their judgment ripens.

This brought Dryden to the third form of readers, the audience capable of appreciating great literature, the audience for which great writers aim. They are those for whom the college and university truly exists.

> I have already named two sorts of judges: but Virgil wrote for neither of them: and by his example, I am not ambitious of pleasing the lowest or the middle form of readers.
>
> He chose to please the most judicious, the souls of the highest rank and understanding. They are few in number; but whoever is happy to gain their approbation can never lose it, because they never give it blindly. Then they have a certain magnetism in their judgment, which attracts others to their sense. Every day they gain some new proselyte, and in time become the Church.

Schools and colleges, should they wish to educate, would aim to please these few, in the hope that they, in time, might become the Church.

The demand for "relevancy" on the part of educationists for their juvenile and adolescent peers, Dryden's lowest and middle form of readers, has been appeased in our schools and colleges. But education is not a matter of being relevant to these tastes. Education is a matter of raising these tastes among those capable of improvement. Many may be bored by literature called great by "self-appointed authorities." They may instead be "turned on" by detective stories, by tales of mysticism and magic, by the intimate personal revelations of the present idols of pop culture. They may demand materials relevant to "women," to "Blacks," to "Mexican-Americans," to "gays," to the "working class," to "Italian-Americans." The list has become endless. But education frees the competent from parochialism and prejudice, it strives to overcome self-glorification and self-adulation. The issue is not new.

Sixty years ago Leon Trotsky refuted the same demagoguery, the same "educationist" appeasement of vulgarity. In the Communist movement (and, to be sure, they did prevail there in the end) there were those who demanded "proletarian" literature. Trotsky responded to the argument that "proletarian" poetry was significant culturally and historically. This he readily admitted, but added:

> this does not at all mean that they are artistic documents. . . . Undoubtedly, the weak, the colorless, and even the illiterate poems may reflect the path of political growth of a poet and of a class. . . . But weak and, what is more, illiterate poems do not make up proletarian poetry, because they do not make up poetry at all.

The study of literary technique, the mastery of language and familiarity with great literature was, Trotsky insisted, a necessary stage in education, "and not a brief one." It was something which is noticed most markedly in the case of those who have not mastered it. Therefore it would be "monstrous" to conclude that mastery was not necessary to workers. Those who insisted,

"Give us something, even pock-marked, but our own," were being false and untrue. A pock-marked art was not art, and was, therefore, "not necessary."

No category of writing or subject matter ought to be licensed on the ground that it appeases some special interest or meets some "felt" need. Such categories violate proportions, they distort standards, and they cultivate the arrogance of small circles. They encourage ignorance. In the same vein Marcel Proust wrote that the idea of "popular" art was ridiculous. The artist can only serve man on the condition he think of nothing except the truth that is before him.

> The grandeur of real art is to rediscover, grasp again and lay before us that reality from which we live so far removed, and from which we become more and more separated as the formal knowledge which we substitute for it grows in thickness and imperviousness—that reality which there is grave danger we might die without having known and yet which is simply our life, life as it really is, disclosed at last and made clear, consequently the only life that is really lived, that life which in one sense is to be found in every moment in every man, as well as in the artist. But men fail to see it because they do not try to get light on it.

Education puts light on it, and opens up to us "the only life that is really lived." Proust wrote:

> The book is only a sort of optical instrument which the writer offers to the reader to enable the latter to discover in himself what he would not have found but for the aid of the book. It is this reading within himself what is also in the book which constitutes the proof of the accuracy of the latter and *vice versa.* . . .

Education is not education if great books, which are the heart of the cultural disciplines, those which offer what the reader would have not have found without the aid of the book, are not read. Education is not for everyone. He who reads great literature, and does not find "the same in himself," will never be educated. But he who never reads this literature suffers the same fate. The curriculum which does not *require* such reading effectively denies the opportunity of education to almost all, and condemns them to be "disadvantaged" forever. Educationists have charged that to isolate literature from "today's social problems" is to "isolate literature from life," and have insisted instead on Trotsky's "pock-marked" literature. In truth, to isolate students from great literature is to reinforce their isolation from life and from understanding.

Those not instructed in the art of reading may, in Gibbon's phrase, be exempted from shame and reproach by the common ignorance of our times. Although the book of nature is open to all, with no other mentor we are reduced to the private circle of our private existence. We are deprived "of those faithful mirrors which reflect to our mind the minds of sages and heroes." More than three centuries ago, Thomas Hobbes confronted the saying, "much usurped of late," that wisdom was acquired not by the reading of books but of men. He responded that there was another saying by which they might truly learn to read one another, if they would take the pains, and that was *Read thy self*. Because of the similitude of the thoughts and passions of one man and thoughts and passions of another, whosoever looks into himself, and considers what he does, when he thinks, hopes, and fears, and on what grounds, will thereby read and know what are the thoughts and passions of all other men upon like occasions. But let one man read another by his actions ever so perfectly, it serves him only with his acquaintances, who are but few. He who would truly understand must do more. He must read in himself, not this, or that, particular man, but mankind. Hobbes concluded:

which though it be hard to do, harder than to learn any Language, or Science; yet, when I shall have set down my own reading orderly, and perspicuously, the pains left another, will be only to consider if he not also find the same in himself. For this kind of Doctrine admitteth of no other Demonstration.

All things cannot be demonstrated to all men. Those capable of learning what is harder to learn than any language or science will never learn it if never confronted with great literature, never tempted or asked to make the effort it requires.

8 The Summary of All Advices

Curriculum is only a part of the difficulty. When the curriculum is structured and language and literature given their proper place the problem of the teacher remains. What standards of performance are demanded and how the material is presented are the crucial questions. Carlyle once gave what he called "the summary of all advices" to a group of students:

> That above all things the interest of your whole life depends upon your being diligent . . . in this place where you have come to get an education! Diligent . . . I mean it to include all those qualities of conduct that lead to the acquirement of real instruction and improvement in such a place.

Nothing is more needed, or more likely to be lacking, than elementary and secondary teachers who understand this. But when diligence is not expected or required, the curriculum and the title of courses matter little. Parents must know more than what is printed in the curriculum. And there is another reason for this. Titles of courses may hide more than they reveal of the content of what is taught. Presentation may subvert the very purpose which justifies the presence of a course in the curriculum.

History, for example, in the elementary and secondary grades, ought to have as its purpose the mastery of as much detailed and objective information as possible of what men have experienced, done, and thought in the past. The knowledge gained is not wisdom, but an escape from ignorance. It does not indoctrinate opinions, but provides a basis for forming opinions. When the teacher has a different agenda, when he orders historical facts to march in well-ordered battalions to the tune of his own private prejudices and chooses texts and materials which conform to his dogma, when he exploits his trust in order to serve his own passions, we are no longer speaking of education.

Writing about a typical textbook, designed in this instance for use in a secondary-school English course, C. S. Lewis discusses the authors' philosophy, and comments:

> In filling their book with it they have been unjust to the parent . . . who buys it and who has got the work of amateur philosophers when he expected the work of professional grammarians. A man would be annoyed if his son returned from the dentist with his teeth untouched and his head crammed with the dentist's *obiter dicta* on bimetalism and Baconian theory.

These "amateur philosophers" abound. They confront every traditional belief with "Why?"—"What good does it do?"—"Who said so?" This is to subvert education itself. If nothing is obligatory for its own sake, nothing is obligatory at all. An open mind about the foundations of either theoretical or practical reason is idiocy. If a man's mind is open on these things, Lewis commented, "Let him keep his mouth shut." At the very least let us not pay him a salary to "instruct" the young. When the "open" mind has dissolved belief in objective reality, only "I want" or "I like" remains. We are familiar with the result. Parents who understand all this should consider Aristotle's precept: "In practical matters the end is not mere speculative knowledge of what is to be done, but rather the doing of it."

Conclusion: The Role of Parents

We recall Philip Rieff's remark that until there are vast numbers of true parents we cannot expect vast numbers of true teachers, or true students. We ought not to expect "a vast number." The hope is that there may be a few. Alfred North Whitehead put it simply: "as to training the most important part is given by mothers before the age of twelve." More than half a century ago D. H. Lawrence described the modern confusion regarding parental responsibility, and gave his advice. He noted that the child who has not learned anything of value from parents will not learn much that is useful in school, and that the child of the parent who is confused about the most fundamental principles can rarely escape serious deformity.

In an essay on primary education Lawrence took table man-

247

ners for an example. He provided us with this dialogue:

> "Miss, if you eat in that piggish, mincing fashion, you shall go without a meal or two."
> "Why?"
> "Because you're an objectionable sight."
> "Well, you needn't look at me."
> Here Miss should get a box on the ear.
> "Take that! And know that I need to look at you, since I'm responsible for you. And since I'm responsible for you, I'll watch it you don't behave like a mincing little pig."

The parent in the right must interfere, otherwise why is the child brought up at all? Lawrence added that parents should never seek justification outside of themselves, never say, "I do this for your good." Parental responsibility is much deeper than ideal responsibility. It is a vital connection. When a child is loose or ugly it is a direct hurt to the parent. The proper parent reacts and retaliates spontaneously. There is no justification save the bond of parenthood. A parent owes the child all the natural reactions it provokes. This is the beginning of true education.

Parental confusion about adult responsibility is widespread, even international Two melancholy examples reflect this. The first: In the summer of 1980, at an Alpine resort in Yugoslavia, the following occurred. Near the shore of a lake a mother duck was teaching her young, who swam behind her imitating her movements. One duckling did not follow the mother's lead and wandered ashore. The mother, quacking angrily, pursued her errant offspring, and when in range began to peck it unmercifully. A group of middle-aged tourist onlookers, including Americans, Belgians, and Swedes, began, first to hoot, then to pelt the mother with stones, in protest against her offensive teaching methods.

Many years intervene between the time when parents do, or do not, impose table manners and such like upon their children, and the time when they do, or do not, exert authority over their college-age offspring. The "educational" issues are constant, parental responsibility continuous. But many a parent who would fully appreciate the absurdity of human adults avenging the battered duckling is filled with doubt about parental authority toward offspring who are of college age. This brings us to our second example.

The wife of the editor of one of our large Northeastern city newspapers writes a syndicated column for adolescents. A mother-confessor to the children who write to her, she seeks to give comfort and support to teenagers struggling to liberate themselves from parents with "outmoded" values. Early in 1980 this columnist printed a letter from a female college student, who suffered because her parents were unhappy that she had moved off campus to share quarters with a boy friend who was not a student. Her parents were not so much shocked as angry. They had skimped and saved to provide her with an education, not to support her Dutch-treat sexual adventures. Our "expert" in these matters instructed the young woman that social patterns and values were changing, and that "this does not mean that parents have to approve of them." She added: "By sending you off to college your parents acknowledge your ability to run your own life." With the inconsistency which characterizes her brand of arrogance, the columnist nonetheless did instruct the "student" how to run her life. She advised her not to cut herself off from the social and extracurricular activities, which are such "a large part of the benefit from the college experience," and was quite firm in declaring that "marriage would be a mistake."

This is official wisdom. Parents under its influence are not likely to have much advice to give to their 18-year-old children, or to have much to teach their 8- or 12-year-old children, or much influence should they try. The presumption here is that other kinds of parents do exist, who are able to understand that "education" is all of one piece, and that parental responsibility lasts for as long, at least, as children are dependent. When parental responsibility is not assumed, the child will never rise far above the environment which the school provides, or accomplish more than it requires, from the beginning to the end of formal education.

During the past 30 or 40 years we have seen the schools assume one responsibility after another hitherto left to parents. This is a cause for shame; it is evidence that we have arrived at a stage in the decline of our civilization at which the family is irresponsible, or incompetent, or helpless, a stage at which parents cannot be expected to train their children properly. When we include as a part of formal education all the influences of family and environment, we realize that we have simply surrendered to mass culture. In the best of circumstances the elementary and secondary schools could only transmit a part of culture, and could transmit this part effectively only if it were to some degree outside the influences of mass culture and tastes. In our society the schools necessarily are in harmony with and reflect majority standards. Parents of higher culture, if higher culture is to survive anywhere, must resist and combat school influences.

Every popular innovative educational theory of the last quarter century, in whatever humanitarian guise it has appeared, has appealed to widespread resentment and rebelliousness against the discipline which excellence demands, against recognition of natural and inevitable qualitative differences in individual human beings, against the hierarchy of values upon which civilization depends. But no majority, no matter how overwhelming, transforms uninformed opinion into truth. In no field of thought is the highest wisdom to be discovered in the notions of average men and women, whether or not these notions are supported and enforced by all the power and authority of the modern state. On the other hand it would be absurd to suggest that we do away with universal suffrage.

Life may be the art of making choices, but in many matters we have no choice. We are given democratic institutions. Blind acceptance of the values and practices which characterize democratic culture is not a necessary consequence of our condition. Writing in 1873, shortly after one of the major steps taken in England in the direction of democratic suffrage, James Fitzjames Stephen noted that the eventual triumph of the idea of universal suffrage was quite certain. He was altogether at a loss to understand why this prospect aroused enthusiastic admiration in anyone. Nevertheless, when asked what he proposed to substitute for universal suffrage, he replied:

> I answer at once, Nothing. The . . . whole stream of human affairs is setting with irresistible force in that direction. The old ways of living, many of which were just as bad in their own time as any of our own devices can be in ours, are breaking down all over Europe, and floating this way and that like haycocks in a flood. Nor do I see why any wise man should expend much thought or trouble to save the wrecks . . . but I do not see why as we go with the stream we need sing Hallelujah to the river god. . . .
>
> No government by a democracy . . . either in its political acts or in the opinions, qualities, and tone of mind which it fosters, ever did or could rise above mediocrity.

In America today each of us need not praise the multitude, study its tastes, assume its prejudices, serve its vices, and approve its injustices. Some, at least, can withstand the dogmatism of democratic ideology, and make decisions based upon different principles than those preached by publicans. Justice demands that inequality be recognized, and in education it must be.

The public classroom can do no more than reflect the contemporary standards of cultureless egalitarian society. Obedience to higher culture will not originate in our schools. True teaching must begin long before the student reaches the classroom, and must continue outside the classroom through all the years of schooling. Without true parents there will never be true students. No one escapes from the kind, or wholly surpasses the degree, of culture acquired during his early years, and when the family fails to play its part we must expect our culture to deteriorate.

Although the revolutionary upheavals which have transformed Europe in this century have spared the United States, fundamental changes have been similar on both continents. When he had achieved power in Russia, Lenin noted that the Bolsheviks had defeated the landlords, the capitalists, and the Czarist bureaucracy, whose culture had been at a miserably low and insignificant level. Nevertheless, he said, "it was higher than ours." Miserable and low as it had been, it had been higher than that of the responsible Communist administrators. Lewis Namier, the historian, addressed the same issue when he observed that all government is based upon some form of oligarchy, and that when these leaders are endowed with the moral values of a religious, national, or class character a basis is provided for the most elementary requirement of a sound society, which we call tradition. Self-made men can continue such a tradition, but cannot, on the strength of being "self-made" create one. He wrote:

> Wars and revolutions have broken up routines, and "intellect" has corroded traditions. . . . The old ruling classes have practically disappeared on the European continent: they perished mostly because they were not equal to their task; but even so their countries are poorer. . . .

And so are we, but those among us still bound by, or even influenced by, the wisdom and authority of the most time-honored traditions and values of our civilization have a responsibility—at least to our own—to transmit at least what we believe.

The primary vehicle for the transmission of culture is the family. In any highly civilized society, different families have different levels of culture, and to ensure the transmission of culture of these different levels there must be groups of families persisting from generation to generation, each in the same way of life. Higher culture depends on it. T. S. Eliot went so far as to suggest that on the whole it would appear for the best that the great majority of human beings should go on living in the locality and class in which they were born. Family, class, and local loyalty all support each other, and if one of these decays, the others will suffer also. There are, and must be, different levels of culture, and the transmission of group culture must be by inheritance. The decay of the family means the decay of the standards of culture, and Eliot anticipated a future period of which it would be possible to say that it will have no culture.

Champions of "equal opportunity" recognized different levels of culture, but disputed the assumption that the transmission of group culture must be by inheritance. They hoped that some mechanism of selection could be found so that every individual would in due course take his place in the highest cultural level for which his natural aptitudes qualified him. The result, had the mechanism been found, is only a matter for conjecture. They placed their hope in public education. Universal education would bring about the rule of a natural elite, and end the injustice of inherited status. This doctrine implied much more than a rectification of such injustice. It posited an atomic view of society. But public education is no longer directed to their purpose. The general will has vetoed "elitism," whatever its source or sanction. The family, defending whatever level of culture it represents, is the last hope.

In matters of education public discussion may ignore the truth and public policy go counter to it. Individual understanding and private convictions are not, therefore, irrelevant. In education the areas of personal choice and decision are still very great. Parents may decide many things according to their own judgment rather than accepting the public consensus, and they may do so without endangering the security or the worldly prospects of their offspring. Indeed, they enhance every worthwhile prospect for their children, including material success, by insisting upon something different. If they understand that distinctions should be made in regard to real differences, that excellence should be recognized, developed, encouraged, and rewarded, they need only have the courage of their conviction to make a difference. Parents of higher culture have a responsibility not only to their own children, but to civilization itself.

"For some time now the evidence

DISCARD
LIBRARY

Politics and the Professors

Studies in Social Economics

TITLES PUBLISHED

The Doctor Shortage: An Economic Diagnosis
Rashi Fein

Medicare and the Hospitals: Issues and Prospects
Herman Miles Somers and Anne Ramsay Somers

Education and Poverty
Thomas I. Ribich

Social Security: Perspectives for Reform
Joseph A. Pechman, Henry J. Aaron, and Michael K. Taussig

Poverty and Discrimination
Lester C. Thurow

Community Control of Schools
Henry M. Levin, Editor

Government Against Poverty
Joseph A. Kershaw with the assistance of Paul N. Courant

American Indians and Federal Aid
Alan L. Sorkin

*Shelter and Subsidies: Who Benefits from Federal
Housing Policies?*
Henry J. Aaron

Why Is Welfare So Hard to Reform?
Henry J. Aaron

Reforming School Finance
Robert D. Reischauer and Robert W. Hartman
with the assistance of Daniel J. Sullivan

National Health Insurance: Benefits, Costs, and Consequences
Karen Davis

The Future of Social Security
Alicia H. Munnell

The Inheritance of Economic Status
John A. Brittain

Inheritance and the Inequality of Material Wealth
John A. Brittain

Politics and the Professors: The Great Society in Perspective
Henry J. Aaron

STUDIES IN SOCIAL ECONOMICS

Henry J. Aaron

Politics and the Professors: The Great Society in Perspective

THE BROOKINGS INSTITUTION
Washington, D.C.

Copyright © 1978 by
THE BROOKINGS INSTITUTION
1775 Massachusetts Avenue, N.W., Washington, D.C. 20036

Library of Congress Cataloging in Publication Data:

Aaron, Henry J.
  Politics and the professors.

  (Studies in social economics)
  Includes bibliographical references and index.
  1. Economic assistance, Domestic—United States.
2. Education and state—United States. I. Title.
II. Series.
HC110.P63A65   338.973   77-91809
ISBN 0-8157-0026-1
ISBN 0-8157-0025-3 pbk.

9 8 7 6 5 4 3 2 1

To Ruthie

338.973
Aa 75 p

Board of Trustees

Robert V. Roosa
Chairman

Louis W. Cabot
Vice President;
Chairman, Executive Committee

Vincent M. Barnett, Jr.
Barton M. Biggs
Edward W. Carter
William T. Coleman, Jr.
Lloyd N. Cutler
Bruce B. Dayton
George M. Elsey
John Fischer
Huntington Harris
Robert W. Heyns
Carla A. Hills
Luther G. Holbrook
Lane Kirkland
Bruce K. MacLaury
Robert S. McNamara
Arjay Miller
Barbara W. Newell
Herbert P. Patterson
J. Woodward Redmond
Charles W. Robinson
Warren M. Shapleigh
Phyllis A. Wallace

Honorary Trustees

Arthur Stanton Adams
Eugene R. Black
Robert D. Calkins
Colgate W. Darden, Jr.
Douglas Dillon
John E. Lockwood
William McC. Martin, Jr.
H. Chapman Rose
Robert Brookings Smith
Sydney Stein, Jr.
J. Harvie Wilkinson, Jr.

THE BROOKINGS INSTITUTION is an independent organization devoted to nonpartisan research, education, and publication in economics, government, foreign policy, and the social sciences generally. Its principal purposes are to aid in the development of sound public policies and to promote public understanding of issues of national importance.

The Institution was founded on December 8, 1927, to merge the activities of the Institute for Government Research, founded in 1916, the Institute of Economics, founded in 1922, and the Robert Brookings Graduate School of Economics and Government, founded in 1924.

The Board of Trustees is responsible for the general administration of the Institution, while the immediate direction of the policies, program, and staff is vested in the President, assisted by an advisory committee of the officers and staff. The by-laws of the Institution state: "It is the function of the Trustees to make possible the conduct of scientific research, and publication, under the most favorable conditions, and to safeguard the independence of the research staff in the pursuit of their studies and in the publication of the results of such studies. It is not a part of their function to determine, control, or influence the conduct of particular investigations or the conclusions reached."

The President bears final responsibility for the decision to publish a manuscript as a Brookings book. In reaching his judgment on the competence, accuracy, and objectivity of each study, the President is advised by the director of the appropriate research program and weighs the views of a panel of expert outside readers who report to him in confidence on the quality of the work. Publication of a work signifies that it is deemed a competent treatment worthy of public consideration but does not imply endorsement of conclusions or recommendations.

The Institution maintains its position of neutrality on issues of public policy in order to safeguard the intellectual freedom of the staff. Hence interpretations or conclusions in Brookings publications should be understood to be solely those of the authors and should not be attributed to the Institution, to its trustees, officers, or other staff members, or to the organizations that support its research.

Foreword

Scholars played a large part in developing and supporting the programs of the Great Society and the War on Poverty. The broad consensus that underlay these programs was shared by scholars who did research on poverty and discrimination, education and training, and unemployment and inflation.

But by the mid-1970s, the political and scholarly tides had changed. A new administration renounced the rhetoric of the Great Society and shifted the emphasis of many programs. Among scholars, new research—much of it supported by the federal government—called old faiths into question. Education and training, for example, seemed to improve the fortunes of the poor less dramatically than many had hoped.

This book describes the initial consensus and its subsequent decline. In various fields oversimplified research gave way to more sophisticated, though not always more accurate, analysis which suggested that policies adopted in the heyday of the Great Society were flawed. The author argues that the Great Society did not fall of its own weight, but rather was eclipsed by external events—the war in Vietnam, the dissolution of the civil rights coalition, and the political defalcations of the Nixon administration. He finds that faiths and beliefs, not research, are the real basis for commitment to social reform. In his view, research tends to be a conservative force because it fosters skepticism and caution by shifting attention from moral commitment to analytical problems that rarely have clear-cut or simple solutions.

Henry J. Aaron, Assistant Secretary for Planning and Evaluation of the U.S. Department of Health, Education, and Welfare, conducted this study while he was a senior fellow in the Brookings Economic Studies program, which is under the direction of Joseph A. Pechman. Having benefited from many incisive and constructive comments on drafts of his manuscript, Aaron is particularly grateful to Edward M. Gramlich, Robert Haveman, Robinson Hollister, Henry M. Levin, Robert Levine, Arthur M. Okun, John L. Palmer, Joseph A. Pechman, George L. Perry, N. J. Simler, Anita Summers, Marshall Smith, Paul J. Taubman, Harold Watts, and Aaron Wildavsky. Research assistance was provided by Carol Gurvitch, Nancy Osher, and Cynthia Nethercut.

Ellen Alston edited the manuscript; Evelyn P. Fisher verified its factual content; and Diana Regenthal prepared the index.

The work on this volume, which is the sixteenth in the Brookings series of Studies in Social Economics, was financed in part by a grant from the Edna McConnell Clark Foundation. The views expressed here are the author's alone and should not be ascribed to the officers, trustees, or staff members of the Brookings Institution, to the Edna McConnell Clark Foundation, or to the U.S. Department of Health, Education, and Welfare.

BRUCE K. MACLAURY
President

December 1977
Washington, D.C.

Contents

1. **Introduction**　　　　　　　　　　　　　　　　　1
   The Common View　*2*
   The Common View Reviewed　*4*
   The War on Poverty and the Great Society　*7*
   Appendix　*10*
   Notes　*15*

2. **Poverty and Discrimination**　　　　　　　　　　16
   Looking Backward　*17*
   OEO, the War on Poverty, and the Great Society　*25*
   Current Views on Poverty and Discrimination　*35*
   Summary　*49*
   Notes　*50*

3. **Education and Jobs: A Swinging Pendulum**　　65
   Naive Hopes and Simple Faiths　*66*
   Loss of Innocence　*72*
   Taking Bearings　*92*
   Notes　*98*

4. **Unemployment and Inflation**　　　　　　　　　111
   A Backward Glance　*112*
   New Facts, New Theories, New Policies　*117*
   Conclusions　*137*
   Notes　*139*

5. **Faith, Intelligence, and Good Works**　　　　146
   The 1960s: Many Currents Join　*147*
   The Currents Diverge　*152*
   Looking Forward　*159*
   Notes　*167*

   Index　　　　　　　　　　　　　　　　　　　179

chapter one **Introduction**

If a modern-day Rip Van Winkle had fallen asleep in the United States in 1965 and awakened in 1976, he would have observed a striking change in the national mood. A country that in 1965 had seemed confident of its military strength and purposeful in its missions abroad, that was embarked on a series of efforts to solve problems that had long troubled a newly ascendant majority of the American people and was dealing at last with a shadowed legacy of racial discrimination, seemed to be moving forward with resolve. But by 1976, Americans, divided and uncertain about what to do abroad and fearful of military inferiority, had become equally despairing of their capacity to deal affirmatively with domestic problems. At every turn Rip Van Winkle would encounter lamentations about the failure of all national efforts to reduce inequality and eliminate poverty, to improve schools, to reduce unemployment and its hardships; he would find a sense that not only had past efforts failed, but future ones were also doomed by the incapacity of the government to act effectively. He might have been tempted to turn over and go back to sleep.

On the other hand, he might become curious and set out to discover what had happened to the faiths so palpable a decade before. Had people simply abandoned their old goals or had events proven them unattainable? This book is offered to readers who share with me the conviction that answers to these questions are among the most important facing those interested in helping the United States to achieve some part of the dreams and hopes its citizens cherished in a more optimistic and perhaps more naive time. The answers must deal with the development and use of ideas and with perceptions of recent history even more than with the history itself, because any loss of faith—and that is what has occurred in the past decade—involves ideas and commitments that are influenced, but not uniquely determined, by events.

An explanation and interpretation of recent efforts to reform education,

1

to end poverty, and to reduce unemployment is readily at hand in the press, on television, and in interpretive magazine and journal articles. This "common view" probably is not held in complete form by anyone, but its elements constitute the basic structure of interpretations by many critics and observers of the New Frontier and the Great Society. It also undergirds the sense among liberals that in recent years important goals have been abandoned and among conservatives that a sense of proportion and proper humility have been restored.

The Common View

According to this common view, the election of John F. Kennedy to the presidency marked the advent to high government positions of a group of political liberals who had been building an agenda of reformist social programs during the 1950s. Dedicated to the perfection and completion of the ideas of the New Deal and to a final assault on official racial discrimination, these liberals looked to John Kennedy to lead the nation to the achievement of goals that Adlai Stevenson had promised so eloquently. Although the terminology had not yet been invented, this group was dedicated to a set of programs that together closely resembled what later became known as the War on Poverty and the Great Society: improved education and training, better housing, expanded health care, and a conscious quest for full employment, all in the faith that serious inflation was unlikely to be a consequence and that some inflation was worth enduring to achieve full employment. An unemployment rate of 4 percent was not an ultimate goal, but only an interim target.

Throughout the Kennedy presidency, however, this liberal group remained frustrated. Concerned about the fragility of his mandate (perhaps also reflecting the weakness of his underlying commitment), Kennedy promoted only fragments of the liberal agenda and was curiously ineffective in securing acceptance even of those items he chose to embrace. He accepted the full-employment target and supported and secured enactment of legislation to create manpower development and training programs and area redevelopment programs, but these represented only minor budgetary commitments.

Two quite independent events changed this picture totally, if temporarily. The first was the incredibly inept and shortsighted response of southern officials to the step-by-step efforts of civil rights groups to dismantle Jim Crow. In a slow-motion ballet, each new effort by civil rights groups seemed to call forth one stupid act of violence or administrative recalcitrance after another from southern officials, solidifying public support for reform. The courts in their turn methodically rejected efforts to stop this movement.

The second event was the assassination of President Kennedy at the very moment when his political fortunes were in the ascendant. In the wake of this unifying event, the Republican Party nominated a weak candidate. No administration since Franklin Roosevelt's first had operated subject to fewer political constraints than President Johnson's.

The new president, by virtue of his own predispositions and the shelf full of programs long supported within his party, chose to declare war on poverty, to expand health, housing, education, and training programs, and to increase transfers in cash and in kind. He converted state and local governments into instruments for achieving these goals by aid formulas that amounted to offers that mayors, governors, and state and local legislators could not refuse.

According to the common view, this one session of liberal legislative happiness enormously expanded the size of the federal sector. An array of new administrative weapons was trained upon problems clearly seen at last after decades of fuzzy perception. The result, liberals hoped, would be full employment, faster economic growth, an equitable distribution of the fruits of growth among previously despised minorities and bypassed segments of the majority, more housing and fewer slums, better health care, especially for the aged and the poor who could not previously afford it, food for those who could not buy it, training for those who could benefit from it, and cash and in-kind assistance for those who could be reached in no other way. The result, conservatives feared, would be explosive growth in the size of the public sector and in its intrusions into the economy and personal liberties. Agencies proliferated. Expenditures increased. Poverty was counted and seen to decline. Hopes were high.

Then something happened. Here the common view splits into two strands that are not entirely consistent, although not directly contradictory. According to one, the programs so enthusiastically sold and indeed oversold were starved in their infancy because the Vietnam War voraciously consumed the fiscal dividend. Programs never grew as planned. As the gap widened between initial promise and the reality engendered by fiscal starvation, enthusiasm gave way to disillusion and a sense of betrayal. Racial divisiveness, marked by assassination, riot, and backlash, replaced the multiracial promise to overcome the legacy of discrimination. To make matters worse, the war in Vietnam came increasingly to absorb the rather limited stock of political energy that even the most activist political devotees can muster, leaving the progeny of the Great Society unloved as well as underfed.

According to the second strand of the common view, the problems were more basic. Not only were the many programs of the Great Society oversold; they were underplanned. Acting in haste while political conditions were favorable, the Johnson administration seemed to feel that enactment of a bill was almost equivalent to solving a problem. Vague legislation was put together, often in strictest secrecy to avoid premature leaks and criticisms and pushed through a dazed Congress, but frequently only after powerful congressional leaders had tacked on favorite ideas of their own.

The result was a deluge of legislation poorly planned, hastily enacted, and beyond the capacities of the federal or state governments to administer. Moreover, much of this legislation called upon the federal government to deal on an individually tailored, detailed basis with the incredibly varied situations in countless separate jurisdictions. The resulting red tape, confusion, and waste revealed the limits of the capacity of the federal government to deal with problems in the small. If all of the legislation had been carefully planned and gradually introduced, everything might still have gone awry; but the actual course of events, according to the common view, almost guaranteed debacle. In the event, money was thrown at problems, especially at problems of the poor, but those problems refused to go away.

Poorly planned, passed in haste, inadequately funded, the programs of the mid-1960s accomplished little according to the common view except to line the pockets of the middle-class professionals hired to dispense services to the poor. Evaluation, a newly developed art, certified the ineffectuality of these programs. Now, sadder but wiser, we confront the wreckage, encumbered by large and costly programs and a budget that is out of control, uncertain about what should be done in the future, and skeptical of the federal capacity to solve any problems. Such is the common view.

The Common View Reviewed

The most striking characteristic of the common view is its very high level of generality. It deals with the War on Poverty or the Great Society as an entity to be evaluated as a whole. It passes judgment on the capacity of the federal government to deal with "social" problems, not with individual tasks. It dwells on the growth of the budget, but avoids statistics and does not concern itself with the components of the budget. It is ironic that those concerned about the failure of "the federal government" to take adequate account of the staggering diversity of local governments and organizations and of the variations in local conditions across the United States commit a similar error in appraising the performance of the federal government as if it were a monolithic entity.

Not surprisingly, so global a view is partly right and partly wrong, partly clear-sighted and partly distorted. On the one hand, critics of federal red tape and regulations can point justifiably to the multiplicity of small grants-in-aid through which Congress has attempted to compel state and local governments to do its detailed bidding in education, health, and other fields, and to futile efforts to regulate the behavior of millions of businesses, individuals, and governmental entities. On the other hand, legislation enacted in the past decade has strengthened the system of cash assistance and in-kind benefits for temporarily or permanently needy households. Even where administratively cumbersome techniques have been used—as, for example, to limit pollution and slow environmental degradation—significant improvements can be noted. Strains in these systems have appeared, but in all cases they can be remedied by revisions or reform of existing programs. A balanced judgment of Great Society legislation would have to be mixed.

Other elements of the common view rest on misperceptions of what actually happened during the last decade. For example, the views that federal expenditures have risen sharply, that the budget is out of control, that the set of aids for the poor has increased enormously, are all contradicted by the facts. The budget measured as a proportion of full-employment gross national product is negligibly larger in 1977 than it was in 1960. In 1960 federal expenditures represented 18.1 percent of full-employment gross national product; in 1970 they claimed 19.0 percent, and by 1977 they had risen to 20.1 percent.[1] But the prices of goods and services purchased by the public sector rose faster than those of other goods and services; as a result, the volume of goods and services purchased with that budget, relative to full-employment gross national product, declined by more than 1 percent of full-employment GNP.[2] This development does not indicate any inherent inefficiency in the public sector, but reflects the same trend that makes the prices of theater and concert tickets and domestic service rise faster than other prices. In each case, the relative cost of services provided largely by labor unaided by machinery tends to increase as wages rise relative to the cost of capital goods. In the aggregate, the federal budget has grown only slightly more rapidly than the rest of the economy, and gives no indication of slipping out of control.

The composition of the budget has changed markedly, however. The portion devoted to expenditures on human resources and transfers—broadly defined to include direct expenditures and grants-in-aid for education and training, health, cash assistance, and in-kind benefits—increased from 6.3 percent of full-employment gross national product in 1961 to 8.7 percent in 1969 and 13.4 percent in 1976. The proportion of these expenditures focused on the poor rose until 1973 and then declined. A decline in defense expenditures from 9.7 percent of full-employment gross national product in 1969 (the peak of the Vietnam War effort) to 5.2 percent in 1976 almost precisely offset increases in expenditures on human resources during that period.

The composition of expenditures on human resources and cash transfers passed through two periods, paralleling the Kennedy-Johnson and Nixon-Ford administrations (see appendix to this chapter for detailed statistics and an explanation of their derivation). During the Kennedy-Johnson years, expenditures focused on the poor as a fraction of full-employment gross national product rose from 0.8 percent (1961) to 1.4 percent (1967) (see figure 1-1). This increase was larger relatively, but smaller absolutely, than the increase in similar programs not focused exclusively on the poor (such as social security), which rose from 5.2 percent of full-employment gross national product in 1961 to 6.1 percent in 1967. The bulk of this latter increase was accounted for by the growth of in-kind assistance. Growth in human resource and transfer programs focused on the poor continued during the first Nixon administration, but was reversed after 1973. Despite the concern about the "welfare mess" of growing rolls and rising budgets, cash and in-kind transfers focused on the poor actually declined between 1973 and 1976, from 1.8 percent to 1.5 percent of full-employment GNP and were about where they had been in 1971. In contrast, cash and in-kind transfers not focused on the poor grew rapidly, rising from 6.6 to 10.0 percent of full-employment GNP between 1969 and 1976.

Perhaps the most striking feature of budgetary evolution during this period was the meager share of the federal budget or of gross national product devoted to education, training, or other services designed to en-

Figure 1-1. Federal Expenditures on Human Resources as a Percentage of Full-Employment Gross National Product, by Target Population, 1961–76

Percent of full-employment GNP

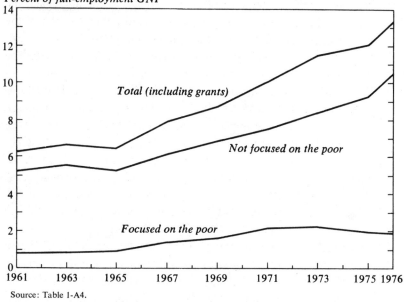

Source: Table 1-A4.

hance earning capacities directly. These expenditures, grouped as "merit wants," never represented more than 1 percent of full-employment GNP or 5 percent of the budget (see figure 1-2). Cash transfers rose as a fraction of GNP, but all the growth occurred in programs such as social security and unemployment insurance that are not focused on the poor. Budget growth was more rapid under Johnson than under Kennedy and this growth slowed little, although its composition changed under the first Nixon administration. The period 1973–76 was one of retrenchment in most expenditures on human resources and transfers (other than social security and in-kind transfers).

In short, the common view embodies an incorrect view of overall budget history and an oversimplified and distorted view of the details.

The War on Poverty and the Great Society

The common view enjoys an intellectual vitality that facts alone are unlikely to diminish. Its vitality derives from at least two sources. The first

Figure 1-2. Federal Expenditures on Human Resources as a Percentage of Full-Employment Gross National Product, by Broad Categories, 1961–76

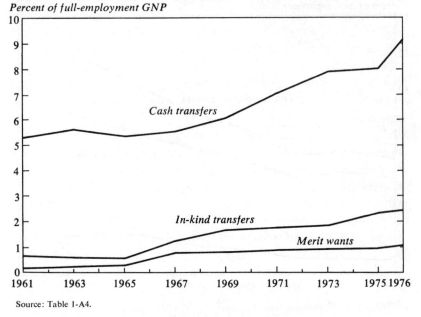

Source: Table 1-A4.

is the destruction—by the war in Vietnam, Richard Nixon's behavior in office, Spiro Agnew's crime, illegal acts by officials of the FBI and CIA, and other evidence of corruption—of the faith created during the Great Depression, World War II, and the period of postwar aid to European countries that the U.S. government was an instrument of beneficent action. This faith, implicit in the rhetoric of liberals and scorned openly by conservatives, never claimed clear majority support, but it enjoyed widespread credibility. Under the multiple assaults of lies, deceptions, and bloodshed that came to be regarded as a waste if not a crime, it expired.

A second source of the vitality of the common view has been a flow of research and evaluation by social scientists in universities, research organizations, and the government itself that undermined naive and simplistic faiths upon which the legislative initiatives of the 1960s implicitly or explicitly rested and that made the bloated claims of the sponsors of such legislation seem inane. In coming to terms with the history of the past fifteen years and with the common view, or with any other interpretation of that period, one must take the measure of the various efforts to evaluate performance during that period. As never before, social scientists were actively engaged in the planning and, later, in the evaluation of the programs of the Great Society. Adherents of the common view can, and do, cite the results of these evaluations in support of their negative appraisals. How good were those appraisals? How much reliance should be placed on them in deciding what to do in the future? These questions must be answered before the common view can be said to rest either on a reasoned disappointment over our collective failure to achieve still-cherished goals or on the specious use of social science to conceal a change of heart about desired outcomes.

This book will examine the attitudes and beliefs that underlie the common view. Because this view is a generalized judgment about actual federal programs, this book does not examine specific programs in detail. Instead it deals with the evolution of attitudes and analyses by scholars and popular writers on the role of the federal government and its capacity to bring about beneficial change in three broad areas: poverty and discrimination, education and training, and unemployment and inflation. In each area, a remarkable parallel change has occurred both in attitudes about the effectiveness of public expenditures and programs and in the prevailing consensus among scholars based on academic research. Chapter 2 describes perceptions of the problems of poverty and discrimination, how these were related to the War on Poverty and other social legislation, how these attitudes changed, and how both the old attitudes and the new are related to such information as we have about the poor. Chapter 3 examines the effect of education on income and earnings. It sketches the attitudes of the early and mid-1960s and indicates how they were related to the programs enacted during that period. Chapter 4 recounts the triumph of policies to achieve full employment during the 1960s, the failure of ideas of structural unemployment to gain a foothold and their subsequent predictive accuracy, the change in ideas about unemployment and the bearing that the new ideas have on the desirable course to adopt in dealing with unemployment.

As will become apparent, the parallel between development of social science and the views of scholars, on the one hand, and developments of public policy during this period, on the other, was striking in each of these three areas. But in many cases, the findings of social science seemed to come after, rather than before, changes in policy, which suggests that political events may influence scholars more than research influences policy. Chapter 5 tries to sort out how, if at all, social science contributed to the evolution of attitudes about public policy and to the evaluation of that performance. I shall suggest that neither the initial acceptance and enthusiasm for aggressive federal efforts to solve social problems nor the present rejection of and reticence about such undertakings are based on reliable information or on scholarly findings or indeed on the actual success or failures of the programs themselves. Both the initial commitment to use national policies to solve social and economic problems and the present distrust of such policies rest largely on preconceptions and faiths whose source lies elsewhere.

Appendix

The course of the human resources budget set forth in figures 1-1 and 1-2 is charted in tables 1-A1 through 1-A4. These tables break down these expenditures into four broad categories. Merit wants include expenditures undertaken by the government to provide recipients with services they would not normally purchase for themselves but which are not provided primarily to boost the income of the recipient. This category also includes governmental programs, such as neighborhood health centers, established in large part to change the technology by which services are provided to some or all recipients. In-kind transfers include expenditures to provide or subsidize the purchase of services, such as food, health care, or housing, deemed necessary for adequate consumption. Cash transfers include all programs that provide recipients with money that they may spend as they choose. A miscellaneous fourth category includes government-provided "public goods," commodities whose benefits are freely available to everyone (such as the services of the Food and Drug Administration), and broad-purpose grants to subsidiary governments, such as Model Cities grants. The distinctions among these four categories are inevitably somewhat arbitrary.

Table 1-A1. Federal Expenditures on Human Resources, by Broad Categories, Selected Fiscal Years, 1961–76
Millions of dollars

Expenditure categories	1961	1963	1965	1967	1969	1971	1973	1975	1976
For the poor									
Merit wants	163	261	719	3,219	4,000	5,989	6,010	7,646	8,502
In-kind transfers	550	368	395	1,156	1,899	4,844	6,562	11,278	11,208
Cash transfers	3,839	4,538	5,022	6,262	8,590	12,139	15,053	12,567	14,756
Total	4,552	5,167	6,136	10,637	14,489	22,972	27,625	31,491	34,466
Not exclusively for the poor									
Merit wants	536	960	1,004	2,419	2,680	3,310	5,311	7,550	9,243
In-kind transfers	2,823	3,060	3,428	8,353	12,794	13,835	15,863	25,179	30,636
Cash transfers	24,971	29,113	30,533	35,785	45,346	62,216	82,741	114,012	143,898
Total	28,330	33,133	34,965	46,557	60,820	79,361	103,915	146,741	183,777
Other	1,075	1,534	1,716	2,983	2,254	3,650	10,974	12,681	14,059
Total, all categories	33,957	39,834	42,817	60,177	77,563	105,983	142,514	190,913	232,302

Sources: *The Budget of the United States Government*, and *Appendix*, alternate years, 1963–77, and 1978.

Table 1-A2. Federal Expenditures on Human Resources, by Broad Categories, Selected Fiscal Years, 1961–76

Percent

Expenditure categories	1961	1963	1965	1967	1969	1971	1973	1975	1976
For the poor									
Merit wants	0.48	0.66	1.68	5.35	5.16	5.65	4.22	4.00	3.66
In-kind transfers	1.62	0.92	0.92	1.92	2.45	4.57	4.60	5.91	4.82
Cash transfers	11.31	11.39	11.73	10.41	11.07	11.45	10.56	6.58	6.35
Total	13.41	12.97	14.33	17.68	18.68	21.68	19.38	16.49	14.84
Not exclusively for the poor									
Merit wants	1.58	2.41	2.34	4.02	3.46	3.12	3.73	3.95	3.98
In-kind transfers	8.31	7.68	8.01	13.88	16.49	13.05	11.13	13.19	13.19
Cash transfers	73.54	73.09	71.31	59.47	58.46	58.70	58.06	59.72	61.94
Total	83.43	83.18	81.66	77.37	78.41	74.88	72.92	76.86	79.11
Other	3.17	3.85	4.01	4.96	2.91	3.44	7.70	6.64	6.05
Total, all categories	100	100	100	100	100	100	100	100	100

Source: Table 1-A1. Figures are rounded.

Table 1-A3. Federal Expenditures on Human Resources as a Percentage of Total Budget Outlays, by Broad Categories, Selected Fiscal Years, 1961–76

Expenditure categories	1961	1963	1965	1967	1969	1971	1973	1975	1976
For the poor									
Merit wants	0.17	0.23	0.61	2.03	2.17	2.83	2.43	2.34	2.32
In-kind transfers	0.56	0.33	0.33	0.73	1.03	2.29	2.66	3.46	3.06
Cash transfers	3.93	4.08	4.24	3.96	4.65	5.74	6.09	3.85	4.03
Total	4.65	4.64	5.18	6.72	7.85	10.87	11.18	9.66	9.40
Not exclusively for the poor									
Merit wants	0.55	0.86	0.85	1.53	1.45	1.57	2.15	2.32	2.52
In-kind transfers	2.89	2.75	2.89	5.28	6.93	6.54	6.42	7.72	8.36
Cash transfers	25.53	26.15	25.78	22.61	24.57	29.43	33.49	34.96	39.27
Total	28.97	29.77	29.52	29.42	32.96	37.54	42.06	45.00	50.15
Other	1.10	1.38	1.45	1.88	1.22	1.73	4.44	3.89	3.84
Total, all categories	34.72	35.79	36.15	38.03	42.03	50.13	57.68	58.54	63.39

Sources: Total budget outlays are from *Economic Report of the President, January 1977*, p. 268; other data, table 1-A1. Figures are rounded.

Table 1-A4. Federal Expenditures on Human Resources as a Percentage of Full-Employment Gross National Product, by Broad Categories, Selected Fiscal Years, 1961–76

Expenditure categories	1961	1963	1965	1967	1969	1971	1973	1975	1976
For the poor									
Merit wants	0.03	0.04	0.11	0.42	0.45	0.57	0.49	0.48	0.49
In-kind transfers	0.10	0.06	0.06	0.15	0.21	0.46	0.53	0.71	0.64
Cash transfers	0.71	0.76	0.75	0.82	0.97	1.15	1.22	0.80	0.85
Total	0.84	0.86	0.92	1.40	1.63	2.18	2.23	1.99	1.98
Not exclusively for the poor									
Merit wants	0.10	0.16	0.15	0.32	0.30	0.31	0.43	0.48	0.53
In-kind transfers	0.52	0.51	0.51	1.10	1.44	1.31	1.28	1.59	1.76
Cash transfers	4.61	4.86	4.58	4.71	5.11	5.90	6.69	7.22	8.27
Total	5.24	5.54	5.25	6.12	6.85	7.52	8.41	9.29	10.56
Other	0.20	0.26	0.26	0.39	0.25	0.35	0.89	0.80	0.81
Total, all categories	6.28	6.66	6.43	7.91	8.74	10.05	11.53	12.09	13.35

Sources: Full employment GNP, derived from series supplied by Council of Economic Advisers, based on a variable full-employment unemployment rate; other data, table 1-A1. Figures are rounded.

Notes

1. Henry Owen and Charles L. Schultze, eds., *Setting National Priorities: The Next Ten Years* (Brookings Institution, 1976), p. 328. Nonrecessionary GNP is used as the benchmark against which to measure changes in the size of the budget for two reasons. First, such expenditures as unemployment insurance rise automatically during recessions but automatically vanish when the recession ends; to include them would make as much sense as to say that a family's income goes up when its house burns down and it collects fire insurance. Second, the decline in GNP during recessions increases the budgetary fraction because it reduces the denominator of the relevant fraction.

2. Ibid., p. 331.

chapter two **Poverty and Discrimination**

In 1960 the problems of economic inequality, poverty, and discrimination were considered to be largely outside the proper realm of public policy. Social security and unemployment insurance, which quietly helped the aged and the unemployed according to outlines laid down in 1935, were exceptions. Then in the sixties inequality, poverty, and discrimination moved to center stage. The view that solutions to these problems were the proper business of government gained currency and temporarily became dominant. Belief in the capacity of government to find solutions to them was widespread. New programs were enacted; new commitments were made.

Then the programs lost support. Some were repealed; others were shifted to new agencies or transferred to state or local control. Meanwhile, data were generated and collected. Programs were evaluated and seemed not to work; many were impossible to evaluate. Scholars analyzed the data and discovered that the problems of poverty and discrimination were a good deal more complicated than most had suspected a decade or so earlier. The faith that complex problems had been understood collapsed. Vigorous action to deal with them lost intellectual respectability. A new and complex understanding of the dynamics of poverty arose that was analytically more satisfying but politically crippling.

This chapter chronicles that evolution. The first section sketches the attitudes about poverty and discrimination that prevailed in the early 1960s and that shaped the War on Poverty and efforts to achieve the Great Society. The second section outlines the growth of these experiments in social welfare legislation and the role research and evaluation played in them. The third section describes present scholarly views on poverty and discrimination.

16

Looking Backward

This section introduces two themes that will recur often in this book: that research reflects prevailing political moods at least as much as it influences them; and that research, insofar as it exercises independent influences on opinions about complex social questions, tends over time to be profoundly conservative in its impact.

Perceptions of Poverty in the Early 1960s

The attitudes toward poverty and discrimination held widely in the early 1960s seem quaint and old-fashioned today. John Kenneth Galbraith had just reminded millions of readers that poverty still survived within an affluent society. "The hard core of the very poor," he reported, "was declining but not with great rapidity."[1] Michael Harrington, a few years later in a much celebrated work, described "the other America," a subnation of the poor, "hidden today in a way that it never was before . . . socially invisible to the rest of us."[2] The allegation by Galbraith, Harrington, and Dwight MacDonald[3] that poverty was neglected seems correct in retrospect. Problems of unemployment, depressed areas, and the aged were or soon would become perennial issues in legislative debates or party platforms; but poverty was rarely mentioned.

If poverty was not a problem in the eyes of the public, it was equally ignored by scholars. A complete bibliography of studies relating to poverty compiled in the early 1960s ran to less than two pages.[4] Official statistics on the extent of poverty were first published in 1965, if one excepts the crude estimates presented in the 1964 *Economic Report of the President.*[5] No detailed information spanning two or more years on a sizable number of families or households was available until the early 1970s.[6]

The only comprehensive statistics available during the 1960s were snapshots of the overall distribution of income. Following these data was like watching the grass grow. They showed almost no year-to-year change in the distribution of income, other than small fluctuations easily explained by the business cycle. They excluded from consideration in-kind transfers, fringe benefits, and accumulations of savings or wealth. And they were rarely accompanied by any explanation of why income was distributed as it was.[7] The bottom fifth of families and unrelated individuals received between 3.0 and 3.4 percent of income between 1948 and 1960, the top fifth between 43.4 and 45.2 percent of income. The bottom quintiles gained when unemployment was low and lost ground when it was high; the shares of the upper quintiles showed the reverse pattern.[8]

As is so often the case, the characteristics of available data influenced perceptions and descriptions. Thus, in the early 1960s poverty was determined by whether cash income exceeded specified thresholds because surveys asked people about cash income, not about assets, in-kind transfers, or fringe benefits. Poverty could be perceived as a relatively fixed state and the poor as an identifiable group because all surveys were cross-sectional snapshots rather than longitudinal motion pictures. Movement in and out of the poverty population, by implication, was difficult and infrequent. For example, Galbraith classified poverty as "case" poverty or "insular" poverty. The former, he asserted, arises because some quality of the individual has kept him from participating in the general economic well-being. The latter arises when a comparatively large number of people desire to live near the place of their birth and that place suffers from hard times. In either case, poverty is "self-perpetuating," and not reduced significantly by economic growth.[9] Harrington is even more explicit. "The new poverty is constructed so as to destroy aspiration; it is a system designed to be impervious to hope. The other America does not contain the adventurous seeking a new life and land. It is populated by the failures, by those driven from the land and bewildered by the city, by old people suddenly confronted with the torments of loneliness and poverty, and by minorities facing a wall of prejudice."[10] Readers familiar with Edward Banfield's description of the lower class may note that, stripped of their sympathies, the factual descriptions of Banfield and Harrington are quite similar. Thus, Banfield characterizes the lower class as lacking a "sense of self," suffering "from feelings of self-contempt and inadequacy," "apathetic or dejected," without "attachment to community, neighbors, or friends," resenting "all authority," "a nonparticipant," and so on.[11] The difference between Harrington and Banfield is simply this: Harrington holds that poverty causes behavioral maladies, Banfield that behavior causes poverty.

This view of poverty was shared by other academics as well. Robert Lampman, who did research on income distribution and poverty before it was fashionable (and who had produced much of the research available before the mid-1960s), summarized these views in an influential book. "Neither past earning experience nor the assets of the poor suggest that a large fraction of the poor were much better off in the recent past than they were in 1959. The expectation for most poor families is continued poverty."[12] Unemployment, an important direct cause of poverty for intact families and an indirect cause—via family dissolution—for broken families, was a particular problem of the "hardcore unemployed," a group of people thought to suffer protracted unemployment.[13] Gunnar Myrdal, author of an impressive study of American race relations, wrote that "something like a caste line is drawn between the people in the urban and rural slums, and the majority of Americans who live in a virtual full-employment economy, even while the unemployment rate is rising and the growth rate of the economy is low. . . . [T]here is an underclass of people in the poverty pockets who live an ever more precarious life and are increasingly excluded from any jobs worth having, or who do not find any jobs at all."[14] Christopher Jencks, a newly minted graduate of Harvard College, wrote that slums would disappear only when there were no slum dwellers, and expressed a fear widely held at the time that the rapid advance of technology was leaving behind the poorly educated.[15] Harrington made the same point with characteristic pungency. "[T]he poor, if they were given to theory, might argue [that] . . . progress is misery."[16]

The consensus of the time seems to have been that full employment might be necessary, but certainly was not sufficient, to ensure the rapid decline of poverty. Such writers as Harrington and Galbraith held that by itself a tight labor market would do almost nothing to help the poor. Others emphasized that economic growth and full employment could help households with potential earners who lived near available jobs. But those not in the labor market—the aged, the disabled, single-parent (then called female-headed) families with small children—and those lacking marketable skills or residing in depressed areas would not be helped adequately by improvements in general economic conditions and would constitute a growing fraction of the poor.[17] The Council of Economic Advisers declared that "rising productivity and earnings, improved education, and the structure of social security have permitted many families or their children to escape [from poverty]; but they have left behind many families who have one or more special handicaps. These facts suggest that in the future economic growth alone will provide relatively fewer escapes from poverty. Policy will have to be more sharply focused on the handicaps that deny the poor fair access to the expanding incomes of a growing economy."[18]

Nevertheless, apart from a group of writers who held that automation had rendered full employment unattainable[19]—and who gained attention from newspapers and magazines and scorn from trained economists in roughly equal proportion—no one felt that the restoration of full employment required basic transformation of the labor market.[20] A few economists argued that automation was tending to create an imbalance between a rapidly shrinking demand for unskilled labor and a slowly contracting supply of such workers.[21]

In fact, the perception was pervasive that poverty was merely one link in a circular chain of misfortunes that led, via cultural and motivational obstacles, to poor health, inadequate education, and limited opportunities, and once again back to poverty through endless cycles, unless some fortuitous event intervened. Racial discrimination strengthened the links in the chain and rendered it even more binding.[22]

Perhaps the most striking characteristic of this view of the poverty cycle is the absence of any mention of the economic system within which it operates. Apart from the problem of high unemployment that the individual is powerless to solve, the poor person was viewed as poor because of shortcomings of his own that may themselves be traceable to his own or his parents' poverty. The person who remained poor when employment was high might not be to blame for his own poverty, if one adopted a sufficiently long perspective, but he could emerge from poverty only if he changed, or was changed, into a person with sufficient skills or motivation to earn an adequate income. This fact was apparently so obvious that it was left implicit in the description of the poverty cycle and was rarely if ever discussed.

Cultural versus Environmental Views of Poverty

What was discussed and heatedly debated were the consequences of intervening at some point in the poverty cycle with some form of external aid: money; access to training, education, or health care; or jobs. Advocates of two theories of poverty—cultural and environmental—contended for adherents.[23]

THEORY. The "culture of poverty" was conceived of as a set of reinforcing attitudes, developed in response to a hostile environment, that would resist change unless (and perhaps even if) the entire environment were altered. A personal orientation toward immediate gratification, the weakness of the nuclear family, and undependability on the job combined to describe a lifestyle that cash assistance, better housing, and access to education, training, or health care would be insufficient to change. The culture of poverty, it was alleged, characterized groups or communities of people, but not necessarily every member of them; and some who were not poor might be carriers of the culture of poverty. In the hands of social anthropologists, such as Oscar Lewis, the culture of poverty was portrayed as a rational and functional response of poor people to the environment in which they lived. But he suggested that as few as 20 percent of the economically poor might be culturally poor.[24] In the eyes of at least one political scientist, Edward Banfield, the culture of poverty was a social malaise.[25] In the eyes of at least one journalist, commenting on the uselessness of welfare, the culture of poverty was utterly pathological: "What is particularly disturbing to social workers, judges, and other public officials is not simply the failure of these people [welfare recipients] to support themselves but the complete breakdown of moral values that is found in a large number of the cases. The homes of many welfare clients are nothing more than breeding grounds for crime, immorality, and severe emotional illnesses, all being subsidized with public money."[26] Michael Harrington cited the famous exchange between F. Scott Fitzgerald and Ernest Hemingway, in which Fitzgerald remarked that "the rich are different," and Hemingway responded, "Yes, they have more money." Harrington then added his view that "Fitzgerald had much the better of the exchange. . . . If this is true of the rich, it is ten times truer of the poor."[27]

The culture-of-poverty view was opposed by the position that poverty was environmental—that antisocial or pathological behavior was not ingrained, but would in general change in short order when the objective conditions in which people lived were altered. This position came naturally to economists accustomed to the analysis of marginal decisions subject to constraints imposed by limited incomes and prices. They tended to argue that the poor, like everyone else, would alter their behavior if the constraints were relaxed—or, to use plain English, if opportunities were enlarged. This position was also held by many sociologists and social psychologists, especially those who considered important the results of surveys that found no significant differences between attitudes expressed by the poor and those expressed by others. According to this rather paternalistic view, if education and training were made available, the poor would take them. If incomes were increased, the poor would spend the increase about as well as the nonpoor, especially if they received advice and counseling. If housing were improved, neighborhoods would become more livable and attractive.[28]

After the debate had cooled, Peter Rossi and Zahava Blum, as if in reply to Harrington, wrote: "That the poor are different and show higher rates of a wide variety of disabilities is seemingly well enough documented: If this is what is meant by a culture of poverty, then the concept has some validity, although perhaps little usefulness. If by the concept is meant something more, then the empirical evidence would not support such a view."[29] Lee Rainwater dryly observed that "the alternative value system of the lower class seems to exist more in the minds of middle-class romantics (and pessimists) than in the wishes of lower-class people themselves."[30]

In retrospect, the debate between the cultural and environmental views of poverty seems to have vanished without leaving significant intellectual residue. The reason may be the failure of either side in the debate to formulate the issues precisely, the lack of evidence (aside from the surveys mentioned above), and the unwillingness of participants to suggest the kinds of tests or information that would resolve the debate. None would deny that experiences condition people's behavior and that eventually such behavior may become habitual. Conversely, few would deny that if conditions change early in a person's life and remain changed sufficiently long, his behavior will eventually change. But one crucial question was not clarified by this debate and one was not even raised. The first concerns the duration and magnitude of environmental changes necessary to alter behavior.[31] The second concerns whether behavioral changes in poor people —the acquisition of more education or training or skills, improved punctuality and dependability, and so on—are sufficient to reduce poverty. If one person climbs out of poverty, is his gain purchased at the price of some other person's decline or are there negligible losses for others? The possibility that the number of badly paid jobs might not decline even if the number of poorly trained or educated workers were reduced was not seriously entertained. Economists had toyed with theories of income distribution that rested on random chance, but such views never enjoyed widespread appeal.[32]

PRACTICE. Whether the debate had any impact on policy seems open to doubt. Two early participants in planning the War on Poverty denied that the culture-of-poverty debate was very important.[33] Others, however, have observed a correlation between positions in the debate and stands on public policy.[34] Herbert Gans noted that "those who argue that the poor share the values of the affluent obviously consider them as ready and able to share in the blessings of the affluent society, whereas those who consider them deficient or culturally different imply that the poor are not able to enter affluent society until they change themselves or are changed."[35]

Rossi and Blum observed that "whereas the subcultural viewpoint stresses the family, the situational viewpoint stresses the occupational system as the point to which the levers of social policy should be applied."[36] Lee Rainwater made the same point, observing that adherents of the view that the poor shared a common American culture tended to support programs that emphasized opportunity and, if these failed, to blame the institutional framework that made poverty. In contrast, those who believed the culture of the poor was distinct from that of the rest of the nation embraced a variety of proposals ranging from such draconian measures as removal of children from the care of their parents to special education programs intended to offset "cultural deprivation," such as Head Start or adult education.[37]

In retrospect, discussions of poverty in the sixties seem remarkably vague and imprecise for at least three reasons. The first was a lack of data. Good statistics on the number of poor at any particular time were unavailable until 1965. Good data on the long-term experiences of people who are poor at any particular time are only beginning to become available now.[38] Second, precise questions about the causes of poverty had not been formulated, much less answered.[39] Third, many ambiguities about the real nature of the problem were left unresolved. Was the problem absolute poverty, relative poverty, or overall inequality? And what was the relative importance of the purely economic factors? Was the problem unequal opportunity or unequal outcomes? Would changes in the *process* by which economic and social rewards were generated be sufficient to end most poverty or was it necessary directly to alter results by providing income in cash or in kind? Few discussions distinguished these questions and neither did the policies adopted to deal with the single perceived problem, "poverty."

Discrimination

Although white poverty in Appalachia was publicized by President Kennedy's campaign, the problems of poverty and racial discrimination were closely linked.[40] Militant civil rights activists were determined to secure enforcement of the Supreme Court decision to desegregate the public schools in the South, so long deferred by the refusal of President Eisenhower actively to support the decision. Other manifestations of Jim Crow were being challenged in the streets, in stores and restaurants, and on public transportation, and simultaneously in the courts, state legislatures, and

Congress. The movements to combat poverty and racial discrimination inevitably blended because everyone knew, and statistics confirmed, that the ranks of the poor were disproportionately black, even if the majority of the poor were white.[41]

But behind the movement against racial discrimination and behind the moral conviction so belatedly dominant that it was wrong to do to blacks what had been so long done to them, there was as much confusion about how discrimination operated in the marketplace and as little study of it as there was about poverty. Racial discrimination had been the subject of one of the most distinguished studies to grace sociology, Gunnar Myrdal's *American Dilemma.*[42] Social psychologists had attempted to understand the pathology of prejudice. But understanding how prejudice operated in the marketplace to deprive its victims of incomes—in other words, how it made them poor—had been almost completely ignored by economists and other social scientists. The connection between discrimination and poverty had not been made by academics, however transparent the mechanisms appeared to the general public.

The first rigorous economic treatment of discrimination, by Gary Becker, drew out the implications of the indulgence by discriminators in a "taste for discrimination" and paralleled in a remarkable way the view expressed by President Eisenhower that the end of discrimination had to await changes in the hearts and minds of discriminators.[43] Eisenhower had answered reporters' questions about his failure to use federal policy actively to enforce the Supreme Court's decision on school desegregation: "I continue to say the real answer here is in the heart of the individual. Just law is not going to do it. We have never stopped sin by passing laws; and in the same way, we are not going to take a great moral ideal and achieve it merely by law."[44]

By applying conventional economic analysis, Becker showed that if one group had a distaste for another, the result was reduced national output and, given certain additional assumptions, higher earnings for workers in the group that discriminated and lower earnings for workers in the group that suffered discrimination. Effects on the victims of discrimination were especially severe if, as seemed realistic, they constituted a minority of the population and lacked capital. An illustrative numerical example, which Becker suggested was realistic, showed that the incomes of blacks could be reduced by 40 percent through discrimination, a number remarkably close to the percentage difference between the earnings of black men and those of white men.[45] The same theory could be used to explain why victims of discrimination might have to pay more than others for consumer goods and housing.[46]

Tastes, whether of the heart or of the head, would have to be changed before discrimination would end. Becker, who published in 1957, like Eisenhower, who remained president for three more years, did not recommend any public policies to end discrimination.

A resounding silence greeted Becker's book. Economists ignored discrimination for at least five more years,[47] and even then people were not yet accustomed to considering what economists had to say on such "noneconomic" questions. Some felt that the lot of American blacks was improving, others did not,[48] but solid information was lacking. A widespread view held that discrimination prodigally wasted the talents of its victims, and that somehow all would benefit if such practices ceased. This view, which was inconsistent with Becker's analysis, found official expression in the 1966 Annual Report of the Council of Economic Advisers, in which the gain from the termination of discrimination was put at $27 billion (then 4 percent of GNP). Although the accomplishment of such a goal would require some resources, the council stated that such "an investment [would yield] important economic as well as social returns for the entire Nation."[49]

It was against such an intellectual background that the War on Poverty was declared. A strongly felt concern with problems previously ignored or deemed to lie outside the ambit of public policy led to action on problems that had not been analyzed or even well defined.

OEO, the War on Poverty, and the Great Society

The promise of a "great society," the declaration of a war on poverty, and the creation of the Office of Economic Opportunity occurred so close in time to one another and overlapped so extensively that it is easy to assume they were identical. In fact, the government programs administered by OEO were only a part of those encompassed by the War on Poverty; and the Great Society included numerous services and benefits for those who were not poor. Like the successive layers of an onion, each was encased by the next. While OEO's expenditures never reached $2 billion, federal outlays for the poor were $15.9 billion in fiscal 1969 and have risen substantially since, although the name has been dropped.[50]

The history of the War on Poverty and the Office of Economic Opportunity has been told many times by partisans and critics[51] and will be told innumerable times again in books and doctoral dissertations. An exhaustive retelling of that history is unnecessary for exploring how that war was affected by and affected the intellectual climate of the time. None of the ideas embodied in the Great Society or the War on Poverty was really new. All had been foreshadowed in the New Deal or Fair Deal, in programs tried abroad, or, as in the case of the Community Action Program, in pilot programs run with foundation support. In fact, most of the elements of the War on Poverty rested on the faith that the establishment of equal opportunity would eventually reduce poverty to a vestigial curiosity.[52] But the commitment to end poverty was new,[53] and it was perceived as new.

The general outline of the War on Poverty is reasonably clear.[54] The first official stirrings that eventually led to its declaration began within the Council of Economic Advisers under Walter Heller during the Kennedy administration. The inauguration of President Johnson began the second phase during which vigorous presidential goading led to both legislative planning within the administration and speedy enactment by Congress. For the first year after it was created in November 1964 as the central planner of the War on Poverty, the Office of Economic Opportunity grew rapidly. New programs were put in place and expenditures began to flow. The costs of the Vietnam War and political opposition to some of its programs stopped expansion of OEO and slowed growth of other components of the War on Poverty. From then until the end of the Johnson administration, OEO encountered a less sympathetic Congress; in 1967 Sargent Shriver, director of OEO, secured a renewal of OEO's mandate, modified and strengthened, and OEO then moved relatively uneventfully to the end of the Johnson administration. During the first Nixon administration OEO maintained existing programs, but it ceased to function as an active force in shaping legislation affecting the poor. More and more OEO occupied itself with evaluation and with experiments in new ways of dealing with poverty. The second Nixon administration liquidated the Office of Economic Opportunity. All OEO programs were either terminated or transferred to other federal or state agencies.

Most of the programs begun by OEO remain in existence, although they have been modified by subsequent legislation. The community action agencies, those local agencies that were to mobilize local and federal resources on behalf of the poor and to enlist their maximum feasible participation in the planning and administration of Community Action Program efforts, now receive federal support through the Community Services

Administration. The legal service program (to provide legal aid to the poor), Head Start (to provide enriched care for preschool children), and other programs continue to receive federal support. OEO training programs were first transferred to the Labor Department. Then principal responsibility for training was given to local governments under the Comprehensive Employment and Training Act, although some federal training programs for special groups were continued.

The War on Poverty was defined officially to include all programs, a significant part of which could be identified as aiding the poor. This official definition encompassed part or all of such traditional programs as social security (old age, survivors, and disability insurance), public assistance, veterans' benefits, public housing, urban renewal, Medicare, and Medicaid. It also included programs operating under the Manpower Development and Training Act and aid to poor school districts under the Elementary and Secondary Education Act of 1965, both of which had been enacted before the War on Poverty was declared. Indeed, only a small part of total expenditures under the War on Poverty represented specific commitments by OEO or increases in programs intended exclusively for the poor (see appendix to chapter 1). In dollar terms, most of the War on Poverty was a by-product of programs intended primarily for the middle class. When attention shifted from the War on Poverty to the war in Vietnam and then away from both, real resources targeted on the poor did not decline. In fact, they continued to increase until the mid-seventies, as shown in chapter 1. Efforts to transform the poor by educating or training them did not increase, however. Instead, aid to the poor was conveyed increasingly through transfers in kind that alleviated the symptoms of poverty but did not deal with its causes.

Rhetorical Excess

Several aspects of the War on Poverty had a major impact upon or were importantly affected by prevailing ideas of the time. The first, justly criticized and much ridiculed, is the flamboyant rhetoric in which the declaration of war on poverty was couched. The metaphor itself is suspect, even if, as Robert Levine observes, likening an effort to help the poor to a war is better than likening it to a crusade.[55] By making his objective "total victory" while refusing to rely primarily on cash transfers, President Johnson made failure inevitable. By assuring Congress that investments in the poor would yield returns "manyfold" greater than their costs, he embraced a faith widely shared at the time and supported by available evidence, but he was stating targets in such a way that they could not be overfulfilled. In the jargon of investors, there was only "downside risk." In prose somewhat less extravagant, but no less explicit, the Council of Economic Advisers wrote, "We pay twice for poverty: once in the production lost in wasted human potential, again in the resources diverted to coping with poverty's social by-products. Humanity compels our action, but it is sound economics as well."[56] The emphasis on the soundness of the investment about to be undertaken had also assured the public that the War on Poverty would not be a raid on the pocketbooks of the middle class. The officials of the Johnson administration obeyed the longstanding, if unspoken, rule of American politics, not to make income redistribution an issue. The gains of the poor were to come from the improved efficiency with which the poor would be able to use their natural endowments. The desire to avoid broader issues of income redistribution was manifest in the way poverty was defined—by a specific threshold unchanging through time, unrelated to growing average incomes.[57]

Ambiguity of Purpose

Second, the prevailing ambiguity about the nature of the problem (poverty or inequality; lack of income or lack of status or lack of power; unequal opportunity or unequal results) was reflected in the War on Poverty. The Council of Economic Advisers listed eleven ways to combat poverty, including full employment; accelerated economic growth; fighting discrimination; better health care, education, and training; regional and community development; and direct cash assistance, but only to the aged and the disabled. Expanded welfare payments or a negative income tax were not officially embraced at that time, probably because of the faith that most people could be made self-sustaining and because of concern that such "far-out" ideas might raise the question the administration so assiduously avoided, income redistribution.

Eventually, the War on Poverty encompassed all of these elements. But it excluded one element strenuously promoted by Secretary of Labor W. Willard Wirtz and then Assistant Secretary of Labor Daniel Patrick Moynihan—a jobs program for employable white males.[58] The initial efforts to incorporate such a program in the War on Poverty were damaged by the suggestion that it should by paid for by an increase in the cigarette tax at a time when the economy was climbing painfully out of a recession and economic advisers were urging a reluctant president to ask for a tax cut. But the decisive reason may well have been the faith that the labor market would provide jobs for the employable white poor if only they were given a modicum of training under the programs of the Manpower Development and Training Act and if demand was sufficiently robust.

Individual programs often had several objectives, as well as a multiplicity of intellectual forebears and political supporters. Moynihan, for example, criticized the Community Action Program for embodying at least four distinct theories: that the power structure should be organized on behalf of the poor, that the power structure should be expanded to include the poor, that the poor should organize to confront the power structure, and that institutions should be set up to aid the power structure.[59] Another observer suggested that the Community Action Program had three broad objectives: to deliver services to the poor, to coordinate the various services to which the poor were entitled in target areas, and to change the institutions that surround and were thought to perpetuate poverty.[60] In practice, more than 1,000 community action agencies assumed a wide variety of forms and adopted various strategies for assisting the poor. The problem with the CAAs was not that they lacked a single intellectually coherent strategy.[61] Rather, the difficulty was first that their objectives were vague and inflated beyond hope of fulfillment by flamboyant rhetoric, and second that the CAAs pursued the inherently divisive objective of increasing the political and economic power of the poor by wresting it from others.

The poverty program, in fact, rested on an ambiguity so profound that it should be called a contradiction. The justification of the War on Poverty was the observation that economic growth becomes progressively less effective in removing households from poverty because, as one of the original officials in the War on Poverty wrote, "economic growth does little or nothing for people not connected with the labor market—such as the aged, husbandless mothers, and the handicapped—many of whom are poor. Furthermore, successive increases in median income . . . move an ever smaller tail of the income distribution across a given income level."[62] But the same writer cited as the first of two main objectives of the War on Poverty "correction of the causes of poverty rather than . . . the alleviation of symptoms. 'Opportunity is our middle name,' the poverty warriors were fond of saying. 'We don't give handouts,' Director [of OEO] Sargent Shriver said on many occasions."[63] The contradiction is obvious: if the poor increasingly consist of those not connected with the labor market, then cash or in-kind assistance is the only short-run solution; if training, education, and full employment are effective in combating poverty, it must be because the poor can be made into self-sufficient earners. The distinction between those in and those out of the labor force is false, however. It is precisely the aged and women, including mothers with children, whose willingness to work is most sensitive to wages and employment opportunities—a sensitivity that was not recognized at the time.[64]

Evaluation

A third central aspect of the War on Poverty derives from the fact that it began just when program evaluation with the tools of economics gained currency. The year after the War on Poverty was declared, the planning, programming, and budgeting system (PPBS) was introduced. Government programs had always passed through an evaluation process of sorts within agencies and in Congress. But systematic efforts to measure and to add up benefits and compare them with costs to see whether programs were worthwhile had been rare outside the Defense Department. Even the Defense Department employed a somewhat less demanding procedure, cost effectiveness analysis. Under this procedure planners sought ways to achieve objectives, taken as given, by the least costly means.

In fact, the most vigorous civilian evaluation programs grew up where the programs of the War on Poverty were concentrated, the Office of Economic Opportunity and the Department of Health, Education, and Welfare.[65] Because of prodding by the administration, the new legislation setting up OEO and other programs required large-scale efforts to evaluate and to measure the eagerly anticipated benefits from the new programs. In the spirit of the times, the new agencies attracted many young economists and other professionals who could simultaneously work on behalf of goals and principles they cherished and apply their newly acquired professional skills. In another manifestation of the spirit of the time, those who planned and fought for the legislation, as well as those who eventually staffed the programs, were confident that analysis would confirm the value of at least a major portion of the new programs; and they were sufficiently naive politically to believe that they could jettison programs found ineffectual without endangering the rest.

Program evaluation was novel and arcane, regarded as science by its predominantly liberal practitioners and ignored or regarded as occult by those unfamiliar with it, including at the time most conservatives. In fact, one of OEO's functions was to experiment with new programs, to run them long enough to determine their effectiveness, to terminate the failures and turn the successes over to regular federal departments, and then to move on to new endeavors. Eventually, a successful poverty program would put itself out of business as its potential clients vanished into the middle class.

Things did not work out that way for several reasons, some political, some analytical. First, certain OEO programs—especially the Community Action Program, Legal Services, and the Job Corps—were under continuous political attack. Political conflict made detached analysis and evaluation of their operations almost impossible because it supported the fear that any negative findings or qualifications of positive findings would find their way into the brief of someone bent on destroying the program.

Second, evaluation of programs contained in the War on Poverty, and indeed of all government programs affecting human resources, has proven extremely difficult. In some cases the benefits from the program cannot be measured with any precision. How could one measure the degree to which a Community Action Agency succeeded in providing new services to the poor or in altering the institutions that affect their lives? One might conclude, as did evaluative studies, that it succeeded in these dimensions while failing miserably in efforts to coordinate the delivery of existing services,[66] but the judgment hinged on qualitative and controversial evidence. How could one evaluate the judgments against landlords or discriminating employers obtained by lawyers through Legal Services? Such judgments may induce people *not* party to the case to change their behavior. Rather narrow tests of management efficiency can be performed and may be useful, but they are insufficient to determine whether such expenditures effectively aid the poor.

Third, a central tenet of the poverty program was that a simultaneous attempt to deal with several manifestations of poverty at once might work where partial methods would not. Only a many-fronted assault might suffice, for example, to change the prospects of blacks in the labor market. Yet most evaluations had to focus on the effectiveness of a particular, rather modest program in achieving some special objective. Did the Job Corps raise subsequent earnings of Corps members? Did Head Start raise test scores? Did Upward Bound, a program to encourage high school students to go to college who would not otherwise do so, succeed in raising college enrollments or rate of completion of college? Because each program operated on a fairly modest scale, it was difficult to sort out its effects from those of the numerous other events and policies impinging on the poor. If effects could be observed only when programs reached a certain scale or if people were affected only when they received a variety of services, there was no way to detect these effects.

Fourth, evaluation ended up being used in rather surprising ways. Head Start received failing marks in its evaluations, but remains politically robust. The Job Corps received mixed marks and may have yielded benefits greater than its costs; nevertheless, it was sharply curtailed. The legal services program could not really be evaluated by the techniques introduced by economists, but despite much controversy and modification, it remains vigorously in existence. Evaluations indicated that Community Action Programs had succeeded, but CAPs became the popular symbol of the failure of the War on Poverty. The college work-study program is one of the most popular higher education programs and has never been evaluated. Manpower development and training, a large and diverse collection of on-the-job and institutional training programs, some of which seemed to work and some of which did not, was transferred to local governments through special revenue sharing. This history suggests that evaluation was only one element, and a very far from decisive one, in the political determination of whether programs should live or die. In short, evaluation was a political instrument to be trotted out when it supported one's objectives or undercut one's opponents', and to be suppressed, if possible, when it opposed one's objectives or strengthened one's opponents'. Far from being an instrument for evenhanded, objective deliberation, evaluation was transmuted into "forensic social science."[67] Moreover, the use of analysis in political debates tended to direct attention to the issues that analysts could cope with, which were not necessarily the central aspects of the program.

An instance of the rise and fall of research for reasons only partly due to its intellectual merit involves a study, published in 1968, that purported to demonstrate that the employment opportunities of blacks were severely limited by their confinement to residental ghettos.[68] This study seemed to have a major impact on public attitudes about employment opportunities for blacks and about ways to improve them. When riots swept the Watts area of Los Angeles, millions of living rooms received television portrayals of a city lacking fast public transportation where a person too poor to own a car could not get to work. The McCone commission, reporting on the causes of the Watts riot and on ways to avoid similar ones, stated:

"Our investigation has brought into clear focus the fact that the inadequate and costly public transportation currently existing throughout the Los Angeles area seriously restricts the residents of the disadvantaged areas such as south central Los Angeles. This lack of adequate transportation handicaps them in seeking and holding jobs, attending schools, shopping and fulfilling other needs."[69] Unfortunately, subsequent research did not support the initial findings or the statements of the McCone commission, at least as a general explanation of why black unemployment is higher than white. Another analyst, using other data, wrote one year later that the geographical separation of blacks "does not seem to be too important"[70] in explaining high black unemployment; and reexamination of the methods used in the first study indicated that the conclusions did not follow from the data used.[71] As time has passed, the idea that blacks experience high unemployment because they are penned in seems to have lost ground. It is doubtful whether anyone today would put much faith in the proposal, widely advocated in the wake of the Watts riots, that transportation subsidies be accorded a major place in combating high unemployment rates of blacks. As so often seems to happen, an idea of a social scientist is seized by laypersons because it accords with views they independently hold. With the passage of time, academic criticism undercuts the analysis and external events move on, leaving the idea, like last year's clothes, a little shabby and unfashionable.

In commenting on the unanticipated uses to which evaluation is put, one observer has noted the irony that "the evaluations and cost-effectiveness studies and experiments started under the Johnson Administration have been used with some success by President Nixon to support his decision to cut back on certain parts of the poverty program."[72] But there is no irony here. What has emerged from experience with formal evaluation and program analysis is an understanding of its profoundly conservative tendency. This fact was briefly obscured when commitments to the War on Poverty seemed strong and when liberals and radicals committed to winning the war were the only ones who performed the evaluations or could interpret them. Inevitably, however, the ability to perform or to understand program analysis spread, and the willingness to cite its results spread even faster. In addition, a disturbing tendency for evaluations to show inconsistent results from training, health, education, and other programs became apparent, leading to the sadder-but-wiser cliché among analysts that "nothing consistently changes anything." The fact that evaluations contained powerful biases toward showing no effects even if they might be present was not clearly recognized at the time. The problem, described in more detail in chapter 3, was that appropriate data were often unavailable and that the models used in statistical analysis were often too naive or simple to pick up the complex relations that might have existed between objectives and the instruments used to affect them. These models generally reflected accurately the theories that practitioners maintained. Statistical analyses frequently refuted these hypotheses, but not the increasingly sophisticated explanations of how programs could help the poor. For example, Head Start was undertaken at a time when experts in early childhood education were speculating that experiences between the ages of two and four decisively influenced later development. Faced with evaluations that suggested the effects of Head Start were modest and transitory, one could criticize the research or revise one's theory; the one thing one could not appropriately do was to argue for the increase of the program. How could those committed to evaluative techniques and the rational application of limited resources to achieve specified goals respond, except with a queasy plea for more research, when evaluations turned up mixed or negative results?

Cash Assistance

A fourth aspect of the War on Poverty that stands out clearly in retrospect was the shift in rhetorical emphasis. At first, the transformation of the poor person was seen as the key to the end of the poverty. This rhetoric supported the transfer payments and in-kind benefits favored in the late 1960s. The poor were initially regarded as an afflicted and relatively stable group, suffering from a kind of disease that they were very likely to transmit to their children if it were not treated with heavy doses of "human capital" (to use the jargon of economists).[73] Cash assistance was initially viewed as possibly necessary for temporary sustenance for the able bodied, but sufficient education and training would leave only those unable to benefit from high employment to be cared for through cash assistance or in-kind transfers. Those with the necessary skills would be able to earn their way out of poverty if unemployment were reduced. Although OEO continued to pursue this strategy, total expenditures on the poor did not follow this pattern. Out of the $16 billion spent on the poor in 1969, less than $3 billion was spent on education and manpower programs, and the addition of community organization and social services leaves the total just over $3.5 billion.[74]

Nevertheless, words triumphed over fact in the mind of the public and even in the writings of scholars who should have known better. Thus, one professor wrote: "The confidence in education inspired by the demonstration that schooling is a major determinant of earnings underlay the basic strategy of the U.S. government's effort to combat poverty. . . . Education and training programs consumed the lion's share of War on Poverty funds."[75]

Current Views on Poverty and Discrimination

The simple picture of the poor as a mass of unfortunates whose destitution persists from year to year, except for the few who can work their way out, remains widespread both among the public and among scholars. But it is not consistent with the facts. More than a decade ago, the Council of Economic Advisers published estimates of the proportion of families poor in any one year likely to be poor the next. Thirty-one percent of those poor in 1962 were estimated to have emerged from poverty by 1963. Then, in defiance of these statistics, but with proper respect for the prevailing image of poverty, the council wrote, "This suggests that the poor include a largely unchanging group of families," just as Harrington had written that the poor were "born to the wrong parents, in the wrong section of the country, in the wrong industry, or in the wrong racial or ethnic group" and that "once that mistake has been made, they could have been paragons of will and morality, but most of them would never even have had a chance to get out of the other America."[76]

New Statistics on Poverty

The statistics supported this view no more than they did the opposing one that poverty was largely transitory. If the same rate of decay continued—an unreasonable assumption because those with least chance of increasing their incomes would have least chance to emerge from poverty and many who left would fall back in—nearly all of those poor in 1962 would escape from poverty in a few years.[77] Even if one recognized that fewer than 31 percent of those remaining poor could be expected to leave poverty in later years and that many of those who left would return, the council's statistics suggested that poverty was transitory for many. It is surprising that the council did not publicly entertain this interpretation, but it is unbelievable that no one else did.[78] The most plausible explanation is that such an interpretation would have conflicted with prevailing ideas at the time and that the statistics contained in the council's report were too weak to confront those preconceptions. They were based on a rather small sample and they covered only two years, so one could not be sure that the 31 percent who left poverty in one year did not return shortly thereafter.

These shortcomings are now being remedied. Based on the first five years of the Panel Survey on Income Dynamics (which is now scheduled to last for twelve years), a major new study has shown that at the end of five years, fewer than half of the people in poverty in the first year remain in poverty. Roughly one-third of those who are poor one year are not poor the next and were not poor the year before. The number of poor is stable because large flows in and out just about balance. Second, of those who leave poverty, somewhere between one-half and four-fifths stay out of poverty for at least a year. Third, most people who leave poverty do *not* do so because of a major change in their family situation, such as marriage or the maturing of children. Fourth, of those who leave poverty, roughly half end up after five years with incomes at least 50 percent above the poverty threshold.[79] A significant fraction of those poor in 1967 had incomes over the six years 1967–72 that averaged above the poverty thresholds, but nearly twice as many were poor at least one of those years.[80] Only about 3 percent of the American population were poor in all six years, but more than one-fifth were poor in at least one of those years.

These statistics admit two complementary interpretations. The first is that the view of poverty prevalent in the 1960s is distorted; a sizable fraction of the poor do not seem to be mired in that state. Many escape from poverty, even if not very far. The group that suffers sustained, long-term poverty is smaller than is commonly supposed. The second is that the pool of people whose incomes periodically fall below the official poverty thresholds is far larger than the poverty statistics suggest. Analysis of these data has just begun, but they seem to indicate that households suffer substantial income variability even after one takes account of their measured characteristics (age, education, race, and so on) and the average incomes they earn over several years. Random events—the business cycle, plant closings, family problems, and, one suspects, interpersonal difficulties on the job—play an important role in the dynamics by which families sink into poverty or rise from it. The problem of poverty is in fact a continuum of problems, ranging from those of households who cannot ever earn as much as the officially designated thresholds, through other families who sometimes earn more but never much more than official thresholds, to a fraction that experiences poverty for a relatively brief time and then emerges from it. Even heads of single-parent families and the disabled spend a good deal of time working. Over half the disabled worked during 1971, and presumably do so in other years as well.[81] Approximately one-third to one-half the mothers receiving aid to families with dependent children work at some point during the year in a full-employment economy. In short, the simple snapshot of poverty that many people carelessly adopted a decade ago has become a complex moving picture.

The Poverty Standard

Any fixed poverty threshold is arbitrary; the problems of being poor are not switched on suddenly when income falls below it and switched off when income rises above it. The particular definition of poverty adopted when official poverty statistics were first published in 1965 has been subject to a steady stream of criticism ever since. It disregards wealth, particularly owned homes. It gives as much weight to a family one dollar below the threshold as to a family thousands of dollars below it, and entirely ignores families with incomes one dollar above it. It ignores unusual and unavoidable expenditures, such as medical costs. It covers a period too brief (as argued above) or too long (because hardship from six months of poverty can be severe for families with few assets). It is fixed in real terms, so that the statistics include only persons suffering from ever-greater relative poverty as average real income rises. It ignores significant amounts of in-kind benefits under an increasing variety of growing federal and state programs. It takes no account of the declining quality of such public services as mass transit when the mass of the population switches to cars.

People who had studied the statistics tended to be impatient with these criticisms during the 1960s because manipulation of the annual survey data then available did not change the snapshot of poverty significantly. Some adjustments, such as the calculation of long-term poverty or the inclusion of in-kind transfers, could not be made with data then available. However one looked at it, blacks were poorer than whites, one-parent families than two-parent families, the aged than the nonaged, the South than the rest of the United States. Some adjustments made marginal differences; counting wealth, for example, made the aged seem less poor compared to the nonaged than they appeared if wealth was ignored.[82] Of perhaps greater significance, the poverty statistics referred only to income, not to poverty in access to such essential services as health or education.[83]

But the gain from having even a flawed standard that had gained wide-spread acceptance was deemed more than ample compensation for such inadequacies.[84]

It has become clear, however, that despite the decline in "officially tab-ulated poverty" during the 1960s, we really do not know what has hap-pened to "poverty." The problem of poverty at any time eventually merges into the more general question of how income should be distributed. This merger of two separate problems must occur if poverty is measured by the proportion of households whose real incomes fall below a stipulated threshold: economic growth ensures that eventually nearly everyone will not be poor even if large groups continue to be regarded as relatively de-prived. Ultimately, the question of the distribution of income must be ad-dressed. In this sense, a major accomplishment of poverty warriors lay in convincing others that, at least for a while, poverty and income inequality were separate issues.

Officially tabulated poverty declined from 22.4 percent of all Amer-icans in 1959, the first year for which poverty statistics were officially tabulated, to 17.3 percent in 1965, the last year before the two wars—on poverty and in Vietnam—became significant, and then to 12.1 percent in 1969. In the succeeding six years, poverty fluctuated as the full-employ-ment potential of the economy grew but was not realized, until 12.3 per-cent were officially counted as poor in 1975. In general, the economic position of blacks increased relative to that of whites, although the differ-ences remained large. Median income of nonwhite families rose from 55 percent of white family income in 1960 to 64 percent in 1970 and 65 per-cent in 1975. The proportion of blacks in poverty declined from 56 per-cent in 1959 to 32 percent in 1969 and to 31 percent in 1975.

The full story, unfortunately, is a good deal more complicated and con-fusing. Some statistics suggest that almost no progress has been made in combating poverty, others that the War on Poverty has been waged and very nearly won. Two facts are discouraging. First, the reasons for increas-ing the income level used to define poverty as the economy grows are com-pelling. Almost no one is poor by the standards of nineteenth century sharecroppers or New England milltowns, but poverty persists. In response to periodic surveys, the income that respondents say defines poverty in-creases about 6 percent for every 10 percent increase in per capita in-come.[85] Whether official statistics should reflect this popular attitude is controversial. Robert Lampman argues that the poverty threshold should not be increased, except to adjust for inflation, on the ground that getting people beyond a fixed target is a rational goal and that after it has been achieved new goals should be set.[86] In contrast, Lee Rainwater derides the idea of a fixed poverty threshold. He notes that the percentage of people officially counted as poor declined nearly 50 percent between 1959 and 1969 and that the extrapolation would suggest the near elimination of poverty by 1980. Rainwater comments: "But we know that is ridiculous. Anyone who argues that in 1973 the poverty problem is almost half of what it was in 1959 is likely to meet with disbelief. His listeners will be quick to point to the undiminished intensity of a broad range of poverty-related human and social problems."[87]

If the poverty threshold is set in relative terms by keeping it equal to a fixed proportion of median family income, poverty declined negligibly between 1963 and 1973, from only 17.1 percent to 15.6 percent of all households.[88] This would seem to suggest that all of the decline in poverty was due to economic growth, as the manna of higher productivity fell equally, but not disproportionately, on the poor.

But this is not true, as the second discouraging fact emphasizes: if poverty thresholds had been based on earnings alone (as a measure of the capacity of families to work their way out of poverty), and had been adjusted only for inflation but not for economic growth, absolute poverty would have fallen between 1963 and 1968, but risen perceptibly thereafter. Fully 31 percent of all households would have been counted as poor in 1963 if only their earnings had been counted. By 1968 this proportion would have fallen to 27 percent; by 1973 it would have risen to more than 29 percent. If the poverty threshold had been increased at the same rate as median income, the proportion of households unable to earn their way out of poverty actually would have increased from 28.2 percent in 1963 to 30.6 percent in 1973. These trends are due to the partially offsetting effects of many events: a rise in unemployment since 1969, a change in the age and sex composition of the labor force, and an increase in the dispersion of earnings.[89]

In at least two respects official statistics suffer from biases that understate the decline in poverty. The most serious is the failure to include as income the value of various in-kind benefits provided by the federal government predominantly for low-income households, notably food stamps, medical benefits under Medicaid and Medicare, and housing assistance under a variety of federal programs, including low-rent public housing. These benefits have been growing more rapidly than any other component of income of the poor, including cash assistance through such programs as social security and public assistance. Furthermore, certain elements of income ostensibly counted in full in the poverty statistics are actually included only in part because they are not fully reported by households; the most notable is public assistance. If incomes are adjusted for the excluded income and for the value of in-kind benefits omitted from the official statistics, the decline in poverty is dramatic. In-kind benefits may be worth less to recipients than their market value, but the effect of including the rapidly growing value of in-kind benefits on poverty is still striking. According to the official statistics, 15.8 percent and 14.6 percent of all families and unrelated individuals were poor in 1968 and 1972, respectively. Statistics revised for underreporting of income and for the value of in-kind benefits indicate that only 10.8 percent in 1968 and 6.6 percent in 1972 of all families and unrelated individuals were poor.[90]

The condition of the poor as indicated by their net incomes is thus getting better faster than the official statistics would suggest. If the value of in-kind benefits is counted as income to poor recipients, these benefits together with cash assistance were sufficient to lift 72 percent of the pretransfer poor over the official poverty threshold in 1972 and filled 83 percent of the gap between their pretransfer income and the poverty threshold.[91]

A complete measure of poverty would include assets as well as income. The distribution of wealth has been getting less uneven. As each person gains work experience, he acquires legal entitlements to social security benefits in the event of disability or death or when he reaches a certain age. These entitlements are wealth in essentially the same sense as ordinary assets (the only difference is that they cannot be traded), but they are distributed far more evenly. Approximately 25 percent of net worth is held by the wealthiest 1 percent of all individuals.[92] Corresponding estimates are unavailable for social security, but it is unlikely that the wealthiest 20 percent of all households possess more than 30 percent of social security entitlements. Between 1950 and 1975, social security wealth increased almost sevenfold, rising from 29 percent of net worth to 94 percent of net worth, and from less than the gross national product to nearly three times gross national product. In short, a form of wealth distributed far more evenly than other assets and more evenly even than earnings has been growing more rapidly than either. The result has been an equalization in the distribution of lifetime capacity to consume that is unrecognized in any official statistics.[93] Offsetting these trends to a considerable extent has been the rapid growth of pension funds, benefits from which will accrue primarily to households with above-average incomes.

These statistics require at least two comments. First, they do not speak for themselves. They can be introduced as evidence for the proposition either that the Great Society and the War on Poverty succeeded or that they failed. On behalf of the former interpretation, poverty has diminished at a prodigious rate and its elimination seems well within reach because of the increasing generosity of cash and in-kind assistance. On behalf of the latter interpretation, the capacity of workers to earn enough to keep themselves and their families out of poverty has not improved and, by the standards of a moving poverty threshold, in fact has deteriorated.

No matter how the statistics are interpreted, they are rather hard on the faiths that underlay the War on Poverty and the Great Society. The purposes of the programs that fall under those headings were multifaceted and included the goal of improving support for those unable to earn enough for themselves. But a leading purpose was to reduce the number of people who earned too little to keep themselves and their families out of poverty. This purpose has not been achieved, in part because full employment has occurred so seldom since 1970 and in part because meager resources were devoted to achieving it (see chapter 1). What has been achieved is a massive increase in cash and in-kind assistance that has made it possible for those unable to earn their way out of poverty to secure a modest living standard.

Discrimination

Something significant began happening to the economic status of black Americans after 1966. After more than a decade of stagnation in the relative earnings of black males,[94] the gap that separated them from white males began to close; median earnings of black males fully employed year round rose from 63 percent of the earnings of white males in 1966 to 72 percent in 1973.[95] Between 1974 and 1975, the ratio of black to white median wage or salary income rose 3 percentage points for men and 2 percentage points for women.[96] The earnings differentials associated with additional schooling, historically much smaller for blacks than for whites, began to narrow.[97]

Three reasons for this change have been suggested. Unfortunately no one knows whether the sudden improvement in the economic status of

black males was due to one or a combination of these three possible causes
and whether these gains will be extended, maintained, or lost in the future.
First, after four years of gradual decline in unemployment rates, labor
markets became very tight in 1965 and remained so for about five years;
this was the longest sustained period of full employment since World War
II, the last preceding period during which the relative economic status of
blacks had shown marked improvement.[98] Second, the federal government
began to use its legal powers to enforce equal employment opportunities
granted under civil rights legislation. The voting rights act may have increased the sensitivity of elected officials to the needs of black constituents
and resulted in fairer hiring practices and an increased flow of public services to them, although it is unclear why such political events would have
immediate and perceptible effects on relative earnings.[99] Third, investments in the education and training of the poor, who were disproportionately black, began to rise significantly in the mid-1960s. These expenditures, however, cannot really have contributed in any direct way to
the economic status of black adults in the late 1960s because they were
too meager and because they were focused largely on children and adolescents. It is true that the educational gap between blacks and whites had
been closing, measured either by years of school completed or by length of
school years, although differences in performance on standardized tests
remained sizable.[100] But this narrowing had been occurring gradually for
decades and cannot explain the abrupt improvements in earnings that began in the mid-1960s.

The economic status of black women relative to that of white women
had been improving for a longer time, as they left household service and
because they tended to remain in the labor force with fewer interruptions
than did white women.[101] The relative economic position of all blacks improved as they migrated from the relatively low-wage South to the higher-
wage North and West.

The result of all these developments was an important improvement in
the relative economic status of blacks. One economist was moved to hail a
"virtual collapse in traditional discriminatory patterns in the labor market."[102] The occupational status of blacks who had recently entered the
labor force approached that of equally experienced whites.[103] Other commentators showed somewhat more rhetorical restraint in describing a situation that left the average black male earning only 66.0 percent as much
as the average white male in 1969, compared with 57.7 percent in 1959.[104]

Others have noted that younger blacks have done relatively better than older blacks for many years but seem to lose ground as they age, raising concern that a similar recession could occur once again.[105] After reviewing a large number of studies, one writer concludes: "After remaining roughly stable during the 1950s and early 1960s, both family and individual income increased rapidly for nonwhites relative to whites during the 1960s. Although the increase was largely due to a tight labor market, the evidence suggests that improvement occurred for many segments of the population *net* of the benefits from the tight labor market. The evidence also suggests that the income gains have been greater for younger blacks, probably due to the substantial increase in the return to schooling for younger blacks."[106] It was clear that something important had happened in the late 1960s.

A simple but profoundly important reversal also has occurred in thinking about racial discrimination during the past decade. The prevailing attitudes of the early 1960s, described above, were simply that economic discrimination occurred because people who made important economic decisions were prejudiced, that with the end of discriminatory attitudes discriminatory behavior would fall of its own weight, that the end of discrimination will benefit just about everybody (most of all, of course, its victims), and that legal prohibitions may make a dent in discriminatory behavior, but not in attitudes. Among economists, the dominant theory of discrimination suggested that the competitive search for profits tends to erode discriminatory behavior.

As a result of analysis and research over the past decade and the lessons learned from civil rights legislation and other legal efforts to combat discriminatory behavior, each of the foregoing propositions would now have to be either qualified or reversed. Much discriminatory behavior can persist even if those making important economic decisions are without prejudice; the competitive search for profits may sustain discriminatory behavior; the end of discrimination will impose rather sizable losses, especially on those persons who now fill occupations from which the victims of discrimination are excluded, and legal prohibitions on discriminatory behavior may change not only behavior, but attitudes as well.[107]

The first preconception of the early 1960s to fall was that the end of discrimination would benefit all. The reasoning behind this proposition had never been made very precise. The estimates of the Council of Economic Advisers of the national gain from the end of discrimination were based on very crude analysis. In an article published in 1971, Barbara Bergmann demonstrated that the termination of discriminatory behavior against blacks would probably reduce the incomes of whites, especially whites with less education than average, who would be thrown into competition with blacks.[108] Such analysis explained the discriminatory behavior of predominantly white construction trade unions;[109] their actions acquired the aura of self-interest, even if they gained nothing in moral stature. The termination of discrimination against women, far more numerous than blacks, it was shown, would have even more far-reaching effects on the incomes of males.

Second, a continuing flow of research showed that differences between incomes of blacks and whites could not be fully explained by any measured differences between them.[110] Blacks were less well educated than whites; their families have less education than do those of whites; proportionately more blacks than whites live in low income regions; and so on. But even after such characteristics have been identified and used statistically to explain the difference in incomes between blacks and whites, a large part of the difference remains unexplained. Additional education was associated with much larger increments in earnings for whites than for blacks; but even if this difference were ignored, whites enjoyed an unexplained income bonus. In fact, when adjustments for IQ, parental education, and occupational status were made, blacks appeared to get about as much education as similarly situated whites, although they ended up with lower occupational status.[111]

Two major explanations for such results could have been advanced: that blacks are inferior to whites in ways not revealed in the statistics—namely, genetically—or that blacks are victims of prejudice.[112] The first explanation, long banished from polite conversation, was briefly readmitted following Arthur Jensen's famous article in the *Harvard Educational Review* in which he argued that most of the differences in school performance between blacks and whites were due to immutable inherited differences in intelligence.[113] The debate over the degree to which IQ was inherited soon became so rancorous that the subject once again ceased to be a subject of polite conversation, although it continued to be debated academically. It now appears that the major piece of genetic research on which Jensen based his article may have been the product of fraud.[114] Only recently has the position clearly been stated that whether IQ is largely inherited has almost no bearing on whether differences between blacks and whites in incomes, in performance on standardized tests, or in almost any other dimension can be altered by conscious policies. A simple analogy establishes this point:

> Height has been proven to be a highly heritable trait in many human populations. The variation in height among Americans, for instance, that can be attributed to environment is almost nil. The variation in height among the Japanese that can be attributed to environment is also almost nil. The current difference in average height between Americans and Japanese is substantial.
>
> But changes in diet (i.e., a single and obvious aspect of environment) have contributed importantly to making each succeeding generation of Americans and each succeeding generation of Japanese taller. The Japanese seem to be growing taller faster. The difference between them may well disappear or even tip the other way. And, within each population, height will have remained just as heritable throughout.[115]

In this analogy, heights of individuals, even more than IQ, are explained by genetic inheritance. Yet the difference in height between populations is amenable to environmental influences. Thus, even if it were true that the IQ of each person largely depended on his genetic inheritance, it still would be true that environmental factors might be largely responsible for the differences between the average IQs of blacks and whites. Whether there are genetic differences between blacks and whites that are relevant to performance in school or in labor markets is an interesting question, but it is doubtful that it can be settled by methods currently available to the social sciences, and however it is settled it has little relevance for issues of public policy.

If blacks are the victims of discrimination—the alternative explanation of the statistical findings—exactly how does discrimination operate? Why has competition among firms not destroyed it? Becker's analysis rests on the presence of tastes for discrimination—in other words, that prejudice and its consequences explain certain kinds of discriminatory behavior by employers, unions, shopkeepers, real estate brokers, and others. Numerous analysts have pointed out, however, that tastes for discrimination should result in segregation—the separation of blacks and whites, or of men and women, in separate work places—but not necessarily in discrimination—the payment of different wages to workers with identical abilities, or the denial of certain jobs to certain workers. Employers with weak tastes for discrimination or none at all would enjoy competitive advantages from employing the victims of discrimination if their wages were below those of others. Workers with weak tastes for discrimination would be sought by employers for integrated work groups. As long as discriminatory wage differentials persisted, nondiscriminatory employers would be able to undersell by hiring victims of discrimination at low wages and would tend to drive out of business employers who indulged their prejudices.[116] In fact, spatial segregation in factories and offices is rare, while occupational segregation is common. One explanation for such occupational segregation might be the indulgence of tastes for discrimination sustained through the maintenance of social distance.[117] Whites might not mind being served by blacks but resent the reverse and have the power to enforce their preferences. Men might not mind working with women, but resent working for them. But the real puzzle is the mechanism by which discrimination persists despite competitive forces.

The puzzle begins to vanish when one considers why employers stipulate that certain jobs require college degrees or five years' experience, and why such requirements are accepted and not regarded as discrimination against those who lack college degrees or who have fewer than five years of experience. The employer is seeking employees who will probably succeed in the job. Not all college graduates with five years of experience will succeed; not all people lacking college degrees or at least five years' experience will fail. In fact, the difference in performance may not be great. But based upon experience or preconception, the employer uses these easily verifiable attributes as signals to tell him whether to hire an applicant. In a very real sense, the possibly sizable fraction of candidates for employment who could do the job but who lack the required attributes are victims of discrimination.[118] The employer, unable to ascertain the true capacities of potential employees except at some cost through such techniques as testing or observation of actual performance on the job, relies on cheap information that he believes to be correlated with subsequent performance. Such easily observable characteristics may include age, sex, education, or race, none of which can be quickly or cheaply altered by the applicant. Other characteristics such as clothing, style of speech, mannerisms, and bearing may serve a similar function, even though they may be altered.

Some such criteria are accepted as legitimate job qualifications; use of others, such as race, is regarded as discrimination. An employer may be right or wrong about his appraisal of particular groups in either case. But indulgence of certain criteria has been judged to have serious, or even catastrophic, consequences and has been made illegal. Some apparently legitimate criteria, such as the use of intelligence in determining who shall receive educational subsidies, may be open to question upon examination.[119] Employers, even if they are not prejudiced, may use race or sex to exclude blacks or other minorities or women from certain jobs if they believe that *on the average* blacks or other minorities or women do less well on a particular job. The differences may be small. Whites may succeed 80 percent of the time, blacks 75 percent; women may average two years before quitting while men average two and one-half. But if breaking in a new employee is costly, even the employer who is utterly blind to the color and indifferent to the sex of his employees may favor whites and men *if he can*.

The simple point is that any easily observed characteristic thought by the employer to be correlated with subsequent performance cannot be ignored except at the sacrifice of profits. The employer may be wrong about the correlation—he may only think that blacks do marginally less well than whites because he has never really checked, just as he may only think that college graduates do better than others because he has never checked—but as long as he thinks that even a small correlation exists and he is able to base decisions on that perception, blacks will be entirely excluded from jobs that they may be only marginally less or equally qualified to fill. Gross results may flow from small differences.

The puzzle vanishes completely when one considers the possible impact of such exclusionary employment policies on subsequent decisions of blacks or women about how much education to acquire or how to plan their careers. A person who knows that chances for a job requiring a college degree are reduced by his race has less incentive to acquire a college degree or perhaps even to complete high school. A woman who is excluded from occupations requiring long and continuous labor force attachment to climb a job ladder has little reason not to leave the labor force to bear and raise children or for other reasons, because she gains little from staying.

In short, important decisions are made on the basis of group averages because accurate information about individuals is costly to obtain. The victims in each case are those who are above the average for their group and quite possibly above the average for the favored group. But in a deeper sense, all members of the disfavored group are victims because their incentives are distorted and because the average among them are denied the chance either to fail or to succeed as the result of luck.[120]

The use of group averages has another unfortunate side effect; improvement in the performance of members of the outcast group will have no effect until some critical point is reached. For example, suppose that male applicants are favored over female applicants for admission to graduate school on the basis that men are likely to use their training for more years than women (because women are believed to withdraw from careers for a few years on the average to bear children). There is no reason to end such policies even if the difference between men and women narrows. A second example is even more troubling. If employers think blacks with high school diplomas are less well trained than whites with high school diplomas and are less likely to perform satisfactorily on certain jobs, then training programs to help black high school graduates will have no effect on hiring policies and no apparent effect on wages or job prospects of trainees until a sufficient number of trainees has been turned out to change the attitudes of employers toward the entire category of black high school graduates. A program that quite effectively raises the capacities of a small minority of black high school graduates may not perceptibly affect wages or job prospects and may be judged a failure. When decisions are made on the basis of group averages, programs that affect only a few individuals cannot be evaluated by looking at the experience of the directly affected individuals; customary evaluation techniques fail.[121]

The existence of discrimination based on group averages, or perceptions of group averages, has three important implications. First, competition may not erode discrimination as the economist's comforting argument of the 1950s and early 1960s maintained; competition may reinforce discrimination. Second, discrimination based on group averages may be rather fragile and quite sensitive to legislative correction. The motive for discrimination based on perceived group averages is economic—the avoidance of unnecessary costs. Laws that prohibit or make costly the use of such group averages can completely destroy the motivation for such discriminatory behavior. One may not have to change hearts and minds; one need only appeal to economic self-interest. This is a sufficient explanation for the apparent effectiveness of affirmative action plans to bar race and sex discrimination.[122] Third, changes in attitudes are likely to follow changes in laws and need not precede them. Attitudes may change immediately if it is discovered that perceptions of group averages were incorrect. Few employers really had much experience with blacks or women in supervisory positions of authority until recently. The changes in attitudes may be deferred until the behavior of the previously excluded groups adjusts to expanded opportunities.

True to its implications, this theory of discrimination is an after-the-fact rationalization for legislation to outlaw discriminatory behavior enacted in the mid-1960s. The theory that underlies it is hard to test and has not been tested. It does not suggest that plain ordinary prejudice and bigotry have ended; it merely suggests that an end to prejudice and bigotry is neither a necessary nor a sufficient condition for reduction of discrimination in the marketplace. It provides a rationale why laws to prohibit discrimination on the basis of race, religion, sex, or age can be effective if they are enforced. To put it the other way, the consensus necessary for passage of the civil rights legislation of the mid-1960s formed despite theories of discrimination that suggested that legislation was being put ahead of attitudes. Only in response to actions whose apparent effectiveness demanded explanation were the intellectual rationalizations forthcoming.

Summary

Understanding of poverty and discrimination has deepened markedly in the last decade. Simple descriptions—a stable population of the poor, discrimination based on attitudes that could easily be condemned—have been replaced or supplemented by complex accounts—a changing population of the poor, discrimination based in some measure on the very motives of profit maximization that underlie the American economic system. The number of people who are sometimes poor is far larger and the number who are always poor is at least somewhat smaller than official statistics suggest. Discrimination depends not only on atavistic prejudices but, in some degree, on economic rationality. We may safely amend Harrington: many of the poor differ from the rest of us only in their lack of money, and many of them one day will leave poverty. But many of the rest of us one day will be poor too.

Opinions vary widely about the degree to which poverty is caused by personal characteristics of the poor or by impersonal characteristics of the job structure. Opinions likewise vary about the extent to which discrimination against blacks, women, and other groups explains the lower pay of these groups; and, of the wage differences attributable to discrimination, no one knows how much is due to simple prejudice and how much to economic decisions soundly or unsoundly based on perceived group characteristics.

In short, oversimplified views that served well as the foundation for political action have been replaced by more complicated analysis that, despite increased accuracy, is likely to generate political confusion.

Notes

1. John Kenneth Galbraith, *The Affluent Society* (Houghton Mifflin, 1958), p. 324.

2. Michael Harrington, *The Other America: Poverty in the United States* (Macmillan, 1963), p. 10.

3. Sar A. Levitan expresses the view that an article by MacDonald was the first to have a significant impact. See *The Great Society's Poor Law: A New Approach to Poverty* (Johns Hopkins Press, 1969), p. 13.

4. Adam Yarmolinsky, "The Beginnings of OEO," in James L. Sundquist, ed., *On Fighting Poverty: Perspectives from Experience* (Basic Books, 1969), p. 37.

5. The 1964 *Economic Report* contained tabulations of the number of families with incomes below $3,000 and below $2,000 over time and for various groups. The same cutoff was used regardless of family size, age, place of residence, wealth, income history, and receipt of certain excluded forms of income or in-kind assistance. Some of these and other shortcomings were corrected in later official statistics and some were not. The first official statistics were published in an article by Mollie Orshansky, "Counting the Poor: Another Look at the Poverty Profile," *Social Security Bulletin,* vol. 28 (January 1965), pp. 3–29. Estimates of poverty had been made in earlier generations, but these referred to periods when income in general was much lower.

6. The lack was not met until the data from the Panel Study of Income Dynamics began to become available. This survey was initially financed by the Office of Economic Opportunity and later by the Department of Health, Education, and Welfare (results are published as available by the Survey Research Center of the University of Michigan in various volumes of *Five Thousand American Families: Patterns of Economic Progress*). It has followed 5,000 families since 1967 and is scheduled to run for ten years. Data from other longitudinal surveys of workers of various ages carried out by the Department of Labor became available at about the same time.

7. That this problem had not vanished even a decade later is attested to by the exasperated comments of a radical economist on a study of income distribution by a conventional economist. "What is missing throughout this study—and in virtually all simplistic econometric studies of this issue—is an attempt to ask what is happening, what the income generating process is. Employment and income are the results of a whole social system. . . . My major objection to this type of study, then, is that it cannot, by design, ask serious questions." Stephan Michelson, "Discussion," *American Economic Review,* vol. 60 (May 1970, *Papers and Proceedings, 1969*), p. 284.

8. These statistics are from Edward C. Budd, "Postwar Changes in the Size Distribution of Income in the U.S.," ibid., p. 251. Similar data were available from the Current Population Survey published each year by the U.S. Bureau of the Census. A controversy has recently enlivened the pages of the *American Economic Review* over whether these statistics give an even approximately

correct picture of how much inequality there is or of how it has changed in the past two decades. Morton Paglin has argued that a good deal of inequality is perfectly natural and should be ignored in measuring the amount of inequality that is socially significant. In particular, the earnings of white males typically follow a life cycle, rising fairly rapidly during the worker's thirties and sometimes during his forties, and then leveling off or declining in his later working years. (The earnings profiles of white females and of blacks of both sexes are much flatter.) Paglin asserts that if adjustments for inequality of income traceable to the life cycle are made, the statistics reveal a decline in the amount of economic inequality since World War II because the component of inequality due to the life cycle has increased while total inequality has remained unchanged. His findings have been severely challenged by critics. See Morton Paglin, "The Measurement and Trend of Inequality: A Basic Revision," *American Economic Review,* vol. 65 (September 1975), pp. 598–609, and the series of comments on this article in ibid., vol. 67 (June 1977), pp. 497–531.

9. *Affluent Society,* pp. 330, 327.

10. *Other America,* p. 17.

11. Edward C. Banfield, *The Unheavenly City: The Nature and Future of Our Urban Crisis* (Little, Brown, 1968), p. 53. Banfield also stresses an inability to defer gratification or otherwise plan for the future as a defining characteristic of the lower class. Not all poor are lower class, however, nor are all members of the lower class poor. Banfield never makes quite clear how one can identify a member of the lower class when one meets him (or her).

12. Robert J. Lampman, "Income and Welfare in the United States: A Review Article," *Review of Economics and Statistics,* vol. 45 (August 1963), pp. 315–16.

13. Unemployment is discussed in chapter 4.

14. Gunnar Myrdal, "The War on Poverty," *New Republic,* vol. 150 (February 8, 1964), p. 14.

15. Christopher Jencks, "Slums and Schools: I," ibid., vol. 147 (September 10, 1962), p. 19.

16. *Other America,* p. 19.

17. For summaries of these views see Joseph A. Kershaw with Paul N. Courant, *Government Against Poverty* (Brookings Institution, 1970); Robert A. Levine, *The Poor Ye Need Not Have with You: Lessons from the War on Poverty* (M.I.T. Press, 1970).

18. *Economic Report of the President together with the Annual Report of the Council of Economic Advisers, January 1964,* p. 72.

19. Ad Hoc Committee on the Triple Revolution, *The Triple Revolution* (Santa Barbara: Ad Hoc Committee, 1964).

20. Henry M. Levin, on the tenth anniversary of the inauguration of the War on Poverty, wrote: "Of course, it was assumed that full employment and prosperity were primarily matters of using correctly the tools of fiscal and monetary policy, so no direct labor market intervention in behalf of the poor was needed other than in the areas of reducing discrimination against minorities and of regional development." See "A Decade of Policy Developments in

Improving Education and Training for Low-Income Populations," in Robert
H. Haveman, ed., *A Decade of Federal Antipoverty Programs: Achievements,
Failures, and Lessons* (Academic Press, 1977), p. 126.

21. See, for example, the testimony on unemployment problems by Charles
C. Killingsworth in *Unemployment Problems,* pt. 3, Hearings before the Senate Special Committee on Unemployment Problems, 86:1 (Government Printing Office, 1960), pp. 1144–54.

22. Harrington, for example, wrote, "Negro poverty is unique in every
way. It grows out of a long American history, and it expresses itself in a sub-
culture that is built up on an interlocking base of economic and racial injustice" (*Other America,* p. 64). "To belong to a racial minority is to be poor, but
poor in a special way" (p. 72). See also Daniel P. Moynihan, "The Professors
and the Poor," in Moynihan, ed., *On Understanding Poverty: Perspectives
from the Social Sciences* (Basic Books, 1969), p. 9.

23. For a description of this debate, see Robinson G. Hollister, *Poor People, Poor Theories, Poor Programs* (forthcoming from the Academic Press in
the Institute for Research on Poverty series).

24. The source of this estimate is obscure. See Oscar Lewis, *La Vida: A
Puerto Rican Family in the Culture of Poverty—San Juan and New York*
(Random House, 1965), p. li.

25. *Unheavenly City.*

26. Ray Moseley, "Detroit's Welfare Empire," *Atlantic Monthly,* vol. 205
(April 1960), p. 46.

27. *Other America,* pp. 22–23.

28. Several studies suggest that income is the most important single determinant of marital stability and that, contrary to prevailing notions, black
families are about as stable as white. See, for example, Myron J. Lefcowitz,
"Poverty and Negro-White Family Structures" (background paper prepared
for the White House Conference on Civil Rights, November 1965; processed),
cited by Elizabeth Herzog, "Is There a 'Breakdown' of the Negro Family?" in
Lee Rainwater and William L. Yancey, *The Moynihan Report and the Politics
of Controversy* (M.I.T. Press, 1967), p. 350. More recently Robert Hampton
has written, "Most studies of marital stability have reported that whites are
more likely to be found in stable marriages than blacks, irrespective of the
measure of stability used. . . . [W]e find that . . . once income, home ownership,
and family size differences are taken into account, all of which are relatively
highly correlated with race, the percentage of black families experiencing divorce or separation is six percentage points less than for whites. This suggests
that it is the economic characteristics of blacks that lead to divorce and separation rates that are as high as or higher than those of whites. Once these economic characteristics are taken into account by regression, we find that the
blacks' rate of marital disruption is *lower* than that for whites." "Marital Disruption: Some Social and Economic Consequences," in Greg J. Duncan and
James N. Morgan, eds., *Five Thousand American Families: Patterns of Economic Progress* (University of Michigan, Institute for Social Research, 1975),
vol. 3, p. 168. For attitudes of a sample of the poor toward work, see Leonard

Goodwin, *Do The Poor Want to Work? A Social-Psychological Study of Work Orientations* (Brookings Institution, 1972).

29. Peter H. Rossi and Zahava D. Blum, "Class, Status, and Poverty," in Moynihan, ed., *On Understanding Poverty*, p. 44.

30. Lee Rainwater, *What Money Buys: Inequality and the Social Meanings of Income* (Basic Books, 1974), p. 10. Rainwater's speculation was supported by Goodwin's findings that the poor and the nonpoor seemed to have similar attitudes toward work. See *Do The Poor Want to Work?* pp. 52, 68, 81.

31. Not until "dual labor market" theories were developed in the late 1960s and early 1970s did economists construct an explanation about how the labor market works in which the behavior of workers—their punctuality, quitting rates, interest in training and advancement—depends on the opportunities open to them. Workers who were denied access to jobs that required punctuality and long periods on a particular job for advancement, it was held, developed into people who were often late to work, quit jobs frequently, and were indifferent to the training or education necessary for advancement. Eventually such behavior becomes habitual, it was argued. Bad jobs make bad workers who then can get only bad jobs. A new vicious circle was conceived in which environment and culture created and reinforced one another within the labor market. See Peter B. Doeringer and Michael J. Piore, *Internal Labor Markets and Manpower Analysis* (Heath, 1971). For a summary and criticism of this literature, see Michael L. Wachter, "Primary and Secondary Labor Markets: A Critique of the Dual Approach," *Brookings Papers on Economic Activity, 3:1974*, pp. 637–80; also Glen G. Cain, "The Challenge of Dual and Radical Theories of the Labor Market to Orthodox Theory," discussion paper 255–75 (University of Wisconsin–Madison, Institute for Research on Poverty, January 1975).

32. In his review of theories of the distribution of earnings, Jacob Mincer remarked, "The models [that emphasize random events] seem rather superficial in focusing on an unexplained category and in the single-minded objective of theoretically reproducing a presumed mathematical form of the aggregative distribution . . . Residual distributions may be best treated in a probabilistic fashion." "The Distribution of Labor Incomes: A Survey With Special Reference to the Human Capital Approach," *Journal of Economic Literature,* vol. 8 (March 1970), p. 6.

33. John G. Wofford wrote, "Little thought, if any, was given by those of us who helped administer CAP [the Community Action Program] to a distinction between poverty (a lack of money) and the 'culture of poverty' (the life style that goes with poverty)." "The Politics of Local Responsibility: Administration of the Community Action Program—1964–1966," in Sundquist, ed., *On Fighting Poverty*, p. 71. In the same volume, Adam Yarmolinsky wrote that among the issues that did not arise in early discussions was much concern about the culture of poverty issue. "[T]he burning sociological issue as to whether there is in fact a culture of poverty was briefly discussed in some of the early sessions with advisers like [Michael] Harrington and [Paul] Jacobs. It did not, however, enter into the construction of legislation except to the extent

that the idea of community action implied a comprehensive attack on all of the interrelated causes of poverty." "The Beginnings of OEO," p. 49.

34. See Hollister, "Poor People, Poor Theories, Poor Programs."

35. Herbert J. Gans, "Culture and Class in the Study of Poverty: An Approach to Anti-Poverty Research," in Moynihan, ed., *On Understanding Poverty*, p. 203.

36. Rossi and Blum, "Class, Status, and Poverty," p. 57.

37. Lee Rainwater, "The Problem of Lower-Class Culture and Poverty-War Strategy," in Moynihan, ed., *On Understanding Poverty*, pp. 249–50.

38. See Frank Levy, "How Big Is the American Underclass?" (University of California, Berkeley, June 1976; processed); U.S. Department of Health, Education, and Welfare, "The Changing Economic Status of 5000 American Families: Highlights from the Panel Study of Income Dynamics" (HEW, May 1974; processed); and Survey Research Center, *A Panel Study of Income Dynamics* (University of Michigan, Institute for Social Research, 1972). Before the *Panel Study* no data were available relating to the long-term experience of poverty households. An earlier analysis of poverty flows by Terence F. Kelly was restricted to a matched (longitudinal) sample of families and unrelated individuals over a two-year period (1965–66). See his "Factors Affecting Poverty: A Gross Flow Analysis," in *The President's Commission on Income Maintenance Programs: Technical Studies* (GPO, 1970), pp. 1–81.

39. Herbert Gans compiled an agenda for research on poverty (published in 1968), consisting of one-line questions, that goes on for several pages. Some of the questions, although important, cannot be answered in any practical way. Many of those that could be answered still have not been. See "Culture and Class," pp. 219–25.

40. "[T]he initial public image of the War on Poverty was disproportionately that of white Appalachia. In the early days of the War on Poverty, the striking photographs were those of President and Mrs. Johnson visiting Appalachian shacks." Levine, *The Poor Ye Need Not Have with You*, p. 33. Nathan Glazer took a flatly contradictory view: "The chief reason why our impoverished population forms a major social problem . . . is because of who they are. . . . It is the civil rights revolution that makes poverty a great issue in America, not merely the fact of poverty." "Paradoxes of American Poverty," *Public Interest*, no. 1 (Fall 1965), pp. 77–78.

41. See "The Problem of Poverty in America," in *Economic Report of the President, January 1964*, chap. 2, and Orshansky, "Counting the Poor."

42. Gunnar Myrdal, *An American Dilemma: The Negro Problem and Modern Democracy* (Harper, 1944).

43. Gary S. Becker, *The Economics of Discrimination* (University of Chicago Press, 1957).

44. "The President's News Conference of May 13, 1959," in *Public Papers of the Presidents of the United States: Dwight D. Eisenhower* (GPO, 1960), p. 388.

45. See Alan B. Batchelder, "Decline in the Relative Income of Negro Men," *Quarterly Journal of Economics*, vol. 78 (November 1964), p. 531.

46. One theory of housing discrimination concluded that blacks would tend to pay more than whites for housing only on the borders of expanding ghettos. See Martin J. Bailey, "Note on the Economics of Residential Zoning and Urban Renewal," *Land Economics*, vol. 35 (August 1959), pp. 288–92.

47. Becker, *Economics of Discrimination* (2nd impression, 1962), p. 2.

48. Elton Rayack, "Discrimination and the Occupational Progress of Negroes," *Review of Economics and Statistics*, vol. 43 (May 1961), pp. 209–14.

49. *Economic Report of the President together with the Annual Report of the Council of Economic Advisers, January 1966*, p. 110.

50. Sar A. Levitan and Robert Taggart, *The Promise of Greatness* (Harvard University Press, 1976), p. 196.

51. See, for example, Kershaw, *Government Against Poverty;* Levine, *The Poor Ye Need Not Have with You;* Moynihan, ed., *On Understanding Poverty;* Levitan, *The Great Society's Poor Law;* Levitan and Taggart, *The Promise of Greatness;* and Sundquist, ed., *On Fighting Poverty*.

52. Robert A. Levine asserts that the goals of equal opportunity and the end of egregiously unequal outcomes were bound together in legislation but not necessarily in logic. See *The Poor Ye Need Not Have with You*, pp. 30–32.

53. See Robert J. Lampman, "What Does It Do for the Poor? A New Test for National Policy," *Public Interest*, no. 34 (Winter 1974), p. 66; and James L. Sundquist, *Politics and Policy: The Eisenhower, Kennedy, and Johnson Years* (Brookings Institution, 1968).

54. The text adopts Robert A. Levine's historical periodization. See *The Poor Ye Need Not Have with You*, pp. 44–45. Also see Levitan, *The Great Society's Poor Law;* and Moynihan, "The Professors and the Poor," in Moynihan, ed., *On Understanding Poverty*.

55. Robert A. Levine observes that "at least it is better to think of the antipoverty effort as a war than as a crusade, in which any setback is a victory for evil, and the moral imperative is to defeat the perpetrators of evil rather than to solve the problem." *The Poor Ye Need Not Have with You*, p. 11.

56. *Economic Report of the President together with the Annual Report of the Council of Economic Advisers, January 1964*, p. 56.

57. Robert Lampman defended this approach explicitly. "Although economists are wont to look to an index of inequality of income shares in comparing the fairness of result of one political economy with that of another, this particular measure has never had any standing among political leaders." "What Does It Do for the Poor?" p. 73. Also, "As I see it, the elimination of income poverty is usefully thought of as a one-time operation in pursuit of a goal unique to this generation. That goal should be achieved before 1980, at which time the next generation will have set new economic and social goals, perhaps including a new distributional goal for themselves." Robert J. Lampman, *Ends and Means of Reducing Income Poverty* (Markham, 1971), p. 53.

58. Levine, *The Poor Ye Need Not Have with You*, p. 49, and Moynihan, "The Professors and the Poor."

59. Daniel P. Moynihan, *Maximum Feasible Misunderstanding: Com-*

munity Action in the War on Poverty (Free Press, 1969), p. 168. Moynihan attributes these four views to the Ford Foundation and Paul Ylvisaker, Richard Cloward and Lloyd Ohlin, Saul Alinsky, and Sargent Shriver, respectively. Moynihan seemed to feel that in this case at least an institution with several objectives or one that uses a variety of means is doomed to confusion, mismanagement, and failure. Why this should be the case when the institution operates through more than 1,000 quasi-independent local agencies, some of which may pursue one strategy, some another, is far from clear. A sympathetic critic might have praised an institution whose task it was to integrate four intellectual traditions where possible or to pursue the one best suited to particular problems.

60. Levine, *The Poor Ye Need Not Have with You,* p. 159.

61. Sundquist cites a remark by Robert A. Levine that "academicians tend to look for single causes for social problems and single cures to solve the problems. They talk too frequently about alternative 'strategies' in which a choice must be made between this way or that way of solving a problem, when in this real world it will take both ways and probably a half dozen others to accomplish anything." James Sundquist, "The End of the Experiment?" in Sundquist, ed., *On Fighting Poverty,* p. 248.

62. Kershaw with Courant, *Government Against Poverty,* p. 22.

63. Ibid., p. 24.

64. For discussions of the negative income tax experiment, see *Journal of Human Resources,* vol. 9 (Spring 1974), pp. 156–278; Glen G. Cain and Harold W. Watts, "Toward a Summary and Synthesis of the Evidence," in Cain and Watts, eds., *Income Maintenance and Labor Supply: Econometric Studies* (Rand McNally, 1973), pp. 328–67; and Stanley Masters and Irwin Garfinkel, *Estimating Labor Supply Effects of Income Maintenance Programs* (Academic Press, forthcoming).

65. The big push for PPBS came from the Bureau of the Budget (subsequently renamed the Office of Management and Budget), not an operating agency. Cost benefit analysis had long been practiced by the Corps of Engineers in selecting among projects, but their procedures left a good deal to be desired from a technical standpoint.

66. Levine, *The Poor Ye Need Not Have with You,* pp. 158–67.

67. The term was originated by Alice M. Rivlin, "Forensic Social Science," *Harvard Educational Review,* vol. 43 (February 1973), pp. 61–75.

68. John F. Kain, "Housing Segregation, Negro Employment, and Metropolitan Decentralization," *Quarterly Journal of Economics,* vol. 82 (May 1968), pp. 175–97.

69. Quoted by John F. Kain, "Housing Segregation, Black Employment, and Metropolitan Decentralization: A Retrospective View," in George M. von Furstenberg, Bennett Harrison, and Ann R. Horowitz, eds., *Patterns of Racial Discrimination,* vol. 1: *Housing* (Heath, 1974), p. 5.

70. Joseph D. Mooney, "Housing Segregation, Negro Employment and Metropolitan Decentralization: An Alternative Perspective," *Quarterly Journal of Economics,* vol. 83 (May 1969), p. 308.

71. Paul Offner and Daniel H. Saks, "A Note on John Kain's 'Housing Segregation, Negro Employment and Metropolitan Decentralization,' " *Quarterly Journal of Economics*, vol. 85 (February 1971), pp. 147–60; Stanley H. Masters, "A Note on John Kain's 'Housing Segregation, Negro Employment and Metropolitan Decentralization,' " *Quarterly Journal of Economics*, vol. 88 (August 1974), pp. 505–12.

72. Lampman, "What Does It Do for the Poor?" p. 74.

73. This point is made forcefully by Levin, "A Decade of Policy Developments."

74. Levitan and Taggart, *The Promise of Greatness*, p. 196.

75. Samuel Bowles, "Schooling and Inequality from Generation to Generation," *Journal of Political Economy*, vol. 80 (May–June 1972, pt. 2), p. S220.

76. *Economic Report of the President together with the Annual Report of the Council of Economic Advisers, January 1965*, p. 163; *Other America*, p. 21.

77. If 31 percent of the poor in one year left poverty the next and stayed out, then of those poor in 1962, 48 percent would be poor in 1964, 33 percent in 1965, 23 percent in 1966, 16 percent in 1967, and 3.5 percent in 1971. Under alternative assumptions the statistics cited by the CEA were consistent with persistent poverty.

78. Harold Watts reports in private correspondence considerable effort within OEO in the late 1960s to determine whether poverty was persistent or transitory. One can also find a few writers who later emphasized actual or possible turnover among the poor. S. M. Miller and Pamela Roby later wrote, "There may be considerable turnover in these bottom groups [those who lag behind the rest of society in one or more dimension of life]. Although we lack data showing what proportion of persons in the bottom groups move in and out of poverty, we do know that a life-cycle pattern is of some importance. . . ." "Poverty: Changing Social Stratification," in Moynihan, ed., *On Understanding Poverty*, p. 78. Stephan Thernstrom wrote in 1968: "[T]here has been . . . a failure to think about poverty in dynamic, or longitudinal, terms; a failure to conceive it as a status that people enter and leave over time, a status of which the social meaning depends, in considerable measure, on the patterns that govern entry into, persistence in, and exit from the status. Thus, a contemporary study that estimates that 10 per cent, let us say, of the citizens in a given society are living in poverty may mean that everyone in the society is impoverished for part, but only part, of his life—the graduate-student poverty model, let us call it—or it may mean that 10 per cent of the citizens are born poor, live poor, and die poor, with no one else ever experiencing deprivation. Obviously, the policy problems posed by these two extreme cases and the solutions that might make sense differ radically. As will be shown later, the massive volume of research that has been conducted on poverty in present-day America provides dismayingly little information about this crucial dimension of the phenomenon." "Poverty in Historical Perspective," in ibid., p. 161.

79. Levy, "How Big Is the American Underclass?" pp. 21, 24–25, 54.

80. The fraction is somewhere between 12 and 36 percent but cannot be

calculated from published tabulations. See Department of Health, Education, and Welfare, "The Changing Economic Status of 5000 American Families," p. 14.

81. See Sar A. Levitan and Robert Taggart, *Jobs for the Disabled* (Johns Hopkins University Press, 1977), p. 4.

82. Burton A. Weisbrod and W. Lee Hansen, "An Income-Net Worth Approach to Measuring Economic Welfare," *American Economic Review*, vol. 58 (December 1968), p. 1325.

83. Lampman, "What Does It Do for the Poor?" p. 68. See also Miller and Roby, "Poverty: Changing Social Stratification," p. 78.

84. Robert A. Levine drew an analogy between the poverty threshold and the distinction between nuclear and conventional weapons. "Nuclear weapons, it was argued, should be used in warfare simply because they were more efficient than their conventional counterparts—more power for a pound. The argument that won out, however, was that the admittedly arbitrary line between nuclear and conventional weapons was a distinction that already existed in the minds of political and military decision makers; once this line was broken, all differences would become differences of degree, and there would be no other accepted line at which escalation could be stopped on the way to the megaton. . . . Thus, although the existing poverty lines are arbitrary both for statistical measurement and for operational purposes, some arbitrary lines are needed and these serve well simply because they already exist as a convention." *The Poor Ye Need Not Have with You,* pp. 18–19. It is not clear what form of holocaust would have resulted from breaches of the conventional ways of measuring poverty. But the value of accepted conventions, even imperfect ones, is undeniable.

85. Robert W. Kilpatrick, "The Income Elasticity of the Poverty Line," *Review of Economics and Statistics,* vol. 55 (August 1973), pp. 327–32.

86. See *Ends and Means of Reducing Income Poverty,* p. 53.

87. Lee Rainwater, *What Money Buys: Inequality and the Social Meanings of Income* (Basic Books, 1974), p. 9.

88. Peter Gottschalk, "Earnings, Transfers and Poverty Reduction" (Mount Holyoke College, n.d.; processed), p. 10.

89. See Benjamin A. Okner and Alice M. Rivlin, "Income Distribution Policy in the United States" (Brookings Institution, 1975; processed); Peter Henle, "Exploring the Distribution of Earned Income," *Monthly Labor Review,* vol. 95 (December 1972), pp. 16–27; Sheldon Danziger and Robert Plotnick, "Demographic Change, Government Transfers, and the Distribution of Income," discussion paper 274–75 (University of Wisconsin–Madison, Institute for Research on Poverty, 1975; processed); Gottschalk, "Earnings, Transfers and Poverty Reduction"; and Robert D. Plotnick and Felicity Skidmore, *Progress against Poverty: A Review of the 1964–1974 Decade* (Academic Press, 1975).

90. Timothy Smeeding, "Measuring the Economic Welfare of Low Income Households and the Antipoverty Effectiveness of Cash and Noncash Transfer

Programs" (Ph.D. dissertation, University of Wisconsin–Madison, 1975), table 8.

91. Plotnick and Skidmore, *Progress against Poverty*, p. 164. Edgar Browning asserts that "when in-kind transfers . . . are counted as income, the average poor family in 1973 had an income that was approximately 30 per cent *above* the poverty line." Edgar K. Browning, "How Much More Inequality Can We Afford?" *Public Interest*, no. 43 (Spring 1976), p. 92. This statement is somewhat misleading, however, as not all poor persons receive aid or the average amount of aid.

92. James D. Smith and Stephen D. Franklin, "The Concentration of Personal Wealth, 1922–1969," *American Economic Review*, vol. 64 (May 1974, *Papers and Proceedings, 1973*), p. 166.

93. Alicia H. Munnell, *The Future of Social Security* (Brookings Institution, 1977), p. 118. See also Martin Feldstein, "Social Security, Induced Retirement, and Aggregate Capital Accumulation," *Journal of Political Economy*, vol. 82 (September–October 1974), pp. 905–26.

94. Orley Ashenfelter, "Changes in Labor Market Discrimination Over Time," *Journal of Human Resources*, vol. 5 (Fall 1970), pp. 403–30. For more up-to-date statistics, see Orley Ashenfelter, "Comment on Black/White Male Earnings and Employment, 1960–1970," in F. Thomas Juster, ed., *The Distribution of Economic Well-Being* (Columbia University Press for the National Bureau of Economic Research, 1977). See also Wayne Vroman, "Changes in Black Workers' Relative Earnings: Evidence from the 1960s," in von Furstenberg, Harrison, and Horowitz, eds., *Patterns of Racial Discrimination*, vol. 2: *Employment and Income*, pp. 167–87; Richard B. Freeman, "Changes in the Labor Market for Black Americans, 1948–72," *Brookings Papers on Economic Activity, 1:1973*, pp. 67–120.

95. U.S. Bureau of the Census, *Current Population Reports*, series P-60, no. 53, "Income in 1966 of Families and Persons in the United States" (GPO, 1967), p. 51, and series P-60, no. 97, "Money Income in 1973 of Families and Persons in the United States" (GPO, 1975), p. 149.

96. The methodology used by the Bureau of the Census in deriving money income statistics was revised in 1975, making direct comparison with previous years difficult. However, the bureau supplied the ratio for 1974 on the new basis from unpublished data. The 1975 data are from Bureau of the Census, *Current Population Reports*, series P-60, no. 105, "Money Income in 1975 of Families and Persons in the United States" (GPO, 1977), p. 246.

97. The literature showing much smaller returns to education for blacks than for whites is voluminous. See Giora Hanoch, "An Economic Analysis of Earnings and Schooling," *Journal of Human Resources*, vol. 2 (Summer 1967), pp. 310–29; Randall D. Weiss, "The Effect of Education on the Earnings of Blacks and Whites," *Review of Economics and Statistics*, vol. 52 (May 1970), pp. 150–59; and Bennett Harrison, "Education and Underemployment in the Urban Ghetto," *American Economic Review*, vol. 62 (December 1972), pp. 796–812. Studies based on recent data tell a quite different story. Finis

Welch estimated that in 1966 an additional year of schooling was worth $650 per year to a black high school graduate with one to three years of experience, but only $460 to a white. For those with four to seven years of experience, the values were $550 and $530, respectively. For those with more experience—that is, for those who had entered the labor force before the 1960s—an additional year of schooling was worth more to a white than to a black high school graduate. In 1959, the value of an additional year of schooling to a black high school graduate with one to four years of experience had been $120, compared with $250 to a white. All these estimates exclude indirect benefits of schooling —through unemployment, for example—which disproportionately increase the value of education to blacks. Finis Welch, "Black-White Differences in Returns to Schooling," *American Economic Review,* vol. 63 (December 1973), p. 903. Others have placed the increase in the relative value of a year of schooling much lower. Haworth, Gwartney, and Haworth estimate that the value of a year of schooling to a black aged twenty-five to thirty-four in 1969 was 60 percent of its value to a white, compared with 53 percent in 1959. Joan Gustafson Haworth, James Gwartney, and Charles Haworth, "Earnings, Productivity, and Changes in Employment Discrimination During the 1960's," *American Economic Review,* vol. 65 (March 1975), p. 165. Welch's estimates are based on years of experience, a closer correlate of earnings than age, and are to be preferred. Leonard Weiss and Jeffrey G. Williamson found that additional education was worth about as much to blacks in 1967 as to whites in 1960. "Black Education, Earnings, and Interregional Migration: Some New Evidence," *American Economic Review,* vol. 62 (June 1972), p. 382. In contrast, see Geoffrey Carliner, "Returns to Education for Blacks, Anglos, and Five Spanish Groups," *Journal of Human Resources,* vol. 11 (Spring 1976), pp. 172–84.

98. U.S. Department of Health, Education, and Welfare, Office of Income Security Policy, "The Impacts of Inflation and Higher Unemployment: With Emphasis on the Lower Income Population," technical analysis paper 2 (Office of Income Security Policy, October 1974; processed); and Edward M. Gramlich, "The Distributional Effects of Higher Unemployment," *Brookings Papers on Economic Activity,* 2:1974, pp. 293–336, both demonstrate that low-income households suffer more than middle- and upper-income households from high unemployment. The corollary, of course, is that low-income households benefit more than middle- or upper-income households from tight labor markets. For each 1 percentage point change in the average unemployment rate Gramlich estimates unemployment of black males aged twenty-five to fifty-four changes 1.7 percentage points. Inflation is shown to have a negligible impact on the distribution of income among income classes, although individuals within income classes may be greatly affected.

99. Richard Freeman has presented evidence that discriminatory denial by state governments of equal access to public education and other services may have contributed to the relative economic decline of blacks following the end of reconstruction. See Richard B. Freeman, "Decline of Labor Market Dis-

crimination and Economic Analysis," *American Economic Review,* vol. 63 (May 1973, *Papers and Proceedings, 1972*), pp. 280–86.

100. In 1940 the median white twenty-five and over had 8.7 years of schooling, the median nonwhite only 5.7 years. By 1960, median attainments for whites and nonwhites were 10.8 and 8.2 years, respectively. In 1975 the median attainments were 12.4 and 11.4 years, respectively, showing a decline in both the relative and the absolute gaps. W. Vance Grant and C. George Lind, *Digest of Education Statistics, 1975 Edition,* U.S. National Center for Education Statistics (GPO, 1976), table 11, p. 14. In southern states, Finis Welch reports that the average days attended per pupil in 1919–20 was 121 days in all schools, but only 80 days in Negro schools; by 1953–54 the average attendance in all schools and Negro schools was 159 and 151 days, respectively. "Black-White Differences in Returns to Schooling," p. 900. According to a 1965 survey, Negroes tested well below whites in all subjects, at all grade levels, and in all geographical regions. By the twelfth grade the lag of blacks behind the average white in the metropolitan northeast was 3.3 and 2.9 years behind grade level in verbal ability and reading comprehension, respectively. James C. Coleman and others, *Equality of Educational Opportunity* (GPO, 1966), pp. 274–75 (referred to as the Coleman Report).

101. Duran Bell, "Why Participation Rates of Black and White Wives Differ," *Journal of Human Resources,* vol. 9 (Fall 1974), pp. 465–79.

102. Richard B. Freeman, "Changes in the Labor Market for Black Americans, 1948–72," *Brookings Papers on Economic Activity, 1:1973,* p. 67.

103. Robert E. Hall and Richard A. Kasten, "The Relative Occupational Success of Blacks and Whites," *Brookings Papers on Economic Activity, 3:1973,* pp. 781–95.

104. Haworth, Gwartney, and Haworth, "Earnings, Productivity, and Changes in Employment Discrimination During the 1960's," p. 162.

105. Weiss, "Effect of Education on Earnings"; Hall and Kasten, "Relative Occupational Success."

106. Ann R. Horowitz, "The Pattern and Causes of Changes in White-Nonwhite Income Differences: 1947–1972," in von Furstenberg, Harrison, and Horowitz, eds., *Patterns of Racial Discrimination,* vol. 2: *Employment and Income,* p. 163.

107. See Ray Marshall, "The Economics of Racial Discrimination: A Survey," *Journal of Economic Literature,* vol. 12 (September 1974), pp. 849–71.

108. Barbara R. Bergmann, "The Effect on White Incomes of Discrimination in Employment," *Journal of Political Economy,* vol. 79 (March–April 1971), pp. 294–313. Preliminary versions of this paper circulated as early as 1965.

109. Analysis by Orley Ashenfelter suggests that unions other than those in the construction trades did not discriminate against blacks more than non-unionized employers. See "Racial Discrimination and Trade Unionism," *Journal of Political Economy,* vol. 80 (May–June 1972, pt. 1), pp. 435–64.

110. Otis Dudley Duncan, "Inheritance of Poverty or Inheritance of

Race?" in Moynihan, ed., *On Understanding Poverty*, pp. 85–110; Alan S. Blinder, "Wage Discrimination: Reduced Form and Structural Estimates," *Journal of Human Resources*, vol. 8 (Fall 1973), pp. 436–55.

111. Bradley R. Schiller, "Class Discrimination vs. Racial Discrimination," *Review of Economics and Statistics*, vol. 53 (August 1971), pp. 263–69. These results agree with those of Duncan.

112. The first explanation is really a special case of the more general possibility that the analyses were improperly done, either because the statistical models incorporated the wrong mathematical form relating income differentials to education, place of residence, or other variables, or because relevant variables were excluded inadvertently from the analysis or are unmeasured or unmeasurable. The omission of genetic differences, such as IQ, would be an example of an unmeasured variable in most of the surveys used in the analyses. The possibility that the research is improperly done—that is, that the measured differences between blacks and whites fully explain the differences between them in income or unemployment—has received almost no attention as the reason why differences between blacks and whites cannot be fully explained. The failure to criticize analytical methods contrasts sharply with the way in which research on the relation between education and income has been reviewed. See chapter 3 below, where shortcomings of analytical methods in the study of the relation between education and income are prominent, and chapter 5, where the reasons for such an inconsistent approach are defended. Irwin Garfinkel, Robert Haveman, and David Betson estimate that 43 to 60 percent of the gap between black and white earnings is due to discrimination in the labor market. See "Labor Market Discrimination and Black-White Differences in Economic Status," discussion paper 403–77 (University of Wisconsin–Madison, Institute for Research on Poverty, 1977; processed), p. 13.

113. Arthur R. Jensen, "How Much Can We Boost IQ and Scholastic Achievement?" *Harvard Educational Review*, vol. 39 (Winter 1969), pp. 1–123. Also see Leon J. Kamin, *The Science and Politics of I.Q.* (Wiley, 1974).

114. See Nicholas Wade, "IQ and Heredity: Suspicion of Fraud Beclouds Classic Experiment," *Science*, vol. 194 (November 26, 1976), pp. 916–19.

115. Felicity Skidmore, "Nature-Nurture Nonsense," *Focus on Poverty Research*, vol. 1 (Spring–Summer 1976), p. 4; she also summarizes recent research by Goldberger. See Arthur S. Goldberger, "Mysteries of the Meritocracy," in N. J. Block and Gerald Dworkin, eds., *The IQ Controversy: Critical Readings* (Random House, 1976), pp. 265–79 (originally, University of Wisconsin–Madison, Institute for Research on Poverty, discussion paper 225–74); Goldberger, "Statistical Inference in the Great IQ Debate," discussion paper 301–75 (Institute for Research on Poverty, 1975; processed); Goldberger and Richard C. Lewontin, "Jensen's Twin Fantasy," discussion paper 341–76 (Institute for Research on Poverty, 1976; processed); Goldberger, "Jensen on Burks," and Goldberger, "On Jensen's Method for Twins," *Educational Psychologist*, vol. 12, no. 1 (1976), pp. 64–78 and 79–82, respectively (both in Institute for Research on Poverty reprint 195).

116. Milton Friedman uses this line of reasoning to maintain that competi-

tive methods are better designed than any other to end discrimination. He does not indicate why discrimination persists. See *Capitalism and Freedom* (University of Chicago Press, 1962).

117. Barbara R. Bergmann, "Occupational Segregation, Wages and Profits when Employers Discriminate by Race or Sex," *Eastern Economic Journal,* vol. 1 (April–July 1974), pp. 103–10.

118. The discussion in the text of the use of race, sex, or other attributes to discriminate among workers, buyers, or sellers is based on a series of studies of statistical discrimination and market signaling including the following: A. Michael Spence, *Market Signaling: Informational Transfer in Hiring and Related Screening Processes* (Harvard University Press, 1974); Edmund S. Phelps, "The Statistical Theory of Racism and Sexism," *American Economic Review,* vol. 62 (September 1972), pp. 659–61; George A. Akerlof, "The Market for 'Lemons': Quality Uncertainty and the Market Mechanism," *Quarterly Journal of Economics,* vol. 84 (August 1970), pp. 488–500; Joseph E. Stiglitz, "Approaches to the Economics of Discrimination," *American Economic Review,* vol. 63 (May 1973, *Papers and Proceedings, 1972*), pp. 287–95; and Stiglitz, "The Theory of 'Screening,' Education, and the Distribution of Income," *American Economic Review,* vol. 65 (June 1975), pp. 283–300.

119. Edward Denison, for example, has observed, "The intellectual community objects if race intrudes into the college selection process and is uneasy if access to higher education depends on parents' income, but it seems content and even pleased when colleges select and retain students on the basis of ability. How often do intellectuals raise a hue and cry because John, graduating from high school with an IQ of 150, scores of 790 on his college boards, and a straight A average, is admitted to Harvard with a scholarship while his classmate Mike, equally diligent and with similar character testimonials, but with an IQ of 100, scores below 400 on his college boards, and a C– average, is admitted nowhere and must enter the labor market with whatever skills he may have acquired? I have not heard it." Edward F. Denison, "An Aspect of Inequality of Opportunity," *Journal of Political Economy,* vol. 78 (September–October 1970), pp. 1195–96. Harry Johnson makes the same point: "If poverty or inequality is considered a problem, one should recognize that the poorest among us, and the one most deserving of help from his fellow men, is the one whom nature forgot to endow with brains—and that the way to make it up to him is not to exclude him from school and tax him to pay part of the cost of educating his intellectually well-endowed and no-longer-poor peer group among the children of poor parents, but to give him money in lieu of the brains he lacks. Superior intelligence or skill is undoubtedly more economically useful than the absence of it, but discriminating in favor of it by fiscal subsidization will not necessarily produce a more democratic and poverty-free or egalitarian society." Harry G. Johnson, "The Alternatives before Us," *Journal of Political Economy,* vol. 80 (May–June 1972, pt. 2), p. S289. Presumably the argument on behalf of discrimination by intelligence is based on the judgment that such discrimination will promote economic efficiency even if it makes the distribution of income less equal, while no such

defense can be made for racial discrimination; and even if it could, most people would regard it as insufficient. See Arthur M. Okun, *Equality and Efficiency: The Big Tradeoff* (Brookings Institution, 1975).

120. The much-quoted statement of Ewald B. Nyquist, New York State Education Commissioner, is apposite. Deploring the fact that not even 1 of 758 school superintendents in upstate districts was female, he remarked, "Equality is not when a female Einstein gets promoted to assistant professor; equality is when a female schlemiel moves ahead as fast as a male schlemiel." *New York Times,* October 9, 1975.

121. George Akerlof presciently warned specifically of pitfalls in analyzing the effectiveness of the poverty program: "An additional worry is that the Office of Economic Opportunity is going to use cost-benefit analysis to evaluate its programs. For many benefits may be external. The benefit from training minority groups may arise as much from raising the average quality of the group as from raising the quality of the individual trainee; and likewise, the returns may be distributed over the whole group rather than to the individual." "The Market for 'Lemons,' " p. 495.

122. Spence, *Market Signaling,* p. 100.

chapter three Education and Jobs: A Swinging Pendulum

"With respect to the distribution of personal income, . . . changes in the investment in human capital are the basic factors reducing the inequality in the distribution of personal income. . . . Modifications in income transfers, in progressive taxation, and in the distribution of privately owned wealth are relatively weak factors in altering the distribution of personal income."—Theodore W. Schultz, "Reflections on Investment in Man," *Journal of Political Economy,* vol. 70 (October 1962, supplement), p. 2.

"I do not know anyone who contends that education reform is a more effective way to reduce the inequality of income than giving the poor more money."—Alice M. Rivlin, "Forensic Social Science," *Harvard Educational Review,* vol. 43 (February 1973), p. 65.

The American public's love affair with education, now more than a century old, has undergone some rather severe strains in the past decade. The beneficent consequences thought to flow from education have been numerous, though frequently vague and often unverifiable, but at least one, additional income, was precise and measurable. In the course of the 1960s the effect of education on income was first taken for granted, then measured and found to be substantial, and finally called into doubt.

The two quotations at the opening of this chapter represent the change of heart among scholars in their view of the impact of education on income, from its high point in the early 1960s as an all-powerful transformer of economic potential to its low point in the early 1970s as an ineffective instrument that had few, if any, predictable consequences. This chapter recounts this transformation in attitudes about education. It describes the initial faith and points out its naiveté, recounts the destruction of that faith by analysis which upon close examination was insufficient either to support or to refute it, and suggests that the vague outlines of the relation between education and economic performance are only now emerging from a haze of conflicting analyses by scholars.

Naive Hopes and Simple Faiths

That education improves the student's chances of high earnings has been accepted for decades. Schooling improves cognitive abilities, changes habits, alters values, and broadens acquaintances. The importance of each of these changes for productivity was thought to be greater for males than for females. Men got jobs; women got husbands. Whatever the mechanisms by which productivity might be increased, the reward for enhanced economic potential would be increased economic reward—in other words, higher income. As a result education was regarded as nearly essential for success in well-paid jobs. In contrast, ignorance and economic deprivation were perceived as causing one another.

A widely cited attempt to put a price tag on the economic value of education in the United States was Paul Glick's estimate that in 1950 a college education was worth $103,000—the difference between $165,000 and $268,000, the lifetime earnings a high school graduate and college graduate, respectively, could expect.[1] This estimate was cited without amendment nearly a decade later by the National Education Association.[2] Similar estimates were presented in 1960 without regard for the criticisms made of Glick's earlier estimates that people with various amounts of education also differed in natural abilities and numerous other characteristics that might affect earnings independently of education.[3]

Other scholars criticized such estimates, but took them quite seriously. One put the value of a college education at $200,000 to $250,000 over a lifetime.[4] Another suggested that the popular estimate of $100,000 was an upper bound for the true worth of college, because college graduates differ from the rest of the population in having more intelligence, coming from higher-income families, and in getting larger inheritances.[5]

The Human Capital Revolution

Meanwhile, many scholars began to study the relation between education and earnings, driven by the powerful new theory of human capital. The organizing principle of human capital analysis was that skills, actual or imagined, are durable and malleable.[6] That is, workers, by spending money on such things as education or training and by forgoing earnings while acquiring them, could increase either their actual productive capacity or the perception of that capacity by employers. As one early contributor put it, "The concept of human capital formation . . . rests on the twin notions that people as productive agents are improved by invest-ment[s] . . . and that the outlays made yield a continuing return in the future. . . . The future increase in labor product resulting from education or from health programs can be quantified to an extent useful for program-ming purposes."[7] This theory has roots going back to Adam Smith and may be traced in the writings of nineteenth century economists.[8] But it blossomed in the late 1950s and early 1960s, initially at the hands of three economists, Theodore Schultz, Jacob Mincer, and Gary Becker. Then dozens of others developed and refined the concept, drawing from it in-ferences about the structure of wages and the behavior of employers and workers.[9]

The centerpiece of analyses of human capital was a collection of esti-mates of the rate of return to investments in human capital, most notably to education. The differences in earnings of people with different amounts of education were compared with the costs of acquiring the additional edu-cation. If the resources devoted to education had been invested, what rate of return on this investment would have been necessary to generate the resulting difference in earnings? Alternatively, the question could be posed somewhat differently: suppose that a sum of money equal to the cost of education had been borrowed at a prevailing market interest rate. By how much would the resulting stream of increased earnings associated with the education exceed the cost of repaying the amount borrowed, plus interest?

However the question was put, education seemed a very good invest-ment indeed, with rates of return equal to or exceeding those yielded by ordinary investments and repaying more than the cost of education plus interest at prevailing rates.[10] The extra cost of going beyond primary edu-cation yielded very high returns, exceeding 20 percent. The return on edu-cation beyond college was smaller, but still respectable. The theory also explained why the rate of return to education was at least as high as the rate of return to other investments: the fact that human capital could not be used as collateral for loans imposed limits on the amount of higher education most people could acquire.[11]

Additional education was associated with much smaller increases in earnings for blacks and for women than for white males.[12] Initially, this discrepancy was explained in one of three ways: discrimination, which de-nied people the capacity to use education; the higher quality of education available to whites, an advantage not captured by the most commonly used measure of education, years of schooling; and, especially, in the case of women, limited freedom to pursue careers. The first and third of these explanations provoked other questions. Why had the quest for profits not led employers to compete and to undercut earnings differentials attributable to discrimination? Why were women paid less than men even for seemingly identical work? These questions went to the foundations of the human capital approach and, indeed, of conventional economic analysis and eventually led some to abandon both.

In their most primitive form, estimates of the rate of return to investment in education represented only slight technical improvements over the crude and naive calculations from the 1950s of the value of a college education. They were technical improvements because they incorporated the important fact that deferred returns are worth less than immediate ones, and because they sometimes, but not always, controlled for some obvious differences other than education that distinguished, say, high school graduates from college graduates.[13]

The major contribution of the human capital literature, however, was not the empirical estimates of the rate of return to education, but the theory that related education to productivity and earnings. By likening education to investment in durable structures or machines, the theory of human capital created a powerful metaphor in which to express the view, widespread among the general public and held quite independently of any academic analysis, that education was a means to self-improvement and social advancement. The independent analysis of education as a force for economic growth contributed to that metaphor.[14]

Because the theory of human capital was stated with some precision, sometimes verbally, sometimes mathematically, it sharpened thought about the role and value of education in three quite distinct ways. First, it yielded a set of insights about the relation between education and earnings, the confirmation of which seemed to support the theory. For example, the theory predicted that in those states where educational attainments of workers varied most widely, earned incomes would also vary most widely.[15] Second, the theory of human capital yielded a set of predictions or inferences about the relation between changes in education and changes in earnings. These predictions were not always correct, and efforts to reconcile the anomalies have led to enrichment of the theory of human capital and the creation of a number of alternative explanations about how education and earnings are related.

For example, many thought that the vast increase in the number of college graduates would reduce the difference between earnings of college and high school graduates. That no such reduction occurred was a major puzzle.[16] Numerous explanations were possible. Demand for college graduates might be rising as fast as supply, although this explanation was circular as demand could only be inferred from the wage differential that increases in demand were supposed to explain. Alternatively, colleges might have been admitting increasingly able students. Selectivity did seem to be increasing,[17] but it was hard to tell whether it could account for the continued high earnings differential. The most satisfactory answer for those who accept the theory of human capital seems to be that there never was any puzzle at all. The increase in college graduates was almost entirely absorbed by graduate schools and government employment during the 1960s and did not reach the competitive wage market until the 1970s, at which time the wage differential between college and high school graduates narrowed perceptibly.[18]

A second puzzle—why women and blacks are paid less than white males with equal education and why the gap between earnings of black and white males failed to narrow despite a decline in the gap between educational attainments of these groups—caused more trouble. Discrimination, the obvious answer, merely labeled the puzzle but did not tell how to resolve it.

Human capital theory also encouraged its users to look at the mechanisms by which education affects earnings. The fact that scholastic achievement as measured by standardized tests was only loosely related to subsequent earnings had been known for a long time. But if such tests were accepted as a good measure of the effectiveness of schools, as many believed, then how could schools have much effect on earnings? The answer was that schools did many things, some of which tests measured and some of which they did not. Moreover, pupils might do well in one area, but not in others. As one scholar wrote, "[T]he output of schools is multidimensional with a vengeance. . . . Moreover, the technologies for the production of each dimension of the output are blatantly dissimilar."[19] In plain English, that meant that the one or two measures of schooling most commonly used in estimating the economic value of education, such as years attended or test scores, could not adequately describe the effects of education.[20] Upon close examination, the theory of human capital was seen to be a good deal less precise and rigorous in linking activities in the school to subsequent earnings than it had at first seemed to be. This developing awareness has taken place gradually over more than a decade and still continues.

Education and Public Policy

Before these intellectual developments occurred, however, the theory of human capital and the widespread set of preconceptions of which it was the academic manifestation saw considerable action in the political arena. Three related issues stand out: economic growth, poverty, and federal aid to education.

ECONOMIC GROWTH. Following four postwar recessions and a period of higher-than-customary unemployment, the issue of economic growth assumed political and intellectual salience in the early 1960s. From the promise of Democratic presidential nominee John F. Kennedy to "get this country moving again" (a promise that included, but was not confined to, economic momentum) through the burgeoning economic subdiscipline of growth models, a sense that economic growth should be deliberately accelerated was widespread. In his Richard T. Ely lecture before the annual convention of economists in 1963, James Tobin expressed a popular view when he argued that a deliberate policy to accelerate growth should be undertaken. One of his discussants, while skeptical about Tobin's reasons for promoting growth, nevertheless agreed that steps should be taken to direct capital to education in order to increase economic growth.[21]

In more popular forums, other economists argued that more should be invested in research and education and less in tangible assets such as factories, structures, and the development of commodities they perceived as useless.[22] Restraining any penchant for understatement, Kenneth Boulding expressed the fear that without a reallocation of 5 to 10 percent of investments to research, education, and development, "it may well be that the problems in social systems created by the enormous changes in physical and biological systems will be too great, and this society, which is a social system, will not survive."[23] Thus, education, in which too little had been invested, as indicated by the high rates of return on it, was a major source both past and potential of economic growth. By increasing expenditures on education it would be possible simultaneously to speed economic growth and to realize a handsome social return.[24]

POVERTY. The returns to additional investments in education if the investments were focused on the poor and the poorly educated seemed to be especially impressive. Estimated rates of return were greatest at low levels of education;[25] education was viewed as the key to improvement in the status of minorities. For example, Kenneth Clark stated unequivocally that "providing more effective education in our public schools for the children of the poor, Negro and white, is the crucial battle in the overall war against poverty and will determine its eventual success or failure."[26] Christopher Jencks, then enamored of the effectiveness of education, wrote: "In the long run there is abundant evidence that this investment [to equalize expenditures on education across income classes] would repay itself by raising taxable income and by cutting expenditures for welfare, unemployment, police and other slum symptoms."[27] Similar views were expressed by the Chamber of Commerce[28] and, officially, by the Council of Economic Advisers.[29]

But poor kids did not seem to do very well in school. The remedy for this difficulty was chosen, according to the preferences of the writer or speaker, from a long list of possible modifications in schools—smaller classes, better trained or more sensitive teachers, different curriculums, changed organization of schools or school systems, and so on through a list of reforms encompassing almost every aspect of the modern public school.

FEDERAL AID. The problem with the reforms, as well as with compensatory education, was that they tended to increase the already considerable financial burden imposed on state and local governments by the need to put up enough school buildings and to hire enough teachers to educate the swollen cohorts of the post–World War II baby boom. State and local governments, already laboring under the fiscal strain of educating more students, seemed unable to accept additional burdens of compensating for the educational deficits of the poor. The goal of identical educational standards and the nationwide benefits of an educated population seemed to justify federal payment for an increased part of the costs of education. Consequently, federal aid to education became a major and divisive issue in the early 1960s. If the issue of federal aid to education had not become entangled with the knotty problem of aid to parochial schools, there is little doubt that a majority of Congress would have supported such aid in the early 1960s—partly to relieve the fiscal burdens caused by the baby boom; partly to relieve low-income communities and states, which had the greatest perceived need to spend heavily on education and the fewest resources to do so; partly to provide federal support for the changes in educational practices necessary, it was thought, to make schools more effective for those groups not benefiting from schooling; and partly to reduce the large disparity in expenditures known to exist among various localities and states and thought to exist among blacks and whites and other groups within the population. Responding to widespread concern that federal aid meant federal control, the Committee for Economic Development declared that "the national interest in good schools everywhere and the national interest in a decentralized school system are not irreconcilable."[30] Several years later, a well-known labor economist sounded the same theme: "The American people are slowly coming to appreciate that the key to economic progress both for the individual and for the nation is the quantity and particularly the quality of the education and training available to present and prospective members of the work force. . . . A major solution is for the federal government to make larger sums available for the support of public education, particularly for those states which are unable to meet a reasonable minimum through their own devices."[31]

But the parochial school issue was inseparable from federal aid to education. Not until 1965 was the political impasse broken by a formula, incorporated in Title II of the Elementary and Secondary Education Act, according to which aid could be directed to school districts on the basis of the number of poor kids. In fact, large amounts of federal aid for education had been given since the Korean War as compensation to school districts for financial burdens imposed by having to educate children from families that did not contribute to the local tax base because of parental connection with the federal government. The appeal of such aid to local school districts, at the same time that other assistance was mired in the swamp of church-state issues, proves once again that in politics form often matters more than substance. Such "impacted areas aid" did not run afoul of the parochial school issue or arouse concern about federal interference with local control of schools, although, like the aid under the Elementary and Secondary Education Act, which at first carried few effective restrictions on use, it might have been expected to raise exactly the same issues.

In retrospect, the most remarkable characteristic of the debate over federal aid to education in the early 1960s was the great importance everyone attached to it. Federal aid to education increased total educational expenditures by only a few percentage points and yet it vied for first place in the list of the most important domestic social legislation.

Loss of Innocence

Americans' faith in the importance of education in determining future earnings existed in two forms—a popular and a scholarly version. They differed primarily in that the latter attempted to base the connection on an articulated theory and to measure the size of the impact with some precision. Both views rested on the perception that education increased productivity by improving cognitive or other skills and that productivity was closely related to earnings. Increase education, and you increase productivity; increase productivity, and you increase earnings. The faith was embodied in legislation creating education and training programs to reduce poverty by increasing the earnings of the poor. Later, when it became apparent that poverty would not yield to the rather meager increments in education and training expenditures by the federal government, analysts came forward with studies showing that the relation between education and earnings *might* be entirely spurious. As will become apparent, they did not show that the relationship *was* spurious, in the sense that they did not offer a single alternative explanation of the relationship that commanded general agreement. The result was a kind of agnosticism. In place of the belief that education had a sizable impact on earnings, a new faith arose that no known change in education could significantly affect earnings on the average.

To understand what happened one must recognize that the initial faith in education was both fatally imprecise and naively simplistic. It did not answer such questions as: Exactly what changes in education would affect earnings? Through what specific channels would such changes occur? Education could be altered in at least three distinct ways. Kids could be kept in school longer—more hours per day, more days per week, more weeks per year, more years; expenditures per unit of time could be increased in any number of ways—by building nicer schools, by reducing class size, by hiring teachers who commanded higher wages, by using more advanced equipment and materials; or the nature of activities within the school could be altered, without any necessary long-run increase in costs, by adopting open or ungraded classrooms, by abandoning marks, by using community resources, by changes in administration or in parental involvement, by devising new curriculums, or by the almost infinite number of educational reforms suggested at one time or another. There was no reason to think that these changes in education would affect all children in the same way or to the same degree. But if their effects were different, it was vital to know what those differences were.

The next step, from education to productivity, was equally vague. It was known that the performance of children differed on standardized tests and that such differences were correlated with a lot of things, including school performance. But it was not clear exactly what aspects of intelligence or motivation these standardized tests measured or how they correlated with productivity. Psychometricians had shown that different tests measure different things that are far from perfectly correlated. It was not known to what degree whatever tests measured was of use on the job. Furthermore, schools changed children in a host of ways not measured by standardized tests. Which were important for subsequent ability on the job? No one could say for sure.

Finally, the belief that education would affect earnings required either that employers base wages on the actual productivity of workers or that employers award jobs on the basis of educational attainment regardless of productivity. Only the former interpretation provided much support for public policies of compensatory education. If the latter interpretation were correct, one person's gain from additional education would be another person's loss. Despite the crucial importance of this distinction, belief in the former interpretation—enshrined in economics as the marginal productivity theory of wages—was accepted as a matter of logic and faith. The theory itself was remarkably vague.[32]

And how exactly was economic performance to be measured? Income might be depressed because of voluntary withdrawal from the labor force or involuntary unemployment, but the implications for economic well-being were rather different. What was the relevant period for measuring productivity—the hour, the week, the year, the lifetime?[33]

Scholars from various disciplines had addressed these questions for some time. Psychometricians tried to identify what tests measured. Educators studied how schools changed children and how changes in schools would change the changes. Economists struggled to measure the effects of education on earnings. But these individual concerns had not coalesced into a force sufficient to confront the faith that increases in education would lead to increases in earnings. In a word, the relationship between education and earnings was a "black box." Event B, higher earnings, followed event A, more education, but the process by which A led to B was not understood. A vague and plausible story asserted that A caused B; this story was accepted by the public and most scholars. But, as became clear in later years, other stories could be told that had very different social, economic, and political implications.

Paradoxically, it was the triumph of those who wished to use education as an instrument for equalizing opportunity through federal legislation that precipitated the demise of the faith. This legislation led to the creation within the Department of Health, Education, and Welfare and the Office of Economic Opportunity of two strong offices of research and evaluation capable of interpreting existing research, authorized to sponsor new research, and charged with the evaluation of the newly created federal programs. In addition, the Civil Rights Act of 1964 called for a survey and report on "the lack of availability of equal educational opportunities for individuals by reason of race, color, religion, or national origin" in public education.[34] The lack was taken for granted; only its magnitude was at issue.

Although hundreds of scholars have produced hundreds of studies on education, earnings, and equal opportunity since the early 1960s, three publications stand as milestones in the decline of the old simple faith in education: *Equality of Educational Opportunity,* the report compiled by a group of scholars under the chairmanship of James Coleman to satisfy the mandate in the Civil Rights Act of 1964; *How Effective Is Schooling?* a review of research on education through 1971 undertaken by a group of scholars from the Rand Corporation; and *Inequality,* by Christopher Jencks and a number of colleagues, a report of conclusions about the impact of schooling and other influences on various aspects of life experiences, including earnings.[35]

The Coleman Report

The survey on which *Equality of Educational Opportunity* was based was undertaken to document generally presumed disparities in the quality of education available to various groups. Just as blacks and certain other minorities were victims of palpable economic and social discrimination, so also, it was confidently believed, they were educated in schools less well financed, staffed, and supplied than those available to whites. It was to measure the size of this discrepancy, not to find out whether it existed, that the Equality of Educational Opportunity Survey was undertaken. The authors of the report went beyond this assignment and attempted to explain observed differences in performance on standardized tests with information about educational resources available from the survey. Thus, the Coleman Report, as *Equality of Educational Opportunity* came to be called, performed two functions: it summarized data on measurable educational inputs available to members of different racial groups in various parts of the country; and it reported the results of statistical analyses relating these inputs and various characteristics of the students to performance on standardized tests, the major proximate, quantifiable indicator of the success of education. The first job was legally mandated; the second was unsolicited.

Publication of the Coleman Report was an intellectual cause célèbre. The large differences between educational resources available to whites and those available to blacks and other minorities that everyone *knew* existed were not found. Whether one looked at age of buildings, class size, teacher characteristics, laboratories, libraries, gyms, availability and age of textbooks, access to special classes in such subjects as art and music, length of school year, curriculum, or any of the many other criteria that would permit one to say schools available to blacks, Puerto Ricans, or Mexican-Americans were better or worse than those available to Orientals or whites, the differences among resources available to these groups were small. What everyone knew to be true was *not* true. It was rather as if Coleman and his colleagues had just returned from the circumnavigation of a world everyone knew to be flat.[36]

If the findings with respect to differences in school and teacher characteristics available to different groups were surprising, the conclusions about the effect of these inputs on tests scores were sensational and devastating. The report confirmed that blacks and other minorities (other than Orientals) scored much lower than whites on standardized tests. It concluded that measurable characteristics of schools and teachers had very little to do with this marked difference in test scores. Rather, the socioeconomic characteristics of peers and family background characteristics of students were far more important. One Harvard professor is reported to have greeted another with "Guess what Coleman's found? . . . Schools make no difference; families make the difference."[37] Most of the variation in test scores was unexplained. The study seemed to imply that policymakers should pay less attention to tangible aspects of education they could control, such as class size, availability of science labs, and curriculum, and relatively more attention to things they could not directly control, such as the socioeconomic characteristics of schools and family background characteristics of students. After a review of research on the effectiveness of schooling that included not only the Coleman Report but also other studies that reached similar conclusions,[38] Averch and coworkers reached precisely this conclusion: "There is good reason to ask whether our educational problems are, in fact, school problems. The most profitable line of attack on educational problems may not, after all, be through the schools."[39]

The "findings" of the Coleman Report were consistent with either a conservative or a radical view of American society, but not with a liberal one. Conservatives could point to the apparent dominant influence of social class and claim that differences lie within the family and cannot be reduced by socially acceptable interventions, that the large amount of unexplained variation in test scores is genetic in origin, or that we were simply ignorant about the determinants of academic performance and should do nothing; in any case, the present order is more or less unchangeable. Radicals could claim that the order is determined through political power and class conflict and that schools merely replicate the pattern of power and of aspiration found in the existing generation. For liberals, the findings were devastating because they denied the possibility of instrumental change.

The report marked the opening of a fascinating academic controversy, still in progress. In part the fascination stems from the paradox that devastating criticisms of the report seem to have done more to spread knowledge about its findings and to increase their influence than could possibly have occurred if it had not been criticized. In some measure this paradox is resolved by the fact that the controversy has pretty much vindicated the factual findings of the report that measured resources available to blacks, whites, and others were roughly equal. At the same time, it has shown that snapshot data of a cross-section of the population are grossly inadequate for analyzing the effect of educational resources on the outcomes of schooling. It also has shown that the apparent ineffectiveness of school inputs in changing test scores may as easily be due to statistical failings of the studies as to genuine ineffectiveness of schools. In part, the paradox is explained by the fact that even critical journal articles and books addressed to questions neglected in the report or treated incorrectly were forced into the procrustean bed formed by the categories and characteristics of the data collected. Like the drunk in the old vaudeville routine who looked for his lost wallet under the lamp post though he had lost it elsewhere, those who denied the acceptability of the report's conclusions were forced to use data whose characteristics and shortcomings very nearly precluded interpretations other than those the report had reached. A notable exception was the scholar who found that computer errors largely accounted for the influence on test scores attributed to classmates.[40]

To understand both the information that the Coleman Report contained and the inferences drawn from it, two key facts about the survey on which they are based must be understood. First, it was and remains a snapshot, not a moving picture, of the educational process. Questions were asked of students, teachers, and school administrators at one particular time, with no attempt to ascertain the types of classmates, school inputs, school organization, or educational policies to which students were exposed in years before the survey. In this respect, the survey resembles census data on poverty, which tell one nothing about the dynamics of poverty, however well they may describe the characteristics of the poor at a particular time. Second, some data on some characteristics of schools and teachers refer to averages for schools or school districts and do not apply to individual classrooms. Furthermore, some schools and some school districts refused to participate in the survey altogether or selectively refused to answer certain questions. In other cases, the responses were inaccurate and the questions may have been inadequate to describe the aspects of school life actually relevant for performance in school or in later life.[41]

This second characteristic of the survey—its lack of detail at the student level and the incompleteness of responses—led a number of writers to suggest that the failure to observe large differences in the availability of school resources to blacks, whites, and others was due to these regrettable shortcomings of the survey as a source of data. Typically, such critics started with strong presumptions that different resources were available to blacks, whites, and others and found the shortcomings of the EEO survey sufficiently serious to undermine the capacity of the Coleman Report to upset their prior beliefs. Nevertheless, none of the subsequent reanalyses of the EEO survey has turned up evidence of bias or mistakes of tabulation sufficient to undermine the basic conclusion that differences between physical school resources available to various racial and ethnic groups in 1965 were small. Furthermore, enough time has now gone by for the production of additional information to call this conclusion into question, even if limited to smaller samples; but none has appeared. The near-equality of resources may have been relatively recent at the time the survey was taken because there is evidence of strenuous efforts, especially in the South, to equalize resources after World War II; but the snapshot character of the survey made it impossible to discover whether such equality was recent or longstanding. In particular, there is abundant evidence of large differences in school years and school expenditures between black and white schools before World War II.[42]

While the factual findings of the Coleman Report have not been overturned, the analysis of how education affects test scores has been picked to pieces;[43] but the process, as just noted, seems only to have driven it deeper into the public consciousness. A number of critics concluded immediately that the report was useless as a guide to policy.[44] The greater sophistication developed since the Coleman Report was issued (much of which came from efforts to understand the report itself) confirms this judgment. The report and the controversy it engendered underscore the pitfalls in drawing hasty policy conclusions from social science research.

Initially critics asked whether Coleman's conclusions followed from the application of valid analysis to the data contained in the EEO survey. By and large, the answer was no. Over time it has become apparent that the important question—do schools have much effect on educational outcomes?—remains unsettled. Some of the shortcomings in the analysis were apparent right away and were the principal contribution of three devastating critiques available shortly after the report appeared.[45] Other problems became apparent only gradually. The statistical model employed was naive and simplistic even by the standards of the time. The information on the economic and social class of students was so poor that the average economic and social class of their peers might have been a better guide to the student's background than the information available about the individual student; as a result the importance of peers as an influence on performance on standardized tests, one of the major findings of the report, was exaggerated.[46] The measure of educational attainment used—standardized tests in five areas—was woefully inadequate for two quite distinct reasons: first, because such tests measure only part of the cognitive development that students undergo and ignore entirely the changes in values, habits, and behavior that schools are intended to and actually do bring about; and second, because such tests are imperfect measures of cognitive development even in those areas they are intended to cover. The measures of school resources referred to the school or the school system and never to the resources available to the classroom or the individual student, and information on whether and how such resources as science labs or libraries were used was completely lacking.[47] So was any description of what went on in the classroom, the actual practices of teachers, and administrative policies. To a considerable degree this lack is inevitable. However important it might be to measure resources actually used if one wants to measure their effectiveness, it is almost impossible to do so. Teachers may use class time for activities that do not and are not intended to raise test scores, and standardized tests are designed not to be sensitive to specific differences in curriculums or texts.[48]

The fact that the survey consisted entirely of data applicable to a given time and contained nothing on the long-term exposure of students to various kinds of school facilities, classes, curriculums, and teachers was noted repeatedly as a serious shortcoming. Nevertheless, analysts almost universally expected to find that school inputs significantly affected educational outcomes; such relationships always showed up in economic studies of the relationship between production and the use of capital and labor in various industries. But while snapshot data are adequate for economic analyses, they are inadequate as a guide to how schools and teachers affect students. Assume, contrary to fact, that the EEO survey had asked exactly the right questions to describe completely the characteristics of students and teachers, the relevant characteristics of schools, and the educational activities that occur within them; that the tests used to measure educational attainment fully described the changes in students that schools bring about; and that all the data referred to individual students, not to schools or school districts. Even if all of those conditions had been satisfied, the data still would have been unable to establish the schools' effects on children, as the following two examples make clear. First, suppose that school administrators followed a compensatory educational policy, providing some extra resources for students who performed less well than average, but that those extra inputs were insufficient to redress the initial imbalance fully. In that event, a snapshot of the school system would show that extra educational resources are associated with below-average performance; more resources, in other words, would appear to damage the student, causing him to perform less well,[49] and the greater the quantity of extra educational resources, the worse his performance.[50] Of course, most of the variation in educational resources does not arise from such conscious decisions. To the extent that it does, however, estimates of the effectiveness of school resources in affecting test scores will be understated.

Second, ignore the possibility that educators may actively use educational resources to help those who lag. Assume instead that the allocation of educational resources is entirely passive. Assume also that educational outcomes as measured by tests depend on expenditures per pupil per year in all grades above kindergarten. If students move among schools with different characteristics, a simple snapshot study of the relation between current spending per pupil and current teacher characteristics, on the one hand, and educational performance, on the other, will understate the effect.[51] In fact, pupils do move surprisingly frequently among schools with different educational practices, different educational resources, and different student bodies. And they typically move once or twice a year from one teacher to another. Any study that ignores such movement may produce biased results.[52]

The use of cross-sectional data in the Coleman Report to specify a process that occurs over time was decried almost immediately,[53] but the full mischief became dramatically clear only recently. Two analysts created a simple model of the educational process, including equations that represented annual promotions and pupil mobility and that incorporated by assumption a positive impact of various educational inputs, including teacher characteristics and per pupil expenditures. They subjected a hypothetical population to this education system; that is, they charted pupils up the educational ladder according to the assumptions embodied in the equations. At a certain point this dynamic process was interrupted and data on a cross-section of students were "collected." The authors then performed the kinds of analyses contained in the Coleman Report. The results resemble those of the Coleman Report; they understate the contribution to educational performance of school inputs, including teachers, and overstate the importance of the student's family background.[54]

The Rand Survey

The impact of the Coleman Report undoubtedly was magnified by the similarity between its results and those of other research being done about the same time. Some of the studies closely resembled the Coleman Report, because they were also based on the EEO survey or on other snapshot surveys that suffered from similar shortcomings. Although the Coleman Report had been criticized severely for being based on cross-sectional data, the repeated failure to achieve from similar data results that looked much different paradoxically had two opposite effects. First, the repetition of similar results made them seem more plausible. Second, the inadequacy of cross-sectional data and of the analytical methods became obvious, as did the meager weight that studies based on such data deserved. Like a dour Cheshire cat, the evidence became so insubstantial that it all but vanished, leaving only a frown behind.

This schizophrenic reaction is embodied nicely in the summary and evaluation of such studies prepared by five scholars at the Rand Corporation, who stated, "[T]here is very little evidence that school resources in general have a powerful impact upon student outcomes, even neglecting the question of which school resources are influential. . . . [T]here is no way to determine whether the absence of results stems from the absence of an underlying relationship between school resources and student outcomes or from a research method that could not find results even if they were actually there."[55] If the analytical methods had been criticized before the studies were issued, their results would have carried less weight. In fact, the criticisms came only after the results had become known and had toppled unsupported faiths in the impact of educational resources on what children learn. So the question was posed: when the results of a study are inconsistent with one's beliefs, should one revise one's beliefs or distrust the studies?

On a few topics the accumulation of evidence was persuasive. General reductions in class size, for example, long a popular method for raising pupil test scores, were shown to cost more than they were worth. Teachers' salaries represent the major part of school budgets, and cutting class size in half nearly doubles educational costs per pupil. Rather dramatic improvements in pupil performance would be necessary to justify such an increase in expenditures, but observed improvements were small or nonexistent. In contrast, the amount of time devoted to subjects, it became apparent, did affect how much pupils learned; and the choice of curriculums helped determine what they learned.[56] Much of this evidence was accumulated long after the Coleman Report.

In fact, the faith that changes in schools can increase learning may end up with a good deal more analytic support than it has yet received. But the process will be far more complex than that considered in the Coleman Report or the numerous other contemporary studies summarized in the Rand study. By recognizing that different aspects of the school environment may affect different children differently, two analysts observed significant effects on learning of those aspects of the school the Coleman Report and other studies found did not significantly affect test scores. This possibility was suppressed by the statistical models used in the previous studies, and, in any case, the data were seldom detailed enough to permit analysts to look at influences affecting individual students, much less follow them through time. Using a unique source of information on individual students and the teaching environments to which they had been exposed over time and statistical techniques that permitted them to discover heterogeneous effects of school characteristics, Anita Summers and Barbara Wolfe found that "the impact of many school inputs on achievement growth varied considerably on different types of students—low-income versus high-income, black versus nonblack, and low-achieving versus high-achieving."[57] For example, students who are below grade level do better in classes with fewer than twenty-eight students, while other students can tolerate classes of up to thirty-three students. Experienced elementary school teachers seem to help high-achieving students, but hinder the learning growth of low achievers. Experienced junior high school English teachers help all students, but especially high achievers, while math teachers with three to nine years' experience are more effective than teachers with less experience or more. And so on.[58]

While this study is based only on a sample of schools from one city, its results raise the possibility that inconsistent findings of previous studies might be reconciled by the fact that particular teacher attributes or classroom characteristics helped some students but not others. One scholar found that the verbal facility of teachers and recentness of their education were statistically significant in explaining test scores of whites but not of Mexican-Americans, but these characteristics changed the performance of students only slightly.[59] A lot might depend on who the students were, how big the classes were, how much experience was involved, and what the subjects were. Experience might be an asset when the content of the subject was changing little and a liability when a drastic curricular change such as the new math was being introduced. The erratic nature of findings about the value of smaller class sizes, various teacher characteristics, new teaching methods and curriculums, and so on led the Rand team to conclude that higher educational expenditures spent in traditional ways are unlikely to improve student achievement.[60] To the extent that the inconsistency of past findings is due to faulty research methods, they say more about the adequacy of analytical methods than about the effectiveness of teachers or schools. They also say something, however, about the ability of the fallible mortals who fill the ranks of school administrators, parents, and other educators to identify what methods work for which children.[61]

Nevertheless, some schools seem consistently to turn out students who do better on standardized tests than do students from other schools. Jencks and Brown report that whether an average student attended one of the eighteen best or eighteen worst high schools from a sample of ninety-one high schools can determine whether the student ends up at the fifty-eighth or the forty-first percentile on standardized tests.[62] Klitgaard and Hall also find similar results from four independent sources of data.[63]

Program Evaluation

While economists and sociologists were analyzing large surveys, the newly created program evaluation offices in the Office of Economic Opportunity and the Department of Health, Education, and Welfare, either internally or with the aid of outside contractors, were evaluating the major new educational programs of the 1960s. The most notable were Head Start, the program to provide preschool education and, in some cases, health care to young children from disadvantaged families; Follow Through, the program of school enrichment for children previously enrolled in Head Start; and Title I of the Elementary and Secondary Education Act, which provided grants to school districts based on the number of children from poor families. These evaluations almost universally reported negligible effects or improvements that faded away after the treatment was stopped. Children in schools aided under Title I remained behind norms for children of the same age or fell further behind. Head Start seemed to produce small improvements in reading readiness, but no improvements beyond the first grade could be discovered. Follow Through may have had some beneficial effects.[64]

These evaluations had considerable influence initially, but once again they were so flawed that one cannot be sure they mean anything at all. On reflection many wondered why anyone ever thought that a brief stint in a special school would permanently transform the school performance of children whose drab lives were otherwise unchanged. Instead of likening remedial early childhood education to a vaccination, one might think of it as a vitamin pill.[65] Viewed in such light, a temporary improvement in academic performance, but nothing more, is all one should expect. The Rand Corporation study noted that "the analyses on which these evaluations are based did not assign treatment and non-treatment children on a random basis."[66] The Rand report continued, "[i]n the Title I surveys the selection of the projects was quite obviously not representative of the country as a whole. . . . spill-over or 'radiation' effects going from the project to nonproject children may contaminate the evaluation," and it cited others who speculated "whether the instructional components associated with compensatory education programs are inadequate or whether the fault lies in the evaluation procedures used to determine their effectiveness."[67]

Scattered evidence lends substance to these doubts. The Rand study found some small-scale studies of compensatory education that indicated it had succeeded. Summers and Wolfe observed beneficial results from Head Start on test scores of third graders.[68] A review of a large number of studies of Follow Through gave mixed results: some indicated that the program succeeded in raising test scores and others indicated no change.[69] Furthermore, a later survey of test scores of students in schools aided by Title I reported that the reading achievement of students increased by more than one year from the beginning of each school year through the *end,* but that the reading achievement of the same students increased less than one year from the beginning of one school year through the *beginning of the next.*[70] The only possible explanation seems to be that students lose ground during the summer when they are not in school, a disturbing finding but one that seems to support a call for more compensatory education, not less. This survey leaves unclear how much of the gain in reading achievement is due to Title I. It does underscore that schools are not the only place where education occurs and that other aspects of the environment, individually or in combination, have a considerable effect on what children learn. Preliminary analyses undertaken by the Development Continuity Consortium indicate that children enrolled in several of the prominent experimental preschool programs other than Head Start showed lower failure rates and required special education less often than did members of a control group.[71] But whatever failings subsequent criticisms may have revealed in the studies of education that proliferated in the mid- and late 1960s, these studies seemed substantial enough at the time to destroy the simplistic, poorly articulated, inadequately supported faith in education so widespread at the start of the decade.

Human Capital Theory on the Defensive

Although far more robust, the intellectual edifice of human capital also came under attack. In the mid-1960s one economist, in a fit of intellectual euphoria reminiscent of the nineteenth century claim that everything had been invented, had proclaimed that "all of us are now convinced that a satisfactory model of income distribution will require reference to investment in human capital—more precisely, a theory of investment decision that brings into play an individual 'demand' curve for investment (showing expected marginal rate of return at each investment level) and an individual 'supply' curve (showing marginal 'interest' cost)."[72] Whether or not this claim is eventually vindicated, it now seems quaintly obsolete. Estimates of the value of education based on the theory of human capital have been extensively criticized and challenged. The estimates were said to be too high because they failed to take adequate account of differences in economically relevant characteristics, some of which were not measured by tests, or because available measures of social class background were inadequate.[73] Others countered that the estimates might as easily be understated because of the inability to measure adequately family background or other relevant characteristics.[74]

The theory of human capital, the academic analogue of the popular faith in education, by now has been joined by a number of alternative explanations of why high income and education go together. One holds that education serves merely to distinguish preexisting abilities, that it screens but does not produce skills. A second holds that academic abilities are largely unrelated to skills relevant for the labor market and that education, in truth, merely legitimizes the hierarchical structure of social and economic relations. In the words of two leading radical adherents to this view, "[T]he emphasis on intelligence as the basis for economic success serves to legitimize an authoritarian, hierarchical, stratified, and unequal economic system of production, and to reconcile the individual to his or her objective position within this system."[75] According to this view, the noncognitive traits schools inculcate—punctuality, working for reward (grades), and so on—are more important than actual skills.[76] The fact that blacks and women benefit less than white males from education is explained by their exploitation at the hands of white males, the stage for which is set by roles assumed and career stereotypes instilled in school. A third explanation holds that education reduces training costs to employers, possibly by much less than the cost of the education itself.[77]

According to the first of these alternatives, a large part of the economic return that adherents of the theory of human capital attributed to education simply arose from the fact that those with the greatest natural abilities or the most advantageous backgrounds tended on the average to stay in school longest. They earned more or achieved higher occupational status than their less well-endowed brethren largely because of superior natural abilities or backgrounds.[78] Attempts were made to deal with this problem by using measures of native ability, such as performance on IQ or other standardized tests, as well as educational attainment to explain income or job status. But even the most painstaking of these attempts could not really lay the matter to rest, because no one could establish that these tests measured any, much less all, economically relevant characteristics.[79] Furthermore, performance on the tests was not truly independent of educational attainments. One could never be sure whether some relevant characteristic, such as drive or fixity of purpose, not measured by tests, was correlated with educational attainment and was actually responsible for both educational attainment and economic success.[80]

Looking back on efforts to determine whether education created or merely recognized preexisting abilities, one analyst wrote, "[I]f both workers and employers are ignorant of individual ability and if schools serve an identification role, I find it hard to conceive of market experiments which distinguish this from a world in which schools produce rather than identify skills."[81] In short, two views of the impact of education with radically different implications for policy had been advanced and there was no way of telling which was valid. If the human capital interpretation was correct, increasing education would increase productivity and earnings; if education merely acted as a screen, increasing education would redistribute income, but not increase it.

The second, or radical, alternative to human capital theory recognizes the same facts as the other views but tells a different story about them. Furthermore, it is embedded in a complex and broad view of politics, history, and sociology inconsistent with the liberal individualist view underlying human capital theory and the other alternatives. Its appeal derives from this breadth and sweep rather than from any superior explanatory power. Radical students of education have emphasized the great, if not dominant, role of noncognitive traits and characteristics, rather than intelligence as conventionally measured, in determining income and social status.[82]

According to the third of the alternative views, schooling serves primarily to reduce the on-the-job-training costs for employers.[83] Employers, in this view, assign individuals with the most education to the jobs that are most productive because they can minimize training costs by doing so. In effect, potential workers bid for jobs using their educational attainments as coin. Their productivity is determined principally by the job they get, and is not inherent in themselves. Because education opens the way to good jobs by signaling employers that the well-educated person is easier to train or by labeling the person as a member of a group previously found to have high productivity, people may be driven to spend more on education than is socially justified. An invisible hand may cause individuals to behave perversely, not in the social interest.[84]

If the job mix does not change, the acquisition of more education by one person means that he will be in a better position to get a good job but only at someone else's expense. This view is summarized by an analogy: "In a way we are describing a game of musical chairs. If there are fewer chairs than there are people, then even if a formerly chairless person obtains a seat he will displace someone who had previously occupied it. To the degree that more education assists him in getting that seat, we will observe a correlation between more education and the probability of obtaining a seat. What we might not observe is the person who is being displaced in the competition. . . . As long as the job competition is composed of more job seekers than there are nonpoverty employment openings, the outcome will always be the same as that of the musical chair game. While new people may find chairs, others will find that they have lost their seats in the competition."[85]

For improvements in education to alter the earnings distribution, the wage structure must change in response to the supply of workers with different educational credentials. While it is known that wage scales have risen for many decades during which educational attainments have increased, no one has produced solid evidence on whether the increase in education caused the change in jobs, the change in jobs caused people to get more education, educational increases and the demand for skills affected each other, or the two events had no direct influence on one another. The conventional interpretation of human capital presumes that the job structure will evolve smoothly and promptly if education increases skills. The view that emphasizes competition for jobs seems to leave the structure of job opportunities unexplained or, at least, beyond the influence of the supply of available skills. The view that education is an instrument to induce acceptance of autocratic, hierarchic, and unequal jobs is generally combined with or flows from a Marxist description of the economy in which the capitalist class simultaneously determines relative wages, technological change, and the amount and kind of education.[86]

The upshot of this long, confusing, and frequently arcane debate is inconclusive. The basic questions remain. Will increases in schooling increase educational achievement? Will increases in educational achievement raise productivity or merely redistribute earnings? The old and naive faiths have fallen victim to analysis, much of which, upon examination, has turned out to be seriously or fatally flawed.

Inequality

Uncertainty about the power of schooling had become fairly apparent when *Inequality* by Christopher Jencks and colleagues appeared in 1972.[87] The book was written to debunk what Jencks felt were the erroneous beliefs underlying national policy during the 1960s. According to these beliefs, "1. Eliminating poverty is largely a matter of helping children born into poverty to rise out of it. Once families escape from poverty, they do not fall back into it. Middle-class children rarely end up poor. 2. The primary reason poor children do not escape from poverty is that they do not acquire basic cognitive skills. . . . Lacking these skills, they cannot get or keep a well-paid job. 3. The best mechanism for breaking this vicious circle is educational reform. . . . [Children may be taught needed skills] by making sure that they attend the same schools as middle-class children, by giving them extra compensatory programs in school, by giving their parents a voice in running their schools, or by some combination of all three approaches."[88]

Jencks argued that each of these beliefs was partly or completely wrong. Poverty, he reported, is not primarily hereditary, but is created anew in each generation, although the children of the poor have a greater chance of becoming poor than do the children of the middle class. Cognitive skills, he suggested, have very little to do with whether a person ends up poor or rich; most variation in income is explained by other factors or is due to unobserved characteristics or chance. Jencks found little evidence that anything the schools do or can do substantially reduces inequality in cognitive performance. Poverty can be eliminated and inequality substantially reduced, he concluded, but only by making the tax and transfer systems more progressive or by changing the wage structure; altering education or otherwise changing individuals would have meager effects.

The most dramatic results of Jencks' study were that only about 15 percent of the variation in income observed among individuals could be explained statistically by their family background (measured by their father's education, occupation, or IQ), by their own intelligence (measured by an IQ test or the armed forces qualification test), and by their own education and occupational status. Fully 85 percent of the observed variation of income, even among brothers, Jencks estimated, was due to factors other than those he measured or to random events—that is, luck.[89]

The publication of *Inequality* was an intellectual "happening." It became front page news, was summarized and reviewed in leading newspapers, and was the subject of most of an issue of the *Harvard Educational Review*. Reactions ranged from enthusiastic acceptance through livid rejection to the suggestion that the book attacked a straw man.[90] Other criticisms went to the statistical methods used in the book, the data to which they were applied, and to the analytic conclusions to which they led.

In fact, the book was subject to many of the same criticisms as the Coleman Report. For one thing, it too relied heavily on cross-sectional data; as a result, accurate estimates of the impact over time of one set of variables on another was impossible. To make matters worse, Jencks's conclusions rest on a linkage of statistical results from several studies, each based on cross-sectional surveys.[91] A recent study based on an examination of brothers supports the likelihood that the influence of educational forces and family background were understated by Jencks; it suggests that between one-third and two-thirds of the variation among individuals in income, occupational status, and education may be explained by characteristics, measured and unmeasured, that are common to members of a given family.[92] Additional work by Jencks and his colleagues also indicates that unmeasured characteristics common to family members may be significantly correlated with later economic and social position.[93] And analysis of the variation in earnings among individuals that takes account of the difference in earning patterns over the life cycle associated with different amounts of education and on-the-job training indicates that about one-third of such variation in earnings is associated statistically with variations in educational attainment alone.[94] As with other estimates based on cross-sectional data, one must enquire whether these estimates are relevant for policy; but they indicate that if one is willing to entertain conclusions based on cross-sectional data, as Jencks is, then the conclusion that only a small percentage of the variation in earnings is associated with differences in education is wrong.

Another criticism commonly directed at Jencks's work was that he chose to employ statistical indicators that tended to make the impact of any change in policy seem small or insignificant. This problem, of which Jencks is acutely aware,[95] can be illustrated with a simple example. Suppose five people have incomes of $5,000, $12,000, $18,000, $35,000, and $60,000, and that through compensatory education these incomes can be changed to $7,000, $13,000, $18,000, $34,000, and $58,000, respectively. According to the measure used most often by Jencks, such redistribution would reduce the inequality by about 18 percent, about the same as the proportion of variation in income explained by the personal characteristics Jencks was able to measure. By some standards such a reduction would be unimportant; the richest person would still earn more than eight times more than the poorest. But the poorest person's income would have risen by 40 percent, the next poorest by 8 percent. If these individuals are taken as representing blocks of 20 percent of the population, then the increase by 40 percent in the incomes of the poorest 20 percent of the population may seem an almost revolutionary change; but it is one that Jencks's methods of statistical presentation treated as minor.

Whether education could achieve such a change and if so whether the cost would be supportable are separate and far more important questions, but unfortunately they are ones on which neither Coleman nor Jencks can shed much light because of the flawed data upon which they relied. The use of statistical measures that made socially significant changes in economic conditions seem trivial was the technical expression of a striking change in the importance accorded two related problems—inequality of opportunity, particularly as symbolized by the gap between blacks and whites, and inequality of results. Jencks and his colleagues explicitly downgraded the problems of the poor in general, and of blacks in particular, relative to a problem that they claimed was far more important—general inequality in the distribution of income. Had a nation not spent a painful decade wrestling with problems of discrimination and poverty, had these problems been fully solved, and had Jencks presented some evidence that overall income inequality was a more serious problem than poverty and discrimination, such a focus might have been understandable. But none of these conditions was satisfied.

The mystery of why focus shifted from equalization of opportunity for groups to equalization of results for the whole population vanishes if one acknowledges that the civil *rights* revolution had been won. In legislatures and in the courts blacks had achieved equality. In the marketplace their disadvantage remained, barely less than before, but it had become clear that the forces of discrimination were in political retreat and morally bankrupt.

Unfortunately, overall inequality had never roused much general concern. Indeed, Jencks cites evidence that people are not distressed by inequality in general, although they are disturbed by poverty and by unequal opportunity.[96] Jencks, in effect, presents evidence that education cannot do something that no informed person had claimed it could do, at least since the euphoric early 1960s (i.e., reduce overall inequality), and pushed to the side its role as one of several instruments for reducing discrepancies among average incomes of blacks, whites, and other groups. Its role in reducing the number of people earning far less than average was downgraded due in part to the use of deficient statistical techniques that badly understated the impact of education on income, and in part to the failure to see through the rhetoric of the War on Poverty and the Great Society to what actually was happening. The poverty program and the Great Society liberal legislation of the 1960s devoted only a small part of incremental resources to education, a fact that was partially obscured by the rhetoric of the time but that was perceived by some even at the height of the War on Poverty.[97]

Jencks accurately and persuasively reported on the massive research that failed to support the faith and rhetoric about the effect of resources on schooling and educational attainment. Unfortunately, this review was linked to a discussion of what determines the distribution of income that will not bear scrutiny. The major contribution of Jencks and other critics of the human capital approach was to underscore how little attention had been given directly to the structure of job opportunities except as they are affected by general employment conditions. This problem is addressed in chapter 4.

Taking Bearings

It is an uninspiring exercise to look back on the writings of the past fifteen years about the impact of education on earnings and about the potential of changes in education to alter those prospects. First there are the popular effusions and simplistic academic writings that do little more than note informally or measure precisely the well-known linkage between educational attainment and earnings. From those writings came an obvious inference—that more education is a powerful instrument for increasing incomes. This inference fitted in nicely with the longstanding American infatuation with education that had led its citizens to spend more on education and go to school longer than the inhabitants of any other country. It provided some rationale for a large number of rather small-scale programs of compensatory education and for some experiments. Some people felt that such programs should constitute a major part of the War on Poverty, and given the rhetorical excesses of the time, some people even believed they did, the contrary facts notwithstanding (see chapter 1).

Beliefs that lived by oversimplification died by oversimplification. Analysts looked at snapshot data and tried to estimate how much progress could be made toward achieving such goals as higher income for the poor by using such instruments as education. They presumed to describe by broad and nonspecific characteristics, such as parental income and occupation and number of years of education or performance on IQ or achievement tests, the infinite and subtle variations among individuals that affect their value to employers. A set of studies resulted that revealed the inadequacies of research methodology more than they documented the ineffectuality of education as an instrument for affecting income. These flawed studies, however, marched forth like soldiers to battle, slaying the naively held preconceptions about the effectiveness of education, before falling themselves to criticism and evaluation. The process partakes of a certain irony.

The problem today consists of choosing among diverse theories, none of which is refuted by available facts, and among empirical findings that seem inconsistent. There is no doubt, and never has been, that at any given time more education is associated with higher income; given the costs of education, the implied rate of return is about as high for education as for ordinary investments. Moreover, returns for black males are now approaching those of white males, in sharp contrast to the situation a generation ago. And the earnings of black women have been increasing relative to those of white women for many years, approaching and in some cases exceeding them. The extent to which these gains by black women are due to the greater commitment of black women to work required by the lower earning prospects of black men remains open to dispute. Women in general continue to earn substantially less than do men, although it is unclear how much of this differential is the result of women's sporadic attachment to the labor force and how much the result of occupational segregation that keeps women from jobs with prospects for promotion. These results are derived from snapshot data and do not by themselves tell any more about the effectiveness of purposeful changes in education in altering incomes than do other cross-sectional studies; but they do describe a change in the distribution of economic rewards among blacks and whites who have acquired different amounts of education.

The fact that more education is now coming to be associated with higher earnings for blacks in the same way it has been for whites provokes a number of questions. Why has this association developed? How can the returns now available to both blacks and whites be reconciled with the frustrating and consistently negative results of studies that seek to measure the effect of what goes on in the schools on test scores or of test scores on income or occupational status? On the one hand, evidence confirms the relation between income and education for whites and increasingly for blacks. On the other hand, few differences among schools seem to have consistent and socially significant effects on how children do on standardized tests; and performance on standardized tests does not seem to have much to do with subsequent earnings.

Vague Outlines

The building blocks for reconciling these conflicting views seem to be at hand. To use them, however, requires that one eclectically incorporate ideas based on human capital, screening, job competition, and radical analysis. With understandable pride and commendable tenacity, many adherents of each of these approaches seem unwilling to admit the usefulness of ideas founded on other views and thereby obstruct understanding, even as they claim to further it. The eclectic view may strike many who are unfamiliar with the academic disputes as little more than common sense.

First, schooling is enormously important in shaping children in a wide variety of ways. It simultaneously inculcates such skills as reading and ciphering; such habits as the ability to stick to a task for an hour or so, or the belief that answers to certain kinds of problems can be found in books; the capacity to follow instructions or participate in team endeavors; many specific kinds of knowledge, much of which is forgotten sooner or later unless it is reinforced; values that are widely held in society, including the importance of competition and the sense that extra rewards for the victors in competition are fair and just; a sense of self, based on one's sex, race, age, and degree of mastery of particular activities, that in some cases broadens and in others constricts aspirations. Some children are more able at various tasks than others, a fact which schools certify and which serves in some measure to screen students and influence their subsequent opportunities.

Moreover, it is becoming increasingly clear that *how* schools proceed does influence what effects they have on children. How long schools devote to particular subjects affects how much children learn about those subjects as measured by standardized tests, and the choice among curriculums helps determine what they learn. It is also clear that how much and what children learn depends on a host of other influences, such as the home, television, peers, health and nutrition (at least in the case of extreme deprivation), and natural intelligence, and that those influences collectively are probably much more powerful than schools are.[98] Furthermore, various aspects of school life affect different children differently; in extreme cases, some may be harmed by practices that help others, causing the average effect to seem insignificant. But the dominant fact about schools is their remarkable uniformity. The number of hours per year spent in school varies only slightly; curriculums are surprisingly similar; objectives, in terms of basic skills, are almost identical.

Second, it is almost impossible for employers to ascertain the actual productivity of any particular worker before he is on the job, and often it remains impossible or very costly even then. Consequently, employers rely on easily ascertained characteristics of potential employees in deciding whether to hire them and, frequently, in deciding whether to promote them. Presumably, employers do not consciously reduce potential profits in deciding which characteristics to use. Their choices may be conditioned by their direct experience, by views they hold but have never checked, or by a sense of propriety about which kinds of workers should hold which kinds of jobs. Among these characteristics, education, race, sex, and age are prominent and can serve in any of three capacities. The view that high school graduates should not be hired for supervisory work, for example, may be based on actual experience, simple prejudice, or fear that employees who are college graduates would resent taking orders from a less well-educated superior. In varying degrees, the criteria used in lieu of the actual productivity of the worker, which cannot be observed, create only a rebuttable presumption that the worker should or should not be hired. Exceptions may be common except in the case of rigidly enforced taboos such as those involving race or sex. And since numerous such characteristics are typically used by employers in making hiring decisions, one can expect that there will be a rather tight relationship between the average education of otherwise identifiable groups and their earnings, while at the same time an enormous amount of variation within groups will be unrelated to differences in education. Thus, education will explain little of the variation in earnings although it is critical in hiring. Employers classify people on the basis of characteristics that define groups, not on the basis of the very large variations in individual, job-relevant attributes that cannot be observed at reasonable cost, except possibly on the job and often not even then.

All these factors help reconcile the apparently conflicting findings of educational research. Education contributes in the long run to aggregate economic growth because it teaches economically relevant skills and because it conditions people to work within and accept the hierarchy, norms, and rules of modern industrial society. It helps explain discrepancies among the earnings of various groups for the same reason. Differences in education help explain differences in èarnings among white males but failed until recently to explain as much of the variation in earnings of black males and of women because of the hangover of racial segregation and the dominance of sex stereotyping in job allocation. Some differences in educational practices, most notably duration and curricular goals, seem to affect performance on standardized tests; these practices and others may affect the myriad outcomes of schooling that are not measured by standardized tests, but there is no way to know. And to the extent that these differences in schools are economically relevant, they are more likely to be relevant for groups than for individuals, because employers may have a feel for the value of, say, white female high school graduates from suburban schools, but are unlikely to have much opinion about the relative value or even be aware of the special intensive course in reading that Mary O'Brien took for the last two years, even if it improved Mary's reading score by five months on the Iowa test. If all Mary's classmates take the same course and gain an average of five months, employers may find out eventually that white female high school graduates from suburban schools are better workers than they used to be and they may gain access to jobs previously reserved for say, white female college graduates. Even then, the wage structure is likely to change slowly, if at all, because of prevailing views about the appropriate structure of relative wages among various kinds of jobs and among different groups of workers. The process by which relative wages of different occupations change is poorly understood, but the recent apparent decline in the extra income associated with a college education suggests that the wage structure is not immutable.

The eclectic view just described incorporates elements from human capital theory, the radical Marxian analysis of education, education as a screen and as a signal, and the institutional view of labor markets. It seems consistent with the principal facts each theory claims to explain that the others do not explain. It lacks simplicity, however—that mark of elegance in the physical sciences that social scientists quixotically continue to seek. It suggests both an important role for and important limits on education as an instrument of social change. To the extent that education changes individual abilities, values, and habits, and to the extent that perceptions of group characteristics are important in determining the economic opportunities of members of those groups, equality of education is necessary for social change but not sufficient, because pure prejudice or social conventions change slowly. It is not sufficient also because other aspects of the environment, notably family or peer group influences, may persist for long periods of time, causing group differentials to continue through several generations. Education is quite unlikely to be used to offset such outside-the-school influences in any clearly compensatory way, however. To use education in this way would be possible if there were certain educational techniques that worked better for disadvantaged groups than for others. In the absence of such techniques, education could be used in a compensatory way only if very much more were spent, and spent effectively, on the education of the disadvantaged groups (not just on a pilot or demonstration basis) or if some educational techniques of demonstrated effectiveness were withheld from the majority of children. The politics of education are such that neither of these two courses will be followed.

Policy Implications

The technical and scholarly debate about the effectiveness of education in altering individual incomes and the shape of the income distribution had an incidental effect on the political debate about the proper role of education in social policy. In the early and mid-1960s education was a salient issue for several reasons: the fiscal problems occasioned by the post–World War II baby boom; the whole set of educational issues affecting blacks, including desegregation, equality of resources, and school effectiveness; and the relation between education and poverty or inequality (though these two problems were seldom distinguished). Education was viewed both as a right (although the content of that right was seldom specified) and as an instrument for achieving other objectives. The contribution of social scientists consisted entirely of an attempt to clarify education's power and its proper sphere as an instrument. By now it should be apparent that that attempt was not successful.

The single-minded focus of analysts on education as an instrument succeeded, however, in diverting attention from education as a right. A number of observers remarked upon this diversion of attention, especially in the courts. James Coleman suggested that *Brown* v. *Board of Education,* the fundamental case on desegregation, would have been more soundly based had the Supreme Court not cited evidence on the effects of schooling, but had instead rested its decision entirely on the proposition that segregation violates freedom.[99] Henry Levin observed that the introduction of social science argumentation by both sides in cases involving educational issues diverts the attention of the courts from basic rights because "courts and policy makers generally find it easier to understand a point of agreement than of contention. . . . Thus, much of the legal debate surrounding the challenge to present methods of financing education does not address the basic unfairness reflected by state arrangements to spend more on the education of children in rich districts than in poor ones. Rather, the prima facie inequities are ignored as the courts are tortured with the convoluted arguments provided by social scientists about whether money makes a difference for 'poor kids.' "[100] Thus, educational research has tended and will continue to act as a conservative influence on educational policy. The inherent complexity of the subject ensures that conflicting evidence will continue to be available to educational policymakers in government as well as to the courts. The political consequence of conflicting evidence, unlike the legal consequence where decisions must be made, is to cause action to be deferred until more evidence is available.

Notes

1. Roger A. Freeman, "Discussion" [of a paper by Gary S. Becker], *American Economic Review*, vol. 50 (May 1960, *Papers and Proceedings, 1959*), pp. 370–71.

2. Ibid., p. 371.

3. Herman P. Miller, "Annual and Lifetime Income in Relation to Education: 1939–1959," *American Economic Review*, vol. 50 (December 1960), pp. 962–86.

4. Seymour E. Harris, "Introduction: Some Broad Issues," *Review of Economics and Statistics*, vol. 42 (August 1960, supplement), p. 22.

5. H. S. Houthakker, "Exchange and Income," *Review of Economics and Statistics*, vol. 41 (February 1959), pp. 24–28.

6. Finis Welch, "Human Capital Theory: Education, Discrimination, and Life Cycles," *American Economic Review*, vol. 65 (May 1975, *Papers and Proceedings, 1974*), p. 63.

7. Selma J. Mushkin, "Health as an Investment," *Journal of Political Economy*, vol. 70 (October 1962, supplement), p. 130.

8. B. F. Kiker, "The Historical Roots of the Concept of Human Capital," *Journal of Political Economy*, vol. 74 (October 1966), pp. 481–99.

9. The classic statements were Jacob Mincer, "Investment in Human Cap-

ital and Personal Income Distribution," *Journal of Political Economy*, vol. 66 (August 1958), pp. 281–302, and Gary S. Becker, *Human Capital: A Theoretical and Empirical Analysis with Special Reference to Education* (Columbia University Press for the National Bureau of Economic Research, 1964). For a general review of economic literature on human capital, see Jacob Mincer, "The Distribution of Labor Incomes: A Survey with Special Reference to the Human Capital Approach," *Journal of Economic Literature*, vol. 8 (March 1970), pp. 1–26; Theodore W. Schultz, "Reflections on Investment in Man," *Journal of Political Economy*, vol. 70 (October 1962, supplement), pp. 1–8.

10. Dozens, if not hundreds, of studies of the rate of return to education have been reported in books, journals, and monographs. Among the earliest and most widely quoted are Becker, *Human Capital*, and Giora Hanoch, "An Economic Analysis of Earnings and Schooling," *Journal of Human Resources*, vol. 2 (Summer 1967), pp. 310–29.

11. Thomas I. Ribich, *Education and Poverty* (Brookings Institution, 1968), pp. 6–7, summarizes these arguments.

12. See, for example, Hanoch, "An Economic Analysis of Earnings and Schooling"; also Randall D. Weiss, "The Effect of Education on the Earnings of Blacks and Whites," *Review of Economics and Statistics*, vol. 52 (May 1970), pp. 150–59, and Becker, *Human Capital*, p. 101.

13. Finis Welch indicts the early human capital literature for the shortcoming of the Glick-Miller estimates of the value of a college education. "The early literature of human capital assumed, perhaps blithely, not only that a causal relation exists [between education and earnings], but that the zero-order association that corrects neither for 'ability' nor 'background' offers an adequate basis for calculations of rates of return and for estimates, based on these returns, of the contributions of increased schooling levels to economic growth." "Human Capital Theory," p. 65.

14. Edward F. Denison, *The Sources of Economic Growth in the United States and the Alternatives Before Us*, supplementary paper 13 (Committee for Economic Development, 1962), pp. 67–79.

15. Gary S. Becker and Barry R. Chiswick, "Education and the Distribution of Earnings," *American Economic Review*, vol. 56 (May 1966, *Papers and Proceedings, 1965*), pp. 358–69; and Barry R. Chiswick, *Income Inequality: Regional Analyses within a Human Capital Framework* (Columbia University Press for the National Bureau of Economic Research, 1974).

16. See Martin Carnoy and Dieter Marenbach, "The Return to Schooling in the United States, 1939–69," *Journal of Human Resources*, vol. 10 (Summer 1975), pp. 312–31; Alice M. Rivlin, "Income Distribution: Can Economists Help?" *American Economic Review*, vol. 65 (May 1975, *Papers and Proceedings, 1974*), pp. 1–15.

17. Paul Taubman and Terence Wales, "Mental Ability and Higher Educational Attainment in the Twentieth Century," in F. Thomas Juster, ed., *Education, Income, and Human Behavior* (McGraw-Hill, 1975), p. 51.

18. Richard B. Freeman, *The Overeducated American* (Academic Press, 1976), p. 14. Freeman's finding that the wage gap has narrowed has been chal-

lenged by Edward F. Denison. See "Some Factors Influencing Future Productivity Growth" (paper delivered at a conference sponsored by the National Center for Productivity and Quality of Working Life, 1976) (forthcoming).

19. Samuel Bowles, "Towards an Educational Production Function," in W. Lee Hansen, ed., *Education, Income, and Human Capital* (Columbia University Press for the National Bureau of Economic Research, 1970), p. 23.

20. Finis Welch remarked, "Frankly, I find it hard to conceive of a poorer measure of the marketable skills a person acquires in school than the number of years he has been able to endure a classroom environment. My only justification for using such a crude measure is that I can find nothing better. Too, I am very agnostic about what 'ability' tests measure. Similar statements hold for measures of home environment. Yet as soon as we open the door to measurement error, we find a completely nebulous world in which almost anything is possible." "Human Capital Theory," p. 67. If, as Welch suggests, anything is possible, it is far from clear how much weight, if any, should be attached to estimates based on such data.

21. James Tobin, "Economic Growth as an Objective of Government Policy," *American Economic Review*, vol. 54 (May 1964, *Papers and Proceedings, 1963*), pp. 1–20. Harry G. Johnson, in commenting on Tobin's analysis, remarked on the presence of imperfections, the removal of which would increase economic growth, but with less governmental interference than a full-blown growth policy. Among these he numbered "social provision of finance for investment in human capital." ("Discussion," ibid., p. 23.) His point, generally accepted among economists, was that students cannot borrow against future earnings to finance as much education as would be optimal because there is no way lenders can compel payment in the event of default and bankruptcy.

22. Alvin H. Hansen, "Automation and the Welfare State," *New Republic*, vol. 144 (April 10, 1961), pp. 10–11.

23. Kenneth E. Boulding, "Better R-E-D than Dead," *New Republic*, vol. 147 (October 20, 1962), p. 16.

24. Although Denison's work, which attributed a sizable fraction of economic growth to education, was used loosely by those who wanted more growth to support increases in educational expenditures, Denison himself was very cautious in suggesting that increases in education would have much effect on growth. Increasing educational attainments one and a half years more than he forecast would raise economic growth only 0.1 percentage point per year from 1960 through 1980. See *Sources of Economic Growth*, p. 277.

25. See both Becker, *Human Capital*, and Hanoch, "An Economic Analysis of Earnings and Schooling."

26. Kenneth B. Clark, "Education of the Minority Poor: The Key to the War on Poverty," in *The Disadvantaged Poor: Education and Employment*, Third Report of the Task Force on Economic Growth and Opportunity (Chamber of Commerce of the United States, 1966), p. 175.

27. Christopher Jencks, "Is the Public School Obsolete?" *Public Interest*, vol. 1 (Winter 1966), p. 19.

28. "To relieve poverty in the United States there is a vital need to close the

educational gap between the poor and the better-off. Children from low-income families in many big cities and in the economically distressed parts of the countryside should receive more and better education. Undereducated, underproductive low-income Americans out of school need remedial programs to increase their productivity and earnings." *The Disadvantaged Poor*, p. 21.

29. "If children of poor families can be given skills and motivation, they will not become poor adults." *Economic Report of the President together with the Annual Report of the Council of Economic Advisers, January 1964*, p. 75.

30. Quoted in "School Study," *Congressional Quarterly Weekly Report*, vol. 18 (February 5, 1960), p. 194.

31. Eli Ginzberg, "Poverty and the Negro," in *The Disadvantaged Poor*, pp. 220–21.

32. For example, over what period is productivity measured? Does productivity refer to groups or individuals? How can the theory apply in the government and nonprofit sectors, which, according to one estimate, employed nearly 27 percent of the total labor force in 1973. Eli Ginzberg, "The Pluralistic Economy of the U.S.," *Scientific American*, vol. 235 (December 1976), p. 26. The vagueness of the marginal productivity theory of wages has been argued by Lester C. Thurow, *Generating Inequality: Mechanisms of Distribution in the U.S. Economy* (Basic Books, 1975), pp. 211–30.

33. The relevant period to use in computing earnings is the technical manifestation of two substantive issues. First, how should leisure be evaluated? This question is important because of the fact that much of the variation in earnings among people is due to differences in hours worked, and much of this difference is voluntary. Second, how should transitory fluctuations in income due to temporary illness, unemployment, or withdrawal from the labor force be handled? In general, use of hourly or daily wage rates makes the return to education seem smaller than when annual earnings are used because the well-educated work more hours per week on the average and experience less unemployment and absence from work due to illness than do the less educated. See R. S. Eckaus, "Estimation of the Returns to Education with Hourly Standardized Incomes," *Quarterly Journal of Economics*, vol. 87 (February 1973), pp. 121–31.

34. Civil Rights Act of 1964, section 402.

35. James S. Coleman and others, *Equality of Educational Opportunity* (Government Printing Office, 1966); Harvey A. Averch and others, *How Effective Is Schooling? A Critical Review and Synthesis of Research Findings* (Rand Corporation, 1972); Christopher Jencks and others, *Inequality: A Reassessment of the Effect of Family and Schooling in America* (Basic Books, 1972).

36. Actually word that the world was round—that outlays per pupil differed relatively little, if at all, at least across economic classes—had been available for some time. James N. Morgan and others had reported that children in the lowest-income families attended schools where per pupil expenditures were only 13 percent below the national average. See *Income and Welfare in the United States* (McGraw-Hill, 1962), p. 306.

37. Godfrey Hodgson, "Do Schools Make a Difference?" in Donald M. Levine and Mary Jo Bane, eds., *The 'Inequality' Controversy: Schooling and Distributive Justice* (Basic Books, 1975), p. 22.

38. See Jesse Burkhead with Thomas G. Fox and John W. Holland, *Input and Output in Large-City High Schools* (Syracuse University Press, 1967), pp. 75–76; and Marion F. Shaycoft, *The High School Years: Growth in Cognitive Skills,* Interim Report to the U.S. Office of Education, Cooperative Research Project 3051 (Project TALENT Office, American Institutes for Research and University of Pittsburgh, 1967), pp. 7-11 and 7-25–26.

39. *How Effective Is Schooling?* p. xii.

40. Marshall S. Smith, *"Equality of Educational Opportunity:* The Basic Findings Reconsidered," in Frederick Mosteller and Daniel P. Moynihan, eds., *On Equality of Educational Opportunity* (Random House, 1972), chap. 6.

41. Christopher Jencks, after an examination of the data collected by the EEO Survey, wrote: "There are a lot of serious problems in the EEOS data. Much of the data is probably inaccurate. Even when the data are accurate in their own terms, they often provide inadequate evidence about both the present state of the schools under study and the likely future lives of their alumni." He concluded, however, that such failings in the data could not possibly account for the insignificant impact on test scores attributed to schools. Christopher R. Jencks, "The Quality of Data Collected by the *Equality of Educational Opportunity Survey,"* in ibid., p. 503.

42. Finis Welch, "Black-White Differences in Returns to Schooling," *American Economic Review,* vol. 63 (December 1973), pp. 893–907.

43. The major critical analyses of the Coleman Report are Samuel Bowles and Henry M. Levin, "The Determinants of Scholastic Achievement—An Appraisal of Some Recent Evidence," *Journal of Human Resources,* vol. 3 (Winter 1968), pp. 3–24; Glen G. Cain and Harold W. Watts, "Problems in Making Policy Inferences from the Coleman Report," *American Sociological Review,* vol. 35 (April 1970), pp. 228–42; and Eric A. Hanushek and John F. Kain, "On the Value of Equality of Educational Opportunity as a Guide to Public Policy," in Mosteller and Moynihan, eds., *On Equality of Educational Opportunity,* chap. 3. See also Marshall S. Smith, *"Equality of Educational Opportunity:* The Basic Findings Reconsidered"; and Donald M. Levine " *'Inequality'* and the Analysis of Educational Policy," in Levine and Bane, eds., *The 'Inequality' Controversy,* pp. 304–25.

44. See the articles by Cain and Watts, Bowles and Levin, and Hanushek and Kain cited in note 43.

45. Ibid.

46. A meticulous reanalysis of EEO's data by Marshall Smith confirmed this criticism. One of the problems was computer programming errors. See *"Equality of Educational Opportunity:* The Basic Findings Reconsidered."

47. Levine, " 'Inequality' and the Analysis of Educational Policy," p. 310. Also see Smith, *"Equality of Educational Opportunity:* The Basic Findings Reconsidered," p. 282.

48. Jencks, "The Quality of the Data Collected," p. 475.

49. This problem is a common one whenever one is attempting to evaluate the impact of some policy that is itself affected by the circumstances or condition it is designed to influence. The problem does not arise in efforts to estimate industrial production functions from cross-sectional data. It does arise in education. If some policy, x, has a positive impact on some objective, y, but is used to the extent that the objective, y, is below some target, any statistical analysis relating x to y must sort out the mechanical relation between x and y (which is positive—more x, more y) from the discretionary use of x to affect y (which is negative—less y, more x). Paradoxical results are possible, like the example in the text, and biased results are likely. For a discussion of this problem in the context of macroeconomic stabilization, see Stephen M. Goldfeld and Alan S. Blinder, "Some Implications of Endogenous Stabilization Policy," *Brookings Papers on Economic Activity, 3:1972*, pp. 585–640.

50. This problem exists even if one attempts to control statistically for other influences on educational outcomes. Members of the group that is below average *after* controlling for such influences will be lower performers than those who are above average after controlling for such influences.

51. One recent longitudinal study supports this point. It suggested that performance in grades two through four was significantly influenced by the characteristics of the pupils' first grade teacher but was unrelated to those of second, third, and fourth grade teachers. See Larry D. Singell and Wesley J. Yordon, "Incentives for More Efficient Education: The Development of a Model," in Bruno Stein and S. M. Miller, eds., *Incentives and Planning in Social Policy* (Aldine, 1973), p. 83.

52. Jencks reports that school characteristics seemed to matter less for sixth grade students who had been in the same school since the first grade than for others. But there is reason to think the background of such students would differ systematically from that of more mobile fellow students. Furthermore, enormous differences in teacher characteristics exist within schools. See Jencks, "The Coleman Report and the Conventional Wisdom," in Mosteller and Moynihan, eds., *On Equality of Educational Opportunity*, p. 108.

53. See especially Hanushek and Kain, "On the Value of Equality of Educational Opportunity as a Guide to Public Policy," and Smith, "*Equality of Educational Opportunity:* The Basic Findings Reconsidered."

54. The underlying statistical reason for these results is that random measurement errors tend to bias estimated coefficients toward zero. Based upon their results, the authors, Daniel F. Luecke and Noel F. McGinn, write: "Our results are consistent with the position that cross-sectional data can tell us little about how a dynamic system has worked in the past, or how it could be made to work in the future. The more complex and more dynamic the system, the less likely are conventional analyses to yield reliable inferences about it. . . . [I]f independent variables change over time in relation to others, the direct effects on the dependent variable are likely to be underestimated. In this study the results tended to exaggerate the direct effect of Family on Achievement, because the stability of Family resulted in a relatively high final-period correlation with Achievement. The direct effect of Teacher on Achievement was

usually underestimated, using contribution to variance as the indicator, since Teacher changes most frequently from period to period. Adding complexity would have resulted in even greater misrepresentations of the dynamic variables, since in multiple regression, the more independent variables one adds the less variance each new variable is likely to explain.

". . . our results suggest that studies which find little or no relationship between educational inputs and achievement may be highly misleading. Our findings suggest that the combination of data and statistical technique most often used is unlikely to reveal such relationships even when they exist." "Regression Analyses and Education Production Functions: Can They Be Trusted?" *Harvard Educational Review*, vol. 45 (August 1975), p. 347.

55. Averch and others, *How Effective Is Schooling?* pp. 48–49.

56. Decker F. Walker and Jon Schaffarzick, "Comparing Curricula," *Review of Educational Research*, vol. 44 (Winter 1974), pp. 83–111.

57. Anita A. Summers and Barbara L. Wolfe, "Do Schools Make a Difference?" *American Economic Review*, vol. 67 (September 1977), pp. 639–52. The finding that disadvantaged students can be helped by particular types of inputs is relevant to the question of equity in intradistrict distributions of educational inputs. See Summers and Wolfe, "Intradistrict Distribution of School Inputs to the Disadvantaged: Evidence for the Courts," *Journal of Human Resources*, vol. 11 (Summer 1976), pp. 328–42.

58. Anita A. Summers and Barbara L. Wolfe, "Equality of Educational Opportunity Quantified: A Production Function Approach," Philadelphia Fed Research Papers (Federal Reserve Bank of Philadelphia, 1975; processed), pp. 10–12. Singell and Yordon, in "Incentives for More Efficient Education," found that during the first four elementary years pupils did better with younger, less experienced, teachers than with older, more experienced, teachers. Whether one should conclude that teacher experience, having shown different effects in these two studies, bears no consistent relation to educational performance, is open to debate. One might conclude with equal plausibility that both studies are valid (i.e., that some teacher characteristics matter for some, but not all, pupils), and seek the unmeasured difference in pupils or teachers that explains such disparate results. Which course one follows depends on one's prior beliefs and the strength with which they are held.

59. Eric Hanushek, "Teacher Characteristics and Gains in Student Achievement: Estimation Using Micro Data," *American Economic Review*, vol. 61 (May 1971, *Papers and Proceedings, 1970*), pp. 280–88.

60. Averch and others, *How Effective Is Schooling?* p. 155.

61. The quest for profits seems not to be a sufficient incentive. Experiments in performance contracting detected no increase in test performance when children were taught by firms whose payment depended contractually on how much students learned. See Irwin Garfinkel and Edward M. Gramlich, "A Statistical Analysis of the OEO Experiment in Educational Performance Contracting," *Journal of Human Resources*, vol. 8 (Summer 1973), pp. 275–305; also Edward M. Gramlich and Patricia P. Koshel, *Educational Performance Contracting* (Brookings Institution, 1975).

62. Christopher S. Jencks and Marsha D. Brown, "Effects of High Schools on Their Students," *Harvard Educational Review*, vol. 45 (August 1975), pp. 290, 292. For reasons that escape me Jencks and Brown chose to emphasize that high schools account for only a small proportion—1 to 3 percent—of the variance in test *scores* while deemphasizing relative standing as trivial. The fact that as late in the educational career as grades ten through twelve high schools can make so great a difference in relative standing would seem to deserve as much emphasis as the findings on variance.

63. Robert Klitgaard and George R. Hall, "Are There Unusually Effective Schools?" *Journal of Human Resources*, vol. 10 (Winter 1975), pp. 90–106.

64. Averch and others, *How Effective Is Schooling?* pp. 100–05, 151.

65. Helen L. Bee, "A Developmental Psychologist Looks at Educational Policy: Or the Hurrier I Go the Behinder I Get," occasional paper (Aspen Institute for Humanistic Studies, Program on Education for a Changing Society, 1976; processed).

66. Averch and others, *How Effective Is Schooling?* p. 106. Under certain circumstances, nonrandom assignment will not lead to biased coefficients. See Glen G. Cain, "Regression and Selection Models to Improve Nonexperimental Comparisons," in Carl A. Bennett and Arthur A. Lumsdaine, eds., *Evaluation and Experiment: Some Critical Issues in Assessing Social Programs* (Academic Press, 1975), pp. 297–317; Arthur S. Goldberger, "Selection Bias in Evaluating Treatment Effects: Some Formal Illustrations," discussion paper 123–72 (University of Wisconsin–Madison, Institute for Research on Poverty, 1972; processed); Arthur S. Goldberger, "Selection Bias in Evaluating Treatment Effects: The Case of Interaction," discussion paper 129–72 (Institute for Research on Poverty, 1972; processed); Burt S. Barnow, "Conditions for the Presence or Absence of a Bias in Treatment Effect: Some Statistical Models for Head Start Evaluation," discussion paper 122–72 (Institute for Research on Poverty, 1972; processed); Barnow, "Evaluating Project Head Start," discussion paper 189–73 (Institute for Research on Poverty, 1973; processed). As Cain put it, ". . . the critical difference for avoiding bias is not whether the assignments are random or nonrandom, but whether the investigator has *knowledge of and can model* this selection process." ("Regression and Selection Models," p. 304.) Barnow was even more pessimistic about the potential for dealing with nonrandom assignment: "An unfortunate drawback of ex post facto analyses is that unless the process by which children were assigned to the treatment groups is known, it is impossible to determine if regression analysis will produce unbiased estimates of treatment effect; it may even be impossible to discuss the direction of the bias. . . . [O]ne must know the selection procedure used before any conclusion can be drawn on whether a given data set will produce biased estimates. . . ." ("Evaluating Project Head Start," pp. 14, 15.)

67. Averch and others, *How Effective Is Schooling?* p. 107.

68. Summers and Wolfe, "Equality of Educational Opportunity Quantified," p. 14.

69. *Follow-Through Planned Variation Experiment: A Synthesis of Findings*, vol. 1 (GPO, forthcoming).

70. Thomas C. Thomas and Sol H. Pelavin, *Patterns in ESEA Title I Reading Achievement*, Research Report EPRC 4537-12 (Stanford Research Institute, 1976).

71. Irving Lazar and others, "Preliminary Findings of the Developmental Continuity Longitudinal Study" (paper presented at the Office of Child Development Conference on Parents, Children, and Continuity, El Paso, Texas, May 23, 1977; processed). For a summary of the results of other recent studies of early childhood, see Thomas W. Hertz, "The Impact of Federal Early Childhood Programs on Children: Executive Summary" (Department of Health, Education, and Welfare, Office of the Assistant Secretary for Planning and Evaluation, 1977; processed).

72. Andre Daniere, "Discussion," *American Economic Review*, vol. 56 (May 1966, *Papers and Proceedings, 1965*), p. 398.

73. Samuel Bowles, "Schooling and Inequality from Generation to Generation," *Journal of Political Economy*, vol. 80 (May–June 1972, pt. 2), pp. S219–51.

74. Paul Taubman has concluded that such variables as parental education, father's occupation, number of siblings, religion, region of birth, and rural upbringing, used in previous studies to control for genetic inheritance and family environment, are inadequate to that task. He finds that the estimated return to education may be reduced by as much as two-thirds if these influences are adequately measured; see Taubman, "Earnings, Education, Genetics, and Environment," *Journal of Human Resources*, vol. 11 (Fall 1976), pp. 447–61. William M. Mason and others, "Models of Reponse Error in Student Reports of Parental Socioeconomic Characteristics," in William H. Sewell, Robert M. Hauser, and David L. Featherman, *Schooling and Achievement in American Society* (Academic Press, 1976), p. 494, report that failure to correct regressions for error in measured status origins will result in biased estimates. This is found to be true even if the status measures are randomly erroneous and of high and equal validity.

75. Samuel Bowles and Herbert Gintis, "I.Q. in the U.S. Class Structure," *Social Policy*, vol. 3 (November–December 1972—January–February 1973, double issue), p. 66. In addition, radical critics of educational policy have compiled extensive evidence that, in their view, supports this contention. See references in Samuel Bowles and Herbert Gintis, *Schooling in Capitalist America: Educational Reform and the Contradictions of Economic Life* (Basic Books, 1976).

76. See Herbert Gintis, "Education, Technology, and the Characteristics of Worker Productivity," *American Economic Review*, vol. 61 (May 1971, *Papers and Proceedings, 1970*), pp. 266–79; Richard C. Edwards, "Individual Traits and Organizational Incentives: What Makes a 'Good' Worker?" *Journal of Human Resources*, vol. 11 (Winter 1976), pp. 51–68.

77. Thurow, *Generating Inequality*, pp. 86–88.

78. The major academic exponent of this view has been Paul Taubman. See Paul Taubman and Terence Wales, *Higher Education and Earnings: College as an Investment and a Screening Device* (McGraw-Hill, 1974). Taubman and

various colleagues find that certain occupations are overpopulated by those with advanced education to a greater extent than estimates based on a decision by workers to maximize income would suggest. He also estimates that about one-third of the returns usually attributed to education are really due to mental ability and other personal characteristics that are discovered, not created, by schools (p. 11).

79. Among the most impressive of these attempts is Zvi Griliches and William M. Mason, "Education, Income, and Ability," *Journal of Political Economy*, vol. 80 (May–June 1972, pt. 2), pp. S74–103. Recent studies of twins lend support to the proposition that no practical, explicit list of variables can account for all relevant genetic and family influences; see Taubman, "Earnings, Education, Genetics, and Environment."

80. See Burton A. Weisbrod, "Comment," *Journal of Political Economy*, vol. 80 (May–June 1972, pt. 2), pp. S139–41. Nathan Keyfitz attributes to Newton the belief that he "was not more clever than other men, but only that he could hold his mind longer on one point." "Can Inequality Be Cured?" *Public Interest*, no. 31 (Spring 1973), p. 96. See John Maynard Keynes, "Newton, the Man," in James R. Newman, *The World of Mathematics*, vol. 1 (Simon and Schuster, 1956), pp. 277–85. John S. Akin and Irwin Garfinkel state, "Unless it is assumed that cognitive development is the only school output that affects future earnings and that achievement test scores measure *all* cognitive development that affects earnings, it is impossible to generalize from the relationship between school expenditures and achievement test scores to the relationship between school expenditures and future earnings." "Economic Returns to Education Quality: An Empirical Analysis for Whites, Blacks, Poor Whites, and Poor Blacks," discussion paper 224–74 (Institute for Research on Poverty, 1974; processed), p. 1.

81. Finis Welch, "Human Capital Theory," p. 68. Henry M. Levin reached identical conclusions: "Whether schools sort according to already-existing characteristics or actually inculcate these characteristics in students cannot be determined without very intensive studies. Possibly both aspects are prevalent but there is no apparent evidence that permits differentiation between the two. Thus, any evidence tending to support the cognitive and noncognitive socialization hypotheses would certainly be consistent with a sorting and selection hypothesis as well." "Education, Life Chances, and the Courts: The Role of Social Science Evidence," *Law and Contemporary Problems*, vol. 39 (Spring 1975), pp. 230–31.

82. Bowles and Gintis, *Schooling in Capitalist America*, and references cited there.

83. For a full exposition of this view see Lester Thurow, *Generating Inequality*. Thurow is careful to state that the "job competition" model is a polar opposite from the "wage competition" model, which closely resembles the standard human capital analysis, and that the truth probably is somewhere between (pp. 75–76).

84. For a thorough theoretical treatment of this possibility, see Joseph E. Stiglitz, "The Theory of 'Screening,' Education, and the Distribution of In-

come," *American Economic Review*, vol. 65 (June 1975), pp. 283–300. R. Joseph Monsen and Anthony Downs make a closely related point: "If all the schools in an entire metropolitan area were financed equally out of one huge district, then such differentiation of expenditure would be harder to achieve, or perhaps impossible. . . . In our opinion, total spending on schools under such circumstances would probably fall. Parents in each sub-area would be unable to improve facilities or change the student-teacher ratio . . . by increasing expenditures, for any such increase would be diluted by being divided among all schools equally. They therefore would have no interest in increasing such expenditures on education" (emphasis omitted). "Public Goods and Private Status," *Public Interest*, no. 23 (Spring 1971), p. 70. See also Richard Freeman, *The Overeducated American*. Paul Taubman and Terence Wales, "Education as an Investment and a Screening Device," in Juster, ed., *Education, Income, and Human Behavior*, pp. 95–121, found that the social returns to education, especially if discounted for screening, are below returns thought to be available on ordinary investments by business, though not necessarily below rates of return available to individuals.

85. Henry M. Levin, "A Decade of Policy Developments in Improving Education and Training for Low-Income Populations," in Robert H. Haveman, ed., *A Decade of Federal Antipoverty Programs: Achievements, Failures, and Lessons* (Academic Press, 1977), pp. 168, 170–71.

86. See Bowles and Gintis, *Schooling in Capitalist America*.

87. Actually the book was written solely by Jencks based on a collection of studies by Jencks and the other authors listed on the title page.

88. Jencks and others, *Inequality*, p. 7.

89. See ibid., pp. 226–27. Jencks had no data on brothers at all, a fact noted at the time by Alice Rivlin ("Forensic Social Science," pp. 73–74) and later underscored by John A. Brittain in *The Inheritance of Economic Status* (Brookings Institution, 1977), p. 13. The attribution of unexplained variation to "luck," Jencks later admitted, was a mistake, but before he did so Nathan Keyfitz wrote, "To suppose that the portion of income variation not explained by the identified variables of schooling, I.Q., and home environment is *objectively* random, is to adopt the statistical model with a wholehearted literalness that embarrasses statisticians," "Can Inequality Be Cured?" p. 94. The point, of course, was the same one made years before by Karl Mannheim on the tendency to misuse statistics in the social sciences, "Instead of attempting to discover what is most significant with the highest degree of precision possible under the existing circumstances, one tends to be content to attribute importance to what is measurable merely because it happens to be measurable." Quoted by Stephan Michelson, "The Further Responsibility of Intellectuals," *Harvard Educational Review*, vol. 43 (February 1973), p. 96.

90. All three positions were taken in the *Harvard Educational Review*, vol. 43 (February 1973). Beverly Duncan enthusiastically commented, "Take as given that the distribution of income among American adults is too unequal. Do we attempt to equalize incomes by attempting to make individuals more nearly equal with respect to education and other characteristics that influence

earning power? Or do we attempt to lessen the range of incomes which an American adult may receive? We have tried the former. Jencks and his collaborators say we should try the latter. They are right." ("Comments on Inequality," p. 122.) Kenneth B. Clark attacked not only the substance of the book, but what he labels its "essentially glib, journalistic, smart-alecky manner" and its "exploitation of Madison Avenue advertising techniques." ("Social Policy, Power, and Social Science Research," p. 116.) Alice Rivlin commented on Jencks's assertion that education is less effective than taxes and transfers in equalizing the income distribution: "But who thinks otherwise? I do not know anyone who contends that education reform is a more effective way to reduce the inequality of income than giving the poor more money. Maybe some enthusiasts in the early days of the War on Poverty sounded as though they thought education were more effective, but they have long since altered their views. . . ." ("Forensic Social Science," p. 65.)

91. Some of the surveys of the impact of educational inputs on test scores and subsequent earnings cited by Jencks (Project Talent in the United States and the Plowden Report in England) were longitudinal in that students initially surveyed were reinterviewed later. But neither survey was longitudinal in the sense that it contained information on educational resources available to children in successive intervals. For the Plowden Report, see *Children and Their Primary Schools*, a Report of the Central Advisory Council for Education (England) (London: Her Majesty's Stationery Office, 1967).

92. Brittain, *Inheritance of Economic Status*. See also Taubman, "Earnings, Education, Genetics, and Environment."

93. Mary Corcoran, Christopher Jencks, and Michael Olneck, "The Effects of Family Background on Earnings," *American Economic Review,* vol. 66 (May 1976, *Papers and Proceedings, 1975*), pp. 430–35.

94. Jacob Mincer, *Schooling, Experience, and Earnings* (Columbia University Press for the National Bureau of Economic Research, 1974). Mincer builds on the fact that earnings of those who undergo more on-the-job training than average start lower and rise more rapidly after termination of formal education and reach a maximum later than do earnings of those who receive less on-the-job training. He estimates that eight to ten years after the end of school, people earn about the same amount regardless of on-the-job training. About one-third of the variation in the logarithm of annual earnings is explained statistically by variations in education for this group; about one-half is explained if the number of weeks worked is controlled statistically. Mincer makes no effort to take into account either intelligence (or academic achievement) or socioeconomic background. If he had done so, presumably the proportion of the variation in income explained by all of these factors would have been well over one-third (one-half if the number of hours worked is included).

95. *Inequality* contains a few paragraphs reporting similar facts about the relation between parental status and years of schooling in five different ways, some of which make schooling sound like an important determinant of income and some of which make it sound trivial. At the end Jencks remarks, "We have presented our data in a number of different ways, but it should be clear that

the problem of interpretation remains a large one." Unfortunately, this example appears on page 358, sandwiched between the last of three dense appendixes and 23 pages of references.

96. Jencks cites the evidence adduced by Lee Rainwater that people described as fair approximately the wage differentials that actually prevailed but seemed prepared to provide support for those who were unable to earn sufficient income. Lee Rainwater, *What Money Buys: Inequality and the Social Meanings of Income* (Basic Books, 1974), pp. 159–78.

97. Thomas Ribich wrote in 1968: ". . . there is little question that the current antipoverty efforts are founded on a belief that simple prolongation of schooling, of present quality, is of secondary importance." *Education and Poverty,* p. 14.

98. However, there is no evidence that *broad* programs to improve health care, nutrition, or housing, or income support for the poor significantly and consistently affect educational outcomes. One possible exception is the small positive impact of income support on school attendance observed in the rural income maintenance experiment. See Charles Mallar and Rebecca Maynard, "An Overview of the Analyses of the Effects of the Rural and New Jersey Income Maintenance Experiments on School Performance and Educational Attainment," MPR Working Paper C–7 (Mathematica Policy Research, 1975; processed). See Henry J. Aaron, *Healthy, Wealthy, and Wise: Backdoor Approaches to Education* (Aspen Institute for Humanistic Studies, 1977).

99. James Coleman, "The Concept of Equality of Educational Opportunity," *Harvard Educational Review,* vol. 38 (Winter 1968), p. 15.

100. Henry M. Levin, "Education, Life Chances, and the Courts," p. 237.

chapter four **Unemployment and Inflation**

Unlike popular and academic ideas about the effect of education on future earnings, which were vague and at least partly correct, views of political leaders and academics in the early 1960s about unemployment and the labor market were more precise and turned out to be demonstrably false in many important respects.

The unemployed, like the poor, were viewed as definable groups. The problem of "hard-core unemployment" absorbed political, journalistic, and intellectual attention, and training programs were designed to solve it. Widespread concern about the impact of automation and structural unemployment caused many government officials and some academics to stress the difficulty of reducing unemployment much below the 5 to 6 percent range that prevailed from the mid-1950s through 1964. Improved training, education, and relocation of workers or regional development were viewed as necessary by some and, with enough aggregate demand, sufficient to reduce the unemployment rate to 4 percent and eventually even lower. In a review of economic policy during the 1960s, one scholar asserted that the attitude among at least some economists "was that within wide limits the norm of 'full employment' was what the nation wished to make it."[1] The penalty for low unemployment would be inflation, but it was anticipated by many to be modest and by some as subject to attenuation through a variety of policies, including training programs to improve the match between the skills workers possessed and those demanded by employers, presidential exhortation, and such informal devices as wage-price guideposts.

With the passage of time, these views were modified or rejected. It became clear that fears about the impact of automation were fantasy; equally exaggerated but opposite fears about the end of economic growth from exhaustion of natural resources and pollution replaced concern over automation. The national significance of the hard-core unemployed was seen

to be minor compared to the difficulties encountered by the "soft-core employed," the millions of workers who had no difficulty finding jobs of
sorts but could not land or keep jobs that held out the prospect of promotion and a decent wage. The idea that unemployment could be reduced to
4 percent or even less if the nation would only tolerate an increase in prices
of a few percent a year lost much academic respectability and political
support. New theories about the operation of labor markets competed with
the old view that labor markets in a rough way recognized and rewarded
the inherent skills of workers. In the late 1960s reformers, concerned that
workers lacked the skills to perform the increasingly demanding tasks a
modern economy required, had urged sympathetic administrations and
Congress to introduce programs to accelerate the acquisition of such
skills. In the early 1970s they were calling for government programs to
upgrade the content, to increase the pay, and to speed the elimination of
low-skill, low-wage jobs whose disappearance had in the 1960s been held
partly responsible for unemployment. Unfortunately, no generally accepted view of labor markets now exists with which to explain the problem
of wage inflation or upon which to base policies to reduce unemployment.

A Backward Glance

In academic and political discussions during the 1960s unemployment,
like Gaul, was commonly divided into three parts—cyclical, frictional, and
structural—according to whether the unemployment was due to a lack of
aggregate demand, to normal labor turnover, or to automation or other
technological change, shifts in the composition of demand, or foreign competition.[2] But other categorizations were common; a survey of the "definitions and terminology describing the major types of unemployment (cyclical, structural, frictional, seasonal, etc.)" prepared for the Joint Economic
Committee in 1961 contained a glossary with fifty-eight different terms
used in various combinations for describing unemployment.[3] The common characteristic of all such categories was that they would enable all
workers without jobs to be classified as cyclically, structurally, or fric-
tionally unemployed.

One could also classify the unemployed into those who could be expected to find work promptly, whether the cause of unemployment was
cyclical, structural, or frictional, and those who could not. Certain people
—notably white prime-age males in economically prosperous areas—fell

into the former category; others—notably women and especially blacks of both sexes and all inhabitants of depressed areas—tended to fall into the latter group, often labeled the hard-core unemployed. Not all women or blacks or residents of depressed areas, of course, were unemployed; but once out of a job, it was perceived that members of these groups tended to experience much longer than average spells of unemployment. As a report of the Chamber of Commerce put it: "Some people are chronically unemployed. Apart from those too old, too sick, or too disabled to work, these people are unemployed primarily because (1) they lack the qualifications needed for available jobs, and/or (2) they lack the basic abilities—such as reading and writing—to qualify for training for jobs"; and the solution for such unemployment followed directly from its description: "To devise solutions for such chronically unemployed people, priority should be given to programs that offer education and skill training that will lead to jobs in the competitive markets."[4]

To abolish cyclical unemployment, it was thought necessary only to ensure sufficient aggregate demand through fiscal and monetary policies. To eliminate structural unemployment, it was necessary to ensure the best possible match between the skills workers possessed and those employers demanded. A variety of government policies would be required to achieve this goal, including education, training, regional development, and measures to protect workers against job loss due to foreign competition. Frictional unemployment was viewed as necessary in a free labor market in which workers shopped for the jobs that best fitted their skills, locational preferences, and tastes among pay, fringe benefits, and working conditions; its reduction below some necessary minimum would lower economic efficiency and work to the long-run detriment of both employers and workers themselves. Its elimination was viewed as impossible because some labor market entrants always would be seeking their first jobs and other labor force participants would be seeking new jobs after having quit or been fired.

Government fiscal and monetary policies could generate sufficient demand to create enough jobs for all who wanted to work, economists proclaimed, but aggregate policies could not ensure that the jobs would be in the right places or require the available skills of workers seeking employment. Consequently, as the unemployment rate declined, it became increasingly likely that the demand for workers in certain areas or with particular skills might exceed supply at going wage rates. First, wages in such areas or for such skills would be increased; then the prices of commodities

those workers produced would begin to rise and the effects would spread
to other sectors, causing a general increase in prices and wages. The extent
and size of such an increase would be greater, the closer the economy was
to general full employment. In short, there would be an inverse relationship between the rate of unemployment and the rate at which prices and
wages would increase. Research on data for the United States and Great
Britain seemed to confirm the existence of such a relationship. This relationship came to be known as the Phillips curve, after the economist who
postulated it. It suggested that the United States could have price stability,
but only if unemployment was sufficiently high—around 5 to 6 percent—
to prevent excessive demand for labor from occurring often or intensely.
Conversely, lower unemployment could be achieved, but, as a result, labor
markets would be so tight that wages would rise faster than productivity;
the result, sooner (if profit margins were maintained) or later (if profits
were squeezed), would be inflation.

The facts were unsettling. After postwar demobilization, unemployment had averaged 4.3 percent from 1948 to 1957, but during the succeeding seven years, from 1958 to 1964, unemployment averaged 5.8
percent. Except for the runup in prices during the consumer binges immediately after World War II and at the onset of the Korean War, prices
remained remarkably stable, rising only 1.5 percent per year at an annual
rate from 1948 to 1956. But inflation, set loose during the mid-1950s,
persisted until unemployment had remained at uncustomarily high rates
from 1957 to 1959. The trade-off between unemployment and inflation
was not precise, but it was disturbing.

To improve what then seemed a rather dismal trade-off, the government
could take a number of steps to reduce structural unemployment—that
due to the imbalance between available skills and the needs of employers.
Where the supply of potential workers was excessive, programs to encourage regional development were advocated and enacted, first focused on
Appalachia, later diffused more broadly under the aegis of the Area Redevelopment Administration. Other proposals, such as relocation allowances to help unemployed workers move from areas of high unemployment, received considerable academic and administration support, but
foundered on political objections best summarized by the remark of one
member of Congress: "Sir, are you asking *me* to vote for appropriations
to help *my* constituents move to some *other* district?" To increase the supply of needed skills, numerous programs were proposed and, it seems,
almost as many were enacted under which the federal government trained

workers or paid for their training. The first major program along these lines was the Manpower Development and Training Act of 1962, but it was followed by a torrent of similar legislation subsumed under the War on Poverty or the Great Society.[5]

Some observers felt that the problem of structural unemployment could be solved only at enormous cost, if at all. Among these pessimists were only a few academic economists but a goodly number of lawyers, sociologists, and other nonspecialists who were impressed with the computer and the technological breakthroughs it seemed to make possible. The problem, as this group perceived it, was that technological change had accelerated or changed in character, causing large numbers of workers to become essentially redundant and unemployable. New words were applied to the phenomenon; cybernation referred to the development of machines to control other machines, automation to the fact that tasks previously performed by people were now performed automatically by machines. In fact, both developments had been occurring since the onset of the industrial revolution (indeed, since the bow and arrow), and the rate of technological advancement as measured by worker productivity had not increased recently.

But in the view of such groups as the Ad Hoc Committee on the Triple Revolution, something new, worthy of being designated as a revolution, was happening, something that invalidated the entire basis of distribution that had until then served to allocate goods among consumers. According to this group, unlimited production was around the corner and there was no way that all previously employed workers could be fruitfully employed.[6]

A less extreme position was taken by economist Charles Killingsworth, who argued only that automation and cybernetics were qualitatively different and quantitatively greater than previous technological change and that they had made structural unemployment more intractable. Moreover, structural unemployment, Killingsworth maintained, would grow in the future as automation proceeded.[7] In fact, adherents of the view that structural unemployment was bad and getting worse were later characterized as "a fairly odd assortment of bed fellows," ranging from the Ad Hoc Committee on the Triple Revolution, through labor market economists concerned about displacement, to conservatives disturbed at the fiscal stimulus advocated by the Council of Economic Advisers and other academic economists.[8]

Professional economists responded to this challenge by inquiring whether there was evidence that structural unemployment had increased during the preceding decade. If it had not, then there was no obvious reason why unemployment rates of 4 percent or less, common in the first postwar decade, could not be achieved again—for example, by tax cuts that would increase private spending. A study by the Joint Economic Committee in 1961 suggested that the increase in unemployment was more likely to have been due to inadequate demand than to an increase in structural unemployment.[9] In 1964, a leading labor economist summarized the views of professional economists with the comment that "to submit the rise-in-structural-unemployment hypothesis to yet another test may strike some as pretty much like subjecting an apparently dead horse to one last thumping."[10] With singular lack of caution, *New York Times* economics reporter Edwin L. Dale, Jr., predicted that "with no new training programs, with no shortening of the work week, with no special manpower policies, with no radical measures like paying people who do not work, this country will get full employment by expansion of demand alone."[11] This view and that of most economists was founded on the belief that with sufficient demand employers would train workers for available jobs or redesign jobs for available workers. Furthermore, the intuition that workers were in the wrong place or lacked the right skills for available jobs was repeatedly refuted by analysis.[12]

With the declaration of the War on Poverty, however, the issue was transformed. The question was not whether structural unemployment had increased, but how to combat it. There was little disagreement that the problem was serious. Unemployment rates of different demographic groups varied widely. White prime-age males enjoyed the lowest rates; blacks, women, and the young all suffered from substantially more unemployment. Cutting across all of these groups, those who lacked education and training suffered higher than average unemployment. Writing from their perspectives in the research office at the Office of Economic Opportunity, Joseph Kershaw and Robert Levine asked for an end to debate between those who stressed structural causes of unemployment and those who stressed demand: "Our thesis . . . is that the disagreement between the structural and aggregate demand theories of unemployment is largely an illusory one; that both increased demand and structural change are necessary support for one another in solving the labor market portion of the poverty problem."[13]

In the rhetoric of the War on Poverty, structural changes primarily meant additions to human capital through education and training, not changes in the demand for low-wage workers or in the composition of jobs. Improved education was necessary to provide new entrants to the labor force with the necessary abilities to read and write and the ability to acquire job-related skills. One observer labeled federal grants to school districts with poor children under the Elementary and Secondary Education Act of 1965 as "the most important manpower policy of all."[14] But a large number of programs, directed to training adults or young people or to encouraging them to remain in school by providing part-time jobs, followed in rapid succession: Job Corps, to provide basic remedial education and training in live-in centers; Neighborhood Youth Corps, to provide money and jobs to adolescents and young adults while schooling continued or after it terminated; job opportunities in the business sector; the concentrated employment program; the work incentive (WIN) program for welfare recipients; and many others. Whether these programs were necessary to permit the unemployment rate to decline below about 5 percent without inflation, as the structuralists suggested, or 4 percent, as maintained by those who stressed the importance of sufficient demand, was clearly less important than that both groups viewed them as necessary to permit full use of economic resources, as important for the prevention of inflation, and as essential for equality of economic opportunity.

The fact of the matter was that enactment of the 1964 tax cut and the later increase in military expenditures associated with the Vietnam War drove unemployment below 4 percent even before the programs of the War on Poverty and the Great Society were fully under way. Inflation rose almost immediately, but concern that it would continue to rise was limited. The various training programs were directed at structural problems in the labor market. The academic and journalistic debate between demand and structural strategies to deal with unemployment was made moot by the political pursuit of both.

New Facts, New Theories, New Policies

No more than five years later, most economists had concluded that the goal of a 4 percent unemployment rate without excessive and perhaps accelerating inflation was unachievable. However, explanations emphasized not the diagnosis initially advanced by the "structuralists," but rather changes in the composition of the labor force and new theories of the relationship between inflation and unemployment. The political goal of 4 percent unemployment, regarded as only a modest interim target when first put forward in the Kennedy administration, had been abandoned because few observers of the labor market thought that an unemployment rate below 5 percent could be achieved in the foreseeable future without triggering rapid inflation; many doubted whether even 5 percent was possible. Moreover, the conviction that training programs or education would bring a more ambitious target within reach seemed to have vanished. One reason for this turnabout was that evaluators had dealt as harshly with government-sponsored training programs as they had with efforts to use education to improve economic opportunities for the poor. As will become clear, these evaluations suffered from many of the same shortcomings. A second reason was that events had invalidated all previous estimates of a simple trade-off between inflation and unemployment. A third reason was the development of a better understanding of the nature of unemployment.

Character of Unemployment

The categories into which unemployment had been classified were intuitively satisfying; it was easy to understand that unemployment could be caused by recession, depressed regions, or job switching. Unfortunately, these causes help little in interpreting the actual experience of the overwhelming majority of the unemployed.[15] Except at very high rates of unemployment, nearly all unemployed workers appear to find jobs after a relatively brief period of joblessness whether they are unemployed because of a cyclical decline in economic activity, because an obsolete factory has closed, because of recent migration to a new city, or because of recently entering the labor market. This seems to be true whatever the initial cause of joblessness and whatever the person's sex, age, or race. A small fraction of the unemployed experience protracted unemployment. Furthermore, members of some groups find it easier to find jobs than do others; the average period out of a job is slightly longer for blacks than for whites, for example. But the difference is nowhere near sufficient to account for the fact that black unemployment rates are about twice white unemployment rates. Young workers of both races and sexes seem to be able to find jobs after shorter spells of unemployment than do older workers, in sharp and paradoxical contrast to the fact that young workers' unemployment typically is manyfold greater than that of prime-age workers.

The large difference in unemployment rates instead seems to be due to two factors that do not fit neatly within the old categories. First, there are enormous differences among demographic groups in the probability of losing a job. White teenage boys, for example, are more than four times more likely than white prime-age males to lose a job either voluntarily or involuntarily; black prime-age males are nearly two times more likely than white prime-age males to lose a job. Women, black or white, are less likely than men of the same race to lose a job, although blacks are more likely than whites of each sex to lose a job. Second, and even more important, there are large differences among demographic groups in the probability of workers who enter the labor force remaining unemployed after the temporarily unsuccessful search for a job.

As a result, most of the differences between unemployment rates of blacks and whites, men and women, young and prime-age workers, can be attributed to the frequency of unemployment; very little is attributable to differences in the duration of unemployment. Teenage nonwhite females, for example, are nearly sixteen times as likely to be unemployed as are white prime-age males. A sizable fraction of the unemployed are temporarily laid off with a fixed date of recall; that is, they have a job but have been furloughed without pay. Many such workers, as well as many who are indefinitely laid off, do not actively search for work.

The picture that emerges is one of a massive lottery, in which people at any given time are in one of three states—employed, unemployed, or not in the labor force. The chances of moving from unemployment into a job differs, but by only a little, from one demographic group to another. But the chances of moving from employment either into unemployment or out of the labor force altogether differ greatly and account for almost all of the differences among demographic groups in unemployment.

These facts are quite inconsistent with the belief, widely held in the 1960s, that the high unemployment rates of blacks, youths, or females were due to the inability to find jobs. Most of the difference seems to be frictional, if one of the formerly popular categories must be used. Something seems to be wrong either with the jobs to which these groups can gain access or with the habits of these groups that cause them to leave employment so often.

These facts should not be construed as suggesting that long-term unemployment does not exist, that those who experience long-term unemployment may not suffer from important disabilities or lack skills, or that the unemployed do not include disproportionate numbers of blacks and other minorities. Indeed, clear-cut evidence demonstrates that the chance of finding a job diminishes the longer a worker is unemployed and that a disproportionate fraction of those unemployed longer than twenty-six weeks are black. The personal catastrophe that protracted unemployment can inflict is beyond question. Both because those with the fewest problems find jobs first, on the average, and because protracted unemployment creates and exacerbates existing problems, the long-term unemployed are more likely than other groups to require assistance in finding and keeping a job.

The point is that long-term unemployment accounts for a very small part of the difference in unemployment rates among demographic groups, and eliminating protracted unemployment completely would reduce total unemployment negligibly. If no unemployment in 1976 had lasted longer than twenty-six weeks, the unemployment rate would have been 6.3 percent rather than 7.7 percent; in 1973, a year of relative prosperity, the elimination of unemployment lasting more than twenty-six weeks would have reduced the overall unemployment rate from 4.9 percent to 4.5 percent.[16] The newly discovered facts, of course, do not indicate whether high turnover rates are due to job characteristics that lead to layoffs or quitting or to worker characteristics that lead to the same results. A recent attempt to determine which cause of high turnover was more important produced inconclusive results.[17] But the stress on these facts marks the end of the neat distinction between the "unemployed" and the "employed."[18]

Another pillar of the old structural unemployment hypothesis crumbled as evidence accumulated that technological change has not accelerated. In fact, it has slowed. Productivity, measured as output per unit of input, rose 2.3 percent a year between 1948 and 1955, but rose only 2.1 percent a year between 1955 and 1969.[19] The computer has not revolutionized the economy, however significant it has been for particular industries. Automation and cybernation, the modish fears of an earlier age, have been replaced by concern over the exhaustion of resources or pollution, which is thought by some to herald the end of economic growth and, in some versions, mass starvation, diminishing worldwide living standards, and other terrestrial disasters. Actual developments will no doubt be less dramatic than the fears of doom through stagnation so extravagantly expressed today, just as they were considerably less drastic than the predictions of doom through technological progress expressed a decade or more ago.

Unemployment and Inflation

Although the reasoning advanced by the structuralists in support of the proposition that an unemployment rate of 4 percent or less could not be achieved without creating inflation has been contradicted by events, the proposition itself has been accepted. It is now generally agreed that unless something else is done to keep prices in check, any attempt to reduce unemployment through aggregate fiscal and monetary policy to levels thought attainable in the 1960s will cause excessive and possibly accelerating inflation. The reasons for this belief are quite diverse and no consensus seems emergent.

According to one line of reasoning, the 4 percent target for unemployment was reasonable when it was advanced in the early 1960s, but it is unattainable today. Conditions are now less favorable, it is alleged, because the composition of the labor force has changed. In particular, the proportion of the labor force composed of women, teenagers, and other young workers has increased.[20] These groups are less productive than are prime-age males, as signified by their low wages. Furthermore, young workers and women change jobs and move in and out of the labor force more often than do men. They generate more unemployment in the process because they spend some time classified as unemployed while they seek work. For both reasons, it is argued, a given number of unemployed workers represents less unemployed productivity and exercises less drag on wage increases than did the same percentage of unemployed workers a decade ago.

To the extent that unemployment, measured in terms of productivity, retards wage increases, a given level of unemployment, measured conventionally, corresponds to a tighter and more inflationary labor market today than was the case a decade ago. Consequently, according to this view, the trade-off between inflation and unemployment is less favorable today than in the past. The wage inflation associated with about 5 percent unemployment is about the same as the wage inflation that was associated with 4 percent unemployment in the past. From the standpoint of inflation, it is argued, the definition of full employment should be revised. Furthermore, experience with inflation at palpable rates during the past decade seems to have made both workers and their employers more sensitive and resulting wage and price decisions more responsive to labor market conditions.[21]

The view that full employment corresponds to a higher rate of unemployment than in the past does not imply that in a social sense the unemployment of women or young workers is less serious than that of prime-age males, although some people support this quite independent proposition. The deprivation caused by the unemployment of a low-wage worker and the damage caused by unfortunate initial contacts with the labor market may be as harmful as that caused by the unemployment of a prime-age male. The point is simply that the change in the composition of unemployment may have one effect on wage stability and quite another on social stability.[22]

This argument can be turned around, however. During the postwar decades, the educational attainment of the labor force has increased markedly. Since unemployment rates for the relatively well-educated are lower than those of the little-educated, this change in the demographic composition of the labor force should have made the attainment of ever-lower rates of unemployment feasible.[23] An obvious, but unsatisfactory, rejoinder to this argument—that the education-specific unemployment rates may have increased, thereby negating the supposedly beneficial effects on unemployment of increased education—raises a troublesome question for those who point to the changing age-sex mix of the labor force to explain why low unemployment has become increasingly difficult to achieve. Why were unemployment rates of the young and of women, already higher absolutely than those of prime-age males in the 1960s, even higher in the 1970s? Why had employers not altered the mix of jobs to take advantage of the available supply of workers? If they did not react to this shift in supply, why would they react to other shifts in supply—such as the growing stock of well-educated workers—by altering the mix of available jobs?

The view that there is a stable trade-off between inflation and unemployment has fallen on hard times. First, no estimated relationship has successfully forecast combinations of unemployment and inflation for very long.[24] Second, although each estimate is rather sensitive to the pattern of wage increases contained in union contracts, the pattern assumed in all studies is arbitrary and not necessarily consistent with fragmentary available evidence.[25]

The view that there is any *stable* trade-off between unemployment and the rate at which wages increase has come in for more basic criticism from those who deny that *any* long-run trade-off exists. The criticism now comes from two directions. One group holds that only at an equilibrium rate of unemployment can stable prices be maintained: at lower unemployment rates wage increases will accelerate and, eventually, so will price increases; at higher-than-equilibrium unemployment rates, prices and wages will decline at ever faster rates.[26] If workers are able to obtain wage increases that exceed productivity growth, prices will begin to rise. Once workers and employers come to expect inflation, all negotiations will take such increases for granted and start there. If labor markets are tight enough to generate wage increases greater than increases in productivity, such increases will be in addition to the commonly expected rate of inflation. Such wage bargains will necessitate ever larger price increases, which then come to be expected, and so on.

The other group holds that the relation between unemployment and wage inflation exists only in the fevered imaginings of economists. Unemployment, it is argued, is determined by overall economic conditions generated by fiscal and monetary policy. Wage increases are institutionally determined by businessmen and workers, who are heavily influenced by customary relative wages. When special events disturb these wage contours, attempts to restore them can trigger protracted wage inflation.[27]

Throughout the history of the Phillips curve, its advocates have been bedeviled by difficulty in explaining the failure of previously estimated statistical relations to forecast accurately the rate of wage inflation associated with any level of unemployment. During the early 1960s, the problem was that wages persistently rose *less* than previously estimated statistical relations suggested. Various explanations were put forward: the alleged success of the wage-price guideposts employed by the Kennedy and Johnson administrations from 1962 to 1966;[28] faulty statistics on unemployment that understated the pool of workers potentially available for work;[29] or, as at least one analyst suggested, both.[30] Labor economists, in fact, were surprised by the size of the increase in the labor force during the period 1961–69 when unemployment more or less steadily declined from 6.7 percent to 3.5 percent.[31] But both of these explanations of the better-than-anticipated performance of the economy accepted the reality of a trade-off between inflation and unemployment.

In the early 1970s, a combination of high unemployment and rapid increase in wages and prices completely defied previously estimated relations. Both adherents and critics of the idea that there was a trade-off between inflation and unemployment tried to assimilate these developments. Adherents pointed to the devaluation of the dollar, which raised the price of imports, to the world food inflation, which boosted food costs at home and stimulated demands by labor for higher wages, and to the tripling of fuel prices triggered by the Organization of Petroleum Exporting Countries as special factors that created an inflationary environment. Faced with these inflationary events, governments tried to fight inflation by curtailing demand, but went far enough only to increase unemployment, not to snuff out the inflation.[32] Unfortunately, this after-the-fact explanation sounded to many like a rationalization of a discredited theory.

These facts were also assimilated by critics of the Phillips curve. Those who held that there exists some natural rate of unemployment viewed the inflation and high unemployment of the early 1970s as the inevitable consequence of attempting for too long to keep unemployment too low. The result was a bad case of accelerating inflation, which only an extended period of economic slack could cure; high unemployment was a regrettable side effect that the economy would have to endure, possibly for a few years, to ensure a complete remission of the disease of inflation. Those who denied that there was any long-run trade-off between unemployment and inflation simply pointed to the facts and let them speak for themselves.

Which of these views turns out to be closest to the truth hinges on the resolution of several analytical questions. How much does previous inflation affect current wage increases? How much do wage increases in one economic sector affect those in another? When inflation has persisted for some time, will both employers and employees assume the continuation of inflation when they bargain for wages and set prices? What events must occur to change those expectations and how long will it take for those events to change inflationary expectations?

On one issue proponents of the Phillips curve have given considerable ground to those who contend that there is a natural rate of unemployment. If a 1 percent increase in prices in a previous period is associated with a less than 1 percent increase in current wages, then a trade-off between unemployment and inflation exists. In that event, a particular rate of unemployment and attendant labor market conditions lead to some estimated increase in wages. If this wage inflation exceeds the growth of productivity, then eventually prices will rise by the difference between the increase in wages and the growth of productivity. As long as this price increase is not fully translated into higher wages, the increase in both wages and prices will settle down to some stable rate. If, however, a rise in prices sooner or later causes the rate of change in wages to increase by the same proportion as prices, then unemployment below some critical level cannot be sustained. Empirical estimates of the proportion of any increase in prices that is translated into wage increases have steadily risen. Initial estimates suggested that wages rise about another 4 percent for every 10 percent increase in prices. As time passed, these estimates rose until wages were calculated to rise about 8 to 9 additional percent for each 10 percent increase in prices; if wages rise a full 10 percent for each 10 percent increase in prices, there is no long-term trade-off between inflation and unemployment.[33] It is apparent that the statistical differences between many of those who insist on a trade-off between inflation and unemployment and those who deny it have become quite narrow. The crucial question—whether these statistical estimates can be used for accurate forecasts—remains unanswered.

Events following the great recession of 1974 were unkind to both views. Wage and price increases both declined markedly from levels reached in 1974 in the face of unemployment that reached 9.0 percent in May 1975. Wages, which had risen 9.4 percent during 1974, rose at an annual rate of only 7.5 percent during the last half of 1975. Prices, which had risen 11.0 percent during 1974, rose at an annual rate of only 7.1 percent during the last half of 1975. But the rate of increase in both prices and wages did not diminish much further in 1976 and 1977 and was forecast to decline only slightly in 1977 and 1978, despite the persistence into 1977 of unemployment rates higher than any that had prevailed in earlier postwar recessions and that exceeded all earlier estimates of the natural rate of unemployment. Why wage and price inflation did not diminish further became a major puzzle for both models of the economic process. History had already posed a similar puzzle. During the depression unemployment rates had exceeded 10 percent for more than a decade and 20 percent for years. Nevertheless, average hourly earnings, which fell from 1930 to 1933, did not fall during the rest of the 1930s.[34] These facts are difficult to reconcile with either the Phillips curve or the natural rate hypotheses.

Manpower Training

Manpower training programs proliferated and expanded in a hectic and confusing fashion during the 1960s. They were intended to help increase economic growth by removing shortages of critical skills, to reduce the threat of inflation by improving the balance between the demand for and the supply of all skills, to assist depressed areas in regaining economic health, and to combat poverty by endowing the poor with skills that would enable them to earn adequate wages. Programs were operated through schools, factories, and community agencies. The result, in the words of one sympathetic critic, was that "few programs were able to operate as efficiently as one might otherwise have expected . . . especially . . . where there were competing programs in the same locality, with each being run on a small and inefficient scale."[35]

Federal management of most training programs enacted during the 1960s has been terminated. State and local governments still operate many of them, supported in large measure by federal funds provided through the Comprehensive Employment and Training Act (CETA), first enacted under the Nixon administration to replace a wide variety of narrowly defined federal grant-in-aid programs with broad categorical grants that would increase state and local discretion and diminish federal control. The debate about this transfer covered many issues: the political pros and cons of federal attempts to achieve narrowly defined objectives that might differ from the desires of state and local governments; the relative solicitude for problems of the poor and of minorities by different levels of government; and the general desirability of having the federal government transfer funds to state and local governments with few or no strings attached. Participants in this political debate cited evidence about the effectiveness of the many federal training programs.

This evidence consisted of the results of many economic studies of the effectiveness of these programs. Government agencies performed some of these studies; private consulting and research organizations carried out most of them.

The results of these studies fall into two categories. First, no perceptible nationwide effect of the training programs on employment or productivity could be discerned, perhaps because the programs were too small in the aggregate.[36] Nor is it clear how training can reduce unemployment unless it causes the substitution of less productive, lower-wage workers for more productive, higher-wage workers or the substitution of labor for capital. Substitution of low-skill for high-skill labor would be desirable, however, because it would delay the appearance of inflationary pressures in the labor markets for skilled workers, where labor shortages first appear during booms, and because it would improve the trade-off between inflation and unemployment. If training programs did improve the trade-off, this effect was overwhelmed by other events, for the trade-off did not in fact improve. Nor did the differences between the unemployment of blacks and that of whites narrow.[37]

Second, many analysts studied the effect of training programs on individual workers. These studies fall into a pattern familiar to consumers of educational research. A few of the programs were unambiguous failures. The work incentive program, for example, an effort to help families off the welfare rolls by offering adults basic instruction on how to get and keep jobs, was later described as misnamed because the welfare system "constituted a notorious disincentive" to gainful employment.[38] For the major training programs, however—those authorized by the Manpower Development and Training Act and the Job Corps, for example—the results were favorable and mixed, respectively. In some studies, under certain criteria, and for some groups the programs were successes; in others, they were failures.[39]

The absence of unambiguous conclusions about the effectiveness of the major training programs has many sources. First, evaluators could choose among various criteria of success, such as higher earnings or reduced unemployment; they could observe the effects of training for a relatively brief period—six months or so—or they could follow the training recipient for a longer time; they could include among the benefits of the program declines in public expenditures on behalf of the trainee, such as reduced unemployment insurance or welfare payments, or they could ignore them; they could attempt to measure, and possibly to assign a cash value to, noneconomic consequences of the training, such as changes in arrests or improvement in family stability. A program that was successful by one criterion might fail by another.

The most difficult problem in evaluating training programs, however, was deciding how to measure their effects. Should the post-training earnings of the trainee be compared with his own earnings before training or with the earnings of similar workers who had not gone through the training program? The first course was obviously unsatisfactory because trainees were never randomly selected and, in any case, the state of the economy of local labor markets, and other circumstances certain to affect job opportunities, were bound to change over time; consequently, one would never know whether the difference in earnings before and after training was due to the special characteristics or circumstances that led to the selection of the particular trainees or to the training. A worker, threatened with the loss of a job using the only skills he possessed, might seek out training, acquire new skills, and obtain a new job. His earnings might go up, down, or stay the same; but any change in earnings would be unlikely to provide an accurate guide to the value of the training.

The second course, the comparison of the change in earnings of the trainees with those of similar workers, was the mark of superior studies. It suffered from similar problems because applicants could not be assigned randomly to training or to a control group. But even if random assignment were possible, evaluations of the impact of training on individuals might fail to detect any effects if employers relied on such gross characteristics of workers as age, race, sex, or level of schooling to categorize workers into groups acceptable or unacceptable for particular jobs. An effective training program would increase the skills of a small proportion of the groups to which trainees belonged; but unless the training caused employers to change these rules-of-thumb, the training would improve earnings of the trainee no more than it would affect earnings of otherwise similar members of the same groups. The trainee might experience some short-run benefits if job placement services were part of the package of benefits that trainees receive. And, indeed, some studies found that employment and earnings increased immediately after completion of training but atrophied until, a year or eighteen months after completion, little or no difference could be observed between the earnings of the trainee and those of members of the control group. Whether these results are due to the widespread use of gross characteristics by employers in hiring or to another explanation—that training is ineffective in raising skills but helpful in finding one a job—cannot now be determined.

Thus, someone convinced of the effectiveness of training programs could argue that the apparent failure of the programs was due to their smallness. He could attribute the failure of evaluations to find higher earnings for trainees than for controls to the use by employers of gross characteristics in hiring; he could cite studies that revealed higher earnings for trainees than for controls as instances where such rules-of-thumb were not so strong as to obscure the presumed beneficent effects of training. One who lacked such faith could claim that training programs, like various educational interventions, were not consistently effective and would not have succeeded even if they had been larger. The crucial point is that there was, and still is, no practical way to determine which of these two explanations of the "facts" is correct. For this reason, decisions about whether to continue training programs and, if so, under which governmental auspices have had to be settled on grounds other than "scientific" evaluation of their effectiveness.

The Labor Market

Economists have carried on a lengthy debate among themselves about the pervasiveness of "rational, maximizing behavior." During the 1940s the debate focused on the behavior of businesses; the issue was whether they maximized profits by setting prices so that the additional revenue from selling one more unit was at least as great as the additional cost of producing one more unit. The technical argument concerned whether businesses were aware of their "marginal cost" and "marginal revenue" curves, the graphs that depicted the mathematical relations from which additional revenues and costs could be calculated. Some held that firms were aware of the extra income and expenditure that producing one more unit would entail. Others held that as a practical matter businesses could not have such detailed information, but in the long run acted *as if* they did, because firms that maximized profits would eventually drive less profitable firms from the marketplace. Still others maintained a variety of competing propositions: that businesses sought to sell as much as they could as long as their profits were satisfactory, for example, or that firms had a multiplicity of objectives among which high profits was only one.

The debate was never settled. The view that businesses maximize profits remained at the core of economic theory for a variety of reasons, one of the more important of which was that it enabled economic theorists to employ the powerful mathematical tool of calculus in drawing inferences that were subtle and suggestive and that were only on occasion conspicuously refuted. The other views have remained alive on the periphery of the profession.

A similar, long-smoldering debate concerning the operation of labor markets flared up during the late 1960s and still rages. The issues bear considerable resemblance to those in the debate over profit maximization. According to the conventional view, workers possess a set of skills determined by genetic endowment, other social and economic influences (such as parental education, religion, or income), education, on-the-job training, and experience. Their productivity in any job depends on these characteristics, and their earnings depend on this productivity. Workers find their way into the job in which their productivity, and hence their real earnings (including not only pay but also working conditions and perquisites), are as high as possible, thus ensuring that the labor force is allocated optimally among available jobs. An excess of workers with a particular set of skills will depress their wages until the demand for workers with those skills equals the supply. In planning what profession to enter and what education and training to acquire, workers are guided by the real earnings they can expect to receive.

A slight variant of this view admits that young people planning careers and older workers contemplating job changes or the acquisition of new skills lack detailed information about the various rates of return but nevertheless act *as if* they had such information. In both variants, however, the labor market operates smoothly, with wages and the number of workers in various occupations adjusting with reasonable speed to prevent persistent shortages or gluts (i.e., extended unemployment) of workers.

This view is supported by indirect, but little direct, evidence. Writing in 1966, Charles Killingsworth observed that "one of the most basic assumptions of the . . . aggregate-demand school . . . remain[ed] essentially unverified," that "when the supply of more desirable kinds of workers gets tight, employers will greatly increase their hiring of teenagers, older workers, nonwhites, and less educated workers and will concurrently engage in wholesale retraining and job redesign programs. . . . There has been virtually no empirical investigation of how employers will respond under present-day conditions to moderate increases in demand; and there haven't even been guesses as to how much private retraining programs and job design might add to unit labor costs and prices."[40] Later work by Okun and Vroman found that tight labor markets have a modest effect on job structure.[41] Michael Piore reported in a study of how industrial plants are designed and processes modified that, in the words of one engineer, "plants 'mold men to jobs, not jobs to men.' " Nevertheless, he concluded that the observed insensitivity of engineers to the supply of various kinds of workers and to their relative wages was probably consistent with cost minimization, because it was just too costly to tailor jobs to the available labor force.[42]

The view that labor markets adjust to available skills has direct bearing on what policies should be adopted to solve the problems of unemployment and low wages for workers now in the job market. If such adjustment occurs, policy should aim to improve the skills of the low-wage workers. If it occurs sluggishly or not at all, policy must increase the demand for occupations for which low-wage workers qualify or can be trained.

Critics of the view that labor markets adjust promptly to changes in the supply of skills, like those of the theory of profit maximization, hold that the world is too complex to permit such nice calculations of the value of individual workers. Instead, the labor market is encrusted with custom and habit, which impede, if they do not block, the processes described in the conventional view. According to this alternative view, the way jobs are structured, the relative wages different classes of workers receive, hiring practices, promotions, tenure and seniority, all are governed by customary behavior that prevents workers from being paid according to their marginal productivity, except by coincidence. Employers find it costly or impossible to measure the actual productivity of individual workers in most jobs; in governments and nonprofit institutions the concept of marginal productivity is hard to define. Workers in government or nonprofit institutions may produce something measurable, but it generally has no clear market value; how much, for instance, is the processing of an application for social security worth? Furthermore, finding and training new workers is costly for employers, and finding and learning new jobs is costly and upsetting for workers. As a result, employees and employers, as if guided by an invisible hand, throw up barriers to minimize these costs of job mobility and, by doing so, make indeterminate the exact wage that they will negotiate.[43] To put it another way, if workers and employers have a long-term, but imprecise, commitment to one another, the worker's marginal value to the firm may be measured over a day, a week, a year, or more, and is probably impossible to estimate precisely.[44]

Critics of the conventional view of labor markets also tend to stress the importance of the job in determining or altering the productivity of the worker. According to one variant, a good part of differences in productivity inhere in jobs that a broad cross-section of the labor force could perform about equally well. According to another, the attributes that jobs require their holders to exhibit are eventually inculcated in the worker. Jobs that require punctuality, precision, and dependability produce punctual, precise, dependable workers. Jobs that permit slack habits produce slack workers who, eventually, are rendered incapable of holding responsible and demanding employment. In either case, productivity is not something workers bring to a job; rather, the job teaches productivity to the worker or confers it on him.

Adherents of the view that businessmen maximize profits have recourse to an argument that adherents of the conventional view of labor markets cannot employ. Firms that do not pursue maximum profits in a competitive market can eventually be driven out of business by aggressive competitors that do. The profit-maximizing firm will exploit cost-reducing opportunities and cut prices in order to enlarge its share of the market. The slack firm will be unable to meet competitive prices and still make a profit and will be forced out of business. But the worker who fails to find a job in which his earnings are as high as possible will not be forced out of business. He will simply get a lower wage than he might be capable of earning.

The crucial question adherents of the conventional view of the labor market had to answer was how workers could be assured of finding the best-paying jobs. If information was hard and costly to obtain, if hiring was dominated by customary procedures that limited access to many jobs, if the wage structure was heavily influenced by differences among jobs that time had rendered legitimate, natural competitive pressures could not be relied upon to direct workers to the best-paying jobs. Workers could not be driven out of business. But they might be trapped in jobs less demanding and less rewarding than those they might perform; the structure of jobs might not respond, or might respond only with considerable delay, to surpluses or shortages of workers with various capacities. Furthermore, it is difficult to reconcile the view that wages adjust promptly and that workers move smoothly into occupations where they have the highest productivity with the palpable facts that, in the aggregate, real wages do not in general decline in the face of high unemployment, and that protracted unemployment of workers with particular skills or in different regions can coexist with labor shortages in other occupations or places. When economists forecast unemployment with econometric models, they typically assume that money wages do not fall if labor is in excess supply—that is, if there is unemployment. When they theorize about labor markets, economists typically assume that real wages adjust to clear the market. These theories are not consistent unless inflation always occurs when unemployment is high, and neither theory readily accommodates the possibility that patterns of relative wages are a dominant influence on wage changes.[45]

The seeming inconsistency among these various perspectives on how labor markets operate may be more apparent than real. The institutional rules and wage rigidity thought by many to be inconsistent with the operation of competitive labor markets may instead be the form competition takes when it is costly for both workers and employers to obtain good information about available skills and job opportunities, when it is costly to find and train new workers, and when switching jobs requires costly adjustments.[46] Job ladders and internal labor markets probably economize on training costs, and seniority provisions are important in securing the cooperation of existing employees in providing on-the-job training to new workers. In the face of variations in demand, the maintenance of rigid wages with fluctuating employment may be preferred by both workers and employers to the maintenance of full employment with fluctuating wages.[47] In the former situation, uncertainty affects only a minority of workers, in the latter, all; and, as previously noted, unemployment typically is briefer than many analysts have supposed.

A number of radical critics have gone beyond suggesting that the failure to consider institutional imperfections mars conventional analysis of labor markets. They hold that wages are not determined and jobs are not allotted on the basis of productivity, but rather to increase the power and wealth of a narrow group of economic and political oligarchs, often identified as monopoly capitalists. They argue that the asserted stability of the income distribution and such problems as discrimination by race and sex, poverty, and, especially, their recalcitrance, can only be explained by the existence of a dominant class pursuing its economic and political interests to the detriment of the powerless.[48]

Although radicals cite many of the same characteristics of labor markets as do other critics of the conventional view of labor markets, they draw conclusions for policy quite different from those of nonradical critics. The radicals hold that there is no hope of reforming the capitalist system because the interests of the dominant capitalist class will ultimately prevail, while other critics share with adherents of the conventional view the perception that incremental reform in labor markets can succeed in improving the fairness and efficiency with which labor markets operate, although they disagree about the desirability of various reforms. The flavor of this difference was keenly perceived by Paul M. Sweezy, who wrote,

What [radical] writers . . . have in common is a total rejection of the whole capitalist-imperialist system and a profound lack of interest in schemes or efforts to reform it (except as they may be related to revolutionary tactics). . . . it should be clear that what is involved here is not really an old-new dichotomy but rather a radical-reformist dichotomy. . . . [Radicals] see the present as the frightful outcome of some four centuries of the history of capitalism, a system the very heart of which is exploitation and inequality and which is now careening out of control toward its final crises and catastrophes. Wars and revolutions are not a matter of preference or choice: they are the inevitable outcome of capitalism's inner contradictions, and the question is not whether they will happen but whether they will finally do away with the system that breeds them. To speak of reforming capitalism is either naïveté or deception.[49]

Both the strength and the weakness of the radical view flow from its emphasis on historic regularities and patterns in the economic system. By stressing such regularities, radicals can draw inferential support for an interpretation that stresses immutable class interests. By downplaying as insignificant changes in economic relations that others regard as profoundly significant, radicals can claim that only superficial characteristics of capitalism have been modified. Thus, the development of the welfare state, the emerging political and economic role of women and of blacks, and the development of trade unionism are all downplayed as tactical concessions by the dominant class to maintain power. The obvious weakness of such a view is that these developments have transformed the lives of most people. To dismiss these changes as insignificant strikes most people as palpably absurd.

Policy Alternatives

Whether or not the alternative nonradical views about the operation of labor markets can be reconciled with the conventional view, it is apparent that such a reconciliation has not yet occurred. As a result, the prescriptions for improving the earnings of low-income workers and for permitting a reduction in overall unemployment without inflation that enjoyed widespread acceptance during the 1960s now face a number of competing prescriptions.

It is relatively easy to design a training program for a worker who is presumed to suffer bouts of protracted unemployment or for groups that have above-average unemployment rates because of a lack of education or skills. But if one holds that the job market is governed by customary relations and that the structure of relative wages depends on the character of the jobs rather than of the individuals who fill them, policies that change people but leave the labor market as it is will do nothing except ensure that those who hold jobs without futures and from which they will soon be laid off have superfluous and irrelevant skills. And from a radical perspective, training programs are certain to fail; they are opiates that deaden their recipients to a recognition of the exploitative nature of the economic system.

The change in perceptions about how the labor market operates and how to characterize the problem of unemployment has led to proposals that government directly alter the demand for low-skill workers, and has caused many to condemn government-sponsored training programs for focusing on the inadequacies of workers who, if anything, are more than adequate for the jobs that are available to them. New proposals include wage subsidies payable to low-income workers or to their employers, public service employment, bonus payments to employers who retain specified people on their payrolls for longer than minimum periods of time, increases in minimum wages, and sheltered workshops.

Minimum Wages

The evolution of attitudes among economists toward minimum wages illustrates the play of these alternative views of the labor market. The general popularity of minimum wages among union officials and members, the general public, and political leaders contrasts with their almost universal condemnation by most traditional economists. Analysts critical of the conventional view are more likely to embrace aggressive use of minimum wages to improve the earnings of low-wage workers. According to the traditional view of labor markets, minimum wages may increase wages for some workers, but force other workers to accept lower wages in other occupations, to leave the labor market, or to suffer unemployment. Wages depend on the value of the skills workers possess; an employer simply will not hire workers whose value to the firm is less than the wage they must be paid. Minimum wage laws can thus injure low-wage workers, the very group they are designed to serve.[50]

Only a slight modification in this view of labor markets is necessary to see minimum wage laws as a potentially useful device for helping low-wage workers. If workers are imperfect substitutes for one another, then employers will respond to minimum wages by trying to replace formerly low-wage workers with other workers possessing different skills. As a result, they will hire fewer low-wage workers, but those whom they continue to employ will receive more pay—fewer of the formerly low-wage workers will be employed, but those who work will be paid more. In that event, total wages paid to workers who earned less than the minimum wage before may increase. This increase may come at the expense of other workers or out of profits. Whether the remaining employees receive more or less pay as a result of an increase in minimum wages will depend on whether the reduction in employment in such jobs is proportionately greater or smaller than the increase in wage rates. In general, the higher the minimum wage relative to the wage that would have prevailed in its absence, the less the chance that workers whose jobs are directly affected by minimum wages will benefit. In addition, of course, workers who lose jobs because minimum wages make it unprofitable for their former employers to retain them may qualify for unemployment insurance benefits and have a significant chance of finding alternative employment.

Some evidence suggests that current minimum wage laws serve to increase the total wages paid to adults who normally hold low-wage jobs (because the wage-increasing effect is proportionately greater than the job-reducing effect) but to reduce the total wages paid to teenagers (because the job-reducing effect exceeds the wage-increasing effect).[51] Advocates argue that minimum wage laws have considerable potential for improving the earnings prospects of low-wage workers. Whether one believes that workers are competing for jobs that they can all perform about as well as one another with sufficient training, or that the structure of jobs and wages is governed more by custom and convention than finely calculated profit maximization, minimum wages may be an effective device for shaking the wage and job structure into a new configuration within which formerly low-wage workers are paid more, and one that is not significantly less productive than the former arrangement.

Public Service Employment

The growing advocacy of federally sponsored programs of public employment reflects a similar change in attitudes. After being used extensively during the Great Depression to provide jobs for the unemployed in the most direct way possible, public employment lost political acceptability and acquired the image of useless make-work. While public employment has come back into favor, the definitions are far from clear. Public employment can consist of direct hiring by the federal government, federal subsidies for state and local hiring (as is done under the Comprehensive Employment and Training Act), or sheltered workshops for those unable to find or keep employment in the private sector. The reasons for the renewed appeal of public employment are also diverse. Some advocates of improved public services look upon publicly employed workers, who might otherwise be collecting unemployment insurance or welfare, as a cheap way of securing some services for payments that would be made in any case. Some view assistance through work as better for the recipient than cash transfer payments. In part, hazy memories of how public employment operated during the depression have been revised; one can as easily reason from the numerous, enduring public works constructed by the Work Projects Administration as from the leaf-raking of the Civilian Conservation Corps. In part, the refusal by many economists and others to accept the conventional view of labor markets has made attempts directly to alter the demand for low-wage workers an appealing alternative, or a necessary complement, to training programs designed to transform low-wage workers themselves.

Unfortunately, the way public employment programs should be designed has received insufficient attention.[52] Should public employment temporarily serve workers who have suffered extended unemployment or should it be a permanent guarantee of a job? Should wage subsidies be paid to low-wage workers? Should wage bill subsidies be paid to employers to induce them to hire low-wage workers? Only after such questions are answered is it possible to decide whether the number of public service jobs should be small or large, limited in number and duration or open-ended, and whether the wages paid on public service employment should be low enough to discourage all but those who held the worst jobs or no job at all from applying or high enough to enable a worker to support a spouse and two children at something above the officially defined poverty standard. Even if wages are set around the minimum wage, millions of workers, who now earn less than the minimum wage, may apply, unless eligibility is limited in some other way; but if such workers are the sole support of even moderate-sized families, they will remain in poverty. If wages are set high enough to enable one earner to support a family of four above the poverty threshold—about 15 percent above the minimum wage—the wage would induce millions of workers who now earn less to switch from private to public employment.

If jobs were temporary, they might reinforce the pattern of repeated bouts of brief employment without chance of progression, the syndrome that recent data on unemployment suggest principally afflicts workers in groups suffering from higher-than-average unemployment. If jobs were permanent, it would be necessary to find a sufficient number of useful jobs for the very large number of potential applicants. Skepticism about the effectiveness of public employment in improving the kinds of jobs to which low-wage workers have access is based on such concerns.[53] Unless public employment shifts the demand for labor toward low-skill workers, it will do nothing to reduce the unemployment rate that can be achieved without causing excessive price increases; without such a reduction the effects of public employment on job opportunities for low-wage workers would not differ from those of tax cuts or other increases in public expenditures.[54]

Conclusions

During the early 1960s a vague consensus marked views about how labor markets work and about the problem of unemployment. The consensus encompassed policies to improve job opportunities for the low-wage worker and, simultaneously, to lower the rate of unemployment that could be sustained without excessively rapid inflation. A certain amount of unemployment—a frictional minimum—was viewed as necessary to ensure both that workers could find the jobs for which they were best suited and that employers could find the workers who could best perform available jobs. Cyclical unemployment was a useless waste that sound management of the economy would terminate. Structural unemployment, the problem found especially in depressed areas and among disadvantaged groups, could be corrected by training and other manpower policies. These programs would bring into the labor force workers who, in effect, were excluded from it by some kind of personal disability.

The seeming failure of training programs to reduce the amount of structural unemployment was signaled by the continuing higher-than-average unemployment rates of blacks (even after one adjusts for educational differences between blacks and whites) and by the inability of the economy to tolerate unemployment rates of 4 percent or less without the onset of severe wage and price inflation; and the failure was certified by the ambiguous and conflicting results of evaluative studies of training programs. The prospects of achieving low unemployment waned; the threat of inflation waxed. In the face of these frustrations, the conventional theory of how labor markets operate was criticized and alternatives were proposed. New information about the frequency and duration of unemployment made clear that the old distinctions among various kinds of unemployment were hard to make when one looked at the actual experience of the unemployed.

As a result of this intellectual turmoil, advocates of a wide range of alternative programs have found support. Those who emphasize training can turn to conventional analysis of labor markets. They can accommodate the new data on duration and frequency of unemployment by claiming that workers with few skills are limited to short-term jobs or ones that hold out no prospects for promotion. But they can only express a faith that if and when low-wage workers acquire skills, the short-term or dead-end jobs they had formerly held would promptly disappear; there is negligible evidence to support (or to refute) such a faith. This same faith—that employers would alter the mix of skills and types of workers they sought to hire to match the available supply—underlay the conviction in the 1960s that adequate aggregate demand would suffice to keep unemployment low without producing unacceptable inflation. Those who emphasize direct job creation can find support in a variety of alternative views of the labor market that cannot be refuted by available evidence.

To keep inflation in bounds, some hold that unemployment would have to exceed the "natural rate" variously estimated at 5 to 6 percent of the labor force. But there is disagreement whether lower unemployment would cause inflation to rise and remain at a higher rate or to accelerate without limit. Still others advocate a variety of measures to reduce inflationary pressures; these measures include a return to something much like the Kennedy-Johnson guideposts,[55] investment incentives, limits on the power of unions, and free use of antitrust, tariff, tax, and regulatory policies to make wage increases that exceed productivity growth unattractive under labor market conditions where such increases now would seem profitable.[56]

Those responsible for economic policy must proceed with this cacophonous intellectual chorus in the background. Milton Friedman has often stated that differences in recommendations for policy among economists stem far more from a lack of knowledge about how the economy works than from disagreement about objectives. It is now apparent that disagreements about values often masquerade as disputes about facts. Friedman's statement is certainly false for the nonexpert, who must decide what policies to support and who inevitably must depend on his own values. Policies to reduce unemployment, to train the unskilled, to change the structure of jobs and wages, and to limit inflation must reflect to varying degrees the strength of commitment to these objectives as well as the analytical conclusions of professional economists.

Notes

1. Edmund S. Phelps, "Economic Policy and Unemployment in the 1960's," *Public Interest*, no. 34 (Winter 1974), p. 31 (emphasis deleted).

2. See Albert Rees, "Dimensions of the Employment Problem," in Arthur M. Okun, ed., *The Battle Against Unemployment* (Norton, 1965), p. 25, for these categories and definitions of them. This three-way division was often increased to four with the addition of "seasonal" unemployment, such as experienced by the northern construction worker in February, the cannery worker between harvests, and so on.

3. *Unemployment: Terminology, Measurement, and Analysis,* Prepared for the Subcommittee on Economic Statistics of the Joint Economic Committee, 87:1 (Government Printing Office, 1961). The quotation appears on p. 3.

4. *The Disadvantaged Poor: Education and Employment,* Third Report of the Task Force on Economic Growth and Opportunity (Chamber of Commerce of the United States, 1966), p. 86.

5. Once again, one should keep in mind that although the number of laws enacted was large and the rhetoric lavished in their support extravagant, the budget expenditures to which they gave rise were modest. See chapter 1.

6. Ad Hoc Committee on the Triple Revolution, *The Triple Revolution* (Santa Barbara: Ad Hoc Committee, 1964). Lest any readers swept up in the

current concern about scarcity think that this description of attitudes in the early 1960s is an exaggeration, the following quotations may persuade them. "The fundamental problem posed by the cybernation revolution in the U.S. is that it invalidates the general mechanism so far employed to undergird people's rights as consumers. Up to this time economic resources have been distributed on the basis of contributions to production, with machines and men competing for employment on somewhat equal terms. In the developing cybernated system, potentially unlimited output can be achieved by systems of machines which will require little cooperation from human beings. As machines take over production from men, they absorb an increasing proportion of resources while the men who are displaced become dependent on minimal and unrelated government measures—unemployment insurance, social security, welfare payments" (ibid., p. 6). And later, in a flight of almost unparalleled idiocy, "Cybernation raises the level of the skills of the machine. . . . [T]he machines being produced today have, on the average, skills equivalent to a high school diploma. If a human being is to compete with such machines, therefore, he must at least possess a high school diploma" (ibid., p. 9).

7. See, for example, Charles C. Killingsworth, "Three Myths of Automation," *Nation*, vol. 191 (December 17, 1960), pp. 467–70; Killingsworth's testimony in *Unemployment Problems*, Hearings before the Senate Special Committee on Unemployment Problems, 86:1 (GPO, 1960), pt. 3, pp. 1144–54; and Killingsworth, "The Bottleneck in Labor Skills," in Okun, ed., *The Battle Against Unemployment*, pp. 32–36.

8. Lloyd Ulman, "The Uses and Limits of Manpower Policy," *Public Interest*, no. 34 (Winter 1974), pp. 87–88.

9. This study received popular coverage through James W. Knowles, "Why Unemployment Stays Up," *New Republic*, vol. 147 (October 20, 1962), pp. 18–19. While he denied that structural unemployment was more of a problem in the early 1960s than it had been in previous years, he put in a plug for programs to train and relocate workers, asserting that expenditures on such programs "will . . . pay large dividends in higher average per capita incomes, a higher growth rate and a reduction in human misery" (p. 19).

10. N. J. Simler, "Long-term Unemployment, the Structural Hypothesis, and Public Policy," *American Economic Review*, vol. 54 (December 1964), p. 985.

11. "The Great Unemployment Fallacy," *New Republic*, vol. 151 (September 5, 1964), p. 10.

12. Simler cites numerous studies that seemed to dispose of one variant or another of the structural hypothesis. See "Long-Term Unemployment, the Structural Hypothesis, and Public Policy," pp. 985–87.

13. Joseph A. Kershaw and Robert A. Levine, "Poverty, Aggregate Demand, and Economic Structure," *Journal of Human Resources*, vol. 1 (Summer 1966), p. 67.

14. Albert Rees, "Economic Expansion and Persisting Unemployment: An Overview," in Robert Aaron Gordon and Margaret S. Gordon, eds., *Prosperity and Unemployment* (Wiley, 1966), p. 345.

15. This section draws on recent research on the nature and causes of unemployment, most notably: Stephen T. Marston, "Employment Instability and High Unemployment Rates," *Brookings Papers on Economic Activity, 1:1976,* pp. 169–203; George L. Perry, "Unemployment Flows in the U.S. Labor Market," *Brookings Papers on Economic Activity, 2:1972,* pp. 245–78; Nancy S. Barrett and Richard D. Morgenstern, "Why Do Blacks and Women Have High Unemployment Rates?" *Journal of Human Resources,* vol. 9 (Fall 1974), pp. 452–64; Martin S. Feldstein, "The Importance of Temporary Layoffs: An Empirical Analysis," *Brookings Papers on Economic Activity, 3:1975,* pp. 725–44; Robert E. Hall, "Why Is the Unemployment Rate So High at Full Employment?" *Brookings Papers on Economic Activity, 3:1970,* pp. 369–409. For a precursor of this view of unemployment, see Edward D. Kalachek, "The Composition of Unemployment and Public Policy," in Gordon and Gordon, eds., *Prosperity and Unemployment,* pp. 227–45.

16. The 6.3 percent and 4.5 percent were derived by subtracting the number of persons unemployed twenty-seven weeks and over from the total number unemployed and dividing by the total civilian labor force. (*Economic Report of the President, January 1977,* pp. 218, 221, 222.) This assumes that jobs are found after twenty-six weeks of unemployment so that the total labor force remains unchanged.

17. Stephen Marston found that personal variables such as race, family status, education, age, and sex were correlated more closely with movements from jobs into unemployment than were job characteristics such as industry of employment, occupation, and part-time work. See "Employment Instability and High Unemployment Rates." Such a statistical exercise cannot settle the question, because much of the collective influence of these variables cannot be assigned uniquely to either set of variables. More basically, however, it is not clear whether Marston's job breakdown is sufficiently fine grained so that given occupation-industry categories can be characterized as good or bad jobs.

18. Robert E. Hall observed that one could "no longer speak of the employed and the unemployed as if they were distinct groups over time, although this mistake still appears in popular accounts of unemployment." "Turnover in the Labor Force," *Brookings Papers on Economic Activity, 3:1972,* p. 710.

19. Edward F. Denison, *Accounting for United States Economic Growth, 1929–1969* (Brookings Institution, 1974), p. 62.

20. This view achieved popular acceptance following an influential paper by George L. Perry, "Changing Labor Markets and Inflation," *Brookings Papers on Economic Activity, 3:1970,* pp. 411–41. The same idea had been advanced a decade earlier as a forecast rather than a description in Harold Demsetz, "Structural Unemployment: A Reconsideration of the Evidence," *Journal of Law and Economics,* vol. 4 (October 1961), pp. 80–92; "Committee Issues Unemployment Recommendations," *Congressional Quarterly Weekly Report,* vol. 18 (April 1, 1960), p. 594; and Thomas Dernberg and Kenneth Strand, "Hidden Unemployment 1953–62: A Quantitative Analysis by Age and Sex," *American Economic Review,* vol. 56 (March 1966), pp. 71–95.

21. Michael L. Wachter, "The Changing Cyclical Responsiveness of Wage Inflation," *Brookings Papers on Economic Activity, 1:1976*, pp. 115–59.

22. See Perry, "Changing Labor Markets and Inflation," p. 438.

23. This argument was put forward by Edgar L. Feige, "The 1972 Report of the President's Council of Economic Advisers: Inflation and Unemployment," *American Economic Review*, vol. 62 (September 1972), p. 512.

24. The succession of articles amending previous estimates in the *Brookings Papers on Economic Activity* forms the most accessible compendium of such revisions.

25. J. C. R. Rowley and D. A. Wilton, "The Sensitivity of Quarterly Models of Wage Determination to Aggregation Assumptions," *Quarterly Journal of Economics*, vol. 88 (November 1974), pp. 671–80.

26. Milton Friedman, "The Role of Monetary Policy," *American Economic Review*, vol. 58 (March 1968), pp. 1–17; and Edmund S. Phelps and others, *The Microeconomic Foundations and Employment and Inflation Theory* (Norton, 1970).

27. John T. Dunlop, *Wage Determination Under Trade Unions* (Macmillan, 1944), pp. 147–48.

28. Gail Pierson, "The Effect of Union Strength on the U.S. 'Phillips Curve,'" *American Economic Review*, vol. 58 (June 1968), pp. 456–67; George L. Perry, "Wages and the Guideposts," *American Economic Review*, vol. 57 (September 1967), pp. 897–904, and comments on this article and Perry's reply in *American Economic Review*, vol. 59 (June 1969), pp. 351–70.

The effectiveness of the guideposts was challenged from the outset, principally by those who believed that market forces, too powerful to be controlled by human actions, determined both wages and prices. For a lucid statement of this view in the context of a critique of the 1972 Report of the Council of Economic Advisers, see Reuben A. Kessel, "The 1972 Report of the President's Council of Economic Advisers: Inflation and Controls," *American Economic Review*, vol. 62 (September 1972), pp. 527–32. Kessel writes, "Precisely how inflation is caused by price and wage increases that are unjustified by competitive market conditions is unspecified. How does monopoly pricing in wage and product markets cause inflation? One will search in vain for an answer to this question in the Report" (p. 528).

29. N. J. Simler and Alfred Tella, "Labor Reserves and the Phillips Curve," *Review of Economics and Statistics*, vol. 50 (February 1968), pp. 32–49. Official statistics excluded those who enter the labor force when job opportunities are plentiful but who remain out of the labor force, and hence are not counted as unemployed, when jobs are scarce.

30. Wayne Vroman, "Manufacturing Wage Behavior with Special Reference to the Period 1962–1966," *Review of Economics and Statistics*, vol. 52 (May 1970), pp. 160–67.

31. Albert Rees, writing in 1966, conceded that "we cannot quarrel with the conclusion that the elasticity of labor supply in response to demand fluctuations is far greater than we suspected a decade ago." "Economic Expansion and Persisting Unemployment," p. 331.

32. Precisely such a relationship was estimated by Nancy S. Barrett, Geral-

dine Gerardi, and Thomas P. Hart, who wrote, "Evidence of short-run compensatory pricing implies that measures to reduce aggregate demand tend to worsen the inflation-unemployment trade-off. But unlike the accelerationist view, our results suggest that the inflationary process will be dampened in the longer run once higher unemployment rates are established." "A Factor Analysis of Quarterly Price and Wage Behavior for U.S. Manufacturing," *Quarterly Journal of Economics,* vol. 88 (August 1974), p. 408.

33. Robert Solow, in commenting on a paper by Robert J. Gordon, had observed that "the accelerationist idea of inflation gets essentially no support from the data. . . . I would suggest that we leave that theoretical question out of our discussion unless somebody has something new to offer." *Brookings Papers on Economic Activity, 1:1970,* p. 42. Two years later Gordon had new results to offer that were much closer to the accelerationist position; see Robert J. Gordon, "Wage-Price Controls and the Shifting Phillips Curve," *Brookings Papers on Economic Activity, 2:1972,* pp. 385–421. Two years later Robert Hall embraced the accelerationist position; see Robert E. Hall, "The Process of Inflation in the Labor Market," *Brookings Papers on Economic Activity, 2:1974,* pp. 343–93.

34. Michael R. Darby has recomputed official unemployment rates for the 1930s and found them to be lower than previously believed; "Three and a Half Million U.S. Employees Have Been Mislaid: Or, an Explanation of Unemployment, 1934–1941," *Journal of Political Economy,* vol. 84 (February 1976), pp. 1–16. Average hourly earnings (which are not the same as average hourly wage rates) fell from 56 cents in 1929 to 44 cents in 1933, but rose to 66 cents in 1940, despite slack labor markets.

35. Ulman, "The Uses and Limits of Manpower Policy," p. 95.

36. Albert Rees estimated that training under the Manpower Development and Training Act and the Area Redevelopment Act had reduced unemployment by only 84,000 by the end of 1964. "Economic Expansion and Persisting Unemployment," p. 343.

37. See Phelps, "Economic Policy and Unemployment," p. 43.

38. Ulman, "The Uses and Limits of Manpower Policy," p. 100.

39. Orley Ashenfelter, "Estimating the Effect of Training Programs on Earnings with Longitudinal Data," and Nicholas M. Kiefer, "The Economic Benefits of Four Manpower Training Programs" (papers presented at the Conference on Evaluating Manpower Training Programs, Princeton University, Industrial Relations Section, May 6 and 7, 1976; processed).

40. "Discussion" [Gertrude Bancroft paper] in Gordon and Gordon, eds., *Prosperity and Unemployment,* p. 252.

41. Arthur M. Okun, "Upward Mobility in a High-pressure Economy," *Brookings Papers on Economic Activity, 1:1973,* pp. 207–52; and Wayne Vroman, "Worker Upgrading and the Business Cycle," *Brookings Papers on Economic Activity, 1:1977,* pp. 229–50.

42. Michael J. Piore, "The Impact of the Labor Market upon the Design and Selection of Productive Techniques within the Manufacturing Plant," *Quarterly Journal of Economics,* vol. 82 (November 1968), p. 619.

43. Peter B. Doeringer and Michael J. Piore, *Internal Labor Markets and*

Manpower Analysis (Heath, 1971), pp. 74–76; Michael J. Piore, "Fragments of a 'Sociological' Theory of Wages," *American Economic Review,* vol. 63 (May 1973, *Papers and Proceedings, 1972*), pp. 377–84.

44. See Lester C. Thurow, *Generating Inequality: Mechanisms of Distribution in the U.S. Economy* (Basic Books, 1975), app. A.

45. The difficulty of reconciling these three processes of wage determination is stressed by Thurow, ibid., pp. 51–54.

46. This possibility is admitted by Michael L. Wachter, "Primary and Secondary Labor Markets: A Critique of the Dual Approach," *Brookings Papers on Economic Activity, 3:1974,* p. 646.

47. See, for example, Donald F. Gordon, "A Neo-Classical Theory of Keynesian Unemployment," *Economic Inquiry,* vol. 12 (December 1974), pp. 431–59; Martin Neil Baily, "Wages and Employment under Uncertain Demand," *Review of Economic Studies,* vol. 41 (January 1974), pp. 37–50; Oliver E. Williamson, Michael L. Wachter, and Jeffrey E. Harris, "Understanding the Employment Relation: The Analysis of Idiosyncratic Exchange," *Bell Journal of Economics,* vol. 6 (Spring 1975), pp. 250–78; and Costas Azariadis, "Implicit Contracts and Underemployment Equilibria," *Journal of Political Economy,* vol. 83 (December 1975), pp. 1183–1202.

48. See David M. Gordon, *Theories of Poverty and Underemployment: Orthodox, Radical, and Dual Labor Market Perspectives* (Heath, 1972); and Samuel Bowles and Herbert Gintis, *Schooling in Capitalist America: Educational Reform and the Contradictions of Economic Life* (Basic Books, 1976). For a sharply critical, but not unsympathetic, examination of radical contributions to the economics of labor markets, see Glen G. Cain, "The Challenge of Dual and Radical Theories of the Labor Market to Orthodox Theory," discussion paper 255–75 (University of Wisconsin–Madison, Institute for Research on Poverty, 1975; processed).

49. Paul M. Sweezy, "Comment," prepared for a Symposium on the Economics of the New Left, *Quarterly Journal of Economics,* vol. 86 (November 1972), pp. 658–60.

50. Numerous studies have been undertaken to measure the reduction in jobs for low-skilled workers caused by minimum wages. See Douglas K. Adie, "Teen-Age Unemployment and Real Federal Minimum Wages," *Journal of Political Economy,* vol. 81 (March–April 1973), pp. 435–41; Marvin Kosters and Finis Welch, "The Effects of Minimum Wages on the Distribution of Changes in Aggregate Employment," *American Economic Review,* vol. 62 (June 1972), pp. 323–32; Thomas Gale Moore, "The Effect of Minimum Wages on Teenage Unemployment Rates," *Journal of Political Economy,* vol. 79 (July–August 1971), pp. 897–902; and Finis Welch, "Minimum Wage Legislation in the United States," *Economic Inquiry,* vol. 12 (September 1974), pp. 285–318.

51. Edward M. Gramlich, "Impact of Minimum Wages on Other Wages, Employment, and Family Incomes," *Brookings Papers on Economic Activity, 2:1976,* pp. 409–51.

52. This lack is being reduced by a study of alternative approaches to em-

ployment programs in progress for the Brookings Institution by John Palmer and Michael Barth.

53. Doeringer and Piore observe, "Public employment programs are likely to expand the demand for low-wage labor in the secondary labor market, which already behaves like a tight labor market, without initiating any corrective mechanisms necessary to overcome instability and to upgrade workers to primary employment. Moreover, a guarantee of work may even aggravate instability on the supply side of the market. Unless such upgrading can be assured, programs directly tied to opening primary employment are preferable." *Internal Labor Markets and Manpower Analysis*, p. 206.

54. Robert E. Hall, "Prospects for Shifting the Phillips Curve through Manpower Policy," *Brookings Papers on Economic Activity, 3:1971*, pp. 692–94.

55. Gardner Ackley, "An Incomes Policy for the 1970's," *Review of Economics and Statistics*, vol. 54 (August 1972), pp. 218–23; and Barrett, Gerardi, and Hart, "A Factor Analysis."

56. Hendrik S. Houthakker, "Are Controls the Answer?" *Review of Economics and Statistics*, vol. 54 (August 1972), pp. 231–34; and George L. Perry, "Stabilization Policy and Inflation," in Henry Owen and Charles L. Schultze, eds., *Setting National Priorities: The Next Ten Years* (Brookings Institution, 1976), pp. 271–321.

chapter five **Faith, Intelligence, and Good Works**

The period from 1964 to 1968, which saw a series of attempts at social reform followed by retrenchment, is unique in American political history. A deluge of legislation dealing with education, training, health care, housing, and numerous other areas affecting incomes and welfare issued forth from Congress. Then the flow ceased, and some of the programs enacted during that period were repealed, scaled down, or delegated to state and local governments with few restrictions to ensure that their original purposes were carried out.

The preceding chapters have described the set of popular attitudes and the generally accepted findings of social scientists in the 1960s concerning poverty, education, and labor markets. The legislation enacted during the 1964–68 period was largely congruent with this popular and scholarly consensus. It may have been this congruence that led President Kennedy to make the remark, now so quaintly dated, that important problems before the nation were technically complex but did not involve ideology.[1] By the end of the decade, and increasingly during the early 1970s, popular uncertainty matched scholarly disagreement about how to deal with poverty and unemployment, how to improve education and build up workers' skills, and how to restrain inflation. Ideological attacks on the liberal consensus came from both conservatives and radicals, whose ranks were swollen by disaffected liberals. The climate of doubt about the capacity of government at any level, but especially of the federal government, to deal with these and other problems was the political manifestation of the vanished consensus.

Why did the legislative outpouring occur? Why did it stop? What lessons does it teach? In particular, how should the new contributions by social scientists be used in reaching judgments about public policies? The answers to these questions go beyond the specific problems addressed so far. They require speculation about the unexamined assumptions, the

146

faiths, that underlie views on specific policies. They demand that basically philosophical questions be addressed: how can accumulation of knowledge about facts and the relations among facts, which is the contribution of social science, help in the formulation of judgments about policy? How does the emphasis on evaluation and research in the formulation of policy affect the evolution of the underlying faiths and values?

The 1960s: Many Currents Join

Each era is the temporal meeting place of attitudes, political and social movements, and intellectual developments, all shaped by demographic trends and historical events deeply rooted in the past. And so it was in the United States during the 1960s.

Depression and War

The dominant historical events relevant to the attitudes of the 1960s are the Great Depression and the Second World War. The former taught that unregulated capitalism could not be counted on to prevent mass unemployment, but that action by government could avert such a catastrophe. Debates go on about whether the depression was caused by government blunders or by processes over which governments exercise little influence. The fact is that the working of capitalism, not the blunders of government policy, was *perceived* as responsible for the economic catastrophe of the 1930s. Moreover, the Keynesian revolution in economic thought responded intellectually to this demoralizing conviction with a remedy for economic instability: adroit regulation by government of total demand through control of taxation, government expenditures, and the money supply. In the United States, President Roosevelt was perceived as having led a partially successful assault on unemployment. While economists, who knew that unemployment remained over 10 percent on the eve of the Second World War, have agreed that Rooseveltian economic policy did little to stimulate the economy, the belief that government had the power to achieve a desired objective—full employment—was unquestioned. The power may have been used too timidly, but few doubted that it was a power for good which, when properly employed, would be efficacious. The Employment Act of 1946 embodied this conviction.

In popular remembrance the Second World War was a bloody, titanic morality play. On one side, evil manifested itself in the Axis powers, per-petrators of aggression and the holocaust, bearers of a repugnant ideology of racial superiority enforced with an efficient brutality unparalleled in modern times. On the other side, one of the Allies, the Soviet Union, more nearly resembled the Axis powers than the Allies in its totalitarian depri-vation of liberty and its use of political murder to suppress domestic dis-sent. Nevertheless, the war was perceived as a crusade to eradicate one particularly odious form of evil, Nazism, and to preserve liberty. Once again, it was the government that organized this virtuous endeavor. And when the war ended, it was the government that was responsible for sus-taining American influence abroad to deal with perceived threats to free-dom and democracy from communist imperialism. Whether the threats were real or imagined, whether the efforts of government were effective in defending others against Soviet threats (as in Berlin) or indigenous left-wing movements (as in Greece or Turkey), and even when such efforts were unsuccessful (as in Eastern Europe or China), the American govern-ment was seen at home as engaged in efforts that were beneficent, even if they were also in America's self-interest.[2]

The view of the state as a necessary agent for good in a hostile world clashed with the traditional American and conservative suspicions of state interference in individual lives. Those who looked to state and local gov-ernments for whatever collective action was necessary to aid individuals in their everyday lives tended to view skeptically claims that the federal government should serve as the instrument for collective action. Doubts about the efficiency of the federal government and concern about the effect of governmental action of any kind, but especially of bureaucratic action by the federal government, on the incentives of individuals and businesses was, and remains for many, a satisfying refutation, deeply rooted in American history, of claims that increased federal responsibili-ties are necessary in the contemporary world. The view that man is in-herently sinful is sanctioned by religious teachings influential throughout American history; a deep fear that the powers of government must be lim-ited because officials may be tempted to abuse them is expressed in many provisions of the Constitution. During the 1950s doubts about the wisdom or effectiveness of using government power to solve domestic problems were voiced in national politics by a popular president. His background as a war hero placed him in an especially favorable position to counter a mood, based in large part on American successes in war, that the federal government was a benign instrument for dealing with problems at home as well as abroad.

The Eisenhower presidency, however, ended with the economy mired in recession. The new administration had campaigned on the principle that economic stagnation was unnecessary, that it knew how to get the country moving again, and that this responsibility could be met only by the federal government. Rather strikingly, however, the new President ignored domestic concerns completely in his inaugural address; instead he heralded the transfer of power to a new generation, tempered by war, and he stressed the foreign obligations of the United States. The faith in the potential of government action to improve conditions at home and abroad, long an element of liberal and reformist ideology, was ascendant.[3] The mood of the times was well expressed by the professor who had done more than anyone else to bring Keynesian economics to the United States: "The progress we shall make in the decades ahead toward a truly high standard of living will depend above all else upon the degree to which we choose to employ the vast powers of a democratic government. . . . More and more the trend toward a 'service' society will be paralleled by the growth of the welfare state."[4]

The Beginning of the End of the American Dilemma

Through a long series of decisions, the Supreme Court had brought to a crisis the issue of civil rights for blacks. Legal rights long denied to blacks had been bestowed; the denial of political rights became an anomaly; economic deprivation, substantially a result of the denial of legal rights and political power, became an embarrassment.

The process was set in motion by judicial action after World War II. Why the courts gradually began to entertain and sustain the assertion of rights they had previously ignored will long be debated. Some suggest that specific social science findings were decisive.[5] Some lawyers hold that the decisions were rooted in the Constitution and that social scientists contributed only the gloss of science to legal reasoning that could have stood alone.[6] But why were rights then discovered that had lain hidden within the Constitution for a century since the end of slavery? The truth is probably mixed. The idea of racial superiority had ceased to be acceptable, in large part as the result of work by a variety of scholars; science converted discrimination from plausible behavior into an atavism. But scientific findings alone are not sufficient to banish racism, as practices in several nations attest. Furthermore, it is difficult to believe that the Supreme Court would have declared school segregation unconstitutional if it were convincingly demonstrated that blacks benefited from segregated schools. Perhaps the successes of the civil rights revolution depended in some part on its timing, coming as it did after the wartime struggle against an enemy that accorded a place of honor to a doctrine of racial superiority. The Nazis gave racism a bad name.

As guardian of the proposition that federal actions should be limited, President Eisenhower had held federal involvement in the civil rights controversy to a minimum, ensuring only that federal court orders were not openly flouted, as in Little Rock. But he resisted far-reaching civil rights legislation. The problem, he repeatedly insisted, lay in hearts and minds. Before they were converted, the problem could not be solved; after they were converted, the problem would not exist.

The activist predilections of the succeeding Democratic administration were held in check by the narrowness of its victory in 1960, the resulting weakness of its political position, and the ebbing, but still considerable, power of traditional southern politicians within the Democratic party. After mixed electoral results in 1962, when the Democratic party lost five seats in the House of Representatives and gained three seats in the Senate, but with auguries favorable for decisive reelection in 1964, the President initiated plans to deal with poverty through a variety of new, reorganized, and coordinated federal programs.

The issues of poverty and civil rights are, of course, logically and factually distinct. But they became joined because the most odious characteristic of poverty and unemployment was their nonrandom character; blacks suffered more poverty and unemployment than whites for a wide variety of reasons, many of which could be traced back to legal and political discrimination. Whether one favored greater general equality or not, one could agree that "[t]he real task of our time was to attack injustice and to change social rules and conduct in order that poverty become and remain a random thing. . . ."[7] Or, as Gunnar Myrdal put it, "Never in the history of America has there been a greater and more complete identity between the ideals of social justice and the requirements of economic progress."[8]

Then the assassination of President Kennedy produced an emotional reaction that, combined with President Johnson's good fortune in being pitted against an unusually weak opponent, led to the electoral landslide of 1964. The nature and quantity of legislation dealing with poverty, cash and in-kind transfers, education, health, housing, and civil rights that followed were determined in no small measure by the political adroitness of the new president.

But major new programs in all these areas were, in the cliché of later years, ideas whose time had come. The faith in government action, long embraced by reformers and spread to the mass of the population by depression and war, achieved political expression in the 1960s. This faith was applied to social and economic problems, the perceptions of which were determined by simplistic and naive popular attitudes and by crude analyses of social scientists.

Social science research was prominent in discussions at the time for two reasons. The first was the intellectual fact that economics and, to a lesser extent, the other social sciences had just developed tools of analysis that promised to add useful information to debates about policy. The advent of quantitative methods enabled social scientists to give specific estimates of benefits and costs, to measure the impact of a policy on some desired outcome. These methods were first applied to military problems by the Rand Corporation and the Department of Defense. Then they achieved official status within civilian departments as the planning-programming-budgeting system (PPBS). The second reason was the unprecedented growth in the numbers of teenagers and young adults, about half of whom were going on to college. To teach the oncoming wave of college students, a huge boost in graduate school enrollments and college faculties was required.[9] A massive increase in the number of persons qualified to do research meant that the voice of academic research would be heard more forcefully than ever before.

The confluence of all these trends explains the gush of legislation on civil rights, education, training, health, and housing that was intended to raise incomes directly with cash assistance or in-kind benefits and to improve the capacity of low-income recipients to support themselves through work. It also explains the enthusiasm and faith, so naive in retrospect, that this legislation would quickly and decisively improve the conditions of the poor in general and of blacks in particular. The depression had lasted a decade, but it had been ended. Military victory in the Second World War had taken the United States less than four years to achieve. Eight years after President Kennedy announced a commitment to put man on the moon, the promise was fulfilled. Perhaps the problems to which the War on Poverty and Great Society legislation were addressed were more difficult but, on the record, progress should have been perceptible and swift.

The Currents Diverge

Moods changed in the late 1960s and early 1970s for three distinct reasons. The first was the loss of faith that government action is a force for good. The second was the *formal* victory of the civil rights movement. The third was the collapse of the intellectual consensus and popular perception about the nature of and solution to the problems that the legislation of the mid-1960s was meant to solve.

Bad Government

Two sets of events made faith in the beneficence of the government seem absurd. The first was the Vietnam War. It siphoned off resources for military purposes that otherwise would have been available for domestic purposes. It also split the liberal coalition that had supported the Great Society. These political consequences damaged the liberal domestic program. But the ideological consequences were catastrophic. The government perpetrated horrors in a foreign land, daily visible on television and described in newspapers and magazines; it then deceived the electorate with misleading reports and outright lies. The faith that the bureaucracy that had waged the Second World War might be big and bumbling but at least had its heart in the right place was gutted as effectively as Vietnamese huts by saturation bombing and other actions taken in a costly and bloody war for which justifications seemed increasingly strained and unbelievable.

Fast on the heels of the end of that war came the scandalous revelations that led to the resignations of Vice President Spiro Agnew and President Richard Nixon. It is hard to imagine a combination of events better designed to undercut the vague presumption that dedicated leaders could achieve benign objectives through government action.

Righted Civil Wrongs

The second cause of the changed mood was the *formal* success of the civil rights revolution. The legal and legislative battles for formal equality for blacks had been won. Legislation was in place prohibiting discrimination in political affairs and economic transactions of all kinds and requiring affirmative action in hiring to undo the effects of past discrimination. By and large this legislation had achieved acceptance. In the South, school desegregation was proceeding under federal court orders. But controversy continued, much of it centered on the desegregation of northern schools and on the issue of busing; much of the antidiscrimination legislation was ineffectively enforced, most notably that requiring affirmative action in hiring and nondiscrimination in housing, and progress in the relative economic status of blacks remained agonizingly slow.

Still, if the campaign to achieve equality before the law, in politics, and in the marketplace is likened to a battle, the front of discrimination had been massively breached and the will of the opposition had been broken; what remained was the long and difficult task of exploiting newly opened opportunities and consolidating gains in order to convert political and legal equality into economic and social equality. Discrimination and prejudice would not vanish, but the cost of indulging in them had been increased. The framework had been established within which blacks might advance if they were able to do well in the ways by which whites had traditionally advanced themselves—schooling and jobs. As a result of this formal success in the civil rights revolution, the goal of making poverty a random thing was at least faintly visible in the distant future.

But a latent ambiguity in the goals of the War on Poverty and the Great Society emerged. Previously, the objectives of equalizing opportunity in the form of legal and political rights had served to advance equality of results, in the form of jobs and income. Achieving the former would further the latter. But if blacks could vote, if legislation prohibiting discrimination was on the books, if resources in schools attended by blacks were roughly equal to those of schools attended by whites, then opportunity had to be defined by conditions within the family or the neighborhood. Equal opportunity was coming increasingly to mean equal housing, equal neighborhoods, and equal income and jobs of parents (to the extent that social policy could directly affect family life). While opportunity had not been equalized, further attempts to do so would require equalization of results; the causation had been reversed.

The effort to come to terms with this new issue of inequality caused two split-offs from the liberal majority of the mid-1960s. Moving to the right, the neoconservatives defended the distribution of income as basically just, although they acknowledged the need to do some tinkering through traditional social welfare programs to help the aged, the unemployed, the disabled, or other beneficiaries of the old New Deal liberalism. Moving to the left, another small group of critics reached the conclusion that the distribution of income was unacceptable because of deeply rooted characteristics of the American economy. They held that more or less radical changes in the operation of labor markets and the distribution of power were required. Many of these radical critics drew considerable inspiration from Marx, but all argued that the reform efforts of the 1960s had failed and that capitalism had to be replaced before the problems of inequality, discrimination, and alienation could be solved.

Both the neoconservatives and the radicals recognized the massive increase in participation by previously silent groups. Neoconservatives became alarmed by the contentiousness and social disruption of the process, by a decline of manners and civility that they regarded as the binding agent of civilization.[10] Radicals, noting that the result of all the conflict was less change than they wished to achieve, blamed the system.[11] The person who has been excluded and sees decisions go against him can blame his lack of voice; the person who is included in the decisionmaking process and sees decisions go against him is likely to perceive selfishness and corruption.

As two disillusioned reformers-turned-radicals put it,

At first the new generation tried to overcome social injustice with the tools of its class: reason, technical knowledge, legal maneuvering, and electoral reform politics. They worked in settlement houses to assist poor people. They went to the South to help blacks obtain their civil rights. They peacefully protested the involvement of U.S. corporations in South Africa. They went abroad in the Peace Corps to aid people in underdeveloped countries. They marched with Martin Luther King and against the war in Vietnam. They patiently tried to introduce reforms in the universities to make them responsive to students. And, finally, they publicized the shoddiness of consumer products and the destruction of the environment. But in all of these activities the newly aroused young people operated on the assumption that the various evils they fought were only imperfections in a basically sound system.

The results obtained by the young activists . . . did not measure up to their expectations. They discovered personally the violence backed up by law and government that was used against blacks; in underdeveloped countries they saw ruling elites cooperating with international business to obstruct the most obviously needed reforms; they saw that their university administrators would resist mild demands with incredible tenacity; they saw how social welfare programs and prisons terrorized and degraded the very people they were supposed to uplift; and, in politics young people found that even if they could rouse a large groundswell against the War and force a President to give up, it did not stop the War. From this experience, they began to wonder if there is not something fundamentally at fault in the system itself.[12]

Liberals expected a reaction to the Great Society from conservatives but were surprised by defection from the left.[13] The essential point, however, was that the coalition united around the civil rights revolution had embraced an agenda of social and economic legislation that transcended civil rights. When formal victory in the civil rights revolution removed it from the agenda of salient political issues, the coalition that had been organized around it dissolved.

The Intellectual Consensus Collapses

A third reason for and expression of the change in the political mood in the late 1960s and early 1970s was the collapse of the intellectual consensus about the nature of and solution to poverty and unemployment, about how to improve education and training, about the nature of the problem of inflation, and about the myriad of other objectives of social welfare legislation. The helplessness of the government before higher-than-acceptable rates of inflation and unemployment and the inability of economists to convince others that both of these problems could be solved simultaneously were particularly important, because they undercut the faith that the government was able to manage economic affairs at home.

Beginning in the early 1960s, an unprecedented amount of research was undertaken on the wide variety of social welfare problems toward the solution of which the Great Society and the War on Poverty were directed.[14] Both the process by which research and experimentation (R&E) is produced and the community within which it is produced have certain characteristics that must be appreciated before the impact of R&E on political events can be understood.

Research and experimentation comes in many guises. It may consist only of tabulations of data not previously available or used; this form of R&E is the most consistently productive and valuable, because it is easily understood and can refute common misperceptions.[15] R&E more frequently consists of statistical estimates of the impact of some variable (such as teacher characteristics or weeks of training) on some other variable (such as test scores or earnings). In this form R&E is harder to understand and results are usually subject to criticism and rejection.[16]

Essentially all R&E is produced by people who are currently in or hope to return to the academic world or whose modes of thinking were shaped by academic customs and habits. This world is highly competitive. Respected positions are few, and access to them is gained in the main by distinguished work done early in one's career. The progress of all science occurs through the discovery of previously unrecognized facts not adequately explained by existing theories and the development of new explanations (i.e., theories) for those anomalous facts. Taken together, these characteristics mean that prestigious positions go to young people able to point out anomalies between facts and existing theories and to develop new theories to resolve the anomalies.

Social scientists, particularly economists, carefully distinguish between ends, values, or tastes, on the one hand, and the means or instruments adopted to achieve them.[17] This distinction cannot be sustained, however.[18] Values and tastes are shaped by experiences, among which economic choices are a significant part. The choice of economic means, therefore, helps alter the tastes by which the efficiency of those means must be judged.[19]

All science imposes certain rules of discourse. They are intended to foster detachment and a willingness to follow where findings lead, to report findings whether or not they agree with one's preferences or prior expectations and hopes. Full achievement of these goals is impossible, but the very existence of the standards imposes a powerful discipline.[20] Still, the intellectual standards of the social sciences may camouflage distortions, selective reporting of results, or more subtle violations of objectivity.[21] Outsiders may be lulled into thinking that issues are being debated with scholarly impartiality, when in fact more basic passions are parading before the reader clad in the jargon of academic debate.[22] Untrained readers are most easily misled, but properly guarded prose may delude trained researchers or even the analyst himself.

Social scientists, in emulation of physical scientists and mathematicians, seek simplicity and "elegance,"[23] though the question whether the problems of social science *can* be solved elegantly remains unanswered. In order to permit simplicity and elegance, problems are separated into components that can be managed and understood.[24] Such abstraction produces theory, apparently detached from reality, that often provokes the layman's scorn. Of greater importance, the impulse to isolate individual influences, to make complex social and economic processes statistically and mathematically manageable through abstraction makes it almost impossible to identify policies that may be necessary, but not sufficient, to achieve some objective. Thus, improved education and training may be ineffective in increasing earning capacity unless steps are also taken to change the mix of available jobs, and efforts to change the mix of available jobs may fail if low-wage workers lack training and education. Either taken alone might fail, when both together might succeed. Research and experimentation would detect the failures but have no way to indicate the hypothetical potential success. A rather vague assumption of such an interrelatedness marked early political rhetoric about the War on Poverty but was wholly absent from the precise, but partial, analyses of its effectiveness performed by social scientists.

Few theories advanced by social scientists can be tested by data from controlled experiments. Instead, theories are developed to answer puzzles thrown up by existing data that were generally produced for other purposes. For example, data on the relation between education and earnings have led to the variety of explanations described in chapter 3; data on the relation between inflation and unemployment have led to the explanations described in chapter 4. A moment's thought makes clear that it is generally prohibitively expensive or simply impossible to generate the kinds of data that would be necessary to refute some or all of the theories on these questions.[25]

The subjects on which analysts do research are influenced by prevailing political interests and preconceptions. One need not be cynical to recognize that research agendas are influenced by the flow of money from government and foundations, which in turn try to use research budgets at least in part to improve decisions on current issues of public policy. They are not immune to currents of intellectual fashion, which are related to prevailing political moods. For instance, the flow of research on human capital responded to, even as it first reinforced and then undermined, the simple faith in education. The research on the ineffectiveness of certain government programs reflected, even as it strengthened, a disillusionment about the potential good to be achieved by governmental action.

Finally, such puzzles as why earnings are distributed as they are and how policies of various kinds would affect the distribution, or what makes prices and wages increase and how to alter that rate of increase, are at least as complex as any addressed in the physical or biological sciences. Underlying these puzzles are all the variations in human personality and the mystery of its development (a puzzle of no small size, itself as yet unsolved), the operation of labor markets involving the decisions of millions of businessmen and tens of millions of workers, and the myriad laws that guide and shape behavior, often indirectly and in surprising ways.

These characteristics mean that any particular set of facts will be consistent with a variety of theories and that it may be impossible or excessively costly to acquire the data that would permit analysts to reject false theories. Which ones will gain currency depends on the mood of the times and will be affected by the persuasiveness or the prestige of their advocates. Moreover, one can count on attempts to extend or overturn existing theories, especially by the untenured.

These characteristics of the people and institutions that produce research and experimentation, of the problems they address, and of the data and scientific procedures they use guarantee that over the long haul R&E will be an intellectually conservative force in debates about public policy. The political liberalism or radicalism of many of those who produce R&E on education and labor markets makes this conclusion paradoxical, but the experience of the last decade supports it. A problem that is both politically and intellectually interesting for a number of years must be difficult and must deal with matters about which people deeply and diversely care. It will typically involve a number of objectives that are hard to define or to measure and that people will value differently. The interactions among the various aspects of the problem are likely to be so numerous and complex as to overload existing capacities of the social sciences. Partial analysis will be carried out but may well fail to detect actions that are necessary but not sufficient to achieve desired ends. Analysts with varying political predispositions will be drawn to the subject and will advance diverse solutions to the puzzles. The incentives of the academic world will encourage people, especially newcomers bent on promotion, to discover facts not consistent with previous theories and to devise new theories to explain them. The difficulty and cost of generating new data adequate to choose among the alternative theories will assure existing puzzles of a long life. Eventually data may be discovered or developed that permit some theories to be rejected definitively. One can be fairly confident, however, that at any given time there will coexist several theories consistent with any given set of facts that are more or less congenial to persons with differing political or philosophical predispositions.

To the extent that R&E operates on general public opinion, defining and redefining the range of topics on which a layman feels there is sufficient consensus to act, conflicting research is bound to have a conservative effect. Only if one feels passionately that a problem is so urgent that some answer, even though it may be wrong, is better than none, will this effect be overcome. Ordinarily, the prudent person will conclude that action should be deferred until the controversial issues have been settled. Or if some decision is imposed, he may put aside the self-canceling research and decide what to do on other grounds.[26] This instinct to delay is likely to be reinforced by the tone of certitude and detachment of those who disagree and by the use of jargon and arcane techniques so common in scholarly discourse. What is an ordinary member of the tribe to do when the witch doctors disagree?

The conclusion to be drawn from this situation can be briefly summarized. The role that research and experimentation played in the demise of the simple faiths of the early 1960s was not accidental. The process by which R&E is created corrodes the kind of simple faiths on which political movements are built; this effect is particularly strong when, as in the late 1960s and early 1970s, the actions of political leaders tend to destroy those faiths and events make them implausible. If government is an agent for good, one may tolerate actions of uncertain effectiveness; but if government is an agent for evil, or even morally neutral, only demonstrably beneficial actions will be tolerated. This corrosive role of R&E was obscured for a while because nearly all of it was produced by analysts who themselves held the simple faiths that underlay the goals of the War on Poverty and the Great Society. Its effects were delayed while a sense of urgent need to act controlled political events. This need, this passion, commanded analysts and others to suggest policies best calculated, given available information, to achieve desired ends. When the passion waned, partly because of external events and partly because of frustration at the apparently mixed results of actual policies, the imperatives of the analytical process won out.

Looking Forward

Doubts about the purposes and certainty about the ineptitude of government have replaced the faith that it is a benevolent and effective instrument for social change. At the same time, victory in the politically unifying battle to win legal and political equality for formerly dispossessed minorities is within reach. The political coalition that produced the outpouring of social and economic legislation in the mid-1960s has split. Social science research, a promising instrument for improving understanding of the social and economic problems, helped undercut the faiths that led to that legislation, and its internal laws guarantee that it will corrode any simple faiths around which political coalitions ordinarily are built.

Some underlying facts suggest, however, that the backlash of the early and mid-1970s may be temporary. First, political and economic conditions are unlikely to permit a decline in the size of the federal budget and may require an increase. Arithmetic laws decree that the share of the budget devoted to national defense, down from 9 percent of gross national product in fiscal 1960 to 5 percent in fiscal 1977, cannot decline as much in the future; decisions on national defense may prevent it from declining at all. Federal expenditures on income security programs are projected to remain at about their present proportion of national product. If a decision is made to adopt some form of national health insurance, health expenditures financed through the budget will increase sharply, even if the sum of privately and publicly financed health expenditures does not rise very much.

Second, despite intense skepticism and disillusionment about government efficiency and honesty, surveys repeatedly indicate that the public wants the federal government to take an active role in solving social and economic problems and has the faith that it can do so. A congressionally financed survey, taken at the peak of the Watergate scandal in late 1973, indicated that the public overwhelmingly believed the federal government can be run efficiently, that a strong federal government is essential for national "momentum," that the federal government should ensure a minimum standard of living for the poor, and that the best government is *not* one that governs least.[27] Another survey of public concern about national issues in 1976 listed thirty-one such issues, ordered according to extent of concern. Among these, "insuring that Americans in general, including the poor and the elderly, get adequate medical and health care" was sixth, "improving our education system" was seventh, inflation was tied for second and unemployment was eighth, while "reducing poverty in this country" was fifteenth. For comparison, "keeping our military and defense forces strong" was eleventh.[28] It is notable that during the eight years of the Nixon and Ford administrations, the size of the nondefense components of the federal sector increased, and the relative importance of expenditures on income security, health, and education and training increased even more rapidly than they had during the preceding eight Kennedy-Johnson years; only the relative importance of programs intended primarily for the poor declined.

In short, the critical questions are likely to remain how government policies can effectively achieve objectives that most Americans feel should be handled collectively and how the results of social science research should be used best to help in that quest. Shaping the answers to both questions are widely held beliefs, altered by national travail and by periodic collective reexamination, that for long periods are taken for granted.

The reputation of government as intrusive and inefficient has many sources. In part it stems from government attempts to achieve hard-to-define and controversial objectives—for example, giving the poor more power through the creation of new political organizations that inevitably reduce the power of some other group. In part it stems from the numerous and conflicting objectives of public programs, no one of which can be pursued single-mindedly—for example, the welfare system is wasteful if it is not focused on the poor but discourages work incentives if it is. In part, government is disparaged because decisions are made in the wrong place —by local governments when the issues transcend localities, or by the national government when local differences are vital. But in large part, the reputation for intrusiveness and inefficiency comes from the excessive use by government of prohibitions, requirements, and regulations—"mandates"—to modify the behavior of fifty states, thousands of local governments, millions of businesses, and tens of millions of people.[29]

Mandates come in many forms. They stipulate how factories and businesses should be arranged for health and safety, how much pollution automobiles may emit, what kind of housing the poor may occupy if they receive housing subsidies, the number, location, and kind of highways that should be built, the kinds of training that workers should receive at federal expense, the kinds of equipment local schools should have, and so on. Given the staggering economic, geographic, cultural, and political diversity of the United States, such mandates are frequently mind-boggling in their complexity or downright inequitable. Complexity arises if rules are tailored to myriads of special conditions. Inequity results if mandates are not tailored to special conditions, for then the same rule produces different effects. Both occur when circumstances are just too varied for even highly complex mandates to encompass fully, or when, through ignorance, ineptitude, or some other failing, the mandate is tailored to only some variations in situations to which it applies. If mandates are sufficiently complex, they become impossible to administer and may be ignored, a situation that seems to have arisen in some state welfare systems.

The alternative to mandates is incentives, typically through subsidies or charges that alter the price of some activity to individuals, businesses, or lower level governments. The scope for incentives is limited, however. We make certain activities illegal, others are obligations, and some privileges are available as a right. By collective decision, for example, we have determined that children in most states shall attend school until they are sixteen, that rape is illegal, that votes cannot be sold, and that people receive pensions when they are old. For matters we have designated as rights, obligations, or crimes, and so removed from the realm of the marketplace, we do not use incentives.[30]

Most members of Congress are lawyers, more accustomed to dealing in mandates that require or prohibit behavior than they are to managing incentives that encourage or discourage behavior. Furthermore, the committee structure of Congress discourages the use of subsidies and charges to achieve substantive objectives. Such legislation must pass through the House Ways and Means and Senate Finance Committees. If committees responsible for housing, education, health, training, safety, natural resources, or any other "substantive" field wish to impose taxes or fees or offer subsidies, they normally must surrender exclusive jurisdiction and may lose all control over the legislation.[31]

Although the tax system is used frequently to encourage or discourage private behavior, it is generally a poor vehicle for providing incentives, especially for the poor. Part of the problem is that deductions inherently reward high-income taxpayers more handsomely than they do low-income taxpayers. A deduction that reduces taxable income $1 saves a person in the 70 percent bracket 70 cents, one in the 14 percent bracket 14 cents, and one who has too little income to be taxable nothing at all.[32] Another part of the problem is that tax provisions are reexamined for continued usefulness less frequently than are direct expenditures for which appropriations typically must be enacted annually and authorizations every few years. More basically, however, the income tax usually is a needlessly complex and inefficient device for influencing specific behavior. For example, if students from low-income families are to be enabled to attend college on a footing not drastically different from that of students from high-income families, direct income-related loans or grants to students from families with low or moderate incomes are simpler to administer and more efficient than a tax credit. In rare cases the tax system is the easiest way to provide a well-targeted incentive. The least controversial example is the investment tax credit, under which firms are rebated 10 percent of the cost of eligible investments through reductions in their tax liabilities. Whether investment incentives are desirable *is* questionable; on grounds of administrative simplicity the advantage of the investment tax credit over direct payments providing the same benefits is not.

Incentives remain attractive instruments for influencing behavior even if the tax code in general is a poor instrument for awarding them. To reduce pollution and economize on energy, for example, charges related to emissions have proven themselves effective.[33] Higher prices are demonstrably effective in inducing measures to economize, and there is no reason to think fuel is an exception. The alternatives—regulations to prevent pollution and exhortations to encourage economical use of fuel—have been cumbersome failures or excessively costly successes. Exhortations work only under the most favorable circumstances, when violators can be easily observed and are subject to social pressure.

Less attention has been given to the use of incentives to improve education, training, and labor markets than to those to reduce pollution and conserve energy, and it is much harder to imagine the character of incentives that would promote the social and economic objectives sought by the legislation of the 1960s. Some do exist. Over 80 percent of federal expenditures to promote higher education support student aid that makes college cheaper, but not free. The funds can be used for programs and at institutions of the students' choice. To promote access of those who cannot now afford education and to preserve choice for all students among varied types of higher education, a strong case can be made for using federal resources to encourage states also to direct aid to students so that they can use it at institutions of their choice, not only at state-financed institutions.[34] Other proposals have been advanced that would leave substantial discretion to individual students, trainees, or businesses. James Tobin has suggested a National Youth Endowment that would provide all youths with drawing rights to defray costs of higher education or vocational training at institutions and for purposes they select.[35] Such a measure would make available to all young people some of the benefits now reserved for those fortunate enough to go to college and receive subsidies, a group that includes all students at state-financed institutions. Some or all of the cost of such a program could be met from a surtax imposed on subsequent earnings of those who avail themselves of the endowment. In another area, to deal with the problem of chronic job instability Lester Thurow has suggested a system of subsidies payable to employers who hire workers with a history of employment instability and retain them as employees for more than a minimum period.[36] All these approaches must be viewed as alternatives to direct government provision of a service.

Whether or not these or other proposals can be converted into workable programs that induce desired behavior in individuals and businesses in the areas of education, training, and labor markets, the proposition that many objectives of public policy can be achieved with less resistance through incentives than they can through mandates or direct government provision of services is attractive. When individuals are induced to alter their behavior in some desired direction by incentives, they need not be compelled to behave in a manner they perceive as contrary to their self-interest. The government need not attempt to establish rules, regulations, and standards for a large and diverse nation. The use of incentives rather than mandates is not a panacea for government inefficiency and unpopularity, however. It promises merely to induce, rather than require, desired behavior and thereby to economize on the limited capacity of government to manage complex enterprises or to make people do things involuntarily.[37]

The Role of Social Science

Social science research on the formulation of social and economic policy is likely to continue to increase. How much research findings influence decisions is a matter of dispute and the channels of influence are diverse. But the trend is clear. Debates about public policy increasingly concern the consequences of public decisions that social science research tries to discover. How will a new welfare system change the amount people work, their divorce or separation rate, family size, school attendance or performance by children of the poor, and the consumption behavior of recipients?[38] How will a program of national health insurance affect the access of various groups to health care, their health, and the cost of health care? How will a program of public employment affect incomes of recipients, the private wage rate for unskilled labor, and the quality of public services? How will a program of cash housing subsidies for the poor affect rents and profits of landlords, patterns of migration, and the quality of housing?

On all these questions and hundreds of others research is being conducted and scholars are producing answers. The quality of the work and of the data on which the answers are based varies from superb to awful, but it is improving. Social science will provide increasing amounts of useful information for people who care about public policy.

As the quality of research improves, how it is used becomes increasingly important. One may dismiss both the scorn of analysts for policymakers who do not act promptly on the latest findings and the scorn of policymakers for analysts whose every pen stroke does not inform tomorrow morning's decision. But one must consider how research should be used. In particular, when a new finding appears that conflicts with previous beliefs, how should it affect decisions?

In any given area of research, many theories are usually contending for acceptance, each of which may yield different predictions of the consequences of a particular policy action. Consider, for example, a decision about whether to liberalize income maintenance through some kind of negative income tax, a children's allowance, or some other scheme. To a degree, this decision may hinge on estimates of the impact of each scheme on labor supply, and one's predictions will depend on which of various estimates of the labor supply behavior of low-income families one accepts, as well as on the credence one gives to all such estimates.

People do not often articulate how they use research findings in reaching decisions, and they are seldom asked to do so. Analysts not familiar with the government decisionmaking process are surprised and often shocked by how small a direct contribution research makes.[39] In fact, the contribution of the social sciences seems to be not so much specific information and conclusions as a perspective, an encouragement to evaluate programs in terms of their demonstrable effects. This finding makes it important to consider alternative ways of fitting analysis into a broader perspective.

In finding that perspective one must attend to recent research, but one must realize that, based on the record, it probably is flawed and will be criticized and possibly rejected, but probably not until after a decision has been made on the policy to which the research is relevant. Today's faddish theory may turn out to be false, and the chance that some other theory may be correct should not be ignored.[40] Given the growing volume and still-primitive character of research and the incentives within the social sciences to search out weaknesses in existing work, few findings that bear on enduring issues of public policy can be expected to remain generally accepted for very long.[41] For these reasons, a social science court, or board, to arbitrate disagreements about the validity of research or to evaluate the implications of research for public policy would be unlikely to be objective. Instead, such a court would serve primarily to give social scientists a much increased, and probably undeserved, voice in political decisions.[42]

One suspects that an awareness of the often precarious objectivity and short life expectancy of most research helps explain why policymakers often place less weight on analytical findings than analysts feel they merit, and why they tend to place most weight on findings that support predetermined positions.[43] Far from necessarily being a sign of intellectual mendacity, such behavior may reflect the fact that the person who finds research in conflict with deeply held beliefs may think errors in the research are more likely than in his preconceptions.[44] A recent survey of government officials revealed that 70 percent agreed with the statement that nonuse of research findings is an example of the general principle that people trust their intuitions about social problems more than anything else. The most striking finding, however, was that agreement with this statement was strongest among those who used research most.[45] Furthermore, social scientists, conditioned by the need to make unreasonable assumptions in order to make complex problems manageable, are apt to forget the necessary abstractions made on the way to results in drawing policy inferences. The policymaker or layman, on the other hand, is more likely to act according to the warning paraphrased from David Hume that "no evidence is sufficient to establish an implausible result unless the unreliability of the evidence would be more remarkable than the result which it endeavors to establish."[46]

This principle also suggests that policymakers or laymen should and do use research findings as only one among many kinds of evidence, including past research and commonsense beliefs, in deciding what public policies to support. They do not, and should not, apply the same tests of statistical significance commonly employed by analysts in testing hypotheses, but rather should act on the weight of all evidence.[47] The analysts can help raise the standards of admissible evidence; they can enrich and deepen understanding of the complexity of problems and the unintended consequences of action.[48] Whether the totality of evidence, of which research findings will be only a small part, is sufficient to support or reject some course of action will, and should, depend on underlying values and perceptions. Thus, for example, one may conclude that programs to provide the needy with health care or food should be presumed effective, even if neither life expectancy nor consumption of B vitamins is increased, whenever these goods are supplied in the quality and quantity that the middle class, by its willingness to buy them, shows it considers worthwhile.[49] As James Sundquist observed, "[T]he country cannot afford to wait until all the analyses have been completed and all the facts are in. Action normally must precede research; it takes the actuality or imminence of action to attract scholars, and the funds required for their support, to an issue. . . . [I]n driving to the Pacific, one need not have a map of the entire route to know that he begins by heading westward."[50]

And so one comes back to the underlying faiths and beliefs on which the valid findings of research must rest. These faiths and beliefs are subject to scrutiny and discussion, although by their very nature they are not the subject of research. They are shaped by commitments at the same time that they inspire commitment.[51] Indeed, the most basic decision—whether to commit oneself to the achievement of some goal—largely eludes rational judgment, but determines how one uses analysis and how one fits thought to action. "It makes all the difference in the world whether a thinker stands in personal relation to his problems, in which he sees his destiny, his need, and even his highest happiness, or can only feel and grasp them impersonally with the tentacles of cold, prying thought."[52]

How serviceable for the 1970s and beyond are the faiths that motivated the reformers of the 1960s? The twin specters of world war and depression, both seemingly banished by government action, recede into the fog of past history, to be replaced in contemporary consciousness by another war without valid purpose or tangible success, by economic and social dilemmas still poorly understood, and by a recognition that modes of government action suitable to the past may be inadequate today. Fear of nuclear catastrophe, initially a source of shared responsibility, has turned to dull awareness. The moods of the post-depression and the postwar years, the sense that humanity must act to improve the world and secure it from disaster while time remains, have ended. The almost mad sense of urgency will not be missed. Now, we can try again to solve many of the problems we tried to solve ten years ago, but as before and as always we must proceed with inadequate research. Nevertheless, sober attempts rationally to solve increasingly complex problems may be advanced if we retain a bit of that sense of mutual obligation and community that flowed from economic catastrophe and the holocaust.

Notes

1. This view, presented to an admiring audience at Yale University on June 11, 1962, was presaged by some comments delivered impromptu at the White House three weeks earlier: "I would like to also say a word about the difference between myth and reality. Most of us are conditioned for many years to have a political viewpoint, Republican or Democratic—liberal, conservative, moderate. The fact of the matter is that most of the problems, or at least many of them, that we now face are technical problems, are administrative problems. They are very sophisticated judgments which do not lend themselves to the great sort of 'passionate movements' which have stirred this country so often in the past. Now they deal with questions which are beyond the comprehension of most men, most governmental administrators, over which experts may differ, and yet we operate through our traditional political system."

John F. Kennedy, "Remarks to Members of the White House Conference on National Economic Issues," *Public Papers of the Presidents of the United States: John F. Kennedy, 1962* (Government Printing Office, 1963), p. 422. For the Yale address, see "Commencement Address at Yale University," ibid., pp. 470–75.

2. After concluding that the depression and the Second World War were dominant influences on general political attitudes, I found that Benjamin Ward had earlier reached identical conclusions on the impact of these events on economists. "[The Great Depression] shook rather definitively any remaining faith in the autonomous, self-adjusting features of the capitalist system. For them it became instead an article of faith that things could easily go very badly wrong. The war, on the other hand, preached a rather optimistic message. A Great Evil had come into the world, and organized effort had brought about its destruction. Furthermore, the instrument for this great triumph of Good over Evil was none other than that peculiarly inefficient government bureaucracy, the United States Armed Forces. . . . The emotional, psychological message from these two great events was a clear one: the world must be managed if it is to work at all, and even the incredibly cumbersome and inefficient bureaucracies that were all that was available could be made to do the job." Benjamin Ward, *What's Wrong with Economics?* (Basic Books, 1972), p. 46.

3. For a critical backward glance at this faith, see Peter F. Drucker, "The Sickness of Government," *Public Interest,* no. 14 (Winter 1969), pp. 3–23. Drucker characterized the appeal of government as follows: "For seventy years or so—from the 1890's to the 1960's—mankind, especially in the developed countries, was hypnotized by government. We were in love with it and saw no limits to its abilities, or to its good intentions. Rarely has there been a more torrid political love affair than that between government and the generations that reached manhood between 1918 and 1960. Anything that anyone felt needed doing during this period was to be turned over to government— and this, everyone seemed to believe, made sure that the job was already done" (p. 4). This quotation, and much of the remaining article, is seriously oversimplified and incomplete, but it expresses well one of the strands of political thought prevalent in the United States in the early twentieth century.

4. Alvin H. Hansen, "Automation and the Welfare State," *New Republic,* vol. 144 (April 10, 1961), p. 11.

5. Kenneth Clark and others have cited the decision of the U.S. Supreme Court in the case of *Brown* v. *Board of Education,* which first found school desegregation unconstitutional, footnote 11 to which cited social science in support of the decision. According to Clark, "This citation demonstrated dramatically that the theories and research findings of social scientists could influence public policy decisions on educational and other social problems." Kenneth B. Clark, "Social Policy, Power, and Social Science Research," *Harvard Educational Review,* vol. 43 (February 1973), p. 113.

6. See the comment by Judge Stephen J. Roth that social science evidence is immaterial in segregation cases if "segregation is caused in substantial part by governmental action," reported by Betsy Levin and Philip Moise, "School

Desegregation Litigation in the Seventies and the Use of Social Science Evidence: An Annotated Guide," *Law and Contemporary Problems,* vol. 39 (Winter 1975), p. 73. John Minor Wisdom, a judge on the U.S. Court of Appeals, writes: "For Professor Edmond Cahn, one of our great legal philosophers, Chief Justice Warren's statement was a truism, 'a fact of common knowledge (e.g. that a fire burns, that a cold causes snuffles . . .).' For him, '[s]egregation does involve stigma; the community knows it does.' Dr. Clark's studies were limited in that they did not isolate the effect of segregated schooling from non-school factors such as the effect of a disadvantaged socioeconomic status or of family background. I tend to agree with Edmond Cahn. I too should hate to think that the constitutional right of Negroes *not* to be segregated in education or in any other segment of American life rested on the social science evidence brought forth in *Brown.*" See John Minor Wisdom, "Random Remarks on the Role of Social Sciences in the Judicial Decision-Making Process in School Desegregation Cases," ibid., p. 138.

7. This quotation is taken from the highly critical discussion of the War on Poverty by Theodore J. Lowi, *The End of Liberalism: Ideology, Policy, and the Crisis of Public Authority* (Norton, 1969), p. 244.

8. Quoted by Kenneth B. Clark, "Education of the Minority Poor: The Key to the War on Poverty," in *The Disadvantaged Poor: Education and Unemployment,* Third Report of the Task Force on Economic Growth and Opportunity (Chamber of Commerce of the United States, 1966), p. 187.

9. With characteristically ebullient overstatement, Daniel P. Moynihan pointed to this youth bulge as decisively important in shaping the tone of the 1960s. "[T]he 1960's saw a profound demographic change occur in American society which was a one-time change, a growth in population vaster than any that had ever occurred before, or any that will ever occur again, with respect to a particular subgroup in the population—namely those persons from 14 to 24 years of age. . . . In the whole of that 70 years, from 1890 to 1960, the total increase in the population of that age group . . . was 12.5 million persons. Then, in the 1960's, it grew by 13.8 million persons. . . . [I]t will grow by 600,000 in the 1970's; it will decline in the 1980's." Daniel P. Moynihan, " 'Peace': Some Thoughts on the 1960's and 1970's," *Public Interest,* no. 32 (Summer 1973), pp. 5, 8 (emphasis omitted). It is striking that this population bulge was also due to the depression and war—the lag in births, due first to economic adversity and then to war-imposed separations, followed by the postwar baby boom, expressing the reaffirmation of family life, often observed after war.

10. Irving Kristol, a leading figure in the group of "old-liberals-turned-conservatives," noted that "people do not know what they ought to think about relations between the sexes, about relations between parents and children, about relations between the citizen and his government. For some individuals, this uncertainty is seen as a creative opportunity. . . . But the fact remains that ordinary people . . . find this state of affairs almost intolerably exacerbating." Irving Kristol, "New Left, New Right," *Public Interest,* no. 4 (Summer 1966), p. 6.

11. Daniel Bell and Virginia Held remarked, "One cliché of contemporary political discourse is that 'the people have no real voice—or, less and less of a voice—in their political affairs.' . . . We believe both assertions to be quite wrong. In fact, the opposite may be true—that there is more participation than ever before in American society . . . and more opportunity for the active and interested person to express his political and social concerns. That very state of affairs leads to a paradox because it is the increase in participation which creates a sense of powerlessness and consequent frustration. . . . A person who is socially conscious wants results, particularly *his* results, and he wants them immediately. But the very fact that there is an increase in the number of claimants leads, inevitably, to lengthier consultation and mediation, and more importantly, to a situation wherein thousands of different organizations, each wanting diverse and contradictory things, simply check each other in their demands." Daniel Bell and Virginia Held, "The Community Revolution," *Public Interest,* no. 16 (Summer 1969), pp. 142–43.

12. Stephen Hymer and Frank Roosevelt, "Comment," prepared for a Symposium on the Economics of the New Left, *Quarterly Journal of Economics,* vol. 86 (November 1972), pp. 645–46.

13. See, for example, Eli Ginzberg and Robert M. Solow, "An Introduction to This Special Issue" [on the Great Society], *Public Interest,* no. 34 (Winter 1974), pp. 12–13.

14. Much of this research was the direct result of the legislation itself, which required that a stipulated fraction of appropriations be spent on research and evaluation. Much was undertaken independently by hordes of academics issuing forth from graduate schools motivated not only by the ethics of scholarship but also by the desire to publish rather than perish. The products of this effort consisted of evaluation reports prepared under government contracts, journal articles prepared by academic scholars—often under government grants or contracts—books, magazine and newspaper articles, and an enormous amount of conversation about the new programs, how they worked and whether they were effective, all couched in a language that literally did not exist in prior decades and that those untrained in the social sciences could not understand. Even those who did not understand the language tried to speak it or write it.

15. One suspects, for example, that the most important contribution social science could make to the public discussion of welfare reform would be to disabuse the general public of its exaggerated estimates of the proportion of the population "on welfare." Lee Rainwater found that among a sizable sample of Bostonians, about half of all respondents thought that 25 percent or more of all people were on welfare; fewer than 20 percent of respondents thought that under 10 percent of the population was on welfare. The actual proportion receiving aid to families with dependent children, food stamps, and supplemental security income in 1974, the year in which Rainwater's work was published, was less than 13 percent. See Lee Rainwater, *What Money Buys: Inequality and the Social Meanings of Income* (Basic Books, 1974), p. 192.

16. The factual findings of the Coleman Report that minorities have access

to roughly the same physical school resources have stood up better than conclusions from regression analysis that school resources do not affect learning.

17. Values are presumed to lie outside the range of economics, which is concerned with the application of scarce means to the achievement of predetermined goals. See Lionel Charles Robbins, *Essay on the Nature and Significance of Economic Science* (St. Martin's Press, 1935); his definition is only one of many. Milton Friedman claims that the discussion of goals is unscientific, that economics must be neutral on ends; see *Essays in Positive Economics* (University of Chicago Press, 1953).

18. Despite this characterization of proper scientific detachment between means and ends, those who have had extensive experience in advising businessmen or political officials point out that in practice the distinction cannot be maintained; the client wants and *needs* advice about objectives as well as the most efficient way of achieving them—i.e., about ends as well as means. Aaron Wildavsky, "The Political Economy of Efficiency," *Public Interest*, no. 8 (Summer 1967), p. 45. See also Ward, *What's Wrong with Economics?* p. 214. Carl Kaysen observes that "the role of the economist in policy formation . . . is almost diametrically opposite to that envisaged in the formal theory of policy-making. . . . He functions primarily as a propagandist of values, not as a technician supplying data for the pre-existing preferences of the policymakers. Some of his propaganda is directed at those participants in political decision-making to whom the advisers are directly responsive, aimed at shaping their values in the direction of the adviser's own. Much of it is directed through his political superiors to other participants in the political process—including the general public—and the adviser becomes, in fact, a supplier of arguments and briefs which seek to gain wider support for economists' political values." Carl Kaysen, "Model-Makers and Decision-Makers: Economists and the Policy Process," *Public Interest*, no. 12 (Summer 1968), p. 83. The same point is made by Ward, *What's Wrong with Economics?* p. 25. To an increasing degree, sociology, political science, and other social sciences are adopting the analytical procedures of economics, and with them this ends-means dichotomy. In any event, this distinction pervades contemporary modes of thought. Roberto M. Unger presents a number of such examples in *Knowledge and Politics* (Macmillan, 1975), in which he argues that these distinctions are artificial and do violence to reality. They include distinctions between theory and fact, rules and values, reason and desire.

19. Benjamin Ward makes the same point: "Learning by doing is not just a matter of improving average performance; perhaps its primary component is the change in attitudes that accompanies an improvement in skill, and in particular the desire to exercise the newly acquired skill. No one who has observed the developing consumption-patterns of such hobbyists as photographers, yachtsmen, or motorcycle racers, can doubt that a quite fundamental and broad pattern of changing tastes accompanies the process, even if he is not forced to endure the changes in their conversational patterns." *What's Wrong with Economics?* p. 125 (emphasis omitted). The argument that tastes cannot

be taken as given is typically advanced by radical economists. Its psychological validity seems beyond challenge, but the implications for decisionmaking are unclear. If tastes are not to form the foundation for market decisions, then individual market preferences must be overridden by political decisions. But why should one suppose that the result of some political decision will be a better guide to the tastes that will result at the end of a market process than are the tastes revealed at the beginning of the process? The preferences people now have seem more worthy of attention than those which someone else thinks they will have in the future. Or, as Abba Lerner put it, "I confess I still find a similar rising of my hackles when I hear people's preferences dismissed as not genuine, because influenced or even created by advertising, and somebody else telling them what they 'really want.' In a rich society like ours, only a very tiny part of what people want is determined by their physical and chemical makeup. Almost all needs and desires are built on observation and imitation." Abba P. Lerner, "The Economics and Politics of Consumer Sovereignty," *American Economic Review*, vol. 62 (May 1972, *Papers and Proceedings, 1971*), p. 258. Even the preferences that will emerge must be evaluated in light of those that exist. On the need for an explicit recognition of the way policies change values, see Laurence H. Tribe, "Policy Science: Analysis or Ideology?" *Philosophy and Public Affairs*, vol. 2 (Fall 1972), pp. 66–110, and Tribe, "Technology Assessment and the Fourth Discontinuity: The Limits of Instrumental Rationality," *Southern California Law Review*, vol. 46 (June 1973), pp. 617–60. See also Ward, *What's Wrong with Economics?* pp. 97–100.

20. As Robert Solow put it, "Many people seem to have rushed from the claim that no social science can be perfectly value-free to the conclusion that therefore anything goes. It is as if we were to discover that it is impossible to render an operating-room perfectly sterile and conclude that therefore one might as well do surgery in a sewer. . . . I think that outsiders underrate the powerful discipline in favor of intellectual honesty that comes from the fact that there is a big professional payoff to anyone who conclusively shoots down a mandarin's ideas." Robert M. Solow, "Science and Ideology in Economics," *Public Interest*, no. 21 (Fall 1970), p. 101.

21. For example, economists tend to disregard as unimportant the processes by which present property holders acquired their holdings and focus on the case for or against inequality as if it were immaculately conceived; political scientists at times seem concerned with nothing but process. Commenting on the claims that social science can be made value neutral, Laurence Tribe writes, "How are such claims to be approached? From the start, some degree of skepticism would seem appropriate, inasmuch as every other language (and the policy sciences are surely languages, at least in part) imposes its own categories and paradigms on the world of experience, every other system of thought its own tendencies on the world of aspiration. I am reminded here of a passage quoted by Michel Foucault, in which Borges refers to the assertion of a certain Chinese encyclopedia that 'animals are divided into: (a) belonging to the Emperor, (b) embalmed, (c) tame, (d) sucking pigs, (e) sirens, (f) fabulous, (g) stray dogs, (h) included in the present classification, (i) frenzied, (j) in-

numerable, (k) drawn with a very fine camelhair brush, (l) *et cetera,* (m) having just broken the water pitcher, (n) that from a long way off look like flies.' As Foucault observes, what we 'apprehend in one great leap' in 'the wonderment of this taxonomy' is not only 'the exotic charm of another system of thought' but—even more pointedly—'the limitation of our own, the stark impossibility of thinking *that*.' " "Policy Science: Analysis or Ideology," p. 76.

22. Scholarly debate is marked by certain rules of common civility, which preserve an aura of gentlemanliness and encourage objectivity. They are occasionally breached, but even the breaches must follow certain rules. One may be scornful or contemptuous, but never emotional. It is bad form to show that one cares and that the object of one's criticism may also be the object of one's anger or hate, or that careless analysis threatens something one cherishes or loves or is undercutting one's faith. The intrinsic and unavoidable importance of style in the presentation of research findings is stressed by Joseph Gusfield in "The Literary Rhetoric of Science: Comedy and Pathos in Drinking Driver Research," *American Sociological Review,* vol. 41 (February 1976), pp. 16–34. He observes, "Art and Rhetoric have not been sent into perpetual exile to live outside the walls of Science and Knowledge. With or without passport, they steal back into the havens of clinical and antiseptic scholarship and operate from underground stations to lead forays into the headquarters of the enemy" (p. 22). See also Joseph R. Gusfield, "The (F)Utility of Knowledge? The Relation of Social Science to Public Policy toward Drugs," *Annals of the American Academy of Political and Social Science,* vol. 417 (January 1975), pp. 1–15.

23. All truly great contributions from the hard sciences and mathematics partake of these two characteristics. Social scientists similarly bestow most respect on the creators of simple and elegant theories. Commenting on this habit of economists, Otto Eckstein remarked, "Our culture has as its philosophical cornerstone, 'Theory should be derived from traditional microeconomics.' Derivation of a hypothesis from the classic micro principle is tantamount to empirical testing, or at least the testing can be safely deferred. There is a lack of purity in other approaches, a sinfulness that the young graduate student is well advised to avoid." "Comments," *American Economic Review,* vol. 59 (May 1969, *Papers and Proceedings, 1968*), p. 163. Benjamin Ward makes a similar point. In economics, "clearcut puzzles, and particularly clearcut consensual solutions to puzzles, are very hard to come by. Instead the ingenuity of the formulations and rationalizations of procedures tend to become the basis for judging the quality of scientific effort. . . . But to the extent that puzzles are not really solved, the system tends to become somewhat circular. The important thing becomes not so much to solve the puzzle as to make an ingenious attempt at solving it within the conventional framework of puzzles." See *What's Wrong With Economics?* p. 19.

24. Robert Solow makes a spirited attack on vague pleas for interdisciplinary research. "When you leave your car with an auto mechanic, it doesn't bother you that he will regard it just as an internal combustion engine on wheels. You don't feel it necessary to remind him that it is also a status symbol,

an object of taxation, and a possible place to make love. Why, then, is it bound to be wrong for economists to regard the economic system just as a mechanism for allocating resources and distributing income, despite the fact that it also plays a role in the determination of status, power, and privilege? Why should economics be 'interdisciplinary?' The answer is, presumably, because otherwise it will make mistakes; the neglect of all but the narrowly economic interactions will lead to false conclusions that could be avoided. The trouble is that the injunction to be interdisciplinary is usually delivered in general, not in particular; it is presented as self-evident, not as a conclusion from the failure of certain narrow undertakings and the success of certain broad ones." "Science and Ideology in Economics," p. 101.

25. The recent social experiments to test the response of recipients to negative income taxes, health insurance, or housing allowances indicate that sometimes data can be obtained experimentally. The cost of these experiments, however, is large—$75 million, $50 million, and $200 million, respectively.

26. Thus, an exasperated Judge J. Skelly Wright scolded both plaintiffs and defendents in *Hobson* v. *Hansen:* "Having hired their respective experts, the lawyers in this case had a basic responsibility, which they have not completely met, to put the hard core statistical demonstrations into language which serious and concerned laymen could, with effort, understand. Moreover, the studies by both experts are tainted by a vice well known in the statistical trade —data shopping and scanning to reach a preconceived result; and the court has had to reject parts of both reports as unreliable because biased. . . . [T]he court has been forced back to its own common sense approach to a problem which, though admittedly complex, has certainly been made more obscure than was necessary. The conclusion I reach is based upon burden of proof, and upon straightforward moral and constitutional arithmetic." Quoted by Henry M. Levin, "Education, Life Chances, and the Courts: The Role of Social Science Evidence," *Law and Contemporary Problems,* vol. 39 (Spring 1975), p. 236, note 56.

27. The responses to specific questions were as follows. "Do you feel your federal government can be run well considering all the problems a big country like this faces today?" Answer: can be run well, 86 percent; can't be done, 8 percent; not sure, 6 percent. "Do you tend to agree or disagree with the following statements made about the way different levels of government should operate in this country? 'The best government is the government that governs the least.' " Answer: agree, 32 percent; disagree, 56 percent; not sure, 12 percent. "The federal government has a deep responsibility for seeing that the poor are taken care of, that no one goes hungry, and that every person achieves a minimum standard of living." Answer: agree, 68 percent; disagree, 27 percent; not sure, 5 percent. "The federal government represents all the people, so should handle the most important matters, such as controlling inflation, avoiding depressions, and achieving world peace." Answer: agree, 88 percent; disagree, 7 percent; not sure, 4 percent. In addition to these responses, however, people felt that as many functions as possible should be turned over to state and local governments because they are closer to the people and because

of the great diversity of the country. They felt that the federal government had become secretive and that elected officials had lost control over bureaucrats. See *Confidence and Concern: Citizens View American Government—A Survey of Public Attitudes,* Subcommittee on Intergovernmental Relations of the Senate Committee on Government Operations, 93:1 (GPO, 1973), pp. 111–13, 115, 399.

28. William Watts and Lloyd Free, *America's Hopes and Fears—1976* (Potomac Associates, 1976), p. 9.

29. The theme of this section is drawn directly from Charles L. Schultze, *The Public Use of Private Interest* (Brookings Institution, 1977).

30. Arthur M. Okun, *Equality and Efficiency: The Big Tradeoff* (Brookings Institution, 1975), pp. 6–22.

31. This division between the tax and expenditure committees has led to a movement to consider "tax expenditures" along with ordinary expenditures in evaluating the scope of federal activity in any field and in designing new programs. For example, housing policy framed without reference to the savings enjoyed by homeowners from the privilege of deducting mortgage interest and property taxes would overlook tax provisions that reduced revenues by $9.9 billion in fiscal 1977, 29 percent more than the $7.7 billion actually spent directly on community and regional development. Health policy made without regard for the deductibility of medical costs in excess of 3 percent of income, expenditures on drugs in excess of 1 percent of income, the first $150 of health insurance premiums, and the exclusion from income of health benefits paid for by employers would omit $7.8 billion in potential revenues forgone in part to defray part of the costs to individuals of health care; the reduction in revenues from these provisions is 19.8 percent of the direct federal expenditures on health. By allowing individuals to deduct charitable contributions, the federal government in effect provides an implicit matching grant for each dollar contributed by individuals, although any direct federal payment to some of these recipients would be unconstitutional.

32. Credits get around this problem, but unless they are refundable to persons with little or no tax liability, they remain ineffective for influencing the behavior of the poor.

33. Alvin K. Klevorick and Gerald H. Kramer, "Social Choice on Pollution Management: The Genossenschaften," *Journal of Public Economics,* vol. 2 (April 1973), pp. 101–46; and Allen V. Kneese and Charles L. Schultze, *Pollution, Prices, and Public Policy* (Brookings Institution, 1975), chap. 7.

34. Robert W. Hartman, "Federal Options for Student Aid," in David W. Breneman and Chester E. Finn, eds., *Public Policy and Private Higher Education* (Brookings Institution, 1978).

35. James Tobin, "Raising the Incomes of the Poor," in Kermit Gordon, ed., *Agenda for the Nation* (Brookings Institution, 1968), p. 92.

36. Lester C. Thurow, *Poverty and Discrimination* (Brookings Institution, 1969), app. I.

37. Far more vaguely than Schultze, Peter Drucker has argued in a similar vein that government should act as a "conductor," drawing on the orchestral

analogy. "I have deliberately used the term 'conductor.' It might not be too fanciful to compare the situation today with the development of music 200 years ago. The dominant musical figure of the early eighteenth century was the great organ virtuoso, especially in the Protestant North. In organ music, as a Buxtehude or a Bach practiced it, one instrument with one performer expressed the total range of music. But as a result, it required almost superhuman virtuosity to be a musician.

"By the end of the century, the organ virtuoso had disappeared. In his place was the modern orchestra. There, each instrument played only one part, and a conductor up front pulled together all these diverse and divergent instruments into one score and one performance. As a result, what had seemed to be absolute limits to music suddenly disappeared. Even the small orchestra of Haydn could express a musical range far beyond the reach of the greatest organ virtuoso of a generation earlier." "The Sickness of Government," p. 18.

38. All these questions have been addressed in recent studies. See *Studies in Public Welfare,* a collection of papers prepared for the use of the Subcommittee on Fiscal Policy of the Joint Economic Committee (GPO, 1972–74).

39. For responses to a survey about the use of research by federal officials, see Nathan Caplan, "The Use of Social Science Information by Federal Executives," in Gene M. Lyons, ed., *Social Research and Public Policies: The Dartmouth/OECD Conference* (University Press of New England for Dartmouth College, 1975), pp. 46–67.

40. Given the fragility of social science results, Robert Packenham observes that "the need for caution is easy to see in retrospect. It is less easy to see in prospect. The historical perspective is sobering. It teaches that much of today's 'discredited' or 'passé' social science knowledge was yesterday's 'latest finding' or 'breakthrough.' Note the quotations [sic] around the first two terms as well as the second two. In other words, if the historical view suggests caution about overreliance on today's fashions, it also warns against premature rejection of yesterday's wisdom. . . ." "Social Science and Public Policy," in Lucian W. Pye and Sidney Verba, eds., *Citizenship and Participation,* forthcoming.

41. As Donald Campbell has noted, "Almost inevitably, the scientist is a partisan advocate of one particular outcome. Ambiguities of interpretation present themselves. Fame and careers are at stake. Errors are made, and not all get corrected before publication, with the hypothesis-supporting errors much less likely to be caught, etc. The puzzle of how science gets its objectivity (if any) is a metascientific issue still unsolved." Donald T. Campbell, "Assessing the Impact of Planned Social Change," in Lyons, ed., *Social Research and Public Policies,* pp. 12–13.

42. The idea of a social science court focused on program evaluation was advocated by Daniel P. Moynihan, "A Crisis of Confidence," *Public Interest,* no. 7 (Spring 1967), p. 9. A broader version was hinted at by Kenneth B. Clark, "Social Policy, Power, and Social Science Research," p. 121. Some of the issues that advocates of a general science court list as likely to be adjudicated involve social, as well as physical or biological, science. See John Noble

Wilford, "Policy Clashes Stir Interest in 'Court' for Science," *New York Times,* February 19, 1976; Walter Sullivan, "Stever Is Confirmed as Head of Science Office and Ford Adviser," *New York Times,* August 10, 1976; "Presidential Science and a Science Court" (editorial), *New York Times,* August 24, 1976; Arthur Kantarowitz, "What a Science Court Can Do" (letter to the editor), *New York Times,* September 21, 1976.

43. There are other reasons as well. Caplan cites three: that social science is too complex to be readily understood, that analysts and "doers" are separated by two distinct cultures, and that policymakers are too busy. See "The Use of Social Science Information by Federal Executives," pp. 56–57. Paul Feldman suggests that economists are ignored because they talk about efficiency or the equity of income distribution, while officials tend to care about whether actual holdings were fairly obtained. See "Efficiency, Distribution, and the Role of Government in a Market Economy," *Journal of Political Economy,* vol. 79 (May–June 1971), pp. 508–26.

44. Henry M. Levin, "A Decade of Policy Developments in Improving Education and Training for Low-Income Populations," in Robert H. Haveman, ed., *A Decade of Federal Antipoverty Programs: Achievements, Failures, and Lessons* (Academic Press, 1977).

45. Caplan, "Use of Social Science Information," pp. 60–61.

46. The paraphrase is from Richard Goode, "Rates of Return, Income Shares, and Corporate Tax Incidence," in Marian Krzyzaniak, ed., *Effects of Corporation Income Tax* (Wayne State University Press, 1966), p. 213. Goode also quotes Hume verbatim: "No Testimony is sufficient to establish a Miracle, unless the Testimony be of such a Kind, that its Falshood (sic) would be more miraculous, than the Fact, which it endeavours to establish . . ." (p. 213, note). Caplan also reported that respondents often rejected "information that was counterintuitive . . . [but] will often uncritically accept information that is intuitively satisfying." "Use of Social Science Information," pp. 60–61.

47. Glen G. Cain and Robinson G. Hollister, "The Methodology of Evaluating Social Action Programs," in Ray Marshall and Richard Perlman, *An Anthology of Labor Economics: Readings and Commentary* (Wiley, 1972), pp. 703–04. Cain and Hollister attribute this approach to Kenneth Arrow.

48. James Q. Wilson, "On Pettigrew and Armor: An Afterword," *Public Interest,* no. 30 (Winter 1973), pp. 132–34.

49. Against this background one can appreciate the frustration of one architect of the poverty program. "Another group [of critics] has fed the belief that poverty programs have failed because they did not meet new standards of 'program effectiveness' that were introduced after 1964. The poverty theme and program-planning methodology both came into the social programs part of the federal budget at the same time—and both with the enthusiastic support of the same high-level appointees of President Johnson. It is ironic that the evaluations and cost-effectiveness studies and experiments started under the Johnson Administration have been used with some success by President Nixon to support his decision to cut back on certain parts of the poverty program. . . .

" 'Results' meant not simply that the poor were getting the same quality of educational and health services as the non-poor, but that these services were meeting some new tests of effectiveness that had never before been applied. In this exercise, the poor served as pawns in contests to reform all governmental policies, contests in which the best became the enemy of the good. Appraisals of the budget against poverty became entangled with discoveries that the links between educational spending and learning, and between medical care outlays and health, are not too clear." Robert J. Lampman, "What Does It Do for the Poor? A New Test for National Policy," *Public Interest*, no. 34 (Winter 1974), pp. 74–75.

50. James L. Sundquist, "Where Shall They Live?" *Public Interest*, no. 18 (Winter 1970), p. 97.

51. Charles Frankel, a philosopher-turned-official, upon return to teaching somewhat overstated the point. "[W]hat one believes is not something independent of one's commitments. It goes along with commitment. Faith is not the prelude to effort. Effort makes for faith." See "Being In and Being Out," *Public Interest*, no. 17 (Fall 1969), p. 51.

52. Quoted from Frederick Nietzsche by Ward, *What's Wrong With Economics?* p. 245.

Index

Aaron, Henry J., 110n
Ackley, Gardner, 145n
Ad Hoc Committee on the Triple Revolution, 115
Adie, Douglas K., 144n
Affirmative action, 48, 153
Age: economic status and, 3, 16, 28, 37, 43; occupational status and, 19, 30, 112–13, 116, 118, 119, 121
Aggregate demand theory, 111, 112, 113, 116–17, 129–30, 138
Agnew, Spiro, 8, 152
Aid to families with dependent children, 37
Akerlof, George A., 63n, 64n
Akin, John S., 107n
Appalachia, 23, 114
Area Redevelopment Administration, 114; programs, 2
Ashenfelter, Orley, 59n, 61n, 143n
Automation, 19, 20, 111, 115, 120
Averch, Harvey A., 76, 101n, 104n, 105n
Azariadis, Costas, 144n

Bailey, Martin J., 55n
Baily, Martin Neil, 144n
Bancroft, Gertrude, 143n
Bane, Mary Jo, 102n
Banfield, Edward, 18, 21
Barnow, Burt S., 105n
Barrett, Nancy S., 141n, 143n, 145n
Barth, Michael, 145n
Batchelder, Alan B., 54n
Becker, Gary, 24–25, 45, 67, 99n, 100n
Bee, Helen L., 105n
Bell, Daniel, 170n
Bell, Duran, 61n
Bennett, Carl A., 105n
Bergmann, Barbara, 44, 63n
Betson, David, 62n
Blacks: economic status, 24, 37, 38, 41–43, 69, 93, 96, 150, 152; educational status, 42, 43, 44, 67, 69, 71, 75, 76, 94, 96; occupational status, 32, 33, 42, 44, 113, 116, 118, 119–20, 138, 150; women, 42, 93, 113. *See also* Civil rights movement
Blinder, Alan S., 62n, 103n
Block, N. J., 62n
Blum, Zahava, 21–22, 23
Boulding, Kenneth, 70
Bowles, Samuel, 100n, 102n, 106n, 107n, 108n, 144n
Breneman, David W., 175n
Brittain, John A., 108n, 109n
Brown, Marsha D., 83
Brown v. *Board of Education*, 97–98
Browning, Edgar K., 59n
Budd, Edward C., 50n
Budget: composition, 6–7, 25, 27, 34–35, 71–72, 117, 160, 163; growth, 5–7, 159
Burkhead, Jesse, 102n

CAAs. *See* Community action agencies
Cain, Glen G., 53n, 56n, 102n, 105n, 144n, 177n
Campbell, Donald T., 176n
CAP. *See* Community Action Program
Capitalism, 133, 147, 154
Caplan, Nathan, 176n, 177n
Carliner, Geoffrey, 60n
Carnoy, Martin, 99n
Cash transfers, 3, 5, 6, 7, 27, 28, 30, 34–35, 39, 41, 136, 151
Central Intelligence Agency (CIA), 8
CETA. *See* Comprehensive Employment and Training Act
Chamber of Commerce, 71, 113
Chiswick, Barry R., 99n
Church-state issue, federal aid to education, 71, 72
Civilian Conservation Corps, 136

Civil Rights Act of *1964*, 75
Civil rights movement, 2–3, 23, 42, 75,
    97–98, 149–50, 152–53
Clark, Kenneth, 70–71, 100n, 109n,
    168n, 169n, 176n
Coleman, James S., 61n, 75, 97, 110n
Coleman Report, 82; data base, 77–78;
    methodological problems, 78–81;
    purpose, 75–76; results, 76–77
College work-study program, 32
Committee for Economic Development,
    72
Community action agencies (CAAs),
    26, 29, 31
Community Action Program (CAP),
    26, 29, 31, 32
Community development, 28
Community Services Administration, 27
Comprehensive Employment and Train-
    ing Act (CETA), 27, 126, 136
Congress, U.S., 4, 5, 26, 30, 71, 150, 162
Conservatives, 2, 3, 8, 30, 77, 115, 146,
    153, 154
Corcoran, Mary, 109n
Cost effectiveness analysis, 30, 33
Council of Economic Advisers, 19, 25,
    28, 35–36, 43–44, 71, 115
Courant, Paul N., 51n, 56n
Cybernation, 115, 120

Dale, Edwin L., Jr., 116
Daniere, Andre, 106n
Danziger, Sheldon, 58n
Darby, Michael R., 143n
Defense Department, 30, 151
Defense expenditures, 6, 117, 160
Demand. *See* Aggregate demand theory
Democratic party, 150
Demsetz, Harold, 141n
Denison, Edward F., 63n, 99–100n,
    141n
Dernberg, Thomas, 141n
Desegregation. *See* Civil rights move-
    ment; Schools
Developmental Continuity Consortium,
    85
Disabled, 19, 28, 37
Discrimination: education and, 23, 44–
    45, 67, 97–98, 152–53; employment,
    45–49; genetic inferiority theory, 44–
    45, 77; group average hiring, 45–49,
    95–97; income and, 41–43, 67–68, 69;
    operation of, 45–49; poverty and, 20,
    23–25, 28; tastes for, 24–25, 45–46;
    termination, 43–45, 149–50. *See also*
    Blacks; Civil rights movement;
    Women

Doeringer, Peter B., 53n, 144n, 145n
Downs, Anthony, 108n
Drucker, Peter F., 168n, 175–76n
Duncan, Beverly, 108–09n
Duncan, Greg J., 52n
Duncan, Otis Dudley, 61–62n
Dunlop, John T., 142n
Dworkin, Gerald, 62n

Earnings. *See* Income
Eckaus, R. S., 101n
Eckstein, Otto, 173n
Economic growth, 3, 70; education and,
    68, 96; poverty and, 19, 28, 29, 38, 39
Education: alteration, 73, 82–83; com-
    pensatory, 71, 84–85, 97; demographic
    variation, 43, 44; discrimination and,
    23, 44–45, 67, 75–85, 97–98, 152–53;
    eclectic approach, 94–97; economic
    growth and, 68, 96; economic value
    of, 66, 69; effectiveness, 32, 34, 44–45,
    73–85, 89–92, 93, 97; federal aid, 6–7,
    27, 34, 71–72, 84, 117, 163; genetic
    inferiority theory, 44–45, 77; human
    capital theory, 34, 65, 66–69, 72–74,
    85–88, 96, 116; incentives, 163;
    income and, 19, 65, 66, 69, 74, 86–88,
    89–92, 93, 95, 96, 97; native ability
    and, 86–87; policy role, 70–72, 96–
    98; poverty and, 30, 34, 42, 70–71,
    89; unemployment and, 111, 113,
    116–17, 118, 122. *See also* Manpower
    training programs; Schools;
    Standardized tests
Education programs, 2, 3, 27; college,
    32; effectiveness, 32, 84–85; enrich-
    ment, 84, 85; preschool, 27, 32, 34,
    84, 85. *See also* Manpower training
    programs
Edwards, Richard C., 106n
Eisenhower, Dwight D., 23, 24, 149, 150
Elderly. *See* Age
Elementary and Secondary Education
    Act of *1965*, 27, 72, 84, 85, 117
Employment: full, 2, 3, 19–20, 28, 41,
    42, 114, 121; job screening effects, 42,
    45–49, 87–88, 95–97, 128, 130–33;
    public service, 136–37; subsidies, 163.
    See also Discrimination; Labor
    market; Unemployment
Employment Act of *1946*, 147
Environment: effect on learning, 45,
    82–83, 85; effect on poverty, 21–22
Equality of Educational Opportunity
    Survey, 75, 77–78, 79, 81. *See also*
    Coleman Report

Equal opportunity, 16, 32, 42, 74–75, 91, 153. *See also* Discrimination
Evaluation. *See* Research and experimentation
Expenditures. *See* Budget

Families: income, 43; influence on learning, 76, 77, 89, 90, 97; poverty and, 19; single-parent, 19, 37
Featherman, David L., 106n
Federal Bureau of Investigation (FBI), 8
Federal government: aid to education, 3, 71–72, 126, 163; corruption, 8, 152; expenditures, 5–7, 25, 27, 34–35, 71–72, 117, 159, 160, 163; growth, 3; program evaluation, 30–34, 84–85, 126–28; regulatory role, 147–51, 160. *See also* Public policy
Feige, Edgar L., 142n
Feldman, Paul, 177n
Feldstein, Martin S., 59n, 141n
Finance Committee, Senate, 162
Finn, Chester E., 175n
Fiscal policies, 113, 121, 123
Follow Through, 84, 85
Ford, Gerald R., 6, 160
Fox, Thomas G., 102n
Frankel, Charles, 178n
Franklin, Stephen D., 59n
Free, Lloyd, 175n
Freeman, Richard B., 59n, 60–61n, 99n, 108n
Freeman, Roger A., 98n
Friedman, Milton, 62–63n, 139, 142n, 171n
Fringe benefits, 17

Galbraith, John Kenneth, 17, 18, 19
Gans, Herbert, 22
Garfinkel, Irwin, 56n, 62n, 104n, 107n
Genetic inferiority theory, 44–45, 77
Gerardi, Geraldine, 143n, 145n
Gintis, Herbert, 106n, 107n, 108n, 144n
Ginzberg, Eli, 101n, 170n
Glazer, Nathan, 54n
Glick, Paul, 66
Goldberger, Arthur S., 62n, 105n
Goldfeld, Stephen M., 103n
Goode, Richard, 177n
Goodwin, Leonard, 52–53n
Gordon, David M., 144n
Gordon, Donald F., 144n
Gordon, Kermit, 175n
Gordon, Margaret S., 140n, 141n, 143n
Gordon, Robert Aaron, 140n, 141n, 143n

Gordon, Robert J., 143n
Gottschalk, Peter, 58n
Gramlich, Edward M., 60n, 104n, 144n
Grant, W. Vance, 61n
Great Depression, 8, 136, 147
Great Society, 2, 4–5, 9, 16, 25–26, 41, 92, 115, 117, 151, 152, 153, 154, 155
Griliches, Zvi, 107n
Group average criterion, 45–49, 95–97, 128
Gusfield, Joseph R., 173n
Gwartney, James, 60n, 61n

Hall, George R., 83
Hall, Robert E., 61n, 141n, 143n, 145n
Hampton, Robert, 52n
Handicapped. *See* Disabled
Hanoch, Giora, 59n, 99n, 100n
Hansen, Alvin H., 100n, 168n
Hansen, W. Lee, 58n, 100n
Hanushek, Eric A., 102n, 103n, 104n
Harrington, Michael, 17, 18, 19, 21, 35, 52n
Harris, Jeffrey E., 144n
Harris, Seymour E., 98n
Harrison, Bennett, 56n, 59n, 61n
Hart, Thomas, 143n, 145n
Hartman, Robert W., 175n
Hauser, Robert M., 106n
Haveman, Robert H., 52n, 62n, 108n, 177n
Haworth, Charles, 60n, 61n
Haworth, Joan Gustafson, 60n, 61n
Head Start, 27, 32, 34, 84, 85
Health care programs, 2, 3, 6, 28, 39, 160
Health, Education, and Welfare, Department of, 30, 75, 84
Held, Virginia, 170n
Heller, Walter, 26
Henle, Peter, 58n
Hertz, Thomas W., 106n
Herzog, Elizabeth, 52n
Hiring. *See* Labor market
Hodgson, Godfrey, 102n
Holland, John W., 102n
Hollister, Robinson G., 52n, 54n, 177n
Horowitz, Ann R., 56n, 59n, 61n
Housing programs, 2, 3, 39, 153
Houthakker, Hendrik S., 98n, 145n
Human capital theory, 34, 65, 96, 116; investment return, 67–68, 86; predictions, 68–69; principle, 66–67; problems, 72–74, 85–88
Hume, David, 166
Hymer, Stephen, 170n

Incentives, 161–64; charges, 161, 162–
63; subsidies, 33, 134, 161, 162, 163
Income: demographic variation, 41–44,
67–68, 69; distribution, 17–18, 22,
38, 39, 65, 91, 96, 97, 133, 153–54;
education and, 65, 66, 67, 68, 69, 73,
74, 86–88, 89–92, 93, 95, 96, 97;
inflation, 113–14, 121–25; minimum
wage, 134–35; poverty standard, 36–
41; redistribution, 28, 90–91;
subsidies, 134; taxes, 28, 65, 89, 162;
wage determination, 74, 129–34.
See also Labor market
Income security programs, 160
Inflation, 2, 117, 155; price, 113–14,
121–25, 138; unemployment and, 111,
113–14, 120–25; wage, 113–14, 121–
25, 138
In-kind transfers, 3, 5, 6, 17, 27, 30, 34,
37, 39, 40, 41, 151
IQ, 44, 45, 86. See also Standardized
tests

Jencks, Christopher, 19, 71, 75, 83, 89,
102n, 103n, 108n, 109n, 110n
Jensen, Arthur, 44
Job Corps, 31, 32, 117, 127
Job screening. See Employment
Jobs program, 28–29
Johnson, Harry G., 63n, 100n
Johnson, Lyndon B., 3, 4, 6, 7, 26, 27–
28, 33, 123, 150–51, 160
Joint Economic Committee, 112, 116
Juster, F. Thomas, 59n, 99n, 108n

Kain, John F., 56n, 102n, 103n
Kalachek, Edward D., 141n
Kamin, Leon J., 62n
Kantarowitz, Arthur, 177n
Kasten, Richard A., 61n
Kaysen, Carl, 171n
Kelly, Terence F., 54n
Kennedy, John F., 2–3, 6, 7, 26, 70,
118, 123, 146, 149, 150, 151, 160,
167–68n
Kershaw, Joseph A., 51n, 55n, 56n, 116
Kessel, Reuben A., 142n
Keyfitz, Nathan, 107n, 108n
Keynes, John Maynard, 107n
Keynesian economics, 147, 149
Kiefer, Nicholas M., 143n
Kiker, B. F., 98n
Killingsworth, Charles C., 52n, 115, 130
Kilpatrick, Robert W., 58n
Klevorick, Alvin K., 175n
Klitgaard, Robert, 83
Kneese, Allen V., 175n
Knowles, James W., 140n

Koshel, Patricia P., 104n
Kosters, Marvin, 144n
Kramer, Gerald H., 175n
Kristol, Irving, 169n
Krzyzaniak, Marian, 177n

Labor Department, 27
Labor market: characteristics, 128–34;
composition, 37, 39, 42, 93, 117, 121–
22, 123; conventional approach, 74,
129–32, 135, 138; customary
behavior approach, 130–32; dominant
class approach, 132–34; educational
level, 122; hiring practices, 42, 45–
49, 87–88, 95–97, 128, 130–33;
manipulation of, 111, 114, 163;
marginal productivity approach, 74,
129–32, 135, 138; poverty and, 19,
29–30, 42, 43. See also Employment;
Income; Unemployment
Lampman, Robert, 18–19, 38, 55n, 58n,
177–78n
Lazar, Irving, 106n
Lefcowitz, Myron J., 52n
Legal services program, 27, 31, 32
Lerner, Abba P., 172n
Levin, Betsy, 168–169n
Levin, Henry M., 51n, 98, 102n, 107n,
108n, 110n, 174n, 177n
Levine, Donald M., 102n
Levine, Robert A., 27, 54n, 55n, 56n,
58n, 116
Levitan, Sar A., 50n, 55n, 58n
Levy, Frank, 54n, 57n
Lewis, Oscar, 21
Lewontin, Richard C., 62n
Liberals, 2, 3, 8, 30, 146, 152, 153,
154–55
Lind, C. George, 61n
Local government: education, 71;
federal grants, 3, 5; manpower
training programs, 27, 32, 125–26
Lowi, Theodore J., 169n
Luecke, Daniel F., 103–04n
Lumsdaine, Arthur A., 105n
Lyons, Gene M., 176n

McCone Commission, 32–33
MacDonald, Dwight, 17
McGinn, Noel F., 103–04n
Mallar, Charles, 110n
Mandates, 161–62
Mannheim, Karl, 108n
Manpower Development and Training
Act, 27, 115, 126–27
Manpower training programs, 2, 117;
administration, 27, 32, 125–26;

effectiveness, 118, 126–27, 128, 138;
    expenditures, 34; incentives, 163
Marenbach, Dieter, 99n
Marginal productivity theory, 73–74,
    129–32, 135, 138
Marshall, Ray, 61n, 177n
Marston, Stephen T., 141n
Mason, William M., 106n, 107n
Masters, Stanley, 56n
Maynard, Rebecca, 110n
Merit wants, 7
Michelson, Stephan, 50n, 108n
Military. See Defense Department; ·
    Defense expenditures
Miller, Herman P., 98n
Miller, S. M., 57n, 58n, 103n
Mincer, Jacob, 53n, 67, 109n
Minimum wages, 134–36
Minorities. See Blacks
Moise, Philip, 168–69n
Monetary policies, 113, 121, 123
Monsen, R. Joseph, 108n
Mooney, Joseph D., 56n
Moore, Thomas Gale, 144n
Morgan, James N., 52n, 101n
Morgenstern, Richard D., 141
Moseley, Ray, 52
Mosteller, Frederick, 102n, 103n
Moynihan, Daniel Patrick, 28, 29, 52n,
    54n, 55–56n, 57n, 62n, 102n, 103n,
    169n, 176n
Munnell, Alicia H., 59n
Mushkin, Selma J., 98
Myrdal, Gunnar, 19, 24, 150

National Education Association, 66
National health insurance, 160
National Youth Endowment, 163
Negro. See Blacks
Neighborhood Youth Corps, 117
Newman, James R., 107n
Nixon, Richard M., 6, 7, 8, 26, 33, 126,
    152, 160
Nyquist, Ewald B., 64n

Occupational segregation, 46
Office of Economic Opportunity (OEO):
    development, 26–27; expenditures,
    25, 34; research and evaluation, 30,
    31, 75, 84
Okner, Benjamin A., 58n
Okun, Arthur M., 64n, 175n
Olneck, Michael, 109n
Organization of Petroleum Exporting
    Countries, 123
Orshansky, Mollie, 50n, 54n
Owen, Henry, 15n, 145n

Packenham, Robert, 176n
Paglin, Morton, 51n
Palmer, John, 145n
Panel Survey on Income Dynamics, 36
Peer groups: impact on learning, 76,
    79, 97
Pelavin, Sol H., 106n
Pension funds, 41
Perlman, Richard, 177n
Perry, George L., 141n, 142n, 145n
Phelps, Edmund S., 63n, 139n, 142n,
    143n
Phillips curve, 114, 123–25
Pierson, Gail, 142n
Piore, Michael, 53n, 130, 143n, 144n,
    145n
Planning, programming, and budgeting
    system (PPBS), 30, 151
Plotnick, Robert, 58n, 59n
Poverty: characteristics, 14, 35–37, 150;
    culture of, 20–23; cycle, 18–20, 34;
    decline, 3, 38, 39, 41; discrimination
    and, 20, 23–25, 28; duration, 36, 37;
    early attitudes, 17–23; education and,
    70–71, 89; environmental, 21–23;
    reduction, 19, 20, 34, 70–71, 89;
    standard of, 37–41. See also
    Discrimination; Unemployment
Poverty programs: criticisms, 27–30;
    development, 3, 16, 26–27; effective-
    ness, 16, 30–34; expenditures, 6, 7,
    25, 27, 28, 34
PPBS. See Planning, programming,
    and budgeting system
Prices, 5–6; inflation, 113–14, 121–25
Productivity: education and, 66, 68, 73–
    74, 87; labor market and, 129;
    marginal, 73–74, 129–32, 135, 138;
    measurement, 74; poverty and, 19;
    technology and, 115, 120; unemploy-
    ment and, 121, 124
Profit maximization: businesses, 128–
    29, 131; labor market, 47, 49, 95,
    129–34
Public policy: development of, 147–51;
    discrimination, 16; economy, 16, 70,
    113–17, 118, 130, 133, 134–37, 139;
    education and training, 70–72, 96–98,
    125–28, 134; poverty, 16, 17, 22, 70–
    71; social science role in, 8–9, 79,
    97–98, 149, 151, 158–59, 164–67
Public service employment, 136–37
Pye, Lucian W., 176n

Radical discrimination. See Blacks;
    Civil rights movement; Discrimina-
    tion; Whites

Radicals, 77, 87, 88, 132–34, 146,
    153–54
Rainwater, Lee, 22, 23, 39, 110n, 170n
Rand Corporation, 75, 81–83, 84–85, 151
R&E. *See* Research and experimentation
Rayack, Elton, 55n
Rees, Albert, 139n, 140n, 142n, 143n
Regional development programs, 28,
    111, 113, 114
Republican party, 3
Research and experimentation (R&E),
    4, 16, 31, 75, 118; characteristics of,
    155–58; data types, 79–81, 90;
    discrimination, 43–45; methodology,
    77–81, 83, 90, 92, 127–28; policy role,
    17, 33, 70, 97–98, 164–67; problems,
    31–32, 79–81, 83, 90, 92, 157–59
Ribich, Thomas I., 99n, 110n
Riots, 32
Rivlin, Alice M., 56n, 58n, 65, 99n,
    108n, 109n
Robbins, Lionel Charles, 171n
Roby, Pamela, 57n, 58n
Roosevelt, Frank, 170n
Roosevelt, Franklin D., 147
Rossi, Peter, 21–22, 23
Roth, Stephen J., 168–69n
Rowley, J. C. R., 142n

Schaffarzick, Jon, 104n
Schiller, Bradley R., 62n
Schools: colleges, 32, 66, 151, 163;
    desegregation, 23, 97–98, 152–53;
    effect on learning, 44, 82–83, 94–95,
    96; federal aid, 6–7, 27, 34, 71–72,
    84, 117, 163; high schools, 83;
    parochial, 71, 72. *See also* Education;
    Manpower training programs;
    Standardized tests
Schultze, Charles L., 15n, 145n, 175n
Schultz, Theodore W., 65, 67, 99
Senior citizens. *See* Age
Sewell, William H., 106n
Sex discrimination. *See* Discrimination;
    Women
Shaycroft, Marion F., 102n
Shriver, Sargent, 26, 29
Simler, N. J., 140n, 142n
Singell, Larry D., 103n, 104n
Skidmore, Felicity, 58n, 59n, 62n
Smeeding, Timothy, 58–59n
Smith, Adam, 67
Smith, James D., 59n
Smith, Marshall S., 102n
Social sciences, public policy role of,
    8–9, 79, 97–98, 149, 151, 158–59,

    164–67. *See also* Research and
    experimentation
Social security, 7, 16, 19, 27, 40
Social welfare programs: attitudes
    toward, 152–55; budget, 5–7; common
    view of, 2–7; development, 2–3;
    effectiveness, 4, 8–9; problems, 3–4,
    7–9; research role, 155–59; trends,
    159–64. *See also* Education pro-
    grams; Manpower training programs;
    Poverty programs; Public policy
Solow, Robert M., 143n, 170n, 172n,
    173–74n
South: black migration from, 42; civil
    rights, 2–3; educational resources, 78;
    poverty, 37; school desegregation, 23,
    152–53
Spence, Michael, 63n, 64n
Standardized tests, 42, 69, 73–74, 75–
    76, 77, 78, 79, 82, 83, 85, 86–87,
    94, 96
State government: education, 71, 163;
    federal grants, 3, 5; manpower
    training programs, 125–26
States' rights issue, 148
Stein, Bruno, 103n
Stevenson, Adlai, 2
Stiglitz, Joseph E., 63n, 107–08n
Strand, Kenneth, 141n
Subsidies, 161, 162; employment, 163;
    transportation, 33; wage, 134
Sullivan, Walter, 177n
Summers, Anita, 82–83, 85
Sundquist, James L., 50n, 53n, 55n, 56n,
    166
Supreme Court, U.S., 23, 24, 97–98,
    149–50
Sweezy, Paul M., 133

Taggart, Robert, 55n, 58n
Taubman, Paul, 99n, 106–07n, 108n,
    109n
Tax system, 28, 65, 89, 117, 162
Teachers, effect on learning of, 82, 83
Technological change, 115, 120. *See also*
    Automation; Cybernation
Teenagers. *See* Age
Tella, Alfred, 142n
Thernstrom, Stephan, 57n
Thomas, Thomas C., 106n
Thurow, Lester C., 101n, 106n, 107n,
    144n, 163
Tobin, James, 70, 163, 175n
Transfers. *See* Cash transfers; In-kind
    transfers
Tribe, Lawrence H., 172n

Ulman, Lloyd, 140, 143n
Unemployment, 18, 34, 39, 42, 147, 150,
    155; causes, 33, 112–16; characteris-
    tics, 118–20; cyclical, 112, 113, 118,
    138; demographic variations, 116,
    118–21, 138, 150; frequency, 119;
    frictional, 112, 113, 119, 137–38;
    hard-core, 19, 111, 112–13; inflation
    and, 111, 113–14, 120–25; insurance,
    7, 16; labor market and, 121; long-
    term, 118, 119–20, 132; natural rate
    theory, 122–25, 138; policy toward,
    116–17; poverty and, 19; reduction,
    111, 112, 113, 137; soft-core, 112;
    structural, 111, 112, 113–17, 120,
    138; types, 112
Unger, Roberto M., 171n
Unions: trade, 44

Verba, Sidney, 176n
Vietnam War, 3, 4, 8, 26, 117, 152
von Furstenberg, George M., 56n, 59n,
    61n
Vroman, Wayne, 59n, 130, 142n

Wachter, Michael L., 53n, 142n, 144n
Wade, Nicholas, 62n
Wage-price guideposts, 111, 123
Wages. See Income
Wales, Terence, 99n, 106n, 108n
Walker, Decker F., 104n
Ward, Benjamin, 168n, 171n, 172n,
    173n, 178n
War on Poverty, 2, 4–5, 16, 22, 38, 41,
    92, 115, 116, 117, 151, 153, 155;
    criticisms of, 27–30; development,
    25–27, 34–35; effectiveness, 30–34
Watts, Harold W., 56n, 57n, 102n
Watts, William, 175n

Ways and Means Committee, House,
    162
Wealth, 17, 37, 40, 65
Weisbrod, Burton A., 58n, 107n
Weiss, Leonard, 60n
Weiss, Randall D., 59n, 61n, 99n
Welch, Finis, 59–60n, 61n, 98n, 99n,
    100n, 102n, 107n, 144n
Welfare payments, 28, 40
Whites: economic status, 23, 24, 42, 44,
    69, 93, 96; educational status, 67, 69,
    83, 94, 96; occupational status, 44,
    68, 112–13, 116, 118, 119; women,
    42, 93
Wildavsky, Aaron, 171n
Wilford, John Noble, 177n
Williamson, Jeffrey G., 60n
Williamson, Oliver E., 144n
Wilson, James Q., 177n
Wilton, D. A., 142
WIN. See Work incentive program
Wirtz, W. Willard, 28
Wisdom, John Minor, 169n
Wofford, John G., 53n
Wolfe, Barbara, 82–83, 85
Women: economic status, 41, 42, 69, 93,
    96; educational status, 67, 69, 96;
    occupational status, 30, 42, 113, 116,
    118, 121; productivity, 66
Work incentive program (WIN), 117,
    126
Work Projects Administration, 136
World War II, 8, 147–48
Wright, J. Skelly, 174n

Yancey, William L., 52n
Yarmolinsky, Adam, 50n, 53–54n
Yordon, Wesley J., 103n, 104n
Youths. See Age

DISCARD

LEADING
FOR INNOVATION

**DRUCKER FOUNDATION
WISDOM TO ACTION SERIES**

ABOUT THE DRUCKER FOUNDATION

The Peter F. Drucker Foundation for Nonprofit Management, founded in 1990, takes its name and inspiration from the acknowledged father of modern management. By providing educational opportunities and resources, the foundation furthers its mission "to lead social sector organizations toward excellence in performance." It pursues this mission through the presentation of conferences, video teleconferences, the annual Peter F. Drucker Award for Nonprofit Innovation, and the annual Frances Hesselbein Community Innovation Fellows Program, as well as through the development of management resources, partnerships, and publications.

The Drucker Foundation believes that a healthy society requires three vital sectors: a public sector of effective governments, a private sector of effective businesses, and a social sector of effective community organizations. The mission of the social sector and its organizations is to change lives. It accomplishes this mission by addressing the needs of the spirit, mind, and body of individuals, the community, and society. This sector and its organizations also create a meaningful sphere of effective and responsible citizenship.

In the ten years after its inception, the Drucker Foundation, among other things:

- Presented the Drucker Innovation Award, which each year generates hundreds of applications from local community enterprises; many applicants work in fields where results are difficult to achieve.

- Worked with social sector leaders through the Frances Hesselbein Community Innovation Fellows program

- Held more than twenty conferences in the United States and in countries around the world.

- Developed eight books: a *Self-Assessment Tool* (revised 1998) for nonprofit organizations; three books in the Drucker Foundation Future Series, *The Leader of the Future* (1996), *The Organization of the Future* (1997), and *The Community of the Future* (1998); *Leader to Leader* (1999); *Leading Beyond the Walls* (1999); *The Collaboration Challenge* (2000); and the *Leading in a Time of Change* viewer's workbook and video (2001).

- Developed *Leader to Leader,* a quarterly journal for leaders from all three sectors.

- Established a Web site (drucker.org) that shares articles on leadership and management and examples of nonprofit innovation with hundreds of thousands of visitors each year.

For more information on the Drucker Foundation, contact:

The Peter F. Drucker Foundation for Nonprofit Management
320 Park Avenue, Third Floor
New York, NY 10022-6839 U.S.A.
Telephone: (212) 224-1174
Fax: (212) 224-2508
E-mail: info@pfdf.org
Web address: www.drucker.org

LEADING

FOR

INNOVATION

and Organizing for Results

FRANCES HESSELBEIN
MARSHALL GOLDSMITH
IAIN SOMERVILLE

EDITORS

JOSSEY-BASS
A Wiley Company
www.josseybass.com

JOSSEY-BASS
A Wiley Company
989 Market Street
San Francisco, CA 94103-1741

www.josseybass.com

Copyright © 2002 by the Peter F. Drucker Foundation for Nonprofit Management,
320 Park Avenue, 3rd floor, New York, New York 10022, www.drucker.org.

Jossey-Bass is a registered trademark of John Wiley & Sons, Inc..

No part of this publication may be reproduced, stored in a retrieval system, or transmitted
in any form or by any means, electronic, mechanical, photocopying, recording, scanning,
or otherwise, except as permitted under Sections 107 or 108 of the 1976 United States
Copyright Act, without either the prior written permission of the Publisher or authoriza-
tion through payment of the appropriate per-copy fee to the Copyright Clearance Center,
222 Rosewood Drive, Danvers, MA 01923, (978) 750-8400, fax (978) 750-4744. Requests
to the Publisher for permission should be addressed to the Permissions Department, John
Wiley & Sons, Inc., 605 Third Avenue, New York, NY 10158-0012, (212) 850-6011, fax
(212) 850-6008, e-mail: permreq@wiley.com.

Jossey-Bass books and products are available through most bookstores. To contact
Jossey-Bass directly, call (888) 378-2537, fax to (800) 605-2665, or visit our website
at www.josseybass.com.

Substantial discounts on bulk quantities of Jossey-Bass books are available to corporations, professional associations, and other organizations. For details and discount
information, contact the special sales department at Jossey-Bass.

We at Jossey-Bass strive to use the most environmentally sensitive paper stocks available
to us. Our publications are printed on acid-free recycled stock whenever possible and our
paper always meets or exceeds minimum GPO and EPA requirements.

Library of Congress Cataloging-in-Publication Data

Leading for innovation and organizing for results / Frances
Hesselbein, Marshall Goldsmith, Iain Somerville, editors.
     p. cm.
Includes index.
  ISBN 0-7879-5359-8 (alk. paper)
  1. Leadership.   2. Organizational change.   3. Technological
innovations.   I. Hesselbein, Frances.   II. Goldsmith, Marshall.
III. Somerville, Iain.
  HD57.7 .L4375 2001
  658.4'092—dc21

2001005165

HB Printing   10 9 8 7 6 5 4 3 2 1   FIRST EDITION

CONTENTS

Foreword   xi
  Frances Hesselbein

The Editors   xvii

Introduction   1
  Frances Hesselbein, Marshall Goldsmith,
  Iain Somerville

**Part I   Leading the People Who Make Innovation
            Happen**

---

1   **We Are All Innovators**   11
    Margaret J. Wheatley

2   **Fleas and Elephants**   23
    Charles Handy

3   **Creative Leadership**   31
    Max De Pree

4   **Changing the Behavior of *Successful* People**   39
    Marshall Goldsmith

5   **Good Work in Business**   57
    Howard Gardner, Kim Barberich

Part II   Creating an Environment That Encourages Innovation

6   **Creating the Culture for Innovation**   **73**
Rosabeth Moss Kanter

7   **The Organization! Is It a Friend or Foe of Innovation?**   **87**
C. William Pollard

8   **To Build a Culture of Innovation, Avoid Conventional Management Wisdom**   **95**
Jeffrey Pfeffer

9   **Innovation in Government**   **105**
Stephen Goldsmith

10 **How Company Culture Encourages Innovation**   **119**
David S. Pottruck

Part III   Changing How You Think About Leadership and Innovation

11 **The Ultimate Creation**   **131**
Jim Collins

12 **Managing to Innovate**   **141**
Henry Mintzberg

13 **Inviting Innovation**   **153**
M. Kathryn Clubb

14 **The Value of "Been There, Done That" in Innovation**   **165**
Dorothy A. Leonard, Walter C. Swap

15 **Leading with Vision, Strategy, and Values**   **177**
Robert E. Knowling Jr.

16 **When 1 + 1 = 3**   **185**
James Burke

Part IV   The Practice of Innovation

17 **Coping with Your Organization's
Innovation Capabilities**   **197**
Clayton M. Christensen

18 **An Innovation Protocol**   **215**
Dave Ulrich

19 **Beware: Innovation Kills!**   **225**
Arie de Geus

20 **Capturing Innovation Power in the
Genomics Era**   **239**
Daniel Vasella

21 **Leading for Innovation and Results in Police
Departments**   **251**
William J. Bratton, William Andrews

22 **Inventing E-Services**   **263**
Ann M. Livermore

23 **Reinventing Innovation: A Perspective
from The Idea Factory**   **273**
John Kao

Index   **285**

FOREWORD

In 1991, when the Drucker Foundation was preparing for its first conference and presentation of the annual Peter F. Drucker Award for Nonprofit Innovation, I called Peter Drucker and said, "In all of your books, you talk about innovation. In the *Practice of Management* (1954), you wrote that business has just two functions: marketing and innovation. We are about to launch the Peter F. Drucker Award for Nonprofit Innovation at our fall conference. Could you possibly give us a definition of *innovation* that would be ours—to use with the award and in all the Drucker Foundation materials?" Peter responded, "I will think about it."

In a little while, the fax machine began sputtering and out rolled Peter's response: "Innovation: change that creates a new dimension of performance." It was the perfect definition for the Drucker Foundation, whose mission—to lead social sector organizations toward excellence in performance—focuses on performance and on helping leaders of change, and whose honorary chairman, Peter F. Drucker, states, "Somewhere in the United States, no matter what the problem, some nonprofit organization is solving it."

The Drucker Foundation has long encouraged leaders *in all three sectors* to manage for the mission, manage for innovation, and manage for diversity. So "Innovation: change that creates a new dimension of performance" became a battle cry, a benchmark, and a call to action. Thousands of nonprofit social sector organizations responded to the challenge of the Drucker Award for Innovation. In a few years, file boxes and then our Web site were filled with amazing examples of innovation that changes lives and builds community; frequently the examples included partnerships and collaborations.

As Peter Drucker looked at the first hundreds of applications for the Innovation Award, he said, "But how does success travel?" This became our challenge—how to share these remarkable examples of real, live, on-the-ground innovation. We began with the Drucker Foundation *News* and our annual Conference on Innovation; then teleconferences began highlighting stirring examples. And now we are pleased to report that success travels by e-mail—every week.

In a weekly e-mail broadcast, the "Drucker Nonprofit Innovation of the Week" goes to thousands of individuals in the United States and around the world, all of them hungry for examples of innovation that works, not theory; they want to see documented successes. There is no charge; a simple request brings the Innovation of the Week e-mail to your computer.

Beyond our walls, the Drucker Award–winning organizations are working with business, government, and other nonprofit organizations to build on their initial success and to broaden and deepen their impact. They have found dramatic ways for their success to travel.

The experiences of the following remarkable nonprofit organizations provide insights on innovation for leaders of change in private, public, and social sector organizations.

• The Computer Clubhouse, the 1997 Drucker Award winner, was founded in 1993 by The Computer Museum (now part of the Museum of Science, Boston) in collaboration with the MIT Media Laboratory. The Clubhouse has served over 1,500 young people who work with adult mentors and use powerful computer tools to develop projects related to their own interests and experiences. The

Clubhouse has gained international recognition among educators and community leaders and serves as a model of how technological tools can support learning, creative expression, and community development. When the Drucker Award was presented in 1997, there were six Computer Clubhouses. In 2001, fourteen Computer Clubhouses serve youth in Boston; Milwaukee; Gum Springs, Virginia; Columbus, Ohio; Bogotá, Colombia; and Esslingen, Germany. In 2000, Intel announced it would partner with the Museum of Science and fund the development of a network of one hundred Computer Clubhouses in underserved communities. The Clubhouse Network at the Museum of Science, Boston, serves as the center of innovation and technical expertise; it provides ongoing support, program guidance, and technical assistance for community-based Computer Clubhouses around the world.

• The 2000 winner of the Drucker Award was aided by the power of the electronic and print media. The SAGE Project in San Francisco is dedicated to helping prostitutes leave the streets and build independent and productive lives free from violence, addiction, and abuse. In the period between 1997 and 2000, SAGE peer educators—former prostitutes themselves—enabled more than seven hundred women and girls to leave prostitution and reclaim their lives.

SAGE founder and executive director is Norma Hotaling, a former prostitute and recovering addict who recognized the absence of services available for women escaping prostitution. "Without treatment, these women and girls are the biggest consumers of medical, criminal justice, and social services in the city," said Ms. Hotaling.

SAGE understood that peer advocates—people who share a given experience and who have changed their own lives—are potent agents of change. "SAGE peer educators have personally experienced the impact of prostitution, domestic violence, abuse, and addiction; they can reach out to women still on the streets or living in abusive relationships in a particularly powerful way," explained Ms. Hotaling. Not only can these peer educators effectively influence the women served by SAGE, but the Peer Educator Training

Program also enables the organization to help an ever-growing number of women and girls by enhancing the skills of current and potential staff.

The story of SAGE's effectiveness was amplified six months after the Drucker Award was presented. Norma Hotaling received the "Use Your Life Award" from Oprah's Angel Network. The award, accompanied by a $100,000 grant, was presented by Oprah Winfrey on the *Oprah Show*. A month later, the SAGE story was told in *Parade* magazine, distributed through 350 Sunday newspapers to an audience of thirty-seven million people across the United States. These notices brought requests for expanded service and offers of help.

• The 1994 Drucker Award went to the Children's Aid Society in New York for its "community school" in Manhattan's Washington Heights neighborhood. The community school model encompasses the full range of social programs and services that all children and families need to flourish. Through community alliances, the model broadens the school's support base to bring in parents, teachers, and the community as full partners. The schools are open from 7 A.M. to 10 P.M., six days a week, twelve months a year. The school becomes a community center. Community school services include an innovative academic curriculum; before- and after-school programs; on-site medical, dental, and eye care; teen programs; parent education; and many more.

To tell a large national audience about the community school model and to help communities across the country adapt it to their own needs, the Children's Aid Society established the Community Schools Technical Assistance Center in 1994. The center has been a first stop for thousands of visitors, including educators, government and business leaders, social service peers, and parent groups. It has worked with the Advertising Council to promote the idea of community schools and to offer information and support to interested localities.

At the end of 2000, over ninety sites were using the community school model or an adaptation of it. These sites are located in the

United States and in Colombia and the Antilles. In New York, the Children's Aid Society oversees nine community schools serving nearly eleven thousand students.

The continued success of the Drucker Award winners is a testimony to their acceptance of the challenge to make success travel and (where possible) to share their learning with other organizations. And as good ideas and practices travel, they cross the borders of nations and move across all sectors. Driven by scarce resources and a great urgency to solve the problems they encountered, these social sector organizations found innovative ways to succeed and to make a difference in the lives of the people they serve. Their success translates to the work we all do, whether we are in a *Fortune* 500 company, a public agency, or a social sector organization. We all seek to achieve great results, and we all need the best tools and ideas to do so.

So when Peter Drucker's two functions—marketing and innovation—are joined together, new results are achieved. The effectiveness of an innovative program serving one community is multiplied when it is expanded and shared with new communities.

From a vision of moving the power of innovation across the country and beyond, we see the shadows of Peter Drucker's wisdom of nearly fifty years ago: two functions—marketing and innovation—enable organizations to further their impact and change lives beyond the local community. Although the wisdom is unchanged, not so for the ways that success travels—from a timid request for definition, to e-mails delivering the innovation of the week, to a corporate-funded network of one hundred Computer Clubhouses, to millions viewing on television and reading in print the story of a winner, to thousands of children and their families being served by community schools. Leadership is needed to support innovation in organizations and communities across the country and the world. It must be leaders who focus on performance and results and then discover all the ways for success to travel.

All of this remarkable effort, with the diverse ways leaders and their organizations have found to move the models, to share their examples, adds up to an energetic response to Peter Drucker's query, "How does success travel?" Our Drucker Award winners demonstrate that success travels in all the ways innovative organizations and their supporters communicate. When our 1998 award winner—the California Transportation Training Institute (training parolees and jobless men and women to become truck drivers)—pondered Peter Drucker's question, their enthusiastic response was, "Success travels by truck."

August 2001   Frances Hesselbein
                                                Easton, Pennsylvania

THE EDITORS

Frances Hesselbein is chairman of the board of governors of the Peter F. Drucker Foundation for Nonprofit Management and is the former chief executive of the Girl Scouts of the U.S.A. She is a member of the boards of other organizations and corporations and is the lead editor of the Drucker Foundation's best-selling books, including *The Leader of the Future*, *The Organization of the Future*, *The Community of the Future*, *Leading Beyond the Walls*, and *Leader to Leader*, published by Jossey-Bass. She also serves as editor-in-chief of the journal *Leader to Leader*. She speaks on leadership and management to audiences around the world in the private, nonprofit, and governmental sectors. She has received fifteen honorary doctorates and was awarded the Presidential Medal of Freedom in 1998.

Marshall Goldsmith is a founding director of the Financial Times Knowledge Dialogue, a coaching network that connects executives from around the world with thought leaders. Marshall has been listed in *Forbes* magazine as one of the five top executive coaches and in *The Wall Street Journal* as one of the "Top Ten" executive educators. He is a leading authority in helping executives achieve positive, measurable change in behavior for themselves, their people, and their teams. He is a member of the board of the Drucker Foundation.

Iain Somerville is a strategy consultant, executive educator, and social entrepreneur. As managing partner of Somerville & Associates, he engages businesses, governments, and community-based organizations in bringing about breakthrough economic and social results. As a former managing partner with Accenture, he founded and led strategy consulting practices and the firm's global business think tank.

LEADING
FOR **INNOVATION**

INTRODUCTION

Peter Drucker has defined *innovation* as "change that creates a new dimension of performance." In today's turbulent times, bringing about such change is one of the greatest challenges leaders face. This book is about what leaders can do to help their people and their organizations achieve this new dimension of performance.

As many of our authors note, innovation does not occur without significant challenge. Many people prefer to do things the way they have always done them, and change is not welcomed. Many innovations will fail; however, all agree that being open to innovative ideas, approaches, and systems is imperative if we are to survive both personally and professionally in today's fast-changing world. This book is for those leaders who will be successful in shaping the future because they are open to new ideas, new approaches, and new mind-sets.

To help today's leaders understand leading for innovation, we have gathered the top authors, practitioners, consultants, researchers, and thought leaders. Each author offers a unique viewpoint about the leadership of innovation. Some chapters explore the past; others cite current trends and theorize about the future. This combination presents an array of insight and knowledge for today's leaders. We hope that *Leading for Innovation* will inspire you, our reader, to make the changes that can make your world a better place.

The book is divided into four parts: (1) "Leading the People Who Make Innovation Happen," (2) "Creating an Environment That Encourages Innovation," (3) "Changing How You Think About Leadership and Innovation," and (4) "The Practice of Innovation." Because this book offers concise explorations of innovation, do not feel compelled to read it by beginning at page one and going straight through. Feel free to begin your journey at any chapter, jump around, pause, reflect, and dive in again. To borrow Peter F. Drucker's advice from his *Management Challenges for the 21st* Century, think about how each chapter affects you and your organization. Then, plan what *action* you will take as a result.

The following will give you an idea of what's ahead as you begin the intellectual adventure of leading for innovation. Part I examines the qualities required to lead innovators. Margaret J. Wheatley, a leader in developing new practices and ideas for organizing in chaotic times, begins this section. She notes that human creativity and commitment are our greatest resources, and she emphasizes that where there is true diversity of opinion, there will be innovation.

Charles Handy combines the experiences of an executive and economist with sage reflections on the changes taking place in the world of work and organizations. He argues that innovation needs to begin *before* a need is felt. Charles encourages large organizations (the elephants) to embrace the innovators (the fleas). Only by working together toward constant reinvention will success be sustained.

Best-selling author Max De Pree shares wisdom and experience from his tenure with Herman Miller, Inc., the great office design innovator. He describes innovation as the search for the "beneficial surprise" and identifies what it looks like from the perspective of both the leaders and the innovators. It is sound and well-proven advice useful for any organization.

Marshall Goldsmith is a leading executive coach with an effective concept for helping successful people improve. He shares valuable insights for understanding the behavior of successful people and offers a simple technique for helping them change the behaviors that hinder their success. This process is a powerful tool for changing ourselves and helping others to change.

Howard Gardner, renowned for his theory of multiple intelligences, and Kim Barberich, a researcher at Project Zero, offer guidance for maintaining a strong sense of values and ethical behavior in the process of innovation. They cite examples of how organizations thrive while doing good works in their community. They also reinforce the need for organizations to be open to errors and to employ the trial-and-error needed for innovation.

In Part II the focus changes from leading people to shaping the environment. What can be done so that a creative culture is developed and reinforced? The chapters provide insight into how organizations, including public agencies, can promote innovation.

Rosabeth Moss Kanter, Harvard scholar, renowned author, and business thought leader, offers insights into how organizations can stifle or encourage innovation. She likens innovation to looking into a kaleidoscope wherein constantly changing patterns and perspectives encourage the insights that lead to innovation. Rosabeth's thoughts will help leaders maintain an environment that promotes the search for new patterns of success.

C. William Pollard, chairman of ServiceMaster, presents a first-person account of how the leaders of an organization built a culture of innovation. They employ a hands-on innovation style and move through risk taking with accountability and tolerance for failure. Safe incubators for ideas and real support from leaders round out the culture, an ideal environment for innovation.

Jeffrey Pfeffer, a Stanford professor, is a leading thinker and author on organizations getting the most from people. He offers advice on what organizations must do differently from past practices to build a culture for innovation. It provides clear direction for leaders of organizations planning to be part of the future.

Stephen Goldsmith, who served as mayor of Indianapolis from 1992 to 1999, brings a public sector perspective to innovation. He changed Indianapolis's city hall from an ineffective bureaucracy to an innovative partner in the service of the community.

David S. Pottruck, president and co-CEO of the Charles Schwab Corporation, closes the section. David offers a story wherein the numbers are considered little more than a consequence of doing the right thing for customer and employee. He illustrates what it means to *live* a value rather than merely *state* it—the power of personally delivering an important message.

The chapters in Part III shift gears from the "doing" activities in the first two sections to "thinking" activities. They will help readers reflect on their views about the relationship between leadership and innovation.

The section begins with a chapter by Jim Collins, management educator, author of *Good to Great*, and coauthor of *Built to Last*. Jim employs a historical perspective to demonstrate why it is *social* innovation and not *technological* innovation that drives the most successful companies, including the pioneering success of companies such as IBM and Wal-Mart.

Henry Mintzberg, management guru and McGill University professor, suggests that we shift our thinking away from *leading* innovation to *managing* innovation. The majority of innovative ideas, he argues, spring forth not from, or because of, a great leader, but because of careful management of the innovation process. Henry begs us to move toward a looped-learning model as the means to innovation.

M. Kathryn Clubb is a consultant in the transformational arts with experience at Northwest Airlines and Andersen Consulting (Accenture). She shows how ongoing dialogue, constructive conflict, and action-based learning are critical elements to leadership in innovation. Kathryn offers leaders a way to both invite and measure the success of innovation initiatives.

Coauthors Dorothy A. Leonard of the Harvard Business School and Walter C. Swap of Tufts University buck the dot.com trend of abandoning experience in favor of youthful exuberance by highlighting the real value of the wisdom that comes only from experience. They show how the success of innovation is improved by adding the perspectives of the *know-what, know-how,* and *know-who* knowledge. Bringing together a team embodying these multiple perspectives is what it takes to generate *creative fusion*.

Robert E. Knowling Jr., chairman and CEO of Internet Access Technologies, offers us a view from a skeptic of the "best practice" schools. Robert points to three main contributions a leader can make to encourage innovation. First is the need to deliver a clear and compelling vision and strategy to the organization. Second is the importance of the leader living the vision and strategy and becoming the teacher of the process. Finally, the leader must ensure that metrics focus people on what is important.

James Burke is a best-selling author and award-winning producer and host of science and technology documentaries, including the *Connections* series. His chapter forces us to reevaluate our perspectives on leadership and to embrace the concept of leader as facilitator. For him, innovation is the way two ideas are brought together to generate something greater than their sum.

The final section, Part IV, presents perspectives on the practice of innovation. The authors share their experience from academia, business, and public service. In addition to their insights, they describe how to maintain the practice of innovation today.

Clayton M. Christensen, Harvard Business School professor and author of *The Innovator's Dilemma*, encourages leaders to evaluate the organization's resources, processes, and values and how they align to the innovations needed. He offers four approaches for creating organization capability and a framework to manage disruptive and sustaining innovations.

Dave Ulrich, an authority in designing human resources systems and professor at the University of Michigan School of Business, offers a process to take innovation from the realm of magic and bring it into the realm of regimen. He presents three premises for what innovation should be about and a protocol for achieving innovation with six distinct phases.

Arie de Geus has followed thirty-eight years with the Royal Dutch Shell Group with award-winning books and articles on innovation. His chapter, "Beware: Innovation Kills," is not a caution against innovation but a warning that those who don't innovate will be killed off by those who do. He provides a historical perspective of the world shift from a land economy to a capital economy, and from a capital economy to the new economy. He concludes with advice for building the organizational knowledge needed to survive in today's economy.

Daniel Vasella is chairman and CEO of Novartis, the global life sciences company. Drawing from his wealth of knowledge in the pharmaceuticals industry, he offers insights on how to effectively manage innovation. In an industry of prolific innovators, it is not enough to encourage innovation, but it is critical to manage the innovation process, to control the costs of innovation, and to speed innovations to market.

William J. Bratton and William Andrews offer a public sector innovation success story from the New York Police Department. William Bratton has been a chief or commissioner of five different police agencies with up to thirty-eight thousand officers and is now a consultant to police agencies worldwide. Their firsthand account illustrates what can be done with minimal resources to energize a workforce, streamline operations, and produce dramatic improvement for the staff and the community at large.

Ann M. Livermore, president of Hewlett-Packard's Business Customer Organization, illustrates a specific innovation: HP's Internet strategy to move into e-services. She also describes how HP is enabling e-solutions to meet very real human needs of hunger and poverty.

John Kao is founder and CEO of The Idea Factory. His chapter cautions us to make innovation a purposeful activity versus a passive one. He shows how we are moving from an economy of scale to an economy of discovery, and therein lies the need to be successful innovators.

We hope that when reading these chapters, you will be open to new ideas, and will take the best from what is given and apply it to your working (and personal) life. Consider the views and practices described. How do they compare with your own ideas? What changes do you want to implement as you, in John Kao's words, "seek the future you prefer"?

Leading for Innovation is our attempt to bring you thinking from the foremost practitioners and thought leaders in all three sectors. All have something unique to offer in examining innovation—a leadership imperative.

As is true for all Drucker Foundation books, all chapters are a contribution of the author, and all royalties are donated to support essential organizations in the social sector as they strive to change lives and build community. We hope you will find in *Leading for Innovation* new perspectives, new energy, and new results as you manage for innovation and find indeed that innovation is change that creates a new dimension of performance!

August 2001

Frances Hesselbein
Easton, Pennsylvania

Marshall Goldsmith
Rancho Santa Fe, California

Iain Somerville
Santa Monica, California

Part I

LEADING THE PEOPLE WHO MAKE INNOVATION HAPPEN

---

1 MARGARET J. WHEATLEY

WE ARE ALL INNOVATORS

Margaret J. Wheatley is president of The Berkana Institute, a charitable global foundation. She was an organizational consultant for many years and also a professor of management in two graduate programs. Her work appears in two award-winning books, Leadership and the New Science *and* A Simpler Way *(coauthored with Myron Kellner-Rogers), plus several videos and articles.*

Innovation has always been a primary challenge of leadership. Today we live in an era of such rapid change and evolution that leaders must work constantly to develop the capacity for continuous change and frequent adaptation, while ensuring that identity and values remain constant. They must recognize people's innate capacity to adapt and create—to innovate.

In my own work, I am constantly and happily surprised by how difficult it is to extinguish the human spirit. Even when people have

Note: This chapter was originally published in the Drucker Foundation journal *Leader to Leader,* vol. 20, Spring 2001, and is reprinted with the permission of Margaret J. Wheatley. Copyright © 2001 by Margaret J. Wheatley.

been given up for dead in their organizations, once conditions change and they feel welcomed back in, these "near dead" find new energy and become real innovators. My questions are: How do we acknowledge that everyone is a potential innovator? How can we evoke the innate human need to innovate?

The human capacity to invent and create is universal. Ours is a living world of continuous creation and infinite variation. Scientists keep discovering more species; there may be more than fifty million of them on earth, each the embodiment of an innovation that worked. Yet when we look at our own species, we frequently say we're "resistant to change." Could this possibly be true? Are we the only species—out of fifty million—that digs in its heels and resists? Or perhaps all those other creatures simply went to better training programs on "Innovation for Competitive Advantage"?

Many years ago, Joel Barker popularized the notion of paradigms or worldviews, those beliefs and assumptions through which we see the world and explain its processes. He stated that when something is impossible to achieve with one view of the world, it can be surprisingly easy to accomplish with a new one. I have found this to be very true. Now that I understand people and organizations as living systems, filled with the innovative dynamics characteristic of all life, many intractable problems have become solvable.

Perhaps the most powerful example in my own work is how relatively easy it is to create successful organizational change if you start with the assumption that people, like all life, are creative and good at change. Once we stop treating organizations and people as machines and stop trying to reengineer them, once we move into the paradigm of living systems, organizational change is not a problem. Using this new worldview, it is possible to create organizations filled with people who are capable of adapting as needed, who are alert to changes in their environment, who are able to innovate strategically. It is possible to work with the innovative potential that exists in all of us and to engage that potential to solve meaningful problems.

We are gradually giving up the paradigm that has dominated Western culture and science for over three hundred years—that of the world and humans as machines. Almost all approaches to management, organizational change, and human behavior have been based on mechanistic images. When we applied these mechanical images to us humans, we developed a strangely negative and unfamiliar view of ourselves. We viewed ourselves as passive, unemotional, fragmented, incapable of self-motivation, uninterested in meaningful questions or good work.

But the twenty-first-century world of complex systems and turbulence is no place for disabling and dispiriting mechanistic thinking. We are confronted daily by events and outcomes that shock us and for which we have no answers. The complexity of modern systems cannot be understood by our old ways of separating problems, or scapegoating individuals, or rearranging the boxes on an org chart. In a complex system, it is impossible to find simple causes that explain our problems or to know whom to blame. A messy tangle of relationships has given rise to these unending crises. To understand this new world of continuous change and intimately connected systems, we need new ways of understanding. Fortunately, life and its living systems offer us great teachings on how to work with a world of continuous change and boundless creativity. And foremost among life's teachings is the recognition that humans possess the capabilities to deal with complexity and interconnection. Human creativity and commitment are our greatest resources.

For several years, I have been exploring the complexities of modern organizations through the lens of living systems. But rather than question whether organizations are living systems, I've become more confident about stating the following: the people working in the organization are alive, and they respond to the same needs and conditions as any other living system. I personally don't require any deeper level of clarity than this. But I'd also like to note that one of the gifts of understanding living systems is that it soon becomes evident that life's processes apply both to individuals and systems. The dynamics of life are *scale-independent*—they are useful to explain what we see no matter how small or large the living system.

The new worldview of organizations as living systems offers many principles for leadership. Each of these principles has affected my work in profound ways. Together they assist leaders to accomplish our greatest task—to create the conditions where human ingenuity can flourish.

Meaning Engages Our Creativity

Every change, every burst of creativity, begins with the identification of a problem or opportunity that somebody finds meaningful. When people become interested in an issue, their creativity is instantly engaged. If we want people to be innovative, we must discover what is important to them, and we must engage them in meaningful issues. The simplest way to discover what's meaningful is to notice what people talk about and where they spend their energy.

In my own work with this principle, I've found that I can't learn what is meaningful just by listening to managers' self-reports or by taking the word of only a few people. I need to be working alongside a group or individual to learn who they are and what attracts their attention. As we work together and deepen our relationship, I can then discern what issues and behaviors make them sit up and take notice. As we work together, doing the real work of the organization, meaning always becomes visible. For example, in meetings, what topics generate the most energy, positive or negative? What issues do people keep returning to? What stories do they tell over and over? I can't be outside the process, observing behaviors or collecting data in traditional ways. I've also learned that I notice a great deal more if I am curious rather than certain.

In any group, I know that I will always hear multiple and diverging interpretations. Because I expect this, I now put ideas, pro-

posals, and issues on the table as experiments to see what's meaningful to people rather than as recommendations for what *should* be
meaningful to them. One of my favorite examples of how easily we
can be surprised by what others find meaningful occurred among
health care professionals who were trying to convince parents of
young children to use seatbelts. But these parents were from a traditional, non-Western culture. They did not see the act of securing
their child to a seat as protective of the child. They saw it as in-
voking the wrath of God. Strapping in a child was an invitation to
God to cause a car accident.

I've learned how critical it is to stay open to the different reactions I get rather than instantly categorizing people as resistors or
allies. This is not easy—I have to constantly let go of my assumptions and stereotypes. But when I listen actively for diversity rather
than agreement, it's fascinating to notice how many interpretations
the different members of a group can give to the same event. I am
both astonished and confident that no two people see the world exactly the same way.

Depend on Diversity

Life relies on diversity to give it the possibility of adapting to changing conditions. If a system becomes too homogeneous, it becomes
vulnerable to environmental shifts. If one form is dominant, and
that form no longer works in the new environment, the entire system is at risk. Where there is true diversity in an organization, innovative solutions are being created all the time, just because
different people do things differently. When the environment
changes and demands a new solution, we can count on the fact that
somebody has already invented or is already practicing that new solution. Almost always, in a diverse organization, the solution the
organization needs is already being practiced somewhere in that system. If, as leaders, we fail to encourage unique and diverse ways of

doing things, we destroy the entire system's capacity to adapt. We need people experimenting with many different ways, just in case. And when the environment then demands a change, we need to look deep inside our organizations to find those solutions that have already been prepared for us by our colleagues.

There is another reason why diversity lies at the heart of an organization's ability to innovate and adapt. Our organizations and societies are now so complex, filled with so many intertwining and diverging interests, personalities, and issues, that nobody can confidently represent anybody else's point of view. Our markets and our organizations behave as "units of one." What this means is that nobody sees the world exactly the same as we do. No matter how hard we try to understand differences, there is no possibility that we can adequately represent anybody else. But there is a simple solution to this dilemma. *We can ask people for their unique perspective.* We can invite them in to share the world as they see it. We can listen for the differences. And we can trust that together we can create a rich mosaic from all our unique perspectives.

Involve Everybody Who Cares

Working with many kinds of organizations over the past several years, I've learned the hard way that participation is not optional. As leaders, we have no choice but to figure out how to invite in everybody who is going to be affected by change. Those we fail to invite into the creation process will surely and always show up as resistors and saboteurs. But I haven't become insistent on broad-based participation just to avoid resistance, or to get people to support my efforts. I've learned that I'm not smart enough to design anything for the whole system. None of us these days can know what will work inside the dense networks we call organizations. We can't see what's meaningful to people or even understand how they get their work done. We have no option but to invite them into the design process.

I know from experience that most people are very intelligent—they have figured out how to make things work when it seemed impossible; they have invented ways to get around roadblocks and dumb policies; they have created their own networks to support them and help them learn. But rarely is this visible to the organization until and unless we invite people in to participate in solution-creation processes. The complexity and density of organizations require that we engage the whole system so we can harvest the invisible intelligence that exists throughout the organization.

Fortunately, during the past ten years there has been pioneering work (by Marvin Weisbord and Sandra Janoff, Robert Jacobson, Kathy Dannemiller, and many others) on how to engage large numbers of people in designing innovations and changing themselves. Yet even in the presence of strong evidence for how well these processes work, most leaders still hesitate to venture down the participation path. Leaders have had so many bad experiences with participation that describing it as "not optional" seems like a death sentence. But we have to accept two simple truths: we can't force anybody to change. And no two people see the world the same way. We can only engage people in the change process from the beginning and see what's possible. If the issue is meaningful to them, they will become enthusiastic and bright advocates. If we want people's intelligence and support, we must welcome them as cocreators. People only support what they create.

Diversity Is the Path to Unity

All change begins with a change in meaning. Yet we each see the world differently. Is it possible to develop a sense of shared meaning without denying our diversity? Are there ways that organizations can develop a shared sense of what's significant without forcing people to accept someone else's viewpoint?

There is a powerful paradox at work here. If we are willing to listen eagerly for diverse interpretations, we discover that our differing perceptions somehow originate from a unifying center. As we become aware of this unity in diversity, it changes our relationships for the better. We recognize that through our diversity we share a dream, or we share a sense of injustice. Then magical things happen to our relationships. We open to each other as colleagues. Past hurts and negative histories get left behind. People step forward to work together. We don't hang back, we don't withdraw, we don't wait to be enticed. We actively seek each other out because the problem is important. The meaningfulness of the issue resounds more loudly than our past grievances or difficulties. As we discover some issue whose importance we share, we want to work together, no matter our differences.

I've been humbled to see how a group can come together as it recognizes its mutual interests. Working together becomes possible because people have discovered a shared meaning for the work that is strong enough to embrace them all. Held together in this rich center of meaning, they let go of many interpersonal difficulties and work around traditional hindrances. They know they need each other. They are willing to struggle with relationships and figure out how to make them work because they realize this is the only path to achieving their aspirations.

People Will Always Surprise Us

Perhaps because of the study of human psychology, perhaps because we're just too busy to get to know each other, we have become a society that labels people in greater and greater detail. We know each other's personality types, leadership styles, syndromes, and neurotic behaviors. We are quick to assign people to a typology and then dismiss them, as if we really knew who they were. If we're trying to get something done in our organization, and things start going badly, we hunt for scapegoats to explain why it's not working. We notice only those who impede our good plans—all those "resistors," those stubborn and scared colleagues who cling to the past. We label ourselves also, but more generously, as "early adopters" or "cultural creatives."

I was recently given a T-shirt with a wonderful motto on the back: "You can't hate someone whose story you know." But these days, in our crazed haste, we don't have time to get to know each other's stories, to be curious about who a person is or why she or he is behaving a particular way. Listening to colleagues—their diverse interpretations, their stories, what they find meaningful in their work—always transforms our relationships. The act of listening to each other always brings us closer. We may not like them or approve of their behavior, but if we listen, we move past the labels. Our "enemy" category shrinks in population. We notice another human being who has a reason for certain actions, who is trying to make some small contribution to our organization or community. The stereotypes that have divided us melt away, and we discover that we want to work together. We realize that only by joining together will we be able to create the change we both want to see in the world.

Rely on Human Goodness

I know that the only path to creating more innovative workplaces and communities is to depend on one another. We cannot cope, much less create, in this increasingly fast and turbulent world without each other. If we try to do it alone, we will fail.

There is no substitute for human creativity, human caring, human will. We can be incredibly resourceful, imaginative, and openhearted. We can do the impossible, learn and change quickly, and extend instant compassion to those who are suffering. And we use these creative and compassionate behaviors frequently. If you look at your daily life, how often do you figure out an answer to a problem, or find a slightly better way of doing something, or extend yourself to someone in need? Very few people go through their days as robots, doing only repetitive tasks, never noticing that anybody else is nearby. Take a moment to look around at your colleagues and neighbors, and you'll see the same behaviors—people trying to be useful, trying to make some small contribution, trying to help someone else.

We have forgotten what we're capable of, and we let our worst natures rise to the surface. We got into this sorry state partly because, for too long, we've been treating people as machines. We've forced people into tiny boxes called roles and job descriptions. We've told people what to do and how they should behave. We've told them they weren't creative, couldn't contribute, couldn't think.

After so many years of being bossed around, of working within confining roles, of unending reorganization, reengineering, downsizing, mergers, and power plays, most people are exhausted, cynical, and focused only on self-protection. Who wouldn't be? But it's important to remember that *we created* these negative and demoralized people. We created them by discounting and denying our best human capacities.

But people are still willing to come back; they still want to work side by side with us to find solutions, develop innovations, make a difference in the world. We just need to invite them back. We do this by using simple processes that bring us together to talk to one another, listen to one another's stories, reflect together on what we're learning as we do our work. We do this by developing relationships of trust where we do what we say, where we speak truthfully, where we refuse to act from petty self-interest. These processes and relationships have already been developed by many courageous companies, leaders, and facilitators. Many pioneers have created processes and organizations that depend on human capacity and know-how to evoke our very best.

In my experience, people everywhere want to work together, because daily they are overwhelmed by problems that they can't solve alone. People want to help. People want to contribute. Everyone wants to feel creative and hopeful again.

As leaders, as neighbors, as colleagues, it is time to turn to one another, to engage in the intentional search for human goodness.

In our meetings and deliberations, we can reach out and invite in those we have excluded. We can recognize that no one person or leader has the answer, that we need everybody's creativity to find our way through this strange new world. We can act from the certainty that most people want to care about others and can invite them to step forward with their compassion. We can realize that "You can't hate someone whose story you know."

We *are* our only hope for creating a future worth working for. We can't go it alone, we can't get there without each other, and we can't create it without relying anew on our fundamental and precious human goodness.

2 CHARLES HANDY

FLEAS AND ELEPHANTS

*Charles Handy was professor at the London Business
School and creator of the London Sloan Programme.
He was an executive with Shell International, an
economist, and chairman of the Royal Society of
Arts. He has authored many books on the changing
shape of work, including* The Age of Unreason,
The Age of Paradox, *and* The Hungry Spirit.

CEOs are not naturally inclined to look to Chairman Mao for
inspiration, but Mao's insistence on the need for constant
reinvention is something they need to contemplate, albeit without
Mao's ruthless methods, if their organizations are going to survive
in a turbulent and changing world. Reinvention, however, is easier
to call for than to accomplish. For one thing, it is subject to the
dilemmas of the Sigmoid Curves.

The first of these curves [Figure 2.1] describes the normal life
cycle of almost anything, anybody, or any organism: a period of
learning or investment, in which inputs exceed outputs, followed
by steady growth that inevitably one day peaks and turns into decline. The only variable is the length of the curve, the time it takes
to reach the various points on the curve.

Figure 2.1. Sigmoid Curves

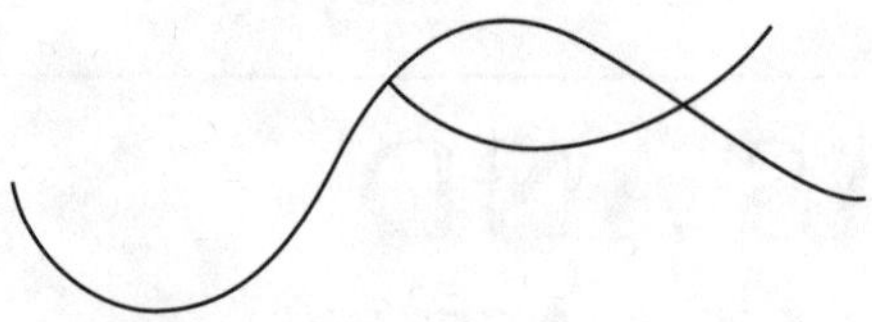

The only way to prolong the life of the body in question, be it an organization or even a career, is to start a second curve. But to allow time and resources for the initial period of learning and investment, that second curve has to start before the first one peaks. You then encounter the paradox of success—when things are going well, there seems no reason to change. "We know how to do it now," people feel, so "don't rock the boat or change the formula." That very reluctance to change ultimately turns success into failure. "Why cannot the status quo be the way forward?" one leader asked me. Sadly, he had to learn the answer by hard experience when his organization disintegrated a few years later.

Long-lasting organizations have to find ways to start second curves before the first curves peak. That's hard to do. It means recognizing, in the midst of a run of success, that it can't last forever and that paradoxically now is the time to start investigating alternatives. It is easier to do that when the need for change is obvious, when the curve is obviously heading downhill. But that is just the time when morale is low, resources are depleted, and leaders are discredited—the worst conditions for any radical thinking. There are earlier, often unnoticed, signs that perceptive leaders can use as a trigger for starting a second curve. Customer or client complaints, if viewed objectively and not defensively, can point to areas where change is needed. Young people, or new recruits, can often see possibilities to which familiarity has blinded those in positions of power.

This prescription, however, requires leaders to blend continuity, the first curve, with invention, the second curve. That, in turn, means finding ways for two very different cultures to live together and to value each other, because both need the other if they are to survive. The second curve needs the resources of the first to support its experiments, and the first curve needs the second to succeed if it is to have any future at all. Sadly, this commonality of interests is not always perceived by either party. "Those Young Turks are all energy but no experience," says one party, while the Young Turks, so-called, mutter about the entrenched attitudes of the Old Guard. Both are right and both are needed.

Put another way, elephants need fleas to keep them alive, to start and then grow that second curve. By *elephants*, I mean the established organizations, be they in business, government, or the voluntary sector. These organizations have a settled way of doing things; they have formalized systems and routines. They deliver efficiency and scale and cultivate predictability, which they see as the key to efficiency. To increase all three, elephants are currently allying themselves with other elephants, swallowing them, marrying them, or organizing friendships, believing that size is safest in a turbulent world. Airlines merge with airlines, banks with banks, pharmaceutical companies with pharmaceuticals. In any industry sector, there may soon be only half a dozen elephants accounting for more than half the output. It would be wrong, too, to imagine that the nonprofit sector could be insulated from the same sort of pressures. All these matings of elephants increase scale and pool resources, but they do not of themselves guarantee a different future, only more of the same if, perhaps sometimes, a little better. For that different future, the elephants need some fleas to grow a second and different curve.

The Alchemist Study

Fleas are the creative individuals or groups. They include small independent businesses or community ventures. Elizabeth Handy and I recently studied twenty-nine typical flea individuals in London, England, who had started their own new ventures—theater companies, small businesses, design communities, and new social ventures. We called them The New Alchemists because of their ability to create metaphorical gold, either from nothing or from desperate situations, the equivalent of base metal. We were interested to discover what circumstances or dispositions shaped them, what influences or happenings made them what they were, and how their capacity for innovation, or alchemy, could be mirrored by others.

The first important thing to note was that these innovators, or fleas, saw themselves as different from other people and destined, in their eyes, to make a difference. They were not conformists, something that on its own makes it difficult to accommodate them in any institution. All the people we studied were, in their own view, unemployable in any organization other than their own. They were not "boss compatible" themselves, however much they might seek to boss others. In other words, independence was a key element in their personality profiles. Fleas, it seems, prefer to live on top of elephants rather than in their bloodstreams. Swallowed by elephants, they die.

The alchemists were also dedicated. Passion was what drove them, whether they were creating businesses, or theater groups, or campaigning organizations. They had to believe in what they were doing, not simply use their talents as a means to an end. Those who had built successful businesses were clearly making small fortunes for themselves, but the fortune was not the initial motivation or even the continuing one. It was the desire to start their own thing, to make a difference in some field that they believed in, that had inspired them. Promises of future wealth or status are therefore not the kinds of things that will motivate such people. What they will want is a cause to commit to, space for independence, and the opportunity to make a difference.

Given dedication and the chance to be different, these individuals were dogged in their determination and in their application. They had what the poet Keats called *negative capability*, the capacity to ride through setbacks and failures and to keep going through all adversities—because they believed in what they were attempting. Any organization using them must also, therefore, be prepared to be equally tolerant when such people suffer reverses or follow trails that come to a dead end—that is how these individuals learn, by trial and as often as not by error.

Harnessing the Fleas

Elephants need fleas such as these to keep them innovating, but fleas cannot easily live in elephants. The inevitable bureaucracy and need for conformity suffocates them, be they individuals or groups. Some organizations put their fleas in separate pens, in what used to be called *skunk works*, only to find, too often, that their innovative ideas are then rejected by the core organization as "not invented here." In a variation of this tactic, some elephant organizations set out to buy successful flea organizations and then incorporate their innovations into their own workings, meanwhile spitting out the original flea creator, who finds corporate life intolerable after independence. Others have turned a part of themselves into a venture capitalist, encouraging and financing would-be fleas to set up their own innovative organizations with the elephant organization's backing, thereby keeping a degree of ownership in any successful innovations. These latter strategies, however, are not readily available to nonprofit organizations, who cannot, by definition, act as conventional venture capitalists, although they can, of course, find other ways of nurturing potential fleas until they either prove themselves or die.

Many organizations look for a more all-embracing cultural approach, trying to create an environment more friendly to fleas by, for instance, rewarding creative ideas from any source or even requiring everyone to spend some 10 percent of the time doing nonessential work. Still others seek to encourage creativity by running seminars with the creative arts—for dancers, actors, or musicians—or by decorating their walls with stimulating arts or employing artists-in-residence. None of these ideas are wrong. They all make it more legitimate to think and act like a flea, but unless the whole culture of the organization is biased toward constant reinvention, these devices are only lip salve, soon to be obliterated by the need for efficiency and the measurements and controls that inevitably follow in efficiency's wake. It is not surprising, therefore, that so many organizations bring in temporary fleas from outside to tickle them behind the ears. These are the strategy and change consultants who find that the easy way to riches is to be a flea on the back of an elephant.

In a perfect organizational world, imported fleas should not be necessary. The only way around it is to build an organization that sees itself as a natural home for fleas. Could elephants be, in effect, federations of fleas, cellular honeycombs of groups of fleas, united only by a common passion for a cause and therefore by a willingness to compromise some of their independence for the mutual advantage of everyone? Such a design principle would invert the traditional logic of organizations, which typically starts from the top and works down. *Federalism* builds from the individual parts to the center, delegating to the center only those things that can only or best be done there.

Federalism—a Home for Fleas

Federalism was originally conceived as a way of combining the independent and the collective, of being both big and small, the same but different. Americans and Germans, Australians and Canadians, Spaniards and Swiss all have federal constitutions, designed to allow independence within a union, but even these do not always see the sense in applying the same principles to their businesses. To the British, federalism is "the F word," a dirty word, one that implies a loss of control to the center. This serious misunderstanding of the principles of federalism will be a handicap in the future development of both their constitution and their economy.

This is not the place for a detailed discussion of federalism. The principles are spelled out in an article by this author for the *Harvard Business Review,* "Balancing Corporate Power: A New Federalist Paper." Suffice it here to say that federalism is a mixture of both centralization and decentralization, centralizing only those things that everyone agrees it would be crazy not to centralize and leaving as much autonomy as is possible to the various states or business groups—the space for the fleas. The retained powers of the center are often the traditional shareholder powers of decisions on new directions, new money, and new people in the key positions. If the strategic, financial, and personnel decisions are taken correctly, the rest should take care of itself, although most federal constitutions, in politics or business, also give the center what has been called "the right to invade" should things seem to be going astray in any of the constituent parts. There is also, in federal institutions, a constitution that sets out rights and responsibilities, a common law or set of rules and a common information system.

Federalism is messy—and political. There are disputes over the allocation of resources. Information is guarded when it should flow freely. There are boundary disputes, necessary compromises, competing lines of accountability. To make it work requires an active understanding of "twin citizenship"—the idea that one can have at least two loyalties, to one's own group and to the larger collective; one can be both a Texan and an American. The lesser loyalty is easy; it is the larger one that requires work, because without it compromise is hard to obtain: Why give up on local priorities for the greater good if you have no interest in that greater good? Hence the critical importance of the talk of *vision* and *values* and the necessity for the top leader to accentuate these in his or her own words and actions. Some distribution of the spoils of success from the center to the states also helps reinforce the idea of a common good.

Properly done, however, federalism allows room for the fleas inside the elephant. ABB tries to restrict the size of its business groups to fifty persons in order to re-create that sense of a small enterprise,

personally led and motivated. In a world of Hi-Tech, Hi-Touch (to use Naisbitt's evocative terms) the touch can easily be neglected, yet fleas rely a lot on trust, trust in those they work with, and trust needs touch to be truly trust. Technology communicates facts but not feelings. Fleas need both for trust to flourish, and few of us can know more than fifty people well enough to gauge their feelings or to know whether they can be relied on. The Alchemists instinctively know this, which is one reason why they are reluctant to grow too big.

Federalism offers a way forward, but it is neither easy nor tidy. Small wonder, perhaps, that many leaders of elephants shrink from it, but without it they have to rely on the perspicacity and farsightedness of those in the center to spot the new trends. It would be easier and less risky to regard their organization as a collection of potential proving grounds, where new ideas could be tried and discarded if found wanting but pursued if thought promising. It is a learning organization, in the sense that the constituent parts tend to learn from one another as they compete to make a difference to the whole. Federalism, in other words, provides the structure for growing second curves without betting the whole organization on one view of the future. For all its difficulties, it is, in the end, a safer bet than any of the alternatives to leading change.

3 MAX DE PREE

CREATIVE LEADERSHIP

Max De Pree is chairman emeritus and former CEO of Herman Miller, Inc., the $2 billion manufacturer of office furniture. He is author of Leadership Is an Art, Leadership Jazz, *and* Letters to Zoe, *and the recently published* Called to Serve, *about establishing and nurturing a competent board for a nonprofit organization.*

King Lear tells us that nothing comes from nothing. So do scientists, for that matter. Everything in the world already exists; whatever seems new is only something old rearranged. So how do we explain innovation? The relatively short history of the United States glistens with innovation. Our open meritocracy has bred and nurtured innovative people with new ideas. Leaders in all sorts of organizations want desperately to encourage creative, innovative persons.

Innovation is a form of change. For the most part our culture welcomes change, but people proposing it do, as you might expect,

---

Note: This chapter was originally published in the Drucker Foundation journal *Leader to Leader*, vol. 20, Spring 2001, and is reprinted with the permission of Max De Pree. Portions of it first appeared in *Leadership Jazz*, published in 1992 by Doubleday. Copyright © 2001 by Max De Pree.

run into barriers. As our society has become more complex, we find important segments of it becoming larger, more structured, more bureaucratic, less nimble, and less hospitable to unusual persons. Leaders can resist hardening of the arteries. Leaders can help unusual people produce innovations—even if it's not out of thin air. But leading creative people in this age of diverse work arrangements and electronic relationships requires leaders themselves to be thoughtfully innovative. The secret, I believe, lies in how individual leaders in a great variety of settings make room for people with unusual and creative gifts and temporarily become followers themselves.

Creative persons stand out from the rest of us. Somehow their contributions affect large groups and move organizations toward something better. John Masters calls them "explorationists" (the most creative people in his organization discover oil and gas). Yet they function, for the most part, outside of or away from organizations. They work in all kinds of places—in cafés, in airports, at home—and they benefit from unusual relationships with the organizations they join. They often have odd reporting relationships, but somehow they instinctively insert themselves into organizations wherever they are needed.

The changes and innovations they bring are often more like leaps than the small steps most of us experience. They think of the world in large terms. They work for institutions or societies or cultures or ideas, not for individuals. Their creativity comes from the novel connections they make between their work and their experience or observations. They are usually curious and need a field in which to exercise that curiosity. Leaders can work to bring the special and creative gifts of these people to bear on the efforts of a group.

Leaders in companies and colleges and banks, in churches and government, in high schools and museums, have already chosen to follow the gifted people who can bring renewal, vitality, and opportunity. Once a leader becomes committed to a new way of dealing with creative people, we can define the process quickly. I would call it a search for beneficial surprise. Traditional education does not prepare us for this. Though familiarity with technology helps us deal with such a search, all the technology in the world won't help us begin to discover the ideas and experiments and failures and successes we will need.

If we are to find new sources and perspectives, it seems to me two questions, if thoughtfully considered, are likely to yield good results. The first looks at innovation from a leader's point of view; the second, from the view of creative persons.

How Does a Leader Approach the Process of Creative Work?

A leader first makes a personal commitment to be hospitable to creative people and a broader commitment to be open to contributions from many quarters. This commitment entails a number of ideas and guidelines. Let me give you some starters.

A leader protects creative persons from the bureaucracy and legalism so ensconced in our organizations.

A leader remains vulnerable to real surprise and to true quality. I do mean surprise—the totally unexpected. I also mean a new level of quality, one that I might not have considered before. Neither of these things is easy; really creative people shake up organizations.

A leader connects creative people to the entire organization. A wise counselor to Herman Miller (the company where I worked for over forty years) once advised a key executive to get to know one of the truly creative designers who worked with the company. The executive failed to set up the meeting. When the counselor asked about the visit, the executive apologized for the delay, admitting that it would do him good. The counselor replied, "I'm not worried about what *you're* missing. The *company* needs you to know this person."

A leader does not demand unreasonable personal or corporate loyalty, understanding that creative persons are loyal to an idea and often appear to others as nonjoiners. I realize that this is difficult;

yet creative persons need breadth of opportunity and the assurance of fair treatment rather than hierarchy and control. Their work rises from discovering and connecting. People remember the story of Archimedes' discovering the principle of displacement while taking a bath, because creative people have insights in all kinds of contexts. Art Fry realized the potential of Post-it notes while singing in his church choir. Hewlett-Packard began in a garage. Leaders understand the potential of connections like these and make it possible for creative persons to discover them.

A leader will be careful about measuring the contributions of creative persons. Return on assets has become a Baal in too many organizations. All things cannot and must not be quantified. Financial and legal matters are truly important, but they do not lie at the heart of our future. Resist the urge to structure all things alike.

We also need to keep in mind that moving up in the hierarchy does not confer competence or wisdom. The discernment and judgment necessary to evaluate true innovation, to doom or give life to good design or breakthroughs in technology, lie with people trained in those fields. I can remember interrupting a discussion among our executive team about the relative merits of a graphic design with the following question: Who here is a graphic designer we trust? Of course, none of us was, and so we called in a competent judge. Sometimes leaders do forget what they don't know.

A leader arranges for projects to proceed along a narrowing path. The majority of data and opinions, dreams and constraints, should be made available at the beginning. Then a leader will narrow involvements and focus responsibilities and begin a careful—but not oppressive—scrutiny of progress and direction. Innovation will never be a democratic event. It's just too risky for groupthink. Majorities seldom vote to change. A small group of accountable leaders and the creative persons involved must take the risk. If you're fortunate enough to come across a truly revolutionary idea, remember what Peter Drucker once said: "When you have a real innovation, don't compromise."

A leader sets an example for openness and imagination and acceptance. Learn to live constructively with eccentricity. Creative people can be great teachers; leaders prepare the classroom. In selecting architects for building projects over the years at Herman Miller, a key question we asked ourselves was, "Who among these very good architects will teach us the most?"

What Do Creative Persons Need to Be Fruitful in the Worlds of Organizations?

Creative persons need access to senior leaders. A leader will let it be known that relationships with creative persons are important, that creative persons are at the heart of the organization.

Creative persons work well in the ethos of jazz. A leader will pick a tune, set the tempo, and start the music—define a style. After that, it's up to the players to be disciplined and free, wild and restrained. Jazz band leaders know how to integrate the voices in the band without diminishing their uniqueness. It matters a great deal how the leader starts the process. In 1977, Herman Miller built a manufacturing facility in Bath, England, which won the *Financial Times* award for the best industrial building of the year. Nicholas Grimshaw, the architect, said at the time that the spirit and quality of the building could never have been achieved without the poetry and constraints in the brief given him by Herman Miller.

Creative persons, like the rest of us, need constraints. The famous industrial designer Charles Eames once called restraints "liberating." And I doubt that Rembrandt ever began a painting on an unlimited canvas. One of the most striking characteristics of the creative persons I know is their ability to renew themselves through constraints.

Creative persons need license to be contrary. Leaders will use the essential contribution of contrary opinion wisely, especially when dealing with creative persons. Cynicism has no place in an organization, but leaders welcome the committed skeptic who wants to be held accountable and demands a share of the risk.

Creative persons need a reasonable chance that their work will see the light of day. Whatever the results are—hardware or software, information or communication—there must be the potential of reality lying ahead as creative persons meander along toward real innovation. They need to know that they will have help in making the results of their work real.

Creative persons need a fundamental level of trust. Industrial designer Bill Stumpf, one of the most creative persons I know, wrote me that a leader's expression of trust creates the grace necessary for him to operate. He also admitted that a leader's trust gave him an added sense of responsibility and pressure. He wanted to see *his* project done right.

The work of creative persons is only a part of a whole; it cannot be taken in isolation. Again Bill Stumpf comes to mind: when a company works with creative persons, it works with their "theories, philosophy, reputation, and talent." I also believe we work with their families, failures, travels, and troubles. Ten years ago, geography would have been on this list; technology is making that increasingly irrelevant.

Creative persons need to work with others of equal competence. Tennis can be played at many levels of ability. We improve only when we are challenged and stretched. This is also the way at work. Things surely go better when we have the chance to work with real competence.

Truly creative persons do not set out to win prizes. They flourish in the process of solving problems. Good work is the goal; recognition is a consequence. Steve Frykholm, an enormously talented graphic designer largely responsible for the Herman Miller image and graphic identity, once won the company's highest award, the Frost Award. He was surprised and pleased when he was named the recipient and told us that his goal had always been to do good design. The prize followed.

Creative persons—like the rest of us—like to be thanked. People who through their unusual gifts bring change and innovation and renewal to organizations need to be identified. Organizations need to know the sources of their vitality; leaders acknowledge these sources with fidelity. A friend of mine noticed buried among the stems in an arrangement of flowers a small tag that read, "Created by number 59." This does not qualify as credit; creativity does not come from anonymous sources.

Both personally and organizationally, the results of becoming a good leader for creative persons are surely worth the effort. Leaders may expect a legacy going well beyond quarterly results. Organizations can expect new windows into territory—both physical and philosophical—that would not open without the gifts of creative persons. Products and services that deliver a truly competitive edge will appear—innovations in the form of beneficial surprises, not merely predictable solutions or designs by committee. Change and renewal and hope will accrue. Higher levels of civility and robust institutional health are possible. Making the effort to be a leader to creative people and learning to follow such people signal both real leadership competence and the understanding that creative work comes from the heart and not from management handbooks.

Creative persons come in all shapes and sizes and fields, from graphic design and architecture to software design and human resources. The best are volunteers. They can find work almost anywhere, and they gauge the quality of their leaders as a way of deciding where they will contribute. Leaders make it possible for creative persons to make something out of nothing—nothing, that is, but expressions of themselves.

Several years ago, the Herman Miller board of directors met in Phoenix. Among other things, we visited an exhibit by the artist Allan Houser, several of whose sculptures the company had purchased. Allan was a marvelous person and had shown us through the exhibit, talking quietly one-on-one with board members. In my best managerial fashion, I asked Allan to speak at dinner that night and tell us something about himself. He replied, "I won't give a speech, but I'll do something." As good as his word, when the time came for him to say something at dinner that night in the Heard Museum, he got up, silently pulled out a flute, and began to play beautiful and haunting melodies from his Chiricahua Apache heritage. None of us even knew that he played the flute. In his creative wisdom, Allan told us who he was. We listened. When he finished, he sat down without a word, and we had learned an important lesson in leadership.

4 MARSHALL GOLDSMITH

CHANGING THE BEHAVIOR OF *SUCCESSFUL* PEOPLE

Marshall Goldsmith is a founding director of the Financial Times Knowledge Dialogue, a coaching network that connects executives from around the world with thought leaders. Marshall has been listed in Forbes *magazine as one of the five top executive coaches and in* The Wall Street Journal *as one of the "Top Ten" executive educators. He is a leading authority in helping executives achieve positive, measurable change in behavior for themselves, their people, and their teams. He is a member of the board of the Drucker Foundation.*

In my role as an executive coach, I am asked to work with extremely successful people who want to get even better. They are usually key executives in major corporations. They are almost always very intelligent, dedicated, and persistent. They are committed to the success of their companies. They have high personal integrity. Many are financially independent. They are not working because they have to. They are working because they want to. Intellectually, they realize that the leadership behavior that was associated with yesterday's results may not be the behavior that is needed to achieve tomorrow's innovation.

Most of us see the need to change the behavior of others. This is one of our great challenges when we try to lead for innovation. We wonder why it is so difficult for people to change. Yet we often have difficulty changing even small aspects of our own behavior! And as we become more successful, change seems even harder. As Charles Handy points out in Chapter Two, the "paradox of success" occurs because we *need to* change before we *have to* change. However, when things are going well we feel no reason to change.

I have recently completed a review of research related to the topic of helping successful people change their behavior. Most research on behavioral change has focused on dysfunctional behavior with clear physiological consequences (for example, alcoholism, drug addiction, eating disorders, and smoking). A substantial amount has been written on *why* successful people succeed. Not surprisingly, very little has been written on the unique challenges involved in helping successful people change. The entire concept is somewhat counterintuitive.

My assumption is that you, the reader of this chapter, are a successful person. You may not be a key executive in a major corporation, but you are probably successful by most socioeconomic standards. My second assumption is that you are managing successful people. I am assuming that many of the people you work with are knowledge workers. And your most valued coworkers are probably there because they want to be, not because they have to be. You frequently have the challenge of helping yourself and helping them make the changes that will take your team to the next level.

What have I learned about helping people like you and your colleagues change? In most cases, even the most successful leaders can increase their effectiveness by changing certain elements of their behavior. (The same is true for us as spouses, partners, friends, parents, and children.) By becoming aware of how we can improve, involving respected colleagues, and following up, we can almost always get better at the behavior we choose as perceived by the people we choose. I have also learned that the key beliefs that help us succeed can become challenges when it is time to change.

Four Key Beliefs of Successful People: Their Implications for Behavioral Change

There are a variety of reasons why successful people succeed; some factors can be changed and some cannot. Every person does not have the *potential* to succeed in every activity. For example, a poor athlete may become better through practice, but physical limitations may prevent this person from ever becoming a professional. As Howard Gardner points out, different individuals have different intelligences that can dramatically affect their potential in different fields.

My review of research focused on the *beliefs* that tend to differentiate more successful people from their peers (who may have similar potential to achieve). Successful people tend to have four underlying beliefs:

1. I choose to succeed.
2. I can succeed.
3. I will succeed.
4. I have succeeded.

Each of these beliefs can be labeled differently (for example, self-determination, self-efficacy, optimism); each increases the likelihood of achieving success, and each is related to and positively correlated with the others. Each belief will be discussed in terms of why it generally leads to success and how it can inhibit change.

I Choose to Succeed

Successful people believe they are doing what they choose to do because they choose to do it. And they have a high need for self-determination. The more successful a person is, the more likely this is to be true. Successful people have a unique distaste for feeling controlled or manipulated. In my work, I have made peace with the fact that I cannot force executives to change. I can only help them get better at what they choose to change. One of the great challenges of coaching (or teaching or parenting) is to realize that the ultimate motivation for change has to come from the person being coached, not the coach. (Margaret Wheatley makes this point very eloquently in the first chapter of this book.)

Having the belief "I choose to succeed" does not imply that successful people are selfish. Many successful people are great team players. It does mean, however, that successful people need to feel a *personal* commitment to what they are doing. They need a sense of ownership. When leaders have a personal commitment to the mission, they are much more likely to achieve results. They lead with their hearts as well as their minds. They are effective in attracting and developing fellow believers who want to get the job done.

"I choose to succeed" is a belief that is highly correlated with achievement. Adding "and I choose to change" can be a very difficult transition. Successful people's personal commitment can make it hard for them to change. The more we believe that our behavior is a result of our own choices and commitments, the less likely we are to want to change.

One of the best-researched principles in psychology is that of cognitive dissonance. The underlying theory is simple. The more we are committed to believing that something is true, the less likely we are to be willing to change our beliefs (even in the face of clear evidence that we are wrong). Cognitive dissonance works in favor of successful people in most situations. Their commitment encourages them to stay the course and not give up when the going gets tough. This same principle can work against successful people when they must *change* course.

A macro-level example of this phenomenon has occurred in Japan. In the 1980s, Japanese managers were widely praised as role models for leadership behavior. The country's economic growth was one of the greatest success stories in the history of business. Books were written, and benchmarking trips were organized so that leaders from around the world could learn from their success, which had a deep impact on many leaders. Business success went beyond financial results and was transformed into national pride in "Japanese management." Leaders were not just proud of what they had achieved; they were proud of how they achieved it.

Unfortunately, the style that worked in the 1980s did not work in the 1990s. Rapid changes in technology, the economy, the role of manufacturing, and the workforce made the Japanese management approach far less desirable. It has taken a decade for many leaders in Japan to admit that their previous approach was no longer working. Many leaders "denied the numbers" for years before accepting the fact that change was needed. The same commitment that had brought a huge success in the 1980s led to a huge challenge by the turn of the century. The leaders who have had the wisdom and courage to let go of the past are the ones who are succeeding in the new Japanese economy.

I Can Succeed

Successful people believe they have the internal capacity to make desirable things happen. This is the definition of self-efficacy and is perhaps the most central belief that drives individual success. People who believe they can succeed see opportunities where others see threats. This comfort with ambiguity leads people with high self-efficacy to take greater risks, achieve greater returns, and try more different things. They do not feel like victims of fate. They believe they have the motivation and ability to change their world. They see success for themselves and others as largely a function of this motivation and ability rather than luck, random chance, or external factors.

There is a positive (and not surprising) relationship between the need for self-determination and what is called internal locus of control. If people believe that the world is largely out of their control and that they are merely cogs in the wheel of life, they do not mind as much being controlled or manipulated. They think that's the way life is. If people feel they can change their world and make it better, they find external control and manipulation much more distasteful.

Although the "I can succeed" belief is generally associated with success, it can (when combined with optimism) lead to what is called superstitious behavior. An illustration of this behavior is the ballplayer who wears his special "game socks" every time he plays because he thinks they cause success on the field. This kind of superstition can lead to difficulty in changing behavior, even when others see it as obviously dysfunctional. Successful people often confuse correlation with causation. They often do not realize that they are successful "because of" some behaviors and "in spite of" others. Superstitious behavior is merely the confusion of correlation and causation. Many leaders get positive reinforcement for the *results* that occur. They then assume that their behavior is what helped lead to these results. Just as successful athletes believe in lucky socks or numbers, or perform rituals before a contest, successful business leaders tend to repeat behaviors that are followed by rewards. They may fear that changing *any* behavior will break their string of successes.

Any human (in fact, any animal) tends to repeat behavior that is followed by positive reinforcement. The more successful people are (by definition), the more positive reinforcement they tend to receive. One of the greatest mistakes of successful people is this assumption: "I am successful. I behave this way. Therefore, I must be successful *because* I behave this way!"

One financial services CEO was viewed as an outstanding leader but as incredibly weak in the area of providing feedback to his direct reports. (This is fairly common for top executives.) He had developed an elaborate rationalization as to (1) why feedback "at my level" was not important, (2) why feedback was a waste of his time, (3) how he had made it this far without providing feedback, and (4) how *he* had never received feedback and it obviously had not hurt *his* career!

Fortunately, this executive had some highly respected direct reports who were both courageous and assertive. He decided to honor their wishes and give feedback a try. After achieving very positive success, he finally admitted that this had been a personal weakness for years. He realized he had been successful in spite of his lack of providing feedback, not because of it.

I Will Succeed

An unflappable sense of optimism is one of the most important characteristics of successful people. Successful people not only believe that they *can* achieve but that they *will* achieve. This belief goes beyond any one task. Successful leaders tend to communicate with an overall sense of self-confidence. In a recent study with Accenture (formerly Andersen Consulting) involving over 200 high-potential leaders (from 120 companies around the world), self-confidence ranked as one of the top ten elements of effective leadership for leaders in the past, the present, and the future.

Successful leaders not only believe they will achieve, they assume that the people they respect will achieve. As was stated earlier, they see success as a function of people's motivation and ability. If they believe that their people have the motivation and ability, they communicate this contagious sense of optimism and self-confidence to others.

Successful people tend to pursue opportunities. If they set a goal, write the goal down, and publicly announce the goal, they will tend to do whatever it takes to achieve the goal. Although this sense of optimism is generally associated with success, it can easily lead to overload if it is not controlled. Successful people tend to be extremely busy and face the danger of overcommitment.

It can be difficult for an ambitious person with an "I will succeed" attitude to say no to desirable opportunities. As of this writing, the huge majority of executives that I work with feel as busy (or busier) today than they have ever felt in their lives. In North

America, this perception was consistent for the last four years of the nineties—a decade that featured one of the longest economic expansions in our history. Most of these executives were not overcommitted because they were trying to save a sinking ship. They were overcommitted because they were drowning in a sea of opportunity.

Successful people achieve a lot, and they often believe they can do more than they actually can. My favorite European "volunteer" client was the executive director of one of the world's leading human services organizations. His mission was to help the world's most vulnerable people. Unfortunately (for all of us), his business was booming. His biggest challenge as a leader, by far, was avoiding overcommitment. (By the way, this is very common for the top human services leaders.) Without externally imposed discipline, he had a tendency to promise even more than the most dedicated staff could deliver. Unchecked, this "we will succeed" attitude can lead to staff burnout, high turnover, and, ultimately, less capability to help those in need.

One of my clients recently completed a study of the graduates of their executive development program. As part of the program, each graduate was expected to focus on behavioral change. They were all instructed in a simple process to help them achieve this change. At the end of the class, over 95 percent of the participants said they would follow the steps in the process (in a confidential survey). One year later, about 70 percent (more or less) followed the process. This group showed huge improvement in effectively changing behavior; approximately 30 percent did nothing. This group showed no more improvement than a control group. When asked, "Why didn't you implement the behavioral change plan that you said you would?" most said, "I was overcommitted and just did not get to it."

I Have Succeeded

Successful people tend to have a positive interpretation of their past performance. High achievers not only believe that they have achieved results, they tend to believe that they were instrumental in helping the results get achieved. This tends to be true, even if the positive outcomes were caused by external events that they did not control.

In a positive way, successful people are delusional. They tend to see their previous history as a validation of who they are and what they have done. This positive interpretation of the past leads to increased optimism toward the future and increases the likelihood of future success.

Although the belief "I have been successful" has many positive benefits, it can cause difficulty when it is time to change behavior. Successful people's positive view of their performance can make it hard to hear negative feedback from others. Successful people consistently overrate their performance relative to their professional peers. I have personally asked over ten thousand successful professionals to "rate yourself relative to your professional peers." Eighty to 85 percent of *all* successful professionals rated themselves in the top 20 percent of their peer group (who were, by the way the exercise was defined, statistically as successful as they were). Professions with higher perceived social status (for example, physicians, pilots, investment bankers) tend to have even higher self-assessments relative to their (equally prestigious) peers.

My favorite example of this characteristic occurred with a group of medical doctors. I told the group that I had done extensive research, which had proven that exactly half of all MDs had graduated in the bottom half of their medical school class. Two of the doctors insisted that this was impossible!

Successful people tend to deny the importance of negative behavioral feedback for three common reasons: (1) the feedback is being delivered by someone they do not see as an equal in terms of success, therefore it doesn't count; (2) they see feedback that is inconsistent with their self-image as incorrect and the other person as confused; or (3) they agree with the feedback but assume that the behavior must not be that important because they are successful.

Helping Successful People Change

In our work with leaders, my firm focuses on helping successful people achieve a positive, measurable, long-term change in behavior. To measure impact, we have completed before-and-after studies with tens of thousands of participants. The steps in the behavioral change process have been developed to work with successful executives. However, these steps can be used to help any successful person change his or her interpersonal behavior.

• *Have the successful person receive feedback on important, self-selected behaviors as perceived by important, self-selected raters.* It is hard to measure effectiveness in changing behavior unless there is a clear agreement on what desired behavior is. Successful people have a high need for self-determination. Ultimately, the ownership of the behavioral change process will have to come from the people who are changing their behavior, not from an internal or external coach.

One reason that successful people tend to deny the validity of behavioral feedback is that they were not involved in determining the desired behavior for a person in their position. The more they are involved in determining what this behavior is, the more likely they are to buy in to the validity of demonstrating it. Successful people are very responsive to help in achieving goals they themselves have set. They tend to resist changes that make them feel judged or manipulated.

Successful people also have a desire for internal consistency. If leaders publicly state that certain behavior is important, they will be more likely to strive to be a positive role model in demonstrating the behavior. From my experience in developing leadership profiles, I have found that most executives develop a great profile of their "desired" behaviors. In most cases, *understanding* what behaviors are desired is not their major challenge; *demonstrating* these behaviors is.

An example of the value of involving leaders in developing their own profile occurred with a CEO client several years ago. When he received feedback from his coworkers (on his own behavior), he looked skeptically at one of the lower-scoring items and asked, "Who was the person that wanted to include *that* item?" I replied, "You!" He then remembered why he wanted to include the item. He also began to face the fact that the real problem was his own behavior, not the wording of an item.

The first reason that people deny the validity of behavioral feedback is "wrong behaviors." The second reason is "wrong raters." If successful people select the raters, they will be much more likely to accept the validity of the feedback. Most executives respect the opinion of *almost all* of their key colleagues. By letting the successful person pick the raters, you can avoid the potential reaction, "Why should a winner like me listen to a loser like him?"

One argument against letting the people we coach pick their own raters is that they will pick their friends and the feedback will not be representative. I have not found this to be true for two reasons. First, almost all of the executives I have met end up selecting raters that are similar to the group I would have selected anyway. The only time they do not want to include someone is if the person is about to leave the company or they have a deep disrespect for this person. I have never had an executive want to exclude more than two raters. Second, when 360-degree feedback is used for *developmental* purposes, the "items for improvement" that emerge from self-selected raters are quite similar to the items that come from other-selected raters.

Bev Kaye, Ken Shelton, and I asked over fifty great leaders and teachers to describe a time when they had learned something that made a key difference in their lives. This led to our book *Learning Journeys*. More than half of the respondents described a situation in which they had received feedback or a challenge from someone they deeply respected. Interestingly enough, most agreed that the same message would not have had much impact if a different person had delivered it. This made us realize that the *source* of feedback and suggestions can be as important as the *content* of the feedback and suggestions. If successful people respect the source of information, they will be much more likely to learn and change.

Successful people usually respond constructively to feedback when they are involved in selecting the behaviors and the raters. When feedback is confidential (raters are not identified), people tend to focus on what they need to improve, not on who did the rating. It is hard to deny the validity of items that we say are important, as evaluated by raters we respect!

• *After receiving feedback, have the person select one or two important areas for behavioral improvement.* I used to suggest that executives pick one to three areas for behavioral change. But our before-and-after interviews (one year after receiving feedback) have let me know that three is too many. Many of the successful people I meet are too busy now. As was mentioned earlier, a main reason that people do not stick with their change plan is overcommitment. I now suggest that two should be the *maximum* number of behaviors to change. Changing *one* high-leverage behavior (that makes the most impact) can create a very positive difference.

Challenge the people you are coaching to work on *only* the behaviors that can make a real difference. I was asked to review the 360-degree feedback of one of the world's most successful "new economy" CEOs. After receiving his confidential feedback, he considered his lowest item (listening) and asked himself, "If I become a better listener, will this make our company a better company? I am busy. Is working to become a better listener the most effective use of my time?" Before he began to work on changing behavior, he checked it out with the board and with people he respected. He then decided that this change was indeed worth his effort. I was greatly impressed with his thoughtfulness and maturity in dealing with his feedback. He had a clear mission and did not want to be distracted by dealing with behavioral change that was not relevant to the achievement of the mission.

If successful people see the connection between their behavioral change goals and their personal goals, they are much more likely to change. They need to understand the difference between "because of" and "in spite of" behaviors. Some interesting research indicates that *the desire to achieve the skills associated with success is more highly correlated with achievement than the desire for success itself*. If the successful people you are coaching see the connection between changing behavior, achieving their vision, and living their values, they will be much more committed to doing what it takes to achieve lasting change.

• *Have the person involve respected colleagues in the behavioral change process*. Ongoing involvement from supportive colleagues is almost always associated with positive behavioral change. Colleagues are much more likely to help if they feel they are respected and their advice is *requested* (as opposed to *expected*).

In involving key colleagues, we teach successful leaders to have brief conversations with each colleague during which they

> Thank each colleague for his or her feedback and express gratitude for the positive recognition that was received
>
> Let each colleague know the one or two areas for improvement that have been selected and why they are important
>
> Ask each colleague to help them by providing constructive, future-oriented suggestions that may help the leader achieve positive, measurable change
>
> Recruit the respected colleague to provide ongoing coaching to help them improve

Findings on the usefulness of this process are very clear. When successful people write down goals, announce these goals to respected colleagues, and involve the colleagues in helping them improve, positive measurable change is much more likely to occur.

• *Teach the successful person's colleagues to be helpful coaches, not cynics, critics, or judges.* Unlike some forms of achievement (for example, academic achievement), behavioral change is dependent on an interpersonal *relationship* that involves more than one person. If successful people feel they are being encouraged and supported by the people around them, they are much more likely to keep trying and to achieve positive, long-term behavioral change. If they feel they are being judged or manipulated, they tend to become hostile to the process and quit trying.

Years ago, I had an experience with this turn-off effect with the CFO of a major computer company. His leadership feedback indicated that he was perceived as being aloof and arrogant. He saw himself as introverted and somewhat shy. (It is not uncommon that introverted, high-level executives are perceived as arrogant.) One suggestion from employees was that he "get off the top floor" and spend more time with the finance staff. On his first visit to practice "management by walking around," he was greeted with sarcastic comments like "What's the matter? Is the air conditioning broken up there?" and "What are *you* doing down here, slumming it?" He found the experience negative and embarrassing. I later discussed this with one of his employees. Although the employee thought this was funny, he did not realize that he was sabotaging his manager's efforts to meet *his* own request for behavioral change.

In our coaching process, we work not only with the executive but with the people around the executive. We do not get paid unless positive, measurable change occurs (after at least one year). The executive does not define whether he or she achieved positive, measurable change; the people around the executive determine it. We help these coworkers help the executive by doing the following:

- *"Letting go" of the past and focusing on the future.* Successful people are much more likely to change by envisioning a positive future than by reliving a humiliating past. Proving that a successful person was "wrong" is often counterproductive and a waste of time. Successful people respond well to getting ideas and suggestions for the future that are aimed at helping them achieve their goals. The analogy used by racecar drivers is "Focus on the *road,* not on the *wall!*" The executive should not be expected to do everything his or her colleagues suggest. Leadership is not a popularity contest. However, well-intended and constructive suggestions for the future are almost always useful.

- *Being a supportive coach, not a cynic, critic, or judge.* Successful people attribute more validity to the sincere recognition of success than to the sincere acknowledgment of failure. Behavioral change is almost always nonlinear. Almost all adults have setbacks when attempting to change behavior. Coworkers need to realize that this is a natural part of the process and to not give up on the executive. We all have a tendency to revert back to behaviors that were correlated with success in the past. The more successful we are, the easier it is to rationalize this return to past behavior. If the executive is encouraged to move beyond setbacks, and the colleagues do not dwell on them, the odds for long-term change greatly improve. The colleagues' goal should be to help the executive feel like a winner when participating in the process of change.

- *Developing a follow-up process that provides an opportunity for ongoing dialogue on selected behaviors with selected colleagues.* Our research on feedback and follow-up has clearly shown that leaders are much more likely to achieve a positive, measurable change in behavior if they consistently involve selected colleagues (through follow-up dialogues) in the change process. These follow-up dialogues are very focused and need take only a few minutes. They can be done by telephone or in person. In one study involving eight thousand respondents in a *Fortune* 100 corporation, only 18 percent of all leaders who received feedback but did no follow-up were rated as a +2 or +3 on increased effectiveness in one year on a −3 to +3 scale. This was no better than a control group who had received no training and no feedback. However, 86 percent of leaders who did consistent (or periodic) follow-up received top ratings on increased effectiveness.

When coworkers are trained to be supportive coaches, the follow-up process provides an ongoing opportunity for constructive suggestions and recognition. It reinforces the individual's public commitment to change. Ongoing dialogue creates a process in which *both* parties are focused on improving the relationship, not on judging each other.

Conducting minisurveys can be a simple and efficient way to measure behavioral change. Minisurveys are usually very short and focus only on the behaviors that have been selected by the person being coached. They are designed so that the raters evaluate behavior that occurs *only* during the coaching period. They focus on the rater's perception of *improvement.* If the executive agrees on the desired behaviors for change, selects highly respected coworkers as raters, takes the process seriously, and follows up, positive change will almost always occur. After receiving the minisurvey results, the executive thanks the raters, involves them in future change, and continues the process. This is almost always a positive experience for the executive and for the coworkers.

In summary, helping successful people change their behavior is both an opportunity and a challenge. Our research has taught us a great lesson: successful people do not change behavior because they take a course. They get better because of their own efforts and the efforts of their respected colleagues. By understanding the unique issues involved in helping successful people change, organizations can get a huge return on investment from their development efforts. There is generally a "normal distribution" curve for most types of achievement. The marginal gain for helping a highly successful person move from the top 5 percent to the top 1 percent may be greater (to the organization) than the gain from helping the average performer move from the top 50 percent to the top 20 percent. This is especially true with high-potential leaders who represent one of the greatest sources of value for the organization of the future. Although much more research needs to be done on this topic, there is a clear body of knowledge that can help make the best performers even better.

5

HOWARD GARDNER
KIM BARBERICH

GOOD WORK
IN BUSINESS

*Kim Barberich is a researcher at the Harvard Gradu-
ate School of Education, where she is a candidate for
the master of education degree. She is working with
Howard Gardner on the Good Work Project, exploring the relationship between ethics and excellence in
business. She is a graduate of Barnard College.*

*Howard Gardner is the Hobbs Professor of Cognition
and Education at the Harvard Graduate School of
Education. He is best known for his theory of multiple intelligences and is currently researching exemplary creators and leaders. Recent books are* The
Disciplined Mind *and* Intelligence Reframed.

Note: The research on business was supported, in part, by a grant from the John
Templeton Foundation for a project titled "The Moral Underpinnings of Endur-
ing Business Success"—principal investigators Howard Gardner (Harvard Uni-
versity), William Damon (Stanford University), and Mihaly Csikszentmihalyi
(Claremont Graduate University). For general support of the Project on Good
Work, we are indebted to the Carnegie Corporation, the Ford Foundation, the
Hewlett Foundation, the Jesse Phillips Foundation, the Louise and Claude Rosen-
berg Jr. Family Foundation, the Ross Family Foundation, and Thomas H. Lee.
Copyright © 2001 by Howard Gardner.

In this chapter, we provide an overview of research that is examining the relationship between cutting-edge work in different domains and a sense of social responsibility for the use and implications of that work.

Being a Good Professional

It has never been easy to be a professional in both senses of the word *good:* technically expert and morally responsible. This difficulty is augmented in a world that is rapidly changing due to technology, globalization, and powerful market forces. Radically altered senses of time and space have placed added strain on the ability to be a good professional—indeed, even to know what are one's responsibilities.

Whereas the notion of an expert professional is relatively straightforward, the idea of the *responsible professional* requires comment. In our view, responsible professionals are persons who rely on moral and ethical principles to guide them, feel a sense of obligation to company and community, and contribute to society. Though it is clearly challenging to carry out work that fulfills these technical and ethical criteria, the ability to execute such work is crucial in our time.

Since 1995, our research team at Harvard University, in collaboration with William Damon of Stanford University, Mihaly Csikszentmihalyi of the Peter Drucker School at Claremont University, and their colleagues, has been looking at the pursuit of good work across numerous domains, ranging from cyberlaw to philanthropy to medicine. We are interested in creators and leaders who are recognized for their achievements in these professional realms. Many of our subjects were nominated, by scholars and peers, as being highly responsible individuals. Through in-depth interviews, we have attempted to identify these professionals' moral and ethical principles, goals, obstacles, accomplishments, and their overall perspective on their professional domain and their place in it. In addition to securing detailed information about these individual practitioners, we have investigated four other elements: the traditional values of their calling; the current institutions where that calling is practiced; the goals of shareholders, in cases of publicly owned companies; and the interests and concerns of stakeholders from the wider community (see Gardner, Csikszentmihalyi, and Damon, 2001).

The first two professional realms that we examined in our study were journalism and genetics. We selected these realms because of their undeniable importance in the world today. Journalists have a great deal to say about what is in our minds, about the *memes*—the units of meaning—that affect us and that we pass on to others. Geneticists have a great deal to say about our bodies (our *genes*) and our health and longevity prospects, as well as about the welfare of our children.

Although we selected these two realms because of the intriguing meme-gene contrast, the two domains turned out to differ on an important and perhaps underappreciated dimension. Geneticists find themselves in a realm that is well aligned: the various parties that are interested in their work are all in substantial agreement about what should be done. More specifically, the individual practitioners, the senior "trustees" of the field, the various institutions in which genetics research is carried out, and the shareholders and stakeholders all desire breakthroughs in understanding that will yield individuals who lead longer and healthier lives.

In striking contrast, journalism emerges as a realm that is massively misaligned. Journalists are guided by one set of principles, the core of their chosen calling; the major institutions in which they work (for example, multinational corporations that own newspapers and broadcast media) have another set of goals and objectives; shareholders are motivated chiefly by a desire for greater profits; and the general readership, either on its own or through manipulation, has an unquenchable appetite for scandal and gossip and—at least at present—very little concern about the larger political, social, and economic events of our time. Not surprisingly, many journalists are depressed and frustrated by their profession: whereas geneticists cannot wait to get up in the morning, journalists look back nostalgically to a Golden Age in the past.

But we also discovered that alignment can occlude problems. If forces are too well aligned, possible dilemmas or problematic issues may be disregarded or viewed as insignificant. In biotechnology companies, we discern an increasing blurring of lines between science and commerce. When the financial well-being of a company is at stake, conflicts may arise regarding who makes the final decision— the shareholders, the managers, or the scientists? If research scientists are vested in the company that they work for, and their findings might increase the value of the company's stock, they may be tempted to speed up the discovery process regardless of possible dangers to patients or research subjects. Any or all of these factors could undermine the alignment, giving rise to research scientists who are as frustrated as the journalists of today.

The View from Business

Recently, we have undertaken a parallel study of business. For this branch of the project, we interviewed two groups of people: individuals nominated, by academics and peers in the business domain, for their entrepreneurial achievements and social responsibility; and individuals selected on the basis of their accomplished reputation in business but not known one way or another for their social responsibility. Most of the individuals we interviewed impressed us as good workers in the sense described previously: both proficient and ethical. Some have created new companies, whereas others have implemented successful changes to already existing organizations. In the aggregate, they see their work as a welcome challenge, they take risks, they sustain their commitment in times of discouragement, and they are more often than not humble about their success. Many have made sacrifices while attempting to maintain an ethical stance. We believe that this population harbors lessons that

could be of use to individuals who are entering business as well as to business workers who may have lost their moral compass.

Until recent reversals in the business community, notably the dotcom downturn, business had appeared to be in alignment at the start of this new century. And it is still a powerful truth that even though we have witnessed some disturbing signals in the economy recently, we have experienced a long period of record growth, during which the American economy has been strong, unemployment has been down, and profits have been at record highs both for those working in the domain and for the shareholders who own stock in prospering companies. At times, it seemed as though *not* being in business was a misfortune. Many economy watchers believe that the recent less benign developments will pass, and the strong economy will continue.

However, even in such good times, good work is hard to carry out, and recent developments have made it clear that no boom lasts forever. There are always obstacles that need to be faced, in both good times and bad times. Profit making and meeting the bottom line are often easier to accomplish by ignoring one's principles. Given the fast pace of many young companies, there is a strong desire to create a business quickly, sell it, and make a bundle rather than to commit to building a solid and enduring organization. In addition, the pressures that traditionally countered untrammeled market forces in the past, like religion, ideology, and government, no longer operate with the same potency. We might say that today there is no *external* check system because the market itself serves as the checking point. This is why it is so important that every individual, regardless of the given profession, learn to develop an *internal* check system—a series of lines that will not be crossed—with an eye toward society and the larger world.

Lessons from Business

Even though they come from different enterprises and diverse backgrounds and have varied lifestyles, our interview subjects share

many of the same guiding principles. These principles, discussed in the following sections, include responsibility to self and others, honesty, accountability, faith in themselves, and thoughtful contribution to society. They rely on them as they go about their business and have succeeded as well in integrating these principles into other parts of their lives. In this regard, they differ from widely held views of business people today. Although many business personnel apparently believe that one must trade moral or ethical responsibility for success, these men and women believe in just the opposite. By the same token, many leaders in business apparently deem their primary responsibility to be the financial health of their company and readily rationalize behavior in accordance with this belief. The professionals with whom we spoke have disdain for peers who suspend their principles in order to fatten the bottom line.

Responsibility

At the heart of being a good professional is a deep-seated sense of responsibility. Responsibility in our participants' lives is parsed as an obligation to oneself, others, the company, the business profession, and society. Although it is unrealistic to expect that all responsibilities can be monitored and honored at all times, the good professional considers one or more of these responsibilities when making decisions and rendering judgments. Such monitoring allows good professionals to measure their actions with a clear and critical eye.

All our subjects understand the need for profit, but they also believe that business should support and develop the people that contribute to it. They feel a deep-rooted responsibility toward everyone they work with; this includes employees, partners, and customers. Michael Murray, former vice president of human resources at Microsoft, wanted to create a workplace where all employees could feel a sense of accomplishment and pride based on their work and at the same time be able to participate in a life outside work that was meaningful and purposeful. Murray firmly believes that the "soft stuff," as he puts it—structuring a successful team, rewarding good

work, being a good leader—is just as essential for the health of an organization as making a profit. Yet even at a company as respected and successful as Microsoft, Murray felt that gaining currency within the company for "human elements" was a challenge. The only way that he felt he could emphasize the importance of these key human issues was to engage senior management in a lively dialogue, so they could begin to understand the significance of these issues with respect to the health of the corporation.

At ServiceMaster, a company that provides outsourcing services—lawn care, landscaping, heating and air conditioning—to customers worldwide, the "development of people" is an important component of the mission statement. To reflect this priority, business decisions are always discussed in light of their effect on individuals who work in the company. When we interviewed the chairman and former CEO of ServiceMaster, William Pollard, he referred to a meeting that he had just held with a manager responsible for the enterprise in a major foreign country. The manager was facing a difficult situation and needed to make some decisions. The meeting focused on possible options for this manager's business unit. Half the time was spent conferring on how these options would affect the business, and the other half of the time was spent discussing how the options would affect people working in that business unit. Pollard underscores the difference between looking at a person as the object of the work and considering that person as the subject of the work. Examining what a change or decision can do to develop and empower an *individual-as-subject* is more important than judging what an *individual-as-object* can do for the company. This consideration promotes hard work and teamwork and is essential for building a strong community within a company.

Honesty and Accountability

The professionals we interviewed deliver the truth when needed and stand accountable for their mistakes. In turn, they expect the same from others. Honesty and accountability are essential for building a lasting and reputable enterprise. Although often requiring more work, these values force one to consider the repercussions of providing poor service or faulty products or of making frankly unethical or immoral decisions.

For many in our sample, honesty and accountability simply come down to doing what is considered the right thing. Michael Hackworth, president and CEO of Aspirian and chairman of Cirrus Logic, both technology companies, lives by a simple ethic imparted to him by his mother. He will not do something that would embarrass him if it were printed in the morning paper. Hackworth admits that being honest and accountable in every business situation can be challenging, especially when one is running a public company. When conditions are good in the company and the stock is up, everything is fine ("aligned" in our terms); but when conditions deteriorate and the stock drops, both executives of the company and shareholders go through hard times.

Business leaders must decide how to deal with the financial markets during a critical time. There is a tendency on the part of many executives to keep quiet and attempt to fix the problem before the stock drops or before it drops further. Hackworth believes, however, that as soon as one knows about impending problems that could affect stock prices, one has an obligation to disclose them. To be sure, the idea of standing in front of one's shareholders and admitting error certainly sounds daunting. Yet Hackworth believes that presenting the truth and fixing the problem, even if the stock drops temporarily, build credibility. As Hackworth put it, the shareholders may not like what you say or even like *you* when you admit error, but after the problem is presented and repaired, they will know that they can count on you. "You have to have a standard that says I'm not going to violate that criteria and I will take the short-term hit, and I will solve the problem then, it's tough, but that's what you have to do."

Hackworth relates that several years ago, he served on the board of a company whose founder boosted shareholder expectations by inflating the company's sales forecast on the basis of possible sales to new distributors. When Hackworth questioned the founder's actions and stated that he could not count sales until the distributor sold the product, the executive stated that as far as he was concerned, it was usual and common practice. Hackworth decided that he could either head up an audit committee at this company or step down from the board. Because the company was running a business akin to Hackworth's and knowing that they would eventually be competitors, Hackworth felt that auditing them would be unethical. He stepped down from the board and was not surprised to read three years later that the company had filed for bankruptcy and the executive was under indictment.

Faith in Business

Even when a domain seems well aligned, there are times when one feels discouraged and pressured. Yet it is often during these times that committed business personnel realize a faith in the profession, the people with whom they work, and their own selves. Often, though not always, this faith is connected to religious principles or ethical precepts that were learned during one's early years.

McDonald Williams, the chairman of Trammel Crow, a commercial real estate company, recalled vividly a difficult period, "a moment of truth," that he had experienced twenty years earlier. At the time, the country had come into a recession, and Williams had a young family, a mortgage, and other responsibilities. Nervous that he had made the wrong decision in working for Trammel Crow, he considered returning to law, where he knew he could make a decent living. In an attempt to come to terms with his struggle, Williams had an "epiphany"—he suddenly remembered why he had entered into business. He valued the people he worked with, and although he felt that external business environments had changed, he felt confident that he could make a difference in his company. Williams believed in himself, the employees in the company, and the company's mission. He stayed on, was soon promoted to CEO, and within several years, the company had turned around dramatically.

Fifteen years later, Williams faced another challenging time as financial hardship recurred. This time, serving as CEO, Williams was embarrassed and knew that he had let many down. Numerous people he had worked with for years and who had profited during the good times left the company not wanting to take any responsibility for its current problems. Williams stayed on because he knew that he had an obligation to get the company out of the red. The earlier epiphany provided him with the faith to keep on working, to mend the problems, and to put the company back on its feet. Williams feels that his faith was "more relevant to my business in tough times than anything else because then your values really were square in your face." In challenging times, Williams discovered, it is imperative to look beyond the moment to a longer time frame, to see yourself as more than your personal career or your net worth. After the hardship, Williams remained as CEO of Trammel Crow and watched the company experience new profit and growth. A few years ago, he stepped aside so that he could work on the renewal of low-income housing in the Dallas area.

Contributions to the Wider Good

For many good professionals, a primary goal in their lives is making a contribution to society. Although this goal may reflect their acquisition of wealth, the individuals with whom we spoke stressed giving back to society and making a difference. In their view, this philanthropy requires more than just writing a check. It also entails donating time and expertise to nonprofit organizations. Our professionals want to use their talent, business expertise, and monetary resources productively and thoughtfully.

Deciding where to donate one's time and money can be complex. When Orit Gadiesh, the chairman of Bain & Company, an international management consulting firm, makes a donation for her company, she wants it to be meaningful. The issue for her is giving money with the ability to also give time so that there is real involvement. This can mean providing a team of employees for a project or getting the whole office to do something together. Either way, Gadiesh says, "I don't think your mind and your heart are really into something unless you're willing to give that."

With his partners, Richard Jacobsen, manager of a real estate development management company, started the California Family Foundation, an institution that deals with educational, housing, and employment issues. Jacobsen and his partners saw a lot of need in their local community; they determined that if they focused their energies and resources, they might be able to do something that would be helpful. In addition, Jacobsen and his partners felt that it would be both challenging and satisfying to take their expertise and resources and put them to work in their community. Today the foundation is over twenty years old and runs a local private school that has 160 students and spans kindergarten through eighth grade. Jacobsen stands behind his belief that all individuals need to give more and still asks, "How do we, . . . those that are equipped, by temperament or whatever else, to be able to function successfully in the market, how do we help those that are not?"

Anita Roddick, founder and cochair of the board of The Body Shop, incorporates her concept of "giving back" into everything she does. In reflecting about how her goals have changed over the years, she says that they "have been reduced and polished to [caring about] what person's life you can affect." Her primary goal is "nothing more than creating a sense of humanity in what [I do] and within the business world." Roddick has accomplished humanitarian work all over the world: she has lived with families in Appalachia, West Virginia, and has worked in refugee camps in Albania. Her conscience is also visible in how she runs her company. During the Gulf War, Roddick had billboards erected denouncing the conflict and had petitions in all her shops demanding its end. Told by senior management that the antiwar sentiment in conjunction with the company name needed to stop, Roddick instead closed down operations for a day and allowed employees the opportunity to debate and discuss the war as well as the company's stance on it.

In fact, Roddick views her company, which she founded in 1976, as "an extension of myself and it was not set up for anything other than to challenge wrongs." She feels that money should be given away strategically—not just handed out but put into foundations with a long-range view. She sees her job as being a moral leader within her organization and doing things that the young people in her company will look up to and be proud of. Despite her continuing efforts to incorporate giving back into her own life, she wonders, "How do you [move young employees] away from a value system of endless increasing wealth to one where humanity, community, is part of the value system?"

Two Caveats and a Conclusion

We believe that the stories of respected leaders like these can inspire and teach others to be good professionals across the various domains of society. It is important, however, to keep two caveats in mind.

First of all, our study relies heavily on the testimony of creators and leaders in different domains. One can reasonably expect that these individuals will describe themselves in a favorable way; and more than once we have discovered, to our regret, that the actions of our subjects did not match their words. We nonetheless feel that the advice can be important, even when it has not always been followed by its dispenser. We therefore describe our study as an examination of good work rather than as an effort to decide who is, in actuality, a good (or a not-so-good) worker.

Second, even—and perhaps even especially—the most impressive professionals have not led perfect lives. We would go further and suggest that being a good professional is a process learned through mistakes and error, properly reflected upon. In many cases, it is only through obstacles and difficult decisions that one learns to develop goals and strategies based on ethical and moral principles. And one learns the most from those individuals who have survived their missteps and are willing to talk about them publicly—even to inquiring social scientists!

Ultimately, we hope to study the nature of good work in a large number of professional domains, as well as in several societies. At a time when market forces are the most powerful and the least opposed in history, it is crucial to think about lines other than the bottom line—the lines that one does not cross even when one could legally do so. We anticipate that guiding principles like responsibility, honesty, accountability, faith, and contributing to society can help many individuals navigate murky waters during times that are exciting but filled with uncertainty.

Part II

CREATING AN ENVIRONMENT THAT ENCOURAGES INNOVATION

6 ROSABETH MOSS KANTER

CREATING THE CULTURE FOR INNOVATION

Rosabeth Moss Kanter holds the Ernest L. Arbuckle chair as Professor of Business Administration at the Harvard Business School. She is an internationally known business leader and advocate for effective change. Her latest book is Evolve!: Succeeding in the Digital Culture of Tomorrow. *Her award-winning best-sellers include* The Change Masters *and* The Challenge of Organizational Change.

Innovation is always a surprise. By definition, it is something no one has thought of before. Its very existence shows that reality is not fixed in predictable patterns. Instead creative new possibilities can emerge in any field, in any industry. Innovators see new patterns in familiar, apparently immutable, situations. It is as though they are looking at the world through a kaleidoscope, which creates endless variations on the same set of fragments. To create a culture for innovation, leaders must distribute virtual kaleidoscopes and encourage their use.

Note: Copyright © 2001 by Rosabeth Moss Kanter.

The Genesis of Innovation:
Kaleidoscope Thinking

Even in light of recent downturns in the technology sector, it's safe to say that new technologies and expanded market possibilities are revolutionizing industries. For consumers, customers, and citizens alike, the global information economy offers more and faster information, fewer geographical constraints, and greater access to world products and services. Trying to run organizations while the system itself is being redefined means we must look at life through a kaleidoscope—to imagine possibilities outside of conventional categories, to envision actions that cross traditional boundaries, to anticipate repercussions and take advantage of interdependencies, to make new connections or invent new combinations.

Fields and industries in the midst of competitive, technological, political, or regulatory upheaval are characterized by a large number of new core concepts—breakthrough stand-alone models or transformational innovations that represent very big twists of very big kaleidoscopes. New core concepts or theories of the business often come from entrepreneurs' bypassing established channels dominated by current players—such as Dell Computer, which innovated by first offering computers through catalogues, building computers to customer orders; Salick Health Centers, which started stand-alone full-service cancer treatment centers, contributing a new model for U.S. health care; Amazon.com, which transformed bookselling through its online Internet virtual bookstores, offering any title, along with information customized to customer preference; or American public education, which has innovated with charter schools. Innovators can build a better office product (high-speed Xerox copiers), or they can build a better way to distribute office products (Staples, among the first office supply superstores).

Every industry, no matter how mature or routinized, can find innovations in the kaleidoscope. Air transportation, for example, is a commodity—the same aircraft, seat configurations, pilot training, interline ticketing, travel bookers. Southwest Airlines found a niche in low-cost services through creativity. Founder Herb Kelleher's core concept for a different kind of airline was augmented by a try-anything mandate to staff that produced numerous small creative differences.

Improvisation is at the heart of innovation. Innovators create value by working on things that are not yet fully known, developing their plan as they discover what emerges from the act of creation. "There is no profit from operating in the realm of the widely understood," former Monsanto CEO Robert Shapiro said. Innovation is inherently improvisational because it is impossible to know how people will react to something they have never seen before, something that has not yet been invented, something that has not yet happened. They can love the initial idea but hate the execution, hate the idea but like what starts to emerge from it. In my book *Evolve!*, I call this the *IKIWISI* Effect. *IKIWISI* (pronounced ick-ee-wis-ee) stands for *I'll Know It When I See It*. We may not always be able to describe the perfect fulfillment of our needs or the perfect solution to our problems, but we certainly know it when we see it. If the play can't be described in advance, it must be performed often in order to take shape from the reactions of those coming to understand it. That's why the best improvisers include members of the audience in a series of quick performances, taking account of each round of reactions to shape the next—like rapid prototyping in the technology world.

Innovation begins with someone being smart enough to sense a new need and then to improvise new methods, products, or services to meet that need. Of course, being "smart enough" comes from focusing time and attention on things going on in the environment that send signals that innovation is needed—perhaps because key stakeholders are getting restless or competitors are gaining ground or technology is changing. Sometimes *changemasters* sense a new appetite because they feel hungry themselves; the concept for on-line auction site eBay came from the desire of the founder's girlfriend to swap Pez dispensers. Tuning into the wider world outside a person's own daily milieu is like filling a kaleidoscope with the bits and pieces that eventually get shaken up into a new mix. Imagination and intuition often depend on fragments of new and different experiences that can then be combined in new and different ways.

Customers, suppliers, and venture partners are important sources of ideas for innovation. IBM CEO Louis Gerstner and former Honeywell CEO Mike Bonsignore both spent a great deal of their time with customers, not at headquarters but in the customers' own environments. At Sun Microsystems, telephone calls to CEO Scott McNealy and President Ed Zander from a new kind of customer— Internet service providers (ISPs)—triggered Doug Kaewert's effort to make changes that would turn ISPs into partners and open new markets. For others, the change sequence begins with challenges. Williams-Sonoma's CEO, Howard Lester, began his conversion to an Internet fan when students at Berkeley's business school challenged his biases. John Chambers of Cisco Systems had a teenager in the office of the CEO for a similar challenge to orthodoxy.

Partners can provide a window on new developments and marketplace changes. The airlines entering into the Star Alliance (Lufthansa, United, Air Canada, Varig, All Nippon, and others) have made learning from one another an explicit goal, as all seek innovation in an industry where it is sometimes hard to distinguish one carrier from another. New kinds of business partnerships with government, community groups, or nonprofit organizations can also stretch thinking in new directions. IBM's Reinventing Education initiative puts IBM engineers, systems integrators, and consultants on significant projects in partnership with public school systems in the United States and countries such as Brazil, Ireland, Italy, and Vietnam to apply new technologies that can transform education; but these projects have also helped IBM teams develop new solutions with commercial applications, such as voice recognition technology based on children's voices or data warehousing for large groups of users.

Immediate experiences of living in a potential user's world make it easier to see new possibilities. Impersonal, arm's-length reports may indicate that there is a problem or an opportunity, but they do not stimulate the mind to see new possibilities. Firsthand experience with power outages in developing countries led the head of a company making electricity-dependent photo identification cameras to see the huge potential for battery-operated cameras even in countries with reliable electricity. Some companies encourage tours of other companies; some take advantage of any way that people discover new possibilities—even on vacation on their own time in foreign countries where they see something they've never seen before. Rubbermaid, which distributes its products through large retailers, uses its laboratory stores to observe consumer reactions to new product prototypes and identify unmet consumer needs.

The more holistic the experience and the wider the view— that is, the more elements of a system that can be included in the kaleidoscope—the more likely that breakthroughs will result, but only if the environment surrounding an innovator makes it possible to act on creative new ideas. Too many leaders say they want innovation but behave in ways that stifle it.

Rules for Stifling Innovation

Lurking behind the virtues of innovation are two painful truths. First, innovation can be a pain in the neck for leaders—a nuisance, a disruption, an inconvenience, and even worse, a risk. Second, it is hard for leaders to predict or control innovation; the innovation process is messy rather than orderly.

It is therefore easier for leaders to praise innovation in theory than to support it in practice. Top managers sometimes ask me questions about innovation that are unintentionally humorous: "We want more innovation. Who else is doing it?" or "We want more innovation. We just don't want to be the first." Even companies known for innovation are more likely to support ideas that fall within existing parameters, such as the pharmaceutical companies with a system for looking for a new drug, getting it approved, and rolling it out to market. In those companies, innovation is the charter for one specific department rather than a wider search for new ideas that might come from any area, level, or geography and might breach existing boundaries or challenge frameworks.

The behavior and attitude of leaders can encourage or stifle innovation. Innovation-stiflers occur everywhere, even in organizations that were founded on innovations but that now freeze their existing assumptions in place. Consider the difficulty that Barnes & Noble faced in creating its own on-line bookstore, barnes&noble.com, in response to the threat from Amazon.com. Entrepreneur Leonard Riggio built Barnes & Noble into the world's largest bookstore chain, filled with numerous innovations that changed industry dynamics. Yet he failed to see the potential of the World Wide Web until pushed into it, and when the company's Internet effort began, it operated defensively rather than bringing new approaches.

Some organizations that claim to want innovation appear instead to operate by an invisible set of guidelines that discourage it— my ten classic "rules for stifling innovation":

Stifler #1. Be suspicious of every new idea from below— because it's new and because it's from below. (After all, if the idea were any good, senior people would have thought of it already.)

Stifler #2. Insist that people who need your approval to act go through several other levels of management first. (Most will fade away before getting back to you.)

Stifler #3. Ask departments or individuals to challenge and criticize one another's proposals. (That saves you the job of deciding; you just pick the survivor.)

Stifler #4. Express your criticisms freely, and withhold your praise. (That keeps people on their toes.) Let them know they could be fired at any time.

Stifler #5. Treat identification of problems as signs of failure, to discourage people from letting you know when something in their area isn't working. (Fear of mistakes will reduce risks.)

Stifler #6. Control everything carefully. Make sure people count everything that can be counted, frequently. (That ensures a tight ship with nothing extra for unproven plans.)

Stifler #7. Make decisions to reorganize or change policies in secret, and spring them on people unexpectedly. (That also keeps people on their toes.)

Stifler #8. Make sure that requests for information are fully justified; don't give it out freely.

Stifler #9. Assign to lower-level managers, in the name of delegation and participation, responsibility for figuring out how to cut back, lay off, move people around, or otherwise implement threatening decisions you have made. And get them to do it quickly.

Stifler #10. And above all, never forget that you, the leaders, already know everything important about this business. (Isn't that why you're in charge?)

This list would be funny if these behaviors were not so typical. I've found them in big bureaucracies, founder-driven companies, and even small nonprofits with "all-knowing" charismatic leaders who manage by whim.

To support innovation, the culture must encourage fast approvals, open communication, cooperation instead of combat across internal units, tolerance for uncertainty, and faith in people to try new things. A few reviews and checkpoints can be a good management tool, especially for ideas that are very risky or require high levels of investments. But routinely moving every proposal through a hierarchy, level by level, is a surefire way to slow things down, discourage any idea that doesn't already fit the organization's direction, and demotivate a potential innovator. In my global e-culture survey, conducted in 2000 as part of the research for my book *Evolve!*, I found that "laggard" organizations that were behind their competitors in embracing new technology were much more likely than innovative "pacesetters" to make slower decisions, particularly about things that were new and different, and to require that these decisions go through many layers.

Some organizations fail to empower even their leaders with the authority to sign off on new ideas quickly. And as I concluded in my earlier work, "powerlessness corrupts"—that is, leaders who themselves feel powerless are not particularly generous in empowering the people around them. (To counter this destructive tendency, many innovation-seeking organizations have eliminated budget approvals for small expenditures, giving leaders flexibility to act without further sign-off within broader limits.) Or sometimes leaders have the authority but pass the buck on risky decisions so that they do not have to bear the consequences. By sending a potential innovator to get approval first from other levels, the leader plays it safe—and sends a message that innovation is too risky, not valued. By expecting the perfect plan or waiting for full information, leaders slow the action. Then rigidity about the appropriate way to execute—insisting that new things be done in traditional ways, that once a plan is agreed to it must remain in effect with no deviations—ensures that only the most conservative innovations will proceed. Arguments that drag on endlessly (even after decisions have been made) or interruptions and distractions that sidetrack the new venture also stop the action.

Insecurity and lack of information discourage innovation. Uncertainty about the future makes it hard to start longer-term projects. People feel controlled rather than empowered, and they proceed cautiously rather than innovatively. Sometimes leaders think that frequent, abrupt changes make people more flexible. But instead, this makes people turn passive. Why bother working on anything new, or anything that will take time to develop, when the organization could change direction unexpectedly at any moment, with no time to prepare for it? *I've Got a Secret* was the name of a television game program popular when I was a child, but as an adult I've seen this game played even more often in large organizations. Traditional bureaucrats jockey for political position; they hoard information and refuse to share it. Of course, information hoarding is much harder and even more dysfunctional in the wake of the Internet, because it is so much easier (theoretically) for everyone to communicate with everyone else, irrespective of level. But the old bureaucratic games have not died. When leaders place restrictions on information sharing, they make it harder for people to generate and develop their ideas.

The casual, free-expression atmosphere of Internet companies (wild colors, personal art on the walls, music on all the time) was often an attempt to stimulate creativity, and it probably did the first few hundred times it appeared. Now it is almost a workplace norm, not an expression of challenging anything. In the e-commerce unit of an industrial company, the venture manager had decorated the facility in what he considered creative style; he spoke repeatedly about wanting to encourage creativity. But then my team watched a meeting that could have taken place in any stifling bureaucracy. The venture head made announcements; the staff sat around looking bored and not saying anything. Colorful walls and pets in the office do not by themselves induce people to challenge assumptions or seek new approaches. It's not the office layout that induces changemasters to step forward; it is the mental layout—whether the person's mind is engaged in a constant search for fresh ideas.

It's the job of leaders to remove the action-stoppers, eliminate the innovation-stiflers, and open minds to kaleidoscope thinking.

Innovation requires courage as well as imagination. Leaders must create cultures in which experiments, questions, and challenges to prevailing models are not just for the courageous few but become the norm for the many.

A Culture for Innovation

Innovation is hard to predict, may occur anywhere, and requires multiple experiments. One study of industrial innovation showed that it took three thousand raw ideas, reflected in three hundred formal proposals, winnowed down eventually to nine large development projects, to produce one commercial success. Pfizer tests over a hundred leads per year in order to find one promising direction for new drug development. Organizations should encourage innovation all the time, everywhere. A strategy for innovation involves activity at three levels of a pyramid:

- At the peak—a few big bets about the future, and thus the biggest investments in product, technology, or market innovation

- In the middle—a portfolio of promising but not-yet-proven experiments, early-stage new ventures, prototypes, or other stand-alone projects

- At the base—a large number of operationally embedded incremental innovations, continual improvements, and early-stage new ideas that boost immediate revenues, take out costs, increase speed, or create a customer success—but even more, suggest a promising new direction for the future

Influence flows in many directions across the pyramid. Big bets influence the domain for experimentation and provide structure for the search for early-stage ideas. Modest ideas up from the bottom can accumulate into a bigger force that turns into new ideas, reaching prototype status. Projects and ideas from one part of the organization trigger new thinking and new opportunities in another part.

Leaders in innovation-intensive organizations give kaleidoscopes to everyone. They empower people to search for new ideas, from constant operational improvements to dramatic breakthroughs. They deploy idea scouts to look for ideas beyond the job, the company, and the industry. I coined the term *far-afield trips* for these tours beyond conventional boundaries to encounter ideas or technologies emerging elsewhere that suggest new opportunities for the company. Time and resources then help the seeds of new ideas blossom. Small budgets—perhaps through a special seed grant fund—can help people take fast action on promising new opportunities without going through the hierarchy, bypassing a lengthy budgeting and resource allocation process. Grant funds help people pursue unexpected opportunities and incubate new initiatives without undermining local line managers. Some proposals might involve stand-alone ventures; others, projects that can be embedded within business units. The seed grant helps fund the creation of a "business plan" that would then either be routed back to the line organization for commitment to develop or qualify for further corporate support. In addition to direct business benefits, this has the side benefit of encouraging more people to think entrepreneurially about creative ways to approach business problems and opportunities.

We expect constant innovation in technology companies—though it is instructive that Sun Microsystems' e-commerce initiative, e-Sun, had to struggle to get acceptance despite Sun's exemplary culture for improvisation. A culture of innovation is not considered as common in much older bricks-and-mortar companies. But British supermarket chain Tesco was first mover to the Internet, not only ahead of retail competitors but also ahead of most other companies of any kind, and its leaders attributed this to its culture. Tesco has built an organizational structure that supports constant change. Its leaders are young, fast, and dynamic. A flattened hierarchy allows their energy to permeate all the way down to the front lines in the form of "hungry twenty-five-year-old store managers," as a leader described them. Store managers are given freedom to take risks (and are expected to perform), which results in Tesco's ability to change on a dime. It puts its money where its mouth is, with a big investment in Web technology compared with competitors. Complacency is avoided by continually setting new targets. Leaders discovered early mistakes in on-line grocery sales— poor customer service, incomplete understanding of skill and staffing requirements, lack of incentives for cooperation across channels— corrected them, and moved on.

A culture for change does not mean doing everything *perfectly;* it means doing everything quickly, learning from it, then doing it *differently.*

Innovators and changemasters are more likely to emerge in companies already open to change. It's a self-reinforcing cycle; those already successful at change create the circumstances that make it easier for people to sense the need for the next changes, because they have opened minds and broken through walls already. Flexible organizations that encourage mobility and are rich in external partnerships are more likely to innovate than rigid, bureaucratic hierarchies. While leaders in lagging companies respond to hints of new developments on the horizon with denial and anger, leaders in pacesetter organizations exhibit curiosity. Imagination is limited when people have conventional wisdom or existing assumptions reinforced by talking only to those who agree with them and think exactly what they think—which locks the kaleidoscope's pattern in place rather than shaking it up.

Many creative experiments, small and large, flow together to make a new strategy possible. Times of uncertainty call for improvisation. Whenever it is impossible to know which model or concept will prevail, it is unwise to make one big bet; it is better to launch many small experiments and learn from the results of each—a hallmark of improvisation. Periods of technological change have always involved numerous creative experiments followed by shakeouts and establishment of an industry standard.

The best companies are prepared for change because they are always preparing for it. That's what helps them create bold transformational leaps. A kaleidoscope, not a computer, is the ultimate weapon to help leaders meet the challenges of the twenty-first century. It represents the ever-changing patterns and endless new possibilities, powered by human imagination, that lie at the heart of innovation.

7 C. WILLIAM POLLARD

THE ORGANIZATION!

Is It a Friend or Foe of Innovation?

*C. William Pollard is chairman of the board of the
ServiceMaster Company, which provides management and residential services and which* Fortune
*magazine called the number one service company
among the* Fortune 500. *The author of several articles and books, including the best-selling* The Soul of
the Firm, *he serves as a director of several public and
private organizations.*

What is there in common between the structure and discipline of an organization focused on results and the freedom
and creativity required for innovative change? Can innovation be
managed as both an art and a science?

Innovation is a creative process. It is uniquely human and often
individualistic, yet it requires the organized efforts of others to be
effective. So without organization, implementation becomes difficult and results are spotty.

Organizational Impediments to Innovation

But we all know that organizational structure and behavior can also
stifle innovation. It can impede the fostering and nurturing of the

entrepreneurial spirit that is so essential to creative change. The systems that are designed for uniformity, for reducing the margin of error, have little elbowroom for mistakes. Layers of management, often thought necessary for orderly review and direction of the organization can, in fact, stifle and limit innovation. Commitment to authority standards, intended for reasonable control, can become bureaucratic and in some cases debilitating. Governance structures can find senior management and the board of directors out of touch with the needs of the creative innovator.

Often these stodgy attributes of organizational behavior are magnified as an organization grows in size. As Jack Welch was reengineering General Electric, he concluded that "size is no longer the trump card it once was in today's brutally competitive world. My goal is to get the small company's soul and small company's speed inside our big company." The message here is more than "small is beautiful." It is, instead, a reminder for all of us that organizations whether large or small are made up of people, not structures and procedures—people who have been born with the potential to create and to change, people who must be empowered and managed if they are to work together to innovate and produce. This is the job of a leader, and leadership can make a difference.

The Role of the Leader

Because the law of entropy is at work in every organization, there is the potential for the creative spirit to decline with each new major increment of growth. The leader must intercept and redefine this indifference curve. The leader must find those strategic intercept points where he or she can cut through the midriff of the organization and encourage the creativity of people who are close to the action and see the need for change and innovation. The leader must cultivate, champion, and then support the new idea. The leader must provide an environment for the development and expression of the entrepreneurial spirit. The leader must empower.

The empowerment of people to innovate, however, does not mean freedom for everybody to do what he or she wants to do. Nor is innovation the recognition and acceptance of every new idea. As innovation and empowerment go hand in hand, they can be managed. *Innovation*, as Peter Drucker has defined it, is a change that creates a new dimension of performance. In so doing, he has reminded us of the continuing need for accountability and results.

But if people are going to initiate change and be accountable for results, they must understand how the organization and its leaders will respond to mistakes and failures. Does the mission of the firm include the development of the innovator, even when the idea or change is not successful?

We all know that not every idea is a good idea. It is painful to shut down innovation when it's not working. Identifying and resolving the pain of a mistake or a failed idea often tests the durability and viability of the organization and its leadership.

Paul Brand, a missionary doctor who served among lepers in India, developed the practice of taking a scalding hot bath once a week. As he felt pain in all of his extremities, he knew that he had not contracted the dreaded disease. To him, pain meant life.

The pain of honestly facing failures and mistakes can mean life for the organization, provided people see a purpose in it all. As the mission of the organization includes the development and growth of people, failure need not be final or fatal. In fact, failure can become that next step of learning, the beginning of another new creative idea.

The Importance of Mission

Our experience at ServiceMaster confirms the importance of mission as an organizing principle. When you visit the headquarters of our firm, you see carved in marble on the lobby wall the four statements that constitute our mission: to honor God in all we do, to help people develop, to pursue excellence, and to grow profitably.

The first two objectives are *end goals;* the second two are *means goals.* As we seek to implement these objectives in the operation of our business, they remind us that every person has been created in the image of God, with dignity and worth and the potential to create and innovate. They also remind us that the work environment can be a place where people grow and develop in who they are becoming as well as in what they are producing.

Although our marble wall conveys a permanency that does not change, if you were to tour the rest of our building, you would notice that nearly all of the work spaces are movable. Most of the walls do not reach the ceiling. All the offices are open and nobody works behind closed doors. Practically everything in the building is changeable and adaptable, just like the markets we serve with their changing demands and opportunities—hence the continuing need for innovation and change.

Of course, we experience our share of mistakes. But because of a stated standard and a reason for that standard, we cannot hide our mistakes. They are flushed out in the open for correction and—in some cases—for forgiveness. Our mission, then, becomes a motivating principle that allows for the risk of failure and encourages learning from mistakes. In such an environment, the leader is reminded that loss does not make someone a loser and that lack of results may be caused by reasons other than the merit of the idea or the desire of people to perform.

One of the best examples in our business of the power of innovation is the largest profit performer in ServiceMaster today. It is a business that lost a lot of money as we first got into it. Few people in the organization expected it to survive. But the people on the front line knew what was wrong and knew how to fix it. Leadership gave them the opportunity to innovate and make the necessary changes. Within twelve months, the business was turning a profit.

Some of the more recent innovative ideas at ServiceMaster have ranged from new business starts, including a venture fund and e-commerce initiatives, to the design and texture of a mop handle and a mop head. Innovation for us must be a continuing process, and there is nothing too small that it cannot be improved.

Sometimes you have to lose before you can win. We can discourage innovation if we pull the plug every time a mistake is made. Conversely, if it isn't working, you have to shut it down. The judgment of waiting, but not waiting too long, is the judgment of the leader who must manage for results. Whatever the decision—to wait, to celebrate, or to bury the dead—there is always the opportunity for personal development and growth, an essential ingredient for any creative and innovative environment.

Knowing When to Go Forward and When to Pull the Plug

But what makes the difference between a good idea and a bad idea? There should be an established process of review and definition that provides a framework for this decision.

First of all, if an idea is worth doing, it's worth doing poorly to begin with. At the beginning, the leader must provide the elbowroom for improving the idea by trying and testing. It is important, however, to move the idea out of the concept stage and into the working-model stage as soon as possible. If the idea works, then it is important to further test it by providing an early exposure to the market. Is there a need? Is there a demand? Will the customer see value? Will the customer buy, and at what price?

I am reminded of a visit I had several years ago with Warren Buffet. During our time together, we discussed ServiceMaster and its various business units, including our expectations for future growth rates. As he often does, he provided some very sage advice as we talked about one of our slower-growing units. He simply said, "Bill, sometimes it's not how hard you row the boat, it's how fast the stream is moving." If early on, the innovative idea is accepted and embraced by the customer, the stream is moving. If not, you may find yourself always rowing upstream with much effort but not much progress.

Not every idea can be tested by the external market. Innovation may also result in a change within the organization. The same principle applies whether the customer is internal or external. Acceptance and performance are essential to success—the earlier the better for the innovative idea.

Beginnings do not last forever, and as you encourage innovation and change, there can be no compromise for seeking and then achieving a standard of excellence. A quality result that can be duplicated in many different environments is essential for effectiveness and success. If the innovative idea does not achieve this standard within a definable period of time, it must be abandoned; otherwise the clutter of the past and the pride of ownership will impede the next generation of innovative ideas.

Some Rules of Thumb to Follow

As we have sought to encourage innovation within our organization, we have learned a few things that might help others in the leadership of innovation and change.

• The potential for the new always requires testing and piloting. Successful new ideas are rarely developed on the drawing board or by a market analysis or focus study group. In other words, get started. Get your hands in the bucket. Understanding the theory and practical application is important to getting every new venture off the drawing board. Get hands-on experience and start serving the first few customers. Too often, ideas are studied and analyzed until they are smothered and suffocated.

• Innovators must have elbowroom for mistakes but also must be accountable and at risk for the results. No firm can afford innovative bystanders. The involvement of innovating and creating must also carry some risk of failure as well as reward for success. Incentives for innovation will not fit the standard compensation patterns of the firm, and unique and different ownership methods will have to be considered and implemented. This has been one of our strong points at ServiceMaster, where we have developed a variety of different ownership plans that not only cover the performance of the company as a whole but also individual units and in some cases individual projects.

• You must have an organizational structure that separates the innovative initiative from the main business and protects the new idea from the crushing big wheel of the firm's operations. New ideas and new businesses don't start with a regular monthly or quarterly track record. No matter how much thought is given to the business plan, there are always variations that are not on the mark. But the expected results over a period of time must be established at the front end of the venture or idea, or the ship will be rudderless.

• You must have supportive senior leadership that is ready to serve and listen but that also has the discipline to bury the corpse of a failed idea. Not every idea will work nor every innovation produce. It is extremely hard for the successful firm to recognize failure. Successes and failures can be a learning experience for the firm and the people involved—provided there is a mission and commitment of the firm and its leadership to the end goal of developing people.

8

JEFFREY PFEFFER

TO BUILD A CULTURE OF INNOVATION, AVOID CONVENTIONAL MANAGEMENT WISDOM

Jeffrey Pfeffer is the Thomas D. Dee II Professor of Organizational Behavior at Stanford Business School. He has authored numerous articles and books, including The Human Equation: Building Profits by Putting People First *and* Hidden Value: How Great Companies Achieve Extraordinary Results with Ordinary People. *He consults and lectures throughout the United States and many other countries.*

It's hard to build an innovative, creative organization that is going to do things better and differently if you essentially do what everyone else does and has always done. Encouraging innovation and learning—I see the two as closely related—is actually reasonably easy as long as you are willing to get beyond conventional management wisdom.

We need to recognize at the outset that innovation and creativity are natural human activities. Remember when you were a child or had young children? Young children naturally explore. They go up to strangers and are eager to investigate the world, including putting all kinds of things in their mouths, until they are trained to behave responsibly. Children are curious, innovative, and eager to learn, and, by the way, they don't need incentives or stock options to stimulate their learning or innovative activity. It's fun, and they do it naturally. As we grow up, we are taught to color inside the lines—unless we are lucky enough to work for Southwest Airlines, a company that wants people, according to one of its famous recruiting ads, who color *outside* the lines. Even as adults, most people are naturally creative and innovative, willing to try new things to solve problems. It takes a lot of hard work to stifle these innovative urges, and, unfortunately, many companies have done so quite successfully.

They haven't done things to stifle innovative activity intentionally or maliciously. It's just that they've decided to follow a number of precepts of conventional, and widespread, management thinking and practice that actually are extremely counterproductive, not only for innovation but for lots of other positive organizational outcomes as well. What that means is that to win at the innovation game—something that is very important given the rapidly decreasing product life cycles and intensifying competition in so many business domains—it is necessary to manage differently. Let's see what this implies for some customary management practices and the associated conventional management thinking.

Deemphasize Individual Accountability

One of the long-standing management principles is that there needs to be individual accountability, that people must be called to account for their *individual* results and performance. This idea forms the basis for management by objectives and for the annual performance appraisal process, the adult version of what happens in school—you get "graded" on your work. The implicit premise is that if you aren't monitored, scored, and ranked, you won't do anything, or at least anything very useful.

What's wrong with emphasizing individual accountability? First, it leads to finger-pointing when things go wrong rather than learning and problem solving. This result is beautifully illustrated in Jody Hoffer Gittell's description of operations management at both American and Southwest Airlines in an article called "Paradox of Coordination and Control," which appeared in the *California Management Review* in spring 2000. At American under Robert Crandall, there was an intense focus on accountability and assigning blame. For every delay, managers were responsible for figuring out which function was responsible. The consequences of this emphasis on accountability were not, however, what was intended. "The system had the unintended effect of encouraging employees to look out for themselves and avoid recrimination, rather than focusing on their shared goals of on-time performance, accurate baggage handling and satisfied customers. 'If you ask anyone here what's the last thing you think of when there's a problem,' said a ramp supervisor, 'I bet your bottom dollar it's the customer'" (p. 103).

In contrast, Southwest Airlines, to encourage problem solving and learning and reduce internal conflict, instituted a *team delay* in the early 1990s that permitted less-precise reporting of the cause of delays. One of Southwest's pilots described the consequences of this approach. "The team delay is used to point out problems between two or three different employee groups in working together. . . . Now . . . you see everybody working as a team. . . . It's been a very positive thing" (p. 104).

Performance appraisals also often get in the way of encouraging innovation. Some managers let the form substitute for other types of feedback, so people don't get constructive guidance on an ongoing basis. Tying performance evaluations to raises means that people don't "hear" what is said during the process, as they are thinking about what it means for them economically. So there isn't much learning or improvement. Giving evaluations according to a curve, as many if not most companies do, sets off destructive internal competition, a subject we will consider later in this chapter. And the whole idea of grading seems degrading.

Many companies, such as SAS Institute, the largest privately owned software company in the world, and even some divisions in General Motors, are giving up their annual individual performance appraisals. These organizations figured out that the appraisals were not a very effective way to accomplish feedback and coaching, even as they absorbed vast amounts of time. As quoted in my book (coauthored with Charles A. O'Reilly III in 2000) *Hidden Value: How Great Companies Achieve Extraordinary Results with Ordinary People*, David Russo, formerly the head of human resources at SAS Institute, has said, "I don't think you can really manage someone's performance. I think you can observe the results. . . . I think you can set short- and long-term goals. And you can sit back and see if it happens or it doesn't happen" (p. 112).

SAS Institute sets high expectations for performance and trust, which then become self-fulfilling prophecies, and gives people the freedom to do what they like to meet those expectations. These wise organizations also recognize the truth of W. Edwards Deming's idea that performance in organizations, which are, after all, interdependent systems, can seldom be attributed to the actions of single individuals. Instead of blaming people for the deficiencies in the system, Deming argued for diagnosing the problem and fixing its root causes.

If you want people to learn and innovate, build a system that encourages teamwork, learning, and trying new things. Get people focused on those goals, not on avoiding blame and assigning responsibility. That's why companies that excel at innovation and learning have management practices and a philosophy that encourage joint problem solving.

Don't Set Quantitative Goals and Overemphasize Budgets

Closely related to the idea of accountability is the idea of goal setting. Yes, I know there is a large literature on goal setting that shows its positive, motivational consequences. But these good effects occur primarily at the individual level when the goals are realistic, people have the training and resources to achieve them, and the goals are sufficiently challenging. In many organizations, budgets become constraints on doing what needs to be done, and performance objectives constrain rather than motivate performance.

These bad effects don't hamper the performance of AES, a global independent power producer that has been enormously successful since its founding in the early 1980s. At AES's power plants, annual budgets are set by a budget task force, composed of people from all departments and levels. The group sets the budget not by looking at some arbitrary financial objectives that need to be achieved but by asking people throughout the plant what they spent last year, on what, and why, and what they need to spend this year, on what, and why, to accomplish their objectives of producing power efficiently, safely, and with as little environmental impact as possible. Plant managers accept these budgets, set by frontline people. What a novel idea! Budgeting by talking to the people who will be subject to the budget. Moreover the budgets are more like guidelines than constraints or fixed objectives that must be met no matter what. This permits AES people the flexibility to respond to challenges and opportunities quickly and easily.

At the corporate level, too, AES has given up the idea of establishing some predetermined set of financial objectives. Think about it. If a company sets a goal of growing profit 20 percent a year, how fast will profit grow? Probably about 20 percent a year. If one year it does better, it will probably "bank" the profit for the next year. If it does worse, who knows what kinds of financial gimmicks the company may try, but the press is filled with financial scandals ranging from booking phantom revenue to trying to hide operating expenses in restructuring charges. AES, around 1995, decided that it wanted to be the leading global power company and then no longer set specific financial objectives. Roger Sant, cofounder and chairman, in an interview for the January-February 1998 issue of *Electricity Journal*, titled "Roger W. Sant—Visionary Internationalist: An Interview with the Chairman, AES Corporation," explained what setting that audacious goal, particularly given the company's relatively small size, did for AES. "'If we're really trying to be the leading global power company, would we have done this or that?' Somehow, just talking that through made it clearer. The company just exploded thereafter. . . . We've decided we don't want a numerical earnings growth goal, because that may be a limitation. . . . It's just dumb to put something down when, once you've unleashed it, you don't really know how far you can go with this capability" (p. 40).

How can you innovate if you can't do anything because of all the constraints, including the constraints of budgets and promises to Wall Street? A colleague was called in by an executive in a publishing firm and asked for help. She had been told by her CEO that Wall Street would value the company more highly if it were perceived as being more innovative. So, in her job in strategic planning, she was given the charge of helping the company become more innovative, but at the same time, she was told not to take too many risks and certainly not to risk missing the quarterly earnings targets. There's the paradox: be innovative but don't depart from our plans, budgets, and standard operating procedures. It doesn't work.

Don't Punish Mistakes

Trying new things, which is what innovation is all about, risks failure. Learning invariably means that people will make mistakes while they are learning. And as they learn and innovate, people will certainly not be as proficient as experts are or as proficient as they would be if they were doing things they already had mastered. Companies that want to encourage innovation and entrepreneurship therefore have to build a forgiveness culture, one in which people are not punished for trying new things.

At IDEO Product Development, one of the most successful product design companies in the world, founder and chairman David Kelley has as one of the company's mottoes, "fail early and fail often." As he points out, this is much preferable to failing once, failing at the end, and probably failing big. The idea of rapid prototyping is to learn by doing, and invariably the early "doing" will be filled with mistakes. But that's how you learn.

At AES, a company that has brought an unusual degree of entrepreneurship and innovation to the normally staid world of electric power, there is definitely an emphasis on forgiveness. As reported in Suzy Wetlaufer's article "Organizing for Empowerment: An Interview with AES's Roger Sant and Dennis Bakke" for the January-February 1999 issue of the *Harvard Business Review*, "It is okay to make most mistakes. We are all human. It's part of AES's values to accept mistakes, as long as people own up to them. . . . The good news about owning up to your mistakes right away is that it is so much easier to move quickly to find a creative solution. You don't sit around wasting time trying to figure out whom to blame" (p. 119).

At SAS Institute, people are encouraged to try new things. In my book, coauthored with Charles O'Reilly, *Hidden Value: How Great Companies Achieve Extraordinary Results with Ordinary People*, David Russo is quoted as saying, "If you're hiring creative people, you give them their head, you tell them that it's all right to take chances, and you mean it, they will do their best" (p. 105). At PSS/World Medical, a large medical supply distributor that grew from its founding in 1983 to have $1.6 billion in sales by 2000, people are promised a soft landing. The company promotes from within, and if someone takes on a position that the person can't handle, that individual gets to go back to the previous job. Many of the people now in senior management have had a soft landing at some point in their careers.

Letting people make mistakes helps create an action orientation, where people learn by trying things and innovation occurs naturally. As David Kelley of IDEO has said, "Enlightened trial and error outperforms the planning of flawless intellects." But to get trial and error and the innovation it produces, you have to encourage people to try—and to fail—without serious consequences.

Ironically, many companies today claim they want learning and innovation, but they don't want anybody to learn or try anything, when that means not being as proficient or making mistakes. The mixed message doesn't work. Innovative cultures let people innovate, with all the associated risks and setbacks. It's as simple as that.

Discourage Internal Competition

Encouraging internal competition is so routine that it is taken for granted. Competition-inducing management practices include forced curve distributions of raises and performance evaluations, so that only some can earn the highest rating or raise; recognition awards given to individuals; contests between departments, divisions, or individuals; and published rankings of unit or individual performance. These practices exist because there is widespread belief that internal competition stimulates higher levels of performance.

And then we wonder why there is so much variation in performance across similar units in the same company and why there is, conversely, so little sharing of best practices and so little internal learning. In one multinational food producer, making the same products with essentially the same machines and raw materials, there was a difference in performance of 112 percent between the best- and worst-performing plants, a situation found in similar studies in a number of industries. In a management approach that emphasizes internal competition, few will be brave enough to ask for help. Asking for the assistance of others sends a signal to everyone that the person asking for help is not as good, and no one wants to be seen as a loser in the internal competition. But even if a person does have the courage to ask for help, why would someone, an internal competitor for raises and evaluations, willingly offer such help?

In today's technologically complex world, launching a new product or service almost invariably entails working across internal organizational boundaries—or silos—to mobilize the various resources and expertise required. Anything that acts to make working across these internal boundaries more difficult inevitably makes innovation and product development more time-consuming and less efficient. That's why Guidant Corporation's cardiovascular division, where more than 50 percent of the revenues are derived from products less than eighteen months old, got rid of individual pay for performance and the internal competitive dynamics it created. Instead the division gives all of its employees identical percentage bonuses if they meet the annual big five research-and-development challenges and the revenue and growth targets. As Peter McInnes, a vice president, noted, "If you tie pay to individual performance . . . it just becomes very hard to manage. You start to get people competing with each other about which department they're going to be in, or which team they're going to be on, or who's going to assess their performance. . . . We just decided we don't want to deal with that."

Ironically, many companies have spent a fortune building intranets and other formal knowledge-sharing structures and systems that they then undermine by developing cultures of internal competition. There is a simple lesson from all of this—fight the competition, not one another. It's much more productive.

The Courage to Be Different

It requires a lot of courage to buck so much conventional manage-ment wisdom and practice, regardless of what the actual evidence shows. That is why sustainable competitive advantage is so difficult to achieve. Everyone wants to earn exceptional returns but to do it by doing what everyone else does and in the same way, too. What our investigation of truly innovative, entrepreneurial, and high-performing companies reveals is that they *don't* do what everyone else does. And they have leaders, at all levels of the organization, with the wisdom and courage to know what to do and to do it. The challenge, of course, is to take these insights and act on them. Knowledge, by itself, is not enough.

9 STEPHEN GOLDSMITH

INNOVATION IN GOVERNMENT

Stephen Goldsmith is special adviser to President George W. Bush on faith-based and nonprofit initiatives and chairman of the board of directors of the Corporation for National Service. As mayor of Indianapolis from 1992 to 1999, he earned a national reputation for bringing innovations to government. He is faculty director of the Innovation in American Government program at Harvard University's Kennedy School of Government, chairman of the Manhattan Institute's Center for Civic Innovation, and a management consultant for Lockheed Martin IMS. He is the editor of The Entrepreneurial City: A How-To Handbook for Urban Innovators *and author of* The Twenty-First Century City: Resurrecting Urban America.

overnment is the custodian of "the public square," the place where all the actors in a particular community—residents, businesses, religious organizations, nonprofit groups, and other social and cultural institutions—compete, cooperate, and work both for their individual good and the good of all. Through its various agencies and departments, government is the means through which laws and regulations are instituted and enforced, and it is also the vehicle through which social problems like crime, poverty, and high taxes are combated. Ideally, government in all its functions is the vehicle through which the voice of the citizens is heard—and then fairly represented in policy.

Yet over the past three or four decades, local, state, and federal governments have grown increasingly bureaucratic. Instead of listening to citizens and helping them solve problems, bureaucrats and elected officials have often imposed policies and interventions that have served to alienate and frustrate citizens—and in many cases to exacerbate social problems. Governments have tried to do too much or do the wrong things—or both. And at all levels, government agencies have grown into clunky, inefficient, and often ineffective bureaucratic machines that have lost their connection to the citizens they serve.

When I took office as mayor of Indianapolis in 1992, the city's bureaucracy was bigger and less efficient than it needed to be, but the overall situation certainly was not bleak. The city had relatively low taxes, its bond rating was good, and city government had a good reputation among its citizens. Nevertheless a closer look revealed signs of trouble.

Like other big cities, Indianapolis was experiencing losses of wealth and population to affluent, safer, lower-taxed suburbs. Poverty in the city was increasing, and the problems associated with it—teenage pregnancy, juvenile crime, drug use, and so forth—were increasingly being concentrated in urban families, creating pressure for more and more government services. Downtown office vacancies were on the rise, and the quality of schools was deteriorating. Many poorer residents felt left out of the city's successes, even disenfranchised. To top it off, the city's roadways and sidewalks were deteriorating, and the chamber of commerce recommended that the city spend $1 billion to repair the aging infrastructure.

Clearly, any significant increase in taxes to meet those challenges would have further compelled those with resources to flee the city. The future success of Indianapolis required that bold changes be implemented, not only in policy but also in the very structure of city government and how it related to its citizens.

Guiding our reform efforts was the following principle: competition drives innovation, and bureaucracies and monopolies restrict it. We relied on the power of the market to create opportunity for people left behind by the mainstream economy and to help reinvent government as well. Competition within a city improves services and drives down costs for residents. Competition with other cities for business creates new jobs and wealth for residents. New opportunity for business opens up the playing field for minority-owned businesses, nontraditional service providers, and new entrepreneurs. And once the doors of opportunity begin to open to those players, a culture of innovation soon follows.

What's more, I knew that the people themselves—both citizens seeking services and frontline city workers providing services—were repositories of innovative ways to meet the city's needs but often did not have a direct line to the decision makers or a way to put their ideas into practice. Those sources of innovation clearly needed to be tapped.

The challenge we faced was twofold: how to create an environment for bold change in the face of a monopolistic bureaucracy that was not facing external pressures to change either from voters or "customers," and how to make those elements of the community that felt disenfranchised feel as if they had a stake in the future of their city. Those goals clearly required that the management-heavy, self-serving bureaucratic system be replaced, that competition be introduced, and that citizens themselves be involved in crafting solutions to their problems.

But we knew change would not occur simply by ordering people to do so. We needed to make city hall realize that if government did not change the way it operated, then the city would soon face serious financial and social consequences. Convincing city employees that the urgency was real, acting fairly with them in tough situations, and rallying the 95 percent of city residents who paid taxes but who did not work for the city were critically important.

As the city's top elected leader, I realized that my role was to make the case for change to all elements of the community, including the bureaucracy, and then to create a culture to accomplish it. I also realized that I needed to facilitate technical changes in the way the city conducted its business. Indeed government appeared to be designed *not* to work, with barriers in place that made success or innovation almost impossible. The financial system, for example, was designed largely to maintain controls and not at all to provide information for managing performance to achieve specific results. And the personnel system was fraught with silly rules, categories, and procedures that hampered effectiveness. Employees, for example, could be disciplined for taking a risk that backfired, but rarely could they find the authority or resources to solve a problem in a new or different way.

A New Vision

To make our case for change, we devised the following vision statement for Indianapolis: "A Competitive City with Safe Streets, Strong Neighborhoods and a Thriving Economy." The concept of competition worked on two levels. For Indianapolis to be competitive with the surrounding region in terms of attracting and maintaining businesses and residents, it needed to keep its taxes low and to ensure that its neighborhoods were safe, vibrant, and economically competitive. And implicitly, given the lack of available funds, the only way for Indianapolis to reach those goals was to shrink the bureaucracy and inject competition into the delivery of public services in order to increase efficiency and save money.

We began with the estimate that city agencies had several layers too many of management, and we assumed that there were 25 percent more non-public-safety employees than were needed. Typically, any change in an established public organization like a government bureaucracy produces a rash of negative reactions from disgruntled employees and interest groups, including the flow of misleading information to the press, so reductions and changes of the magnitude that we were suggesting were certain to be met with tremendous resistance.

We therefore knew that we needed to convince the majority of citizens and city employees of the pressing need for change *now*, even though the situation had not yet become dire.

We also needed to make the case to city workers that the proposed changes would actually work to their benefit—to empower them, if you will, to do their jobs more effectively. We needed to make the case to those in poorer neighborhoods that a drop in city hall budgets would not mean a drop in services or a shirking of government's responsibility to help them solve their many problems. And we needed to make the case to the business community that our investment in long-neglected neighborhoods would work to their direct benefit.

While driving one day, I found the symbol we needed: a large billboard on which the mayor of the nearby city of Anderson was urging citizens to move to his city in order to save property taxes. The message was clear: if our city's taxes were raised any higher, its tax base was in serious jeopardy. We reproduced the billboard for city employees, held news conferences highlighting it, and hosted conferences on the effects to the city of losing businesses and citizens.

Making the Case to Poor Neighborhoods

Complementing our efforts to win over city workers was an all-out effort to convince residents in the most neglected areas of the city that they, too, had something to gain. Conventional wisdom held that these low-income residents would protect city employees and the status quo—an impression left over from the era when city hall was the employer of last resort.

Our goal was to demonstrate to these residents that when city hall paid more than it should for inferior services, poor people were the most adversely affected, because the services typically were worst in the neighborhoods with the least political clout and wealth. We also knew that we had to make the benefits of change immediately tangible to those in the poorest neighborhoods. In dozens and dozens of meetings across the city, we described how the savings won from shrinking the bureaucracy and opening up the provision of services to outside competition would be used to repair roads, parks, police stations, sidewalks, and the like in these long-neglected neighborhoods—an effort that became known as Building Better Neighborhoods. We also assured neighborhood leaders that they would be included in the planning of projects and that they would have ample opportunity to provide input and advice on where to spend the money.

Concurrently, we told residents of poor communities that we wanted to change the way that city government related to their neighborhoods, and we made a concerted effort to convince them that the new system would work to their advantage. Over time, the old system of municipal government had become functionally specific and geographically general, so that no city employee felt ownership for a particular area of the city. Consequently, leaders of poor neighborhoods typically had to fight their way through the buck-passing of city hall bureaucracies to gain the ear of an official. To give the neighborhoods greater clout, we assigned to each neighborhood a specific employee who was responsible for maintaining ties with that neighborhood. By providing neighborhood leaders with an advocate for their causes at city hall who could give them access to the inner working of government and pertinent information about their communities, we encouraged poor residents to have a stake in the changes that were taking place. The approach dramatically changed the thinking of the employees and the neighborhood leaders, opening up both groups to collaborative ways to solve problems.

Introducing Competition to Agencies

As mayor, I had personally hired only about fifty of the city's five thousand employees. Even if they all were exceptional managers and totally aligned with my goals, they still would not have had the ability to shake up the bureaucracy enough to make a significant difference. So we decided that we needed to independently and concurrently inject elements of managed competition into the systems of government to create the pressure and environment for change.

To that end, I created an office in the mayor's suite—which I called the Enterprise Development Office—and asked a small group of talented professionals to scour city government and nominate projects for competition and outsourcing. The group would present an idea to an agency, and the agency would reply about the benefits and drawbacks of changing the current system. These discussions accelerated change.

What the enterprise group soon discovered, however, was that the tools of government—most specifically, its financial accounting methods—neither supported innovation nor allowed for managed competition. Traditionally, government financial systems have nothing to do with management. Instead financial information is collected mostly for political and bond-rating purposes, and there is no systematic way to evaluate cost as defined by actual work activity. If competition was to spark innovation in government agencies, then a new approach to financial management and a new tool, *activity-based costing* (ABC), would be necessary.

The ABC goal is to define not just the obvious costs of labor and material but also the less obvious costs of fixed assets and depreciation on machinery and capital equipment, as well as the indirect costs of support services that make a particular work activity possible. The result of such an accounting tool is that direct comparisons can be made between public and private bidders for the same contract.

We also realized that we had to devise new performance measures. In government, the measures of performance tend to be whether the budget is balanced, whether the rules are followed, and whether the process is corruption-free. All these standards, of course, are reasonable and desirable, but the ultimate measures needed to be outputs and outcomes—the level of citizens' satisfaction with consumer services, for example, or the number of people successfully placed into jobs. So with the help of an outside consultant, we created performance measures for each government activity. The metrics of government, if they include quality and cost, can drive innovation. Indeed the process of bidding out and competing for work forces officials to focus on outcomes—for example, how many abandoned cars can be towed per dollar, or how much water cleaned, or how many roads repaired. Performance bidding and measurement acted as a catalyst for change.

As in other fields, new technologies can provide government employees not only with a tangible reason for change but also with an excuse to totally reengineer the way government conducts its business. To motivate city employees to think and act differently, we insisted that departments place one new application a week on the Internet. As old paper forms were confiscated and replaced with digital information, change became obligatory. And as the ABC system began to look at outputs per dollar spent, investments in technology from a department's budget became far easier to justify. Directors began to look at performance and to amortize the technology to see if the long-term benefits would outweigh the costs. What's more, we allowed directors to petition for internal "venture" capital if they could make a case for an investment that when amortized would make sense in terms of productivity or customer service.

Some Clear Results

Under our plan, private companies were not the only ones to compete for contracts; government agencies competed too—and often won. To aid them in their efforts, the city provided workers with private consultants to help them prepare their proposals and offered incentive pay when city workers outperformed their contracts. In addition, we never laid off union workers as a result of competition; instead we found them jobs with our contractors or trained them for new jobs elsewhere.

With a new culture of competition taking root, and new accounting tools in place, we began to see some innovative results—and some significant cost savings. By opening up to competition such municipal services as wastewater treatment, trash collection, street repair, printing, abandoned-vehicle disposal, and parking enforcement, we were able to save more than $420 million. Moreover we helped other units of government in Indianapolis—the U.S. Navy, for example—use competition to save millions of dollars.

Our efforts to thin the bureaucracy and reward efficiency and success meant that city employees were freer to institute the innovations that they thought were needed. Historically, the work environment for government employees has been one in which decisions about work processes and resources are made at the top, with very little input from frontline workers. Employees are classified and promoted through a large number of narrowband skill groups, and compensation is time based, with little or no regard for performance.

But when arbitrary management levels are stripped away, performance incentives are offered, and departments come together as a team to prepare bids to provide services, amazing things can happen. Using the newly developed accounting tools, workers were able to identify sources of inefficiency and work to eliminate them. In preparing competitive bids, for example, the employee union exposed as untenable overhead the overstaffing of middle managers and wasteful equipment practices, and the garage mechanics were able to significantly reduce their costs while enhancing the quality of the service they provided.

Ultimately, the introduction of competition meant that employees were given more discretion over how they did their work, broader job responsibilities, and an opportunity to share financially in their achievements. This led to the rise of several innovative ideas—the solid waste (garbage) workers, for example, demanded that computer terminals be placed next to the time clocks so they could see the actual complaints and then be able to e-mail the mayor directly with suggestions on how to improve the quality of their service. Making city workers true partners in the effort to cut costs and improve services turned their initial hostility to the proposed changes into enthusiasm for them.

Perhaps the best way to summarize the value of our competitive strategy is to quote a letter by a local union president, Steve Quick, that was published in the *Indianapolis News* in 1996, four years after we began our efforts:

> City workers are empowered now to do their jobs better. We participate in the purchase of equipment, materials and tools [and] even had a say in designing snowplowing and trash collection routes. Goldsmith got rid of ineffective or unnecessary supervisors and kept managers who had better skills and abilities to work with workers to get things done. As a result, the number of grievances is way down. . . . What distinguishes Indianapolis is the hard stuff—increased communication, better (not more) management, empowerment of workers, incentives rather than threats, and an attempt to be a real partner in the process.

We also knew that in order to solve the serious problems that were plaguing our most troubled neighborhoods, we needed to show the leaders of those communities that we were willing to become real partners with them as well. In fact, we knew that if we could empower citizens—that is, give them the resources and power to effect change and the structure to do so—then together we would be able to arrive at innovative and effective solutions to many of the city's problems.

Solutions to social problems that are imposed by government tend not to work, and the most innovative ideas—and not coincidentally the most effective ones—come from the bottom up rather than from the top down. In most cases, the citizens themselves know what is best for them and their own neighborhoods. The role of a good leader, therefore, is to promote the development of responsible, citizen-generated solutions by giving citizens the capacity to make a real difference in their communities.

Although we knew that citizens were capable of coming up with innovative solutions to social problems, we also knew that they could not do so very effectively without some guidelines, structure, and assistance. In all of the various programs that we introduced, we let residents know that if they wanted to receive funding or have their proposals seriously considered, then they needed to work through a local organization. Requiring that citizens work through such organizations not only gave us a way to track any funding or activity that we directed to a neighborhood but also provided a vehicle for residents to work together, develop common aims, and negotiate among themselves the kinds of programs they wanted to implement. To help those organizations succeed, we sponsored leadership-training sessions, appointed coordinators whose job was to navigate the complex system of licenses and permits required for virtually any activity, and established a neighborhood resource center.

In 1997, we launched the Front Porch Alliance, a partnership of city government with churches, religious organizations, and other neighborhood groups, as a way to bridge the unnecessary divide between municipal government and faith-based organizations. We knew that faith-based and neighborhood organizations could dream up innovative programs to deal with social problems and then implement them much more effectively than government could. They could change lives and improve communities, and we wanted to support them in that effort.

Our promise to Front Porch was not primarily a financial one, although we did secure some resources to support the alliance. Instead

we helped the group navigate city hall's red tape and build the partnerships in the community at large that would help it achieve its
mission and have the greatest impact. The results were astounding.
In two years' time, the alliance forged partnerships with more than
five hundred churches and other organizations, including public
schools, in the Indianapolis area. Through its teen abstinence, summer camp, and other programs, it served thousands of Indianapolis
youth, and it also coordinated such innovative programs as Adopt-
a-Block, in which thirty churches "adopted" more than sixty city
blocks. In addition, fifteen churches maintained thirty city parks.
The alliance turned crack-cocaine alleys into community gardens
and vacant warehouses into transitional housing, and it instituted
innovative juvenile-justice and public-safety initiatives in partnership with various city agencies.

Faith-based and community groups were helped in another way
as well. Just as we had suspected, contracting out government services opened the economic arena for bids—and contracts won—by
faith-based and other neighborhood groups. That in turn led to
some rather innovative arrangements. In 1999, for example, we received a mowing contract bid from Wheeler Enterprises, a nonprofit
joint venture between the multibillion-dollar ServiceMaster Company and Wheeler Mission, a hundred-year-old Indianapolis homeless shelter. Their bid was superior to any others we received, and
they won a $150,000 contract.

Wheeler Enterprises employs homeless and other poor individuals who have sought help from Wheeler Mission, which provides
them with a host of personal supportive services. The partnership
draws on the expertise of ServiceMaster in contract management
and landscape business management. Together they deliver quality
service while helping people with multiple barriers to employment
reach self-sufficiency.

Their contract with us enabled them to leverage other opportunities. They purchased a window-washing company to add to their
portfolio of services, and less than two years after starting, they em-

ploy more than twenty people and generate $500,000 in annual revenue. In the process, they have helped people learn to work, kick drug habits, begin saving money, and reconcile with their families. An enterprising environment, as it grows, attracts new kinds of innovative ventures, such as Wheeler Enterprises, which create economic value at the same time they are solving some of our most entrenched social problems.

Innovations such as these could only have been achieved by breaking down the old monopolistic bureaucracy and introducing the notion of competition into the business of government. Over eight years, our efforts produced countless innovations and real, measurable results: a drop in the non-public-safety workforce of 50 percent, more than $450 million saved through outsourcing services, a big decline in customer complaints, and more than $1.2 billion invested in the city's aging infrastructure without raising taxes. What's more, the very structure of city government was changed, with citizens becoming more directly involved and with the line between "public" and "private" made far less distinct, to the benefit of all.

New and more effective ways of doing the business of government can best be encouraged by putting in place the elements for competition, supporting workers and citizens in their efforts to solve problems, updating outmoded or ineffective measures of performance, and demanding that agencies and neighborhood organizations produce results. Our success in Indianapolis demonstrates that if such a strategy is applied elsewhere, the future of innovative city government is bright.

10 DAVID S. POTTRUCK

HOW COMPANY CULTURE ENCOURAGES INNOVATION

David S. Pottruck is president and co-CEO of the Charles Schwab Corporation. Named one of the top fifty CEOs by Worth *magazine (April 2001), top twenty-five managers of the year by* BusinessWeek *(January 2001), and Executive of the Year by the San Francisco Business Times (January 2001), he is on the board of governors of the National Association of Security Dealers and is a trustee of the University of Pennsylvania. His most recent publication (coauthored) is* Clicks and Mortar: Passion-Driven Growth in an Internet-Driven World *(Jossey-Bass, 2000). Prior to joining Schwab, he was a senior vice president with Shearson/American Express.*

We are living in one of the most innovative ages in history. Why do I say this? Because I believe that despite the ups and downs of many Internet firms, technology and the Internet have helped to create the most competitive business arena that has ever existed. Even small companies now have a global reach. If you have a vision, and are willing to work hard and adhere to sound business values and principles, the rewards can be staggering.

As a result, the amount of innovation we are seeing today is breathtaking. The creation of this new marketplace has unleashed incredible amounts of creative power. The result is a fast-paced and exhilarating business environment that has helped to create the largest economic expansion in U.S. history. Working in this arena is much like running the rapids—on a nonstop basis.

Succeeding in this economy requires all of our best efforts. The successful company must innovate ahead of the curve, not only to prosper but to survive. Without a primary focus on innovation, a cutting-edge firm can become obsolete almost overnight. Larger, established firms can be even more vulnerable to sacrificing the future by clinging too long to the status quo.

That is why I believe that today's vital challenge for companies and leaders is to create an environment that nourishes innovation. How is this done? When I have conversations about how to best create and sustain an innovative environment, I generally share our experiences at Charles Schwab.

Traditional Business Values

We launched Internet trading in 1996. By 1998, we were widely recognized as the world leader in on-line investing. Our Web site is now the busiest in our business. In the first quarter of 2000, when stock market trading volumes were at an all-time high, we had as many as ninety-six thousand simultaneous Web sessions and transacted $25.1 billion in securities through Schwab.com each week. Although this number has vacillated with the ups and downs of the market, we are prepared for future expansion.

I mention these numbers not for bragging purposes but to point out that our cyberspace strategy has received a solid marketplace endorsement. It has passed the test of winning against competition and demonstrating a successful business model that makes money and grows. This brings us to the question of what exactly is Schwab's strategy for creating the environment in which continuing innovation can flourish.

We have found that the key to success in the new computer- and information-driven economy is basically the same key that opens doors in the old bricks-and-mortar economy. Quite simply, we have found that despite its earthshaking and revolutionary nature, the Internet respects and rewards traditional business values and principles. We have found that when these foundational values (which I will discuss later in the chapter) are solidly in place and solidly embraced by a company's workforce, a firm maximizes its ability to innovate ahead of the curve and enjoy prolonged success.

Note the word *prolonged*. There is no disputing that some Internet firms come out of nowhere and experience incredible initial success. Yet as we have seen, many disappear quickly. Why? I believe that in many cases it is because the main objective is to grow fast and achieve an IPO—to make as much money as quickly as possible for the founders rather than build a great company that succeeds because it meets customer needs better than any competitor. I don't mean to take anything away from these companies. Certainly many are built on truly great ideas—visions, in fact—and their success has come at the price of very hard work and a willingness to take significant risks. Many of these companies embody the entrepreneurial spirit at its most dynamic.

Yet it is also true that many startups capitalize on their initial innovation without creating the environment that supports continually innovating for the future. As a result, they can quickly be overtaken by new innovators. At Schwab, we bet our future on the belief that the business values and traditions that allowed us to innovate in the bricks-and-mortar world would also serve us well in cyberspace—with some modifications to transform our business culture for the future.

What Is Company Culture?

A good way to grasp the concept of *company culture* is to think of a firm as a minicivilization. All civilizations have a group of animating beliefs and values that give meaning, purpose, and direction.

These beliefs constitute culture. The United States, for example, is centered on the beliefs and values found in our Declaration of Independence and our Constitution. If you reduce those beliefs down to their essence, you might say that our national animating principles are "equality before the law" and "life, liberty and the pursuit of happiness," among others.

At Schwab, our company culture is built around chairman and co-CEO Chuck Schwab's seemingly simple yet profound questions: How do we best serve our customers? How do we build the most useful and ethical (not necessarily the biggest or most profitable) financial services firm in the world?

We took that principle to the Internet, where it continued to guide our interactions with customers and our innovations on their behalf. But the fact is, Internet technology is still in its infancy. We're literally inventing technology as we go. And quite frankly, sooner or later, technology is going to screw up. That's when you have to know the true meaning of the word *mortar*. It's about the element that holds it all together—it's about people. You've got to have great people on board, especially in this period when technology is still evolving. Great people help clients get through the frailty and newness of cutting-edge technology, and it takes great people to figure out how to make the new technologies work in a user-friendly and high-value way.

I recognize that this all sounds very simple. But the fact is, creating and sustaining a company culture requires discipline and the willingness to sometimes sacrifice short-term profits in order to ensure long-term success. It's not always easy, as I will illustrate shortly. First, however, let's take a closer look at why culture is vital to establishing an innovation-nurturing environment.

Permanence, Direction, Identity

We have found that a strong corporate culture provides employees with a sense of stability, belonging, and serving a higher purpose—

in our case, serving others. When these needs are met, I believe that people are much more likely to innovate at the top of their abilities. I should also say that I am continually amazed by the high level of innovation and contribution that employees are capable of if they are supported and inspired by a strong company culture—and are encouraged to participate in innovation.

That's the overview. Now let's take a closer look at why culture is vital.

- *Culture offers a sense of permanence.* Change is not only inevitable but also is often unsettling, especially when it is unexpected and relentless. Our employees know, however, that our company's purpose and values are unchanging, even as procedures and practices are constantly being redefined and no matter how fast and furious the market pace may be. This appears to many as a paradox, that a stable culture and set of corporate values is what enables employees to manage through the rapid-fire changes required for today's business leaders.

- *Culture provides a sense of direction.* Culture is not only a foundation of core beliefs but also serves as a compass. We cannot see into the future, of course. But if we are guided by solid principles—principles that have worked in the past—we can move forward with assurance that we can also succeed in the future. This shared, guiding vision focuses our employees, holds our company together, distinguishes us in the eyes of customers, and inspires and shapes our innovations.

- *Culture helps us find our natural allies.* When we are hiring new people, we look for those whose personal values mirror our organizational values. A shared philosophy is vital because you cannot write personnel policies to keep up with an accelerated pace of change. An employee should have a strong inner sense of how our values apply to business situations. This greatly reduces the threat of internal dissonance and nurtures our ability to innovate on behalf of our customers.

- *Culture provides a marketplace identity*. Our customers know Schwab is an ethical, service-based company because we really have provided them with the best and most ethical financial services in the world. Our employees radiate this philosophy during every interaction with customers. We often refer to this as "doing well by doing good," and it is a linchpin of our company. It connects our employees with our customers and benefits both groups immensely. We listen to our customers because, otherwise, how can you tell if you're meeting and exceeding their wishes?

Culture creates the stable environment in which innovation can flourish. But there are two aspects to culture: creating it and sustaining it. Now let's look at how we have sustained our culture—and adapted it to the new economy.

Leading for Innovation

There's a popular Washington expression that holds that "people are policy." In other words, you can publicly embrace noble principles, but if your team isn't dedicated to advancing those principles, they really don't make any difference. That is why we take extraordinary steps to ensure that our company culture is embraced by our entire team, from the boardroom to the mailroom.

First, let's talk about the business leaders. The CEO who wants to be a true leader must be the most vivid example of the culture at work. Only then can the CEO inspire passion in the rest of the team.

How is this accomplished?

Rule one: Inspiring business leaders must never treat essential corporate beliefs and values as if they are mere slogans. It must be apparent that those at the very top not only believe in the company's principles but live them. Let me give an example. I have talked with Chuck Schwab for hours without ever hearing him mention profits. Most of his inspiring and animated discussions start with references to "a chance to serve others," "a chance to make a difference," "a chance to change the world."

Chuck is very clearly propelled by these core beliefs. Of course he is concerned that the company is financially successful. We spend a lot of time on the analytical parts of our business. But he always talks in terms that if the company's culture is strong—if our dedication to customers and employees is unwavering—then the innovations that create stronger growth and profits will follow. He radiates that belief, and this has had a hugely positive effect on our entire workforce, myself very much included.

Rule two: A few people are apparently born with great leadership ability, but for most of us, leadership is a learned behavior. It is much more difficult to master than a set of management behaviors, and its payoff is far, far greater. When a leader creates the right culture, he or she gives an organization a lasting competitive advantage. Having a culture that promotes high performance and innovation at all levels is ultimately more essential than any single business plan, which is often quickly forgotten or, even more often, quickly outdated by changes in the marketplace. People and cultures achieve much more than any team of managers or planners could ever envision.

Rule three: Innovation is not only energizing and inspiring; it is fun. It creates heroes who embody aspects of the culture and vision. It creates the special stores that older workers share with the newer ones to extend the culture. All of these factors, in turn, provide support and encouragement for leaders to take the next bold step forward.

Emphasize Creative Roles

Chuck Schwab has also recognized that moving from bricks to clicks requires some fine-tuning of company culture. Like many established firms, we found it necessary to work hard to inspire employees to shift more of their focus toward innovation and knowledge sharing. We continually stress their vital creative role and encourage them to speak up and share their insights, visions, and knowledge. For companies making the transition from the bricks-and-mortar world, this is especially important.

Blending technology and the Internet into everyone's job can be scary and unsettling. I remember how our employees, as used to change as they are, resisted at first, fearing that the Internet would eliminate their jobs. In fact, it eliminated most of the clerical parts of their work, making their jobs more interesting, more valuable, and higher paying.

Dick Notebaert, CEO of Ameritech, has a valuable insight into the business leader's responsibility to nurture innovation. "When innovation is ingrained into your culture, you're living your brand. It's just a way of life. You do things with your customers because you're trying to look at it from their perspective, not yours." Like Chuck Schwab, Dick reminds us that innovation is customer driven. Lines of communication between a company and its customers must therefore be strong and dynamic. This means that the front-line employees who have the greatest contact with customers have a process for identifying and developing their best ideas about how to respond to customer requests and needs for better products and services.

Inspiring your team to innovate is a large task. We have made a commitment to letting employees at every level know that they are valued, that they are part of a larger vision that depends on them for success. We don't accomplish this merely by e-mail and phone calls. Sometimes the expenditure of old-fashioned shoe leather— and airline miles—is what the task requires.

Let me give a few examples.

Better Than a Memo

As we expanded our European operations several years ago, I was very proud of our team. It was doing a great job. At the same time, however, I knew that these new managers were unfamiliar with how strongly we felt about company culture. I am so convinced that culture is central to long-term success that I flew to England to meet with these employees. During our meeting, I discussed the importance that we placed on customer service and company culture. Then I closed the meeting with a question-and-answer session, which included a question of my own: How many of these team members would share our discussion with their workers?

No one raised a hand.

When I asked why not, the consensus was that sharing this information simply wasn't necessary. The managers knew what was expected, and that was all that really mattered. Their staffs just needed to focus on doing their job.

Then I turned the question on its head. Was it, I asked, really necessary for me to fly in from San Francisco to meet face-to-face with them to discuss these issues? After all, I could have e-mailed them a memo.

They immediately understood. They recognized that I took the trouble to fly in because we value, very highly, both our employees and our company culture. I wanted them to understand, in no uncertain terms, how vital both are to our company's success. My presence transmitted this in a way a memo never could. It also gave me a chance to listen and learn from their reactions.

We did much the same thing, on a vastly larger scale, in 1999, convening our entire workforce of thirteen thousand on a Saturday to hear Chuck and me discuss our corporate values and philosophy. This meeting (with five thousand employees gathered in San Francisco and the others linked by satellite) cost us $6 million, but it was more than worth every dollar. Among other things, we saw an immediate reduction in our attrition rate, which dropped from 13 percent to 11 percent. Because every percentage drop saves us $15 million, we spent $6 million and saved $30 million.

One other point—a CEO must embody a corporate culture and inspire employees to innovate, but he or she must also attract and keep the best innovators that can possibly be found. Although this does not qualify as a great revelation, there is a new wrinkle. The

Internet has made the technologist a central character in a company's success. Yet all too often, an adversarial relationship can arise between business leaders and technologists. Managers must recognize the fundamental difference between the way people on the business side look at the world and the way technologists see things.

Business leaders tend to think in broad and sometimes fuzzy terms. This is vital to innovation and should be encouraged. At the same time, those who actually develop the technology that exploits business opportunities must primarily be precise and concrete thinkers. Their part of the company vision is figuring out where the nuts and bolts go in order to make the vision take off and fly.

Our approach has been to cherish the technologist, without whom many innovations would never get off the drawing board. They are very much partners, a point we emphasize by having our hugely talented chief information officer report directly to the co-CEO. Believe me, the technologists recognize this—and appreciate it. To win in cyberspace, all of us need as many allies—and as few adversaries—as possible.

We are living in the Golden Age of Innovation. I cannot imagine a more exhilarating—or challenging—experience. The good news is that cyberspace really does reward traditional business values. At the same time, it will punish—quickly and severely—those who don't build and sustain the kind of company culture that provides stability and nurtures innovation.

Part III

CHANGING HOW YOU THINK ABOUT LEADERSHIP AND INNOVATION

11 JIM COLLINS

THE ULTIMATE CREATION

Jim Collins operates a management research laboratory in Boulder, Colorado. He is author of Good to Great: Why Some Companies Make the Leap . . . and Others Don't *and coauthor of* Built to Last: Successful Habits of Visionary Companies. *Previously, Jim was a faculty member at the Stanford University Graduate School of Business, where he received the Distinguished Teaching Award in 1992.*

E veryone knows that innovations—innovative products, innovative technologies, innovative services, innovative *things*—separate great organizations from their mediocre counterparts. And everyone knows that a key role of a leader in any great organization is to create leading-edge innovations or to lead other people to do so.

Well, "everyone" is wrong.

Note: Copyright © 2001 by Jim Collins (jimcollins@aol.com). Portions of this chapter were extracted and adapted for the Drucker Foundation from Jim Collins's articles that appeared in *Inc.* magazine.

Following Can Be
Better Than Leading

Great organizations do not necessarily make innovation a central part of their vision or strategy. They are just as likely to be followers as they are to be leaders with pioneering products and leading-edge services.

IBM, for example, grew from a one-building small business into one of the largest corporations in the world primarily because of its professional sales force, not because of its pioneering innovations. In the early days of the computer industry, IBM lagged so far behind Remington Rand (which had the UNIVAC, the first commercially successful large-scale computer) that people called its first computer "IBM's UNIVAC." In the 1960s, Burroughs clearly had more innovative computers than IBM. And in the personal computer explosion, the IBM PC was anything but innovative. It was primarily an agglomeration of standard components with the IBM name on it. Yet IBM's mainframe and later its personal computer standards triumphed.

Similarly, Boeing did not invent the commercial jet. De Havilland did with the Comet, but it lost ground when one of its early jets exploded in midair, not exactly a brand-building moment. American Express dragged its feet into credit cards, not introducing its first card until eight years after the early leader, Diners Club—hardly leading-edge behavior. Taking advantage of Diners Club's billing and bookkeeping problems, American Express built not a more innovative service but a more reliable service. Nucor did not invent the mini-mill; it got into the business thirty years after others had pioneered the innovation. Starbucks did not invent the high-end coffee chain; Peet's preceded it. General Electric did not innovate the AC electrical system; Westinghouse did, and GE copied. Wal-Mart did not invent discount retailing; Sam Walton lagged years behind other leaders. Nordstrom, McKinsey, Marriott—none of these great companies made innovation a core value.

History is full of now defunct companies that were the early innovative leaders in their fields. In fact, being the pioneering innovator of a new idea seldom proves to be a sustainable advantage and usually proves to be a *liability*. VisiCalc, for example, was the first major personal computer spreadsheet. Where is VisiCalc today? Do you know anyone who uses it? And what of the company that pioneered it? Gone; it doesn't even exist. VisiCalc eventually lost out to Lotus 1-2-3, which itself lost out to Excel. Similarly, the first portable computers came from now dead companies, such as Osborne computer. Today we primarily use portables from companies such as Dell. Look at all the innovative Internet companies that have recently failed. They were first. They were innovative. And most will not end up as great companies, if they end up as companies at all.

Certainly, some great companies—notably Sony, Johnson & Johnson, Merck, and 3M—did make innovation into a core value as they grew into great companies. So you *can* have innovation as a core value and be great. But this fact remains: only about half of the enduring great companies in *Built to Last* had innovation as a central part of their ethos as they grew up.

The same pattern continues in our new research. My research team and I recently completed a five-year study to answer the question, "Can a good company become a great company, and if so, how?" Of 1,435 companies that appeared on the *Fortune* 500 from 1965 to 1995, only eleven demonstrated a verifiable shift from sustained mediocrity to sustained excellence, defined by performance relative to the general market. In systematically studying these eleven in contrast to a set of comparison companies that failed to shift from good to great, leading-edge innovation simply does not show up as a distinguishing variable. Only about half of the good-to-great companies focused on pioneering innovations as a key strategy, and only half of those were more innovative in products and services than their comparison counterparts.

So now, you are probably wondering, Why on Earth am I writing this chapter in a book on innovation? Because, despite all of the

aforementioned, leading for innovation *is* an essential variable—
but not innovation in the way we normally think of it.

All of the leaders who build enduring great organizations from
the ground up or who turn good organizations into great ones—
without exception—pursue the most powerful and profound form
of innovation: *social innovation*.

Social Innovation Is
the Truest Innovation

Social innovation—or what I like to call *innovation squared*—makes
all first-order innovation and human productivity possible in the first
place. The invention of constitutional government, private property
as a social mechanism, money, public stock ownership, the corporation, the free-market economy, public education—all of these social
innovations—are ultimately more significant than the invention of
the personal computer, the telephone, the automobile, the jet airplane, or the Internet. The greatest of all inventions is human organization and society—the ultimate tool for achieving human
objectives. Boeing jets, 3M Post-it notes, Federal Express, universal telephone service, the Sony Walkman, the Hewlett-Packard
200LX pocket computer—none of these would have been possible
without the invention of human organization and continual innovation in the practice of management.

Let me use my own experience in the world of rock climbing to
illustrate the power of social innovation to drive human progress.
In the past thirty years, climbing has seen gigantic leaps in accomplishment. Sheer, overhanging rock faces once deemed impossible
now get climbed by fifteen-year-old kids as "warm-ups." It took
forty-seven *days* to climb the south face of El Capitan on the first
ascent in 1958; the current record stands at less than five *hours*. Although technical innovations, such as sticky shoe rubber, contributed to climbing progress, the primary drivers were in fact social
innovations. The decision to include the names of first ascension-
ists in guidebooks fueled a fierce competition among climbers to

push standards and establish new routes. The radical social innovation to work climbs from the "top down" rather than using the conventional approach to work from the "ground up"—which is essentially reverse-engineering a climb—shattered a social convention and led to a quantum leap in standards. These and other social innovations, such as international climbing competitions, drove technical innovation, not the other way around.

Taking this concept to an organizational level, I'm asking you to shift your attention from product and technology innovation to social innovation. Think of it this way: What was Thomas Edison's greatest invention? Not the light bulb. Not the phonograph. Not the telegraph. I agree with many Edison observers that his greatest invention was the modern research-and-development laboratory—a social invention. What was Henry Ford's greatest invention? Not the Model T, but the first successful large-scale application of a new method of management to the automobile industry—the assembly line. What was Walt Disney's greatest creation? Not Disneyland or Mickey Mouse, but the Disney creative department that to this day continues to generate ingenious ways to make people happy.

If you want to create a great organization, don't make the mistake that the leaders of Apple Computer made in the late 1980s. After the remarkable success of the Macintosh computer and the departure of Steve Jobs, Apple's leaders spent their time trying to come up with the next insanely great innovation. Apple's CEO, John Scully, became the personal product champion for innovating the Newton, a precursor to the now ubiquitous Palm Pilot. Instead of trying to become product visionaries, Scully and his associates should have spent their time being social inventors, designing an environment that would be the seedbed for many insanely great innovations over decades to come. They should have been more like William McKnight of 3M or George Merck of Merck—leaders who never came up with a single product innovation themselves but instead created perpetual motion machines, fueled by social inventions (like "bootleg time," wherein 3Mers get 15 percent free time to tinker around, or Merck's pioneering of an industrial research process that allowed scientists to fully participate and publish in the scientific community rather than keep their work secret). Apple failed to become a truly innovative company like Merck or 3M because its leadership failed to pay attention to the most important form of innovation, namely social innovation.

Now you might be wondering, but what about Apple's comeback with the iMac in the late 1990s? Good question. Apple did finally return to creating insanely great products, with the reentrance of the Grand Master of Insanely Great Products himself, Steve Jobs. But the real question is this: Will Steve Jobs apply his genius to social innovation and make Apple the ultimate creation, or will he simply ignite some innovative product development? If the former, Apple may indeed—finally—make the transition from a company with innovative *products* and a visionary leader to a truly innovative *company*. Otherwise Apple will languish once again, after the Grand Master leaves.

We frequently confuse the notion of a great organization with the notion of a great and innovative leader, who happens to have an organization at his or her disposal. Indeed many so-called great companies are not companies at all. They are a platform for a single remarkable individual, a "genius with a thousand helpers."

A classic case of the genius-with-helpers model is Microsoft, with Bill Gates, as is the early Apple with Steve Jobs. But there are hundreds of other examples, companies that rose and fell with one great genius, who hired lots of able help, but that then declined after the departure of the genius visionary: Polaroid with Edwin Land, Westinghouse with George Westinghouse, DEC with Ken Olson, Netscape with Jim Clark.

Being Innovative in the *Way* You Lead Is What Matters

In the social sector, we can see the same pattern. Compare for example the NBC Orchestra of New York and the Cleveland Orchestra. Under Arturo Toscanini—a genius with hundreds of capable helpers—the NBC Orchestra became one of the most visibly innovative orchestras in the 1940s and 1950s. It was the first to embrace broadcast technology, first in radio, then television. It shattered long-entrenched traditions of restraint, introducing an almost rock-and-roll flavor to some of its concerts. But after Toscanini died, the orchestra completely disintegrated and doesn't even exist today.

Now look at Cleveland. Cleveland is perhaps the most consistently excellent orchestra in the United States and one of the very best in the world. George Szell, Toscanini's counterpart at Cleveland, beginning in 1946, focused on less-visible innovations, channeling his energies into creating a culture unique among American orchestras. Instead of focusing publicity on star performers, he celebrated the achievements of the entire orchestra. Instead of viewing businesslike accountability and artistic creativity as incompatible, he blended them together, one playing off the other like yin and yang. Most important, he built a culture that endures beyond any single individual. As Greg Sandow (2000) observed in a feature article for the *Wall Street Journal,* you can listen to three generations of Cleveland directors conducting Beethoven's Ninth, dating back over four decades, and no matter who the conductor, "the musicians play each note with radiant care" (p. 24). And to this day, leaders of the Cleveland Orchestra focus first on perpetuating a set of values that institutionalize excellence and innovation, not on creating a platform for a single genius to strut his stuff.

To lead for innovation, then, does not mean leading the creation of innovations per se or being a towering innovative genius yourself. *Rather, it means being innovative in the way you lead, manage, and build your organization.* Consider the success of the Homeless Outreach Program (HOP) in Los Angeles. Michael Neely, recipient of a Frances Hesselbein Community Innovation Fellowship, founded HOP based on two simple observations. First, for many, homelessness follows from a deeper root cause such as mental illness, drug addiction, or severe alcoholism. Second, while a homeless person suffers on the street, a well-funded program designed specifically to address that person's root problem often sits not far away, with excess capacity. So Neely's idea was to create an organization whose mission is not to "solve the homeless problem" but to serve as a bridge to educate homeless people about the existence of these programs and to get them into treatment for their root problems.

But the real source of HOP's success lies not in the innovative concept (as beautiful as it is) but in the way Neely has gone about building and managing the organization. He is a social innovator par excellence. His most radical innovation comes in staffing the entire organization not with "experts" and social workers but with ex-homeless people. Just as some organizations require a college degree, HOP requires a street degree; you must have had the practical experience of living on the streets. This even applies to Neely himself, who spent two years homeless on the streets of Los Angeles before founding HOP. To keep your job at HOP, you have to live a clean, responsible life, serving as a visible role model for other homeless people. If you have child payments, you have to make them. If you have a substance problem, you've got to stay clean. Neely has turned HOP into the elite corps of ex-homeless people in Los Angeles, almost like the Marines.

To reinforce the elite status of being part of HOP, Neely came up with the idea of the yellow shirt—a bright jersey with HOP emblazoned across the front and back. When someone walks down the street wearing a yellow HOP shirt, they get a respect that they have probably never experienced in life. The only way you can get a yellow shirt is to have it bestowed upon you by the rest of the staff, after an intense trial period of work. And no person outside of HOP can ever get a yellow shirt. The mayor of Los Angeles? Nope. The governor of California? Sorry, but no. The president of the United States? Not even. The only people who can wear the yellow shirt are those who earn it, by having been on the street, gotten off the street, and made it through the staff cut at HOP.

Those who create great organizations are early adopters, if not outright creators, of progressive management practices and mechanisms. They are like Procter & Gamble, which experimented with employee stock ownership in the late 1800s, *a hundred years* before such practices became commonplace. They are like Nordstrom, which encouraged salespeople to use their own best judgment in serving the customer, a full fifty years before the word *empowerment* was invented. They are like W. L. Gore, which experimented in the 1950s with Abraham Maslow's self-actualization concepts and a loosely coupled "lattice" organization structure, decades before these ideas were taught at business schools. Even today, W. L. Gore is a bit radical, in giving its people the power to, in essence, fire their boss, if they feel their boss is not adding value as a leader.

As we head into the new century, leaders will need to be even more innovative in how they construct and build their organizations. They will need to create mechanisms that are as radical to modern organizations as the invention of constitutional government with decentralized democratic power was to the creation of the United States in the late 1700s. What will these new mechanisms be? I can't possibly predict. That's the whole beauty of creative invention: it's inherently unpredictable. And it's up to you to apply your creative energies to creating exciting new methods and mechanisms of management.

So look at the way you spend your time. Are you creating the next great innovation, or are you creating an environment that stimulates innovation? Are you focused on what to do when your current activities become obsolete, or are you focused on building a unique culture that cannot be copied? Are you busy inventing gadgets or busy experimenting with social inventions? The next wave of enduring great institutions will not be built by technical or product visionaries but by social visionaries—those who see their organization, what it stands for, and how it operates as their ultimate creation.

12 HENRY MINTZBERG

MANAGING TO INNOVATE

*Henry Mintzberg is Cleghorn Professor of Manage-
ment Studies at McGill University in Montreal and
visiting scholar at INSEAD in Fontainebleau, France.
His research focuses on management, organization,
and strategy formation. He is the author of ten books,
including* The Structuring of Organizations,
Mintzberg on Management, The Canadian Condition, Strategy Safari, *and* Why I Hate Flying.

We talk a great deal about innovation, yet all too often we do
not manage to innovate—in both senses of the expression.
I would like to lay the blame here on "leadership" and the strategies and structures it promotes. Perhaps it is time to revert to mere
management, reconceived and reviewed.

Enough "Leadership"

In a literature that exaggerates everything, *leadership* (alongside
change and *globalization*) stands out. We crave leadership like children lost in the wilderness, convinced that if only the great hero

will appear, all our problems will magically disappear. Perhaps the opposite keeps happening because of these very cravings.

True leaders build for the long run; they stimulate the engagement of others by personal example. So they would not accept a bonus that singles themselves out, especially one that rewards efforts in the short run. By that token, we do not seem to have many leaders in our large publicly held corporations.

The separation of leadership, its isolation as something apart—individual and heroic—works against innovation. The heroic leader has to generate the great strategy, in order to gain the attention of the press and financial community so as to drive up the stock price. As a result, we get strategies as dramatic acts: the huge merger, the massive expansion, and so forth. Yet much of this hardly seems to be strategic at all. *Big* is not a strategy and *global* is not a vision. Worse, it is often antithetical to innovation, which requires careful, dedicated, and enthusiastic attention to detail—to the specifics of products and services and markets and materials—by all kinds of people in the organization. These people are not merely implementers; they are strategists too, because any really good idea can change a company—and an industry.

For example, an engineer working with Pilkington Glass got an idea for a new process to make float glass. With the support of the senior management, he worked on it for the better part of a decade. It eventually remade the company and the industry. Yet read the typical strategy textbook, and you will discover that manufacturing processes are not strategies. Strategy is about playing chess with pieces called *products* on boards called *markets*. It is supposed to be disconnected from processes down on the ground, where innovation happens.

To be innovative requires the freedom to act, in places where the detailed knowledge is held. Complex innovation usually also requires that the action be collective, in free-flowing teamwork. Yet heroic leadership centralizes; it puts undue attention on one individual and thereby implicitly disempowers everyone else—often within the rhetoric of "empowerment." Asked in an interview with *Across the Board* in 1995 if the members of the Harvard Business School "Class of '74," about whom he wrote a book, were "team players," John Kotter responded, "I think it fair to say that these people want to create the team and lead it to some glory as opposed to being a member of a team that's being driven by somebody else" (p. 80). That is not teamwork! Wanting to run the team—having to run the team—is the antithesis of teamwork.

People who lead innovative organizations behave quite differently, in my experience: they work quietly to draw out the energy in everyone else. In the words of a Japanese colleague, Kaz Mishina, they exercise "leadership in the background." These managers encourage processes that inspire people and foster teamwork, and this in turn produces the interesting innovations that become strategic.

Many years ago, Peter Drucker distinguished managers from administrators, who, he said, only work within the constraints. More recently, leaders have been distinguished from mere managers on much the same grounds. Now we seem to be headed for heroes, as distinguished from mere leaders. I would like to suggest that we return to the mere managers, so that we can tone down the rhetoric and appreciate how processes like innovation take place.

Distinguishing Innovation

We seem to confuse innovation much like we confuse leadership; the more we emphasize it, the more we trivialize it. The more we obsess ourselves with it, the less of it we seem to get.

This is probably because of our attitude to another of those fine words of management: *change*. We talk so much about change that we become numb to its absence. Contrary to the claims of what seems to be almost every speech and popular article written in this field over the last thirty years, we do not live in times of great change at all (and it is pretentious of us to believe that we can be the judge of that).

Most of the things around us are not changing. Look around yourself right now, and ask what you see that has changed significantly in recent years. The nature of your clothing? Your furniture? The car you drive? (The Ford Motor Company used this four-cycle internal-combustion technology almost a century ago.) The signs on your highway? (If you are driving in the United States, even in Silicon Valley, you use a system of measurement that was surpassed by a better one two centuries ago.) The airplane you are in? (The Comet flew with that technology in 1952.) The laptop on your desk? (The software probably yes, the hardware perhaps not for some years.) Your mobile telephone? (Sure.)

The fact is that we notice what *is* changing—something is always changing, now it happens to be information technology—and ignore the rest. Or perhaps—more accurately—we pretend the rest is changing too. In other words, we confuse *adaptation* with innovation. Oreo cookie ice cream. Or a new automobile shape, which elicits all kinds of excitement even though it performs precisely the same function in precisely the same way. We confuse fashion with innovation too.

Figure 12.1 plots the stages of design as an industry develops, from initial conception on. As has been widely documented, after usually great variety in the early life of the industry—as in automobiles a century ago and perhaps electronic publishing today—most industries settle down to a *dominant design:* that four-cycle internal combustion engine, for example, or blue jeans. Innovation, or we should say *invention*, virtually stops (or shifts to process technologies—how to make the standard product more efficiently). Eventually adaptation, more than innovation, does pick up, and so we get that new automobile body, as well as Oreo cookie ice cream.

Of course, off to the side, in niche markets, innovation may continue: we have had Wankel engines and now ones that combine battery power with gasoline firing. There are also some industries

Figure 12.1. Stages of Design

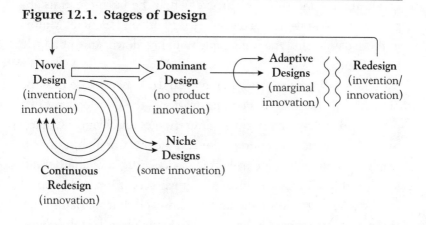

that never settle down but continue to produce a steady stream of innovation—as in software or filmmaking (at least concerning the content if not the processes of production and distribution), also pharmaceuticals, perhaps, which emerge as a steady stream of dominant designs. And every once in a while, a dominant design is reconceived through radical innovation (again, really invention, which may have started as adaptation or niche design): Pilkington's float glass process, for example, or quartz technology that changed the inside of watches.

Conventional approaches to management, including, I believe, heroic leadership, may be fine for dominant designs and adaptations of them. The work is divided into coherent categories, as in an assembly line, and the whole process is driven from the so-called top. Indeed organizing in this way almost ensures that an accepted design will remain dominant, because it does not really allow anyone to readily see the big picture. Most people are working in the little categories, and those on top of it all, so to speak, may be too distant to see any picture clearly. Hence we had decades during which the American automobile companies threw their designs "over the wall," from one category to another—styling to engineering to fabricating to assembling, and so forth—while innovation was reduced to adding fins and shifting chrome. Then the Japanese firms appeared with teamwork—a discovery for Ford and General Motors in those days!—and the walls came tumbling down, at least a little bit of them.

Teamwork is necessary when a good deal of expertise must be brought together for complex innovation—the development of a new mobile telephone or the organization of an Olympic Games. Simple innovation, in contrast, for your next toy or T-shirt, for example, can often be done by heroic leadership, but of a rather different sort: the inventor-entrepreneur who comes up with a novel idea in a field that he or she understands well. But we hardly lack for creative entrepreneurs with novel, simple ideas. It is the stimulation of teamwork needed to create truly complex innovations that is the problem.

Innovation Structure

Ask for a picture of almost any organization, and someone will hand you "The Chart": managers stacked on managers with nary a mention of real products and services, let alone the people who create them. What an awful image!

If you insist on seeing some picture to understand the operating processes, they might draw you a *chain*—everything shown as one step after the other in linear sequence, as in the *value chain* that has become so popular. A fine way to depict an assembly line perhaps, but no way to see new product development or any other process involving innovation. The chain is designed for stable, established processes, not for innovation. It is just the thing for those administrators who work within the constraints, maybe even for heroic leaders removed from everything else. The chain might also work in a pharmaceutical company, at least for the development of some new molecule into a marketable product through a series of well-defined tests. But it hardly fits the research process that gave rise to that molecule in the first place.

Figure 12.2. The Chain Chart

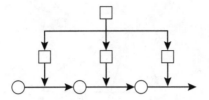

The fact is that the chart and the chain go together, right under heroic leadership, for over each link of the chain, on "top" of every step of the way, as shown in Figure 12.2, sits a manager, and over all of these managers sits a "top" manager. A manager for each and a manager for all. In other words, we make the chart by laying a chain of command over the chain of operations.

That top manager is supposed to see the big picture and come up with the strategy that connects all the pieces together—hence the need for heroic leadership. The trouble is that leaders are usually ordinary human beings, maybe even administrators at heart, rendered weaker by the myopia that comes from believing themselves to be on top of things. All too often, the only thing they are on top of is the chart. Put differently, the big picture is not there for the seeing; it has to be put together out of all the little details. As a consequence, heroic leadership, distant from the details, all too often ends up as dramatic leadership, full of sound and fury, while everyone sits below waiting for something truly significant to happen. We don't get innovation out of that.

In fact, we know what we get innovation out of: not chains, but *webs:* free-flowing networks—like structures in which people interact easily and informally. That is what allows them to resolve the tricky problems that arise during complex innovation. We accept this, yet we accept those charts too. The trouble is that the two don't go together: you can't put a web under a chain.

Figure 12.3. The Web

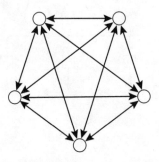

Repositioning Management

Take a look at the web depicted in Figure 12.3. Where does management come in? Where do you put it? Think about this for a minute.

Putting management on top would be silly, disconnecting it from the rich activity of the web. Putting management in the middle would not make much more sense, for that would just draw all the communication to one central point, diminishing the free flow of ideas. There is only one obvious answer. Management of the web has to be *everywhere*. In a literal sense, it has to be out of the office, down from the suite, on the floor, in the studio, with the customers, and wherever else real things are happening. It has to move around, literally and figuratively, in order to facilitate collaboration and energize the network. Management that is not everywhere in the web is nowhere.

But there is another part of the answer that is less obvious. Management also has to be *everyone*. The process has to be shared, as different people take natural responsibility for different aspects of the innovative process. Whoever draws things together, whoever takes initiative, whether it be scientist, planner, or salesperson, becomes the de facto manager for a time. Does that mean there is no role for conventional managers in the web? Not at all. It means that they have to manage in unconventional ways—at least by the standards of today's heroic leadership.

Two anecdotes from IBM illustrate the contrast. A few years ago, *Fortune* magazine wrote, "In four years Gerstner has added more than $40 billion to IBM's share value" (April 14, 1997). How extraordinary. All by himself!

More recently, an article by Gary Hamel, "Waking Up IBM," in the July-August 2000 issue of the *Harvard Business Review* suggests how some of this was actually done—specifically how IBM got into the e-business. Gerstner is hardly mentioned in this story, except at one point, almost parenthetically—but appropriately. Upon hearing about the initiative, he appreciated it immediately and encouraged it. In other words, he exercised good management (or should we say good judgment), not heroic leadership. Of course, he may well have set the tone in the corporation that enabled such a thing to happen in the first place. But that too is hardly heroic, let alone dramatic. It is merely what effective managers do.

Otherwise the process was driven—led—by two people far removed from formal leadership, a "self-absorbed programmer," who had the initial idea and had to beat all sorts of people over the head to get them to understand it, and a staff manager, who picked up the ball and somehow, with hardly any resources, stitched together the loose team of people who made it happen.

This, of course, is a classic "skunk works" story, not chainlike but one that unfolded in fits and starts, dependent on the building of a network of almost casual but energized relationships. We have all heard such stories many times. Why, then, do we insist on throwing chains of command on top of weblike processes, as some sort of wet (heavy-metal) blanket? Isn't it time we thought differently about management?

Energizing Management

Two little models of management are presented in Figures 12.4 and 12.5, a strategic model, called the *driven chain*, and an energizing model, called the *learning loops*. One is not better than the other,

Figure 12.4. Strategic Model—The Driven Chain

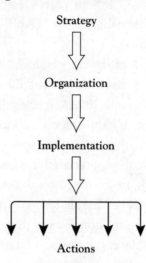

Figure 12.5. Energizing Model—The Learning Loops

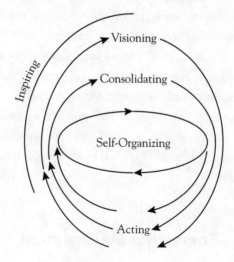

unless you wish to stimulate people to take their jobs seriously and do interesting things.

The strategic model is linear: it drives *strategy* down a chain to *organization* and then to *implementation*, which is supposed to manifest itself in a set of decomposed *actions*. Here leadership deems; everyone else acts. Notice the assumptions: the CEO *is* the corporation, everyone else being a "human resource"; that leader is a lone wolf, ultimately responsible for everything; leading means making the great decisions, formulating the grand strategies, doing the big deals; implementation follows as something apart. This may be a great way to build a dam when a hundred thousand workers have to carry rocks on their head and dump them in place (as I once saw on television), maybe also to drive that pharmaceutical molecule through development. But it is no way to stimulate innovation. Nor, perhaps, to win a war. As quoted in Smalter and Ruggles's article, "Six Business Lessons from the Pentagon," which appeared in the March-April 1966 issue of the *Harvard Business Review*, Robert McNamara, as secretary of defense at the start of the Vietnam War, said, "We must first determine what our foreign policy is to be, formulate a military strategy to carry out that policy, then build the military forces to conduct this strategy" (p. 170).

The energizing model depicts the role of management in an entirely different way. Management does not sit on top and pronounce. It surrounds process, energizes it, facilitates it, and infuses it by getting personally involved, so that people feel inspired to do good things. There is no place to start in this model, nor in the world of complex innovation, because all of this is loops within loops. *Self-organization* is key, but that is helped by a *consolidation* of experience that may eventually appear as *vision*—after the facts, as a consequence of them. Here, in other words, strategy emerges. The self-organizing stimulates *acting*, which causes reassessment of organizing, which evokes new visioning, and so on.

Such managing is better described as caring than curing—in other words, based on careful and continuous attention, not sudden and intermittent intervention. This managing is inspiring too, but not empowering, because it is based on respect for people who already know what they have to do and get supported in doing it. They don't have to be empowered.

We don't need heroic leadership, certainly not in the world of complex innovation. Merely managing to innovate should be good enough.

13 M. KATHRYN CLUBB

INVITING INNOVATION

*M. Kathryn Clubb has assisted clients as a strategy
and leadership consultant, managed a consulting
practice, and fostered executive development for over
twenty years. Most recently, she was the managing
partner of executive development at Andersen Consulting. She previously held several management positions at Northwest Airlines. She currently works as
an independent practitioner and consultant.*

Circumstances today conspire against leaders. Blurring boundaries between competitors and allies, rapid change, and the
inexorable march of new technology create vertigo in even the most
grounded executive. Most of those promoted to top jobs have en-
viable track records. So why do many very experienced, very dynamic individuals who seem to have what it takes still struggle? The
past is no longer a trusted guide to the future for senior executives.
Bold actions, innovations, and market-making moves are required
for success. However, for many executives, the very behaviors and
actions that catapulted them into high-level positions are barely
a starting point for future innovation and success. As the business

environment has changed, so have the components of effective leadership, leaving many executives struggling to lead their companies effectively.

The dilemma for executives is to find ever new ways to lead and to deliver results in a fluid, rapidly changing environment. To succeed, leaders must be willing to overhaul their perspective and skill set—both of which have served them well, albeit in different circumstances—and break the habits and mind-sets used to frame issues and actions in the past. Leaders need to lead the way in discarding long-held assumptions about how the world works and in accepting new constructs. To invite and lead innovation, what should leaders do more of, and, perhaps more important, what should they leave behind?

Understand Human Nature

First, develop a new understanding of how human nature works and why people think and act the way they do. This is a first step toward exploding limitations that keep leaders, their top teams, and their organizations from being as innovative and effective as possible.

We like to think we tackle a new challenge with objectivity. In actuality, our actions rise from years of unconscious mental programming, built almost exclusively on biases, assumptions, or ideas related to prior circumstances. These mental models may have limited relevance to and may even interfere with addressing today's possibilities. The logic is straightforward. To achieve different results, we must take different actions. Because our actions are shaped by how we see the world, to do something different we must see something different. We must question the assumptions and mental models we use to see the world, frame our thinking, and determine action. Innovation depends on it.

Although simple in the abstract, making a clean break with learned biases and behavior takes effort. Behavioral science has shown that an action, even taken once, becomes a habit that guides future action even when the results are poor. Examples are legion of leaders' sticking with a personal or organizational course of action even as changed circumstances doom the approach to failure. Additional research shows that the very threat of change causes people to cling to current patterns of action. Under perceived threat, actions—of individuals, teams, and organizations—are almost always automatic and dominated by primitive *fight or flight* reactions.

Many leaders believe that the answers to today's problems *do* lie in past actions and successes. Consider their typical responses to change initiatives: "We've always done it this way." "That's the culture around here." "It's always worked for me before." None looks at whether circumstances are different now. In fact, the degree and speed of change in business and technology make it risky to substitute mere memory—even an extensive, well-organized memory—for genuinely new thinking.

Finally, innovation only happens with learning. Although failure and setbacks provide the best opportunities to learn and change one's thinking, acknowledging that either has occurred puts leaders in a seemingly vulnerable position. The wrath of the board and shareholders, not to mention the loss of employee confidence, is simply too much to risk.

For individual leaders, this means

- Examining and challenging their own assumptions and mental models

- Understanding and overcoming their automatic reactions to perceived threats

- Being willing to be leader *and* learner

Adopt a Strategy Geared to Action

Abandon the notion that leaders can plan their way to success, and instead adopt a directionally correct strategy geared to action and adjustment by all employees.

The death knell of comprehensive multiyear strategic plans tolled throughout the last few years, as discontinuous technology change and shifting competitive rules became the norm. Indeed such plans may even blind leaders to new opportunities and tie up resources on projects that no longer make financial sense. As Sir John Browne of BP Amoco says, "No advantage and no success is ever permanent. The winners are those who keep moving." Instead of developing and managing toward a detailed plan, leaders need to articulate vivid images of the future, communicate the rationale, and encourage employee action. Dennis Bakke, CEO of the global, successful independent power producer AES, takes this approach: "We try a bunch of stuff, we see what works, and we call that our strategy." For most companies, this may be too radical, but effective leaders know that they must make space for experimentation and innovation.

There will always be people who crave certainty and detailed marching orders. But leaders must train themselves and their employees that too much direction actually limits individual innovation and speed. Leaders must demonstrate that directional strategy can guide company success, leaving selection of specific paths to executives across the company. The North Star provides an apt analogy. It offers a constant point from which to chart a course but does not obviate the need for the captain and crew to make decisions based on current sailing conditions.

So a directionally correct strategy, one that has a solid foundation but permits flexibility, can guide a company to accomplish great things. If the direction is clear and inspiring enough, employees will seize emerging opportunities and assume personal responsibility for keeping the ship on course. Leadership's challenge here is to "keep moving," to remain confident, even as the future remains uncertain and failures are inevitable as employees innovate.

For individual leaders, this means

- Creating pictures of the future that incite employees to action

- Fostering an environment where innovation and experimentation and all its results (positive and negative) are embraced as learning

- Having the ego strength to move from a style of "confident and certain" to "confident and uncertain"

- Giving up the patriarchal leadership role of having all the answers

Promote Team Behaviors Conducive to Innovation

Raise the standard of what happens when people work together, and develop new skills for encouraging innovation.

Everyone agrees that effective leadership teams are and will remain essential to organizational success. But few companies benefit all they might from teams because they set the bar too low—using teams merely to align tasks, to ensure only the absence of overlaps and gaps between team members' responsibilities. Team members, particularly members of executive teams, frequently work independently. That's unfortunate, because innovation is a more probable result when team members challenge, corroborate, and build on others' work, insights, and expertise rather than just aggregate results. Why do executive teams operate at less than full creative and innovative capacity? For several reasons:

- Executive teams share all the human foibles of individuals. In-group settings and outdated, irrelevant, or harmful assumptions about situations and people get in the way of productive working relationships. The political, emotional, and rational agendas within executive teams are real and can undercut genuine efforts at collaboration, innovation, and risk taking.

- The time required to reach the common interpretation needed for the synergistic action for broad-scale innovation is rarely available. Agendas are full and top teams are focused on other urgent activities without regard to longer-term implications.

- Most executive measurement-and-rewards systems, especially in the United States, recognize individual achievements and generally discourage risk taking. Teams may embrace the philosophy of team-based measures, but when times get tough, many executives revert to holding someone individually accountable, undercutting any incentive to maximize team results. Executives must lead and inspire those networks rather than be threatened or challenged by them.

- Bold ideas and action no longer belong solely to executives. Especially when a company is undertaking significant market, organizational, or cultural shift, innovation must emerge at all levels of the organization, making executives part of a larger leadership network that changes as conditions dictate.

Real innovations are blind to traditional organizational boundaries and rules. The responsibility of the CEO or executive team, then, includes teaming behaviors conducive to innovation. At its highest level, teaming means that all team members can be counted on to make decisions on behalf of the others and consider implications beyond their own domain. Such synergy requires superior skills among team members, specifically *ongoing dialogue*, *constructive conflict*, and *action-based learning*. The leader's role here is to notice helpful and harmful patterns of behavior and set the standard for superior teaming.

Ongoing Dialogue

Imagine an executive team making a decision that is truly innovative with implications across the company, including how people do their work. Two things are important: how the team makes the decision *and* how deeply team members understand the actions required and the implications of the decision. Like many teams, this one may debate and seemingly make decisions only to find that agreements aren't kept outside the meeting room. What's wrong? Either the decision-making process or the shared understanding of the decision is flawed. Effective dialogue, characterized by suspending judgment, articulating assumptions, listening, being curious, reflecting, and having patience, can limit such disconnects and accelerate taking action. To effectively move from innovative ideas to action requires hearing all views and examining all perspectives to understand the complexity of the situation and the appropriateness of the solution. Shared understanding breeds consistent actions. Mixed levels of understanding engender mixed actions.

Effective dialogue may seem to demand an enormous investment of time from the executive team. However, two points are important to consider:

- Making good decisions and keeping them made is more efficient in the long run, requiring less rework and adjustment as actions proceed.

- Learning these dialogue skills takes time. As the executive team becomes more skillful, the team becomes more efficient, while deepening the trust people have in one another and accelerating team effectiveness. The more important the innovation, the more important creation of shared ownership.

Constructive Conflict

The ability to generate and weigh the merits of alternative or even conflicting ideas plays a role in achieving innovation. Constructive conflict among executive team members—checking assumptions, voicing reservations, generating lots of alternatives—can prevent weak ideas from gathering momentum and can inculcate a deeper understanding of and commitment to the decisions. Unfortunately, in most corporate cultures a lot of energy is spent avoiding conflict or even the appearance of conflict. Some organizations overtly pride themselves on how quickly everyone aligns around an idea. They forget the counsel of General George S. Patton, who is reported to have said: "If everybody is thinking alike, then somebody isn't thinking."

Recent research has found that a key characteristic distinguishing high-performing teams from lesser-performing ones is the ability to generate more options. This requires time for expansive thinking and idea generation before narrowing options through analysis and evaluation. Unfettered generation of alternatives produces not only more innovative ideas but also a way to build understanding and ownership in a group.

Action-Based Learning

Experience is the best teacher in corporate environments. But experimentation to develop innovative solutions has yet to take root in the business community. Three things are generally required to embrace action-based learning:

- Put a learning spin on mistakes or take the fear out of making mistakes. Ben Zander, music director of the Boston Philharmonic, says, "How fascinating!" when the sound produced was not as expected. Expressing curiosity rather than blaming invites learning.

- Take the right action for the moment. Rarely must the next step be "bet the farm." Testing new actions or ideas in one part of the business can limit organizational risk.

- Act before it is comfortable. Even when the decision has been properly made and all perspectives and facts uncovered, uncertainty lingers. The only way to see the result is to take the first step.

Leaders must lead by doing and communicate that they are trying something new, for good, articulated reasons. Acknowledging their own trials and learning also signals to employees that experimentation is valued, encouraging a more innovative, action-oriented environment throughout the organization.

For individual leaders, this means

- Setting a new standard for teaming, and investing time and attention to make that new standard a reality.

- Acknowledging not knowing or not having the answers. What does the question imply? How many ways could we answer the question?

- Encouraging sufficient, creative dialogue on actions that require broad ownership and common interpretation.

- Acknowledging publicly lessons learned through setbacks and surprises.

Make Sure the Organization Has Both Structure and Adaptability

Create an environment that encourages innovation in support of the organization's goals and is flexible enough to change.

An organization is a fabric of structures, practices, norms, informal rules, and culture that influences behavior. Consistency and synergy among these elements increase the likelihood of achieving the directional strategy. Two powerful factors influencing company success are the organizational structure and performance measures and the incentives—two well-known *change levers*. They are important, but the key to using each to encourage innovation is to uncover unstated assumptions and embedded beliefs that may no longer apply.

Most corporations unconsciously overemphasize organizational structure, believing that it clarifies purpose and responsibility.

Organizations invent structures and imbue them with meaning and authority, translating over time into permanence and rigidity. Organizations are nothing more than agreed-on patterns of activity and communication that warrant routine review to ensure that they are serving, not inhibiting, organizational purpose.

As organizations flatten and people job-hop, structure has lost much of its potency to clarify purpose and a path to career success. Structure is necessary, just like the skeleton in people, but it reveals little about how the company really works and is never the whole story. To support innovation, work environments must become more fluid and adaptable to shifting situations. Leading thinking about organizations envisions a more organic structure than the hierarchical forms currently in use. The future organization will undoubtedly be more oriented around *energy sources* (tasks, ideas, or people) that quicken the pulse of organization.

Performance metrics and incentives affect every employee, but many companies fail to develop measures that both match current business reality and motivate desired results and behavior. Learning how metrics affect the business takes time. People generally perform as measured, and the unintended impact surfaces only after the chosen metrics have been in place for some time.

Some companies are experimenting with metrics to influence other conditions as well. For example, the Men's Wearhouse has developed metrics that encourage a team approach to sales. While paying commissions to individuals based on sales, Men's Wearhouse also monitors transactions for each salesperson in a store to see whether salespeople are sharing walk-in traffic. The company is serious about this; it fired a top-selling salesperson who undercut the team approach. What was the impact? Same-store average sales and transactions per employee rose after his departure. What's the lesson? Look not only at the results but also at the behaviors that metrics are encouraging.

For individual leaders, this means

- Examining supporting mechanisms and determining whether they are really supporting innovation

- Taking a learning approach toward metrics, and altering them to support changing internal and external conditions

---

Today's leaders must deliver big results while navigating an ever-changing, volatile business climate. Success depends largely on their willingness to change how they approach their job—assumptions used to define opportunities, extent of reliance on a team for innovation, comfort with setting directional strategies and giving employees the authority to invent new ways of achieving them, and attention paid to creating an environment that motivates innovation. Although change takes effort and tenacity, the possibilities of innovation provide enormous rewards for leaders.

14 DOROTHY A. LEONARD
WALTER C. SWAP

THE VALUE OF "BEEN THERE, DONE THAT" IN INNOVATION

Dorothy A. Leonard is the William J. Abernathy Professor of Business Administration at Harvard Business School, where she has taught since 1983. Her research, teaching, and consulting focus on the management of knowledge and innovation, with particular emphasis on communication and human behavior. Author of two books, Wellsprings of Knowledge: Building and Sustaining the Sources of Innovation *and (with Walter C. Swap)* When Sparks Fly: Igniting Creativity in Groups, *she has also published over 100 articles, book chapters, and field-based cases.*

Walter C. Swap is professor of psychology at Tufts University, where he chaired the Psychology Department and was Dean of the Colleges. His research interests include group dynamics, attitudes and attitude change, altruism, and creativity. He is coauthor (with Dorothy A. Leonard) of When Sparks Fly: Igniting Creativity in Groups, *and the editor of* Group Decision Making, *as well as the author of numerous articles in scholarly journals.*

I n the Western world, we are programmed to believe that *new* always equals *better*. For years, we have seen triumphs of new technical, scientific, and medical knowledge. It is not surprising, then, that our faith in the power of infant industries or technologies sometimes overshoots reality. In our infatuation with the new, we forget that innovation often involves the creative recombination of extant ideas with new ones and the fusion of existing expertise with new knowledge. In fact, the wisdom of those who have "been there and done that" can add creativity and impulse to new endeavors—if the fusion of knowledge is managed for innovation.

Creativity, as we have written in our 1999 book, *When Sparks Fly: Igniting Creativity in Groups,* is a process of developing and expressing novel ideas that are likely to be useful. *Innovation* is the embodiment of such ideas into valued new products, processes, or services. In this chapter, we focus on the front end of the creativity-innovation process, where the composition of the founding team and the interactions of its members critically influence the paths taken toward success or failure. We draw on recent observations from an acknowledged hothouse for innovation, California's Silicon Valley, where we spent months interviewing and observing creative groups starting up some of the new businesses that are forming the new economy. These groups typically combine the technical wizardry of founders who are making their first forays into entrepreneurship with the expertise of experienced entrepreneurs turned coach or mentor. The difficult, eclectic, exhilarating partnerships between these groups of individuals offer interesting insights into the creative process and some object lessons about the value of expert mentoring for innovation of any kind, in any organization.

Designing a Group for Creativity

Popular advice for managers who wish to think out of the box, create new paradigms—choose your cliché—is to assign people to the problem who know nothing about prior attempts, "because they won't know it can't be done." There is a certain logic to this advice. Our thinking is often constrained by rigid assumptions, lack of vision, or timid aspirations. However, the mix of hindsight and foresight represents one type of intellectual diversity that can aid the creative process. The collision of ideas that arises from blending varied perspectives can lead to the consideration of more options—and then better decisions. These varied perspectives may come from different *know-what* (from experience or education), *know-how* (from thinking-style preferences or from using different processes), and *know-who* (from personal networks). In the Silicon Valley start-up businesses, we find team members drawing on all three sources of diversity.

For example, the Generation-X entrepreneurs building businesses on Internet real estate have a better grasp than their elders, in general, of possible market appeal and uses of the Web. But they often lack even the most elementary knowledge about legal and accounting processes (know-what), the sequencing of steps in the start-up process (know-how), or contacts to recruit and raise money (know-who). Nor have they enough management experience and political savvy to handle interpersonal problems with partners, directors, or staff or to negotiate with vendors, investors, and customers. If you follow the progress of a successful Silicon Valley start-up from its inception in the dorm room of a few twenty-somethings until it hits the front page of the *Wall Street Journal* (preferably as a success story), you will find a surprising number of behind-the-scenes actors with gray hair. Scott Cook had Bill Campbell's wisdom to help him at Intuit, and Randy Paynter at tiny Care2 could rely on Fern Mandelbaum to guide him through the start-up process. These mentors and coaches are usually former entrepreneurs who provide hard-won expertise in the process of innovation because they know what doesn't work as well as what does. By coaching inexperienced entrepreneurs, they help fuel the phenomenal amount of innovative activity always present in Silicon Valley today.

This melding of entrepreneurial expertise with New Age know-how is an example of what we call *creative fusion*. Creative fusion is critical for innovation because it is impossible for one person to have enough depth of expertise in enough different fields to originate a full menu of options from which to select. This is increasingly true in an ever more complex world. We just don't have many Leonardo da Vincis around anymore—and today even he would likely have to work as part of a team. So rather than dismissing experience as the enemy of innovation, consider blending different kinds of expertise for greater innovation. Some of the dotcom failures that we have witnessed in the recent past make a good case for the importance of creative fusion. The gray hairs might have saved the crewcuts from learning the bitter lessons of their inexperience.

Let us digress a moment to consider how people gain expertise. This process limits the ability to quickly transfer that expertise from master to understudy and thus dictates the design of creative teams.

The Nature of Expertise

True expertise, as contrasted with competence, takes about ten years to develop. Of course, history provides some examples of true in-born genius, but even chess prodigy Bobby Fischer required nine years of intense preparation to become a true expert. Even the most gifted must practice, practice, practice: there are no expert-to-novice mind-melds to short-circuit the process. This is not to say that anyone can develop expertise through diligence; rather, between two people of equal natural ability, the one who becomes more expert is the one who engages in the activity more, be it music composition or law or entrepreneurship. Expertise is developed through learning-by-doing.

Second, experts make decisions largely through the recognition of patterns, situations they have encountered before that they can integrate with information from the current context. They then can extrapolate from the patterns to anticipate and evaluate the results from various alternative actions. Listen to an expert coach for start-up businesses, Fred Luconi, talk about how he helps:

> You have these models that you carry around. . . . You have hired, promoted and fired hundreds of people in your life, you have seen the way it looks during the interview, you have seen the way people do and don't tell you certain things in the referencing process; you have seen how people are either political or nonpolitical. . . . Entrepreneurs confuse people who are interested [in their products or services] with people who actually put down money and buy. . . . After awhile, you say about a given situation: "that's going to be one of these"; . . . you can project what's going to happen. You have to have lived through all of those to have a gut sense of which things have a chance of succeeding, which are going to be difficult and which are impossible. If you don't have [a mental] model, you don't have a framework to react instinctively. You have to be careful to make sure your models are up to date and they are still relevant. . . . But the more you see, the more it's the same. . . . There are differences, in the current economy clearly—that's what makes it interesting. . . . But there are an awful lot of [familiar] dynamics going on.

It is always possible, of course, that experts will extrapolate incorrectly, misguided by a few familiar cues into believing that they have identified a well-known pattern. But such errors will occur only when the ground well trodden by the experts has in fact fundamentally shifted because of technological, social, or economic change—and they are insensitive to the shift. Seasoned entrepreneurs who have "been there," observing perhaps thousands of patterns, become experts in the *process of innovation,* which is inherently flexible and open to constant learning, so their expertise leads them to expect change.

These two characteristics of expertise—the ten-year rule and pattern recognition based on experience—both constrain the ability to transfer expertise. One might think that experts could simply provide rules to guide novices, but it is very difficult to reduce an expert's knowledge to a set of general rules, as so much depends on context. Experts can certainly provide rules of thumb. Coaches for start-up teams have a remarkably similar set of admonitions for budding entrepreneurs, for example, "focus, focus, focus." However, experts realize when exceptions must be made, that such general rules don't fit every situation. When, for example, would exclusively focusing on one particular market be premature? Only the expert recognizes the context, the pattern that directs the application of the rule—or suggests exceptions. Moreover, an expert is not always able to articulate the reasoning behind a conclusion, as it is not a linear process of logically connecting a string of assumptions, causes, and effects but a recognition of a familiar, holistic system. Expertise therefore has many tacit dimensions that are hard to separate from the person—and that makes it hard to transfer.

Because the nature of expertise sets limits not only on how many different kinds of expertise any one person can possess but also on how quickly expertise can be transferred, we see many different models being tried for accelerating innovation by *assembling* experts, then *fusing* their knowledge to create new products, services, or companies.

Assembling Expertise for Creative Fusion

The starting point for assembling the diverse sources of expertise that promote divergent thinking and therefore likely lead to innovative options is know-who—the knowledge networks available to the core innovation team. There is great value in being able to reach beyond the insular bounds of an organization to pull in disparate knowledge assets from outside, and the inhabitants of Sili-

con Valley seem to have their antennae constantly up for new contacts to enrich their individual communities. In the United States,
we are moving toward identifying more closely with our professional
clans than with any particular organization—that is, a technically
capable individual is likely to move from corporation to corporation, sometimes with a few selected professional acquaintances,
without any expectation of spending more than a few years with any
one business. The social capital that develops in this peripatetic career is an important asset because the personal network defines one's
ability to reach beyond one's own knowledge base to access different forms of expertise. In one promising young company, the CEO
asks prospective hires a question he regards as critical to understanding the applicant's knowledge assets, "Who do you know?" The
CEO wants to know whether prior work and personal experiences
provide the applicant with a rich knowledge network. Even more
important is finding out if the applicant actively nurtures the network—not just to exploit it but also to contribute knowledge to it.
The wider the access represented by the aggregated individual networks of the employees, the greater the potential for innovation
within the company.

Entrepreneurial teams use their cumulative know-who to col-
lect the right blend of expertise—either informally or with the help
of assembly houses being set up specifically for the purpose. The
need to stake claims in the new-economy land rush spurred growth
in the informal, cottage industry of *mentor capitalists*, although there
have always been "smart angels" around to coach entrepreneurs.
Mentor capitalists differ from venture capitalists in that they aggregate in informal groups instead of formal partnerships, invest
their own money rather than monies from a pooled fund, and usually invest—if ever—only after they have spent time working with
the start-ups. As one mentor capitalist told us, "Engagement comes
first—then money, rather than vice versa, as with the venture capitalists." These experienced, "cashed-out" entrepreneurs have
enough money and time to coach inexperienced entrepreneurial

teams, and they constitute themselves in groups of complementary skill sets. If one is especially good at structuring early processes, another may be able to guide the discovery of the market "sweet spot." Much (but not all) of the knowledge flows in one direction: experienced coaches to entrepreneurs, partly because mentor capitalists and venture capitalists alike have the power of the purse, and investments must be protected by sound business strategies. However, the coaches provide resources and guide the *process of discovery* more than they directly advise about courses of action. In the final analysis, decisions about the nature of the business have to be made by the entrepreneurs themselves.

Most striking is the variety of roles that these coaches play in the innovation process. True, some of these roles can be found in the history of many successful innovations—including those inside large organizations. Like any good innovation sponsor, the coach provides resources as well as protection for a while for the fledgling endeavor and helps in strategy. However, these entrepreneurial coaches dig into their personal experience to give a remarkable amount of psychological support and—even more important—to guide the process of sculpting the business concept from its original form into one more likely to succeed. Because innovation necessarily involves enormous uncertainty, the coaches work tirelessly with their teams to try, test, and learn—to experiment within focused bounds with different versions of the product and various classes of customer. In one of the small start-ups we have been observing, under the guidance of two mentor capitalists the business concept shifted from business-to-consumer to business-to-business, the customers changed from a public-safety market to insurance and auctions, and the hardware part of the business was abandoned— all in the space of six months. The coaches thus guided their team away from the shoals upon which so many Internet start-up businesses foundered.

Guided by experience, the coaches always *expect* multiple iterations of the business concept, plan for its evolution, and are not discouraged by exploratory probes. This expertise in the *process* of innovation is enormously helpful in accelerating the maturation of the entrepreneurs and their endeavor. And although the protégés certainly do not become experts overnight, they are fairly launched on entrepreneurial careers.

During 1999 and 2000, we saw the startling growth (and sometimes almost immediate demise) of businesses that purport to provide all the in-house expertise needed to jump-start new businesses. These *incubators* or *accelerators* represented a wide range of models, ranging from those who were mostly landlords, giving entrepreneurs physical space and a few basic services in exchange for equity, to those that, like the mentor capitalists, provided hands-on coaching and access to people with decades of experience in business. One-stop shopping for innovation! Inexperienced entrepreneurs obtained help with polishing their presentations for venture capitalists, recruiting, legal issues—all kinds of professional services. The ultimate test of any such knowledge assembly for the purpose of innovation is the quality of the expertise aggregated. Certainly, the provision of aggregated services can aid and even accelerate the launch of a new business. However, even those that still exist have dropped the name *incubator* and have changed their own value propositions, at least in part because they lacked expertise. If designed with enough access to experienced entrepreneurs, accelerators may be a creative fusion model for other innovation situations, such as spinouts from large companies and mergings of acquired companies, but the concept is still evolving.

Managing Creative Fusion

One of the challenges to managing creative fusion is that experts have to work together in an atmosphere of mutual respect and trust, or else heat rather than light will be the result. In the case of our Silicon Valley start-ups, the coaches have to respect the fact that these barely postpubescent entrepreneurs have some expertise too.

They actually have years of experience with precursors of the Internet, with playing and modifying video games, with programming,
and with their immersion in a culture of on-line exchange. Years
from now, their current expertise will prove to have been shallow
as society grows an entire new on-line ecology, but today they know
as much as anyone about this evolving world. And for their part,
the inexperienced entrepreneurs have to realize that their knowledge is insufficient for growing a business, regardless of the brilliance
of their ideas. Not only has human behavior not been fundamentally altered by the latest greatest technology (and therefore their
elders have some wisdom about managing people), but there are
some essential and immutable patterns to shaping ideas and building businesses.

We found that the more successful and lasting teams were ones
in which mentors and protégés shared values and objectives. For example, they had to agree whether they were building a business for
quick sale—or for long-term value. And given that the primary motive was to build something of lasting value, founders generally had
to accept the high likelihood that they would eventually have to
step aside in favor of more experienced managers. The matching
process was intuitive and voluntary, unlike some official mentoring
programs in companies, where the partnering is forced. (Research
suggests that mentoring always works best when mentor and pro-
tégé mutually select.) Both coaches and entrepreneurs talked about
the necessity for "good chemistry."

Because the objective of creative fusion is innovation, none of
the experts is likely to be able to exactly predict the ultimate outcome of their endeavors—or even to lay out the exact steps to success. Rather, creative fusion requires a collaborative process of
mutual learning-by-doing. Experts engaged in the process of innovation have to conduct joint explorations of the new space with
their junior partners, drawing not only on their own deep knowledge but also on that of their fellow explorers. The experts have to
teach one another and learn from one another. They have to be

concerned with the process of efficient, smart experimentation. Guiding this learning process is what the best innovation coaches do so well. Rather than trying to *tell* the entrepreneurs exactly what will result from a given action, they ask questions until the entrepreneurs see the pitfall themselves. Or the coach will launch the entrepreneur on a voyage of self-discovery: "Go talk to the customers," or "Go see my friend X, who has twenty-five years' experience in this kind of retailing."

Silicon Valley culture has supported intelligent risk taking since the early days of Hewlett-Packard, and stories abound about both flops and triumphs—sometimes by the same entrepreneur. This nurturing, mentoring attitude is by no means soft, however. It is performance based, and the mentors can be brutal in their assessments. Deliver or you are out (or deliver and you may delay the inevitable CEO succession as the company scales). But mentor capitalists also appreciate the value of *failing forward*—regarding failure as a learning experience rather than a disgrace (so long as it isn't endlessly repeated). Many of the coaches have a few scars from their own falls from grace. Their balance between encouragement and honest evaluation separates the innovation stars from those who have neither the talent nor the heart for the race.

This kind of mentor-protégé relationship is so obviously critical in starting new businesses that one wonders why it is so rare in other innovation situations. There are many instances, of course, of sponsors in large organizations who support and shield innovative subordinates. But the deliberate, well-established innovation apprenticeship served by inexperienced entrepreneurs in Silicon Valley seems in a class by itself.

Lessons from the Valley

We derive two general lessons from the observations of Silicon Valley start-ups and the relationship between mentors and inexperienced entrepreneurs. The first is that experience-based expertise has great value for creative fusion, yet its power is underestimated in many innovation situations. The second is that expert innovators can pass along their knowledge best by guiding others through the experience of self-discovery. Although there is no shortcut to gaining expertise, practice, experimentation, and exploration guided by knowledgeable people who have "been there and done that" do accelerate learning. All managers who wish to enhance the innovative capability of their organizations could profit from emulating the Silicon Valley apprenticeships.

15 ROBERT E. KNOWLING JR.

LEADING WITH VISION, STRATEGY, AND VALUES

Robert E. Knowling Jr. is chairman, president, and CEO of Internet Access Technologies. Previously, he was chairman, president, and CEO of Covad Communications, executive vice president of US West, vice president of network operations for Ameritech, and lead architect on Ameritech's reengineering breakthrough development team. He serves on the board of directors for Hewlett-Packard, Ariba, Broadmedia, and the Juvenile Diabetes Foundation International.

I'll admit it—I'm a little leery of management change consultants and experts, who have inundated the market with scores of books and an endless train of seminars that attract corporate leaders searching for the ultimate answer to leading and managing the organization. The endless pursuit to find the miracle solution simply points to the reality that there isn't one solution that fits everyone. Most leaders create their own style by distilling the "best practices" of mentors, peers, and sometimes management consultants. So here is my best-practice strategy for leading a company to success.

Start with a Clear Vision and Strategy

It must start with clarity around vision and strategy in order for any management process to have any chance for success. It can't be just clarity at the top level; it must be clear and strong enough to be internalized throughout the rank and file. The leader must articulate a compelling vision and a strategy to achieve that vision at all levels. In addition, the organization's commitment to the vision and strategy must be supported by the leader with a commitment of resources, a reward and recognition system that is aligned with the strategy, and management attention to the various elements of the strategy. And all of these things have to be visible to the employee body at large. How often have you heard the woes of the CEO who can't find any traces of the corporate vision at the front line of the organization? Just because the strategy updates are facilitated via typical management retreats once or twice a year does not mean that the vision has been embraced by employees, which begs the question of just how committed the senior leaders of the boss are and why they have failed to communicate very important visions and strategy information to the rank and file. People emulate their leaders, and if the vision is not real with the boss, then it's not real with the subordinate. The absence of a motivating vision and a strategy to achieve business success yields a company that has questionable focus and purpose. In fact, the enterprise is probably operating in a state of transactional behavior that only achieves success through luck, or they have the great fortune of operating and existing in a market with pent-up demand. In either case, the success is momentary and unsustainable.

My career has spanned two *Fortune* 500 firms where I served in several managerial capacities and eventually in the most senior executive positions. In addition, I've been the CEO at two start-up firms. The approach to visioning and developing the strategy has been the same regardless of the size of the enterprise or the type of business. I start the visioning process with my direct report team. I typically spend a few days with the senior team talking about what we want our company to look like in five years. How successful will our business be? What will the corporate culture be like? How will the business be viewed in the industry? Thinking about what future success looks like is the catalyst for visioning. In this session we take the time to put some stakes in the ground around vision and strategy. To do that, I put every member of the team through a writing exercise. I ask them to write an article about the business as if it would be read in a major business publication such as *Forbes*, *Fortune*, or *Business Week*. The only ground rule is that for the purpose of the exercise, it is now five years later, and I want them to envision the state of the business and how success has been achieved. I then have the senior leaders stand up and read their stories to the rest of the team. Based on their envisioning of the future and my own article, I go off on my own and prepare a collective view of the future. From that visioning session, I now have the groundwork to craft the vision for the organization. The strategy that follows the vision is then fairly easy to create, as everything that we do has to move us closer to the aspirational goal of what we want the business to become.

Formulate a Common Set of Values

The next component I normally address is the formation of shared values. Here again, the senior leaders and I spend time off-site, away from the business, debating our respective points of view on what the shared values should be. Our attention to this is perhaps one of the most important things that we do as a leadership team. These values should represent the criteria by which we will make hiring choices, promote people, reward and recognize people, and—one of the most important considerations—evaluate the performance of individuals.

The next step is a little trickier. You have to figure out how to introduce the values to the organization without this looking and feeling like "another program." To that end, I like to bring the entire executive team of directors and above together for a two-day meeting where the vision, strategy, and values are presented, discussed, and experienced. During the strategy session, we allow the strategy to be debated in a spirited fashion. One of the dangers in doing this is that the strategy could change as a result of the input, and the leader has to be prepared for that. In one case, the input only enhanced what we had agreed on as a senior team.

For example, we put a lot of clarity around our product offerings, yet we also made the tough choice of not putting energy around one product that Wall Street was excited about more than we were. In another example, one of the values that we established was the commitment to the communities in which we conducted our business. My fear was that of all the values, this one had the least chance of being embraced. So during the session, we took everyone out for an extended visit to a school to work one-on-one with the kids. The experience was powerful. Lives were touched. The company made a long-term commitment to this school, and its students will be forever changed. The lives of over 150 executives were opened to a new realm of commitment and consciousness, but even more important, the buy-in to the value was more than just words.

The director-and-above group is then given a chance to go back and replicate the two days of strategy, alignment, and focus in the business with their people. In fact, this process of bringing the management team together and training them to teach and coach their teams through the same experience is a common practice that I embrace. It provides consistency in messages, and it's a great leadership development tool.

Invest in People

Incidentally, I should highlight another value that has been endorsed at each company I've led: "investing in the development of our people." How many organizations can assert that their managers can get up in front of their people and teach? Couple that with the fact that the teachable points of view are about vision, strategy, and values and what they mean to the leaders of the organization. This has been a very rewarding business practice, as it will turn line managers into coaches and leaders.

Once you do these kinds of things in the leadership-and-development arena, you can't let this become a onetime event. Jack Welch of General Electric has ingrained in my mind that repetition is key to learning and embracing change. For this reason, I make it a habit to bring leaders together to ensure consistency in messaging, focus, and alignment.

As I said at the beginning, my management methodology can be summed up best as a compilation of best practices that I have taken the liberty of adopting from various leaders whom I have admired over my professional career. A best practice that I have borrowed from Jac Nasser, the CEO at Ford, is to communicate occasionally with the entire workforce via e-mail. I was impressed that Nasser makes this commitment to the employees at Ford every Friday, regardless of where he is in the world. The methodology is very random, and although the message can be a state-of-the-business update on one day, I also use this vehicle to address rumors or talk about why the stock price is rising (yes, people want a reason for why things are going so well) or falling. (Perhaps more attention is paid to my notes when the stock price is falling.) I've used the process to thank the entire company for stellar performance or just to wish people a safe and happy Halloween. Labor Day has special significance to me, so I want to always send out a note that day. I never miss Mother's Day or Father's Day to salute the great men and women in the company for all their hard work and personal sacrifices in helping me build the company. This single action has taken my relationship with my employees to a different level of trust, engagement, and openness.

I also use Jack Welch's nine-cell succession-planning model to regularly assess our high-potential performers and to plan rotational assignments for people in the business. This GE best practice is replicated all the way down to frontline management. I like to do two succession reviews per year at every level in the business. Speaking of levels, I like to have a three-layer structure throughout my companies, and that is a best practice that I learned from the best CEO I ever had the pleasure of working for, Dick Notebaert, the former CEO of Ameritech. I could talk about dozens of traits in my management methodology that I have copied from Dick. He has taught me more about how to lead with courage and conviction than anyone.

Use a Common Set of Metrics

The last perspective that I would offer is that the leader must align the business around a common set of metrics that will ensure business success.

I routinely follow up the vision, strategy, and values workshops with a workshop focusing on *value drivers*. This is a concept that I learned from Larry Seldon, a finance professor at Columbia School of Business. Larry is renowned for his work with several great firms in his concept of value drivers, which means that there are probably three to five metrics in a business that when aggregated spell out the success or failure of the business. In a package goods industry, the value driver can probably be summed up into a few metrics, like cases produced per day/cases delivered per day/cases boxed per day/cases sold per day. In a service delivery business, the metric could be items installed or delivered per day/items processed per day. An airline might find merit in getting everyone focused on seats filled per flight and on-time departures. When you take these metrics and add them up, they can easily be translated into revenue; sales; cost; earnings before interest, taxes, depreciation, and amortization (EBITDA); and so forth. The key is that the high corporate metric has to be something that can be disaggregated to mean something to the frontline employee and supervisor. This provides the organization the opportunity to see how what they do every day at the front line of the business really counts. It is tragic when employees have no idea how their performance mattered for that day. Again, in this workshop, we prepared leaders with the data and information so there can be total alignment in the business at every level. The charge for the group is to go back into the organization and teach the concepts to their subordinates.

There are no silver bullets in innovative leading, and there are no canned recipes for leading and managing change. Vision, strategy, and the embracement of values fuel an organization, and one must never forget the human connection in that process. My tour of duty in leading a business has been very rewarding, and although there are lows mixed in with the highs, building a business with integrity, purpose, and care requires that you embrace and support the human issues. Larry Bossidy of Allied Signal probably said it best: "I bet on people, not strategies."

16 JAMES BURKE

WHEN 1 + 1 = 3

James Burke has produced and hosted television series for the BBC and others on the history of science and technology for thirty years. He has received the Royal Television Society's Gold Medal and an Emmy nomination. The author of eight best-selling books, he writes a monthly column in Scientific American *and is a frequent lecturer at corporations and universities.*

As the pace of technological innovation and its social consequences have quickened over the centuries, managing change has presented a growing challenge for several reasons: the basically serendipitous process of innovation, our view of knowledge (what it is, who gets it), and above all the increasingly interactive nature of the community. This complexifying situation adds to the already difficult problem of planning from inside the box. Not only is your field often diversifying in unexpected ways, but growing interference (from what used to be unrelated external factors) has added to the confusion.

How Knowledge Advanced Historically

A fairly typical historical example of this process illustrates how difficult it can be to second-guess events accurately: in mid-nineteenth-century England, as the lighting and heating market begins to saturate, coal-gas manufacturers are looking for ways to diversify. At the time, they are dumping tons of coal tar, the by-product of gaslight production. A separate (and until this moment, unrelated) problem is the disastrous effect of malaria on British colonial administration staff in India. The best antimalaria drug, South American quinine, is rare and expensive. Finding ways to transplant and relocate the cinchona plant (from which quinine is extracted) might be the coming business opportunity to watch for. However, in search of an alternate (and cheaper) source of the medicine, chemist William Perkin is seeking a way to make artificial quinine from the free coal tar by-product being thrown away by the gaslight makers. He fails to do so but instead accidentally derives the first artificial aniline dye. Dyes may be the new major business opportunity to watch for, until a German medical researcher accidentally drops some of the new colorant into a petri dish containing a culture and discovers that the dye preferentially stains and kills certain bacilli. Chemotherapy goes on to develop a world market. But who could have foreseen it? Gaslight makers knew nothing about quinine botanists, who knew nothing about dye chemists, who knew nothing about bacteriologists.

The history of technology shows, I believe, a clear-cut route back to the origin of these kinds of esoteric complications. The first and most basic trigger is the prehistoric flint tool. Its first application changed lunch from berries and dirt to mammoth filet mignon and at a stroke generated the hierarchical decision-making structure and division of labor that still organize the modern world. At the top, a man-with-a-plan (a leader) emerged, who organized the hunt, aided by executives who carried out the strategy required to trap and kill the animal, using hunting and butchering tools provided by the tribe's flint-knapping lab technicians. With the consequent major improvement in diet, the community survived and multiplied. And as the population grew larger, it became reliant for food on the success of the technicians in developing more effective tools and (when the community eventually became big enough to need room to expand into the hunting grounds of other groups) more effective weapons.

Key in the development of these artifacts was the simultaneous emergence of the means to teach flint-tool manufacture with language, which, like the toolmaking activity it mediated, was precise and sequential. In time, under the Greeks, language itself became a tool for cutting up thought (through the process of logic, with which you could innovate by putting two things you knew together to reveal a third thing you didn't know—for example, stars give off light; light comes from fires; *ergo* stars are on fire).

Fast-forward to the eventual ripple effect of these simple beginnings. In the West, by the late fifteenth century the man-with-a-plan is a government or early capitalist venture, run by the small (1 percent) literate minority and serviced by an even smaller number of logic-wielding descendants of the flint-toolmakers: noodler specialists in botany, medicine, agriculture, theology, astrology, architecture, engineering, hydraulics, metallurgy, and little else. Each noodler discipline is incomprehensible to the others, and all are organized into guilds to keep what they know secret from everyone but guild members. All of these specialists are to a greater or lesser extent dependent on what few examples of ancient Greek knowledge have earlier been imported to medieval Europe from sources in the Arab world.

Then Columbus rediscovers America, and things go to hell in a handbasket—first, because America isn't in the Bible (so what's it doing there?), and second, neither are all those new transatlantic animals and plants (so who created them?). If neither of these questions can be satisfactorily answered, how trustworthy can any knowledge be? The epistemological rug has been pulled out from under.

The New Noodlers and New Ways of Advancing Knowledge

In the intellectual panic that follows, French noodler René Descartes comes up with a way of thinking problems through without error by reducing each to its simplest component parts. Descartes' reductionism kick-starts science and the modern world of hi-tech arcana, where success has come to mean this: knowing more and more about less and less and inventing vocabulary so esoteric that only the infield specialists can explain what it means and in this way become indispensable. Thanks to Descartes, knowledge proliferates and differentiates. By 1970, for instance, the single, medieval discipline of botany has split to become botany, biology, organic chemistry, histology, embryology, evolutionary biology, physiology, cytology, pathology, bacteriology, urology, ecology, population genetics, and zoology (and since 1970, who knows . . .).

Today, as a result of this constant fissioning of knowledge and expertise into sub- and sub-sub-disciplines, even the noodlers don't know what's going on at the next workbench, where people are scratching their heads at matters so esoteric that nobody else knows what they're up to, until their gizmo hits the marketplace. Faced with the resultant avalanche of unexpected innovation, the average modern-technology user, both corporate and individual, too often reacts like the depressive who gets a few days away from the clinic. He goes to the beach to get himself a tan. A couple of days later, his psychiatrist back at the hospital gets a postcard from the depressive. The message on the card reads much like the average user's reaction to high rates of technological change: "Having a wonderful time. Why?"

Things are not helped by the lingering predilections of most modern businesses for the trick invented in the eighteenth century by British economist Adam Smith: the division of labor—which dealt brilliantly with the threat of chaos and confusion in manufacturing when the new steam-power, factory production capabilities met head-to-head with the manual, cottage industry techniques of the earlier agricultural age. Over the intervening two-and-a-half centuries since then, the division of labor has served all aspects of industry well by divisionalizing corporate activity in the classic reductionist way.

However, the coming information technologies will rapidly make the division of labor obsolete, as networking makes it easier for individuals to make valuable use of the *penumbra* (the shadowy area) of informal experience that surrounds each individual's core competence. In a reductionist world, separated (thanks to technological limitations) into isolated silos of expertise, only core competence was valid. There was no technology (and perhaps also no need) to make use of the more experiential talents of the individual.

It is nearly always in these shadowy areas, located around the individual's discipline focus, that innovation emerges. The basic process of innovation seems to be the way in which novelty occurs when things, or ideas, overlap, coming together in new ways. When that happens, the rules of math change, and 1 + 1 = 3 occurs, to make the result more than the sum of the parts. A simple historical example illustrates the idea: the nineteenth-century German engineer Wilhelm Maybach, working for Daimler, puts together the perfume spray and gasoline and comes up with the carburetor.

This juxtapositional event should be no surprise, as it appears to conform with the operating mode of the extraordinarily interactive human brain, composed of one hundred billion neurons, each linked by up to fifty thousand dendrites, each capable of linking to fifty thousand other dendrites, indicating a possible total number of ten trillion cerebral connections. This means that the number of ways a signal (a thought) can go in the brain is greater than the number of atoms in the known universe. Data in the brain seem to be connected all with all.

The evolutionary value of such a system is obvious: its immense connective potential makes it easy to run scenarios in real time so as to make the kind of decision that could in some cases be survival-critical. Less life-or-death versions of these exercises are variously described as "innovative" or "imaginative" thinking.

According to major thinkers like Einstein, innovative ideas tend to be generated when the brain is operating in what might be called *penumbra mode:* defocused rather than concentrated in the linear style initially triggered by the nature of language, reinforced by Descartes' straight-line reductionism, and facilitated by technologies designed to operate in similarly sequential ways.

Unfortunately, in capturing these innovative products of the brain, so that they might profitably be put to use, corporations and communities have tended to act in ways (reasonable enough, given the contemporary system limits) that stifle the inventive process at birth, because if any new idea works well, to keep it safe, it is protected by being institutionalized. If the idea enhances profits, or potential market growth, or community well-being, the last thing anybody wants to do is to put it at risk. So it is ring fenced. This, ironically, protects it from the very same unstable, indefinable, unquantifiable, risk-associated environment from which it has emerged. In plain language, companies and communities take innovative risks in order to develop ways of enhancing their output, and as soon as they have succeeded in this attempt, they stop taking risks. Conformity is then encouraged, and the status quo is maintained.

Even in the past, however, ring-fenced, institutionalized thinking was always vulnerable to external factors. Living behind their secure mental walls, entities were often blind to the dangers approaching them from outside until too late. Nineteenth-century gaslight manufacturers ignored the coal tar experiments mentioned earlier and concentrated on improving the performance of their product with new manufacturing techniques and add-ons, such as higher-illumination gas mantles, until they were suddenly driven right out of business by electric light.

For most of history, this kind of occurrence has not caused wide-ranging and catastrophic consequences. Given the generally limited forms of communication at the time, ripples spread slowly, if at all (in an extreme example, news of Columbus's rediscovery of America took nearly twenty years to reach Poland). But today, as information technology begins to remove all limitations of space and time, we need to rethink modes of operation designed for structures in which change came slowly and in many cases have existed unaltered for more than 150,000 years.

Leadership itself may be a valid example of this. When, historically, the aim of the group was a focused, single task, concentrating the activities of all group members on one aim (catching an animal, producing a printed book, operating a mine, selling a single product type), the traditional, decisive characteristics demonstrated by leaders were essential. Leaders have always led primarily because they possessed knowledge that the rest of the group lacked. In deep time, their capabilities may have sprung from little more than a superior ability to recognize spoor or from a thorough acquaintance with the local hunting terrain. Through history, as the body of knowledge increased, the group assisting the leader remained small, thanks to the extremely limited technology available for use. In consequence, the decisive process remained essentially unchanged. In the early days of capitalism and print, corporate and community actions remained relatively simple, and aims were limited.

With this history of scarcity as our inheritance, we have come to regard the qualities represented by leadership as highly desirable but—above all—as relatively rare. However, in a sense, the concept of leadership can be seen as a product of the same technological limitations that also severely limited general access to knowledge, because in the country of the blind, the one-eyed man is king. When 99 percent of the community were by force of circumstance illiterate and innumerate, leaders were by definition exceptional and outstanding. It became accepted as a law of nature that the few led, and the many followed. In a slowly changing environment, leadership involved principally the ability to make long-term decisions. By the beginning of the (still slow-paced) twentieth century, the sheer productive power of industrial technology brought leaders of the strategic type to their apotheosis in multinational corporations and ideological structures that were so massive and centralized that they split the world between them.

How Knowledge Will Advance
in the Future

Meanwhile, in spite of continual growth in the individual leader's power, throughout the centuries small amounts of knowledge were gradually diffusing outward and downward, primarily as the result of advances in communications, which provided access to greater and greater numbers of people. Today the recent, sudden, and unprecedented explosion of information technology has radically altered the situation. Evolution has become revolution. The massive increase in individual empowerment made possible over the last decade, first by telecommunications and then by computing, has had a centrifugal, fragmenting influence. This has been reflected in the breakdown of political blocs, the erosion of confidence in the political institutions, and the extraordinary growth of the influence of the individual entrepreneur and the individual customer. As people demand greater customization of product, their relationship with their suppliers becomes more one-to-one than ever before. Corporations are already preparing to establish thousands of individual relationships with their customers, as the age of mass production and mass behavior fades into history. In such a situation, it becomes imperative to enfranchise corporate individuals in order to enable them to make decisions previously reserved to their superiors in the hierarchical pyramid and to provide access for them to any and all sources of relevant data necessary for use in their transactions.

The same diffusional process is also beginning to affect the political and social arena, as technology opens up government to scrutiny and reveals the old representative political process for what it is: an eighteenth-century answer to the eighteenth-century problem of bad roads and no telecommunications.

Corporations and social institutions that do not respond to the new obligation to release power outward will find themselves rejected in the marketplace and the ballot box. As we move into the twenty-first century, and technology taps the awesome potential talent of the penumbra of nearly five billion previously disfranchised intelligences on the planet, the Paleolithic concept of single-issue, top-down leadership needs to be redefined. The old reductionist division of labor, which solved problems one at a time, will not be able to keep pace with the demand for simultaneity and flexibility in the new dynamic business and political environment.

In this new world of personal empowerment, the all-seeing visionary leader, pointing the way to the future, is an obsolete anachronism to be replaced perhaps by facilitators, acting as mentors rather than commanders. Knowledge is power, and for the first time it is becoming freely available to the many rather than the few.

Part IV

THE PRACTICE
OF INNOVATION

17 CLAYTON M. CHRISTENSEN

COPING WITH YOUR ORGANIZATION'S INNOVATION CAPABILITIES

Clayton M. Christensen is professor of business administration at the Harvard Business School and is the author of The Innovator's Dilemma: When New Technologies Cause Great Firms to Fail. *His research and teaching interests center on the management of innovation and finding new markets for new technologies. He consults for many of the world's leading corporations on these issues.*

Warnings are all about us that the pace of change is accelerating. The amount of information available to managers—as well as the amount of work and judgment required to sort the important from the less important—is increasing exponentially. The pervasive emergence of the Internet is exacerbating these trends.

This is scary news—because when the pace of change was slower, most managers' track records in dealing with change weren't that good. For example, none of the minicomputer companies such

Note: This chapter was originally published in the Drucker Foundation journal *Leader to Leader*, vol. 21, Summer 2001, and is reprinted with the permission of Clayton M. Christensen. Copyright © 2001 by Clayton M. Christensen.

as Digital, Data General, and Wang succeeded in developing a competitive position in the personal computer business. Only one of the hundreds of department stores, Dayton Hudson, became a leader in discount retailing. Medical and business schools have struggled to change their curricula fast enough to train the types of doctors and managers that their markets need. The list could go on. In most of these instances, seeing the innovations coming at them hasn't been the problem. The organizations just didn't have the capability to react to what their employees and leaders saw, in a way that enabled them to keep pace with required changes.

When managers assign employees to tackle a critical innovation, they instinctively work to match the requirements of the job with the capabilities of the individuals they charge to do it. In evaluating whether an employee is capable of successfully executing a job, managers will look for the requisite knowledge, judgment, skill, perspective, and energy. Managers will also assess the employee's values—the criteria by which the person tends to decide what should and shouldn't be done.

Unfortunately, some managers don't think as rigorously about whether their *organizations* have the capability to successfully execute jobs that may be given to them. Often, they assume that if the people working on a project individually have the requisite capabilities to get the job done well, then the organization in which they work will also have the capability to succeed.

The purpose of this chapter is to offer a framework to help managers confronted with necessary change understand whether the organizations over which they preside are capable or incapable of tackling the challenge.

An Organizational Capabilities Framework

Three classes of factors affect what an organization can and cannot do: its resources, its processes, and its values. When asking what sorts of innovations their organizations are and are not likely to be able to implement successfully, managers can learn a lot about capabilities by disaggregating their answers into these three categories.

Resources

Resources are the most visible of the factors that contribute to what an organization can and cannot do. Resources include people, equipment, technology, product designs, brands, information, cash, and relationships with suppliers, distributors, and customers. Resources are usually *things*, or *assets*—they can be hired and fired, bought and sold, depreciated or enhanced.

Resources are not only valuable, they are *flexible*. An engineer who works productively for Dow Chemical can also work productively in a start-up. Software that helps UPS manage its logistics system can also be useful at Amazon.com. Technology that proves valuable in mainframe computers also can be used in telecommunications switches. Cash is a consummately flexible resource.

Resources are the things that managers most instinctively identify when assessing whether their organizations can successfully implement changes that confront them. Yet resource analysis clearly does not tell a sufficient story about capabilities.

Processes

Organizations create value as employees transform inputs of resources into products and services of greater worth. The patterns of interaction, coordination, communication, and decision making through which they accomplish these transformations are *processes*. Processes include not just manufacturing processes but also those by which product development, procurement, market research, budgeting, employee development and compensation, and resource allocation are accomplished.

Processes are defined or evolve de facto to address specific tasks. This means that when managers use a process to execute the tasks for which it was designed, it is likely to perform efficiently. But when the same seemingly efficient process is employed to tackle a very different task, it is likely to prove slow, bureaucratic, and inefficient. In contrast to the flexibility of resources, processes are inherently inflexible. In other words, a process that defines a *capability* in executing a certain task concurrently defines *disabilities* in executing other tasks.

One of the dilemmas of management is that by their very nature, processes are established so that employees perform recurrent tasks in a consistent way, time after time. To ensure consistency, processes are meant *not* to change—or if they must change, to change through tightly controlled procedures. The reason good managers strive for focus in their organizations is that processes and tasks can be readily aligned. The alignment of specific tasks with the processes that were designed to address those tasks is, in fact, the very definition of a focused organization. It is when managers begin employing processes that were designed to address one problem to tackle a range of very different tasks that an organization manifests slow, inefficient, and bureaucratic behavior.

Values

The third class of factors that affects what an organization can or cannot accomplish is its values. The term *values* carries an ethical connotation, such as those that guide decisions to ensure patient well-being at Johnson & Johnson or that guide decisions about plant safety at Alcoa. But in this framework, values have a broader meaning. An organization's values are the criteria by which employees make prioritization decisions—by which they judge whether an order is attractive or unattractive, whether a customer is more important or less important, whether an idea for a new product is attractive or marginal, and so on. Prioritization decisions are made by employees at every level. At the executive tiers, they often take the form of decisions to invest or not invest in new products, services, and processes. Among salespeople, they consist of day-to-day decisions about which customers to call on and which to ignore, which products to push and which to deemphasize.

The larger and more complex a company becomes, the more important it is for senior managers to train employees at every level to make independent decisions about priorities that are consistent with the strategic direction and the business model of the company. A key metric of good management, in fact, is whether such clear and consistent values have permeated the organization. This is an important theme in two of the most powerful and popular books on management, Jim Collins and Jerry Porras's 1994 book, *Built to Last*, and Thomas Peters and Robert Waterman's 1982 best-seller, *In Search of Excellence*.

Clear, consistent, and broadly understood values, however, also define what an organization cannot do. A company's values must by necessity reflect its cost structure or its business model, because these define the rules its employees must follow for the company to prosper. If, for example, the structure of a company's overhead costs requires it to achieve gross profit margins of 40 percent, a powerful value or decision rule will have evolved that encourages middle managers to kill ideas that promise gross margins below 40 percent. This means that such an organization would be *incapable* of successfully commercializing projects targeting low-margin markets—even while another organization's values, driven by a very different cost structure, might enable or facilitate the success of the very same projects.

The values of successful firms tend to evolve in a predictable fashion on at least two dimensions. The first relates to acceptable gross margins. As companies add features and functionality to their products and services in an effort to capture more attractive customers in premium tiers of their markets, they often add overhead cost. As a result, gross margins that at one point were quite attractive, at a later point seem unattractive. Their values change.

The second dimension along which values can change relates to how big a customer or market has to be, in order to be interesting. Because a company's stock price represents the discounted present value of its projected earnings stream, most managers typically feel compelled not just to maintain growth but to maintain a constant *rate* of growth. For a $40 million company to grow 25 percent, it needs to find $10 million in new business the next year. For a $40 *billion* company to grow 25 percent, it needs to find $10 *billion* in new business the next year. The size of market opportunity that will solve each of these companies' needs for growth is very different. An opportunity that excites a small organization isn't large enough to be interesting to a very large one. One of the bittersweet rewards of success is, in fact, that as companies become large, they literally lose the capability to enter the small, emerging markets of today that will be tomorrow's large markets. This disability is not because of a change in the resources within the companies—their resources typically are vast. Rather, it is because their values change.

Those who engineer mega-mergers among already huge companies to achieve cost savings, for example, need to account for the impact of these actions on the resultant companies' values. Although their merged research organizations might have more resources to throw at innovation problems, they lose the appetite for all but the biggest market opportunities. This constitutes a very real *disability* in managing innovation.

The Capabilities to Address Sustaining or Disruptive Technologies

One of the most important findings in the research summarized in my 1997 book, *The Innovator's Dilemma: When New Technologies Cause Great Firms to Fail*, relates to the differences in companies' track records at making effective use of sustaining and disruptive technologies. *Sustaining technologies* are innovations that make a product or service better along the dimensions of performance valued by customers in the mainstream market. Compaq's early use of Intel's thirty-two-bit 386 microprocessor instead of the sixteen-bit

286 chip was an example of a sustaining innovation. So was Merrill Lynch's introduction of its cash management account.

Disruptive innovations, in contrast, bring to market a new product or service that is actually *worse* along the metrics of performance most valued by mainstream customers. Charles Schwab's initial entry as a bare-bones discount broker was a disruptive innovation, relative to the offerings of full-service brokers. Early personal computers were a disruptive innovation, relative to mainframes and minicomputers. PCs were disruptive in that they didn't address the next-generation needs of leading customers in existing markets. They had other attributes, of course, that enabled new market applications to coalesce, however—and from those new applications, the disruptive innovations improved so rapidly that they ultimately could address the needs of customers in the mainstream market as well.

In a study of sustaining and disruptive technologies in the disk drive industry, my colleagues and I built a database of every disk drive model introduced by any company in the world between 1975 and 1995—comprising nearly five thousand models. For each of these models, we gathered data on the components used, as well as the software codes and architectural concepts employed. This allowed us to put our finger right on the spot in the industry where each new technology was used. We could then correlate companies' leadership or laggardship in using new technologies with their subsequent fortunes in the market.

We identified 116 new technologies that were introduced in the industry's history. Of these, 111 were sustaining technologies, in that their impact was to improve the performance of disk drives. Some of these were incremental improvements, whereas others, such as magneto-resistive heads, represented discontinuous leaps forward in performance. In all 111 cases of sustaining technology, the companies that led in developing and introducing the new technology were the companies that had led in the old technology. It didn't matter how difficult it was, from a technological point of view. The success rate of the established firms was 100 percent.

The other five technologies were disruptive innovations—in each case, smaller disk drives that were slower and had lower capacity than those used in the mainstream market. There was no new technology involved in these disruptive products. Yet *none* of the industry's leading companies remained atop the industry after these disruptive innovations entered the market—their batting average was *zero*. *The Innovator's Dilemma* recounts how dynamics like those we observed for disk drives—the interplay between the speed of technology change and the evolution in market needs—precipitated the failure of the leading companies to cope with disruptive innovations in a range of very different industries.

Why such markedly different batting averages when playing the sustaining versus disruptive games? The answer lies in the resources-processes-values (RPV) framework of organizational capabilities described earlier. The industry leaders developed and introduced sustaining technologies over and over again—111 of the 116 new technologies were sustaining ones. Month after month, year after year, as they introduced improved products to gain a competitive edge, the leading companies developed processes for evaluating the technological potential and assessing their customers' needs for alternative sustaining technologies. In the parlance of this chapter, the organizations developed a *capability* for doing these things, which resided in their processes. Sustaining technology investments also fit the values of the leading companies, in that they promised higher margins from better products sold to their leading-edge customers.

Conversely, the disruptive innovations occurred so intermittently that no company had a routinized process for handling them. Furthermore, because the disruptive products promised lower profit margins per unit sold and could not be used by their best customers, these innovations were inconsistent with the leading companies' values. The leading disk drive companies had the *resources*—the people, money, and technology—required to succeed at both sustaining and disruptive technologies. But their processes and values constituted disabilities in their efforts to succeed at disruptive technologies.

Large companies often surrender emerging growth markets because smaller, disruptive companies are actually more capable of pursuing them. Though start-ups lack resources, it doesn't matter. Their values can embrace small markets, and their cost structures can accommodate lower margins. Their market research and resource allocation processes allow managers to proceed intuitively rather than having to be backed up by careful research and analysis. All these advantages add up to enormous opportunity or looming disaster—depending on your perspective.

Managers who face the need to change or innovate, therefore, need to do more than assign the right resources to the problem. They need to be sure that the organization in which those resources will be working is itself capable of succeeding—and in making that assessment, managers must scrutinize whether the organization's processes and values fit the problem.

Creating Capabilities to Cope with Change

A manager determined that an employee was incapable of succeeding at a task would either find someone else to do the job or carefully train the employee to be able to succeed. Training often works, because individuals can become skilled at multiple tasks.

Despite beliefs spawned by change-management and reengineering programs, processes are not nearly as flexible as resources are—and values are even less so. The processes that make an organization good at outsourcing components cannot simultaneously make it good at developing and manufacturing components inhouse. Values that focus an organization's priorities on large customers cannot simultaneously focus priorities on small customers.

For these reasons, managers who determine that an organization's capabilities aren't suited for a new task are faced with three options through which to create new capabilities:

- Acquire a different organization whose processes and values are a close match with the new task.

- Try to change the processes and values of the current organization.

- Separate out an independent organization and develop within it the new processes and values required to solve the new problem.

Creating Capabilities Through Acquisitions

Managers often sense that acquiring rather than developing a set of capabilities makes competitive and financial sense. Unfortunately, companies' track records in developing new capabilities through acquisition are frighteningly spotty. Here, the RPV framework can be a useful way to frame the challenge of integrating acquired organizations. Acquiring managers need to begin by asking, "What is it that really created the value I just paid so dearly for? Did I justify the price because of the acquisition's resources—its people, products, technology, market position, and so on? Or was a substantial portion of its worth created by processes and values—unique ways of working and decision making that have enabled the company to understand and satisfy customers and develop, make, and deliver new products and services in a timely way?"

If the acquired company's processes and values are the real driver of its success, then the last thing the acquiring manager wants to do is to integrate the company into the new parent organization. Integration will vaporize many of the processes and values of the acquired firm as its managers are required to adopt the buyer's way of doing business and have their proposals to innovate evaluated according to the decision criteria of the acquiring company. If the acquiree's processes and values were the reason for its historical success, a better strategy is to let the business stand alone and for the parent to infuse its resources into the acquired firm's processes and values. This strategy, in essence, truly constitutes the acquisition of new capabilities.

If, however, the company's *resources* were the primary rationale for the acquisition, then integrating the firm into the parent can make a lot of sense—essentially plugging the acquired people, products, technology, and customers into the parent's processes as a way of leveraging the parent's existing capabilities.

The perils of the ongoing DaimlerChrysler merger, for example, can be better understood through the RPV model. Chrysler had few resources that could be considered unique in comparison with its competitors. Its recent success in the market was rooted in its processes—particularly in its product design process and in its processes of managing its relationships with its key subsystem suppliers. What is the best way for Daimler to leverage the capabilities that Chrysler brings to the table? Wall Street is pressuring management to consolidate the two organizations so as to cut costs. However, if the two companies are integrated, it is very likely that the key processes that made Chrysler such an attractive acquisition will not just be compromised, they will be vaporized.

This situation is reminiscent of IBM's 1984 acquisition of Rolm. There wasn't anything in Rolm's pool of resources that IBM didn't already have. It was Rolm's processes for developing PBX products and for finding new markets for them that were really responsible for its success. In 1987, IBM decided to fully integrate the company into its corporate structure. IBM soon learned the folly of this decision. Trying to push Rolm's resources—its products and its customers—through the same processes that were honed in IBM's large-computer business caused the Rolm business to stumble badly. This decision to integrate Rolm actually destroyed the very source of the original worth of the deal. How much better off they would have been had IBM infused some of its vast resources into Rolm's processes and values!

DaimlerChrysler, bowing to the investment community's drumbeat for efficiency savings, now stands on the edge of the same precipice. Often, it seems, financial analysts have a better intuition for the worth of resources than for processes or values.

In contrast, Cisco Systems' acquisitions process has worked well—because, I would argue, it has kept resources, processes, and values in the right perspective. Between 1993 and 1997, most of its acquisitions were small companies that were less than two years old: early-stage organizations whose market value was built primarily on resources—particularly engineers and products. Cisco has a well-defined, deliberate process by which it essentially plugs these resources into the parent's processes and systems, and it has a carefully cultivated method of keeping the engineers of the acquired company happily on the Cisco payroll. In the process of integration, Cisco throws away whatever nascent processes and values came with the acquisition—because those weren't what Cisco paid for. On a couple of occasions when the company acquired a larger, more mature organization—notably its 1996 acquisition of StrataCom—Cisco did *not* integrate. Rather, it let StrataCom stand alone and infused its substantial resources into the organization to help it grow at a more rapid rate.

Creating New Capabilities Internally

Companies that have tried to develop new capabilities within established organizational units also have a spotty track record. Assembling a beefed-up set of resources as a means of changing what an existing organization can do is relatively straightforward. People with new skills can be hired, technology can be licensed, capital can be raised, and product lines, brands, and information can be acquired. Too often, however, resources such as these are then plugged into fundamentally unchanged processes—and little change results. For example, through the 1970s and 1980s Toyota upended the world automobile industry through its innovation in development, manufacturing, and supply-chain *processes*—without investing aggressively in resources such as advanced manufacturing or information processing technology. General Motors responded by investing nearly $60 billion in manufacturing *resources*—computer-automated equipment that was designed to reduce cost and improve quality. Using state-of-the-art resources in antiquated processes, however, made little difference in GM's performance, because it is in its processes and values that the organization's most fundamental capabilities lie. Processes and values define how resources—many of which can be bought and sold, hired and fired—are combined to create value.

Unfortunately, processes are very hard to change. Organizational boundaries are often drawn to facilitate the operation of present processes. Those boundaries can impede the creation of new processes that cut across those boundaries. When new challenges require people or groups to interact differently than they habitually have done—addressing different challenges with different timing than historically required—managers need to pull the relevant people out of the existing organization and draw a new boundary around a new group. New team boundaries enable or facilitate new patterns of working together that ultimately can coalesce as new processes—new capabilities for transforming inputs into outputs. In their 1992 book, *Revolutionizing Product Development*, Steven Wheelwright and Kim Clark call these structures *heavyweight teams*. Not just Chrysler but companies as diverse as Medtronic in cardiac pacemakers, IBM in disk drives, and Eli Lilly with its new blockbuster drug Zyprexa have used heavyweight teams as vehicles within which new processes could coalesce.

Creating Capabilities Through a Spinout Organization

The third mechanism for creating new capabilities—spawning them within spinout ventures—is currently in vogue among many managers as they wrestle with how to address the Internet. When are spinouts a crucial step in building new capabilities to exploit

change, and what are the guidelines by which they should be managed? A separate organization is required when the mainstream organization's *values* would render it incapable of focusing resources
on the innovation project. Large organizations cannot be expected
to freely allocate the critical financial and human resources needed
to build a strong position in small, emerging markets. And it is very
difficult for a company whose cost structure is tailored to compete
in high-end markets to be profitable in low-end markets as well.
When a threatening disruptive technology requires a different cost
structure to be profitable and competitive, or when the current size
of the opportunity is insignificant relative to the growth needs of
the mainstream organization, then—and only then—is a spinout
organization a required part of the solution.

Just as with new processes, business based on new values needs
to be established while the old business is still at the top of its
game. Merrill Lynch's retail brokerage business, for example, is
today a very healthy business—and the firm's processes and values
for serving its clients work well. The disruption of on-line brokerage looms powerfully on the horizon—but any attempt Merrill
management might make to transform the existing business to succeed in the next world of self-service, automated trading would
compromise its near-term profit potential. Merrill Lynch needs to
own another retail brokerage business, which would be free to create its own processes and forge a cost structure that could enable
different values to prevail. It must do this if it hopes to thrive in
the postdisruption world.

How separate does the effort need to be? The primary requirement is that the project cannot be forced to compete for resources
with projects in the mainstream organization. Because values are
the criteria by which prioritization decisions are made, projects that
are inconsistent with a company's mainstream values will naturally
be accorded lowest priority. The physical location of the independent organization is less important than its independence from the
normal resource allocation process.

In our studies of this challenge, we have never seen a company succeed in addressing a change that disrupts its mainstream values absent the personal, attentive oversight of the CEO—precisely because of the power of processes and values and particularly the logic of the normal resource allocation process. Only the CEO can ensure that the new organization gets the required resources and is free to create processes and values that are appropriate to the new challenge. CEOs who view spinouts as a tool to get disruptive threats off their personal agendas are almost certain to meet with failure. We have seen no exceptions to this rule.

A Structural Framework for Managing Different Types of Innovation

The framework summarized in Figure 17.1 can help managers exploit current organizational capabilities when that is possible and create new ones when the present organization is incapable.

The left axis in Figure 17.1 measures the extent to which the existing processes—the patterns of interaction, communication, coordination, and decision making currently used in the organization—are the ones that will get the new job done effectively. If the answer is yes (toward the lower end of the scale), the new team can exploit the organization's existing processes or capabilities to succeed. As depicted in the corresponding position on the right axis, functional or lightweight teams are useful structures for exploiting existing capabilities. Conversely, if the ways of getting work done and of decision making in the mainstream business would impede rather than facilitate the work of the new team—because different people need to interact with different people about different subjects and with different timing than has habitually been necessary—then a heavyweight team structure is necessary. Heavyweight teams are tools to create new processes—new ways of working together that constitute new capabilities.

Figure 17.1. Fitting an Innovation's Requirements with the Organization's Capabilities

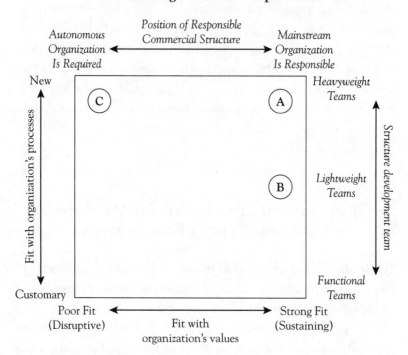

Note: The left and bottom axes reflect the questions that the manager needs to ask about the existing situation. The italicized notes at the right side represent the appropriate response to the situation on the left axis. The italicized notes at the top represent the appropriate response to the manager's answer to the bottom axis.

The horizontal axis of Figure 17.1 asks managers to assess whether the organization's values will allocate to the new initiative the resources it will need in order to become successful. If there is a poor or disruptive fit, then the mainstream organization's values will accord low priority to the project. Therefore, setting up an autonomous organization within which development and commercialization can occur will be absolutely essential to success. At the other extreme, however, if there is a strong, sustaining fit, then the manager can expect that the energy and resources of the mainstream organization will coalesce behind it. There is no reason for a skunk works or a spinout in such cases.

Region "A" in Figure 17.1 depicts a situation in which a manager is faced with a sustaining technological change—it fits the organization's values. But it presents the organization with different types of problems to solve and therefore requires new types of interaction and coordination among groups and individuals. The manager needs a heavyweight development team to tackle the new task, but the project can be executed within the mainstream company. This is how Chrysler, Eli Lilly, Medtronic, and the IBM disk drive division successfully revamped their product development processes. When in region "B" (where the project fits the company's processes and values), a lightweight development team, in which coordination across functional boundaries occurs within the mainstream organization, can be successful. Region "C" denotes an area in which a manager is faced with a disruptive technological change that doesn't fit the organization's existing processes and values. To ensure success in such instances, managers should create an autonomous organization and commission a heavyweight development team to tackle the challenge.

Functional and lightweight teams are appropriate vehicles for exploiting established capabilities, whereas heavyweight teams are tools for creating new ones. Spinout organizations, similarly, are tools for forging new values. Unfortunately, most companies employ a one-size-fits-all organizing strategy, using lightweight teams for programs of every size and character. Among those few firms that have accepted the "heavyweight gospel," many have attempted to organize all development teams in a heavyweight fashion. Ideally, each company should tailor the team structure and organizational location to the process and values required by each project.

The Danger of Wishful Thinking

Managers whose organizations are confronting change must first determine that they have the resources required to succeed. They then need to ask a separate question: Does the organization have the processes and values to succeed? Asking this second question is not as instinctive for most managers because the processes by which work is done and the values by which employees make their decisions have served them well. What the RPV framework adds to managers' thinking, however, is the concept that the very capabilities of an organization also define its disabilities. A little time spent soul-searching for honest answers to this issue will pay off handsomely. Are the processes by which work habitually gets done in the organization appropriate for this new problem? And will the values of the organization cause this initiative to get high priority or not?

If the answer to these questions is no, it's OK. Understanding problems is the most crucial step in solving them. Wishful thinking about this issue can set teams charged with developing and implementing an innovation on a course fraught with roadblocks, second-guessing, and frustration. The reason why innovation often seems to be so difficult for established firms is that they employ highly capable people and then set them to work within processes and values that weren't designed to facilitate success with the task at hand. Ensuring that capable people are ensconced in capable organizations is a major management responsibility in an age such as ours, when the ability to cope with accelerating change has become so critical.

18 DAVE ULRICH

AN INNOVATION PROTOCOL

Dave Ulrich is professor of business administration at the University of Michigan, a consultant to the Fortune 200, and the author of over ninety articles and book chapters. His books include HR Scorecard, Results Based Leadership, Organizational Capability, The Boundaryless Organization, *and* Human Resource Champions. *He has been listed by* Business Week *as one of the top ten educators in management and is on the board of directors at Herman Miller.*

A play has a script that guides how actors perform on stage. A sports team has a playbook that specifies how players execute a diagrammed play. A pilot has a checklist to ensure flight safety before and during a flight. A script, a playbook, and a checklist serve as protocols to predict successful action.

Leaders who desire innovation need and deserve an *innovation protocol*. This protocol enables leaders to make informed choices that increase the probability of successful innovation. In this chapter, I present minicases of leaders seeking to innovate, then suggest resolution to the cases based on innovation premises and an innovation protocol.

Case 1   A high-tech firm depends on new products to compete. The half-life of new products in this industry is increasingly falling, and success requires a pipeline of new products. Innovation success will be tracked through a *vitality index*, which represents the percent of revenue from products produced in the preceding three years.

Case 2   The CEO of a traditional firm focused on products has decided that in the new economy, the firm must adopt a new strategy and channel of distribution. The firm hopes to become more customer-centric as measured by revenue per target customer and to increase customer share as measured by lifetime share of customer expenditure in the products and services that the firm offers. It also hopes to have more intimacy with customers around the world through Web-based relationships.

Case 3   A staff member in a firm needs to innovate in the type and quality of support work delivered (for example, in finance, focusing on economic value-added; in manufacturing, on lean manufacturing; in IT, on a new enterprise resource planning system; in HR, on competence-based hiring). The updated staff work requires an investment of time and resources and should enable the firm to better reach its business goals.

These minicases illustrate the range of innovation. Innovation means letting go of old behaviors and policies and adapting new ones. Learning to forget becomes almost as difficult as learning to adapt. Employees naturally become wedded to products, strategies, or programs that they create, and innovation requires abdicating the past to originate the future. Innovation is more than creativity.

To help leaders innovate in these three related cases, I will suggest three lessons learned about innovation and propose an innovation protocol that provides discipline to the innovation process.

Premise 1: Innovation Matters

Innovation is critical to growth. There is no such thing as a mature business; every business must find ways to grow and expand its products, services, and reach. Innovation focuses on share of opportunity—it's about what can be, more than about market share or what has been. Innovation focuses on creating the future rather than relying on past successes. Innovation matters because it fosters growth; it excites employees by focusing on what can be; it anticipates customer requests and delights customers with what they did not expect; it builds confidence with investors by creating intangible value.

Leaders who focus on innovation constantly ask, "What's next?" in all domains of their business. They recognize the ever shorter half-life of most organizational processes (half-life is when 50 percent of current work processes are out of date because of new knowledge). In each of the three cases outlined earlier, leaders apply this lesson by articulating and measuring the value or outcome of innovation in terms of new products, strategies, or programs.

Premise 2: Innovation Is Multifaceted

Innovation occurs in many business domains. In the three mini-cases, innovation occurs in product or service offerings, business strategy, and administrative processes.

Innovative product offerings include revolutionary new products or product extensions (for example, features, performance, or functionality). Business strategy innovation changes how the enterprise makes money (for example, services more than products), where the enterprise does business (for example, new geographies), how the enterprise goes to market (for example, new channels), how the customers experience the firm (for example, brand), or how the firm services customers (for example, eBay). Administrative innovation occurs when new processes are introduced in finance, IT, marketing, HR, manufacturing, or other staff systems.

Leaders who recognize the array of innovation possibilities have passion for change. They encourage newer, better ways of doing all aspects of business. They relentlessly challenge the status quo. They surround themselves with people who constantly attempt to do work in new ways.

Premise 3: Innovation Is a Culture, Not an Event

Innovation events occur when new ideas are tried; *innovation culture* occurs when new ideas become ingrained in the way work is done. Product innovation is an event when a new product comes to market; a product innovation culture occurs when a pipeline of new products continually flows. Strategy innovation is an event when a business plan is drafted and publicized; a strategy innovation culture occurs when leaders continually make new business choices. Administrative innovation is an event when a new process is introduced; an administrative innovation culture occurs when new programs are sought and continually implemented.

Leaders who build an innovative culture encourage challenging more than accepting, questioning more than settling for pat answers, curiosity more than comfort, rebels more than bureaucrats, problem identification more than problem solution, sharing information more than hoarding information, and demanding more than passively responding. These cultural attributes collectively create a firm identity that communicates innovation as a firm brand to both employees and customers.

Because innovation matters, has many facets, and depicts a firm's identity, leaders who institutionalize innovation need a protocol. Protocols identify decision points that leaders may follow to ensure success. Accountants follow accepted standards as a protocol to ensure accuracy and reliability in reporting financial data. Lawyers follow routines as a protocol in preparing their legal briefs and arguments. Architects have accepted standards or protocols that they must adhere to in turning ideas into blueprints. Leaders may also follow a protocol in ensuring innovation. An innovation protocol ensures repeatable success by stipulating a definitive process that can be both learned and applied.

Protocol 1: Idea Generation

Innovation originates with ideas—fresh ideas, different ideas, out-of-the-box ideas, streams of ongoing ideas. Leaders inspire new ideas by focusing on customers, encouraging risk takers, and forming alliances.

Most product and strategy innovation comes from gaps or holes in existing customer expectations. *Outside-in innovation* occurs when leaders have the capacity to define target customers and analyze their unmet needs in new ways. General Woods identified the impact of freeways in the United States as a forerunner of suburbs, where people could live apart from where they work. With this insight, he was able to invest in Sears stores in suburbs, where people lived, rather than in urban areas, where they worked. *Customer-pulled innovation* draws on customer panels, where leaders use focus groups of current and future customers to determine unmet needs. Motorola has used high school students to determine that they wanted colored telephones and pagers to match their daily attire. Engineers who focused on the pager and cellular technology had no clue that customers might prefer a host of color-coordinated phone services. Identifying target, or lighthouse, customers who lead the industry, engaging in ongoing dialogues with these customers, and creating ways to meet unmet customer needs become sources of idea generation. The ultimate innovation partner is the customer who participates in exploring, discovering, and anticipating new products.

Within even staid and traditional firms, iconoclasts exist. These individuals don't accept that work should be done a certain way because it has been done that way before; they are passionate about learning opportunities, and they often experiment with new approaches. Begetting innovators from iconoclasts is not an accident. It requires hiring people with both technical competence and innovation courage; it means creating organizational space where they are allowed to innovate and experiment without undue reins; it means stealing time from existing projects to invest in future opportunities.

New ideas often come from alliances with sources of knowledge. Innovative leaders form alliances with places where ideas come from—for example, universities, research centers, and research consortia. Passing the idea test by focusing on customers, encouraging iconoclasts, and forging alliances ensures a continual flow of ideas.

Protocol 2: Impact

Not all ideas lead to successful innovation. Creativity means new ideas; innovation means that new ideas have impact. To move from ideas to impact requires rigorous filtering. Innovation leaders require both objective and subjective data for the following screens:

- *Strategic fit.* Will the idea fit within the existing strategy of the business? Will it be consistent with the identity and core competencies of the firm? Will it be credible for our firm to pursue this idea?

- *Potential value.* Will the idea be commercial? Will there be possible financial margins or other impact to justify further investments?

- *Opportunity size.* Will the idea be large enough to pursue? Will there be sufficient demand for the product or service created?

- *Competitors.* Will the firm be able to distinguish itself from competitors with the product or service? Who else is working on the idea, and can the firm learn from and leapfrog them? Will the innovation be able to distinguish the firm from competitors in ways that are meaningful to users of the innovation?

- *Employee passion.* Will the firm find employees who have both passion and competence to do the innovation? Will there be sufficient employee excitement about this innovation?

Leaders may filter product, strategic, and administrative ideas through these screens with both objective and subjective data to turn ideas into impact. These assessments prioritize product, strategic, and administrative ideas worth pursuing.

Protocol 3: Incubation

Ideas that pass the impact screen merit additional attention through *incubation preserves*, where experiments occur. Experiments may be set up where ideas are piloted, tested, and adapted. Product incubations may include target customers who validate new products or services. Strategic incubations may include customers or investors who confirm strategic assumptions. Administrative incubations may be experiments with groups of employees to determine the viability of the administrative action.

Innovative leaders create these incubation preserves, where pilot tests ensure proof of concept (whether the innovation makes sense to a customer or employee audience), technological feasibility (whether the firm has knowledge to create innovation), and resource accessibility (whether the firm has resources to pursue the innovation).

Successfully passing through the incubation protocol encourages further investment. However, failures from pilots are equally important because they focus future investment. Incubation pilots should have as many failures as successes so that prioritized investments may be made.

Protocol 4: Investment

Ideas that pass the incubation test deserve further investment. These ideas may then be field-tested to ensure sustained value. To launch a product innovation requires marketing, R&D, manufacturing, sales, and service resources. These resources allow products or services to be assessed with a large audience of consumers to determine breadth of market potential. To launch a strategic investment requires strategic clarity around product portfolios, distribution channels, and geographical scope. Administrative investments require talent (people to do the job), finances (money to design and deliver the innovative program), and technology (data sources to monitor the innovation). As these resources are committed, innovation reaches critical mass. Marshaling these resources comes as leaders build governance mechanisms to ensure focused investment.

Some innovations may be governed at a distance through alliances or joint ventures. In these cases, the firm takes a financial or knowledge equity position in the innovation but does not control it. In these virtual network organizations, innovations may occur as resources from multiple firms combine. The risk is that the innovation remains the property of the alliance rather than the firm and that knowledge is not transferred to other units in the firm. If the innovation remains outside the main body of the firm, the new innovation may lack full impact.

Other innovations are governed through the corporation's setting up an internal venture capital group that sponsors new ideas. These innovations become corporate experiments, supported by corporate resources. These corporate innovations attempt to affect the entire organization, adapting how the entire enterprise operates.

Other innovations are governed by pockets of excellence within a business. When a business unit experiments, it creates a pocket of excellence that may then be infused throughout the whole enterprise.

Protocol 5: Integration

Innovation requires integration of new ideas into old. With product innovation, this means that new products and services both complement and cannibalize the old. With strategic innovation, new business models become commonplace throughout an enterprise. With administrative innovations, practices that worked in one division must become integrated across an enterprise.

Leveraging innovation across an enterprise comes through moving talent—by having innovators move across businesses or geographies and operate in a career mosaic throughout the enterprise. Leveraging innovation also comes when incentives encourage sharing of information and ideas. In one firm, 20 percent of the bonus pool was allocated to individuals not within the leader's chain of command. This pool of money allowed leaders to reward individuals outside of their hierarchy who shared information. Leveraging innovation comes when task forces, training programs, and teams include people from multiple divisions and geographies so that information can be shared. Leveraging innovation avoids a "not-invented-here" culture, and leaders encourage those who both share and borrow ideas.

When leveraging occurs, innovations become integrated into ongoing business operations. The test of integration is the extent to which innovations flow across business, division, function, and geographical boundaries. Successfully passing the integration test ensures that innovations in any one unit of a business transfer to the whole enterprise and that innovations in one time period are shared over time to build cumulative learning.

Protocol 6: Improvement

Innovation does not end but evolves. It requires successive improvement, in which lessons learned are constantly codified, adapted, and implemented. Leaders committed to innovation improvement constantly monitor the innovation. Product innovations have life cycles. As the life cycle for a new product slows, it behooves leaders to encourage ideas for a new round of product innovation. Strategic innovations also must evolve so that successful strategies in one time period or business evolve when new business conditions arise. Administrative innovations also have a life cycle, in which improvement in the administrative system must continually evolve.

Leaders committed to improvement of innovation have a monitoring process to constantly check if the innovation is creating value, if tweaks for the innovation are possible, and if the innovation might be adapted from successes or failures. Innovation leaders often build in ongoing monitoring processes, in which they have quarterly or semiannual reviews of product, strategic, or administrative innovations, where questions about the rate of innovative change are evaluated.

Summary

To make product, strategic, or administrative innovation happen, leaders must recognize that innovation matters and make it part of their priority. They must recognize that innovation occurs in diverse settings and create an innovation culture beyond an innovation event. To create this culture, leaders may deploy an innovation protocol with six phases, each of which has a series of questions that must be answered in the affirmative to move forward to the next phase. With the discipline of an innovation protocol, product innovations occur regularly, with new products replacing old; strategic innovations occur, with new models of competition emerging; and administrative innovations are designed and implemented continually. Innovation becomes less magic and more regimen.

19 ARIE DE GEUS

BEWARE: INNOVATION KILLS!

Arie de Geus was with the Royal Dutch Shell Group for thirty-eight years, retiring as group planning coordinator. He has advised governments and private institutions. His publications include "Planning as Learning" in the Harvard Business Review *and* The Living Company, *which received the Edwin G. Booz prize as "the most innovative business book of the year 1997."*

The surefire and ultimate result of birth will be death, but the great uncertainty during a lifetime is how quickly death will follow birth. Innovation is one of the causes of short corporate lifetimes. It leads to the sudden death of many entrepreneurs and ignorant bystanders and results in very short average life expectancies for companies.

This high death rate and its social and human costs are not inevitable, however. This chapter examines the role of profit maximization and postulates that giving management priority to the optimization of people is a better way of ensuring long-lasting business success, especially in the new economy.

Innovation and the Maximization
of Shareholder Value

Peter Drucker has been fascinated with innovation ever since he started writing books in the early fifties. He links it with entrepreneurship, which, he says, is neither a science nor an art. It is a practice—and innovation (or the knowledge that is the outcome of the innovation) is a means to an end. "Entrepreneurs innovate. Innovation is the specific instrument of entrepreneurship."

Which "end" is Drucker talking about? As a good Austrian economist, he links it up with Schumpeter's *creative destruction*. Through innovation, the entrepreneur creates a dynamic disequilibrium, which gives him opportunities and brings destruction to the others. Unfortunately, in this process not only the ignorant bystander dies but also, according to Drucker in his 1985 *Innovation and Entrepreneurship*, among entrepreneurs, "The casualty rate is high and the chances of success or even of survival seem to be quite low—especially, in such highly visible areas of innovation as high tech" (p. 25). The latter observation is confirmed by Clayton M. Christensen in his 1997 book, *The Innovator's Dilemma*, the subtitle of which is *When New Technologies Cause Great Firms to Fail*.

Christensen and Drucker outline a hard reality, one confirmed by two studies that showed that the average life expectancy at birth of commercial companies in the developed world is abominably low and seemingly coming down (to 12.5 years!) Indeed there is a lot of creative destruction. Is that inevitable or a good thing? Is it the corporate equivalent of Darwin's survival of the fittest? Companies do not only consist of entrepreneurs. Usually, lots of other people are involved, both inside and outside the company—sometimes entire local communities or geographical regions. The death of a company is not gratuitous; witness some of the areas around the Great Lakes or parts of the Midlands in the United Kingdom. In addition, business produces most of a country's GNP: the health of the business sector as a whole is vital for the health of the country.

Fortunately, true as the Drucker-Schumpeter picture may be, there are, as always, exceptions to the rule. A study done during my time with Royal Dutch Shell showed that some companies are very long-term survivors. At least forty-five of the world's major commercial corporations have survived the storms of creative destruction, sometimes for centuries. In so doing, they have even succeeded in overcoming the high odds of dying in successive technological waves. So how did they do this, and what lessons are there to be learned for both the ignorant bystanders and the entrepreneurs who cause the storms of creative destruction? If innovation is a practice, as Drucker says, how can we make sure that this practice will be applied across the board? And not only by today's management but also by a succession of many generations of leaders, owners, and managers? In other words, why do certain companies succeed in institutionalizing innovation and survival for more than just one or two management generations?

Both Drucker and Christensen go in search of practices to enhance the chances of survival. Drucker says that entrepreneurship needs to be systematic, and it needs to be managed. He says that as the tool of entrepreneurs, innovation is capable of being learned and practiced. Christensen, also, maintains that there are managerial solutions to the dilemma. Unfortunately, so far, there is little evidence that these practices work. More than one-half of newborn companies die before they are ten years old. Very few weather the storm of creative destruction. To me, it raises these questions: How does the learning that Drucker mentions take place? And why is it that it becomes part of the institutional behavior pattern during many generations in only a few companies? Why are some companies superior learners in the sense that they have a long history of adapting and thriving through successive storms of creative destruction?

We know that part of the answer is in the way these latter companies think about themselves. Both the Shell study and the work of Jim Collins and Jerry Porras in their 1994 book, *Built to Last*, indicate that these successful learners define themselves and set their

priorities quite differently from the majority of commercial corporations. One major difference is that those companies see themselves as communities with a characteristic culture or ideology,
which they combine with a pragmatic pursuit of profits. They certainly do not see themselves primarily or uniquely as economic units
to produce profits and value for entrepreneur and shareholder.

By contrast, in today's society, a consensus exists that business
is about profits and that management has no choice but to maximize profits or shareholder value as its top priority—preferably at
the shortest possible notice. It is rare, nowadays, to hear voices like
Dave Packard's, the late cofounder of Hewlett-Packard, saying that
"a company doesn't exist simply to make money." The law in most
countries gives the holder of shares in a limited-liability company
the power to enforce the maximization of profits and shareholder
value as top priorities. And that is what they do. Even in companies that by nature have other priorities, such as cooperatives, mutuals, or partnerships, some carpetbagging members will try to divide
the commons: "to take it all and to take it now." No thanks is given
to previous generations that did the building and little thought to
succeeding generations that may need the fruits.

Surprisingly, this seems to be also the credo of many new-
economy companies. "Surprisingly," because these companies are
clearly work communities based on people and have little capital
investment. They desperately need high learning and innovation
abilities, yet they have a legal setup as if they are nineteenth-
century industrial enterprises based on capital assets. Their employees receive some of the company's shares—not for weighing
their private capital but because the continued input of their human
talents is the only basis of the company's enduring success. This success is then measured by the price at which these notional shares
are sold. So what happens after the successful sale of the shares or
the IPO? On the one hand, does it produce a number of wealthy individuals facing the fate of a star tennis player? "Done it all at thirty-
five, so what are we going to do with the remaining forty-five years

of our life?" On the other hand, what will we do with the company? Its shares are now in the hands of people who did put up substantial capital sums but who are not members of the work community that is the only source of that company's enduring success. Finally, what should be the priorities of the people who happen to be the responsible management of the company after the sale or IPO? Should they be managing the company again for maximum profits at the shortest possible notice?

On the basis of historical evidence, these behavior patterns of the new-economy company are unlikely to lead to high survival rates. And in fact, we have already seen huge numbers of these once-promising start-ups crash and burn. Putting (individual) profits before people and before the interests of the (work) community as a whole was no recipe for success in the old economy. Could it be that the future and the new economy are different? It's beginning to be clear that the answer is a resounding *no*.

And what is this new economy anyway?

The Demise of the Old Economy

There is little doubt that once again we are living through a storm of creative destruction.

Twenty years ago, the talk was about the postindustrial society. The words *postindustrial society* seemed to suggest that makers of things would not find a place in that society. Future prosperity would be found in the production of services rather than material goods. Interestingly, by the mid-1980s, the original worry had disappeared from the press headlines. There was still a concern that the world around business was turbulent, but the theme was different. The headlines changed from "postindustrial" to "We are moving into the Information Age" or the "Knowledge Society" and lately into the "New Economy."

Any distracted, busy manager looking at these headlines could just think that all the talk is, indeed, about a new technology. And

Schumpeter is right: a new technology is a threatening, unpleasant experience for a lot of companies. Many companies actually die on the wave of a new technology. But long-, well-established companies would not unduly worry about it. If you are three hundred years old like Mitsui or two hundred years old like Du Pont, you would not worry about new technologies because you have seen so many come and go. You have seen steam being replaced by the internal combustion engine. You have seen the advent of chemicals. A company like Du Pont was actually able to ride on the chemical wave and flourish. A new technology can be an opportunity. That company would therefore not necessarily change the way it runs the business. So what change in the world would require a company to be run in a different way than it was used to? When would its managers have to sit up, innovate, and change their ways and their priorities in order for their company to survive and thrive?

In this light, let us look at the new economy to try to define its distinguishing characteristics. What does it mean for a company to be successful as a business in such a new economy?

A Historical Perspective

To answer those questions, allow me to use the language of economics, that most maligned of sciences, which still has a lot to offer in this debate. Economics handbooks give a short and interesting definition of what business is about. This definition goes as follows: "Business is about the production of goods and services by combining three production factors—land and natural resources, capital, and labor."

Unfortunately, economics textbooks rarely show that over long periods of time, these three production factors do not carry the same weight in the process of producing goods and services. So let us allow historians into the debate. From their books, it becomes clear that in early or pre-medieval times land was the dominant production factor. That had consequences. In pre-medieval society, those who had land were rich and powerful, and those who did not were poor. There were very few rich people and lots of poor people.

It also had consequences for the managerial methods employed for the production of goods in that pre-medieval society. Land is a finite production factor; there is only so much of it. Successful landowners who wanted to increase their production had to get hold of more land. Generally, they would find that somebody else was already sitting on it. So we should not be surprised that the managerial methods in the pre-medieval society were characterized by violence. Success was measured by the size of landholdings and the ability to hold on to them. And the other two production factors were either not existent (capital) or subordinated in a literal sense: feudalism, even slavery (labor).

The Rise of Capitalism

Then about five hundred years ago, two miracles happened in northern Italy and in Flanders. First, production had begun to exceed the immediate needs for consumption. As the science of economics teaches us, when production is higher than consumption, the difference between the two is called *savings*. The second miracle was that these savings found their way into the productive processes of the times rather than into the lifestyle of the land-based elite. Ships became bigger. Voyages became longer. Mines became deeper. Machines were added both to the mines and the workshops of the medieval tradesmen. Textiles developed into an industry in Flanders.

A shift was taking place in the three production factors: capital was being added to the processes of producing economic goods.

The results were spectacular. Adding capital to natural resources increased output manyfold. In economic terms, it meant that because capital became such a success factor, obviously everybody engaged in the process of producing goods in that society had to get hold of capital. The demand increased quickly and soon exceeded the available savings. Capital became the scarce production factor. But at the same time, it was the production factor that a tradesman or an entrepreneur needed to be more successful than or as successful as his competitors. Capital became the production factor that was most critical for success.

The shift in the production factors in the fifteenth century went in parallel with a quantum jump in technology: the invention of the printing technique by Gutenberg in Germany. The result was that the societal propagation of accumulated human knowledge became more precise and faster. In his 1990 book, *Bionomics* (p. 8), Rothschild estimates that it became fifty times faster than before. A lot of knowledge all of a sudden became available to infuse in the process of producing goods and services. That had consequences.

First of all, those who had capital were the new rich, who gradually also became more powerful in society at large. Those who did not were poor. As an economist, I would date the beginning of the capitalist era in that period. *Capitalism* starts when capital takes over from land as the dominant and most critical production factor. Some of the elite of the land-based period still hung in there. In many countries, even today, land and those who own it are still king. But it is clear that power in the Western world shifted to the new capitalist rich over the next five hundred years.

The managerial methods obviously had to be very different from the managerial methods of the feudal society. The optimization of capital became top managerial priority instead of the optimization of land. To optimize capital, the manager, the leader, or the owner of the enterprise has to make the maximum use of whatever capital is available in order to remain competitive. Second, to keep access to the supply of capital, they have to ensure that the capital supplier gets the maximum remuneration.

This situation lasted about five hundred years. It still existed when I was a student at what is nowadays called Erasmus University in Rotterdam in the early 1950s.

Capital Is No Longer the Scarce Resource

Since the 1950s, the Western world has gone through a period of unsurpassed capital accumulation. In North America, in Europe, and in Japan, we have had a half-century during which GNP grew 600 percent. Of this constantly growing GNP, society saved between 20 and 30 percent each year. Most of these savings were institutional—through pension and insurance premiums, and so forth. It led to a financial resilience of banks, insurance companies, pension funds, and the like that was unsurpassed in the history of mankind. Total assets of U.S. banks, mutuals, and pension funds surpassed $10 trillion in 1999. Alongside these accumulated savings in the hands of institutions, the wealth controlled by individual millionaires is now estimated at $16 trillion.

So the stock of capital in the world in these last fifty years has increased beyond imagination. At the same time, something else happened: a manyfold increase in the velocity with which that money circulates in the world—notably as a result of the abolition of capital controls. The supply of a good is the multiplication of its stock times the velocity of circulation. My hypothesis is that these developments led to a situation at the beginning of the 1980s whereby the capital market changed from a seller's market to a buyer's market. In the last fifteen to twenty years, capital has no longer been the scarce production factor. Capital has now the same status as the natural resources of the land-based period: it is a commodity like iron ore or wheat. It has to be marketed actively, and it is available for anybody who is able to pay its market price. The evidence has been visible since the early 1980s.

Since the early 1980s, the suppliers of capital have had to engage in aggressive marketing through the packaging and repackaging of credit products to push the excess supply into the market. The competition has heated up to supply not only governments and businesses but even unwitting individuals, for instance, with credit cards they did not ask for. Banks are regularly taking excessive risks and gearing up the supply of capital by leveraging the assets-to-equity ratios into the twenty-five to thirty-five range to compensate for razor-thin margins with higher volumes.

Capitalism in its economic definition finished in the 1980s!

The New Economy

Nowadays the knowledge that is produced in the heads of the people who work together in the process of producing goods and services is the critical production factor that is producing economic value in the new economy.

The evidence is clearly visible for anybody who wants to see. Look at the *Fortune* 500 list: Who is going up and who is coming down? Going up are capital-poor, brain-rich companies: they are communities of people—software firms, IT firms, and auditors. Could anyone have imagined the rise of law firms? Law firms used to live in nice little town houses and have five partners. Or the rise of advertising and media businesses? They are among today's winners.

Again, as in the fifteenth century, the shift in the dominant production factor is accompanied by a quantum jump in technology. This time, it is the microchip revolution. The microchip, like the Gutenberg printing press, increases immensely the speed and precision of the societal propagation of knowledge. And again the business results are spectacular—as are the consequences in society at large.

In a society where the critical production factor shifts to people, wealth and power are shifting to those with access to knowledge, the *new rich*. Those who have no access to knowledge are the *new poor*.

In economic terms, it means that because knowledge—and human talent in general—is the determining success factor, every company engaged in producing economic value has to get hold of talent. The demand for it is increasing fast and in many places is exceeding supply. Human talent is becoming the scarce production factor, and at the same time it is the production factor that an entrepreneur needs to have to be more successful than or as successful as the competition. So it is no surprise that in 1998 McKinsey published a study under the title of "The War for Talent," and the *Economist*, on March 25, 2000, quotes a venture capitalist as saying, "There is no shortage of venture capital or bright ideas, but there is a serious shortage of people with the ability to execute the ideas. Those firms that cannot get the right people will probably fail" (p. 101). Sure, companies die fast, but the talented people find jobs almost immediately. Unemployment figures remain low or are still coming down in many companies.

The managerial methods that worked in the capitalist period will have to shift. The managerial priority of the brain-rich, capital-poor company is to create a work company that is learning faster and better than the competition. It means the optimization of people rather than the optimization of capital. Optimizing people has two elements. First, the manager, the leader, or the owner of the enterprise has to make the maximum use of whatever talent is available in order to remain competitive, which means increasing the learning abilities of the work community as a whole. Second, the manager, leader, or owner has to ensure access to the supply of talent and retention of those that are already there. The latter is not exactly the same problem as maintaining access to the supply of capital in the capitalist period. Access to capital is mostly an economic proposition, which can be solved by maximizing the return on capital. Retention of human talent is not simply a matter of ensuring the maximum remuneration, as the fifty-year-old research of Maslow and McGregor shows convincingly. Notwithstanding the $20 million "club" for Hollywood stars, £1 million salaries at the British Broadcasting Corporation, $50 million transfer fees for soccer players, and the explosion in top-management remuneration, there are serious retention problems that clearly cannot be solved by merely increasing salaries, bonuses, share options, and perks. So how are companies going about solving these problems?

First of all, the surviving companies of the capitalist period have a difficult time in this transitional period. More than ever, learning will be the key to competitive success. It is to be expected that many of them will not weather the present storm of creative destruction with a management generation that is steeped in the control theories of the capitalist period, with large stocks of capital assets that might confuse them into thinking that those assets are still the essence of their existence—rather than people—and into believing that the maximization of shareholder value is still the managerial top priority.

But the companies born in this new epoch have no excuse. They are clearly communities of people with relatively little capital, producing goods and services that are successful in the market only to the extent that they incorporate better ideas than their competitors. Their managerial attention surely must shift to this: How can I maximize both the availability and the use of the available brainpower in my company, my community?

The first obvious step is to get human talent and brains to join the company, and to retain them. Among the practices we see employed nowadays are (often in this order)

1. Hiring (senior) people from the outside

2. Making acquisitions

3. Offering deferred stock options

4. Developing human resources internally

The results are the opposite of those intended. A recent McKinsey study, *The McKinsey Quarterly 2000* (vol. 3), found that "half of those who graduated in the 1971–1990 period left their first jobs within three to five years, and among those who graduated from

1991 to 1993, more than two-thirds did. Recent graduates receive, on average, 30 new offers a year" (p. 5). Junior staff members who come in with the acquired companies often depart in large numbers for rival firms. The remedy usually applied by the company is to offer yet more money.

Developing human resources internally is not done or not done very well. In the McKinsey report "The War for Talent," published in *The McKinsey Quarterly 1998* (vol. 3, pp. 44–57), the results of a survey showed that only 3 percent of the 6,000 executives occupying the top 200 positions at 50 large U.S. corporations agreed that their organizations developed talent quickly and effectively. This situation is in marked contrast with the finding of Collins and Porras in *Built to Last* that in seventeen hundred years of combined life span across long-lasting and highly successful companies, only two of those companies went outside for a CEO.

So, sadly, the expectation must be that the present storm will continue to kill a lot of companies, both old- and new-economy ones. Indeed there is a lot of innovation and a lot of creative destruction. I do not think that it is inevitable or a good thing, but the necessary shift in managerial thinking and priorities to prevent it from happening is not yet visible.

20 DANIEL VASELLA

CAPTURING INNOVATION POWER IN THE GENOMICS ERA

Daniel Vasella is chairman, CEO, and head of the executive committee of the health care company Novartis. He previously was an attending physician at the university hospital in Bern, Switzerland. He is a member of the board of directors of Credit Suisse, the supervisory board of Siemens AG, and the international board of governors of the Peres Center of Peace. He is also a member of the board of directors of Associates of Harvard Business School and the Rockefeller University.

The twentieth century closed with high technology dramatically altering the way we live and work. Entering the twenty-first century, which promises to be the century of biology and information technology, we can expect sweeping changes in managing our health care, based on remarkable discoveries in the biology of the human being.

Many questions have been raised about what lies ahead, which scientific breakthroughs and what innovations will transform our lives and what their impact will be. Novartis is looking ahead to a new decade in which we will experience a revolution in the scientific foundation of our business, as our work is intimately intertwined with the scientific exploration in genomics.

The importance of our future success will depend on our ability to manage our company with a focus on innovation. This commitment to innovation permeates many areas of our business, but it is especially critical in our R&D activities. The key success factors behind the pharmaceutical industry's ability to provide differentiated drugs to customers are very strong innovation, both in discovery research and through access to expertise in biotechnology, and superb functional execution, particularly in R&D development but also in marketing and sales. Although technology tools have an important role in driving discovery and helping us manage a vast amount of data, people are also vital to innovation. Being an innovator means not only having a distinctive research department but also having employees who pursue product innovation aggressively at all levels, both inside and outside their immediate product area.

The Changing Landscape of Our Industry

Novartis has many of the tools in place and holds the expertise to be at the forefront of innovation and drug discovery. But the environment of our industry is rapidly changing. We have to keep a sharp external focus on the competition and on the emerging needs of our customers. This will allow us to identify, develop, and commercialize new ideas, generated both internally and externally.

We are witnessing an impressive shift in demographics, with the balance tilting especially in developed countries toward the older population. The proportion of people over the age of sixty-five is likely to double over the next three decades. This creates an imperative for medicines targeted to diseases for which the older population is at risk, such as cancer and neurodegenerative and cardiovascular diseases.

Patients are becoming increasingly empowered, as they are better informed about products, new discoveries, and health care options. This trend is accelerating due to the Internet. If we look at the United States, estimates are that there are more than fifty thousand health care Web sites. Of the ninety million Americans who have access to the Internet, more than two-thirds have used it to search for health information. In Europe, patients and their families can also find information about their health problems on Web pages and through health portals, which link to a number of different sites. Some portals, for example, offer information about a condition and available drugs, in addition to providing a self-assessment questionnaire to evaluate one's risk, and a bulletin board for patients to exchange personal experience about their medical conditions and treatment options. We will see a further increase in consumer portals in Europe that offer information about medical conditions and drugs. This will increase the ability of patients to be full partners with their doctor regarding health care decisions.

The Challenge of Discovering New Drugs

The costs of drug discovery and development are escalating every year. Today it takes eight to twelve years for one new medicine to come to market, and still only one in every ten thousand substances actually reaches the market. The investments required for developing an innovative new drug have risen over the past two decades tenfold, to an estimated average of around $800 million.

In a recent survey, pharmaceutical industry leaders expressed the opinion that new technologies should begin to lower costs as enhanced technology tools improve the industry's ability to select higher-quality medicines and targets. By the end of this decade, the industry anticipates that it will experience a 65 percent increase in the number of medicines entering clinical development. This could quadruple the yield of new compounds brought to market annually.

The overall time to market for new drugs is expected to be reduced by a third over the next ten years. This could be accomplished as the pharmaceutical industry uses increasingly public and private gene databases and tools such as bioinformatics and computational chemistry to accelerate the design and development of critical new drug leads. The ultimate goal is to identify successful compounds sooner that offer the greatest value to patients. Scientific excellence and creativity are key to modern drug research, but there are other elements. Due to the multidisciplinary processes and the novel technologies employed, discovery and development—and therefore innovation—must be professionally managed. There needs to be a focus on high-value research programs, maximum efficiency, and productivity.

Our Approach to Innovation Management in Research

To optimally exploit the opportunities in pharmaceutical research, we are focusing on

- *Prioritization of targets*. The exponential increase in the number and types of potential drug targets makes it necessary to select targets according to disease priorities and *drugability* (that is, the ease of finding druglike molecules).

- *Speed and productivity*. In order to achieve optimal speed, our drug discovery processes must be multi-parallel and based on a "drug discovery engine" with large-scale capabilities. Furthermore we need to instill a culture that encourages discarding failing targets quickly and picking new ones. All of this will contribute to enhancing the productivity of our R&D

activities by increasing our speed to market and therefore ensuring our continued success in an ever-increasingly competitive environment.

- *Talent.* To attract and retain the best talent is a major challenge, especially when competing with academia and focused biotech companies. In order to be successful in this respect, we make sure that we have a comprehensive and interactive array of technology platforms in place. At the same time, we foster an attractive scientific environment based on smaller entrepreneurial units.

- *Technologies.* We have access to state-of-the-art technologies with applications to important biomedical problems, including technologies such as genomics, proteomics, cell biology, engineering, computation, and combinatorial chemistry.

- *Alliances.* To complement our in-house innovation effort, we enter into collaborations with world-leading biotech and academic groups. These relationships are driven by our desire to have access to leading discovery technologies, to novel external disease targets and therapeutic leads, to key intellectual property, to top scientific groups, and to the exploration of novel diseases and scientific hypotheses.

Prioritization of Targets

Rather than simply looking for drug targets, we focus on prioritizing targets. In order to do so, we first must analyze and understand the competitive marketplace. This includes a review of Novartis's capabilities and position in the market compared with other players. It is also essential that we assess the market potential and the value of current and future therapies, along with the impact of illness and the social cost of diseases.

Our next challenge is to use optimally the vast amount of data generated by the sequencing of the human genome and to study the functions of the genes. Novartis is unique in having an integrated approach that includes a broad array of technology platforms and significant bioinformatic power.

Our resources are focused on gaining leadership in *functional genomics*, the field of science that is targeted to understanding the function of a particular gene and to learning how to modulate the gene function. This is the crucial step for discovering therapies that can treat and cure disease. We therefore have set up a dedicated in-house functional genomics group and also have established the Genomics Institute of the Novartis Foundation (GNF), which has one of the largest privately funded functional genomics programs.

Functional genomics relies on a set of interacting technologies at our disposal, including the following:

- *Differential display.* In order to understand the differences in gene expression in normal and diseased cells and tissues, researchers have developed the differential display technology. It can provide important clues as to which genes are involved in disease onset and progression. Advances in micro-array and gene-chip technologies are helping to further the "high-throughput" capacity of this approach.

- *Proteomics.* Proteomics is an important and complementary approach to other genomics tools, which aims to produce high-resolution protein maps for a given organism. Understanding both how proteins interact with one another in biochemical networks and which of these molecules are the key players in diseases will

provide valuable knowledge for developing new
therapies.

- *Model organisms.* The genetic and biochemical path-
  ways and mechanisms of yeast, fruit flies, worms, and
  mammals share similarities. The study of these organisms, therefore, can provide valuable information and
  insight into the function and dysfunction of genes and
  proteins in human beings. The relative ease with
  which these models can be studied in the laboratory
  makes them attractive to drug discovery.

- *Bioinformatics.* The vast amount of gene sequence and
  related data generated by the Human Genome Project,
  for instance, requires an increasing number of highly
  sophisticated informatics tools to store, manage, and
  analyze data in a meaningful and timely way.

Speed and Productivity

To increase our productivity in drug research, we are taking the following steps:

- Engaging in target validation throughout the drug discovery process

- Implementing multiparallel drug discovery processes

In addition to these concrete actions, we need to capture productivity improvement opportunities through scientific synergies
and economies of scale and scope across our entire R&D organization. This implies the creation of an integrated research organization
facilitating the exploitation of synergies between therapeutic areas.
Furthermore we must continue to increase our internal and external investments in critical technologies, such as multiparallel screening, bioinformatics, and knowledge management.

Internally, we can speed up the selection of candidate compounds and the clinical proof of concept by strengthening the coordination between our research and development departments. At Novartis, we have established "Proof of Research in Development" (PRIDE) teams, which are responsible for rapidly testing compounds in research to prove their value and potential for further development. By extending the scope of the current PRIDE teams, we can further build capability that extends from lead optimization in research through phase one in clinical development. This will enable us to bridge the critical interface between research and development.

Externally, we are developing more partnerships with leading-edge biotech entities. One example is the collaboration we have set up with Vertex to support discovery activities in the field of human *kinases*. Kinases are proteins that are able to switch cell activities on and off and are therefore believed to play a crucial role in many different disease states, such as cancer, diabetes, rheumatoid arthritis, and cardiovascular diseases. Vertex, which is a leader in kinase research, will help us accelerate our time lines and increase our success rates in the early phases of development. Although we have enhanced our productivity over the past few years, we still have ambitions to improve further. The type of relationship that we have established with Vertex extends the work we are doing in-house. It brings synergies to our own drug discovery activities and, at the same time, gives us access to novel compounds from external sources.

Attracting and Retaining the Best Talent

A sizable R&D budget provides Novartis with access to the latest technologies and thereby helps us offer positions that compare competitively with academia, which has been traditionally the first option for top scientists. However, that critical mass can be both an advantage and a disadvantage. Scientists prefer to work in smaller size units, where they can have a sense of ownership and account-ability for their projects. Organizational considerations in R&D are therefore paramount. We are evaluating our research organization to accomplish the following:

- Maximize creativity and innovation.

- Ensure ownership and clear accountability.

- Minimize bureaucracy.

- Foster entrepreneurship through performance-related incentives.

The GNF in La Jolla, California, is one model that illustrates how we are accomplishing this. This institute is headed by Professor Peter Schultz, who has been described as "part entrepreneur, part research administrator, and part organic chemist." The GNF structure is one in which scientists can also hold academic positions. Schultz typifies this, serving as a director of several start-up companies and running a forty-person lab at Scripps Research Institute at the same time that he heads GNF. He describes GNF as being between a university and a biotech–pharmaceutical research operation.

The advantage and attractiveness of our GNF model is that it is unique in bringing together all the new research tools under one roof, using them synergistically to explore gene function. This would not be possible in a university setting, because of the dedicated resources and focused efforts that are necessary to mount a research operation of this scope. Similarly, biotech companies are not as effective as the GNF model, as they are usually centered on one technology or product area. GNF has the advantage of being somewhat like a new "Bell Lab" of biology, with an outstanding technological infrastructure and a small team working in tight collaboration. The GNF model is only one example of how we are selecting and fostering entrepreneurial and innovative talent.

New Health Care Solutions and Implications for Individuals

The new wave of genomics will greatly increase the proportion of therapies that modify, cure, or prevent disease processes by identifying the causative process and intervening in it. This will be a fundamental change in medical care, offering considerable added value over today's therapies, which largely provide only symptomatic relief.

The importance of genetics is especially increasing in the study of cancer. Today there are 369 biotech drugs in development, and 47 percent of them target cancer. One recently launched Novartis compound illustrates how rational drug design can help discover new therapies. This compound (Gleevec) was developed for the treatment of chronic myelogenous leukemia (CML). This particular type of leukemia is caused by a chromosomal translocation, which is essentially an exchange of genetic material between two different chromosomes. The result of this translocation is the production of an abnormal protein that causes an uncontrolled proliferation of the leukemic cells. Gleevec has been designed specifically to block the function of this protein. The precision of the drug's targeting differentiates it from other cancer treatment. Clinical results have shown that 80 to 90 percent of patients respond to Gleevec therapy. By targeting a specific cause of cancer, one can discover and develop a therapy that impedes the cancer without harming normal cells. For patients, this is revolutionary in terms of improving survival rates and reducing side effects.

Knowledge of genes and their function is already changing the way we categorize and treat diseases. Diseases with similar symptoms may have different underlying molecular pathologies, requiring different treatment strategies. More accurate classification of diseases could lead to so-called individualized medicines, allowing doctors to tailor therapies to subsets of disease and to individuals. In each person, a small variation in genetic makeup can influence whether a medicine will work or whether it will cause side effects.

Conclusions

The discoveries in genomics taking place today will facilitate the development of more effective medicines, enabling us to solve individual health care needs more quickly. R&D at Novartis is actively being managed to foster innovative new solutions in health care. Innovation is not limited to research. Throughout the company, we are striving to build a flat organization with strong entrepreneurial values, based on processes for encouraging "out-of-the-box" thinking. We will make sure that our business plans capture maximum value from innovative opportunities. Leadership in innovation as well as performance management will substantially contribute to our long-term success.

21 WILLIAM J. BRATTON
WILLIAM ANDREWS

LEADING FOR INNOVATION AND RESULTS IN POLICE DEPARTMENTS

William J. Bratton has been chief or commissioner of five different police departments. At the New York City Transit Police, he restored morale and established a patrol strategy that eventually cut subway crime by more than 80 percent. At the NYPD, he remotivated an underperforming organization to successfully reduce neighborhood crime. He is now a police management consultant.

William Andrews was special assistant to Commissioner Bratton at the NYPD, responsible for shaping and communicating the commissioner's message to thirty-eight thousand police officers and five thousand civilian employees. Previously with the New York City Transit Police and principal author of their 1991 Plan of Action, he is currently a police management consultant.

Until recently, few people would have associated police departments with the word *innovation*. To outsiders, and especially to criminologists and other scholars, police departments appeared to be conservative bureaucracies, slow to adapt to rapidly changing realities in the communities where they did their work. Many of these scholars even came to the conclusion that police couldn't do much about preventing crime, which was said to be driven by social and economic factors beyond police control. Police departments were seen as reactive entities that were called in after crime had done its damage to take reports and investigate. They might be able to control crime at the margins, scholars argued, but they would never be able to develop innovative programs to actually prevent crime or to drive down significantly the amount of crime in any given community.

What my team and I accomplished during my tenure as New York City police commissioner should change that perception forever. I came in as commissioner in 1994 with the unwavering belief, in contrast to the prevailing wisdom of the 1970s and 1980s, that we could cut crime through focused problem-solving efforts. Police can control criminal and disorderly behavior to such an extent that they can change the behavior of many crime-prone individuals. With well-organized, highly focused police agencies applying innovative techniques to fighting crime and to managing their own operations, I saw the potential for American police departments to achieve declines in crime of 30, 40, and even 50 percent.

If I had one overriding goal at the NYPD, and at the other police departments I have headed, it was to establish an atmosphere of creative innovation. As a lifelong police officer and police administrator, I know perfectly well that most police departments don't encourage or value innovation, cultivating instead conformity, complacency, and even timidity among police managers. But I also have met countless police officers and managers in my career who are bold, inventive, decisive, and eager for the big challenges of restoring order and safety to urban communities. My job as a police executive was to bring those people to the fore and let them run. Theodore Roosevelt, who preceded me as the civilian head of the NYPD by almost exactly a hundred years, defined my credo as a manager when he wrote, "The best executive is one who has sense enough to pick good men to do what he wants done and self restraint enough to keep him from meddling with them while they do it."

In 1994 and 1995, we turned the NYPD into a hotbed of innovation, opening the organization to its own ideas and the talents of its own people. Since then, the department has cut crime in New York in half and homicide by nearly 70 percent. The crime drop was even larger in the toughest, most crime-ridden neighborhoods, where peace and order were restored to virtual war zones. I believe that successful crime fighting on the streets began with successful management changes in the offices and precincts of the NYPD. We had to free the organization from itself before it could begin to free the city of crime and criminals.

In managing five police departments ranging in size from one hundred to thirty-eight thousand officers during my twenty-six-year police career, I have learned a lot about organizations. I am convinced that in many public and private enterprises, the organizations themselves—their structure, their management, their culture—stand in the way of their people and therefore of their success. Nowhere is this truer than in police departments, where frustration is almost a way of life among rank-and-file cops. They want desperately to make a difference—they became cops to make a difference—but their departments throw roadblock after roadblock in their paths, turning what should be a vital, engaging, people-oriented job into a deadening bureaucratic routine. The idealism that most young cops bring to the job slips predictably into cynicism. I think the same kind of frustration can be found in many other public agencies and private businesses. A lot of organizations are assemblages of human creativity and energy struggling to get out. These organizations have the human resources to achieve their goals. They just don't know how to use them.

The organizational leader's job is to energize and motivate the organization, to take all that human capital and put it to work. A good leader becomes both the driving force behind organizational change and the symbol of it. Change emanates from the leader. With the right leader, a low-performing organization with a scattershot focus and an inability to perform its central missions can be transformed into a dynamo of human energy, intelligence, and innovation.

In accomplishing this transformation, the leader performs four broad functions: developing and communicating the vision, building the management team while inspiring both managers and the workforce, streamlining the corporate structure, and holding the organization's managers accountable for reaching its goals.

Vision and Communication

Revitalizing organizations—and especially service organizations like police departments—is both a leadership and a communications challenge. To break the stranglehold of low-performance habits, the leader must develop a vision of where the organization is going and what it can potentially achieve and then communicate that vision to the organization's members. The best way of doing this is to find and motivate other leaders within the organization who share the vision or can be converted to it and who then help spread the word. At every level, moving the organization forward is a question of people communicating with people about goals, values, strategies, and methods. The bigger the organization, the more important this process is.

But to do all this, the top leader has to share power. The micromanager, who tries to control every aspect of the organization, and the organizational bully, who tries to intimidate subordinates into better performance, are both going to fail, especially in large organizations. To propel a large organization forward, the leader has to enlist literally hundreds of coleaders at every level. The leader has to share both the vision and the power with these many allies because only they can use the power to make the vision a reality.

Working in police departments has given me a great appreciation for human capital. That's because police departments don't have much to work with other than their people. A fleet of cars, a bunch of run-down precinct buildings, a crime lab, a radio dispatch system, and a few high-tech toys are pretty much the extent of the physical assets. You have to improve those assets to help your people work better, but your real task is to motivate, energize, and redirect the human capital. In police departments—as in many other organizations—the human capital is a rich resource, a repository of knowledge, skill, and experience that you couldn't buy at any price. Getting it working for you—really working for you—is what leadership is all about. What is often called *morale* is nothing more than the shared sense in an organization that the human capital isn't going to be wasted, ignored, and belittled. Workers at every level in every organization are just waiting for the opportunity to be a part of something they can believe in. Once they believe, they'll give you their best efforts and their best ideas as a gift.

A successful master plan for revitalizing organizations should be a cooperative effort with workers rather than a top-down attempt to force-feed or bully them. Every organization has a core group of people with original ideas and untapped talents. Some are in leadership positions, and some are not. A successful leader reaches deeply into the organization to find these people. As part of a department-wide reengineering initiative at the NYPD, we institutionalized the team effort, assigning twelve teams to analyze virtually every aspect of our operations. In a six-month planning process, these teams came forward with some of the most innovative and progressive ideas we developed. At some point in the process, the agenda slips from the leader's control, and like a conductor during a great performance of his orchestra, the leader is riding the music like everyone else. I love those moments most of all, when the organization begins to set its own agenda, and the many leaders I have cultivated and encouraged at every level come into their own and take charge.

Choosing and Leading Your Team

I entered four of the five police departments that I have run as a stranger. Building a winning team in an organization that you are unfamiliar with is one of the biggest challenges a new leader faces.

You have to learn to judge managers quickly and accurately. You have to learn to mix and match the skills and personalities of your top executives for maximum effectiveness. You have to learn how to develop and cultivate the best middle managers, a second tier of talent (and the organization's future leaders), to support the efforts of the executive staff. By developing middle management, you are also helping to ensure that the changes you are making will have a lasting and deep effect on the organization long after you are gone.

Although I usually bring in a few outsiders wherever I go and am not averse to cleaning house when the situation requires it, I much prefer to work with and cultivate the people I find. Opening up an organization is like opening up a Christmas present. You discover great riches inside of talented and often underutilized people.

It's not uncommon for managers to erect hierarchical barriers to a detrimental degree. I have known CEOs who considered it the height of efficiency to limit the number of their direct reports to ten people or fewer. It becomes almost a fetish for them and their gatekeepers to keep people away from them. That's not an effective way to run a modern organization. The CEOs who operate this way are managing up, not down. They are clearing their desks and their schedules for the big brain work that they are supposedly going to do after they have gathered information from their ten rarefied sources. It's as if they believe that the whole purpose of the organization is to provide them with free time. Although they might deceive themselves into believing that they don't need contact with people in the organization, people in the organization—especially the middle managers—very much need contact with them.

I have always used planning meetings to develop management talent, especially middle managers. My philosophy is to cast a wide net; you never know what you will find. So when the organization was facing an issue, I would bring in ten or twelve experts from around the department to meet with me. These were orderly meetings, but they were also intellectual free-for-alls, with the participants encouraged to speak their minds. The meetings are quite a contrast to a lot of management meetings I've seen in police organizations, where people practically sit at attention waiting to be called on to speak their piece and then sputter it out as if they were afraid of using too much of the boss's time. What's the boss's time for, if not to cultivate the skill and enthusiasm of the managers in the field? Brainstorming is best done with a lot of brains in the room. That insight was the foundation for Compstat, the award-winning management system that we developed at the NYPD and that I will discuss later in the chapter under accountability systems.

I'm also a great believer in "battlefield promotions." When people show initiative, perseverance, and competence in the field, reward them. I found my best managers in the middle and at the bottom of the vast management cadre at the NYPD. Their promotions sent a signal of opportunity to their fellow managers. The old NYPD, like many multilayered bureaucracies, promoted its top managers by seniority and the old-boy network. I rewarded initiative, risk taking, and achievement. The second- and third-ranking executives in the NYPD today were mere precinct commanders in 1994, decades away from rising to their current jobs under the old system. In seven years, they rose through the new NYPD because of what they could do, not whom they knew.

It's important to be consistent and controlled in your relationships with all these managers. There is nothing more counterproductive in management than temper tantrums. Sometimes it's necessary to lower the boom. Most times it's not. People who have failed usually know it without your shouting in their faces. You can make your disappointment just as clear without a tirade, and you can make it work more effectively. Instead of feeling abused and trampled on and therefore resentful, your subordinates can walk away with a painful sense that they have let you down and a renewed determination to do better. The shouters in management are indulging their own needs and abusing their power. I turned around one of the largest public bureaucracies in the United States without raising my voice.

Streamlining the Structure

Organizations get top-heavy. It's a natural evolution. People want to be managers, and managers want to promote their protégés to managerial positions. Slowly but surely, more and more people rise to the top. The organization starts inventing new layers of management for all the new managers. The new managers start inventing self-justifying ways to oversee and interfere with the fundamental work of the organization. Before long, the organization is maintaining an army of naysayers, second-guessers, and hangers-on who aren't contributing much to the basic work and who may even be damaging it. It's a Leaning Tower of Pisa, ready to topple over.

In government, we call it the bureaucracy, but there's a bureaucracy in business too, just as large and just as pervasive. It defends its prerogatives and turf fiercely. One of the best ways to overcome it is by making the right structural changes. Eliminate the superfluous, overstaffed divisions of your management corps, and you will go a long way toward eliminating the worst abuses of the bureaucracy, including the self-justifying, defensive atmosphere, the endless paper chase, the fear of failure, and the often punitive and abusive management style.

I use a rule of thumb: when an organization is more than three or four layers deep, it's time to pare away some of the fat. As a CEO, whenever possible, you don't want to be more than four steps from your basic unit of production or service. In large police departments, the basic unit is the precinct. That's where most police patrol is directed from. That's where the detective squads, which investigate most crimes, are housed. The precinct is the place where a police department's most important work gets done.

The old NYPD had a wedding cake structure that insulated top management from its seventy-six neighborhood precincts. If you worked in headquarters where the bosses got to know you, your career could take off. If you were out in a precinct, you'd be lucky if they had ever heard of you. The top managers distrusted whatever and whomever they didn't know, so the precinct commanders were given very little latitude or actual authority. Even an outstanding precinct commander's performance against crime would go largely unnoticed because nobody was monitoring that kind of success. But a corruption scandal or a mishandled community incident could set a career back years. The precinct commander's job was all downside risk; there was no real way to succeed and a dozen ways to fail. It wasn't an atmosphere that inspired risk taking or creativity.

We restored the precinct and the precinct commander to the center stage in the NYPD. I made it clear to the middle managers of the organization that they should be spending their middle years in the precincts. That was the place to shine. That was the place to advance. We eliminated one entire layer of management, freeing up experienced management personnel for precinct assignments. I was telling the young managers of the NYPD to go out and make their marks in the precincts.

But I was also making it possible for them to do so. The management superstructure overseeing the precincts had spewed out rules for years: precincts will not execute search warrants; precincts will not conduct plainclothes drug operations; precincts will not conduct anti-prostitution operations; precincts will not turn out more than 10 percent of their personnel in plainclothes; and so on, and so on. The truth is that the precinct, the basic unit of service in the police department, was being undercut by its own management.

We ended all that. We gave precinct managers a new vision of precinct policing, the resources they needed, and the freedom to execute the vision within local contexts. The good ones leaped at the chance, and the precincts become a natural arena for team building. Cops like to do police work. Stinging a drug dealer with a buy-and-bust operation, catching a john soliciting sex, executing a search warrant at the apartment of a gun dealer, or even using a decibel meter to stop someone from blasting a car radio—these are interesting jobs compared with regular patrol, even if the hours are worse and the danger is greater. They are also team activities that give the workers a shared sense of purpose and a renewed sense of energy. In the old NYPD, a timid management corps foreclosed all of this energy and activity because they were afraid someone was going to make a mistake. They were right about the mistake. They were making it themselves.

Accountability Systems

Lack of accountability can be a problem in any large organization, but it is the hallmark of police departments. In most departments, the chain of command doesn't enforce accountability. Passing the buck is refined to an art form. Perhaps believing that they are delegating authority, police managers hand off problems with dexterity to the next level of supervision. A problem will march right down the chain of command from chief to inspector to captain to sergeant and finally to the cop who has to try to solve it in the streets. Blame moves in the same direction. People don't want to take responsibility because the organization has no track record for rewarding people who do. Taking responsibility only gets you into trouble. Success is something you stand next to after it has happened. It's not something you go out and seek.

The Compstat process, the NYPD's now famous crime control meetings, built a system of accountability in the NYPD. In an organization that had never used crime data to direct its daily operations (amazing, considering that the primary role and obligation of a police department should be to prevent crime), we developed a weekly crime report that displayed crime incident and arrest data for every precinct in the city. Using this report, the NYPD commanders could watch weekly crime trends with the same hawklike attention that corporate managers pay to profit and loss. Crime statistics became the department's bottom line and are the best indicator of how police are doing, precinct by precinct and citywide.

The next step was our award-winning innovation, the Compstat crime strategy meetings. In a five-week cycle, we brought in every borough command, consisting of about ten precincts each, to do what had never been done in the NYPD before—talk with the department's top commanders about precinct crime problems and how to control them. For the first time in the NYPD's history, the chief of department and other top officials were sitting across from the precinct commanders wanting to know what their problems were, what their strategies were, and what their progress had been since the last session.

As the Compstat meetings grew more sophisticated, we began computer-mapping the crime patterns and displaying the maps on large overhead screens. You could see the clusters of shootings, robberies, burglaries, and car thefts. We also mapped arrest and patrol activity and compared crime incidents with police response. If the two didn't match up, you knew you were doing something wrong. We did the same thing with time-of-day graphs, which showed us when the crime spikes were occurring. We compared those data with our deployment patterns. People talk about the interactive use of computers. Compstat actually does it. It's an age-old organizational problem: Are you putting your resources where the problems are? Compstat's maps helped make sure that we were.

Compstat also enforced cooperation among the NYPD's many bureaus and units. The precinct commander and the detective squad commander were being grilled at the podium, but every other relevant police commander for that area of the city was also present, including narcotics commanders, warrant enforcement commanders, vice unit commanders, and all the other commanders of special units and task forces. The simple device of having them all in one room, talking about specific crime problems, cut the Gordian knot of the NYPD bureaucracy. There was no more paper chase, no more months of delay, no more "send us a report and we'll get back to you." The chief of department and the deputy commissioner for operations brokered solutions to current crime problems on the spot. The police department was doing what it's supposed to do: quickly assessing crime patterns, rapidly responding to what it has learned, and relentlessly analyzing outcomes. New York City criminals never knew what hit them.

Compstat also turned out to be a very effective way to communicate within the organization. Although strategic guidance flowed down to the precincts, many of the individual tactics to accomplish the strategies flowed up from precinct commanders, detective squad commanders, and rank-and-file police officers and detectives. In the five-week Compstat cycle, the effectiveness of every new tactic or program was rapidly assessed. Failed tactics didn't last long, and successful tactics were quickly replicated in other precincts. The gathering of field intelligence, the adapting of tactics to changing conditions, the close review of field results became a continual daily process rather than an annual or biennial event. The NYPD was suddenly able to make fundamental changes in its strategic approach in a few weeks rather than a few years.

As Compstat evolved, it added representatives from various other criminal justice agencies, including corrections officers, prosecutors, parole officers, and federal and state law enforcement officials. The enlarged Compstat encouraged better coordination, cooperation, and cross-fertilization of ideas across jurisdictional and specialty lines. Working with this wider group, we sought and often achieved an atmosphere of continual creativity and innovation in responding to developing crime and disorder patterns. Innovation, once a rarity in the NYPD, had become day-to-day reality in the nation's largest police department.

22 ANN M. LIVERMORE

INVENTING
E-SERVICES

*Ann M. Livermore, president of Hewlett-Packard's
Services Business, is responsible for helping customers
reinvent their businesses to gain competitive advantage. She is responsible for professional services,
financing, and marketing. With Hewlett-Packard
for nearly twenty years, she is on the executive council. Fortune magazine has named her the eleventh
most powerful woman in American business.*

We all know that the global economy is currently undergoing
a shift as profound as the shift from the Agrarian Age to the
Industrial Revolution. As the Industrial Age transforms into the Information Age, we're seeing massive changes in the way business is
conducted, much of it thanks to the growth of the Internet. It's a
whole new ball game—one in which flexibility, quick thinking, and
quick action are required. Established businesses are reinventing
themselves, and brand-new start-ups are developing innovative new
business models.

In this chapter, I'd like to provide a bit of a case study and tell
you how Hewlett-Packard—a sixty-two-year-old company—is reinventing itself to take advantage of new opportunities in the marketplace and to deliver the best possible customer experience.

Every company needs to have an Internet strategy today. That's not just true for start-ups; it's true for established companies as well. In May 1999, HP made an inventive move in the marketplace by launching *e-services* (http://www.hp.com/solutions1/e-services/), our Internet strategy. But what began as HP's Internet strategy developed into a journey of invention that has affected every part of the company.

First, let me explain how we developed the e-services strategy. We knew that we wanted HP to drive the next generation of computing, so in January 1999 we went into think tank mode with about ten people. We locked them in a room and blacked out the windows. Four members of the team were from HP; the other six were thought leaders from various sectors of the technology industry.

We talked with our customers. We dug deep in HP Labs. We talked with industry watchers, and we talked with key technology and Internet strategists inside and outside of HP. We looked at what worked well on the Net, and we examined the Net's shortcomings. We looked at new business models and how they might evolve. We looked at the role telecom companies, service providers, and others would play as the major catalysts for this new world. We looked at what was preventing companies from getting the full value out of their information technology (IT) investments. But most of all, our goal was to examine the next logical evolution of the Net. And a central thread emerged: a world of interconnected services—e-services.

The Logical Evolution of the Net

In the history of the Internet, the granddaddy of Internet companies, Netscape, had led the way in showing us how to use Internet technology to bring business processes on-line. These on-line processes not only increased efficiency but also helped improve both the top and bottom lines of a business; this was what IBM later termed *e-business*. Other first movers—the Amazon.coms and the

Schwabs of the world—figured out how to sell goods and services on the Net and got *e-commerce* off to a running start. And even though e-commerce has certainly taken some hits recently, it is clear that it is here to stay and will remain a key element for just about any business with goods and services to sell.

At HP, we saw these first two major developments—e-business and e-commerce—as the essential foundations that were necessary before e-services could take hold. E-business enabled us to share information and make business processes available over the Net; e-commerce made the exchange of goods and services for money possible over the Net.

The next logical step was to catalyze this whole infrastructure so that it could support billions of new information appliances and trillions of new transactions and make it fundamental to the economics of business and society. This is where e-services fit in. So what exactly is an e-service?

We define an *e-service* as any asset that is made available via the Internet to drive new revenue streams or create new efficiencies. In other words, they help you make money or save money. Or they make a specific task or process easier for you to complete.

E-services can be applications, computing resources, services, processes, or information. They can conduct a transaction, complete a task, or solve a problem. They can be used by people, applications, businesses, or even devices. What we saw when talking to the folks in HP Labs was that there are now more than forty times more devices with chips in them than there are personal computers. This includes intelligent devices such as your mobile phone, your pager, your printer, your personal digital assistant (PDA), your watch, or your car. These products become more valuable when they have services wrapped around them. And e-services not only allow companies to wrap services around products, but they also enable these devices to talk to one another. Software can talk to software. Some e-services will be aggregated on Web sites. Others will work behind the scenes, invoked automatically.

Here are a few examples of e-services:

- Business-to-business e-services (such as bill payment and presentment, automated supply-chain management, procurement, and modular enterprise resource planning)

- Computing e-services that give companies much more flexibility in managing their IT infrastructures (infrastructure on demand, outsourced storage, directory services, and data mining)

- Pay-per-use consumer e-services tightly woven into daily life (financial-planning e-services, vacation-planning e-services, relocation e-services, traffic-routing e-services)

Unlike today's large, proprietary e-business and e-commerce systems, these e-services are highly modular, and each service functions as a building block for other e-services.

In the near future, we see the emergence of a marketplace that dynamically brokers e-services. HP is developing the technology, called *e-speak* (http://www.e-speak.hp.com/), that creates a new breed of intelligent services and appliances. Using the Linux model, we've made the e-speak source code freely available on the Net so that any software developer can download it and work with it. E-speak technology makes it possible for services to advertise their capabilities and then interact with other e-services to complete a transaction or task on your behalf. Requests for services can be automatically brokered, bid, and transacted on the Net, from any device.

It's important to remember that nobody talked about e-services two years ago. Now everybody talks about them. HP is defining the language in this space. E-services have become HP's strategy—driving R&D investments, product plans, and sales-and-marketing spending. It's clear that e-services are the next big wave of growth, and we've aligned our entire company around them. What's more, we're inventing ways to take e-services to the next stage.

The Three Vectors

When we take a closer look at e-services, we see that they involve not just the services themselves but also the intelligent devices that deliver those services and the always-on Internet infrastructure—wired or wireless—on which those services are powered. The intersection of these three vectors—e-services, intelligent devices, and always-on Internet infrastructure—is where transformational, market-making opportunities exist. Let's look at the three vectors.

The first vector is e-services. Any process can be turned into a service and delivered over the Net. And any process that is inefficient *will* be turned into a service and delivered over the Net. It's only a question of time, and this is a marvelous opportunity for every enterprise.

The second vector is intelligent, connected devices and environments. HP invented the first information appliance, by the way. It was the handheld calculator, which we first delivered to customers in 1972. This has evolved into the Jornada (http://www.hp.com/jornada/), HP's handheld PC that runs a complete Web browser with full 128-bit encryption for security. Intelligent devices will proliferate, not consolidate. They will become almost anything and everything—printers, calculators, scanners, digital cameras, mobile phones, wristwatches. The Web-enabled Swatch watch will be delivered soon. So using intelligent devices to access e-services isn't way out in the future. It's here.

The third vector is Internet infrastructure. An always-on Internet infrastructure is needed to support these trillions of e-services and billions of devices. That infrastructure has to be incredibly reliable and secure, easily managed, and highly available. It needs to be like a utility—a computing utility—always there, always on.

Computing as a utility is something HP has pioneered for fifteen years, and now we are at the point in time where it really is possible—as an e-service.

So HP works in all three of these vectors. But it's the intersection of the three that represents our unique competitive advantage. Our strategy is to work at the intersection of these three vectors and help companies transform their businesses—and their industries—so they can serve customers better. As usual, we won't work alone. We'll partner with companies that can help us exploit that intersection. We're known for being a great partner. That's an important differentiator in the Internet economy, where partnerships are key to success.

At the Intersection: Printing E-Services

Think about the potential of this intersection strategy. If you look at HP's printing business, it's about a $20 billion a year business. And we have lots of market share—more than 70 percent. Printers are a ubiquitous intelligent, connected device for HP.

We used to think that our $20 billion printing business was a product business. We now understand that we have about 3 percent of the available market opportunity—because all of a sudden, we're thinking about printers as intelligent devices that enable a whole set of e-services that can be delivered over an always-on infrastructure. When you look at the intersection of printers, e-services, and infrastructure, that $20 billion printing business becomes a $100 billion market opportunity.

For example, take an inefficient process, such as standing in line at the post office to buy stamps. Well, now that process is an e-service delivered over the Web and accessed by a ubiquitous information appliance—the printer. Other printing e-services include newspaper printing e-services and ticket e-services.

HP has turned the printing and imaging market upside down by reinventing the role of printers and printing. Instead of being simply "peripherals," printing and imaging equipment is now a platform for delivering services, bringing both individuals and organizations greater value and utility. This is a great example of how HP is helping to make the Internet work for customers rather than the other way around.

You can also download Web content on your mobile phone, point it at an HP printer, and print. We invented technology that enables any information appliance to print without wires.

Printing e-services are just one example of how HP is playing at the intersection of intelligent devices, e-services, and always-on infrastructure to transform industries and improve the customer experience. Think about all the other industries and all the other processes that can be transformed in that intersection.

Inventing for the Common Good

Much of the excitement in today's business landscape revolves around new business models that the Internet has enabled. Let me close this chapter by giving a few examples of how e-services are enabling new business models that help solve some of the world's problems, such as hunger and poverty. HP has a vision of a world where the Internet works for people instead of people having to work the Net, a world where technology is truly for everyone, not just the elite.

Giving back to the community has always been a part of HP. In fact, one of HP's founders, Dave Packard, expressed the company's philosophy in his book, *The HP Way*. He said, "The purpose of the HP company is to improve the welfare of humanity. . . . the purpose of the company is contribution." HP has always cared about contribution to the community in addition to contribution to customers and contribution to the bottom line.

Two projects we're working on, the LINCOS Project and the Grameen Bank Project, help developing countries pursue sustainable economic development that has a minimal impact on the environment. These projects also plan to provide telemedicine and other e-services that improve the quality of life.

The LINCOS Project is bringing Internet connectivity and information technology into areas of the developing world that are currently poorly served, starting in Central America and environs. The technology sits inside what's called a LINCOS unit, which is a refurbished metal shipping container that contains computing and printing equipment, a cell phone base station, and a satellite connection to the Internet. E-services and applications being developed include telemedicine, environmental analysis, education, communications, banking and financial services, e-commerce, and videoconferencing and entertainment.

Each community that has a LINCOS unit will have a local board of advisers. This board will coordinate services with the local community, including the government, businesses, and the general public. The LINCOS units are therefore intended as genuine "digital town centers." We anticipate that the physical technology that LINCOS brings to a community will eventually be supplanted by purely private, commercial infrastructure. We hope that the community center aspect of the LINCOS units may remain, however, by providing open public access, regardless of income, to the Internet.

The Grameen Bank Project, which is located in Bangladesh, focuses on telemedicine and financial e-services. The telemedicine e-service aims to improve the birth process for both mother and baby. Delivery death rates in Bangladesh are among the highest in the world. A telemedicine e-service will connect communications units in remote villages with a central hospital. The equipment at the remote end will include a fetal health monitor and some ultrasound imaging capability, as well as equipment necessary to obtain the vital signs of the mother. The equipment will be such that it can be operated by a technician who can be trained specifically for these tasks, with no other medical training necessary. HP will enable additional image-based, health-related data transfers. Hospital staff will review the data and offer advice to the patients.

The financial e-service targets money transfers. Getting money from one place to another in Bangladesh by mail is slow and unreliable. Because there is no wire-line telephone service available in remote areas, this e-service uses mobile phones to provide a secure, fast, and reliable way of conducting money transfers electronically, in conjunction with Grameen Bank's existing financial services.

Here's another example that's closer to home. In the United States, HP, along with America's Second Harvest, sponsors ResourceLink (http://www.resourcelink.org/), a project that uses e-services to deliver food to charities that need it. ResourceLink acts as a virtual warehouse where businesses can donate first-quality products, surplus products, or discontinued products to certified charitable organizations.

Today billions of dollars worth of goods are discarded because manufacturers cannot easily find charities that can take large quantities of goods. Nearly a hundred billion pounds of consumable food are destroyed annually in the United States alone. We have some of the most efficient food producers in the world, yet billions of pounds of food go to waste. We also have great distribution capability, much of which goes unused every day. And we have people in need who don't have enough to eat. Now *this* defines an inefficient process—excess food, excess distribution capability, people who don't have enough to eat. Supply is not reaching demand. HP took this inefficient process and turned it into an e-service called ResourceLink. ResourceLink matches donor companies with charities in real time, thus eliminating the time and costs of finding a good use for the products. The service also links to transportation company partners that provide no- or low-cost shipping.

Creating a more efficient way in which suppliers can donate their surplus goods has provided the ultimate win-win scenario: suppliers solve a business problem of slow-moving inventory and generate substantial tax deductions, and charities receive much-needed items to assist them with their mission of helping people develop highly productive lives.

Kraft, Pillsbury, General Mills, Nabisco, and dozens of other major manufacturers are using ResourceLink in their donation efforts. ResourceLink will expand over the next year to include donations of surplus apparel and building materials.

I hope I've given you a sense of the current business landscape and what HP is doing to succeed in it. This is an economy and a marketplace that have demanded inventive thinking like no other time in history.

When I say "inventive," I mean

- Turning problems upside down and looking at them from new angles

- Taking the initiative to create the future—rather than just responding to it

- Accepting radical ideas when approaching a problem

With e-services, we're fortifying the culture of radical ideas that began sixty-two years ago when Bill Hewlett and Dave Packard entered their garage to invent useful and significant things. Invention is truly at the heart of HP. Helping companies invent. Helping people invent. Whether we're working with a large multinational corporation, a service provider, an Internet start-up, an individual consumer, or a developing nation, HP is committed to inventing the technologies and solutions and business models that help them thrive in the Internet economy.

23 JOHN KAO

REINVENTING INNOVATION

A Perspective from The Idea Factory

John Kao, dubbed a "serial innovator" by the Economist, *is founder and CEO of The Idea Factory, which offers new methodologies for embedding innovation in corporations. He wrote* Jamming, *a Busi*nessWeek *best-seller. He is also a psychiatrist, jazz pianist, Tony-nominated producer, former Harvard Business School faculty member, and founder of Ealing Digital, a next-generation studio for new media.*

When I give speeches these days, I often start with two questions. First, I ask for a show of hands. I ask, "How many of you feel that innovation, however you understand it, is fundamental for the future of your company?" Anywhere between 80 and 99 percent of the audience usually raises their hands. Then I ask the second question, "How many of you believe that your company has a system for innovation that satisfies three simple tests? First, your people know that the system exists; it's not a state secret. Second, it works pretty well, whatever that means to you. And third, on some basis, no matter how irregular, it leads to the realization of value on an ongoing basis for your organization."

I have never had an audience—whether from Silicon Valley, Tokyo, the public sector, or the *Fortune* 500—in which more than 2 percent raised their hands to the second question. That illustrates a key dilemma regarding the corporate practice of innovation: on the one hand, we all want it; on the other hand, few if any can point to systematic practices that express corporate innovation through the realization of value in a reliable and continuous fashion. In short, there is a vast gap between the aspiration to innovation and its reality.

A Lack of Existing Processes to Practice or Measure Innovation

It may be instructive to contrast this state of affairs with how other organizational priorities are handled. In the field of finance, for example, the typical firm has well-established systems. There is a chief financial officer, a person responsible for budgets, and a planning cycle. You know where your money is, or at least you should! Analogous systems exist for dealing with human resources, consisting of on-line human resource information systems (HRIS), personnel managers, and benefits plans. It's all reassuringly concrete.

In contrast, few organizations have a designated *innovation process owner* or *chief innovation officer*. The relevant metrics for return on innovation, or ROI, are usually lacking. Innovation processes lack a physical container or platform within which the new and unproven may be shielded from the established and cynical. Innovation itself is not tangible form; it is virtually impossible to locate the embodiments of an integrated, purposeful, strategically relevant innovation system within most organizations.

Innovation practices that are in step with the speed, uncertainty, and volatility of the new economy are still a promissory note in this day and age. Until we go beyond brainstorming or simply tweaking a new product development process, we will never arrive at the promised land of strategic innovation. Knowing that innovation is critical isn't enough. "Getting it" is one thing. "Getting it done" is quite another.

The practice of innovation needs to be reinvented precisely because if there is any attribute that best defines the so-called new economy, it is the imperative of innovation. The imperatives of the new economy demand it—requiring speed, pushing new forms of winner-take-all competitive dynamics, introducing business models that involve the creation of standards. And hovering over all these factors is the accelerated transformation of technology—for example, the Internet itself is a powerful form of innovation technology in its ability to disintermediate the relationship among capital, talent, and ideas, giving surprising strength to new innovators.

In an era in which everyone clamors for innovation, it is paradoxically harder to find. The word itself is in danger of becoming a synonym for *good*. No one wants to be "uninnovative." As such, innovation becomes the answer offered to every business question. Is it about cutting costs? Retaining key people? Aligning personnel and organizational goals? Creating greater efficiency? Realizing disruptive innovation? Changing the nature of the game we are playing?

If the agendas for innovation are diverse, so are the proposed remedies. It's like the story of the blind men and the elephant. Innovation is . . . ideation and brainstorming. It is . . . enhanced product development and product development funnel. It's about . . . culture. Compensation. And so forth, and so on.

Innovation is so important that the word itself is groaning under the weight of expectations placed on it. Yet as a systematic practice, it remains obscure. Few understand how to implement innovation, and increasingly, the traditional engines of innovation are breaking down.

For example, incubators have proliferated recently as the latest innovation panacea, bottling creative energies and shielding them from an unsympathetic environment. As of 2000, there were 50 incubators in Singapore; 150 in London. Probably there are far fewer today. The current value-added of incubators rests for the most part with readily replicable, easily commoditized offerings for which the best and brightest ventures are understandably reluctant to surrender equity. A question looms over the sustainability of the incubator business model.

Venture capital is broken. Classical venture capital involved cool people writing checks to other cool people to start cool companies. Today, in an era of billion-dollar funds, the game is about efficient capital allocation, while the ratio of thinking to execution increasingly shrinks in the face of constrained human bandwidth. Company building or investment banking? It's sometimes hard to tell the difference.

As a further example of the innovation "gap," traditional corporate venture departments have difficulty going outside of what they know to what is disruptive and game changing. Managers tend to traffic less in foresight for the future than in the politics of the present. The struggles around who will get to create the officially anointed future obscure a richer level of dialogue around what is unexpected but potentially more valuable.

Amid the chaos of the innovation "field," it is imperative that concrete practices be developed and the conceptual frameworks underlying innovation redefined, for we are not interested in coming up with a new toaster or a new "me-too" dotcom company, but rather in realizing the strategic value from large-scale, competitively significant innovation platforms and systems.

A New Model

Innovation in the new economy requires a new model. At my company, The Idea Factory, we call the process *innovation aggregation*— the systematic integration of large-scale components crucial for innovation: talent, capital, intellectual property, personal and corporate relationships, innovation methodologies, foresight tools, and the ability to link resources in diverse geographies and disciplines.

An *idea factory* provides a context for innovation that allows this integration to take place.

Although the idea factory concept is itself a work in progress, if I could offer a prediction at this point, I would say that within the next five years, many organizations will have such explicit, embedded innovation systems. They will have a chief innovation officer or (in the current argot) an *innovation process owner*. They will have well-documented practices and systems for innovation, by which I don't mean a set of specs or a big industrial mechanism for spewing out ideas. They will have physical places and virtual spaces in which the work of innovation takes place.

I will offer another prediction, which is that the new disciplines of corporate innovation will come from unlikely sources. In my work over the past few years at The Idea Factory, I have spent time with (and recruited) industrial designers, cultural anthropologists, improvisational actors, theater directors, digital designers, and cognitive psychologists, among others. If we are to reinvent innovation, we must be open to knowledge from the periphery of our understanding and not merely reaffirm the tired "wisdom" of the mainstream.

To embrace innovation encompasses a number of fundamental design questions. Innovation is the path by which we seek the future we prefer—not the future that we're going to get, but rather the future we want. Firms typically have talent, ideas, resources, brands, history, competencies—assets galore. But large questions beckon. What is the path you wish to take? What is needed to get where you want to go? What is the future of desire? Innovation fits with a designer's definition of *design:* the ability to move from the existing to the preferred.

Most important, we need to understand the concept of an *innovation system*. I define it as an integrated set of processes, policies, and tools that link corporate strategy to new sources of value (products, services, processes) in order to create sustainable competitive advantage.

The challenge of designing an innovation system, a robust set of innovation practices that allow the journey to the preferred, is complex and rich with issues. For some organizations, it opens up a veritable Pandora's box; once you start talking about innovation, a number of core organizational issues surface whether you want them to or not. If you take innovation seriously within an organization, it touches every aspect of how business is done. It's about leadership, organizational structure, knowledge management, corporate purpose and values, norms regarding collaboration, and strategy processes. The purpose of an innovation system is to embrace these disparate agendas and align them, building the linkages and frameworks that embed innovation throughout the organization.

Innovation touches everything. An innovation system requires an examination of the organization in a holistic manner, which is why most organizations have a tough time grasping the agenda. Innovation is not simply about slathering a little rhetoric onto the organization and into your corporate communications documents. Virtually every business now says somewhere in its annual report that it strives for innovation and supports the work of its talented people. And much of the time, this amounts to nothing more than meaningless public relations. It's the minimum requirement for organizations to be politically correct. What we need instead is a lot more than the "mascara" of innovation. We have to talk about the hard work of creating deep capabilities within the organization, capabilities that, once established with tremendous effort and patience, don't go away and instead confer competitive advantage over long periods of time.

What makes this difficult is that the models we have of innovation are dictated by a form of economic logic that although not dead has certainly been superseded in many ways by the logics at the heart of the new economy. In a sense, we are always shifting between two forms of economic logic, from *economies of scale* to *economies of discovery*. Economies of scale reward manufacturing-oriented businesses that achieve scale, long production runs, and the learning-curve effects that come with them. These lead in turn to lower costs, higher margins, more profits, enhanced competitiveness, further scale, more factories, until all of a sudden you're the Ford Motor Company. The economies-of-scale organization is of necessity hierarchical and control focused, as is the mind-set of its managers.

Economies of discovery, which in my opinion are characteristic of the new economy, work quite differently. Instead of efficiency, we strive for originality, for what will change the game. Instead of hierarchy and control, the focus of management must be on collaboration and enabling what is new. Instead of cost-effectiveness, we must strive for investment in the future and experimentation with no certainty of return.

Every organization, I believe, needs to master both forms of economic logic. Obviously, when you go to your brain surgeon, you don't want the surgeon getting inspired while trying to extract your tumor. You want the surgeon to know how to do the job and to carry it out quickly. We all want benchmarks to get the job done more efficiently. But this does not lead to disruptive, game-changing innovation, the stuff of which organizational renewal and competitiveness under conditions of uncertainty are all about.

This is an important point because in times of stability, economies of scale make absolute sense. In search of long production runs, you tweak the machines, they vibrate a little and then calm down, so that more product spews out, and then you do a little production line adjustment, and you keep getting more valuable "stuff" out the other end. But the present era of instability requires wholesale reinvention. It is not enough to simply tweak the machine. And reinvention means a willingness to embrace the unexpected, the surprising, the uncertain, in the interest of creating new forms of demand and value. It's about "brave new world" versus "better faster cheaper."

New Types of Strategy, New Ways
of Thinking and Doing

To get there, we need new disciplines of strategy. There must first be an intimate connection between strategic thinking and innovation. Strategic planning must coexist with strategic foresight. Innovation then becomes an answer to a set of strategic questions. Strategy is useless without innovation; innovation is directionless without strategy. Second, we must develop robust innovation processes. These are not simply about ideas. Ideas are the easy part! Every organization needs a process for design around ideas, which creates the right kind of prototypes and experiments that in turn engender creative collaboration and iterative experimentation around the idea.

We also need a new sense of the scope of innovation. We have to look at it far beyond products and services to new ways of seeing and shifting perspective, so that a new vision, a new set of possibilities, can emerge. It may involve new ways of delighting customers or simply finding out about customers. Clearly, innovation is also about new ways of doing things, new processes, and new ways of making sense of the environment. We only see what we have eyes to see. Institutions only acknowledge the reality defined by their processes. They can't see beyond their version of the visible spectrum.

So how do we step outside of our existing, limited approaches to innovation?

One path that The Idea Factory has explored is to investigate the value of new disciplines and perspectives drawn from design, theater, and systems thinking.

Design is an innovation process that is not about figuring out a specification and then filling in the blanks. Design is the ability to create interim understandings of what you want that you apply effort to transcend. Specifically, it's a process of prototyping, which is modeling or simulating your best current understandings precisely and correctly, so you can share them with people of different discipline bases and perspectives. That will also allow you to break that prototype and iterate, prototype again and iterate, until you get to some desired outcome that you could not necessarily have predicted in the beginning.

Most designers understand that when you start with a question like how to improve a toaster, the way that you arrive at being able to say "I like that end point" is a process that could not be predicted. It's like the musical art and discipline of jazz. You have to achieve a balance between structure and freedom to get to a desired end point. It's not simply about beginning with engineering specifications and then proceeding to a desired end point through flawless execution. You do arrive, but then you also exclude all other potential options in your haste to arrive at a known destination. Design is about enabling any relevant idea, without a road map that guides the journey to the exclusion of what might be genuinely new and valuable. In this sense, design is inherently a process for getting to unpredicted outcomes. This is why a rich direction for the reinvention of innovation lies in the application of design disciplines to the prototyping of business models, organizational structures, corporate cultures, customer experiences, and other facets of business process.

The second discipline used by The Idea Factory is theater. We often hear the complaint from companies, "We spent all this money on strategy, but nothing changed, nothing happened." It is clear that in order for an organization to embrace innovation, people have to take risks. This means that they have to be really committed to doing something new, because taking risks means that there may be unpleasant consequences as well as pleasant outcomes.

You have to have a way of enabling people to shift their perspective so they see why something is important and develop the commitment to pursue a new horizon. So if, for instance, I hand you a memo that says we're going to have an event called the French Revolution, and here are five reasons why it is happening, please check here if you're interested in participating, it's not an exciting experience. But if I take you to a revolutionary theater, and I tell you about the evil that has occurred in our history, and I immerse you in symbolism and vivid colors, you may get very excited and want to do something dramatically different. This underlies the significance of why one of Mao's first priorities when he took over China was to establish firm control over the country's storytelling apparatus: film, publishing, and theater. Whoever controls the dream owns the future.

Theater goes back to the Greeks. The purpose of theater was to transform your moral perspective in the deepest sense. Moral perspective implies dealing with large, fundamental questions such as, What is the good life? What is most important? How should the collective be governed? These are transcendent issues, just as relevant to a multinational company as to the Greek *polis*. Theater, seen in this sense, becomes a crucial and unique form of social prototyping, a public shared space within which the telling of stories leads to shared meaning and emotional experience that changes something profoundly. It sets an agenda for the modern enterprise: how to create new kinds of communication tools and meaning-carrying vehicles that allow change processes to become revolutionary in the best sense. By that, I mean not just sharing content but also creating a context around the content that allows it to come alive.

The third and final leg of the new innovation tripod involves systems: the notion that the innovation process isn't simply a painfully explicit end-to-end product development approach or an episodic ideation process, but rather a management approach that requires the design of integrated, continuous, and persistent organizational systems. In our language, this is about designing a custom idea factory for a particular organization. To be systematic about innovation encompasses a variety of organizational design issues. Many companies think that if they have one optimized venture development process and one funding mechanism, then they're done. I would argue that they've just started. These days, companies that are great at innovation need to do many things, including what is redundant, messy, overlapping, and inefficient. Companies need to have an innovation portfolio, not just an innovation strategy.

At The Idea Factory, we sit down with management and audit innovation practices. We work to understand what the current innovation practices are and what they need to be for the company to achieve its desired set of outcomes. One needs to think through how to build such an innovation system, with everything from the tools of compensation, resource allocation, and organizational structure to the communication systems and leadership style. We would also argue that if you get serious about innovation, you're committing yourself to a long and broad road, because innovation touches everything about a company, how it behaves and operates.

The knowledge that organizations have is often much less valuable than the knowledge they wish they had—if they only knew what it was. That is key to the kind of reinvented innovation processes we seek. Three sets of tools inform how we help companies get outside of their established perspectives to what is new and potentially valuable.

First are disciplines of strategic foresight—the ability to take imaginative leaps into the future and then come back to the present in the search for appropriate execution. Scenario planning and experience design can support such leaps through processes that differ fundamentally from classical strategic planning—drawing a line from yesterday through today in an effort to arrive at tomorrow. Planning and foresight are both necessary, and in the appropriate balance. Most organizations have a great deal of planning but little foresight.

A second source of new thinking comes from customer-centered design, involving processes that surface the often implicit or tacit dimensions of a user's wants and needs. One requires the skill set of a trained ethnographer to observe behavior and induce patterns of desire that might not have been otherwise apparent.

Organizations can also animate their innovation processes by a considered reexamination of their core purpose, mission, and values. Often a clue to the reinvention of innovation in a particular organizational context comes from the reframing of this all-important cultural DNA.

To arrive at the promised land of innovation, companies must develop new kinds of capabilities. We believe in the importance of physical environments that support innovation, that make innovation practices concrete, that support and generate persistence around knowledge creation processes. These are places where knowledge can not only be generated but also deepened—a container for exploration, a studio for collaboration, a context for birthing the new. This container may extend to the virtual dimension as well. IT—nominally "information technology"—will increasingly be viewed as "innovation technology," a set of ways to support collaboration as well as knowledge processes that support organizational innovation.

At its heart, the reinvention of innovation requires developing systematic practices that have persistence, that invite collaboration, and that act as a magnet to convene networks of talent and resources. This is what we mean when we refer to an idea factory and what we have implemented at The Idea Factory. Reinventing innovation within an organization requires transformation. It is a process that involves patience, an agnostic attitude that is willing to try new things, and a pragmatism that is always asking, "So what?" It is a journey across uncharted territory to reach unknown goals that could not be more essential to the future of all organizations.

INDEX

A

ABB, 29
Accelerator businesses, 173
Accenture (Andersen Consulting), 45, 153
Access: of innovators to leaders, 35; to the Internet, 270
Accountability: and blame, 97–98, 158, 260; in business, 63–65, 96–97, 158; deemphasizing the innovator's, 96–98; and ownership by innovators, 92–93, 247
Accounting tools, changing, 111–112
Acquisitions, to add organization capabilities, 206–208
Activity-based costing (ABC), city government, 111–112
Adaptation or innovation, 144
Administration innovation protocols, 219–224
Adopt-a-Block programs, 116
AES, 99–100, 101, 156
Aging populations, rise in, 240–241
Air Canada, 76
All Nippon, 76
Alliances: idea generation, 76, 220, 243, 262, 268; innovation investment, 222

B

Bain & Company, 66
Bakke, D., 156
Bangladesh, e-services in, 269–271
Barberich, K., 3, 57
Barker, J., 12
Barnes & Noble, 78
"Been there, done that" and innovation, 165–176

Amazon.com, 74
Ambiguity and uncertainty, accepting, 43, 156–157, 160, 279
American Airlines, 97
American Express, 132
Andersen Consulting, 45, 153
Andrews, W., 6, 251
Animals, research, 245
Antiwar debate, 67–68
Apple Computer, 135–136
Apprenticeships, Silicon Valley, 166–168, 170–176
Archimedes, 34
Arts, creativity in the, 35, 37–38
Arts, transformational, 281–282
Aspirian, 64
Automobile industry, merger problems, 207

Behavior, superstitious, 44
Behavioral change: number of areas for, 50–51; overcommitment and, 45–46, 50
Behaviors, "because of" and "in spite of," 44, 51
Beliefs, of successful people, key, 41–47
Beneficial surprise. *See* Surprise
Benefits: of helping successful people, 54–55; of leading innovation, 37
Best practice, 5
Bidding for municipal services, competitive, 111–112
Bioinformatics, 245
The Body Shop, 67–68
Boeing, 132, 134
Bonsignore, M., 76
Bossidy, L., 183
Brainstorming meetings, 256–257, 264
Brand, P., 89
Bratton, W. J., 6, 251
"Brave new world" versus "better faster cheaper," 279
Browne, J., 156
Budgets, avoiding predetermined, 99–100
Buffet, W., 91
Building Better Neighborhoods campaign, 110
Bureaucracies. *See* Environments, organizational
Burke, J., 5, 185
Burroughs, 132
Bush, G. W., 105
Business concepts and theories, innovative, 74
Business, definition of, 230
Business-to-business e-services, 266

C

California Family Foundation, 67
Campbell, B., 167
Cancer causes, drugs targeting, 248
Capitalism, the history of, 231–234
Case studies, range of innovation, 216

Causation, and correlation, 44, 51
Chain charts, 146–147; driven, 149–150
Chambers, J., 76
Change: accepting the need for, 43; a culture for, 84–85, 280–284; innovation confused with, 144; innovation as a form of, 31–32; the lack of significant, 144; making a case for, 108–109; organization capability for coping with, 205–211; the pace of, 144, 185, 190, 197–198, 204; performance bidding a catalyst for, 112; and repetition, 181; success beliefs which may inhibit, 41–47; success and the timing of, 24, 40, 154
Change process: encouraging participation in, 16–17, 97; feedback and the follow-up, 53–54; personal investment in the, 16–17, 48, 54–55; strategies, 280–284
Changemasters, 75–76
Charities, donations to, 116–117, 271–272
Charles Schwab Corporation, 4, 120–128, 203
Charts, organization, 146–148
Checklist. *See* Innovation protocols
Chief innovation officer (innovation process owner), 274, 277
Childbirth, telemedicine for, 270
Christensen, C. M., 5, 197, 226–227
Chrysler, 207, 209, 213
Circulation of capital, 233–234
Cirrus Logic, 64
Cisco Systems, 208
Citizenship, twin, 29
Clark, J., 136
Clark, K., 209
Cleveland Orchestra, 136–137
Clubb, M. K., 4, 153
Coaching: by colleagues and peers, 52–54; of executives, 3, 39, 52–54; by mentors, 167–168, 171–175; the process of, 52–54

E-services: for the common good, 269–272; definition of, 265; and Internet evolution, 264–267; printing, 268–269; the three vectors of, 267–268

E-speak technology, 266

Ethic and behavior, 58, 62, 66–68, 89–90, 124

Evaluation of innovation, by professionals or executives, 34

Experience: conventional wisdom and, 95–104; and expertise, 168–170; knowledge and, 5; the value of, 165–176

Experimentation, encouraging, 160–161, 172–173

Expertise, the nature of, 168–170; value of, 175–176

Explorationists, 32

F

Failure and setbacks: assigning blame for, 97–98, 158, 260; and becoming good professionals, 64, 65–66, 68–69; honestly facing, 64–65, 89, 101; innovation incubation, 221–222; learning from, 90–91, 160–161, 175; not punishing, 100–102; tolerance for, 27, 53; and trial-and-error innovation, 100–102

Faith in business, 65–66

Faith-based community groups, 115–117

Families, 270

Fashion and innovation, 144, 275

Federal Express, 134

Federalism, and innovation, 28–30

Feedback: denying the importance of negative, 47, 49; and performance evaluations, 97–98; providing or avoiding, 44–45; receiving behavioral, 48–50; respected sources of, 48–50, 51–52

Field tactics, 83, 257, 262

Financial hardships. *See* Hardships, financial

Financial systems, 274; and company

resource allocation, 208, 210–211; e-services for, 270–271; government, 111

Fischer, B., 168

Fleas, and elephants, 25

Focus groups, 219

Ford, H., 135

Ford Motor Company, 144, 146

Forgiveness, company emphasis on, 101

Framework for managing innovations, RPV: disruptive and sustaining, 6, 202–205, 211–213; and organization capabilities, 211–213

Front Porch Alliance, 115–116

Frustration, professional, 60, 253

Fry, A., 34

Frykholm, S., 36

Funding new ideas. *See* Charities, donations to; Costs

Fusion, creative, 168; assembling expertise for, 170–173; managing, 173–175

Future: focusing on the, 53; planning and innovation, 155–157

G

Gadiesh, O., 66–67

Gardner, H., 3, 41, 57

Gates, W. (Bill), 136

General Electric, 88, 132, 181

General Motors, 98, 146, 209

Geneticists, 59

Genius-with-helpers leadership model, 136

Genomics, functional, 244–245; health care implications of, 248

Genomics Institute of the Novartis Foundation (GNF), 244, 247

Gerstner, L., 76, 149

Geus, A. de, 6, 19, 225

Gittell, H., 97

Goldsmith, M., 3, 39

Goldsmith, S., 4, 105, 114

Good work in business, 57–69; caveats about studying, 68–69;

lessons from, 61–68; responsible professionals, 58–60

Goodness, relying on human, 19–21; *See also* Social innovation

Gore & Associates, W. L., 139

Government: current problems in city, 106; encouraging stakeholders in reform of, 108–110; functions of, 105–106; innovations in, 105–112; introducing internal competition in, 111–112; invention of constitutional, 29–30, 139; police department innovations in, 251–262; reform challenges, 106–108; release of power by, 192; results of innovations in, 112–117

Grameen Bank Project, 269–270

Greek theater, 282

Grimshaw, N., 35

Grocery business, the, 83–84

Growth, rate of company, 202

Guidant Corporation, 103

Gutenberg, J., 232

H

Hackworth, M., 64–65

Half-life of organizational processes, 217

Hamel, G., 149

Handy, C., 2, 23, 40

Handy, E., 25

Hardships, financial: and faith in business, 65–66; honestly facing, 64–65

Health care: medicines, 248, 270; *See also* Pharmaceuticals industry

Health care industry changes, 239–240, 248, 270

Heavyweight teams. *See* Teamwork

Help: asking for, 102–103; the human desire to, 19–21; through charities, 116–117, 271–272; *See also* Social innovation

Herman Miller, 2, 33, 35, 36, 37

Heroic leadership model, the, 136, 141–143; and organization structure, 146–148, 151

Hewlett, W. (Bill), 272

Hewlett-Packard, 6, 34, 134; inventing e-services at, 263–272

Hierarchies. *See* Environments, organizational; Organizations, large

History: and the new economy, 230–231; of technology, 186–187, 188–191, 232

Homeless outreach programs, 116–117, 137–138

Honesty, in business, 63–65, 89, 101

Houser, A., 37–38

Human capital, 254–255

Human genome research, 244, 245

Human nature: importance of human issues and, 62–63; and novel thinking, 189–190; and pattern recognition, 169–170; understanding, 154–155; *See also* Need, human

Human resources: and incentives, 97–98, 101–102, 181–182, 257; organizations with rich, 254–255; scarcity of, 235–237; systems for, 274

Humanitarian work, 67, 116–117, 137–138, 269–272

Hunger, innovations to reduce, 6, 271–272

I

IBM, 76, 132, 149, 207, 209, 213, 264

The Idea Factory, 7, 281, 283, 284; innovation aggregation model, 276–280

Identity, organization culture and, 124, 138, 228; as an innovation culture, 218

IDEO Product Development, 101, 102

IKIWISI Effect, the, 75

Improvement, behavioral, 50–51

Improvisation, and innovation, 35, 75, 84–85, 281

Incubator businesses, 173, 221–222, 275–276

Independence: for innovation,

259–260; of innovators, 26, 33–34; of successful people, 41–42, 48

Indianapolis: mayor's innovations in, 4, 107–112; results of innovations in, 112–117

Individual-as-subject versus individual-as-object, 63, 138, 180–182

Individualized medicines, 248

Individuals, creative. *See* Creative persons

Individuals working in business: benefits of company culture to, 122–124; budgeting by listening to, 99; daily performance of, 183; deemphasis on accountability of, 96–98; emphasizing creative roles of, 125–126; enfranchising, 192–193; identical rewards for, 103; importance of, 122, 180–182, 222; personal communication with, 126–128; qualifications of, 167, 198; recruitment and retention of, 234–235; responsibility for, 62–63, 125–126; soft landings for, 101–102; technologists, 127–128

Individuals working in government: challenges facing, 107–108; change and winning over, 108–109; and competition, 111–112; innovations by, 113–114; police departments, 251–262

Individuals working in nonprofit organizations, 138

Information: functional genomics, 244–245; health, 241, 248; police department and crime, 260–262; sharing or hoarding, 80–81, 223, 254–255

Information age, the, 189, 229–230, 263

Infrastructure: improving municipal services and, 112–117; NYPD Compstat, 260–261; problems as opportunities, 77; technological, 247, 260–261

Innovation: at three levels of a pyramid, 82; and business strategy, 142, 155–157, 178–179; components, 276; and constructive conflict, 159–160; creating the culture for, 73, 82–85; and creative fusion, 168; distinguishing, 143–146; four rules of thumb for, 92–93; as fun, 125; and the human brain, 189–190; and improvisation, 35, 75, 84–85, 281; and kaleidoscope thinking, 74–77, 83–85; management practices counterproductive to, 96–103; minicases, three, 216; as multifaceted, 217–218; as a natural human activity, 96; organizational impediments to, 77–82, 87–88, 96–103; planning and active, 155–157, 255; as regimen or magic, 5, 224; six phases of achieving, 5, 219–224; social versus technical, 134–136; sources of ideas for, 76, 162, 253, 277; and stages of design, 144–145; structural framework for managing types of, 211–213; and structure, 146–147, 161–163, 247, 253, 258–260; as surprise, 32–33, 73, 279; ten rules for stifling, 77–82; three premises of, 5, 217–219; and wishful thinking, 213–214

Innovation aggregation model, the, 276–280

Innovation capabilities of organizations. *See* Organization capability for innovation

Innovation, definitions of, 166; concepts confused with, 143–146, 275; Drucker's, 1, 89

Innovation process owner, 274, 277

Innovation protocols, 215, 219–224; idea generation, 219–220; impact screen, 220–221; improvement, 223–224; incubation, 173, 221–222, 275–276; integration, 223; investment, 222

Innovation squared, 134

Innovation systems: innovation aggregation model, 276–280; lack of, 274–276; strategies, 280–284; *See also* Innovation protocols

Innovations: acceptance and performance, 92; disruptive or sustaining, 202–205, 211–212, 276; following or leading, 132–134; improvement of, 223–224; leveraging, 223; and making connections, 33–34; organization capabilities and requirements of, 211–213; ownership and accountability for, 92–93, 247; pioneering, 132–133; practical testing of, 92, 117; pursuing or abandoning, 91–92, 93; relationships between separate, 186; six phases of protocols for, 219–224; unsuccessful companies with, 132–133

Intel, 202

Internet business: approaches to, 78, 209, 264; the innovative environment of, 119–120; spinout organizations for, 209; and traditional business values, 121, 210

Internet service providers (ISPs), 76

Internet, the: always-on infrastructure of, 267–268; city government use of, 112, 260–261; health information availability, 241; logical evolution of, 264–267

Invention and continuity, 24–25

Investment: in innovation, 222; in people, 122, 180–182, 222; personal, in the change process, 16–17, 48, 54–55

J

Jacobsen, R., 67

Jacobson, R., 17

Janoff, S., 17

Japan, leadership models in, 42–43

Jazz, the creative environment of, 35, 281

Jobs, S., 135, 136

Johnson & Johnson, 133

Journalists, 59–60

K

Kaewert, D., 76

Kaleidoscope thinking, 74–77, 83–85

Kanter, R. M., 3, 73

Kao, J., 7, 273

Kaye, B., 49

Kelleher, H., 75

Kelley, D., 101, 102

Kinases, human, 246

Knowledge: alliances with sources of, 220, 222, 243, 277; and expertise, 168–170; history of advancement of, 186–187, 232; know-what, know-how, and know-who, 5, 167; new ways of advancing, 188–191; for organizational survival, 6, 227, 279; and power, 192–193; proliferation and differentiation, 188; wealth and access to, 234–235

Knowling, R. E., Jr., 5, 177

Kotter, J., 143

L

Labor, division of, 188–189, 193, 231–232

Land, E., 136

Land and wealth, 6, 230–231

Leaders: attention to spinouts from, 211; creation of organization culture by, 124–125; empowering decision making by, 80; four transformational functions of, 254–262; great organizations or great, 136–137; heroic model of, 136, 141–143, 146–148, 151; history of technology and, 186–187, 191, 230–237; innovation stifled by, 77–78; and innovators, 33–35, 37–38, 88–89; moral, 66–68; as symbols of organizational change, 253–254; tantrums by, 257; and understanding human nature, 154–155

Leading innovation: benefits of, 37;

and core company beliefs, 124–125, 278; following or, 132–134; managing or, 4, 137–138; strategies for, 33–35, 155–157, 254–262

Learning: about metrics, 162–163; accepting mistakes during, 100–101, 160; action-based, 160–161; by doing, 174–175; encouraging, 95–96; and expertise, 168–170; from experience, 165–176; and innovation, 155; *See also* Teachers

Learning loops model, 4, 149–152

Leonard, D. A., 5, 165

Lester, H., 76

Leukemia, drugs targeting, 248

Life cycles: of innovations, 224; of organizational processes, 217

Life expectancy of organizations, 225, 226–228; and the human resources shortage, 235–237

Life processes, scale-independent, 14

LINCOS Project, 269–270

Listening: budget-setting by, 99; improving, 50; to colleagues' feedback, 51–54, 99; to colleagues' stories, 19; to customers, 76, 124, 126, 219–220; to poor city neighborhoods, 110; to unique perspectives, 16, 272, 281–282; *See also* Communication

Livermore, A. M., 6, 263

Looped-learning model, 4, 149–152

Loyalty: group and larger collective, 29; to ideas, 14–15, 33–34, 217

Luconi, F., 169

Lufthansa, 76

M

Machines, treating people as, 13, 20, 189

Management practices: avoiding conventional, 95–104; in city government, 111–112; counterproductive to innovation, 96–103; driven chain, 149–150; energizing, 149–152; of heroic leadership, 136,

141–143, 146–148; innovation in, 138–139; and innovation structure, 146–148, 161–163; learning loops, 149–152; streamlining, 258–260

Managing innovation: by avoiding conventional wisdom, 95–104; leading or, 4, 141–143; the narrowing path of, 34

Mandelbaum, F., 167

Mao Zedong, 23, 282

Maps and graphs, Compstat, 260–261

Margins, gross, 201

Markets: capital, 233–234; and industry innovation and design stages, 144–145; speed of innovations reaching the, 6, 78, 80, 242–243, 245–246; spinout organizations for different, 210; and stock fluctuations, 64, 66, 181; for sustaining and disruptive technologies, 203–205

Marriott, 132

Maslow, A. H., 139, 235

Masters, J., 32

Maybach, W., 189

McGregor, D., 235

McInnes, P., 103

McKinsey & Company, 132, 235, 236–237

McKnight, W., 135

McNamara, R., 151

McNealy, S., 76

Meaning: and common metrics, 182–183; company culture and, 122–124, 138, 228; creativity engaged by, 14–15; diversity and shared, 18; of innovation, 217

Measuring: behavioral change, 54; the contributions of innovators, 34, 162–163; government performance, 112, 117; system for innovation, 274–276; *See also* Metrics

Medicines. *See* Pharmaceuticals industry

Medtronic, 209, 213

Meetings: company vision and values development, 179–180, 264; face-to-face, 126–128, 256–257; police department, 256–257

The Men's Wearhouse, 162

Mentor capitalists, 171–172

Mentors, 167–168, 170–175

Merck, 133, 135–136

Merck, G., 135

Mergers, organizational, 25, 202, 206–208

Merrill Lynch, 203, 210

Metrics, performance, 5, 162; government, 112; using a common set of, 182–183

Microchip revolution, the, 234

Microsoft, 62–63, 136

Miller, Herman, 35

Mintzberg, H., 4, 141

Mishina, K., 143

Mission: the importance of, 89–91, 127; reexamination of, 283–284; and shared goals, 97, 254–255

Mission statements: company contributions, 269, 272; components of, 63; new city vision, 108–109

Morale, 255

Motivations of innovators: and goals, 36, 98, 216; iconoclastic, 219–220; meaningfulness, 14–15, 217; passion, 26, 220, 221; real results, 36, 117; self-initiated, 42

Motorola, 219

Municipal services. *See* Government; Indianapolis

Murray, M., 62–63

Music and creativity, 35, 37–38, 136–137, 281

N

Naisbitt, J., 30

Nasser, J., 181

Natural resources, economy based on, 230–231

NBC [Symphony] Orchestra, 136–137

Need, human: E-services to satisfy, 266, 269–272; innovation before feeling a, 2, 23–24; for reinventing innovation, 273–276; sensing a, 75–76, 283; for "soft stuff," 62–63, 101–102; speed of technology change and evolution of, 204

Neely, M., 137–138

"Negative capability," 26–27

Neighborhoods: benefits of change to, 109–110; empowering, 114–116

Netscape, 136, 264

Networks: knowledge, 170–173; virtual, 222; web, 147–148

New Alchemists, the, 25–27

New economy, the, 6, 234–237, 279; historical perspective on, 229–234

New York Police Department (NYPD). *See* Police departments, innovation in

New-economy companies: profit priorities of, 228–229; *See also* Silicon Valley; Start-up companies

Nonprofit organizations: innovation in, 137–138; *See also* Individuals working in non-profit organizations

Nordstrom, 132, 139

Notebaert, R. (Dick), 126, 182

Novartis, 6, 239–240, 243–244, 246, 248, 249

Nucor, 132

NYPD. *See* Police departments, innovation in

O

Old Guard attitudes, 25

Olson, K., 136

Openness to innovation, 1, 33, 279

Optimism, 43–44

O'Reilly, C. A., III, 98, 101

Organisms, model, 245

Organization capability for innovation, 197–214; and acquisitions, 206–208; change and creating, 205–211; four approaches to, 6; and the human resources shortage,

235–237; and innovation aggregation, 276–280; internal creation of,
208–209, 213; and internal diversity, 15–16; and new strategies and
disciplines, 280–2894; RPV framework analysis, 198–202, 204; in
spinout ventures, 209–211, 213;
structural framework for managing,
211–213; and wishful thinking,
213–214; *See also* Innovation
systems
Organizations: citizens working
through local, 115; effective use of
technologies by, 202–205; good-to-
great, study of, 133–134; importance of diversity in, 15–16;
innovation at many levels of, 82,
158, 255, 256; innovative structure
of, 146–148, 161–163, 211–213,
247; as interdependent systems, 98;
life expectancy of, 225, 226–228; as
living systems, 13–14; now defunct
pioneering, 132–133; processes and
inflexibility of, 199–200, 205, 206,
209; resources and flexibility of,
199, 206–207, 210–211, 255;
streamlining, 258–260; and sustaining and disruptive technologies,
202–205, 211–213; three-level
structures of, 82, 182, 256
Organizations, large: centralization
and decentralization in, 29, 210;
company culture of, 121–122; decision making in, 201; discouraging
internal competition in, 102–103;
as elephants, 2, 25; and federalism,
28–30; and fleas (innovators), 26–
27; and hierarchy, 79–80, 88, 93,
249, 279; separation of innovative
initiatives within, 93, 208–209,
210
Osborne Computer, 133
Outsourcing, city government,
111–112, 117
Overcommitment by successful people, 45–46, 50

P
Packard, D., 228, 269, 272
Paradigms, changing, 12
Paradoxes: of coordination and con-
trol, 97; of success, 24, 40, 154, 202
Participation in the change process,
16–17
Partners, venture, 268; ideas from, 76
Passion, of innovators, 26, 220, 221
Past, the: learning from, 95–104,
165–176; letting go of, 24, 43, 53;
positive interpretation of, 47; *See
also* History
Patients, empowerment of, 241
Pattern recognition based on experi-
ence, 168–170
Patton, G. S., 160
Pay bonuses for individuals, 103, 223
Paynter, R., 167
Peers. *See* Colleagues and peers
Peet's Coffee and Tea, 132
Penumbra mode thinking, 190
Performance appraisals, 97–98
Performance incentives, 113, 247
Performance objectives, avoiding
quantitative, 99–100
Perkin, W., 186
Peters, T., 201
Pfeffer, J., 3, 95
Pharmaceuticals industry, 6, 209, 213,
239–240, 242–247, 248, 249;
changes, 240–241, 244–245; drugs
development, 241–242; prioritiza-
tion of drug targets, 242, 243–245
Philosophy. *See* Mission; Values
Pilkington Glass, 142
Polaroid, 136
Police departments, innovation in,
251–262; and structure streamlin-
ing, 258–260; and teamwork,
255–257
Pollard, C. M., 3, 63, 87
Porras, J., 201, 227, 237
Portfolio, innovation practices, 283
Positive reinforcement, 44–45
Pottruck, D. S., 4, 119

Poverty, innovations combating, 116–117, 137–138, 271–272

Power industry innovations, 99–100, 101, 156

Precincts. *See* Police departments, innovation in

Principles: moral and ethical, 58, 66–68, 89–90; *See also* Good work in business

Printing e-services, 268–269

Printing press revolution, 232, 234

Problem solving: cutting crime through focused, 252; encouraging, 16–17, 97

Proctor & Gamble, 139

Product innovation protocols, 219–224

Professionals, good: contributing to society, 66–68; faith in business of, 65–66; geneticists and journalists, 58–60; honesty and accountability of, 63–65; sense of responsibility of, 62–63

Professions: information age, 234–237; knowledge from other, 277; *See also names of specific industries*

Profit making: and company resource allocation, 208, 210–211; emphasis on goal of, 228; and ignoring principles, 61; numerical goals for, 99–100, 201

Project on Good Work, 57

Promotion of individuals: and "battlefield" initiative, 257; and performance appraisals, 97–98; rotations and succession, 181–182; and soft landings, 101–102

Proof of Research in Development (PRIDE) teams, 246

Proteins, drugs targeting, 248

Proteomics, 244–245

Protocols, 215, 218; six phases of innovation, 219–224

Prototyping, design, 144–145, 280–281

PSS/World Medical, 101–102

Public education: commitment to, 180; innovation in, 74, 76

Public sector innovation: Indianapolis city government, 107–117; New York Police Department (NYPD), 6, 251–262

Q

Quantification evaluations, influence of, 34, 99–100, 201

Questions, monitoring. *See* Innovation protocols

Quick, S., 114

R

Raters, behavioral feedback, 49–50, 52–54

Recycling surplus goods, 271–272

Reinvention, and the Sigmoid Curves, 23–24

Remington Rand, 132

Research and development, pharmaceuticals, 241–242; innovation management in, 242–247; technologies, 244–245

ResourceLink, 271–272

Responsible professionals, 58–60

Results of innovation: lack of processes measuring, 274–276; measurable city government, 117; positive reinforcement for, 44; real, 36

Retail business, innovation in, 74, 83–84, 162, 219

Rewards for individuals, 103, 158, 223

Riggio, L., 78

Risk-taking: courage for, 104, 220; and decision making, 80; discouraging, 158; and innovative projects, 34, 92, 175, 190

Rock climbing innovations, 134–135

Roddick, A., 67–68

Role models, change and consistency of, 48–49

Rolm, 207

Roosevelt, T., 252–253
Rothschild, M., 232
Royal Dutch Shell Group, 6, 225
Rubbermaid, 77
Ruggles, R. L., 151
Russo, D., 98, 101

S

Salary levels, rise in, 235–236
Sales forecasts, honest, 65
Salick Health Centers, 74
Sandow, G., 137
Sant, R., 100
SAS Institute, 98, 101
Schultz, P., 247
Schumpeter, J. A., 226, 230
Schwab, C., 122, 124–125
Scientists, attracting and retaining,
    243, 246–247
Scripps Research Institute, 247
Script. See Innovation protocols
Scully, J., 135
Seed grants, for innovations, 83
Seldon, L., 182
Self-confidence, 45–46
Self-determination. See Independence
Self-efficacy, 43–45
Self-organization management,
    151–152
ServiceMaster, 63, 89–91, 93,
    116–117
Shapiro, R., 75
Shareholder goals, profit maximiza-
    tion, 228
Shelton, K., 49
Sigmoid Curves, 23–24
Silicon Valley: creative groups in,
    166–168, 170–175; lessons from,
    175–176
Size: as antithetical to innovation,
    142, 202; goals for company, 100,
    268; opportunity, 202, 220,
    268–269; organization, 87–88; trust
    and group, 30; See also Markets;
    Organizations, large
Skepticism, 35

Skunk works, internal, 208–209, 213;
    See also Spinout organizations
Smalter, D. J., 151
Smith, A., 188
Social capital, 167, 171; human and,
    254–255
Social innovation, 282; and con-
    tributing to society, 66–68,
    269–272; technological versus, 4,
    135; as the truest innovation,
    134–136, 269–272
Social problems, innovative venture
    effects on, 116–117, 137–138,
    271–272
Social science research on good work,
    57–69
Social status, 47
Society. See Social innovation
Soft landings policy, 101–102
"Soft stuff," the, 62–63
Solution-creation process participa-
    tion, 16–17
Sony, 133, 134
Southwest Airlines, 75, 96, 97
Specialization, history of, 186–187;
    and new ways of advancing knowl-
    edge, 188–191
Spinout organizations, 93, 208–211,
    213
Stability and change, 123
Stakeholders: city workers as,
    108–109; in innovation, 217; poor
    city neighborhoods as, 109–110
Standing in line, no longer, 268
Staples stores, 74
Star Alliance (airlines), 76
Starbucks, 132
Start-up companies: growth markets
    capabilities of, 205; managing cre-
    ative fusion in, 173–175; profit
    making by, 228–229; Silicon Valley,
    165–176
Stereotypes, listening counteracts, 19
Stock value fluctuations, 66, 181;
    honesty and accountability about,
    64

Stories: "five years from now" success, 179; listening to people's, 19

StrataCom, 208

Strategic fit, 211–213, 220

Strategic planning: clarity of vision and, 178–179, 254–255; and innovation, 142, 155–157, 216, 261–262, 280; innovation protocols, 219–224; and strategic foresight, 283

Stumpf, B. (Bill), 36

Success: and ethical or moral responsibility, 62, 66–68, 124; and good management, 149; the paradox of, 24, 40, 154, 202

Successful people: behavioral feedback from colleagues of, 48–50, 51–54; contributing to society, 66–68; four key beliefs of, 41–47; helping behavioral change by, 40–41, 48–54, 154–155

Sun Microsystems, 76, 83

Superstition, 44

Surplus goods donation matching service, 271–272

Surprise: the beneficial, 2, 32–33; innovation as, 73; listening and, 18–19; openness and vulnerability to, 33, 279

Survival, organizational, 6, 279; long-term, 227

Sustaining technologies, 202–205, 211–213

Swap, W. C., 5, 165

Szell, G., 137

T

Talent (human), recruitment and retention of, 235–237, 243, 246–247

Tantrums, avoiding, 257

Teachers: creative people as, 35; managers as, 180–181; and mentors, 167–168, 170–175; See also Learning

Team delay analysis, 97

Teamwork: in city government, 113–114, 255–257; conducive to innovation, 157–161; for creative fusion, 173–175; designing groups for creative, 166–168; encouraging, 97–98, 113, 117, 146, 158; executive, 157–158; heavyweight, 209, 211, 212, 213; and internal competition, 102–103; pharmaceuticals research, 246; in police departments, 255–257, 259–260; in sales, 162; versus leadership, 143

Technologies: functional genomics, 244–245; interactive computer use, 260–262; investing in, 209, 266; police department Compstat, 260–261; sharing software, 266; surviving changes in, 230; sustaining and disruptive, 202–205, 211–213

Technologists: cherishing, 127–128; and entrepreneurs, 166

Technology: community connectivity, 270; history of, 186–187, 232; information age, 189, 234

Technology companies, 228–229; innovation in, 76, 83, 132–133, 134; Silicon Valley, 166–168, 170–176

Telemedicine, 270

Tesco, 83–84

Thanks: for creative persons, 36–37; for feedback, 51

Theater and social prototyping, 281–282

Thinking: kaleidoscope, 74–77, 83–85; mechanistic, 13, 20, 189; penumbra mode, 190; wishful, 213–214

3M, 133, 134, 135–136

360-degree feedback, 49

Time: expertise development, 168; good professionals giving, 66–67; for innovation, 78; overcommitment of, 45–46, 50

Toscanini, A., 136–137

Toyota, 208–209

Trammel Crow, 65–66

Trial-and-error innovation. See Failure and setbacks

Trips: far-afield, 83; to see company individuals, 126–128
Trust: in creative people, 36; and group size, 30

U

Ulrich, D., 5, 215
Union workers, city employee, 113, 114
United Airlines, 76
"Units of one," 16
Unity: and commonality of interests, 25; diversity as the path to, 17–18

V

Value drivers, 182
Values: formulation of shared, 179–180; humanity and community, 66–68, 180, 270; innovation as one of core, 133, 278; living rather than merely stating, 119–128; market forces versus internal, 61, 69, 201; old and new business, 210; an organization culture of shared, 123–124, 127–128, 174, 223, 228; and organizational decision making, 200–202, 205, 206; reexamination of organization, 283–284; traditional business, 120–121
Varig, 76
Vasella, D., 6, 239
Venture capital: as broken, 276; entrepreneurs, 166; partners, 76; within city government, 112, 117
Vertex, 127–128, 246
Vietnam War, 151

Vision statement: developing a clear, 178–179, 254–255; for Indianapolis, 108–109
Vulnerability, to surprise and quality, 33, 279

W

W. L. Gore & Associates, 139
Wal-Mart, 132
Walton, S., 132
Waterman, R., 201
Web networks, 147–148, 268–269
Weisbord, M., 17
Welch, J., 88, 181
Westinghouse, 132, 136
Westinghouse, G., 136
Wheatley, M. J., 2, 11, 42
Wheeler Mission, 116–117
Wheelwright, S., 209
Williams, M., 65–66
Wireless technology, 267, 269, 271
Woods, R. E., 219
Workers. *See* Individuals working in business
Worldviews, changing, 12, 263

X

Xerox, 74

Y

Young Turks, attitudes of, 25

Z

Zander, B., 160
Zander, E., 76

The Drucker Foundation Future Series

All Three Volumes in a Slipcover Case
Boxed Set   ISBN 0-7879-4696-6 $80.00
PaperbackSset   ISBN 0-7879-5370-9 $49.00

Business Week Best-Seller!
The Leader of the Future
New Visions, Strategies, and Practices for the Next Era
Frances Hesselbein, Marshall Goldsmith,
Richard Beckhard, Editors

World-class contributors offer insights into the future
quality of our lives, businesses, organizations, society, and
the leadership required to move us into the exciting
unknown.

Hardcover   ISBN 0-7879-0180-6 $26.00
Paperback   ISBN 0-7879-0935-1 $18.00

Now in Paperback!
The Organization of the Future
Frances Hesselbein, Marshall Goldsmith, Richard Beckhard, Editors

"Required reading. If you don't use this book to help guide your organization through
the changes, you may well be left behind."
                                        —*Nonprofit World*

Hardcover   ISBN 0-7879-0303-5 $26.00
Paperback   ISBN 0-7879-5203-6 $18.00

Now in Paperback!
The Community of the Future
Frances Hesselbein, Marshall Goldsmith, Richard Beckhard,
Richard F. Schubert, Editors

"This book of essays is full of rampant idealism. Its authors share a desire to better
the world through their ideas and actions."
                                        —*Christian Science Monitor*

Hardcover   ISBN 0-7879-1006-6 $26.00
Paperback   ISBN 0-7879-5204-4 $18.00

FAX	CALL	MAIL	WEB
Toll Free	Toll Free	Jossey-Bass Publishers	Secure ordering at:
24 hours a day:	6am to 5pm PST:	989 Market St.	www.josseybass.com
800-605-2665	800-956-7739	San Francisco, CA 94103-1741	

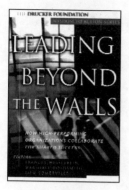

Leading Beyond the Walls

Frances Hesselbein, Marshall Goldsmith,
Iain Somerville, Editors

from the Drucker Foundation's Wisdom to Action Series

"There is need for acceptance on the part of leaders in every single institution, and in every single sector, that they, as leaders, have two responsibilities. They are responsible and accountable for the performance of their institution, and that has to be concentrated, focused, limited. They are responsible however, also, for the community as a whole. This requires commitment. It requires willingness to accept that other institutions have different values, respect for these values, and willingness to learn what these values are. It requires hard work. But above all, it requires commitment; conviction; dedication to the Common Good. Yes, each institution is autonomous and has to do its own work the way each instrument in an orchestra plays its own part. But there is also the 'score,' the community. And only if the individual instrument contributes to the score is there music. Otherwise there is only noise. This book is about the score."

—Peter F. Drucker

Increasingly, leaders and their organizations work in ways that extend beyond the walls of the enterprise. These partnerships, alliances, and networks allow organizations to achieve new levels of performance. At the same time, they create new challenges. Leaders "beyond the walls" must be adept at building and maintaining relationships, comfortable in working with individuals and organizations they cannot control, and able to move beyond the old preconceptions.

Leading Beyond the Walls presents insights from over twenty-five thought leaders from all three sectors, exploring the challenges and opportunities of partnership as well as the unique practices and perspectives that have helped individuals and organizations become more effective.

Paperback   ISBN 0-7879-5555-8 $16.50

FAX
Toll Free
24 hours a day:
800-605-2665

CALL
Toll Free
6am to 5pm PST:
800-956-7739

MAIL
Jossey-Bass Publishers
989 Market St.
San Francisco, CA 94103-1741

WEB
Secure ordering at:
www.josseybass.com

Leading in a Time of Change

A conversation between Peter F. Drucker and
Peter M. Senge

Peter F. Drucker, Peter M. Senge, and Frances Hesselbein

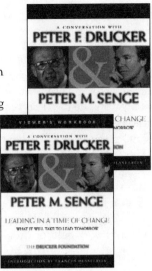

Sit at the table with the visionary leaders who are setting the agenda for organizational leadership and change.

The Drucker Foundation presents a conversation with Peter F. Drucker and Peter M. Senge, hosted by Frances Hesselbein. In this dynamic package—which includes a video and companion workbook—two great minds of modern management share their wisdom on how leaders can prepare themselves and their organizations for the inevitable changes that lie ahead.

Watch the video and witness a remarkable conversation between Peter Drucker and Peter Senge as they talk about the importance of learning to lead change for all organizations. Using the principles presented in this stimulating video and workbook, you can help transform your organization into a change leader. In their discussion Drucker and Senge reveal how you can:

- Develop systematic methods to look for and anticipate change.

- Focus on and invest in opportunities rather than problems.

- Phase out established products and services.

- Balance change and continuity.

- Motivate and retain top performers and create a mind-set among employees that embraces positive change.

The companion workbook will be an invaluable aid in making strategic decisions. It will also serve as a fundamental resource for planning and implementing changes within your organization. This extraordinary package is an ideal tool for executive retreats, management training, and personal leadership development.

42-minute video with companion Viewer's Workbook ISBN 0-7879-5603-1 $195.00

FAX
Toll Free
24 hours a day:
800-605-2665

CALL
Toll Free
6am to 5pm PST:
800-956-7739

MAIL
Jossey-Bass Publishers
989 Market St.
San Francisco, CA 94103-1741

WEB
Secure ordering at:
www.josseybass.com

Lessons in Leadership

Peter F. Drucker

Over the span of his sixty-year career, Peter F. Drucker has worked with many exemplary leaders in the non-profit sector, government, and business. In the course of his work, he has observed these leaders closely and learned from them the attributes of effective leadership. In this video, Drucker presents inspirational portraits of five outstanding leaders, showing how each brought different strengths to the task, and shares the lessons we can learn from their approaches to leadership. Drucker's insights (plus the accompanying *Facilitator's Guide* and *Workbook*) will help participants identify which methods work best for them and how to recognize their own particular strengths in leadership.

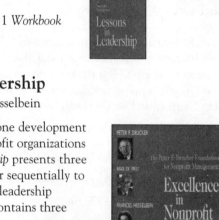

1 20-minute video + 1 *Facilitator's Guide* + 1 *Workbook*
ISBN 0-7879-4497-1 $95.00

Excellence in Nonprofit Leadership

Peter F. Drucker, Max De Pree, Frances Hesselbein

This video package is a powerful three-in-one development program for building more effective nonprofit organizations and boards. *Excellence in Nonprofit Leadership* presents three modules that can be used independently or sequentially to help nonprofit boards and staff strengthen leadership throughout the organization. The video contains three twenty-minute programs: (I) *Lessons in Leadership* with Peter Drucker (as described above); (II) *Identifying the Needs of Followers*, with Max De Pree and Michele Hunt; and (III) *Leading Through Mission*, with Frances Hesselbein. The video comes with one *Facilitator's Guide*, which contains complete instructions for leading all three programs, and one free *Workbook*, which is designed to help participants deepen and enrich the learning experience.

1 60-minute video + 1 *Facilitator's Guide* + 1 *Workbook*
ISBN 0-7879-4496-3 $140.00

FAX	**CALL**	**MAIL**	**WEB**
Toll Free	Toll Free	Jossey-Bass Publishers	Secure ordering at:
24 hours a day:	6am to 5pm PST:	989 Market St.	www.josseybass.com
800-605-2665	800-956-7739	San Francisco, CA 94103-1741	

The Drucker Foundation Self-Assessment Tool

Since its original publication in 1993, the best-selling *Drucker Foundation Self-Assessment Tool* has helped and inspired countless nonprofit boards, executives, and teams to rediscover the direction and potential of their organizations. This completely revised edition of the *Self-Assessment Tool* now offers even more powerful guidance to help organizations uncover the truth about their performance, focus their direction, and take control of their future.

The *Self-Assessment Tool* combines long-range planning and strategic marketing with a passion for dispersed leadership. It allows an organization to plan for results, to learn from its customers, and to release the energy of its people to further its mission. The *Process Guide* by Gary J. Stern provides step-by-step guidelines and self-assessment resources, while the *Participant Workbook* by Peter F. Drucker features thoughtful introductions and clear worksheets. Participants will not only gain new insights about their organization's potential, but also forge strategies for implementation and future success.

Multiple Uses for the *Self-Assessment Tool*

- *The leadership team*—the chairman of the board and the chief executive—can lead the organization in conducting a comprehensive self-assessment, refining mission, goals, and results, and developing a working plan of action.

- *Teams throughout the organization* can use the *Tool* to invigorate projects, tailoring the process to focus on specific areas as needed.

- *Governing boards* can use the *Tool* in orientation for new members, as means to deepen thinking during retreats, and to develop clarity on mission and goals.

- *Working groups from collaborating organizations* can use the *Tool* to define common purpose and to develop clear goals, programs, and plans.

Process Guide　　　　Paperback ISBN 0-7879-4436-X　$30.00
Participant Workbook　　Paperback ISBN 0-7879-4437-8　$14.00

1+1 SAT Package = 1 *Process Guide* + 1 *Participant Workbook*
ISBN 0-7879-4730-X　$35.00 **Save 20%!**

1+10 SAT Package = 1 *Process Guide* + 10 *Participant Workbooks*
ISBN 0-7879-4731-8　$95.00 **Save 40%!**

FAX	**CALL**	**MAIL**	**WEB**
Toll Free	Toll Free	Jossey-Bass Publishers	Secure ordering at:
24 hours a day:	6am to 5pm PST:	989 Market St.	www.josseybass.com
800-605-2665	800-956-7739	San Francisco, CA 94103-1741	

Leader to Leader

A quarterly publication of the Drucker Foundation and Jossey-Bass Publishers

Frances Hesselbein, Editor-in-Chief

WINNER
1998
MAGGIE AWARD
1998
APEX AWARD

Leader to Leader is a unique management publication, a quarterly report on management, leadership, and strategy written by today's top leaders *themselves*. Four times a year, *Leader to Leader* keeps you ahead of the curve by bringing you the latest offerings from a peerless selection of world-class executives, best-selling management authors, leading consultants, and respected social thinkers, making *Leader to Leader* unlike any other magazine or professional publication today.

Think of it as a short, intensive seminar with today's top thinkers and doers—people like Peter F. Drucker, Rosabeth Moss Kanter, Max De Pree, Charles Handy, Esther Dyson, Stephen Covey, Meg Wheatley, Peter Senge, and others.

Subscriptions to **Leader to Leader** are $199.00.
501(c)(3) nonprofit organizations can subscribe for $99.00 (must supply tax-exempt ID number when subscribing). Prices subject to change without notice.

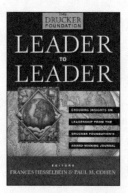

Leader to Leader

Enduring Insights on Leadership from the Drucker Foundation's Award-Winning Journal

Frances Hesselbein, Paul M. Cohen, Editors

The world's thought leaders come together in *Leader to Leader*, an inspiring examination of mission, leadership, values, innovation, building collaborations, shaping effective institutions, and creating community. Management pioneer Peter F. Drucker; Southwest Airlines CEO Herb Kelleher; best-selling authors Warren Bennis, Stephen R. Covey, and Charles Handy; Pulitzer Prize winner Doris Kearns Goodwin; Harvard professors Rosabeth Moss Kanter and Regina Herzlinger; and learning organization expert Peter Senge are among those who share their knowledge and experience in this essential resource. Their essays will spark ideas, open doors, and inspire all those who face the challenge of leading in an ever-changing environment.

For a reader's guide, see www.leaderbooks.org

Hardcover 402 pages   ISBN 0-7879-4726-1 $27.00

FAX	**CALL**	**MAIL**	**WEB**
Toll Free	Toll Free	Jossey-Bass Publishers	Secure ordering at:
24 hours a day:	6am to 5pm PST:	989 Market St.	www.josseybass.com
800-605-2665	800-956-7739	San Francisco, CA 94103-1741	

The Collaboration Challenge

How Nonprofits and Businesses Succeed Through Strategic Alliances

James E. Austin

Presented by the Drucker Foundation

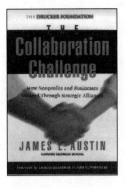

In these complex times, when no organization can succeed on its own, nonprofits and businesses are embracing collaboration for mutual benefits. Nonprofits are partnering with businesses to further their missions, develop resources, strengthen programs, and thrive in today's competitive world. Companies are discovering that alliances with nonprofits generate significant rewards: increased customer preference, improved employee recruitment and morale, greater brand identity, stronger corporate culture, expanded good will, and innovations strengthened by testing.

In this timely and insightful book, James E. Austin demonstrates how to establish and manage strategic alliances that are effective and mutually beneficial. He provides a practical framework for understanding how traditional philanthropic relationships can be transformed into powerful strategic alliances. Readers will find key lessons drawn from more than fifteen collaborations, including Timberland and City Year; Starbucks and CARE; Georgia-Pacific and The Nature Conservancy; MCI WorldCom and the National Geographic Society; Reebok and Amnesty International; and Hewlett-Packard and the National Resources Center. From his anlaysis, nonprofit and business leaders will learn how to:

- Find and connect with high-potential partners

- Ensure strategic fit with a partner's mission and values

- Generate greater value for each partner and society

- Manage the partnering relationship effectively

Perceptive, powerful, and practical, *The Collaboration Challenge* offers valuable insights on the process of creating and sustaining successful strategic alliances between nonprofits and businesses.

Hardcover   ISBN 0-7879-5220-6 $25.00

FAX	CALL	MAIL	WEB
Toll Free	Toll Free	Jossey-Bass Publishers	Secure ordering at:
24 hours a day:	6am to 5pm PST:	989 Market St.	www.josseybass.com
800-605-2665	800-956-7739	San Francisco, CA 94103-1741	www.leaderbooks.org